Breaking the Curse

The Real-life Adventures
of the U.S. Secret Service Agent
Who Tried to Change Tomorrow

Life is good!

Jan Marie Ritter
With Bob Ritter

C/P
Calvert Press

CALVERT PRESS

9440 Old Solomons Island RD #445
Owings, MD 20736
Http://www.calvertpress.com/

Manufactured in the United States of America

ISBN 978-0-9888502-0-0

Library of Congress Control Number: 2013902015

Cover photo courtesy of Ronald Reagan Library

DEDICATION

This book is dedicated to the men and women of
the U.S. Secret Service and their families—
past, present, and future.

"Desperate people are dangerous people."

Bob Ritter

CHAPTERS

AUTHOR'S NOTE

In the past, a number of books have been written about the legendary United States Secret Service (USSS). Some of these were written as overviews of the Secret Service and its rich history. The overwhelming majority have been written as memoirs by former agents, who related their fascinating careers. None has been authored from the perspective of an agent's spouse. This book fills that void.

It *highlights* a perilous period for the Secret Service—from 1972 to 1982. During that time, five assassination attempts took place against persons protected by the USSS (protectees)—more than any other era. Four of the five attempts were directed against presidents—the other against a presidential candidate. Two of the attempts were partially successful in that protectees were wounded. The operating procedures of the Secret Service had been put to the test by would-be assassins. Not only were questions raised, but also the future of the Secret Service was in jeopardy.

During much of this dangerous epoch, my husband was directly involved in the protective mission of the USSS—especially protective intelligence (PI). He regularly related his activities, concerns, and ideas to me. He had knowledge and understanding of the real Secret Service that only an insider could gain. Participating firsthand in notable incidents and events, he is one of only a very few who know the *full* truth surrounding the assassination attempt on President Ronald Reagan.

He also knows the facts regarding the "Libyan hit teams," which purportedly entered the United States to assassinate President Reagan—as well as other *secrets* of the Secret Service. Some never before published information will be brought to light.

This book was almost not written. For many years, my husband did not wish to revisit many of these memories. In a post 9/11 world, it is important that this story be told. If history is shaded and recorded inaccurately, some lessons will not be learned, and others will not ring true. Preventable mistakes will occur again. Unfortunately in the endangered world we live, future mistakes could be very costly—especially in human lives.

Revealed in this volume will be the *past* inner workings and culture of one of the world's elite organizations—during its most critical time. Insight gained can still be relevant today. We'll particularly look into the unpublicized and fascinating area of protective intelligence. Believing that PI offered the best hope for preventing the assassination of President Reagan—supposedly predestined by "Tecumseh's Curse"—my husband sought to improve its capabilities. Strategies for predicting dangerousness in individuals are explored. We can change our tomorrows.

There's also coverage of pre-1970s USSS protective history. Included is a new look at the assassination of President John F. Kennedy in regard to Lee Harvey Oswald. We'll analyze Oswald's behavior and mental state. Despite all the investigations into the JFK assassination, some little-known, provocative information will be brought to print.

At the same time, this is foremost the personal love story of a young couple, who embarked on a shared journey through life. Being married to a very dedicated Secret Service agent presented many challenges since I wanted a happy family life—and a rewarding career too. The demands made on my husband by the Secret Service greatly affected me—and the relationship we had. Balancing the needs of the Secret Service with each other and our family became a major concern.

Some words of caution: It should be remembered that we will be returning to the Secret Service of a bygone era. Today's Secret Service is a different organization. It's much improved with more people, cutting edge technology, and better organization and procedures.

Additionally, my husband has kept his trust not to reveal any of the embarrassing *private* life moments of a protectee—learned through the close access protective agents are granted in order to properly perform their duties.

Most importantly, while every effort has been made to scrupulously write the truth, this book relates *our* opinions and experiences as remembered by us. The views expressed here do not necessarily reflect those of the United States Secret Service or any other governmental organization.

Quotations were derived from our best memories of the actual conversations. For privacy reasons, some names and other identifying details have been changed. Nothing written here is meant to harm *any* individual or organization.

With these precautions in mind, please join us as we relive an exciting yet troubled time—as my husband and his fellow agents try to break Tecumseh's Curse. There'll be fun and adventure—along with some sorrow and disappointment.

Jan Marie Ritter

BREAKING TECUMSEH'S CURSE

Chapter 1

3-30-81

I'll *never* forget when I heard the news. It was mid-afternoon Monday, March 30, 1981. An overcast sky with drizzle enveloped the Washington, D.C. area in a lining of gray. My class of fourth and fifth graders was reading silently at their desks. Setting an example, I was reading too. My thoughts drifted between the fantasies of the novel, the remaining school day, and the coming evening with my family. Only an occasional cough or shuffling of feet interrupted the calm. It had been a productive and quiet start to the week—as quiet as a suburban Maryland elementary school could be.

Suddenly, the classroom door swung open with an alarming creak, snapping me back to reality. In darted Principal Jo Fisher; she headed straight for my desk. It wasn't unusual for Jo to visit classes, but this time her face expressed worry and concern—in an intensity I hadn't seen before. Reaching my side, she leaned down close to my ear and softly asked, "Jan, is Bob working today?"

The unusualness of the question along with her troubled look made me immediately apprehensive. My husband, Bob Ritter, was a special agent with the United States Secret Service (USSS). He had been in federal law enforcement for about nine years and was currently stationed in Washington at the Secret Service Intelligence Division (ID).

Fearing what Jo might say next, I almost didn't want to answer. Holding back some anxiety, I summoned enough nerve to reply, "Yes, Bob works just about every day." In an instant, Jo's face turned pale with distress; her head slumped toward the floor. The hardback dropped from my hands, landing on the desk with a clunk. "What's wrong, Jo?" I clamored.

Jo took a deep breath as she raised her head. Her eyes met mine, and she quickly turned her head to the side—trying to shield me from the increased concern her face displayed. Jo's next words fell from her lips straight to my heart. "There's been a shooting involving the president, and some people have been injured. Go to the media center. I'll watch your class."

A sense of dread seized me as I ran—heart pounding furiously—all the way to the school's media center. Inside, I found some of our support personnel crowded around the sole television set—with eyes fixed to the screen. One of the ladies from the cafeteria staff was holding her hands to her head and letting out a wail—in shock and disbelief. News was breaking of an assassination attempt on President Ronald Reagan—at the Washington Hilton Hotel.

At first, the news coverage was spotty and left much to the imagination. Later that afternoon, video taken during the incident appeared on the networks. Terror overtook me like a speeding bullet. This wasn't a Hollywood thriller; this was all too real. President Reagan was coming out of the hotel toward his limousine, smiling and waving to the crowd. Without warning, gunshots rang out; pandemonium ensued. Some people near the president were hit. My heart skipped a beat; one was a Secret Service agent. During the first quick take, this agent resembled Bob in general features. It was my worst nightmare come to life. Thankfully, it appeared that the president was unharmed.

Even though I knew Bob had most likely *not* been assigned to the Washington Hilton that day, I held my breath until the video segment was re-played, and I was positive the agent wounded was neither Bob nor anyone I recognized. Although sad for those injured, I involuntarily gasped with relief. My display of thankfulness was noticeable and understandable to those in the room. They were aware of my husband's occupation, and several hugged me with compassion for my emotions.

I was grateful I hadn't seen Bob in the video. Only 69 days before, he had worked the *same* arrival/departure area. Bob had been the Secret Service Intelligence Division advance agent for the presidential inaugural ball held at the Washington Hilton. Bob considered it the *most dangerous* site in D.C. for the president; therefore, he had specifically asked for the assignment. He wanted to ensure that an agent fully aware of the security vulnerabilities at that location would be handling the protective intelligence duties. Bob had been worried about the protective survey changes the USSS had made at the Washington Hilton during his tenure at the Washington Field Office (WFO). Bob's warnings had been prophetic.

As the TV was switched between channels that afternoon, all networks were initially reporting that the president had *not* been injured. This raised our spirits. Later, more horror unfolded, as the networks corrected earlier bulletins regarding the president. The president *had* been injured and was undergoing emergency treatment at George Washington University Hospital. In addition, it was reported that a Secret Service agent, a Metropolitan Police officer, and White House Press Secretary James Brady had also been wounded.

School dismissal had brought a surge of classroom teachers to the media center, as word of the assassination attempt spread. Everyone wanted to learn the latest news. Some asked me if Bob was involved in the incident. I told them it was my belief that he was working at Secret Service Headquarters as an Intelligence Division duty agent. All were very concerned, and I was appreciative of the support and comfort they gave.

The replaying of the video became overwhelming—particularly the chilling sight of Mr. Brady's motionless head lying in a pool of his own blood. I had to turn away and couldn't watch any longer.

Leaving the media center, I went to look for Jo. I wanted to thank her for her kindness and concern. She was now holding down the school's office while intently following the news via radio. When Jo saw me, she turned down the volume and searched my face—looking for telltale signs regarding Bob. I related that I hadn't seen Bob in any of the news footage. It was my belief that he hadn't been at the Hilton. She was relieved to hear that bit of good news. We sadly discussed the turnaround of reports regarding the president. We were devastated that he had been shot.

Attempting to get my mind off the tragedy, I told Jo I was going back to my classroom to work on my lesson plans. She replied sharply: "No, you should go home *now*. Carrie and Robbie will need you to sort this out." Of course, she was right. My 11-year-old daughter and 6-year-old son would need answers to their questions and easing of any fears caused by the tragic news. This was *not* a normal day.

I hurried to my car and drove to my son's after school caregiver while thinking of how best to handle the situation. Fortunately, Robbie was not aware of the shooting. The caregiver, a friend and neighbor, had purposely shielded Robbie from the news. I would do likewise until both of my children were together.

Once home, I kept Robbie to his normal routine. Bursting through the front door, Carrie arrived a short time later. She ran to me with outstretched arms and a puzzled look. While we were still embraced, she said in an uncertain tone: "Mommy, something about Daddy's work was on TV. The teachers told us about it."

"I know, honey," I replied.

Carrie and I got Robbie, and we went to the family room and settled down on the floor in front of the television set. I told them as calmly as I could: "A terrible thing happened today. A bad man has shot our president along with some other people. Dad's okay, but a Secret Serviceman, just like Dad, was one of the people hurt."

I turned on the television, and we watched the news coverage and videotape of the attempt. I explained what they were seeing. Afterwards, both Robbie and Carrie looked at me with astonishment, and Carrie exclaimed: "That's what Daddy does! It's not fair that he would have to be shot for the president."

It suddenly occurred to me that my children didn't really understand what their father did for a living. They had only seen Bob in the work setting of White House tours, Christmas parties, Easter egg hunts, and other fun activities.

Hugging my children tightly to comfort them, I said: "Yes, Secret Service men and women work hard to keep the president safe. It can sometimes be dangerous—like today, but good people have to stand up to bad people. Your dad knows what he's doing, and we don't need to worry about him. He'll be okay."

I turned the TV off, so Robbie and Carrie wouldn't become permeated with the graphic images of real-life violence. They went to their rooms for homework and reading, while I headed to the kitchen to prepare dinner.

I knew there was no need to set a place for Bob. Although he was working the 7:00 a.m. to 3:00 p.m. shift, the attempt on the president's life would necessitate him being held over. The best I could hope for would be a telephone call from Bob, letting me know his situation. It would be reassuring to hear his voice.

While making dinner, I listened to the radio to stay abreast of the president's surgery and the condition of the others injured. The roller coaster ride of emotion continued. It had been announced that James Brady had died. Deeply saddened by the news, I rejoiced when Mr. Brady's death was retracted. Reports now listed him as alive but unfortunately gravely wounded.

The Secret Service agent wounded was identified as Tim McCarthy. I remembered the name as an agent Bob had shared hotel rooms with— during an overseas trip of Secretary of State Henry Kissinger. Bob had mentioned that he and Tim were members of the same college social fraternity—at different universities. I felt sorry for Tim's family and wondered if he was married.

Every time the phone rang, I dropped what I was doing (in hope it was Bob) and ran to grab the receiver. Each time, it was a family member or friend inquiring about Bob and the assassination attempt. I briefly told them what I knew and that I appreciated their concern. I apologized for having to keep the calls short; I needed to leave the phone free—for whenever Bob could call.

Later that evening, Bob did telephone; it was a great relief to hear from him and to confirm his safety. His calm and confident voice was quite a contrast to the confusion and uncertainty of the television and radio coverage. Since the attempt on President Reagan's life, Bob had worked nonstop at the ID duty desk. He had no idea when he would be able to come home. Bob told me he loved me and missed me. He asked me to give the kids his love and to kiss them goodnight for him.

I remarked how unbelievable it was that the assassination attempt had taken place at the Washington Hilton—the very site that Bob had been worried about. His reply: "It was a dangerous spot. Honey, I have to go now. See you when I get home. Love you."

I immediately told Robbie and Carrie of Bob's call. As I put them to bed, we said a prayer for Bob, President Reagan, Mr. Brady, Agent McCarthy, and the injured Metropolitan Police officer, who was identified as Thomas Delahanty. I kissed the kids goodnight and sent along Bob's love.

Restlessly and anxiously waiting for Bob to arrive, I passed the remainder of the evening on the living room sofa. Several times, I arose to my feet when I heard a car approaching—only to be considerably disappointed when it didn't stop. Finally, I heard Bob's car pulling into our driveway. I met him at the door with a kiss and an embrace.

Bob was exhausted. The collar to his wrinkled dress shirt was unbuttoned; his tie hung out of the breast pocket of his suit jacket. He was slumped over and moved slowly. Bob had gotten up at 4:30 a.m. in order to arrive at Secret Service Headquarters for the 6:45 a.m. relief of the midnight shift.

"Do you want something to eat?" I asked.

In a hoarse voice, Bob answered: "No thanks, I'll wait till breakfast. I just want to get some sleep."

"What time do you have to go in tomorrow?"

"Regular time," he replied.

We went to our bedroom where I helped Bob off with his clothes. After collapsing onto the bed and closing his eyes, he found enough energy to say: "It was close. We almost lost the president today. It looks like everyone is going to be okay—except Secretary Brady. He's in a bad way. It shouldn't have happened. I wish I could have been there. It shouldn't have happened."

I had many questions, but mercifully I let Bob rest. In spite of his long day, the Secret Service was still requiring him to be back at 6:45 a.m. I set his alarm and snuggled with Bob in bed. It was good to have him safely home and close to me. I gave him a goodnight kiss and told him I loved him. Bob didn't respond; he was already asleep.

Earlier in the day, I had thought the unthinkable—of what it would be like to lose Bob forever—as I watched the video of the shooting. As I lay in bed—still restless—the fear suddenly returned like a dagger to my heart. I tried to suppress it. I thought of the life that Bob and I had made together the past 11-plus years. We had two wonderful children and shared a loving relationship. We had worked hard, sacrificed, and persevered. We had accomplished much and shared many joyful memories. Nevertheless, I wasn't happy with my life and not sure about the future. Sadly, a problem had been growing inside me for some time. It was the source of bizarre contradictions.

For now, I just wanted to thank God for keeping Bob safe. I calmed myself by remembering the journey Bob and I had taken, and the first time we met.

Chapter 2

Chance and Romance

It was late January 1967—the start of the spring semester of my freshman year in college. In the news that month, the National Aeronautics and Space Administration (NASA) suffered a tragic setback in the Apollo space program, which aimed to land a man on the moon by the end of the decade. Fire erupted during a launch pad test at Cape Kennedy. Astronauts Gus Grissom, Edward White, and Roger Chaffee were killed. Overseas in Vietnam, the build-up of U.S. combat troops continued as opposition to the war grew at home.

At the University of Maryland at College Park, Bob and I were among the many hundreds of students who signed up to take Spanish I. It was good fortune that we were both assigned to the same session of the many offered.

When I entered the classroom on the first day of Spanish, I was attracted to a tall, good-looking guy. Since he gave me a warm smile, I sat down next to him. We introduced ourselves and hit it off immediately. We were at ease together—as if we were old friends.

As our next classes were in the same direction, Bob and I walked together and enjoyed pleasant conversation. As we made our way across campus, people kept saying hello to Bob. With some wonder, I remarked, "You sure know a lot of people."

"I'm in a fraternity and some organizations," Bob modestly replied. Later, I found out Bob was an upperclassman and respected campus leader. He was the president of his fraternity, a student court judge, men's league representative, a class officer, intramural referee, and more. He had been elected to Kalegathos (inter-fraternity honorary), Omicron Delta Kappa (national leadership honorary), and Who's Who in American Colleges and Universities.

As the semester progressed, I looked forward to our brief time together. Bob impressed me with his friendliness, good manners, and intellect. It appeared that he liked me too, and I hoped he would ask me out on a date. I thought it would be fun and even imagined it *might* lead to romance.

About mid-semester, while the professor was taking roll at the beginning of class, a prophetic thing happened. My maiden name, *Janet Rehkemper*, came immediately before *Robert Ritter* on the class list. When the professor came to my name, she accidentally transposed my first name with Bob's last name. She called out, "Janet Ritter," which was met with laughter by the other students.

The professor and I were both embarrassed. She corrected herself, while I blushed and timidly answered, "Here."

Smiling, Bob leaned toward me and whispered, "Sounds good."

This boosted my hope that Bob *had* noticed my feminine qualities, and I might get a date with him. I considered telling Bob that it sounded good to me too. I didn't because he might have thought me too forward. Actually, I didn't especially like my last name. It was often mispronounced and confusing. Some people thought my name was *Janet Raykemper*; others believed it was *Janet Rae Kemper*.

As I thought about the roll call mistake, it occurred to me that my monogram initials would remain the same—an odd thought to pop up. The romantic side of me believes it was destiny. Although I didn't know it then, it was the first time I was called by what would become my married name.

The semester continued, but our conversations never got around to dating or relationships. I wondered why I hadn't sparked Bob's romantic interest. When the semester ended without being asked out by Bob, I was disappointed. I thought he must have a steady girl.

June through August 1967 became known as the "Summer of Love," as hippies flocked to the Haight-Ashbury section of San Francisco in search of the counterculture movement. Songs from the Beatles album *Sergeant Pepper's Lonely Hearts Club Band* dominated the radio airwaves. The Six-Day War between the Arabs and Israelis broke out abroad, and urban unrest raged at home.

During the summer recess, I came across one of Bob's fraternity brothers who lived in my neighborhood (District Heights, Maryland). Mentioning that Bob and I had taken a class together, I remarked that Bob seemed very nice and asked if he had a girlfriend. His fraternity brother candidly replied: "Bob doesn't have a steady. He dates around quite a bit."

Gosh, what a blow to my ego! Maybe Bob thought I was in a relationship. There was also the complication that I lived at home my freshman year and commuted to campus. I was upset at myself that I hadn't said more to Bob to indicate my interest. I certainly wanted to be with him in a social setting. If I ever ran into Bob again, I would be sure to let him know my feelings.

Unfortunately, my chances of having another course with Bob were not good. My major was music, while Bob majored in government with a history minor. At a college the size of the University of Maryland, we might never see each other again.

I moved on campus my sophomore year. Living in a dormitory exposed me to more university life, and new friendships developed. I dated several guys—enjoying the social opportunities available. It was fun, but I found no one with whom I wanted a special relationship. I still dated my high school sweetheart too, but knew we would never be more than good friends.

One day about midway through the fall semester, I was crossing the university mall heading for a class in the music building. All of a sudden—about 40 yards in front of me—I thought I recognized Bob. He was walking with a girl, and they were moving away from me.

Hurrying in their direction, I was excited to realize: It was Bob! My heart raced. I caught up and grabbed him by the arm, while pulling myself close to his side. I gave him a big smile and a warm greeting. As Bob recognized me, a smile came over his face. "Hi, Jan—what a nice surprise. It's been some time. How have you been?"

"Great," I replied. "I moved on campus and live at Somerset Hall. I love it here—especially the social life. I'm not dating anyone in particular—just looking to have some fun. I miss you in Spanish." I squeezed his arm a little tighter, while I said with some emotion, "It's *really* nice to see you."

Bob then introduced me to his friend, Carol. She was a gorgeous blonde and smartly dressed. Her makeup was perfect and her perfume divine. She looked like she had just stepped out of a beauty salon. I could tell by the pin on her sweater that she was a Tri Delta (one of the best sororities at Maryland). Feeling diminished in her presence, insecurity overtook me like an express train at a rail crossing. I was still gazing at her when Bob continued: "Jan, it's great that you moved on campus. You can fully experience all the university offers. The extracurricular activities provide something for everyone."

Composing myself, I turned back toward Bob and nodded my head in agreement. Then I stroked my long, blond hair with my free hand, while offering Bob my best "starry-eyed" look. I was going to be sure to send him signs I was interested.

Bob smiled again and said: "We're on our way to the Student Union [building] for a break. Would you like to join us?"

"I'd love to, but I have a class. We're reviewing for an exam."

"Okay, maybe next time. Take care and good luck in your exam."

As I said goodbye, I immediately second-guessed myself for turning down the invitation. What was I thinking? It was an important class and exam, but this was a chance to be with Bob. I suppose I would have felt like the odd person. I might have been unconsciously fearful that I couldn't match up to Bob's beautiful friend—although I had never flinched from competition before. In any case, I had just blown a chance to be with Bob socially. I was upset at myself! I couldn't believe what I had done.

Disheartened, I tucked away my books and started walking toward the music building. Looking back, I saw Bob and Carol talking and smiling as they made their way. He was carrying her books, and I wondered what their relationship was. If Bob was dating women like Carol, it was no wonder that he wasn't interested in me. I started to believe that Bob and I would never be more than acquaintances.

Several days passed. Then one evening, while I was busily studying in my dorm room, the house telephone rang at the end of the hallway. One of the girls called out, "Janet Rehkemper."

I got up from my desk and went to the doorway. "Yes," I replied.

"The receptionist says you have a visitor in the lobby."

"Ask who it is please." I didn't want to be disturbed, and I suspected my visitor was a guy who had been making some recent advances toward me. I had been trying to show him—in a nice way—that I wasn't interested, but he hadn't been taking the hints. I was afraid he had stopped by.

I was thinking of an excuse when the girl turned toward me again and yelled, "Bob Ritter." The name reverberated through my brain. I couldn't believe my ears. *Bob* was downstairs! What was he doing here? And asking for me!

"Tell the receptionist I'll be right down!" I screamed. Racing to my dresser to freshen up, I was startled by the reflection in the mirror. My long hair had been twisted and clipped up on the back of my head, and I was wearing old clothes—all for a comfortable evening of study.

My roommate, Joanne, had also heard the news. She hurried to my side while crying out: "Bob Ritter! That's the guy from last year you ran into the other day."

"Yes, and I look terrible."

I hurriedly changed clothes, while Joanne frantically worked on my hair. I put on some makeup and a touch of perfume. Joanne gave me the once-over, nodded her approval, and headed me off to the lobby. The transformation was worthy of any quick change of costume I had done in high school plays.

Bob, waiting on a couch in the dorm lounge, arose when I approached. "Hi, Jan. Hope I didn't disturb you?"

"Oh, *no*," I replied. "I was just studying. It's good to take a break and to see you again."

"Good, please sit down." Bob waited until we were both seated. Then he continued: "I don't know if you're doing anything a week from this Saturday, but I'd like to ask you out. A fraternity brother of mine is getting married, and I would like you to be my date. I wanted to ask you in person."

I was surprised and thrilled. As I already had a date with my high school boyfriend for that Saturday night, I asked Bob the time of the wedding. "The ceremony starts at noon, and the reception follows at about 1:30 to 5:30 p.m. It's at Andrews Air Force Base [AAFB]."

"I'd love to," I enthusiastically replied. "Can you pick me up at home? I live about 10 minutes from Andrews and was planning to spend that weekend off campus. And, I have a prior commitment that evening so would need to be home by 6:00 p.m."

"Sure, no problem, I have my own car. All I need is directions." I gave Bob directions, and we finalized the other arrangements. After saying good night, I returned to my dorm floor where I excitedly filled in Joanne and some other friends on the good news. I was extremely happy that Bob had *finally* asked me for a date. He did it in such a sweet and charming way. I could hardly get back to my studies; my mind filled with anticipation.

I felt a little guilty I hadn't told Bob the complete reason I wanted to be home by 6:00 p.m. If there had been a conflict, I would have canceled the prior date in order to go with Bob. Since there wasn't, I felt obliged to keep it. For some reason, I found it hard to end things with my old boyfriend. Maybe I didn't want to hurt him. I told him I was dating at college, so we weren't going steady anymore. He continued to ask me out, and I continued to see him. He might have thought he could still win me over, and we would eventually marry—someday. But I knew in my heart that wasn't going to happen.

The big day drew near. I went home on Friday afternoon. I was on top of the world. I had a date with Bob, and my grades were doing well.

The next morning, I was dressed and ready to go by the pickup time of 11:30 a.m. Soon it was 11:45 a.m., and Bob had neither arrived nor called. I was worried. When 12 o'clock came and went with no sign of Bob, I became doubly worried.

My brother, Gene, didn't help matters by goading: "He's not coming. You might as well go take that dress off. Shot down!" Now, I was not only worried but also thoroughly upset. If Bob didn't show for the date, I knew that I would never be able to live down the embarrassment—and the disappointment.

At last, Bob arrived at about 12:15 p.m. He hurried up the walkway and saw me through the glass storm door. I was not happy. Opening the door for Bob, I returned his greeting and smile with silence and a chilly expression. As soon as Bob got inside, he started to apologize, saying he had gotten lost.

My mom and Gene were seated nearby. Without accepting Bob's apology, I turned toward them and introduced Bob. My mom remarked, "So, you had some trouble finding our house."

"Yes, ma'am, it's hard to believe someone as smart as Jan—could give such bad directions." My mom and Gene broke out in laughter.

When Gene stopped laughing, he added: "Yeah, I know what you mean. One time, Janet and I were trying to find a place. I was driving; she was navigating; we were getting nowhere. I finally looked over, and she was reading the map upside down!" There was another round of laughter at my expense—even Bob joined in.

My ears started to burn. Bob must have sensed the embarrassment building inside me for he quickly said: "No, I was just kidding. It was entirely my fault, and I again apologize for keeping Jan waiting." Bob turned to me with a choirboy look and flashed his dark brown eyes. "*Please forgive me, Jan*," he pleaded.

I looked at Bob. He was handsome in his midnight-blue, three-piece suit, button-down-collar shirt, and traditional-striped tie. He had a nice smile and athletic physique. He was smart and classy. And I adored the scent of his English Leather cologne. This man had possibilities. Plus, he had apologized and taken full blame. How could I be upset at him?

"No apology is needed," I said. "It can be tricky to find our house—especially if you're not from the area. We'd better be going. We're late for the wedding."

As we walked to Bob's car (a chestnut-colored 1964 Plymouth Sport Fury), he gave me an approving look and commented: "Jan, that's a lovely dress. You really look nice." I thanked him and returned the compliment. It felt good to be noticed, and he sounded sincere.

Bob and I arrived at the AAFB Chapel and quietly sat in the rear. We had missed most of the wedding. Soon, the ceremony ended with the recessional of the bride, groom, and wedding party. While standing for their exit, I imagined what my wedding day would be like. Most importantly, I wondered who would be walking with me—arm in arm.

We gathered outside the church with the rest of the guests. Bob introduced me to several people. Everyone was saying how beautiful the wedding was. Bob would give me a wink and enthusiastically agree.

The reception was held at the AAFB Officers' Club. I was very familiar with Andrews. My dad had served in the Air Force and was stationed at Andrews at the time of his death. I was an Air Force "brat" and had many memories of AAFB. It was quite a coincidence that Bob and I would have our first date there.

The reception was wonderful. A lively band played both rock-'n'-roll and soul music. Bob and I danced a lot. It felt good to be in his arms during the slow dances. I met more of Bob's friends, and they all seemed very nice. Bob was a well-mannered gentleman. Our conversation was lively and pleasant. Bob was charming, and he made me feel special. It was a fun-filled, enjoyable afternoon. Things could not have gone better, and I was sorry to see the reception end.

Bob and I were invited to the home of the groom's parents for an after-reception party. Not wanting to leave Bob, I thought about breaking the date with my former boyfriend—but I couldn't. I wouldn't have been able to catch him in time. I reluctantly told Bob that I still needed to be home by 6:00 p.m.

On the drive back, Bob thanked me for going with him and said he had a fun time. Gently placing my hand on his shoulder, I spoke with sincerity: "I had a great time too. I really wish we could have gone to the party."

Arriving at home, Bob got out and hurried over to my door, to open it for me. After helping me out of the car, he slid an arm around my waist and escorted me to the front door. Looking into my eyes, Bob said: "We're having a fraternity party next Saturday night in D.C. Would you like to go?"

"Sure."

"Great, I'll call you tomorrow to set things up."

Bob leaned his head toward mine, while gently pulling me closer. Our lips met for a kiss. It was soft and sensuous. A kiss had never felt better. My body tingled. I didn't want to let go of Bob, yet my old boyfriend would soon be here. We said goodnight, and I watched Bob drive off.

My old boyfriend took me to the movies—*Cool Hand Luke* starring Paul Newman. Still thinking of Bob, I couldn't get interested in the film. Its dark theme was quite a comedown from earlier in the day. I wanted the film to end, so I could go home and call my girlfriends. I wanted to tell them how nice my date with Bob had been. Most importantly, he had asked me for a second date!

After the movie, I asked my ex-boyfriend to take me directly home. The feelings I was developing for Bob gave me courage to do what was overdue. Pulling up to my house, my old boyfriend slid over and tried to put his arms around me. I curtly responded, "Please, not tonight" while drawing back at the same time.

Surprised, he retreated and asked, "What's wrong?"

After a long pause, I turned to him and firmly stated: "The romance has gone out of our relationship. It would be better if we stopped seeing each other."

He tried to get me to reconsider, but I held firm. I got out of the car and didn't look back. I felt an immediate sense of emotional relief. I was now totally *free* to date Bob and others.

Bob had aroused sensations in me that I hadn't experienced before. Looking back now, I realize that I was transitioning from adolescence to womanhood. A new stage in my life was beginning. I eagerly anticipated my next date with Bob—to explore these emerging feelings.

The week passed slowly as I waited for Saturday night and my second date with Bob. I didn't see him on campus. He called several times to check arrangements and to say hello. Hearing Bob's voice on the phone would have to satisfy me till date night. I welcomed the opportunity to learn more about Bob and to see if my feelings for him would intensify.

Although I was hopeful Bob and I could develop a serious relationship, I tried not to get carried away. This was only our second date and *very* early in the game. I knew that I needed to take one-step at a time. If I let my heart leap ahead too fast, it could end in heartache.

At last, Saturday night arrived, and Bob picked me up at the dorm—on time. Since I wanted Bob to drop me at my mom's house after the party, I signed out for an overnight. I took a small suitcase with me, containing some laundry to wash at home and class notes to study. Bob carried it for me.

As we were leaving the dorm, we ran into a girl who lived on my floor. She looked naughtily at Bob, the suitcase, and me. Then she asked, "Jan, you got something on for tonight?"

Introducing my friend to Bob, I reminded her about the fraternity party. Her eyes rolled as she replied, "I meant after the party."

"Bob's taking me home after the party; I'll be back at the dorm Sunday evening."

Bob grinned, as he had already understood that my friend was joking that some hanky-panky might be afoot. When I realized the inference, I became a bit embarrassed and said, "Really, this is just some stuff for home."

"All right then, you and Bob have a fun time." She gave me a wink and went into the dorm.

Bob's fraternity, the Delta Sigma chapter of Delta Tau Delta (DTD), rented the party room in an old Washington nightclub in the Northeast section of the city. As the legal drinking age was 18 in D.C. for beer and wine, most fraternities held their parties in the District. The University of Maryland was a dry campus and the state drinking age was 21. Bob was 21, and I was 19.

We entered the smoky, dimly lit club and headed for the back—passing a row of elderly men seated at the bar. Several turned to us and smiled when Bob respectfully greeted them, "Good evening, gentlemen; how's it going?"

Bob then whisked me down a rickety flight of stairs to the basement party room. Neon beer signs covered the walls, and the smell of beer and hot-buttered popcorn filled the air. About 30 people had already arrived; they were scattered about the tables.

The party was casual. Guys wore shirts, sweaters, and slacks. The gals wore dresses or skirts with blouses or sweaters. In one corner next to the popcorn machine, a keg of beer had been tapped. A seven-piece soul band was just finishing a sound check. I had been to fraternity parties before, but this one seemed special. I looked at Bob and smiled, as I anticipated a fun evening.

Bob escorted me around the room and introduced me to his fraternity brothers and pledges (probationary members). In turn, they introduced me to their dates. Bob got us a couple of beers and some fresh popcorn from the machine. We picked a table and sat down.

More people arrived, and I saw some folks that I had met at last Saturday's wedding. The room lights were dimmed, and the band started out with an instrumental number, "Soul Finger." Couples headed to the dance floor. This was heaven! Being with Bob was a big part of my heightened sensation and enjoyment.

Before the night was over, nearly 100 people filled the party room. Some of the girls wore Delt fraternity pins. This meant they were "pinned"—in a committed relationship to the guy they were with. Bob's fraternity pin was different from everyone else's. His pin had a ruby and pearl border, and a small gold gavel hung from it. Bob explained that only the reigning chapter president was permitted to wear a jeweled pin.

During the evening, I became acquainted with some of Bob's closest fraternity brother friends. They seemed genuinely interested in me. I was made to feel welcome and enjoyed genial conversation with them and their dates.

Bob and I had fun dancing, and it was pleasurable to be together. When the band's singer belted out Percy Sledge's "When a Man Loves a Woman," Bob and I pressed close to each other, and I melted in his arms. It was a perfect evening; I wished the night would never end.

The last dance, Otis Redding's "These Arms of Mine," came all too soon. It felt good being close to Bob; I wouldn't let go of him after the song ended. I kept an arm around him, while we walked over to thank the band. The room lights rose, and we helped with the clean up. Bob met with the fraternity's treasurer to co-sign the checks for the band and club. Then Bob and several other brothers checked that everyone who was driving was fit to drive.

After Bob completed his duties, we started out to his car when Don Furtney, a fraternity brother who had been at our table, asked if we wanted to get a bite to eat. Don had graduated from Maryland and was working in D.C. as an insurance adjustor. His girlfriend had traveled from out of town to make the party. Bob looked at me, and I responded, "It's fine with me."

Don smiled as he said: "Great, I know an all-night place. Follow me." After a long drive into Virginia and out U.S. Route 1, we arrived at a shiny-silver diner with a big neon sign on top. As we entered, we were greeted by the sound of crackling grease and the sight of grey smoke puffing up from the grill. The aroma of hot coffee, cheese steaks, hamburgers, and seasoned fries wafted through the air. The place was as crowded and noisy as the service was slow, yet Bob and I enjoyed every minute. It was good to be with each other, and Don and his girlfriend were charming companions.

We chatted and joked the entire time. When the food finally arrived, it was freshly prepared and tasty. I thought it sweet of Bob to hand feed me some of his fries after I said they looked good. Returning the favor, I gave him some of my club sandwich. We were having such delightful conversation and fun that we all lost track of the time.

Suddenly, Don looked at his watch. "Man, it's almost 2:30."

Horrified, I blurted out, "Don, please tell me you're kidding."

"Okay, Jan, I'm kidding. But my watch still shows it's almost 2:30 a.m."

Bob looked at his watch and cried out, "Oh, no!"

Grabbing Bob's arm, the words exploded from me: "It'll be after 3:00 when you drop me off. My mom's going to have a stroke. Then she's going to kill me!"

"Jan, take it easy. We'll be all right. Let's call your mom now and tell her what happened."

I sharply cut Bob off by exclaiming: "We can't call my mom! She's sleeping. If the phone rings now, she'll think something's wrong. If she learns I'm out this late, I'll be in trouble forever!"

Bob apologetically replied: "Jan, this is my fault. I should have had you home by a decent hour." Bob shook his head a couple of times—upset at himself. Suddenly, confusion showed on Bob's face. "Wait a minute. Won't your mom be waiting up for you and worried?"

"No, earlier in the week, I told her I'd *probably* be dropped back at the dorm. I didn't decide to go home until this afternoon. She wasn't really expecting me. What am I going to do? I've missed curfew at the dorm, and I can't go home this late. Even if I tried to sneak in, my mom is sure to hear me and wake up."

"Why don't you guys crash at my place?" Don suggested. "Jan, Bob can drive you back to the dorm tomorrow."

Looking at his watch again, Bob retorted, "Don, it is tomorrow."

I knew Bob would be a perfect gentleman, yet this brought reservations of propriety to mind—caused by my Catholic upbringing. I had gone to a parochial school and an all-girl Catholic high school. My mom and the nuns had taught me well. There was an awkward silence, as I was still thinking of an answer and a way out of the dilemma.

Bob sensed my predicament and offered: "Jan, I have an idea. Let's drive back to D.C. and do some sightseeing. Some of the memorials never close. Later in the morning, we'll get some breakfast, and I'll take you back to the dorm when it reopens."

I gave Bob a huge look of relief and thankfully said: "That's a great idea. Let's do that."

We paid the check and headed to our cars. Along the way, Don mischievously started to sing the old Ricky Nelson song, "It's Late." Don had a big grin on his face and rendered the lyric in his unmistakable Pittsburgh-Pennsylvanian accent. We couldn't help but laugh, and my worries disappeared.

Back in D.C., Bob and I drove by the Capitol Building, Library of Congress, Supreme Court, and Union Station. Then we connected with Massachusetts Avenue and saw the many foreign embassies along Embassy Row. From Massachusetts Avenue, we traveled south to the Treasury Building, White House, and the Old Executive Office Building.

Next, we drove past the Department of State and then to the Washington Monument grounds. We walked arm in arm up to the Monument. It was a clear, starry night with a chill in the air. I kept telling Bob I was cold, so he would grasp me as close as possible. We sat on a bench and enjoyed the view of the National Mall.

Returning to the car, we went to the Jefferson Memorial. After visiting the memorial, we briefly strolled along the tidal basin. It was picturesque—even though the cherry trees were bare.

After another short drive, we took in the Lincoln Memorial and then walked down to the Reflecting Pool. Standing at the edge, we tossed in coins while making silent wishes. Impulsively, one of my wishes was that Bob and I would develop a romantic relationship. That particular coin magically skipped along the water in the moonlight. I couldn't believe it! Was it a sign? I watched Bob, while he finished tossing his coins. I wondered what his wishes were; I hoped one included me ...

Our next stop was in East Potomac Park. Bob parked the car at Hains Point where the Washington Channel and Anacostia River meet the Potomac River. Bob tuned the car radio to an oldies music station. A song I wasn't familiar with was playing. Bob was raised in the Philadelphia-South Jersey area and knew popular music. "What's the name of this?" I asked. "It's a pretty melody."

" 'I Only Have Eyes for You,' by the Flamingos." He turned toward me and continued, "It's a pretty song—but not as pretty as you."

"Oh, stop! You're just saying that."

"No, I really mean it. It's not a line. You were the prettiest girl at the party tonight."

I gave Bob an affectionate look and said in an appreciative tone: "Thank you. That's very sweet."

Pointing out to the moonlit water beyond Hains Point, Bob teasingly asked: "Jan, do you see the submarines? If you look closely, you can see the ripples they make on the surface."

"Yes, they're really *making time* tonight," I answered with mock sincerity. Bob looked at me and laughed. I slipped off my shoes, swung my legs up on the sport seat, and slid over the console next to Bob. Nestling up to him, I laid my head on his shoulder.

Bob put his right arm around me as he said: "I love Washington. It's such a beautiful and inspiring city. I want to work here after graduation."

"At what?" I asked.

"Work for the federal government in law enforcement."

"Really—law enforcement," I remarked with surprise.

"Yes, eventually for the FBI or Secret Service. I want a public service career—one with action. Your major is music. What do you want to do?"

"I'm actually thinking of switching to early childhood education. Once, I had thoughts of a musical career. But I really love children and would like to work with them. That would probably be a more realistic and satisfying career."

"My mom and sister are teachers," Bob responded with pride. "That's a worthy profession—like law enforcement."

During our conversation, Bob and I learned much about each other. Amazingly, there was nothing that we disagreed about. We continued to find out that we were remarkably compatible.

I raised my head toward Bob and gave him a kiss on the cheek. He kissed me in return; I loved every second. Eventually the moon and stars began to disappear, as the sun rose with its light becoming higher and brighter. I felt the warmth of the sun and Bob's strong embrace.

Earlier, I wished that the night wouldn't end. That wish was granted. Although a new day had arrived, Bob and I were still together, and the thrill of our Saturday night date continued. It was a wonderful feeling.

Driving out of the city via the Eleventh Street Bridge, we headed east toward Maryland along Kenilworth Avenue. We stopped at a pancake house in Riverdale, Md. We had a good breakfast and talked some more. We were more tired than we wanted to admit. It was time for Bob to take me to my dorm.

We were driving back to school and had stopped for a red light. I was resting with my eyes closed. Suddenly, Bob said under his breath: "Jan, there's a police car alongside us at the light. The officer is staring at us."

"What!" I straightened up and looked over. "It's my brother Art!"

"You're kidding, right?"

"No, he's a county policeman. He works this area."

The light changed and both cars pulled off. I waved to Art and smiled. He nodded his head and smiled back. Then he looked quizzically at Bob. Finally, he pulled away and sped down the road.

"Did he know you were out on a date last night?" Bob asked with concern. "He might think ..."

"Don't worry," I interjected. "If anything comes of this, I'll tell Art we were just out for breakfast."

We arrived at Somerset Hall. Bob walked me to the door and carried my suitcase. He apologized again for not getting me home. I told him not to worry; I had a great time and really enjoyed myself. He said he did too. We shared one more kiss and said goodnight. Bob promised to call me that afternoon.

I signed in at the desk and carried my suitcase upstairs. By now, I was *really* wishing I had never brought it with me. I was just about to my room when someone called my name from down the hall. It was the same friend I had run into Saturday evening—while leaving the dorm. She hurried to me and asked, "Jan, I thought you weren't coming back until tonight?"

"Change of plans. I decided to come back early," I replied.

"How did your date go?"

"Okay—he's very nice."

"Don't kid me. I can see it in your eyes. You're falling for him."

"Well, maybe a little," I admitted. "We've only had two dates. I don't want to look too far ahead. I don't know how he feels."

"I think he *really* likes you."

I thanked her for the encouragement and hoped to myself that she was right. I entered my room and was relieved to find my roommate still asleep.

Although I wanted to share all that happened, I knew I was too tired. I dropped into bed and thanked God for bringing Bob and I together. I had just had the most incredible night of my life and prayed that Bob and I would continue into a meaningful relationship.

Chapter 3

Romance and Love

That Sunday afternoon, I awakened to the realization I had truly lived an incredible night. It wasn't a dream. I found several of my girlfriends and excitedly told them about my evening with Bob. They were thrilled for me.

Later that day, Bob telephoned and again told me how much he had enjoyed our date. He asked me out for the following Saturday night; I eagerly accepted. He then invited me to study with him that evening—at the university library.

Picking me up at the dorm, Bob carried my books, while we walked to McKeldin Library. He took me to the library stacks—where books are neatly stored on rows of shelves from floor to ceiling. The musty smell of old bindings and yellowing paper overwhelmed the scent of my perfume.

Also within the stacks were small enclosures; each containing a desktop and a couple of chairs. We chose a location, sat down, and spread out our work. The space was tight, but I wasn't complaining. It was nice to be close to each other. "I come here a lot," Bob whispered. "It's quiet and free from distractions—mostly used by graduate students doing research. It's a great place to study." Bob was right. We spent several productive hours in the stacks.

Before going back to the dorm, we stopped at the Student Union for milkshakes. After getting our shakes and finding a quiet table, Bob tilted slowly back on his chair as he remarked: "The library is one of my favorite places on campus. To me, it's not just a repository of the past, but our best hope for the future."

"Best hope for the future," I inquired.

"If we don't know the errors of the past, we'll keep making the same mistakes—over and over. I enjoy history—especially the biographies of historic figures. We can learn from their successes and failures."

"Wow, you're really into this," I replied.

"Yes, every challenge I'll face in my life has already been met by someone in the past. I don't want to make their mistakes. Studying what they did will help me make better decisions. The lessons of history are relevant for our future—possibly our survival. I really think our country is at an important crossroads. We're in the nuclear age, and we've got a lot of problems at home and abroad. We have to choose our actions wisely."

"How could I apply this to my field?"

"In a way, you already are. You're at the university taking a degree program and working hard to acquire the accepted knowledge. You're not using *trial and error* as a learning tool."

"You're really a deep thinker," I said admiringly. "Can we study together again? Maybe some of it will rub off on me."

"Sure," said Bob, "anytime."

As we walked back to the dorm, I thought how Bob had impressed me with his intelligence and other qualities. So far, he was everything I wanted in a man.

We continued to date during the final months of 1967 and into the spring semester of 1968—mostly going to fraternity parties and campus activities. At times, we watched television in the lounge at my dormitory. A new comedy series, *Rowan and Martin's Laugh-In*, became one of our favorites. At Bob's fraternity house, we viewed the National Football League (NFL) Championship game. Vince Lombardi's Green Bay Packers defeated the Dallas Cowboys 21-17 in the "Ice Bowl," the coldest NFL game in history. Game time temperatures at Lambeau Field in Green Bay dipped to 13 below zero with a wind chill of minus 36. Bob and I continued to have fun and enjoyed being together—regardless of the occasion.

The year 1968 was an important time for Bob and me. The events of 1968 along with our growing personal relationship would greatly influence the rest of our lives. Although Bob hadn't asked me to be his steady, we were dating regularly. I was increasingly turning down dates to keep my social calendar open for him. There was more and more romance in our dates. Nevertheless, I was wondering why Bob hadn't asked me for a committed relationship.

One Saturday evening, Bob arrived early at my house to pick me up for a fraternity party. I was still putting on makeup, so Bob waited in the living room and chatted with my mom. When I was ready, I joined them. Instead of escorting me to his car, Bob asked me to sit next to him on the sofa. To my surprise, he took my hand and said: "I have something special on me. If you can find it, it's yours."

Going through Bob's pockets with fervor, I found his wallet and removed it. Bob laughed and said, "No, Jan, you can't have my wallet." I continued my search and felt a small clump in the inside breast pocket of Bob's fraternity blazer. I pulled out the object and discovered it was a gold chain and lavaliere (charm) made of the Greek letters of Bob's fraternity (ΔTΔ).

The look of surprise on my face turned to a wide-open smile. I held the chain to my neck, while Bob fastened the catch. Then he declared: "Jan, I offer this Delt lavaliere as a symbol of the special feelings I have for you. I ask you to be my girl and to wear it as an expression of that commitment."

Instantly, I replied, "Silly, I've already stopped dating other guys." I hugged Bob and gave him a kiss on the cheek. My mom smiled and offered her congratulations. She liked Bob too.

During the next several months, we spent increasing amounts of time together. My close friends thought us to be a perfect match and several predicted love. One evening, we were having dinner at Ledo Pizza, an Italian restaurant and sports bar near the university. It was one of our favorite spots and served the best pizza in the area. We were having a fun time and enjoying each other's company. To our surprise, an elderly couple stopped at our table on their way out. They smiled at us, and the lady asked, "Are you two married?"

"No," I answered. "We've been dating about five months."

The lady remarked: "You remind us of ourselves when we were young. You two seem very happy together. It raises our spirits to see such a nice young couple, especially nowadays—with hippies and protestors everywhere."

Then the gentleman added: "We've been married 37 years. I hope you can be as happy as we've been. Good luck."

We thanked them for their kind comments, and they continued on their way. Bob remarked with some amazement: "They thought we might be married. Isn't that something?"

"As a matter of fact," I responded, "people see the affection we have for each other. My friends think we make a great couple. What do your friends think?"

"They think the same. They all like you. Sometimes, I think we've known each other forever."

"Yes, me too! The first time we met; I felt as if we were old friends seeing each other again. Do you believe in déjà vu?"

Bob thought for a moment and replied, "That it's psychological illusion—to feel we've experienced the same event before."

"How about destiny?" I asked.

"I don't believe in predestination; we have free will to determine our lives. History has shown that individuals can have tremendous influence on shaping events. Assassination is a good example. A lone assassin can murder a prominent political figure. That single act can have far-reaching consequences on history. Look at the Lincoln and Kennedy assassinations. Anyway, education and hard work are the keys to my destiny."

Reaching over the table and taking Bob's hand, I said: "The romantic in me would like to think we were destined to meet. Maybe we were lovers in a past life."

Bob grinned as he squeezed my hand in return. "Jan, I sure hope I shared a past life with you. I bet we had fun. Right now though, I'm enjoying the here and now."

"I am too." Flashing a flirtatious look, I extended my leg under the table to rub against Bob's leg.

Several weeks after that, almost prophetically, I received a phone call at my dorm from Bob. It was Thursday evening, April 4, 1968. "Jan, have you heard? Martin Luther King Jr. has been shot!"

"Oh, no!" I cried out.

"It happened in Memphis, Tennessee."

"This is horrible," I said.

"Jan, I'll pick you up in 10 minutes. We can follow the news at the fraternity house." Arriving at the Delt house, Bob and I crowded into the already packed television room. The network news departments were interrupting regular programming to provide what was known about the shooting. At about 8:15 p.m., the tragic news we had feared was announced. Dr. Martin Luther King Jr. was dead. Bob grimaced as he remarked, "The cities are going to explode."

"You think they'll be riots?" I asked with concern.

"I'm afraid so," Bob answered. "Civil disturbance has been on the rise the past several years. We've had violence from Watts to Harlem. Last summer, the destruction in Newark and Detroit alone caused over 50 deaths and tens of millions in damage. Dr. King's loss is tragic. He was our nation's conscience on civil rights. There's going to be a lot of rage."

We continued to watch that evening as history unfolded before our eyes. It was reported that Memphis Police were looking for an unidentified white male who was seen running from where the deadly rifle shot was fired. Bulletins of disturbances in Memphis and Harlem, New York were aired. President Lyndon B. Johnson addressed the nation and pleaded for calm.

Later, the first reports of trouble in Washington, D.C. were broadcast. It started at 14th and U Streets, NW, in the Shaw neighborhood. The area was settled by freed slaves after the Civil War and took its name from Shaw Junior High School. The school was named for Colonel Robert Gould Shaw, the white officer who commanded the African-American 54th Massachusetts Volunteer Infantry Regiment during the Civil War. This unit gained fame for its courageous charge of Fort Wagner at Charleston, South Carolina. During the battle, Col. Shaw was killed and over 250 men of the 600-man regiment were killed, wounded, or captured.

From the late 1800s, Shaw was a thriving center of black commerce and culture. It was home to jazz great Duke Ellington and other black high society. Through the years, the "Black Broadway" area of Shaw featured African-American entertainers such as Washingtonian Pearl Bailey, Baltimore native Cab Calloway, Billy Eckstine, Louie Armstrong, Ella Fitzgerald, Louis Jordan, Dizzy Gillespie, Washington native Marvin Gaye, the Supremes, Smokey Robinson, the Temptations, and many others.

As word of the shooting spread, crowds formed at the busy intersection of 14th and U. When it was announced that Dr. King had died, the crowds marched through the business district demanding that stores close in respect for the fallen civil rights leader. Next, troublemakers began to break windows. The crowds turned into mobs; looting began, and fires were set.

As it was getting late, Bob dropped me back to the dorm. I fell asleep listening to the escalating events via an earphone plugged into a tiny transistor radio. Disc jockeys and civic leaders were appealing for folks to go home and to stay calm. The radio stations were playing hymns.

By early Friday morning, April 5, firefighters had succeeded in extinguishing the flames, while police had restored order. The streets were cleaned, and it was hoped that the worst was over. It was decided to keep D.C. schools open that Friday, and school officials planned tributes to Dr. King. By midday however, disturbances had broken out along the 14th Street, NW, 7th Street, NW, and H Street, NE corridors. Looting and arson were breaking out faster than civil authorities could contain. Schools, the federal and district governments, and businesses began to close early.

That afternoon, Bob and I were sitting in the lobby of the Delt house, discussing the worsening situation. A fraternity brother of Bob's entered the room, looking pale and shaken. "What's wrong, Jay?" Bob asked.

"I just got back from work. Things are *really* bad in D.C."

Bob glanced at me and added, "Jay works part time at the Hecht Company [department store] warehouse on New York Avenue."

"Wow, that's close to the riot area," I said.

"Yeah, too close!" Jay exclaimed. "I was working back in the warehouse— not knowing what was happening—when a couple of black co-workers came to me at about 1:30 p.m. They told me I'd better get home. Since it was a mild day, I had driven to work with my convertible top down. As soon as I get out of the parking lot, some kids start throwing rocks at me. I'm driving along New York Avenue, trying to get my top up, and it gets stuck in mid-air. It would have been funny—if it hadn't been so scary."

"Jay, are you all right?" I asked.

"I think so, but my car's damaged."

The three of us went into the TV room where we learned that Mayor Walter Washington had issued an emergency proclamation for the District of Columbia. A curfew would go in effect at 5:30 p.m. The sale of gasoline, liquor, firearms, and ammunition was restricted. The federal government was asked for assistance in restoring order. President Johnson responded by mobilizing the D.C. National Guard and by ordering active duty troops into the city.

That evening from the third-floor sundeck of the fraternity house, we could see huge clouds of smoke billowing up from D.C. Within the hue of flames, it eerily looked as if the city had been bombed. We learned from news reports that the first troop units were being deployed. They assisted police in quelling arson and looting. Troops also provided added protection for firefighting personnel.

During Saturday, April 6, things started to improve. More troops arrived to take up positions throughout the city. Television coverage showed troops and machine gun nests on the Capitol and White House grounds. James Brown, "The Godfather of Soul," came to Washington at the request of President Johnson. The evening before in Boston, Massachusetts, Brown had given a concert that helped that city avoid violence. Wherever Brown appeared—radio, television, on the streets, or in concert—he spoke against the violence and was a calming influence.

President Johnson declared Palm Sunday, April 7, a national day of mourning. By that afternoon, law and order had been restored to most of the riot areas of D.C. Government officials made plans to return the city to something approaching normalcy. Schools, the government, and businesses would reopen on Monday—on abbreviated schedules. The curfew would continue but not begin until 6:00 p.m.

On Tuesday, April 9, funeral services for Dr. King were held in Atlanta, Georgia. No more major incidents occurred in D.C., although troops would remain for days to come. The military occupation of Washington by over 15,000 troops was the largest since 1932. In that year, thousands of World War I veterans (known as the Bonus Army) encamped in Washington, trying to get Congress to pay a cash bonus that had been promised. When they refused to leave town, General Douglas MacArthur was dispatched with regular Army troops. The veterans were routed from the city.

The death and destruction throughout the nation attributed to the 1968 rioting was staggering. Disturbances had broken out in over 100 U.S. cities. The cities hit hardest included Washington, Baltimore, and Chicago. In the District alone, over 1,200 buildings were destroyed with a reported 27 million dollar property loss. Over 6,100 people were arrested. Of the hundreds injured, 13 people died—mostly victims of the fires that ravaged entire city blocks. Not since the British burned Washington in 1814 (War of 1812) had such devastation been seen in the nation's capital.

Bob understood that discrimination, poverty, drugs, and despair fueled lawlessness in our inner cities and that Dr. King's assassination was the explosive catalyst for the recent rioting. Yet, it made no sense to Bob that rioters would destroy their neighborhoods. "Why would they burn down their own homes, stores, and culture?" Bob asked.

Shaking his head, Bob continued: "Waxie Maxie was a piece of black history. Now it's gone." Bob had been a regular at the store, located on 7th Street, NW. It opened in 1938 and had been one of the only record shops in the country to specialize in jazz and blues recordings. Ahmet Ertegun, the founder of rhythm and blues label Atlantic Records, had been a steady customer at the D.C. shop during his early years. Ertegun's father had been the Turkish Ambassador to the United States.

"Local landmarks destroyed in flames; neighborhood businesses and housing leveled. It's going to kill those areas," Bob warned. "It's counterproductive. I suppose some want rebellion, revolution, and black separatism. That isn't the way to go. It's a dead-end street."

Controversy developed regarding the handling of the D.C. riots. Business owners felt that police had condoned the looting by not taking aggressive enough action. Early on, Federal Bureau of Investigation (FBI) Director J. Edgar Hoover had suggested that looters be shot. Bob and I both agreed that you don't shoot people unless your life is in danger. How many more lives would have been lost if D.C. officials had followed Hoover's suggestion? In most people's estimation, the police and military showed proper restraint in the use of deadly force.

The semester moved on and the days became warmer. Several weeks later on a gorgeous spring day, Bob took me to the university dairy bar for ice cream cones. We sat on the grass in the mall and enjoyed our treats, while birds playfully chirped and fluttered about. Bob finished his cone first and pulled something from his pocket—slyly keeping it hidden in his hand.

He peered into my eyes as he said: "Jan, you're beautiful, smart, and everything I could want in a girl. I cherish our time together and have deep feelings for you." Opening his hand to reveal his fraternity pin, Bob continued, "I will be the happiest man on campus if you will be my pin mate."

I screamed with joy and leaped over toward Bob to hug and to kiss him. In my enthusiasm, I spilled ice cream on his shirt.

Bob grinned and said, "I'll take that as a yes."

"Yes, yes," I affirmed. "Where do I wear it?"

"Right over your heart," Bob answered.

After Bob pinned it to my blouse, I gave him another kiss and said, "Bobbie, I'm so happy!" I started calling him "Bobbie" as a pet name. I still used "Bob" when talking about him to others.

We went back to my dorm, and I brought all the friends I could find to the lobby. They shared our joy and offered congratulations. It was one of the happiest days of my life. I started to believe: Bob just might be the one—I would share the rest of my life with.

That weekend at the Delt fraternity party, everyone congratulated us. I beamed with pride, as Bob's pin sparkled on my blouse. I was especially moved by comments from some of Bob's closest friends, like Andy Balo. Andy caught me in a lone moment. "Jan, congratulations, Bob's crazy over you. He's never pinned anyone before. I've always said the girl he pins will be the girl he marries. You guys make the perfect couple. I'm envious of him but happy for both of you."

The social highlights of the spring semester were the fraternity formal held at a famous inn in Virginia and the junior class prom held at the Washington Hilton Hotel. Both events were wonderful. At the prom, we were seated at the head table since Bob was a class officer. We enjoyed dinner, dancing, and the fabulous stage show of Little Anthony and the Imperials.

The evening ended on a sour note, however. After the last dance, Bob continued to hold me in his arms. "Jan, when final exams are over, I have to go to New Jersey for the summer. I promised a friend I'd help him run a swim club."

I felt like my heart had just been ripped from my chest. It was devastating news! "No, please don't go," I urged. "Work down here. I don't want you to leave." Bob had worked the previous summer in Maryland, and it never occurred to me—especially since we were pinned—that we would be apart.

"Jan, you know I want to stay, but I gave my word some time ago."

"He'll understand. Tell him to find someone else," I pleaded.

Bob held me tighter. "He's already tried to find someone else. No one good has been available for months. Believe me, if there was any other way."

Bob had been a varsity athlete in high school and had graduated fifth in his class of over 400. He had worked at swim clubs in both New Jersey and Maryland and had earned an excellent reputation. Bob's friend wanted him to be his assistant manager and the head swim team coach. Although Bob now wanted to stay in Maryland, he had given his word. Bob was loyal to his friends; they could count on him.

Final examination week arrived at Maryland. I was still unhappy about Bob leaving for the summer but needed to concentrate on my finals. It was Wednesday morning, June 5. I was just getting up when my roommate, Joanne, arrived back from an early breakfast at the dining hall. She was in tears.

"Joanne, what's wrong?"

"Bobby's been shot!" she sobbed.

For a couple of heartbeats, I froze in terror, as I immediately thought of Bob. Then, quickly realizing that she couldn't have been referring to Bob, I asked, "Bobbie who?"

"Bobby Kennedy! He was shot!" Joanne shrieked.

"I'm so sorry," I said. I rushed to Joanne to console her. She had been a big supporter of New York Senator Robert F. Kennedy's run for the 1968 Democratic presidential nomination. Bob and I were also favoring Robert F. Kennedy (RFK). He had entered the race on March 16, following a close contest in the New Hampshire primary between President Lyndon B. Johnson and antiwar-candidate Senator Eugene McCarthy of Minnesota. McCarthy had finished a close second to Johnson.

Criticism of President Johnson's handling of the Vietnam War correlated to his drop in popularity. Earlier in the year, attacks were made throughout South Vietnam in the Tet Offensive. Even the grounds of the U.S. Embassy in Saigon were penetrated. Although a military defeat for the North Vietnamese and Viet Cong (guerillas in the south), the operation was a psychological success. More Americans doubted U.S. assessments that we were turning the corner in Vietnam.

On March 31, President Johnson surprised the nation by announcing that he had decided not to seek reelection. Vice President Hubert H. Humphrey entered the race as Johnson's heir apparent. Due to the nominating process used then, the vast majority of delegates to the Democratic National Convention were *not* chosen by voters in primaries. Most delegates were chosen by party leaders. Humphrey had garnered the support of these delegations and was the front-runner. He chose not to enter any of the remaining Democratic primaries.

California was the last major Democratic primary before the convention. It was crucial for Kennedy to win the state, so he could mount a convention challenge to Humphrey. On June 4, California voters gave Kennedy the win he needed.

After giving his victory speech in the ballroom of the Ambassador Hotel in Los Angeles, Kennedy exited the stage to a rear service hallway. It was a little after midnight on June 5. The hallway connected to a kitchen pantry that led to another room where a press conference would be held. While traveling through the pantry and shaking hands with hotel workers, Senator Kennedy was shot by Sirhan Sirhan, a Palestinian immigrant who was upset at Kennedy's support for Israel. Sirhan emptied a .22-caliber revolver at Kennedy, hitting him three times. Kennedy was mortally wounded and died in the early morning hours of June 6.

Bob and I considered what might have been. "Do you really think Kennedy could have won the nomination?" I asked.

Bob thought a bit before he replied: "Kennedy had momentum from his win in California. If he had been able to pick up some delegation support and prevent Humphrey from winning on the first ballot, Kennedy stood a chance. If not, then he might have gotten on the ticket as vice president. The problem is we'll never know," Bob lamented. "Once again, an assassin has changed our future."

As a result of Robert F. Kennedy's assassination, Congress authorized the Secret Service to protect major presidential and vice presidential candidates and nominees. Bob welcomed the change. Senator Kennedy had no *professional* protection with him and was an easy target.

Finals ended, and Bob left for home. I hated to see Bob leave, but he promised to visit me when he could. Back in New Jersey, Bob worked six days a week with Sundays off. Even though he telephoned regularly, our separation was terribly difficult.

Several weeks passed before Bob was able to return to Maryland. He came down on a Saturday afternoon following a morning swim meet. We were so happy to see each other. I didn't realize until then: I could miss someone that much.

We went to the Bayou, a nightclub in the Georgetown section of D.C., and spent the evening in each other's arms. Afterwards, Bob dropped me home, and he stayed the night at the fraternity house. On Sunday, we visited

Greenbelt Park in Greenbelt, Maryland and enjoyed a picnic lunch. Bob drove back to New Jersey that evening. It was hard to say goodbye. We kissed and embraced for at least 10 minutes—before I finally let him drive away.

Bob returned to Maryland the next several weekends. He drove down after the Saturday morning swim meets and went back Sunday nights. I was miserable during the long and lonely days and nights between his visits. Phone calls helped to ease the loneliness a little, but they were a poor substitute for not being able to see and to touch each other. The calls were only a Band-Aid to my heart; I needed Bob to heal it.

Then, the swim season moved into the invitational and championship period. Bob would be tied up with meets that lasted all weekend. Faced with the prospect of not seeing each other for several weeks, Bob invited me to New Jersey for a couple of days. He arranged bus transportation and a hotel room for me.

On the ride up, I thought seriously about our relationship and examined my deepest emotions. I came to the realization: I had fallen in *love* with Bob. This was the man I wanted to marry. Yet there were many unanswered questions.

Foremost, when would Bob be ready to even consider marriage? Bob had switched his field of study from the sciences to government and history at the end of his sophomore year. He had decided that he would rather be in law enforcement and maybe go to law school, instead of becoming a research scientist. These two career choices had attracted him since childhood—with science finally losing out. Because of the switch in majors and prerequisites to required upper-level courses, Bob still had several more semesters until graduation.

As the Maryland and Delaware countryside rolled by, I contemplated our future. Should I tell Bob of my love, or should I just let things continue as they were? I wondered what Bob's true feelings were. Did he see me as a prospective wife? Would he go to law school? It might be years before Bob would be ready for marriage.

The bus motored north over the Delaware River Memorial Bridge into New Jersey. Looking down to the water far below, I saw an expanse of uncertainties between Bob and me. I decided not to tell Bob the results of my self-reflection. For the time being, I would keep my deep love for him a secret.

Later, the bus exited the New Jersey Turnpike and after a few more miles pulled into the station. Through my window, I saw Bob waiting anxiously for me in the arrival area. I was excited to see him and looked forward to a fun visit. Although I anticipated some romantic moments, I never could have guessed what would transpire in the next several hours ...

Hurrying down the aisle to the front of the bus, I could hardly wait for the driver to open the door. After leaping off, I made a dash for Bob, which ended in each other's arms. I kissed him dearly and cheerfully screamed, "Bobbie, it's *so* good to be here with you."

We remained embraced as Bob replied with emotion, "I've missed you too."

We retrieved my suitcase, and Bob drove me to the hotel. After I checked in, Bob helped me to my room. As soon as he put my bag down, I playfully dragged him toward the bed. We toppled onto it, and I kissed and caressed him. I couldn't keep my hands off Bob.

Suddenly, Bob sat up on the edge of the bed and pulled me alongside. A serious look came over his face. He put his arms around me, squeezed me tightly, and said: "Jan, these long separations are tough to take. When we're apart, a piece of me is missing. When I'm with you, I feel complete. I know there's a difference between being in love with love—and being in love with you. Jan, I'm in love—with *you*."

Then, Bob took my left hand and asked: "Will you marry me? I want to share my life with you. You can take all the time you want for an answer. This is one of the most important decisions you'll ever make. It certainly is for me. My fate is in your hands."

I couldn't believe my ears! I was stunned—absolutely stunned. We had developed an intimate relationship, but Bob's marriage proposal was completely unexpected.

It didn't take long for me to answer: "Yes, I will. You must have been reading my mind. I love you Bobbie. I've never been so sure of anything."

Bob displayed a brief look of relief and smiled broadly. Reaching into his pocket, he presented a sparkling, pear-shape diamond engagement ring. Bob placed the ring on the third finger of my left hand. Once more, I was stunned. "Bobbie, it's beautiful! When did you get this? What a surprise," I said with sincere astonishment.

"I'm glad you like it. I picked out the diamond and setting last week. It was ready yesterday. I think I got the size right. If it doesn't fit, we can have it resized."

"No one's taking it off my finger," I warned. "Bobbie, it's perfect. You couldn't have gotten a nicer ring. We're going to be married. Hooray!"

Later that evening, Bob took me to a nice restaurant to celebrate the occasion. I proudly displayed my engagement ring for all to see. I found myself taking frequent, admiring glances at it too. I was delighted with the ring, yet more important was what it symbolized—the love and commitment Bob and I shared—and our future together.

Bob had only told a few close friends that he was planning to ask for my hand in marriage. Bob hadn't even told his parents. They were on an extended vacation in Europe, and Bob only had an emergency contact number for their cruise ship via radiotelephone. He would wait until their return and tell them in person. I wanted to call my mom to tell her the news, but Bob suggested that we talk over some things first.

We discussed our future, especially when we wanted to marry. I warned Bob, "You know our parents will want us to wait—until we both graduate."

Bob gave this some thought. "Yeah, you're probably right. They'll want us to have our degrees on the wall first. That would be the logical thing to do. But with all that's been happening, I don't want to wait a couple of years."

"I don't either," I said in total agreement. "I have an idea. I've been thinking of switching from music to early childhood education. How about I take some time off from school? I think I can teach in parochial school with two years of college. I can see if I really want a teaching career. With the income, we could get married and not have to depend on our parents for money."

Bob considered my offer and asked, "Are you sure you want to do that?"

"Yes, I want to have a career, and this will help me decide which way to go. And we can start our life together. I believe getting married to the person you love and having a family is one of the most important things in life. I'd like to have our children when we're young. They can grow up and be out on their own, and we'll be free to do what we want."

Bob grinned as he replied, "Sounds good."

"Bobbie, I *really* love you and want to be with you. I know we can do this."

A determined look appeared on Bob's face as he said: "Okay, sometimes you have to let your heart make decisions. I have a friend who teaches in a high school near the university. I can substitute teach there and go to school at night. With both our salaries, we'll be able to support ourselves and be financially independent. It'll be hard at times, but we'll have fun and lots of memories to tell our children."

"And grandchildren," I added.

"Let's set a date," Bob said.

I suggested November 23, and Bob replied, "That's the day after your birthday."

"Yes, it is. I would like to have a nice church wedding and that should give us time for the arrangements. It's a Saturday and also the soonest we can marry after I turn 20. I don't want you to have to marry a teenager!"

Bob laughed and said in jest, "That's fine with me—but understand for future years—I'm only going to buy one present to cover both your birthday *and* our anniversary."

"That's okay—as long as it's an *expensive* one," I jokingly replied.

In a reflective tone, Bob expressed: "When I finish my work here, I'm returning to Maryland. I'll get an apartment near the university. We can live there after we're married. I think we're set—for now."

I leaned over the table and gave Bob a kiss. I couldn't believe the good fortune that had blessed me. Only hours before, I had decided to keep my love for Bob a secret. Then, I had more questions than answers for our relationship and future. Now, we were engaged and had marriage plans.

I looked forward to married life. Bob was the smartest man I knew and had all the attributes I could ever want in a partner. I realized that we had some challenges in our future, but I wasn't worried with Bob at my side. In fact, I couldn't have been happier; I had found the love of my life!

Upon further consideration, I decided not to tell my mom of my engagement until I returned home. It would also be better to tell her in person my intention to take a hiatus from school, so Bob and I could marry in the fall.

On the bus trip back to Maryland, I eagerly contemplated our future wedding. I wrote down whom I wanted for bridesmaids. It would be fun to look for my gown and their dresses. I thought it appropriate for Bob and me to have the ceremony at the University of Maryland Chapel. Bob would know a good place for the reception. There were many things to do. As soon as Bob returned to Maryland, we could make arrangements in earnest.

Arriving home, I excitedly told my mom the good news and showed her my engagement ring. She was happy about my betrothal to Bob but became upset when she heard our proposed wedding plans. Her mood changed in an instant. I had anticipated some reluctance, but was dismayed when she dismissed Bob's and my wishes outright.

She made it clear that I wouldn't be marrying anyone—*until I graduated college.* I tried to reason with her by countering: "Mother, Bob and I are old enough to decide what we want to do. We love each other; we're going to make this work. The most important thing in the world to us now is that we go through life together. I don't want to lose Bob."

"If Bob truly loves you, he'll wait. You're not dropping out of school. Get that out of your mind," she stated emphatically.

"Mother, I'm not dropping out. I'm taking a break to begin my professional life. This will help me decide if I want to change majors. I *am* going to graduate. Before that, I'm going to marry Bob. That's more important to me now. We want to be together."

"We'll see about that," she said definitively.

I asserted: "Yes, we will. Bob and I aren't children!"

Throwing her hands up in despair, my mom retired to the kitchen where she busied herself. I had put up a good front but couldn't have been more worried that Bob's and my plans had received a mortal blow. I feared Bob would back out of an early marriage date—when he hears of my mom's steadfast disapproval.

I went to my room, closing the door behind me—okay, maybe I *slammed* it. Sitting on my bed thinking of how my hopes had been dashed, I finally got up enough nerve to telephone Bob. As soon as I heard his voice, I started to sob a little. Bob responded, "I hope those are tears of joy I hear."

"No, my mom is forbidding me to marry until I graduate." I then related the entire encounter with my mom.

Afterwards, Bob remarked: "At least she was happy with our engagement. That's a positive sign."

"A positive sign," I screamed sarcastically into the phone. "She's not happy about it now!"

"Okay, Jan—calm down. We'll work it out. For now, don't mention our engagement or marriage plans to anyone. Don't say anything more about them to your mom. Let's stay off her radar screen. I'll talk with your Mom when I get down there. Don't worry."

"Don't worry! Bobbie, I want to marry you as soon as we can. I don't want to wait a couple of years!"

"Same here, honey. Cheer up. I promise we'll get married this year or early next year—even if we have to elope."

"Seriously, do you really mean it?" I asked in a subdued, pleading tone.

"Yes, *really*, just hang in there. I'll be done here and back to Maryland in a couple of days. Things will work out."

"Bobbie, I love you."

I was feeling much better after my talk with Bob. My spirits were raised. Bob had affirmed that we would be marrying within the next six months or so—regardless of my mom's objections. For the next several days, I avoided any confrontations with my mom and behaved as the perfect daughter in all respects. I looked forward to Bob's return to Maryland.

Chapter 4

Love and Marriage

Bob finished his summer job by mid-August and returned to College Park. After dropping off his belongings at the fraternity house, Bob drove over to see me at my home. It was good to be together again.

Bob wasted no time in setting up a meeting with my mom. He called her at work and asked if we could take her out to dinner that evening. He also mentioned that he would like to discuss some things with her. She accepted the dinner invitation and agreed to talk with Bob when she got home—at about 5:00 p.m.

I spent the next several hours nervously awaiting her arrival. In contrast, Bob was calm the entire time and unusually quiet and reserved. I tried to discuss the situation with him, but he kept telling me not to worry. Bob did say that he wanted to talk with my mom alone. He thought it better if I didn't take part. I reluctantly agreed.

Sitting on the living room sofa, Bob flipped through magazines for a while. Then, he placed his hands behind his head and relaxed back into the couch. He appeared to be contemplating the coming talk with my mom. Bob would surely need his best effort—and maybe a miracle too.

I was very concerned. In fact, I had become sick to my stomach. I figured the stress was getting to me. It was an emotionally difficult time. My mom meant the world to me, and I loved her dearly.

After my dad died when I was 13 years old, my mom had been both mother and father to me. She had gone to work after my dad's death to provide the income needed for our family—in a clerical position with the telephone company. I respected her for that and valued her judgment; nevertheless, I was ready to move forward with my adult life. At the same time, I wanted her approval and certainly did not want to be estranged from her in any way.

As time passed that afternoon, concern turned to despair. Even though my mom had become more lenient in the years after my dad's death, I felt she would not agree to my marriage plans. I feared that Bob and I would have to disregard her parental authority and elope.

By 5 o'clock, much tension had built inside me; I was apprehensive and now almost certain that their talk would not go well. Like an overinflated balloon, I was ready to pop from the pressure. Pacing back in forth by the living room window, I drew back in fear when I saw my mom pull into the driveway. I ran to Bob like a schoolgirl with a bad report card. I hugged him, gave him a kiss, and wished him good luck. Now, I was happy that I wouldn't be taking part in the discussion.

Bob greeted my mom at the door with a wide smile and a hello. He then embraced her. She smiled and said: "Well, hi, Bob. Welcome back."

"Thank you. It's good to be back. Jan and I are happy that we can take you to dinner. I know you must be tired from work, so there's no rush. We're at your convenience."

"Good, I'd like to sit down, take my shoes off, and rest some. And we can talk."

"Sure," Bob agreed. He then pulled out his wallet, handed me some cash, and asked: "Jan, will you please drive my car to the car wash and get it gassed up too? And ask the attendant to check under the hood and have him check the tire pressure."

"Okay," I replied.

While escorting me to the door, Bob winked at me and added: "Thanks, Jan. It'll be nice to go to dinner in a clean car."

I squeezed Bob's hand and whispered, "Love you," in his ear.

I went to the gas station first and got a fill up and everything checked like Bob asked. The whole time, I couldn't help but wonder and worry what was going on back at the house. I didn't think Bob would be able to change my mom's mind. For me, it had become a hopeless situation.

The line at the carwash was long. During the wait, I tried listening to the radio to get my mind off things. It didn't work. I finally got through the carwash and went to a nearby shopping center to find a pay phone. I thought it best to call Bob to see if he and my mom needed more time alone. More importantly, I wanted to find out how things were going. The suspense was enormous.

I said a silent prayer and summoned some inner strength. My hand shook a bit as I dialed the phone. My mom answered, and I asked to speak with Bob. I was relieved that my mom didn't sound upset. This rekindled some hope. Following what seemed like an eternity, Bob came on the line, and I anxiously exploded with: "Bobbie, how's it going? Do you need more time? I see she hasn't thrown you out of the house. Are things okay?"

In a deadpan voice, Bob replied, "*Yes*, Jan, go ahead and get the hot wax."

Perturbed, I complained: "Bobbie, I've already been to the carwash. At a time like this, you're worrying about hot wax!"

"*Yes*, Jan, it's *okay* if they steam the wheels."

Suddenly, it dawned on me that Bob wasn't able to talk freely, but was still trying to give me a sign. I followed with, "Bobbie, if things are okay with my mom, answer yes."

"*Yes*, Jan, that's fine."

"Oh, Bobbie, I love you! See you soon." Apparently, things were going well—or as good as could be expected—under the circumstances. I became excitedly optimistic but wanted to stay cautiously levelheaded—until I could get the details from Bob.

On the drive home, I reflected on our romance. Bob and I had been dating for nine months. We had been semi-secretly engaged for less than a week, and wanted to marry in three months. I suppose some might think us impetuous, yet I knew every step in our relationship was thought out and not taken lightly. I couldn't have been surer that Bob and I truly loved each other and belonged together.

I arrived home and parked Bob's car at the curb. Seeing my return, Bob met me at the sidewalk. I frantically grabbed him by the arms and forcibly shook them as I asked: "What did she say? Bobbie, I've been so worried. Tell me what happened."

Sighing with relief, Bob answered: "Your mom isn't overjoyed that we're going to marry in November, but she finally gave her blessing. She'll support a church wedding and reception. She's accepting—with protest—that you're going to take a break from school—*only until I finish*."

"Wow, Bobbie, how did you do it? What did you say? I can't believe it."

"Jan, your mom and I agreed to keep the details of our conversation between her and me. That way we felt we could be more frank with each other. I also made her some personal, private promises."

"You did. What kind of promises?"

"Jan, like I said—personal and private ones."

"Well, I guess I understand. The important thing is: We're getting married soon, and my mom is okay with it!"

"Yep, we're on our way! Tonight we can celebrate our engagement with your mom. Tomorrow we can start checking out wedding arrangements, and you can help me find an apartment. We've got a lot to do."

We shared a kiss and walked arm in arm to the house. I kept wondering what Bob had said to my mom. An hour before, I had thought his attempt would be to no avail. What a relief that Bob was able to persuade my mom. It would be years before I would learn the specifics of the conversation they had.

That evening at dinner, the three of us discussed the coming wedding. My mom let me know that I would have to be responsible for the immediate planning, as she would be too busy at work to offer much help. I brought up what I would like for the wedding and reception; she would nod her head between bites of food or make short comments. Yes, there was much to be done the next three months.

Bob came over to my house early the following morning, and we wrote our engagement announcement. I typed them, while Bob addressed the envelopes and affixed stamps for mailing to the newspapers. Luckily, when Bob and I were pinned, I had some professional photos taken. There were still enough small prints to include one with each announcement.

I was again feeling sick to my stomach, but we needed to make arrangements for our wedding and reception. First, we stopped by the university. Being a campus leader, Bob knew administrators and other support staff. We quickly reserved the university chapel and a clergyman friend of Bob's for Saturday, November 23.

Next, we checked the reception room and catering menu at a nearby hotel in Wheaton, Maryland. It was perfect, so we arranged for a contract to be sent to my mom. I was relieved that the site was available for our chosen date.

Later that afternoon, we drove to Riverdale, Maryland to check out an apartment for Bob. We found a nice one-bedroom unit. Bob put down a deposit and signed a lease. He would need to find some furniture and other household goods. This would become our first home.

It was a long day and a good start, but we still had to accomplish the following: prepare the guest list, order and mail out invitations, hire a band, determine the wedding party, select a wedding dress and formal attire, pick out flowers, and get a marriage license. Additionally, Bob needed to submit an application for substitute teaching. Bob would also have to register for evening courses at the university. We both looked forward to letting our family and friends know of our engagement and wedding plans. We would be busy in the coming weeks.

We continued to make progress on all fronts, but I continued to feel nauseous. I went to the university health clinic and was diagnosed with a "stomach bug." I was told to rest and to drink plenty of fluids. They wouldn't give me any medication.

When the illness persisted, I went to the health clinic at Andrews AFB. After a long wait, I was called into a small examination room. It was cold and antiseptic looking. An uninviting examination table, with tissue paper strewn over it, filled most of the Spartan-like room. Shiny metal implements lined a counter top—like soldiers in formation. Meanwhile, the nurse checked my vital signs and all appeared normal.

Later, a young-looking doctor entered with my medical records in hand. A stethoscope protruded from the breast pocket of his lab coat, which was embroidered with his name in script. After giving a quick hello, he sat down and reviewed my files for a minute or two. Then he asked, "Miss Rehkemper, you've been nauseous for several days?"

"Yes, doctor. I've been nauseous with vomiting and don't seem to be getting any better."

He directed me to sit on the end of the examination table where he physically checked me and asked medical questions. When he was done with the examination, he picked up my medical records again, and I noticed him shifting his eyes between the files and me. He sat back down, and without looking up from my medical folder, he asked, "Is there a chance you might be pregnant?"

"I guess it's a possibility. I've been having sex with my boyfriend. But I really think I've got something. I've been stressed lately and tiring myself out too."

The doctor jotted some quick notes and still without looking up, he asked, "Have you missed your period?"

"I might be a little late. I haven't thought about that. I've been so sick in the stomach and so busy."

The doctor wrote some more notes in my file and said: "Well, we'll run some tests—just to rule out all possibilities. I'll give you something for your stomach distress. You'll need to give a urine sample, and we'll take some blood too. We should know something soon."

I was sure that I wasn't pregnant and drove home not thinking much about it. When Bob called later and asked me how the appointment went, I just told him they were running some tests to find the cause of my illness. I didn't mention anything about pregnancy. I had dismissed that possibility.

A day or two passed, and I wasn't any better. In fact, I was worse. I called Andrews for my test results. I sure hoped they had discovered what was wrong. After a few minutes, the doctor came on the line. "Miss Rehkemper, I have your test results. Your blood counts are fine. Everything looks normal." There was a brief pause. The pitch of his voice lowered as he continued, "You did have a positive reading in the pregnancy test."

"Excuse me. What did you say?"

"You tested positive in the pregnancy test."

"Are you sure you've got the right file?" I asked in disbelief.

"R-e-h-k-e-m-p-e-r," he spelled out, "Janet M."

"Yes, that's me. But I'm not pregnant."

"Your pregnancy test was positive. The test is reliable. I see no indication of an infection or other problems. You're most likely experiencing morning sickness. You did mention that you were sexually active."

There was dead silence on my end of the phone. I was dazed. I hadn't just been sick in the morning. I was feeling miserable much of the time. I hadn't given the idea of being pregnant any serious consideration. Now, it was registering in my brain that I was pregnant and varied feelings erupted.

"Miss Rehkemper, are you there?"

"Yes, doctor. This is just such a surprise."

"You'll need to follow-up with an obstetrician," the doctor advised.

"Okay, thank you."

After hanging up the phone, I took some time to reflect. I wanted to have a family, but I wondered how Bob was going to take the unexpected news. Next, I worried what my mom's reaction would be. I was pregnant and going to have a child; I felt blessed but was afraid this might worsen the current situation.

Later that afternoon, Bob called to check on me. I told him I had my test results and that the Doctor had *even* ordered a pregnancy test. "What did they find out, honey?" Bob asked with sympathy in his voice.

I thought I'd get right to it. "The rabbit died!"

"What?" Bob said with more than a hint of nervousness.

"The rabbit died!"

"Funny, Jan, you're such a kidder. Anyway, rabbits aren't harmed in pregnancy tests, even positive ones. All the little furry creatures at Andrews are A-OK. So what did they find out—for real?"

"Bobbie, I'm pregnant."

"Seriously," Bob soberly replied.

"Yes, Bobbie, we're going to have a baby. You're going to be a father."

Bob, after a suspenseful pause, said in a soft, reflective tone: "Wow, I'm going to be a father. We're going to have a child."

"Bobbie, if you change your mind down the road and no longer want to marry me, I don't want you to feel you can't reconsider because I'm pregnant. I want you to marry me because you love me—not because you feel you have to."

"I'm not changing my mind. I love you, and we're getting married," Bob stated emphatically. "A child will be a lot of responsibility for us. But I'll do my best. We'll be okay."

"I know you love me. I also didn't want you to think you had to get married *now*—no matter what. It was something I felt I had to say. I don't want you to feel pressured."

"Jan, he or she is always going to know that they were wanted and loved, and that his or her parents truly love each other," Bob promised.

A couple of tears came to my eyes as I said, "Bobbie, I love you." Bob's words had touched my heart. I was very lucky and blessed to have fallen in love with a man like Bob. It would always be reassuring to know that Bob and I had already decided to marry *before* we learned of my pregnancy. There would never be any doubt to our love and to our desire to marry each other.

Even though I still wasn't feeling well, Bob came over that evening, and we went out for dinner and celebrated. Later that night, I told my mom of my pregnancy. She was disappointed in me but didn't say much. Her displeasure was tempered by the fact that she had already reconciled that Bob and I were marrying and that I would be taking a break from school to work. It also helped that my mom had gotten to know Bob and liked him very much.

The situation was different for Bob. His mom and dad had finally returned from their European trip. When they left, Bob and I were just pin mates. Less than a month later, Bob and I were engaged and making plans to marry in November. Bob would be taking night courses in the fall, and we were going to have a baby. Bob had a lot to tell them—*maybe too much.*

I had only met Bob's parents once, earlier in the year, when they were traveling through Maryland. Now they would become my mother and father-in-law. Bob decided to drive home, so he could tell his parents the news in person.

After welcoming his parents back, Bob asked about their trip. He listened, smiled, and nodded with approval as his parents related the high points of their enjoyable vacation. At the same time, apprehension came over Bob, while he awaited the opportunity to tell his parents about us. The moment finally arrived when time stood still. Bob's mom asked, "What's new with you?"

Bob inhaled deeply and replied with the understatement of his life, "Well, I've been busy since you've been gone."

"Busy," Bob's mom said in an inquiring tone.

"Yes, taking stock of my life and making some solid plans for the future."

"Uh-oh," Bob's dad blurted out with some anxiety.

Bob continued: "Jan and I are deeply in love. Our separation this summer has caused us to realize that we want to be together—for now and forever. In these crazy times, she gives me hope for the future. She's been the missing part of my life."

"Robert, I know she's a fine girl. But *please*, you still have to finish college. You'll have time for this later," Bob's mom chided.

"I asked Jan to marry me, and she accepted. We're making plans for a November 23 wedding in Maryland."

"You're kidding, right?" Bob's mom replied.

"No."

"You need to wait until you graduate," Bob's mom stated authoritatively.

"Don't worry. We've got things worked out. I can take my remaining courses at night and be a substitute teacher by day. She's going to work too, so we'll be able to support ourselves."

"No, you need to wait. Then you'll have your degree and be able to get a real job. And Janet should graduate too. You'll have plenty of time to marry after you get your education," Bob's mom advised.

"We've thought this out carefully, and we know we can do it. And I've got some more great news. You're going to be grandparents. Jan just found out that she's pregnant with your first grandchild."

"You've been busy all right," Bob's dad remarked with surprise and displeasure.

When the full measure of the news sunk in, Bob's mom and dad were angry. Bob's dad was suspicious that we planned the pregnancy to force a marriage before graduation. Bob assured his parents that wasn't the case.

They also worried that marriage and a child would cause us not to finish college. Bob impressed on them how much we wanted and needed our degrees. There was no way we were not going to graduate. Bob concluded with: "Jan and I are young and in love. That's different than being foolish and in love. We'll make you proud. Trust me."

Bob returned to Maryland and his apartment in Riverdale. We continued with our wedding arrangements and started job searches. It was near the end of August 1968.

In the evening on Bob's 1950s vintage black and white TV, we watched the Democratic National Convention from Chicago. Inside the International Amphitheater, there were heated arguments over credentials, the seating of delegates, and the Democratic Party platform—as to the Vietnam War and social reform. Vice President Humphrey's support of Lyndon Johnson's Vietnam policies carried the day.

Outside, protesters clashed with police and National Guardsmen. Demonstrators were in turn choked with tear gas and clubbed to the ground. Violence seemed to be taking over America.

With Robert Kennedy's assassination, Humphrey easily received the presidential nomination. He chose Maine Senator Edmund Muskie to be his running mate. The convention closed with the Democratic Party in disunity and the city of Chicago in shame.

We finished our wedding arrangements by the end of September and excitedly looked forward to our marriage. I worked as a salesgirl for a dress shop at Prince George's Plaza in Hyattsville, Maryland. I decided to wait until after our child was born to apply for a teaching position. Bob became a substitute teacher at Parkdale Senior High School in Riverdale, Maryland. It was decent money and good job experience. He had enrolled in night school and was receiving straight "A's." Everything was coming together for us.

Soon, it was Tuesday, November 5, 1968. The first presidential election that Bob could vote in saw Republican Richard M. Nixon defeat Hubert H. Humphrey by a popular vote margin of about 500,000. Maryland Governor Spiro Agnew became vice president. Agnew had come to Nixon's attention during the Baltimore riots that followed the King assassination earlier in the year. Agnew had taken a tough law and order stance and was put on the Republican ticket to appeal to Southern voters. In an ironic twist, Nixon-Agnew failed to win Maryland, which ended up in the Democratic column.

After hearing the election results, Bob couldn't help but again wonder what might have been. If Dr. King hadn't been assassinated, neither the April riots nor the backlash from them would have occurred. If Robert Kennedy would not have been assassinated, he *might* have been our new president or vice president.

The day before our wedding finally arrived. It was also my 20th birthday. We planned a party for 5 p.m. at my mom's house. We would celebrate my birthday with the members of the wedding party. Then, all of us would go to the university chapel for the wedding rehearsal.

Before the party, Bob would pick up our marriage license at the county courthouse in Upper Marlboro, Maryland. We had gone there several weeks before, filled out the application, and paid the fee. In Maryland, marriage licenses were issued by the Clerk of the Circuit Court. Bob got off work and headed for the courthouse. During the drive, our clergyman's last reminder rang out loudly and clearly in Bob's mind, like an alarm bell. "Make sure you don't forget the marriage license. I won't be able to officiate the wedding without it."

Upper Marlboro was a small, sleepy Southern Maryland town. Bob entered the old, stately courthouse through massive wooden doors. His quick footsteps echoed between the marble floors, paneled walls, and high plaster ceilings. At the counter for the clerk's office, Bob presented his driver's permit for identification to the lady working the window and said he was there to pick up our marriage license.

Searching through a big wire basket, the clerk pulled out a couple of documents with a note attached by paper clip. One of the documents was the marriage license, the other the original application. After reading the note, she looked at Bob and asked, "Where's Janet?"

"Getting off work and picking up some food for a party we're having. Today's her birthday, and tomorrow we're getting married."

"She needs to sign the application. I can't release the license until she does."

Bob glanced at his watch and saw it was just after 3:00 p.m. "Ma'am, what time do you close?"

"Four o'clock sharp."

"Are you open on Saturday?"

"No."

"Ma'am, she was here in person and filled it out. We submitted it, and the application was accepted. No one called us or anything!"

"I'm sorry; she missed a signature line. Can you contact her? There's a pay phone outside the office of the justice of the peace. You can get change at the snack bar."

Bob got change and hurriedly found the pay phone. It was an old style wooden phone booth. Bob didn't bother to sit down or to close the door. He quickly dialed my work number. Bob explained the problem to the store's manager. Telling Bob that I had just left, she asked him to hold, while she tried to catch me in the parking lot. The shop's manager returned with the bad news that she was unable to find me.

Next, Bob called my house several times, but there was no answer. He exited the phone booth with head low in frustration. Bob blamed himself for not coming to the courthouse earlier in the week. Despair was setting in. Maybe we wouldn't be getting married tomorrow.

Two men had been standing together nearby. One was wearing a gray-pinstriped suit, which highlighted his graying temples. He carried a brown leather briefcase and wore horn-rimmed glasses. Taking a couple of steps toward Bob, he said: "I couldn't help but overhear your problem. I'm an attorney and know most of the circuit court judges. Let's see if we can find one in chambers. Maybe he can help you."

"That would be great," Bob said with the hope of a man seeking an eleventh-hour reprieve. "I'd really appreciate it. Thanks."

The other man introduced himself as a bail bondsman. Both men led Bob to the receptionist's office for the circuit court judges. The attorney asked the receptionist if a certain judge was in and available. She buzzed his office and the judge agreed to see the trio. Bob was already dressed in a suit and a tie for my party and the rehearsal. Bob thought that to be fortunate since he was now seeing a judge on business.

As they walked to the judge's office, the attorney comforted Bob: "We're in luck. I've known the judge for many years. He's a good man, and I'm sure he'll help us."

Arriving at the judge's open door, the attorney gave a couple of quick courtesy raps. The judge invited the men in, and after an exchange of pleasantries, they sat down around the judge's large American-walnut desk. Bob gazed around the room, noticing the judge's robe hanging on a coat tree as well as walls covered with degrees and awards.

The judge asked the lawyer, "Do I need to have a representative from the state's attorney office step in here?"

"No, your honor, it's not a criminal matter," the attorney assured. Gesturing toward Bob, he continued: "This young man is to be married tomorrow. He and his fiancé previously came to the clerk's office and filled out a marriage license application. In the excitement, she missed signing one of the lines. They won't let him have the license, your honor. Unfortunately, she's unavailable until after close of business today. We're hoping that an accommodation can be made under the circumstances."

The judge looked at Bob and asked, "How old are you and your fiancé?"

"Your honor, I'm 22 and Jan turned 20 today. It's her birthday." Bob pulled out a picture of me from his wallet and handed it to the judge.

"She's lovely. You're a lucky young man," remarked the judge.

"Thank you, your honor".

"Tell me about your wedding plans."

"This evening was to be our wedding rehearsal, and we have a 4 o'clock wedding scheduled for tomorrow at the University of Maryland Chapel. After the reception, I have a honeymoon planned for the tidewater area of Virginia."

The judge smiled. "I went to University of Maryland Law School in Baltimore. Do you go to Maryland?"

"Yes, your honor, I'm finishing my degree in night school."

The judge handed back the picture and stated: "Young man, raise your right hand. Do you solemnly swear that the information you and your fiancé entered on the marriage application is truthful, so help you God."

"I do."

The judge telephoned the clerk's office and directed them to release the license. The judge told Bob to bring me in to sign the application after our return from the honeymoon. The judge, puzzled as to why the bondsman was there, asked if he needed anything.

"No, your honor, I just wanted to see how this was going to turn out and to offer any support I could. I also thought his fiancé might need me—if he *didn't* get the license."

"How's that?" asked the judge.

"She'd probably kill him and end up in jail!"

Everyone had a good laugh, *except* Bob. He knew he had just dodged a bullet with his name on it. Bob rose and thanked the judge as well as the other two men. All offered their best wishes to Bob and me.

Bob arrived at my mom's house with license in hand. I *shuddered* when Bob related the courthouse story. We had come very close to a fiasco. I asked Bob what we would have done had he been unable to get the license. I worried about everyone from out of town, the deposits for the reception, etc.

Bob said he would have asked the minister to conduct an *unofficial* ceremony at the chapel. The reception would follow as planned. On Monday, we would go to the courthouse, get our license, and have the justice of peace perform a civil ceremony. Then, we would be off on our delayed honeymoon. Certainly that would have been better than postponing the wedding, but thank heaven it wasn't necessary. It was good fortune that the attorney had overheard Bob, that he offered help, and that a sympathetic judge was found. To me, it was still another sign that our marriage was meant to be.

The birthday party was fun. Bob's best man, Charlie Sockwell, left the party early in order to coordinate the wedding rehearsal. Upon Bob's and my arrival, I noticed the minister looking at us with what I thought was a troubled look. Throughout the rehearsal, he appeared nervous and uneasy. Right before the point in the rehearsal—where vows would be exchanged— the minister asked Bob for the marriage license. Bob handed over the license. After perusing it, the minister placed the license between the pages of his Bible and continued with the remainder of the ceremony.

Before we left the chapel that evening, the minister announced that he wanted the bridesmaids and ushers to arrive the next day by 3:00 p.m. Then, he took Bob and me aside and said, "I would like you two here by no later than 3:30 p.m." Holding out the marriage license, he looked solemnly and directly into my eyes alone and stated: "I want you to know that I signed your marriage license but didn't date it. *What we did tonight fulfilled the legal requirements.* Of course after tomorrow's ceremony, that will be the official union and date I'll fill in."

Bob and I glanced at each other and then the minister. Neither of us knew what to say. Bob finally thanked the minister for everything and told him we'd see him tomorrow. On the drive to the rehearsal dinner, I commented to Bob: "Did you think that was a little strange at the end? And the minister seemed nervous all evening."

"Yes, I don't know what was wrong. I've known him for several years and have never seen him like that. We should be the nervous ones. He's done this before; we haven't."

The next afternoon, my mom and I drove to my brother Art's apartment—about 10–15 minutes from the university. Art's wife, Betty, was one of my bridesmaids and would help me dress for the wedding. I brought my wedding gown, accessories, makeup, hair spray, and suitcase of clothes and essentials for the honeymoon. My mom took candid snapshots. The big day had finally arrived.

After showering, I just couldn't get my long hair dry. Betty and I kept working on it and lost track of the time. Then, we heard Art bellowing through the bedroom door: "Let's go in there. We're going to be late."

"Art, we can't get my hair dry."

"Well, do something with it. We have to get going; it's 3:45. In case you've forgotten, you're supposed to get married in 15 minutes!" Wanting everything to be perfect, I waited until my hair was dry and styled the way I wanted. When Betty and I finally emerged at 3:55 p.m., Art shook his head and grumbled: "Man, are we going to be late. I sure hope traffic isn't bad."

"Art, how do we look?" I asked.

"Fine, move it on out to the car."

Meanwhile from their vantage point at the front doors of the chapel, Bob and the wedding party were anxiously watching the street for our arrival. All of the guests had arrived and been seated. The minister came to Bob and asked that the wedding party start to form the processional line. The minister motioned to the groomsmen to start pairing up with the bridesmaids. Suddenly, the minister stopped, grimaced, and asked, "Where's the bride?"

"Probably late getting ready or traffic problems," Bob answered. "She's coming with her brother and his wife."

Shaking his finger at Bob, the minister scolded, "I had asked that she arrive here not later than 30 minutes before the start of the ceremony."

"I know. I'm sorry. I'm sure they'll be here any minute," Bob said apologetically.

The minister pulled Bob to the side and stated in a dead-serious tone: "This isn't good, Bob. You might want to prepare yourself in case she's gotten cold feet. It happens more than you'd think."

Bob had a good laugh before he replied: "No, they're just running late. I appreciate your concern, but she's totally committed to our marriage."

"Well, sometimes the groom is the last to know," cautioned the minister.

"Believe me; she's as happy and as sure as can be. She really wants this."

The minister appeared unconvinced. At 4:05 p.m., he told Bob in private: "It's past the starting time for the ceremony. They might not be coming. People change their minds."

By 4:10 p.m., the guests in the chapel were looking at their watches and back at the rear doors, wondering about the delay. Some had noticed that my mom had not yet been seated. Now, even Bob's face showed concern. The minister, holding his bible in one hand and touching Bob's arm with the other, advised, "Bob, we need to start thinking of what to say to the congregation."

"I guess we can say they're running late, and we apologize for the delay."

"No, I mean we might have to consider ..."

Just then, one of the bridesmaids cried out, "I think I see her!"

Bob turned toward the street and saw Art's sea-foam-green Oldsmobile Cutlass pulling to the curb in front of the chapel. "Yes, it's them," Bob yelled excitedly.

Relieved, the minister looked up to the sky and called aloud, "Thank you, Lord!"

That evening at the reception, Bob related to me how the minister was concerned that I wasn't going to show for the wedding. Adding this to his odd behavior the night before, we began to wonder about him. The best man, who was seated with us at the head table, overheard our conversation and started to laugh uncontrollably. Bob, sensing something was up, turned to the best man and said in an accusatory tone, "Okay, Sockwell, what did you do?"

"When I went over early to check on the rehearsal, I saw the minister and just couldn't pass up the opportunity."

"What opportunity, Charlie?" Bob asked sternly.

"To tell him that Jan had told me in confidence that she had last minute misgivings about the marriage and didn't know if she could go through with it or not."

"Charlie, you didn't!" I exclaimed.

"Yes, but I didn't know you were going to be late for your own wedding," Charlie said with more laughter. "That really must have set the minister off."

Later, Bob took his new brother-in-law Art by the arm and remarked with joking irony: "Thanks for your services today—especially in getting my bride to the church on time. Your punctuality had a lot to do with the smoothness of the ceremony. You made this an afternoon I'll *never* forget."

Art threw up his hands and smiled as he jovially replied: "Hey, she couldn't get her hair dry. Welcome to married life. Get use to it!"

At the end of the evening, we said goodbye to our family and friends. They pelted us with rice, while we walked hand in hand to Bob's car. As we drove off on our honeymoon, I snuggled alongside Bob and thought how happy I was. We were finally husband and wife, and our wedding day was all I had hoped for. Bob was the man of my dreams. I was pregnant with our child and looked forward to our married life. Being married added an exclamation mark to our love, and we were ready to take on the world.

Chapter 5

Marriage and Beyond

Returning from the honeymoon, my first challenge was turning Bob's apartment into our home. The only furnishings we owned were a mattress with bed frame, a small chest of drawers, a dinette set, a couple of lamps, and a bookcase. For entertainment, we had a TV, a stereo with FM radio, and Bob's collection of books and records.

Relatives helped by offering some of their old furniture. We were given a sofa, an easy chair, coffee and end tables, lamps, a triple dresser, and a desk with chair. Fortunately, we had received pots, pans, dinnerware, silverware, linens, and other essentials for wedding presents. I made some curtains and hung a few pictures. Things started to look better.

In the spring of 1969, my sister-in-law Betty threw a baby shower for me. The gifts were a much-needed blessing. Family and friends also gave us used baby items like clothes, toys, and a crib. The kindness and generosity shown to Bob and me during those difficult financial times will *never* be forgotten.

With Bob making $17.50 a day as a substitute teacher and me earning only $2.00 an hour in retail sales, I had to plan our household budget to the penny. Our rent was $100 a month plus utilities. In 1969, gasoline was 35 cents a gallon. Bread cost 29 cents a loaf; eggs were priced at 59 cents a dozen, and milk was $1.10 a gallon. In spite of the low cost of living, we struggled to make ends meet each and every month. Our budget became even tighter when I quit my job several weeks before my due date.

Then in June 1969, we were blessed with the birth of our beautiful daughter, Caren. Our schedules became busier with the added responsibilities of parenthood, but we didn't mind. Our baby was a precious addition to our lives; the contentment we felt overshadowed our sacrifices. We had become a family.

When school ended for the summer, Bob took a position as pool manager and swimming team coach at a club in Bethesda, Maryland. I stayed at home with Caren and applied for a teaching position for the coming school year. On television in the evening, Bob and I laughed along with classic comedy reruns like "The Honeymooners" and "I Love Lucy."

Like most everyone else on Earth that summer, we witnessed one of mankind's greatest technological achievements—the historic lunar landing. On July 20, 1969, the lunar module Eagle separated from the orbiting Apollo 11 command module Columbia. Astronaut Neil Armstrong piloted the lunar module toward the surface of the Moon with Astronaut Edwin "Buzz" Aldrin calling out altitude and velocity data. We were in awe when Armstrong radioed: "Houston, Tranquility Base here. The Eagle has landed."

Later that evening, Armstrong descended from the lunar module and spoke some of the most famous words in history, "That's one small step for man, one giant leap for mankind." It was almost unbelievable. From Bob's vintage, vacuum-tube TV set, we watched "live" video transmissions from the Moon. With hope for our future, Bob turned to me and said, "If we can land men on the Moon, we can solve the problems of Earth."

In September, I started teaching second grade at St. Jerome School in Hyattsville, Maryland. I discovered that I enjoyed teaching and truly wanted a career in early childhood education. Bob continued to substitute teach by day and to take college courses by night. Although we had little money, we lived on love, while we worked for our future. It was wonderful to be married and to have a child. We made sacrifices for our daughter and each other, and that added to our maturity.

On the national scene, the Vietnam War continued to divide and define our nation. It was an ever-growing cancer on our national character—no matter which side you were on. At about the time Bob and I were celebrating our first wedding anniversary (November 1969), we were shocked to hear of an atrocity that had occurred in Vietnam the previous year. It was reported that over 300 unarmed civilians (mostly women, children, and the elderly) were gunned down by American soldiers in the Vietnamese village of My Lai. Bob and I wondered how Americans could do this.

Then on April 30, 1970, President Nixon announced on television that U.S. combat forces were invading Cambodia to attack Viet Cong sanctuaries. This was seen by anti-war groups as a widening of the conflict. A national student-faculty strike was called. Protests erupted on college campuses across America.

Even the University of Maryland (UM) saw disruptive demonstrations. Anti-war protestors rallied on the mall and marched to the armory, which housed the UM offices of the Reserve Officers' Training Corps (ROTC). After causing havoc in the armory, militant demonstrators descended on nearby U.S. Route 1, closing it down to traffic. Maryland State Police used tear gas to clear the thoroughfare. Eventually, the Maryland National Guard was called up to quell the continuing violence, which had forced the university to close.

Bob liberally interpreted and supported the constitutional rights of freedom of assembly and speech, but drew the line at violent acts. He feared that the fury of the civil rights unrest of the 60s was spreading to the anti-war movement. "Let them demonstrate as much as they wish," Bob said. "But don't infringe on my right to attend classes. They're using violence to shut things down. I'm all for political change, but they're trying to start a revolution."

Tragically, student protests turned deadly at two college campuses. On May 4, 1970, nine students were injured and four were killed when Ohio National Guard troops opened fire on demonstrators at Kent State University in Kent, Ohio. Two students were killed and nine were injured on May 15, 1970, when police shot up a residence hall at Jackson State University in Jackson, Mississippi.

The University of Maryland reopened; Bob spoke out in student forums against the recent violence. He suggested petitions, marches, voter registration, working in political campaigns, lobbying, and other peaceful activity. There were other issues at stake at the university besides the Vietnam War. Bob saw a new wave of student and faculty leaders come to power; some put national issues over everyday student and faculty concerns.

Later that May, Bob received a strange call at our apartment. A man identifying himself as "Mr. Lydecker" said he wanted to meet with Bob regarding a business proposal. Mr. Lydecker wouldn't discuss details over the phone but assured Bob the opportunity would be "right down your alley and good money." Curious, Bob agreed to meet Lydecker at the fraternity house.

Lydecker arrived for the appointment attired in a tailored business suit. He carried an expensive leather briefcase, the type that was secured with straps and brass buckles. He was slim and of medium height. By the appearance of Mr. Lydecker's facial features and graying, curly hair, Bob thought Lydecker to be in his mid-40s.

Mr. Lydecker leaned toward Bob and asked, "Is there a place we can talk in private?"

"Sure, we can use the library." Bob escorted Lydecker to the fraternity's library and closed the door behind them. Bob and Mr. Lydecker sat down at the end of a long conference table.

Looking around the room for a moment, Lydecker commented, "You have a nice collection of law books here."

"Yes," Bob agreed, "former Supreme Court Justice Tom Clark gave them to us. He was a Delt at the University of Texas. He comes out here from time-to-time. His son, Ramsey, was Attorney General in Johnson's administration."

"Tom Clark is a good American. I know Ramsey all too well. Too bad he wasn't more like his dad," Lydecker replied with a grimace.

"Mr. Lydecker, what can I do for you?"

"Bob, I was told you're someone who loves America—that you stand up for your country and what we're doing in Southeast Asia. I represent some patriotic Americans who are troubled by what's been happening at our colleges and universities.

"We'd like you to organize a major event—something that would show large-scale student support for the war. You could schedule it for the fall and work on it over the summer. With the proximity of the university to Washington, a well-planned event could garner major media coverage. We might even be able to get Vice President Agnew to attend.

"Whatever you need in expenses I can get. All you have to do is come up with a plan and carry it out. Of course, we'll have money in there for you. We'll make it worth your while."

"For whom would I be working?"

"Bob, the folks backing this are philanthropists and patriots. They wish to remain anonymous. I would be your contact for this enterprise."

Bob thought for a moment before relating: "I don't know. I already have a full-time job lined up for the summer. And to be honest with you, while I support our armed forces and a violence-free campus, I don't support our Vietnam policy."

A surprised look came over Lydecker. "Why not?" he asked.

"We became involved with the vestiges of colonialism and guerrilla warfare. It's not in our strategic interest to embroil ourselves in foreign wars of nationalism or religious extremism. Since John Foster Dulles and the Eisenhower administration, we have mistakenly made Vietnam a domino in the Cold War. Too many people in South Vietnam don't support the government in Saigon nor the religion of its leaders. We can't win these types of conflicts. We need to learn not to walk into quicksand."

When Bob arrived back at the apartment, he told me about the meeting with Lydecker. "So you turned him down?" I asked.

"Yes, he wanted me to think about it for a few days. When I asked for a number to contact him, he said he'd contact me. That's when I told him I wasn't interested. He was a little too secretive. I didn't like the idea of taking money from unknown sources. I don't have the time anyway."

In January of 1971, Bob received his Bachelor of Arts degree from the University of Maryland. At graduation, an assistant dean sought Bob out to congratulate him. The dean remarked that Bob had earned more credit hours than anyone at the university could remember! This was due to Bob switching majors and taking as many electives as possible. Also, a professor of Bob's offered him a slot in a Ph.D. program. Bob declined graduate school. He was honored by the offer but wanted to get me back to college. We needed to finish the other half of the graduation promise we made to our parents.

Now that Bob had his degree, he would find a better paying job than substitute teaching and one with health benefits. This would enable me to quit my job at St. Jerome. I could return to the University of Maryland full time and attain my degree.

Bob accepted a position as an administrative assistant with the Prince George's County Council. Working with the chairman of the council and the council's attorney gained Bob some good legal experience. Bob became a favorite of the council and particularly Councilman Sam Bogley, who was an attorney. Sam wanted Bob on his staff. He offered to help Bob into law school and to arrange for Bob to clerk for a prominent judge. Bob respectfully turned down the gracious offer as well as a position with Councilwoman Gladys Noon Spellman. In later years, Sam Bogley would become the Lieutenant Governor of Maryland and Gladys Spellman would be elected to the U.S. House of Representatives.

Bob enjoyed his work for the council but wanted the excitement and satisfaction of law enforcement. Everyone was recommending that Bob go into law rather than law enforcement. In spite of this, he applied for a police officer position with the United States Park Police (USPP).

While waiting for that job to open, Bob transferred from the council to the county's housing code office. Although it was a step backwards in prestige and pay, Bob saw code enforcement as a good introduction to law enforcement. As an inspector, Bob investigated complaints and issued violations for unsafe conditions in homes and apartments.

He also represented the county in front of the appeals board and was placed in charge of a special project. Traveling throughout the Bowie, Maryland area, Bob ordered dilapidated, unsafe buildings to be demolished. He gained experience in title searches and other legal matters. After the project, the town of Bowie commended Bob.

Several retired Washington Metropolitan Police Department (MPD) officers worked in the housing division. Bob became especially friendly with Clyde Shippe and Harold Burwell. Both had been experienced detectives, and Bob loved to hear them talk about investigation, police work, and their remarkable careers.

The first time we met Clyde and his wife for dinner, Clyde showed Bob where to sit in a restaurant—never with his back to the door. Clyde would tell Bob lessons learned from his MPD career. Clyde would let out a hearty laugh and end his tips with, "You won't learn that in rookie school."

On another occasion, we stopped by Harold Burwell's residence. Harold liked to impart his wisdom in the form of animated anecdotes. He reached into his pocket and dropped nine pea-size, metal balls on the brass top of his coffee table. I thought they were ball bearings. They made a thud when they hit and then noisily rolled around the tabletop with several falling onto the floor.

Harold had gotten our attention. Gazing at us with dark, piercing eyes, he began, "Whenever I heard that someone was threatening to do me harm— because I was investigating them or an accomplice—I'd go looking for them.

"When I found them, I'd step out of the car with my riot gun like this." Harold held his arms to his chest as if he was cradling a shotgun. "I'd walk up nice and close. I'd keep my right hand on the gun and reach into my left pocket and pull out that double-ought buckshot. I'd roll them around in my hand a bit." Harold flexed his huge left hand in front of us. "Then I'd tell them the word on the street was they were out to get me. I'd ask if this was true. If it was, I was loaded for bear, and we could settle this now. If not, they could come down to headquarters with me, and we could talk."

On another occasion, Harold told Bob: "The quickest way to close cases is to get the suspect off the street and get them talking. Use psychology and establish a relationship. After you recite the Miranda warning, get them talking and keep them talking. Don't give them time to think or to develop a story. Convince them it's in their best interest to tell what they know—now. If they lie to you, be firm and let them know that isn't going to help them. Keep at them as long as you can until you get the truth. You're giving them a chance to clear their conscience and make things right."

Then, Harold playfully threw a right jab at Bob and continued, "I never used the rough stuff." Harold, tapping a finger to the side of Bob's head, added, "You can do better mind against mind.

"And try not to make them think they need an attorney. Once they ask for an attorney, you have to stop the questioning, and you missed your opportunity for a confession."

U.S. Park Police called Bob in for an interview. They offered him a spot in the next police school—contingent on a clear background investigation and medical examination. Bob filled out the security forms and mailed them back. He made an appointment for his physical at the D.C. Police and Fire Clinic located at the Washington Hospital Center.

Bob wanted to become a Park Police officer, as they had an excellent reputation and were a federal force. Once on board, it would be easier for Bob to transfer within the federal government, and the USPP time would count toward his total federal service.

Bob probably could have been hired as a U.S. Treasury law enforcement agent with his academic record, Prince George's County experience, and stellar background. Yet, he first wanted the training and experience of police work. He believed this would make him a better agent and person in the long run.

Park Police had jurisdiction throughout D.C. like Metropolitan Police officers and primary jurisdiction on federal lands administered by the National Park Service. This included commuter parkways, urban and rural parks, as well as our national monuments and memorials. Bob would become experienced in all aspects of police work—patrol, investigation, security, and protection.

At this point, Bob wanted to spend a couple of years in USPP and then transfer over to the U.S. Secret Service as a special agent. Bob was eliminating the Federal Bureau of Investigation (FBI) as a future possibility. The FBI required a degree in law or accounting, and we couldn't afford to send Bob to law school now. I still had another full year of college for my bachelor's degree.

The scheduled date for the Park Police physical arrived. Bob took the day off from his housing inspector job and went in for the appointment. When I arrived home that afternoon from my classes at Maryland, one look at Bob's face told me something wasn't right. We exchanged a kiss, and I immediately asked what was wrong.

"I didn't pass."

"What, you're as healthy as an ox!"

"Yes, but the doctor thinks I have a cyst in my abdomen that could cause problems down the road. He's recommending exploratory surgery. It's elective surgery on my part, but he won't pass me until I have it done."

"So you have it done," I replied as cheerfully as I could.

"It's major surgery with weeks of recovery. By the time I have the procedure and recover, I'll have missed the upcoming police school."

"Bobbie, I know this is a setback, but you'll become a Park Police officer. It's just going to take some more time and effort."

Several days later, Bob received a call from the Park Police personnel office. Bob had passed the background investigation, but his failed physical had been reported. The personnel officer seemed surprised when Bob said he was planning to undergo the elective surgery. No one had ever submitted to major surgery in order to become a Park Police officer. The personnel officer wished Bob good luck and told him to call back after the operation.

Bob's surgery was scheduled for the morning of May 15, 1972. We arrived early to fill out the paperwork. Bob was taken to a hospital room where he put on a gown. He appeared nervous and uneasy; I thought Bob was concerned about the upcoming surgery. He kept looking out the window—as if he longed to be back outside.

"Don't worry," I said. "Everything is going to be fine."

"I'm not worried about the surgery. When I was five years old, I got a bad case of scarlet fever. I was rushed to the emergency room with a high temperature and almost died. I spent several weeks in the hospital; it was a terrifying experience."

"Wow, the mortality rate was pretty high for scarlet fever back then," I remarked.

"Yeah, things were different in those days," Bob continued. "Antibiotics weren't as good. I was kept in a straightjacket tied to the rungs of the hospital bed's headboard. They told my parents it was a preventive measure, so I couldn't get out of bed.

"My arms were sore from the blood they were taking all the time. My mom and dad could only see me for about 15 minutes a day. They made my parents burn my baseball and football card collection and other stuff that couldn't be disinfected. Since then, I've never been hospitalized. Being a patient again is bringing back some bad childhood memories."

"You'll be fine. Think good thoughts."

"The only good thing to come out of that nightmare was an interest in science and technology. Doctor Salk was an inspiration."

"The Doctor who developed the polio vaccine?"

"Yes, he was one of the physicians who attended me. He was in the Philadelphia area doing research, and my parents permitted him to use my blood."

"So that's why you thought about being a research scientist."

"Yeah, or fly around all the time solving mysteries like Sky King," Bob said with a laugh.

"You wouldn't have been happy being a scientist. You need adventure."

I hugged Bob and told him I loved him. As they wheeled him away to the operating room, I thought about Bob's close call as a child. I thanked God for keeping Bob safe then and asked that he continue to watch over Bob.

Turning on the television in Bob's hospital room, I watched soap operas to pass the hours. That afternoon, Bob was brought back to the room after recovery. I could see that he was in a great deal of pain. Later, the doctor stopped by and notified us that the operation was successful. The doctor wanted to prescribe some narcotic painkillers for Bob, but he refused them. The Doctor thought Bob would change his mind in a couple of hours—when the anesthetic wore off. The physician left a prescription, but Bob never did use it. He took only nonnarcotic pain medications.

We watched some TV, and I hoped it would help get Bob's mind off the pain. Suddenly, the show we were watching was interrupted for a special news report. Alabama Governor and presidential candidate George C. Wallace had been shot at an outdoor campaign rally in Laurel, Maryland—about 20 miles east of the hospital. Wallace had been in Maryland for some last minute campaigning for the Democratic presidential primary, which was scheduled for the following day. A Secret Service agent, an Alabama state trooper, and a bystander were also wounded.

After finishing his speech, Governor Wallace left the stage to shake hands with the crowd. Wallace was working his way along a rope line—flanked by Secret Service agents. Out of nowhere, a male subject, wearing dark glasses, pointed a handgun at Wallace and emptied it before the assailant could be subdued. The shooter looked to be a supporter of Wallace. He had short hair and was wearing a patriotic red, white, and blue shirt adorned with a Wallace button.

"We've been to that shopping center!" Bob exclaimed. "It looks like they set up a stage in the parking lot."

"Yes, we've been there a couple of times," I agreed. "Wow, isn't that something."

Bob quickly assessed in his mind what we had just seen and commented: "It looks bad for Wallace. He went down and didn't move. There's blood coming down his arm and a big bloodstain on his shirt. The agents didn't stand a chance. It happened too fast."

More information was disclosed throughout the evening. Governor Wallace had been taken to Holy Cross Hospital in Silver Spring, Maryland. We were about 10 minutes away at the Washington Hospital Center.

It was getting late and time for me to go home for the night. As I was leaving, I reminded Bob that he had just had major surgery and that he needed rest. He shook his head in acknowledgement but continued to follow the coverage of the assassination attempt—especially the video of the shooting.

When I arrived back at the hospital the following morning, the Wallace assassination attempt was still the top news story. The shooter was identified as Arthur Herman Bremer, a 21-year-old unemployed janitor from Milwaukee, Wisconsin. Governor Wallace survived but was paralyzed below the waist. A .38-caliber bullet had severed his spinal cord. The other three persons hit were expected to recover.

Bob looked at me and excitedly said: "I've been studying the news footage. The agents did everything humanly possible. No one could have reacted any faster. The answer is in the crowd."

"In the crowd?" I echoed back to Bob.

"Yes, they need agents on the other side of the rope line. They could parallel the person they're protecting. They would have a chance of spotting and stopping a potential assassin."

"Bobbie, it was a big crowd. How could you move within it?"

"You only need to cover the first couple of rows. The crowd is worried about pressing forward to shake hands. One should be able to slide across the grain of the crowd. I think it would work."

In another one of those coincidences of life, my brother Art had left Prince George's County Police in 1970 to join the Secret Service. Art was a special agent in the USSS Special Investigations and Security Division (SI&SD). With that in mind, I suggested to Bob, "Maybe you should talk to Art."

"I'd better wait. I need to get Park Police under my belt and get into the Secret Service. Then, I'll have the additional knowledge, experience, and credentials to be able to refine something like this and present it in a way that's not presumptuous. Besides, I've got until 1980," Bob said with a smile.

"Why until 1980?" I asked.

Bob answered with just two words, *"Tecumseh's Curse."*

"Tecumseh's Curse—what's that?" I asked with healthy curiosity.

"Honey, sit down and make yourself comfortable. I'll tell you the tale of Tecumseh's Curse."

Chapter 6

Tecumseh's Curse

Eagerly, I slid the hospital room chair next to Bob's bed and dropped into the seat. I was intrigued about Tecumseh's Curse.

With a twinkle in his eye, Bob began: "As a child, I was fascinated by history—especially American history. I read everything I could and enjoyed visiting historic places. The lives of historic figures appealed to me, and I was especially attracted to the 'what ifs' of history."

"The 'what ifs,' " I expressed with a little frustration.

"What if Lincoln wouldn't have gone to Ford's Theater? What if Stonewall Jackson hadn't been mistakenly shot by his own troops? What if Archduke Ferdinand *hadn't been* assassinated? What if Hitler *had been* assassinated in 1939?"

"Yes, but Lincoln did go to the theater," I remarked with the impatience of someone who had just battled rush hour traffic.

"That's why I studied historical events in a scientific approach. What could have been done to prevent an event or to cause a different outcome. Our recorded past is *not* an assortment of random events. There's cause and effect. History lives and continues as we speak. What happens next is rooted in everything that has come before us. What we did last year, last month, yesterday, and today can determine what will happen tomorrow."

"Bobbie, you should go back to Maryland and get a Ph.D. You have a gift for this type of stuff."

"Yes, but it's drawn me to the action side of the equation and to law enforcement—especially assassination and the Secret Service. It first began when I watched some shows as a kid. There was a film called *The Tall Target*—about an assassination plot against Lincoln—when he was traveling to Washington for his 1861 inauguration. Lincoln was secretly routed through Baltimore at night to prevent an attack by Southern sympathizers. It appealed to my sense of action and adventure. The other was a TV show about Tecumseh's Curse. It presented a challenge that intrigued me."

"Bobbie, tell me about Tecumseh's Curse!"

"Okay, honey, it stems from folklore. In 1808, Shawnee Chief Tecumseh and his brother, The Prophet, founded an Indian settlement at Tippecanoe in the Indiana Territory. Tecumseh wanted to unite the Indian people to fight the westward expansion of white settlers. Tippecanoe was the capital of their tribal confederation.

"In 1811, Tecumseh was in the South recruiting warriors when the governor of the territory, William Henry Harrison, decided to act. He raised an army and marched to Tippecanoe with the intent of settling the matter by treaty or force. Harrison's men camped outside the Indian village upon word from The Prophet that he wished a meeting. Tecumseh had warned his brother not to engage the white man until the Indian alliance could be strengthened.

"In spite of Tecumseh's warning, his brother led a surprise attack on Harrison's campsite the following morning. Casualties were heavy on both sides, and the Indians finally withdrew. The Prophet was disgraced, and he eventually fled to the Northwest Territory as the other tribes scattered. The next day, Harrison entered the deserted settlement and burned it to the ground.

"Chief Tecumseh returned to find his capital in ashes and his dreams of an Indian nation shattered. Upon this tragic fate, legend has it that Tecumseh called on the gods to curse Governor Harrison and his people. The gods answered Tecumseh with prophecy. Harrison would one day become the Great White Chief, but he would die soon after. Each Great White Chief chosen every 20 years after Harrison would also die in office. This would be punishment for the white nation and serve as a reminder of the sorrow of the Indian people.

"Tecumseh and his followers would fight for the British in the War of 1812. Harrison was given command of the U.S. Army in the Northwest. Tecumseh was killed in battle in 1813 by troops led by General Harrison.

"After the war, Harrison returned to public life in Ohio and served in the U.S. House of Representatives and the U.S. Senate. In 1840, he successfully ran for the presidency on the campaign slogan, 'Tippecanoe and Tyler, Too.' He gave a long inaugural address on a cold, blustery day, and it rained as he rode on horseback in his inaugural parade. Newly elected President Harrison caught a cold that turned into pneumonia. He died about a month later. Harrison was the *first* president to die in office. Tecumseh's Curse had begun."

"That's eerie," I remarked.

"Yes—and the curse continued. Twenty years later, Abraham Lincoln was elected president, and the Civil War erupted—pitting North against South. Lincoln was reelected in 1864. Just five days after Lee's surrender at Appomattox Court House, President Lincoln was assassinated at Ford's Theater by John Wilkes Booth on April 14, 1865. Booth had originally planned to kidnap Lincoln to aid the Confederacy. After the downfall of the South, Booth became more embittered and sought revenge. He might also have held an irrational hope that the assassination of the president and others might rekindle the war. President Lincoln was the *first* president to be assassinated.

"Next in 1880, James Garfield—the last president to be born in a log cabin—was elected. Less than four months after taking office, President Garfield was shot in a Washington train station by Charles J. Guiteau. Garfield died of his wounds a couple of months later.

"Guiteau was a religious fanatic, who was turned down for a consular position. He believed that God told him to kill President Garfield. Garfield was the *second* president to be assassinated.

"In 1900, President William McKinley was reelected to a second term. His first term was notable for U.S. intervention in Cuba and the Spanish-American War. McKinley's imperialistic sentiments led to the annexation of the Philippines, Guam, and Puerto Rico.

"In 1901, President McKinley visited the Pan-American Exposition in Buffalo, New York. Leon Czolgosz, a fanatical anarchist from the Midwest, traveled to Buffalo to assassinate the president. McKinley stood in a receiving line, greeting the public and shaking hands with them. Czolgosz wrapped a handkerchief over his right hand to conceal a revolver—as if his hand was injured. Upon reaching the front of the line, he extended his left hand for the handshake. At the same time, he pressed his revolver hand into the president and fired two quick shots. McKinley died eight days later, becoming the *third* president to be assassinated."

"Bobbie, was it a Tecumseh handker*chief*?"

"That's cute, Jan—really cute. Continuing with the curse, Warren G. Harding was elected to the presidency in 1920. He was leading the U.S. in its recovery from World War I. In 1923, Harding was advised that some of his appointees were using their government positions for personal gain. On the eve of the corruption scandals, Harding left Washington to take a trip out West. During his visit to San Francisco, Harding died suddenly of a heart attack.

"Next, President Franklin D. Roosevelt was reelected to an unprecedented third term in 1940. He had led the U.S. out of the Great Depression with his New Deal. He would lead the U.S. during the crucial years of World War II and again won reelection in 1944. President Roosevelt would continue in office until 1945 when he died of a cerebral hemorrhage.

"And in 1960, John F. Kennedy became the youngest *elected* president. He was also the youngest to die in office. JFK met his destiny in Dallas on November 22, 1963—your birthday."

"Yes, that's one birthday I'll never forget. It was a Friday. Everything was canceled. What a terrible time," I remarked.

Bob's face took on a sad yet determined look. "Let's hope our nation never has to go through that again—JFK, Martin Luther King, and RFK. It's too late to help them. Yet we can learn from those mistakes. History doesn't have to repeat itself. We can break Tecumseh's Curse."

"So, all presidents elected every 20 years since 1840 have died before completing their terms?" I asked incredulously.

"That's right. Starting in 1840 with William Henry Harrison, the hero of Tippecanoe, every president—elected or reelected in a year ending in zero—died in office. Of those seven presidents, four were assassinated."

"That's unbelievable," I said. "It also says something about our society. But Bobbie, you don't believe in curses—do you?"

"No, but I do believe in patterns of history. Patterns that show a sitting president is going to die about every 20 years—mostly by assassination. These assassinations can be studied for the purpose of prediction and prevention. Socio-scientific analysis can be made. The results can suggest successful strategies. We can't change the past, but we can change our *tomorrows*."

"Well, if anyone can figure it out, you can," I said in admiration. I believed that Bob could accomplish most anything—once he set his mind to the task.

Chapter 7

Into the Force

Bob spent another night in the hospital before being discharged. Since our wedding day, this had been the longest we'd been apart overnight. It was good to bring him home.

Bent over at the waist in pain, Bob had a hard time making it up the stairs to our apartment. It was emotionally difficult for me to see him in such distress. Even our neighbors commented that Bob appeared to be suffering.

During his recovery, Bob closely followed his Doctor's orders, which included daily exercises and walking. It was a painful regimen. Eventually the incision healed, and Bob could walk straight and tall again. He became stronger, while he worked his way back into shape.

The hard work paid off; Bob was subsequently released by the D.C. Police and Fire Clinic as fit for duty. The USPP scheduled Bob for the next police school. He was excited and looked forward to the future.

Bob had several fraternity brothers on the force. One of them, Dick Furbish, invited Bob to ride along on a midnight tour of duty. Dick was a graduate of the University of Maryland and also had aspirations of becoming a federal agent.

Bob arrived at the USPP Greenbelt Substation, while Dick was inspecting his assigned police car prior to patrol. Dick's beat was a stretch of the busy Baltimore-Washington Parkway. He was walking around the car, checking the running and emergency lights as Bob approached.

Motioning to the open rear door, Dick told Bob to jump in the back of the cruiser (patrol car). As soon as Bob was in the rear seat, Dick swiftly slammed the door shut. An impish grin came over Dick's face. Then, he began to laugh aloud. Bob realized that the interior door handles and window cranks had been removed. All police cars are set up that way, so subjects can't get out on their own.

Dick stuck his head through the open driver's window and called back to Bob, "I'm going to turn on the dome light and make you ride around in the back all night—like you're under arrest."

"You do, Furbish, and I'll scream police brutality."

"Quiet—or I'll slap the cuffs on you!"

A moment later, Dick, still displaying a mischievous grin, opened Bob's door. He shook Bob's hand and warmly congratulated him for his appointment to USPP. He directed Bob to move to the right-front seat.

The patrol car was a full-size Chevrolet sedan with a powerful 454-cubic-inch engine. It was painted in the light green that Park Police used. Bob observed the two-way radio, emergency light and siren controls, and the microphones for the radio and public address system. Lying on the front seat was a clipboard, portable radio, and a huge multi-cell flashlight.

Dick climbed in and pointed the cruiser out of the parking area. In a couple of minutes, they were on the ramp leading to the northbound lanes of the B-W Parkway. Dick put his foot down hard on the accelerator; the four-barrel carburetor responded with a deep *whoosh* as the cruiser sped into the night. Bob was pushed back into the seat, and a chill ran down his spine. This was the exhilaration of police work.

Dick made several traffic stops and imparted some good advice as to their safe handling. Making his points in a witty manner, Dick was a smart and savvy officer. They talked through the night about police work. Bob was an eager learner and firm believer that knowledge was the key to safety and success.

Suddenly, the dispatcher called Officer Furbish's patrol car number on the radio. Dick replied and was notified that an accident had been reported on his beat. Switching on the emergency lights and siren, he drove into the grass median separating the north and southbound lanes. The accident was in the opposite direction. Dick yelled for Bob to tighten his seat belt. After the opposing traffic had yielded, Dick headed the cruiser up the parkway at a high rate of speed. Cars slowed and pulled to the right as the police vehicle whizzed by

Arriving at the accident, they observed that a vehicle had run off the road into a ditch. Its headlights were still on and the driver's door was open. The operator was sitting sideways in the seat—with his head drooped over and his legs hanging out of the car. Dick pulled the cruiser off the parkway to the shoulder. He cautioned Bob to stay in the car and to touch nothing. Grabbing his flashlight and portable radio, Dick leaped out of the cruiser and ran to the scene.

Bob already knew the 10-code that police use; he was able to follow the radio traffic between Dick and the Park Police dispatcher. Dick reported that the subject appeared uninjured and was refusing any medical assistance. Suspecting the driver to be intoxicated, Dick requested a unit to transport the subject to the substation for a breathalyzer test. A unit replied that they were en route. Dick also asked for a tow truck to pull the car out of the ditch and to carry it to the impound lot. Then Bob heard another voice over the two-way radio. That unit was stating that it was responding to the scene also.

Immediately, Dick dashed over to the cruiser and yelled to Bob: "Get out of the car! Go stand over there." Dick pointed to an area well off the side of the roadway near the woods. "Don't say anything. I'll explain later."

Dick ran back to the intoxicated subject, while Bob headed to the tree line, which bordered the parkway. Soon, another Park Police cruiser arrived, and an officer with sergeant stripes on his sleeves exited the vehicle and walked over to the scene. He conversed with Officer Furbish for a moment, and then they helped the driver out of the vehicle. They attempted to administer a field sobriety test to the driver, but he couldn't stand.

Several minutes later, a "caged unit" arrived. This vehicle had a wire screen separating the rear seat area from the front. Dick placed the subject under arrest and advised him of his Miranda rights. The park policemen helped the subject to the transport unit. It was at this time that the sergeant first noticed Bob standing along the perimeter of the parkway. The sergeant pointed to Bob and asked Officer Furbish, "Was that guy in the car too?"

"No, he was hitchhiking on the parkway, and I was transporting him off when the call came in."

"Have you run him through WALES [Washington Area Law Enforcement System] and NCIC [National Crime Information Computer]?"

"No, he's a local, who's just trying to get home."

"Well, run him just to be sure—while we've got the transport unit here. He could be giving you a story."

The sergeant and Dick walked over to Bob. Dick said in a stern voice, "Let's see some ID."

Bob answered, "Yes, sir." He reached into his pocket, pulled out his wallet, and presented his driver's permit to Dick. The sergeant kept a watch on Bob, while Dick went over to his cruiser to name check Bob for wants and warrants.

Dick returned a short time later, telling the sergeant, "He's 10-74 [negative]."

"Give him a ticket for hitchhiking and escort him off the parkway on your way back to the substation." Then, the sergeant turned to Bob and warned: "If we see you out here again, you're going to be arrested. Understand?"

"Yes, sir." Bob replied.

The sergeant departed as the tow truck arrived. The vehicle was pulled up the embankment and towed off to the substation. Dick and Bob followed in the Park Police cruiser. Once they were underway, Bob looked at Dick and asked, "What was all that about with the sergeant?"

"My regular sergeant called in sick. That guy's from another district—just covering for tonight. My sergeant wouldn't care if you were riding along. The other sergeant has a reputation of being a 'hard ass.' I didn't want to take any chances."

Back at the substation, Dick dropped Bob off at his car. Bob thanked Dick for the first hand look at USPP and exited the patrol car. As Bob was unlocking his car door, Dick yelled, "Hey, you forgot something." Bob turned back toward Dick who declared, "I need to write you a ticket."

"What!"

"All right, I'll let you off with a warning. But the next time I see you on *my* parkway, you'd better be in uniform." Dick chuckled as he drove the cruiser off to the police parking area. A sense of satisfaction came over Bob. The day was near when he would proudly wear the Park Police uniform.

Chapter 8

USPP

The origins of the U.S. Park Police date back to 1867 when park watchmen were hired to provide security for the Washington Monument grounds. In 1880, a federal appropriations act granted the park watchmen police authority similar to that of the Washington Metropolitan Police Department. Congress passed permanent legislation authorizing police powers in 1882. Soon afterwards, the park watchmen became known as the United States Park Police. Congress made that designation official in 1919. By 1972, the USPP was a modern police force of over 400 sworn officers.

Prior to Bob's police school, the U.S. Park Police trained their officers in the USPP academy at Jones Point in Alexandria, Virginia. In 1970, it was decided to consolidate the training of all federal law enforcement personnel, except those of the Justice Department and the military. A Consolidated Federal Law Enforcement Training Center (CFLETC) was established as a bureau of the Treasury Department. It was located at 1310 L Street, NW, Washington, D.C.

The upside of Bob's surgery and delayed entry into the USPP was that by June of 1972, the CFLETC was ready to take on its first class of police trainees. Bob thought it fortunate that he would have the opportunity to attend the new school. It would be based on the latest concepts.

One evening, we were discussing Bob's coming transition from county housing inspector to federal police officer, while he browsed the newspaper. Suddenly, a story caught his eye. "Look at this; there was a burglary at the Watergate!"

"Really," I replied. The Watergate was a complex of buildings situated along the Potomac River in Northwest D.C. The complex consisted of condominiums, offices, and a hotel. One of Bob's fraternity brothers had bought a residential unit at the upscale development. We had attended a party there.

"Yeah, five guys were caught in the act by MPD."

"Gosh, that seemed to be a pretty safe place," I remarked.

Several weeks later, Bob and his fellow USPP recruits reported to Park Police Headquarters at 1100 Ohio Drive, SW, D.C., located in East Potomac Park. They were sworn in and welcomed to the force. Bob was finally on board and was looking forward to the coming training.

CFLETC Police School Number 1 consisted of U.S. Park Police, National Park Service rangers (law enforcement specialists), and Bureau of Indian Affairs Police. The 12-week course covered interviewing, arrest techniques, marksmanship, vehicle operation, searches, first aid, report writing, evidence, law, testifying in court, and crowd control.

Checking in at USPP Headquarters each day, the Park Police trainees were bused to the CFLETC. Being from outside the metropolitan area, the National Park Service (NPS) and Bureau of Indian Affairs (BIA) personnel were housed in a hotel near the school. Besides the CFLETC, the building at 1310 L Street also contained the Foreign Missions Branch of the Executive Protective Service (EPS) and the USSS Transportation Section.

Bob was impressed with the quality of instruction at the CFLETC. The police school was directed by Al Turner, who had been an agent with the Bureau of Alcohol, Tobacco, and Firearms (ATF). Al had a storied past and had helped to train the original sky marshals. With a hands-on approach, Al taught several of the courses and was always good for an anecdote or two. The pearls of wisdom Bob gleaned from Al and the other instructors were a nice supplement to the course material.

Each evening, Bob would come home and enthusiastically recap the training highlights of the day. I learned many things about law enforcement—some of which I could apply to everyday life. For example: never assume. Know what happens when you assume? You make an "ass" out of "u" and "me." Another less colorful but still useful piece of information was that every good report should answer the questions: who, what, when, where, why, and how. And there was the "Kiss" principle: Keep it simple stupid!

Although Bob learned much in the classroom, the practical exercises and role-play scenarios were always his favorites. The CFLETC used role-playing techniques for reality training. In these exercises, students were asked to behave as if the event was actually occurring. Settings were realistically created, and role players interacted with the trainees.

For the summer of 1972, the use of role play to simulate real-world situations and responses was fairly advanced for police training. The federal government spared no resources in creating a first-class police school that could serve as a model for state and local agencies. At times, experienced law enforcement personnel and even professional actors were utilized as role players. A clinical psychologist was an advisor on some of the exercises.

Several of the roll-play simulations elicited some heated responses from the trainees. On one occasion, Bob related with concern: "Today, we had a practical exercise with role players as demonstrators. It got out of hand for a couple of guys."

"Tell me more," I said enthusiastically.

"A ranger and a Park Police officer both lost it in a crowd control situation [demonstration]—especially the ranger. A role player cursed and taunted him. The ranger got all red in the face and attacked the role player. He had to be pulled off the guy."

"Gosh, do you think he just got caught up in the exercise or what?"

"He's very excitable, and his buttons were pushed. It's probably a good indication of what he would do in real life. Hopefully, he can work on it before then. Training isn't just learning new facts and procedures; it's learning about one's self too."

"And what are you learning about yourself?" I asked.

"Through training feedback and self-examination, I'm recognizing my strengths and weaknesses. That's a good basis to use for personal improvement—to become a better officer and person."

The weeks flew by. Bob immersed himself into the training, and he willingly studied and analyzed every topic. Having an aptitude for law enforcement, Bob did well in the classroom and practical exercises.

Marksmanship and driving were two of Bob's favorite subjects. The CFLETC utilized the U.S. Secret Service training facility at Beltsville, Maryland for firearms instruction. To reach it, the trainees were bused out New York Avenue to the Baltimore-Washington Parkway. After exiting at Powder Mill Road, a short drive led to the gate and entry road of the USSS Training Center. Nestled in the woods was a modern concrete building that contained classrooms, indoor pistol ranges, offices, and gunsmith shops. Nearby were outdoor pistol and rifle ranges and "Main Street, U.S.A."—a small town mock-up used for USSS motorcade and presidential protection training.

After a day of classroom training on firearm marksmanship and safety, the recruits were ready for one of the two indoor pistol ranges. Each 25-yard range, located in the basement of the main building, contained 12 firing positions and featured automated target carriers, variable lighting, and dual timers. All shooting stations had foldaway benches and barricades. The Secret Service ranges were state of the art, and the range instructors, selected from the Executive Protective Service, were top-notch.

The first order of business, following a review of range safety, was dry firing exercises. In these, an unloaded revolver is pointed down range. After cocking the hammer with the thumb (single-action shooting), the shooter aims at the target and squeezes the trigger so that the falling hammer does not disturb sight alignment. The shooter should not know the exact moment the gun will fire. If one does, then the subconscious mind will brace the body against the anticipated recoil. This produces a "flinch" with corresponding loss in accuracy.

After being checked out on dry firing, the trainees advanced to live-fire training. First up was the Standard Qualification Course (SQC), which is fired in single action. To emphasize correct sight alignment, bull's-eye targets are used. Analysis of the target can be a good diagnostic tool. For example: If the student hits in the top left or top right quadrant of the target, it's usually due to anticipating the shot and flinching.

For range guns, the Secret Service used Smith & Wesson Combat Masterpieces (Model 15)—.38 Special revolvers with four-inch barrels and adjustable sites. The SQC is a 30-shot course with each target placed at 50 feet for the three stages. The first sequence, slow fire, consists of 10 shots on one target in five minutes. For timed fire, the shooter fires 10 shots on one target in two 20-second strings of five shots each. During rapid fire, the shooter fires 10 shots on the final target in two 10-second strings of five shots each.

Since the six-shot Combat Masterpiece needed to be loaded with only five rounds for each stage of the SQC, the trainees learned that a Smith & Wesson cylinder rotates counterclockwise as viewed from the rear (loading end). This is opposite of Colt revolvers, which rotate clockwise. To load either make for five shots, one just has to leave an empty cylinder chamber under the hammer. But if you were in a police situation with only one round of ammunition left, it might save your life to know how to load that last round, so it rotates under the hammer for firing.

After a couple of days on the SQC and everyone qualifying, the trainees were introduced to double-action combat shooting via the Practical Pistol Course (PPC). In double-action shooting, the hammer is not manually cocked as in single action. The trigger is pulled through the entire range of motion for firing double action.

For the PPC, the class moved to the outdoor pistol range. Being a combat course, a man-size silhouette target is used. The course totals 60 rounds, which are shot at four different distances: 7, 15, 25, and 50 yards. Twelve rounds are shot at both the seven and 15-yard stages. Eighteen rounds are shot at the 25 and 50-yard stages.

In the PPC, trainees are required to shoot some segments with their non-dominant hand. They must also reload from a bullet pouch and pants pocket, and shoot from barricade positions. After several days of practice, Bob was shooting an expert rating in the course.

To celebrate his success, Bob purchased a Smith & Wesson Chiefs Special (Model 36). It was a .38 Special five-shot revolver with a two-inch barrel. Bob planned to use it as an off-duty weapon. Being lighter and smaller than the Park Police duty handgun, the Chiefs Special would be more readily concealable. Bob also used the Chiefs Special to practice at home. He taped a small bull's-eye target to our dresser mirror and dry fired for about 20 minutes each evening. After one session, Bob looked at me and joked, "The guy in the mirror is always as fast as I am."

Bob let me try some dry firing on one occasion. After briefing me on safety, he demonstrated proper stance, and showed me how to grip the gun. I raised the gun and pointed it toward the target, while Bob advised:

"The two most important things to remember are sight alignment and trigger control. Center the front sight blade, so it's level with the top of the rear sight and directly in the middle of the rear sight notch. While maintaining that sight picture—with the trigger finger only—apply straight to the rear, constantly increasing pressure to the trigger until the hammer drops. Don't *jerk* the trigger; let it be a surprise."

I tried, but I would yank the trigger, and the gun would lurch in every direction except where originally aimed. Bob continued to work with me as my arm wobbled, and the gun continued to move on firing. After 10 minutes of this, I eagerly but naively asked Bob: "What do you think? Will I be able to protect myself when you're off working nights?"

Bob looked at me, shook his head, and sighed, "Only if I get you a shotgun!"

CFLETC driving instruction was conducted at an old airfield on federal land at the Agricultural Research Center in Beltsville, Maryland (near the USSS Training Center). Next to the strip, a trailer had been set up as a classroom. Training was conducted in defensive and high speed driving. Who wouldn't enjoy racing a powerful police cruiser around a closed track? Several of the students got carried away and consistently plowed through the traffic cones that marked the course—drawing the ire of the instructors who had to reset them.

In those days, vehicles didn't have anti-lock brakes and traction control. It was impossible to hit the brakes hard without locking up the wheels. When the wheels of a vehicle stop rolling, the tires lose friction with the road, and a skid can ensue—especially in a turn. Turning the steering wheel will have no affect on the direction of the vehicle.

Bob learned to stay off the brake pedal as much as possible. When he had to brake, he used the technique of "stab braking." This consisted of rapidly pumping the brakes on and off. While the brakes are depressed, the vehicle will slow. When the brakes are released, the wheels will roll again. During the periods of rolling friction, the operator can regain steering control.

With their big engines, the police cruisers were heavy in the front end. Their rear wheels could spin upon acceleration and lose grip with the road. They were tough machines to master in high-speed turns, and the trainees learned things like coefficients of friction, oversteering, understeering, and countersteering.

At the time of Bob's police school, we still lived in Riverdale, Maryland. One Saturday, Bob took me to the old Engineering and Research Corporation (ERCO) factory and airstrip located on the northeast side of town. The ERCO complex was built in the late 1930s.

From 1937–1947, ERCO developed and manufactured a small civilian aircraft named the Ercoupe. It was innovative for its time and featured a design that was spin-proof and easy to fly. During World War II, ERCO produced gun turrets for U.S. bombers.

By 1972, the main factory had long been closed. Only a few sections of the complex showed any activity, being leased by local businesses. The airstrip was still in decent condition, and Bob used it to show me some of the things that he learned during the driving course.

After awhile, I got behind the wheel, and Bob instructed me in skid control. I got Bob's car up to a good speed and purposely tried to skid during some turns. Bob wanted me to get the feel of recovering from a skid. He cautioned, "If caught in a skid, get off the gas; stay off the brakes and quickly turn the steering wheel in the direction you want to go." I also learned that I might have to turn the wheel back (countersteer) to prevent skidding in the opposite direction.

We worked on it, but I spun out several times and even ran off the paved surface in one of those instances. It was eye opening to see the limitations of both car and driver (me). During my runs, a man and his son were in a nearby field flying a model airplane. I know it must have been a peculiar sight: a young blonde running the wheels off a 1969 Plymouth Valiant four-door sedan. Each time I spun out, the man would look over and shake his head. Bob finally yelled out the window, "I'm teaching her some driving techniques."

The man bellowed back, "Maybe you ought to hire a professional!"

Bob dropped his head, turned to me sheepishly, and said: "I think that's enough for today. Let's go back to the main building and park. It's better to prevent the situation anyway. Drive the speed limit. Reduce your speed in wet and icy conditions. Remember what you and your car can and cannot do."

It was pretty good advice, as my car couldn't do much anyway. It was an old British import—a 1959 Morris Minor 1000. Its four-cylinder engine put out 37 horsepower—only 13 more than my then tender age of 24!

We had brought a picnic lunch with us, so we found a nice spot to lay out a blanket. After lunch, we walked around the outside of the old factory and poked our heads through broken windows and wherever we could. The now quiet assembly line sections of the factory stood like old soldiers at ease. It was fun to imagine what the plant was like in days gone by, especially during the bustle of wartime production.

Bob and I enjoyed historical sites; we had visited many throughout the Middle-Atlantic states. Bob's passion for American history imbued me with a new interest in our national heritage. It was a pleasurable way to spend our leisure time, and we always learned a thing or two. Plus, it was affordable for a young married couple on a tight budget.

For the past 18 months, we had lived on Bob's salary alone because I returned to college full time. Once again, Bob was starting a new job at a low salary. The Park Police, Capitol Police, Executive Protective Service, and Washington Metropolitan Police were all on the same pay scale. As the positions only required a high school diploma—though many officers had

military experience, other creditable experience, and college degrees—
Congress set a low entry salary. There wasn't much left for take home pay
after deductions for health insurance, retirement, tax withholding, etc. Out
of necessity, I frugally watched the expenses for our family of three.

Graduation day arrived for the CFLETC Police School, and it was time for
the Park Police officers to move onto their specialized training. Bob said
goodbye to the rangers and BIA officers, who were returning to duty
assignments across the country.

Bob particularly held the BIA Police in high esteem. Underneath their
dark features and rugged, chiseled looks, Bob discovered noble hearts and
spirited minds. Projecting strength and courage, these proud American
Indians were responsible for law enforcement and public safety on vast
reservations. It was not uncommon for their patrol beats to encompass
hundreds of square miles. Patrolling most often alone, backup officers
could be many miles away, if available at all. Bob would miss their
inspiration and earthy philosophy.

The first half of the six-week Park Police specialized course covered USPP
operations and procedures. In the classroom, Bob and the other Park
Police rookies also studied the U.S. Criminal Code, D.C. law, and the laws
of Virginia and Maryland.

Federal parks and parkways in the national capital region exhibited
concurrent jurisdiction. This meant that violators could be charged with
U.S. or D.C. violations in the District, and U.S. or state violations in
Virginia and Maryland. Officers might have to testify in a variety of
different courts. There was much to learn.

In the evenings of late August and early September, Bob took breaks from
his studies to watch the 1972 Munich Summer Olympics with me. We were
amazed by the seven-gold-medal performance of U.S.A. swimmer Mark
Spitz.

Then, on September 5, 1972, eight heavily armed Palestinian terrorists
(members of Black September) infiltrated the Olympic Village. Two
members of the Israeli Olympic Team were killed outright and nine were
taken hostage. The terrorists demanded the release of several hundred
Arab prisoners held by Israel plus the release by West Germany of two
members of a terrorist group, the Red Army Brigade.

After failed negotiations, the terrorists asked to be flown to Egypt. West
German authorities set an ambush for the terrorists at a military airfield.
During a supposed transfer of the terrorists from helicopters to a Boeing
737 airliner, West German police snipers opened fire. In the tragic shootout
that ensued, all nine of the Israeli hostages were killed along with five of
the eight terrorists and a West German police officer. The deficiencies of
this operation led to the founding of the anti-terrorist unit GSG 9 by West
Germany.

Back in school, the trainees were sent to Harpers Ferry, West Virginia for a week of specialized training conducted by the National Park Service. It was a nice break from D.C. Bob caught a ride to Harpers Ferry with a classmate. At the end of the training on Friday, I drove up in Bob's car, so we could tour the area and have a weekend escape. My mom was watching our three-year-old daughter.

Harpers Ferry is a small town surrounded by scenic rolling hills where West Virginia, Maryland, and Virginia meet—and the headwaters of the Shenandoah and Potomac Rivers flow. In 1859, the abolitionist John Brown seized the federal armory at Harpers Ferry. Brown intended to use the captured arms to start a slave uprising in Virginia. Local militia had become aware of the action. They mounted a counter-attack, which forced Brown and his men to seek cover within a fire engine house located on the arsenal grounds.

U.S. Army Colonel Robert E. Lee met and commanded a force of Marines that had been dispatched from Washington. Upon Brown's refusal to surrender, the Marines attacked the building—capturing Brown and his men. Brown was convicted of treason and hanged.

During the Civil War, the armory at Harpers Ferry was destroyed. But the engine house (which became known as John Brown's Fort) had a strange odyssey. The building was bought by an entrepreneur, who dismantled it and shipped it to Chicago. It was reconstructed and exhibited at the 1891 Columbian Exhibition. In 1895, the fort returned to Harpers Ferry. Since its original location had been covered by a railroad embankment in 1894, the fort was situated on a farm outside of town. In 1909, Storer College bought the building and moved it to its campus in Harpers Ferry. The National Park Service acquired the structure in 1960; in 1968 the NPS moved John Brown's Fort to a site near its original 1859 location. It became the major attraction of the area.

As I hadn't seen Bob for a week, I was looking forward to our reunion and mini-vacation. The drive up had been pleasant, and the weekend promised excitement and fun. It was a beautiful, early fall day, and the foliage displayed leaves of spectacular hues—as if brushed from nature's palette of autumn colors.

Upon meeting Bob at the motel, I was surprised to find him quiet—yet disturbed. He had called me the night before, sounding upbeat and excited about our coming weekend. Now, something was wrong. "What's the matter?" I asked.

"I saw a guy die before my eyes today. I couldn't save him. It was a dangerous situation too."

My heart beat rapidly, while it sank in my chest. Instantly, all thoughts of my "beautiful day" vanished. "Oh, no! Bobbie, what happened? Was he one of the officers in your class?" I cried out with emotion.

"No, he was a civilian. We were on lunch break. Three classmates and I were in a car—driving through Harpers Ferry. All of a sudden, a woman came running out of her yard and into the street. She was screaming and waving her arms—almost hysterically. The driver slammed on the brakes.

"The lady yelled that a man had just fallen from a ladder at the back of her house. He was hurt and needed help. I thought his bad luck was about to change, as the four of us had recently taken advanced first aid training, and one of the guys had been a combat medic in Vietnam.

"I'm the first one out of the car, and I start to sprint around the side of the house. The driver stays to park the car. Another grabs the lady, intending to calm her and to take her inside, so they can call the rescue squad. The other officer follows me around the house; he's about 10 yards behind me.

"I reach the back yard and see a tall extension ladder up against the rear of the house. Nearby in some large shrubs, I see a guy lying motionless. Reaching him, I start to move some of the branches out of the way, while bending down to offer assistance. Suddenly, the officer behind me yells, 'Freeze, Ritter, don't move! There's a power line near the left side of your head. Don't move! I'm coming.'

"The officer came up behind me and pulled me out of the bushes. It was only then that I saw the broken end of a 'live' electrical cable, next to where I had just been. It was the end attached to the utility pole, so it was still energized. If I had come in contact with it, it could have grounded through me."

I grabbed Bob and held him dearly. "Bobbie, I'm so glad you're okay. Thank God for the officer's alertness and quick action!"

"Yeah, the officer had it together. It was a *very* dangerous situation. I owe him. One of the other officers said we both deserve a commendation. Hey, I'm just happy to be here."

"Bobbie—the man who fell—what about his injuries?"

"Honey, he had been electrocuted. It goes to show that you have to be really careful when coming upon an accident scene. You know what we learned in school: Never assume! I thought the guy had only fallen from a ladder.

"We found out later; he was installing a TV antenna for the lady. He had all of the elements of the antenna out and was carrying it up over his head, while he climbed the ladder. When he got to the roof, the antenna touched the power supply going into the house. In this old town, the power lines aren't insulated. He caught a big charge. With the shock, the man was knocked off the ladder. The antenna fell on the flat roof, so we didn't see it. When the cable snapped from the heat generated, the live end fell down along the house and snagged in the overgrown shrubs. The cable was fairly well camouflaged until I started to move some of the branches."

"What happened after the officer pulled you away?" I asked.

"We carefully dragged the man from the bushes to a safe area. Then we checked his vitals. His pulse was weak, and we observed burn marks on his clothes and body. It was now obvious to us that he had been electrocuted. We gave him CPR. We were doing good and kept his blood circulating. We could still feel a pulse when the rescue squad arrived on the scene."

Bob paused for a moment. He turned away to compose himself. "Bobbie, I know it's hard. What happened next?"

"The rescue squad arrived and took over. We were still giving mouth-to-mouth respiration and chest compressions. They moved us aside and hooked up an oxygen mask. That's when—I'll never forget it—the life started going out of his eyes. They dilated and slowly turned glassy, and he had no pulse. He was gone."

"Bobbie, you did your very best. You couldn't have done anymore. I'm proud of you and the others. You all deserve an award."

"I just keep thinking that we could have done more. The guy who was the combat medic thought that we should have kept giving CPR."

"Bobbie, after the rescue squad arrives, it's their responsibility. The guy probably wasn't going to make it—no matter what. He wasn't careful in the first place, and he paid with his life. It's terribly sad, but it happens. You're going to see more of it—as a police officer. Don't let it get you down."

Some of the anguish in Bob's face was replaced with determination. He replied: "You're right, honey; I shouldn't take it personally. But I have to learn from this. For the past four months, we've done role-play exercises. We're shot with blanks and stabbed with rubber knives. No matter what mistakes we make, we get to go home, and there's always a tomorrow. Today was *real*. In life and death situations, you don't get second chances. I have to be more aware of the 'big picture.' My mind focused that this was a routine fall. That was only one of the circumstances that had occurred. I have to do better. *Expect everything and be ready for anything.*"

After hearing Bob's last remark, even with the sadness and seriousness of the situation, a smile came to my face. I hugged Bob and gave him a kiss. Then, I warned, "Bobbie, you're starting to sound like Inspector Clouseau [of *Pink Panther* fame]."

We enjoyed a nice weekend together. At the same time, I could tell Bob was redoubling his awareness and thought processes to be prepared for anything. Bob was already the most careful and cautious person I knew. Yet he had come within inches of losing his life. And down deep inside, he felt that he had failed in preventing the death of another.

As a lifeguard, Bob had made successful rescues in his time. The latest event had shaken his world—and mine. I knew that Bob would be encountering dangerous situations as a police officer. Yet for the first time, it hit me like a shockwave—*that he might suddenly be taken from me.* I didn't know what I'd do without Bob in my life. I comforted myself by renewing my faith. I believed that God had different plans for us.

For the remaining Park Police training, Bob became an even more serious student. The incident at Harpers Ferry acted as a catalyst. It caused him to rethink his personal career goals. From then on Bob just didn't want to be the best he could be, he wanted to be the best *anyone* could be. As if the assigned work was not enough, he checked out library books on a wide range of topics—including rescue and emergency procedures. Bob was an avid reader. While I read novels, Bob chose biographies and reference works in an unending quest for knowledge.

The last several weeks of specialized training were most enjoyable for Bob, as it featured many days away from the classroom. One day was spent at the U.S. Park Police supply section, located at the National Park Service Brentwood Maintenance Yard in Northeast D.C. Lining up outside the building, the rookies were let in, one at a time, for the issuance of uniforms and equipment.

Once inside, the rookies passed through a series of stations, being measured, fitted, and supplied as needed. Behind a long counter, uniforms hung on racks, while bins and boxes were filled with all sorts of police equipment. Bob was issued a dress blouse, winter coat, shirts, pants, belts, and shoes. For the selection of summer and winter uniform caps, the supply officer put a tape measure around Bob's head and advised, "You look like a 7⅛." Grabbing one from a box, he tossed it over the counter to Bob.

After trying on the cap, Bob remarked: "It feels a little tight. Can I try a larger size?" The supply officer handed Bob a 7¼. After placing it on his head, Bob immediately said: "Yeah, this feels better. Let's go with this."

"You don't want it too big," the supply officer warned.

"Why not?" asked Bob.

Suddenly, the supply officer leaned over the counter. With one swift motion, he grabbed the uniform cap by the bill and forcibly thrust it down over Bob's ears and eyes. Bob couldn't see anything. Had this been a violator, Bob would have been vulnerable to a follow-up assault. "Okay," Bob replied, "I'll go with the 7⅛."

At the time of Bob's class, the only guns in Park Police inventory were old Colt revolvers. The guns were well used and older than the officers who would be carrying them. Bob and another officer expressed concern that modern ammunition, loaded hotter to produce faster bullet velocity, might cause the vintage wheel guns to malfunction. Replying that new Smith & Wessons were on order, the supply officers issued the Colts.

At the remaining supply stations, the officers received holsters, nightsticks, riot batons, duffel bags, riot helmets, handcuffs, mace, raincoats, rubber boots, and assorted other gear. It took Bob several trips to bring all of his issued items up to our apartment that evening. He modeled his new apparel for me, and I was surprised as to how much I liked Bob in uniform.

Returning to the USSS indoor range at Beltsville, Maryland for more firearms and driving instruction, Bob and his fellow classmates were introduced to "night firing." In this course, range lights are dimmed to simulate conditions of low visibility—encountered during evening and midnight shifts.

A friendly rivalry existed between the various police forces in the District of Columbia. Although brothers and sisters underneath the uniform, the patches on their sleeves set them apart for bragging rights as to D.C.'s finest. The Metropolitan Police Department referred to park policemen as "grasshoppers." This nickname dates back to the early 1900s when the Park Police wore green uniforms patterned after German foresters. To Park Police, the abbreviation MPD jokingly stood for "Many Police Dummies." Not to be left out, the Executive Protective Service needled both—when an opportunity presented itself.

In the CFLETC Police School, the Park Police wore old clothes at the range and were part of a class that also included rangers and BIA officers. Now, the Park Police were in uniform and an identifiable group. The EPS chief range officer lost no time in stirring up trouble. During the first running of the Night Firing Course (NFC), he announced over the range public address system: "Okay, U.S. *Parking* Police, the other day we had an EPS rookie group in here, and they all shot expert on this course. Let's see what you can do. We'll shoot the course first under medium light conditions, so you can work on form. Then, you'll shoot the course under low light conditions, approximating a D.C. alley on a dark night. Finally, we'll bring out the flashlights, and you'll shoot in total darkness, except for clicking your flashlights on and off—only during the instant of firing. This stage will simulate searching a Park Service warehouse at 2:00 a.m.—after a burglar turns the lights out on you. Your command to draw and fire will be when you see the target turn and face you. Let's proceed."

Suddenly, the range was plunged into complete darkness to the howls of the Park Police. The first running of the course was supposed to be done at medium light levels, for familiarization and form. The range was now pitch-black.

The chief range officer barked out the command: "On the line with six rounds load and holster your weapon. If you drop any ammunition, *do not* pick it up or move from your position." The occasional sounds of rounds falling on the concrete floor could be heard accompanied with some swearing, while the officers fumbled in the dark. Finally, everyone completed loading and the chief range officer continued: "Is the line loaded? The line is loaded and ready. When target turns, draw your weapon, fire one round, and reholster your weapon."

Next, there was a swishing sound as the target carriers turned to face the paper-thin silhouette targets toward the shooters. Bob drew his weapon. With his best form, he squeezed off a round into the black hole that the range had become. Other shots rang out too, but not from all of the 12 shooting positions. Some of the officers had not fired before the targets swished back to the side position and the ceasefire was sounded. Out of the darkness, groans and moans could be heard, and one of the Park Police officers called out: "Hey, I couldn't see my target. Turn the lights up some!"

The EPS chief range officer fired back: "Concentrate and pay attention to the turning target. Aim your weapon as an extension of your arm. There's plenty of light out there. Your eyes will adjust."

To that reply, somebody yelled out of the blackness, "Bullsh-t!"

"Who said that?" boomed out of the range loudspeakers.

From another shooting position came, "If there was plenty of light, you wouldn't be asking!" Eventually the lights were raised, and the shooters, becoming acclimated, started doing better.

Between firing stages, one of the rookies sarcastically told a range officer, "So I don't qualify in night firing—big deal—I guess I won't have to work midnights."

"The EPS range officer replied, "Yeah, and you won't have to worry about working days either." By the end of the day though, all but two officers had qualified.

Later that week, the Park Police traveled to the USSS outdoor range to fire the Shotgun Course. The Remington Model No. 870 pump shotgun was utilized. The course totaled 30 rounds shot at three different distances: 50, 25, and 10 yards. Rifled slugs and No. 4 buckshot were used for the course. The officers learned the proper procedure to load the magazine. They also fired from loading rounds directly into the breech of the shotgun. The Remington 870s had a bruising kick when firing 12-gauge rifled slugs from the shoulder position. Bob concentrated on sight picture and letting each shot be a surprise.

The final days of driving instruction focused on traffic stops, high-speed driving, and pursuit driving. These were dangerous aspects of everyday police work—especially when officers treat them as "routine" and become careless. An officer can be killed or seriously injured by persons stopped for traffic violations. The occupants of the vehicle could be wanted felons or might have just robbed a convenience store. Officers can also be struck by passing motorists. High-speed chases can be dangerous to officers, violators, and innocent civilians.

The academy fostered good judgment, which was a vital key to safety. Traffic stop scenarios were run that put the trainees in jeopardy at every opportunity. The officers learned never to let their guard down. Bob's new credo of "expect everything and be ready for anything" certainly applied here.

The officers trained on the skid pad before moving to the pursuit course. The skid pad was a circular area with traffic cones around the circumference and center. Water and oil were mixed on the asphalt to create slippery conditions. Students had to navigate around the inside of the circle for 90 seconds without hitting the brakes, spinning out, or knocking over a cone. They learned to control the vehicle using only the steering wheel and accelerator. Experiencing vehicle dynamics and controlling vehicle motion would help the officers to stay out of trouble in high speed and pursuit driving.

Besides excellent driving skills, pursuit driving requires full-time concentration on the road and surroundings. On the Beltsville track—like a television chase scene—engines roared; tires squealed; sirens blared, and emergency lights flashed. The rookies sped around the course in pursuit of violators who failed to pull over. Instructors on the ground used portable radios to distract the officers with simulated police transmissions. Good peripheral vision and an ability to stay focused were a must.

At the end of the session, the tough Park Police training sergeant paced around the classroom, critiquing the students somewhat caustically. To an officer who didn't pass, the sergeant said: "You need to come out here again. You're going to be walking a beat for a long time, if today is any indication."

When it was Bob's turn, the sergeant scowled as he said: "Officer Ritter, you drive like an old lady! While you have a natural feel for high speed driving and are smooth and calm, you consistently underestimate your ability and don't drive to your limits. You should be going faster out there. I sure hope I don't have to wait for you when I need backup."

Bob, never shy to defend his beliefs, replied: "Sarge, I can't help you if I get in an accident while responding to your call. During responses and pursuits, we also have a duty to safeguard pedestrians, other drivers on the road, and even the violator. I'm not going to overestimate their abilities. The punk I'm going to be chasing isn't driving a specially set-up police cruiser. He's had no high-speed training. He's scared, maybe hopped up on drugs. I don't want to chase him to the point where he's becoming a deadly menace to innocent bystanders and himself. I'll back off.

"One of my runs today was a stolen car scenario. Crime statistics show that most often these are kids who are joy riding; most are too young to have an operator's permit. Pushing them at unsafe, high speeds in busy urban areas doesn't seem to be worth the risk in my judgment. If they plow through a red light and kill a mother and her carload of children, what kind of police action is that?

"Taking dangerous risks and putting the public in jeopardy, especially for minor infractions, doesn't add up. If we make the apprehension on a juvenile, the judge does nothing. The kid is put on probation. When he turns 18, it's like it never happened—no record. Why should I risk turning a slap on the wrist into a death sentence for someone?"

The sergeant was taken back a bit with Bob's rapid-fire yet sincere response and seemed to be at a momentary loss for words. Before moving to the next student, the sergeant softly commented: "Maybe you're right. Maybe we should all drive like you. At least you're thinking."

Other highlights during the remainder of specialized training included visits to Saint Elizabeths Hospital (nicknamed St. E's), the D.C. Morgue, Central Cell Block (CCB), D.C. Superior Court, and National Park Service monuments and memorials. The rookies were given behind the scenes familiarization tours. At St. E's, they also attended a seminar on the recognition, handling, and treatment of abnormal persons.

Founded by an act of Congress in 1852, St. Elizabeths was the first federal mental asylum. Mental health advocate Dorothea Dix worked for its establishment to treat mentally ill soldiers, sailors, and D.C. residents. Opening its doors in 1855, it was originally named the Government Hospital for the Insane (GHI).

During the Civil War, the complex spawned additional wards for the care and treatment of soldiers injured on the battlefield. Both Union and captured Confederate soldiers were treated. Those treated for non-mental conditions objected to being patients at a complex known as the Government Hospital for the Insane. They started to refer to the compound as "St. Elizabeths"—after the original colonial name for the tract of land that the facility was built on. In 1916, Congress officially renamed the GHI to Saint Elizabeths Hospital (*no* apostrophe).

By 1972, St. E's had developed into a sprawling campus of over 100 buildings on over 300 acres of land. It was one of the foremost psychiatric institutions in the world. Its distinguished history included the development of pioneering treatments and therapies.

One of St. E's earliest residents was would-be presidential assassin Richard Lawrence. On January 30, 1835, President Andrew Jackson was leaving the Capitol Building after attending the state funeral of South Carolina Congressman Warren Davis. From behind a column stepped unemployed house painter Richard Lawrence—with pistol in hand. At close range, Lawrence took aim and pulled the trigger. The hammer fell on the percussion cap of the single-shot derringer, producing a small bang, but the gunpowder did not ignite. The president moved toward Lawrence. From a pocket, Lawrence grabbed a second derringer—pulling the trigger at point-blank range. This pistol miraculously misfired too! The 67-year-old Jackson, with cane in hand, flogged Lawrence to the ground. Old Hickory had to be restrained from inflicting severe bodily harm on Lawrence.

Afterwards, Lawrence's guns were checked and found to be in good working order. As it rained on the day of the attempt, the ignition system and/or gunpowder might have gotten wet and that was the reason the pistols failed to discharge, or the percussion caps might have been defective. At the time, many believed that "divine providence" had spared Jackson from being harmed.

A hundred years later in 1935, the Smithsonian Institution—which had Lawrence's pistols in its collection—decided to test fire them. Experts placed the odds of both guns misfiring at 125,000 to 1. On the first try, each pistol fired and discharged its round with lethal force.

Lawrence was prosecuted by U.S. Attorney Francis Scott Key, of "Star-Spangled Banner" fame. Lawrence, an English immigrant, claimed that Jackson had killed Lawrence's father in the War of 1812. Additionally, Lawrence accused the president of conspiring to prevent the payment of money due Lawrence. Fired from his last job, Lawrence blamed that on Jackson too. None of the assertions were true. Finally, Lawrence believed that he was actually King Richard III (dead since 1485) and therefore not subject to American law. Lawrence was judged insane and was institutionalized in several hospitals. He was transferred to the GHI when it opened in 1855 and died there in 1861. He remains at St. E's to this day, buried in an unmarked grave.

The nation reacted with outrage to the attempt on Old Hickory's life. It was the first assassination attempt on a U.S. president. Assassination was part of the intrigues and treachery of Europe with its dictators and kings. It was a shock to the American public that their popularly elected leader could be the target of an assassin's bullet.

It was also the beginning of another concept in U.S. history: assassination conspiracy. President Jackson believed that political opponents had put Lawrence up to the attempt. Jackson blamed elements of the rival Whig Party, which wanted to prevent him from closing the National Bank. No credible evidence was presented to support the alleged conspiracy. Richard Lawrence was obviously insane and probably acted alone.

Another infamous resident of St. Elizabeths was presidential assassin Charles Guiteau. On July 2, 1881, Guiteau shot President James A. Garfield in the old Baltimore and Potomac Railroad Station (current site of the West Wing of the National Gallery of Art). Guiteau used a Webley British Bulldog .44-caliber revolver. A bullet struck the president from behind and lodged within his chest.

Garfield was taken to the White House where he was examined by his personal physician in consultation with other doctors. They needed to know the exact location of the bullet before deciding how to proceed. If the bullet punctured an organ, surgery would be needed to remove it to stop internal bleeding and other distress.

X-rays had not been discovered, so the only method of finding the bullet was to explore the wound with fingers and metal probes. This led to risks also, as continued probing could cause further injury and infection. Unable to discover the location of the bullet, the president's doctors could only watch Garfield and hope for the best.

The newspapers of the day published front-page accounts of this medical dilemma. Distinguished doctors and other learned individuals were interviewed. Their opinions and suggestions were printed, and a national debate ensued over what to do.

In one of these articles, Simon Newcomb, a scientist at the U.S. Naval Observatory in Washington, D.C., related his research with wire coils charged with electricity. He discovered that when metal comes close to an energized coil; a very faint hum is produced at the spot in the wire nearest the metal. Unfortunately, Newcomb said it was much too faint a sound to be of use to physicians attending the president.

Reading Newcomb's statements in the newspaper, Alexander Graham Bell offered his assistance. The two men collaborated, and a device was produced (the first metal detector). It consisted of Newcomb's electrical coils attached to Bell's telephone invention, which would amplify the hum.

Trying the apparatus in the laboratory, it accurately located bullets placed in sacks of grain and sides of beef with a degree of precision that could detect the bullet within the president. With success in the lab, Bell received a White House appointment. On July 26, 1881, with the president's doctor assisting, the detector was moved over Garfield's body. Unfortunately, a steady hum was heard on the receiver no matter where the detector was placed on Garfield.

After additional attempts with the same result, Bell returned to the lab to check the machine. Once again, the device performed satisfactorily. Bell even tested the machine at the Old Soldiers' Home in Washington where it accurately located a bullet known to be still lodged inside a Civil War veteran.

With this success, Garfield's physician was persuaded into giving Bell one more chance. Inexplicably, it was a repeat performance. No matter where the detector was placed over the president, a steady hum was heard—with little variance in intensity.

Later, it became known why the machine was ineffective. Just before the shooting, the White House had changed over to new mattresses. They came from the factory with the latest innovation: coil springs. Being such a new design, Bell had no idea that metal springs were hidden throughout the mattress beneath the stricken president.

The president's doctor would not allow further use of the machine. He had already decided that the bullet did not need to be removed. President Garfield lingered on until September 19, 1881, when he died from suspected blood poisoning. It has been speculated that the president was infected when the wound was first explored with fingers and probes.

With the death of the president, Guiteau was charged with murder. He had been undergoing psychiatric examination at St. Elizabeths. Guiteau believed, irrationally, that he had been largely responsible for Garfield being elected. After the new administration took office, Guiteau had personally demanded an appointment to an ambassadorial post as a patronage reward. He was repeatedly tuned down and finally told by

Secretary of State James G. Blaine to leave and never to return. Following this incident, Guiteau came to the belief that he had been commanded by God to strike down the ungrateful Garfield.

The examining psychiatrists at St. Elizabeths thought Guiteau to be medically insane. His lawyers wanted to argue the insanity defense. The resulting trial was heavily covered by the media and became one of the most famous of its day.

During the trial, Guiteau exhibited much bizarre behavior. He criticized his defense team, solicited advice from spectators in the courtroom, and wrote poems for his testimony. Going against his attorneys' advice, Guiteau maintained that he was "legally" insane at the time of the shooting but not "medically" insane.

Guiteau thought he would be found not guilty and released. Believing that the media and public adored him, he made plans for a lecture tour and an 1884 run for the presidency. The jury rejected Guiteau's defense and found him guilty of murder. He was hanged on June 30, 1882.

In 1883 as a result of Garfield's assassination, Congress passed the Pendleton Act, which reformed the federal civil service. Before this time, federal workers were hired in a "spoils system" of political patronage. Government jobs were given to the supporters and friends of the party who controlled the White House. Now, most appointments to the civilian workforce would be based on merit and competitive examinations. The law also protected federal employees from demotion or firing due to political reasons and prohibited them from being pressured to support the party in power. A Civil Service Commission was established to implement the act.

Attending the seminar at historic St. Elizabeths, Bob found a new interest in abnormal behavior. It was at this time that he began to frequent area used bookstores. Purchasing books on psychology, assassination, and the Secret Service, Bob added to his already sizeable reference library. He wanted to develop personal strategies for the prediction of dangerousness in individuals.

Being most interested in Washington landmarks, I was excited when Bob's academy class visited the Park Service monuments and memorials. It was interesting to hear Bob relate all the insider information he learned. The trainees spent several days becoming familiar with some of our most famous national treasures, like the Washington Monument.

Construction of the Washington Monument (known as the Monument) began in 1848. A private citizens group started raising money for the project in 1833. The federal government donated the land. The original design of noted architect Robert Mills depicted a circular, colonnaded Greek temple with a 600-foot obelisk rising from its center. The building would contain statues of Revolutionary War heroes, and the entrance would be topped with a statue of Washington driving a triumphal chariot. The society decided, in a cost cutting measure, to erect only an obelisk.

From 1848–1854, construction proceeded steadily to the 152-foot level. In 1854, construction was virtually halted due to a lack of funds. It wasn't until well after the Civil War in 1876 that Congress authorized the federal government to finish the Monument. The project was turned over to the Army Corps of Engineers, and construction resumed in 1880. By then, the original vein of white marble used to face the Monument had been depleted. This necessitated the use of different marble to finish the structure. Growing an average of 80 feet a year, the Washington Monument was completed in 1884. One can readily see the difference in color between the earlier and later marble.

Visiting the Monument, Bob's class inspected its little-known basement, which contained the mechanical equipment needed for heating, cooling, and dehumidification. Walking around the Monument's base, they noted the banks of floodlights, within the circle of 50 American flags (one for each state). These powerful lights emitted more than 92-million candlepower of illumination. Projecting majestically about 555 feet into the sky, the Washington Monument—ablaze with sunshine by day and illumination by night—appeared to watch over the nation's capital with the spirit of our most beloved founding father.

Pointing to the observation windows near the top of the Monument, the training officer amused the class by recounting a spectacular stunt that occurred in the early years of the Monument. On the morning of August 21, 1910, Washington Senators catcher Charles "Gabby" Street caught a ball thrown from one of the Monument windows, located just above the 500-foot level. It was estimated that the ball was traveling at over 100 miles per hour and with some heavy pounds of force when caught. That afternoon, Street caught legendary pitcher Walter "The Train" Johnson in a 3-1 win over the Detroit Tigers.

After the 70-second elevator ride to the top, the officers enjoyed panoramic views through the observation windows. Originally just cutouts in the walls, iron bars were installed in the openings after several suicides in the 1920s. The throwing of objects through the gaps became a continuing problem. There were occasional incidents of people unfurling banners through the openings. Eventually, the bars were removed and safety glass windows installed.

Descending the 898 steps in the shaft, the rookies took notice of the 190 memorial stones lining the interior granite walls. The carved blocks of stone were presented by countries, states, cities, and various societies. Since the obelisk opened in 1888, vandalism of the stones has been a *monumental* problem. Tourists have chipped away at the blocks for souvenirs. Silver letters were even removed from the stone presented by the state of Nevada.

During the walk down, the training officer related two of the biggest mysteries of the Monument. In 1854, a memorial stone was given by Pope

Pius IX. The marble block was taken from the Temple of Concord in Rome and was inscribed "Rome to America." Before it could be embedded, the papal stone was stolen from the Monument grounds.

Authorities suspected members of the American (Know-Nothing) Party. The Know-Nothings were anti-foreign immigration and anti-Roman Catholic. The Know-Nothings claimed they "knew nothing" about the theft. Without any hard evidence to the contrary, the Pope's Stone, as it became known, was not recovered.

In 1892, divers working off Long Bridge on the Potomac River (current site of the Fourteenth Street Bridge) found an unusual stone. When they brought it up, the inscription matched that of the missing Pope's Stone. The engineer in charge locked it in a work shed until experts could verify the find. That night, someone broke into the shed, and the stone was stolen for a second time. It has never been seen since.

The second unsolved mystery occurred in late 1934. A thief stole over 100 gold-plated, platinum-tipped lightning rod points from the top of the Monument. A complete base-to-top cleaning was being completed that year. Scaffolding had been erected for the workmen to access the top. Somehow, the daring burglar managed to scale the scaffolding and to remove the expensive points without being noticed. The case remains unsolved to this day.

Pausing at several spots on the descent, the training officer—pointing to the iron stairway—briefed the rookies on some of the tragic history of the Monument. A woman jumped to her death in 1915 from the 480-foot landing. In 1924, at the 400-foot level, another woman fell to her death. Her three-year-old child had slipped on the stairs, and in coming to the youth's aid, the woman fell through the double guardrails. To prevent similar accidents, an additional guardrail was added in 1927 with a metal grill covering all three guardrails.

Next on the visitation schedule was the Lincoln Memorial, designed by architect Henry Bacon along the lines of the Parthenon in Athens, Greece. Congress authorized the memorial in 1911, and ground was broken in 1914. With Lincoln's son (Robert Todd Lincoln) in attendance, it was dedicated on Memorial Day, May 30, 1922, by Chief Justice William Howard Taft and President Warren G. Harding.

The Greek revival architecture of the Lincoln Memorial featured a design motif that pays homage to the states. The 36 Doric columns of the memorial represent the 36 states of the Union at the time of Lincoln's assassination in 1865. Above the columns is a frieze that names these 36 states in bas-relief along with the year each joined the Union. The 48 states in the Union at the time the memorial was designed are displayed on the attic walls, which rise from a flat roof.

Bob's class was provided access to areas of the memorial that were off-limits to tourists. Atop the roof—almost 100 feet high—the officers took in breathtaking views of Memorial Bridge, Arlington National Cemetery, and Arlington House (Custis-Lee Mansion), all situated to the west. The Reflecting Pool, Washington Monument, Mall, and Capitol dome—as if arranged by the heavens in planetary alignment—appeared in a grand axis to the east of the Lincoln Memorial.

During their rooftop stop, the rookies were told how the Lincoln Memorial became the only location in Washington to be fired upon in World War II. At the time, an anti-aircraft battery was stationed on the roof of the Department of Interior Building (located at 18th and C Streets, NW). The gun was accidentally fired, and a .50-caliber bullet hit the memorial along its roofline. If one looks closely, a faint trace of the repair can still be seen near the Maryland sculpture.

Inside the memorial chamber, the officers were cautioned to protect the statue of Lincoln and the two inscribed stone tablets at all cost. The Daniel Chester French designed sculpture of a seated Lincoln stands 19 feet tall. It rests on a pedestal over 10 feet high. On the north wall of the chamber, literally carved in stone, is Lincoln's Second Inaugural Address. The tablet on the south wall is inscribed with Lincoln's Gettysburg Address. In the past, protestors have climbed the statue, and vandals have spray-painted graffiti on the chamber walls.

Underneath the main floor, stands the foundation for the memorial. In this vast area hidden from outside view, the Park Police stage officers and vehicles for quick response during mass demonstrations and other large events. Nicknamed "The Cave" due to the remarkable stalactites and stalagmites that grow there, the area is not open to the public. The formations are caused by water seeping into the foundation from cleaning and acid rain. This dissolves the calcium contained in the foundation cement, which reforms as stalactites and stalagmites. In the 1970s, one stalactite was over several feet long!

In the remaining days of Park Police training, orientation visits were made to the Jefferson Memorial, Kennedy Center, Ford's Theater, and other National Park Service sites. Soon, the new officers would be policing some of our most revered national icons.

Chapter 9

On the Street

Marking the successful completion of the six-week academy, the U.S. Park Police graduation ceremony also denoted a rite of passage. Combined with the CFLETC police school, the officers had undergone 18 weeks of demanding training and were now officially ready to join the ranks of the force.

Wives, girlfriends, and parents proudly gathered in the auditorium at Park Police Headquarters (HQ) to pay honor to their loved one's achievement. Sitting in the front rows in pressed dress uniforms with shiny leather and polished brass, the officers would soon embark into the concrete world of police work. From now on, there would be no instructors nearby; there would be no role-playing. Actions would have real-life consequences.

Officials praised the class for being the best-prepared officers in Park Police history. With a growing number of civil rights complaints against law enforcement agencies, the federal government had made a strong commitment to standardize and to improve the instruction of its enforcement personnel. Bob's class of uniformed officers was the first to receive the enhanced training. It would be up to them to reflect well on the new curriculum by becoming capable and effective officers.

Not being able to attend the CFLETC graduation made the Park Police ceremony even more special for me. As the officers were called to receive their certificates, it was nice to finally put faces to the names that Bob had been mentioning. After the ceremony, Bob introduced me around the room, and I witnessed firsthand the camaraderie that had developed. It was an additional pleasure to personally thank the officer who had prevented Bob from being harmed at Harper's Ferry. He was a knight in blue armor to me.

I also met Flip Hagood, one of Bob's Park Police training officers. After congratulating Bob, Flip continued that it was a pleasure to have had Bob in the class. Turning to me, he remarked how well Bob had done in the training and that it had been difficult to choose the recipient of the top officer award. It had come down to Bob and the officer who did win the coveted honor.

Overhearing this conversation was the lead Park Police training sergeant, who joined us. As if he didn't want to make direct eye contact with Bob, the sergeant looked to the side a bit, as he said: "Yeah, Bob, I owe you an explanation. If we went on total scores, you probably would have won. I overruled that though. I had to give it to Jim. The guy's a former MPD officer, who transferred to us. If it had been up to me, he wouldn't have had to take the course. He already went through the MPD academy and is an experienced officer."

"Sarge, I understand," replied Bob. "There's no shame in losing to Jim. He's a proven, solid officer."

"I knew you'd understand. I want you to know it had nothing to do with you as a person. If I get back to the street, I'd be proud to serve with you."

Later on the drive home, I asked Bob, "Are you disappointed?"

"About what, honey?" Bob answered.

"Not winning the award."

"No, I didn't think about it much. Jim's a great guy. I enjoyed the training, and I'm ready for the streets. I learned a lot. That's reward enough."

"Well, it helped that you were paid too, so I could keep food on the table!" I quipped. Bob smiled with agreement, but I knew full well that he would have done it for free. At this stage of Bob's life, family, friends, and career were paramount. Next in importance was the pursuit of knowledge. Learning facts and putting them to practical use gave Bob a sense of heightened well-being—as if he were unlocking the secrets of the universe. Scholarship was an important human trait that Bob relished.

The 18 weeks of training and Bob's prior jobs had spoiled me. I was used to Bob working days with weekends off. Now, he would be starting shift work with Wednesdays and Thursdays off. This would be Bob's last free weekend for quite some time. We decided to enjoy it with a trip to the historic triangle of Virginia (Williamsburg, Jamestown, and Yorktown).

Arriving home, Bob quickly changed out of his uniform and into casual clothes. Now that Bob was a full-fledged officer, he was required to be armed within the District of Columbia and on lands administered by the National Park Service. Bob had the authority to arrest violators for misdemeanors and felonies committed in his presence and for felonies with probable cause (a reasonable belief).

Carrying his off-duty Chiefs Special in an "inside-the-pants holster," Bob placed the holster within the waistband and secured it by fastening the loop of the holster around his pants belt. As the weapon needed to be concealed in public places, Bob had to start wearing bulky jackets, even indoors, or he had to leave his shirttail out over the holstered weapon. Bob had always been a sharp dresser. It took some time for me to adjust to this new style—necessitated by his police duties.

Removing his badge from the uniform, Bob pinned it to the front of his leather commission book, which contained his Park Police photo identification. He placed the credentials in his jacket pocket and snapped a pouch of spare ammo to his belt. When carrying a concealed weapon, having your police ID readily available is important to identify yourself to violators and other police. Bob's primary jurisdiction was at National Park Service sites, and we had several of those on our weekend itinerary.

When traveling, we preferred the older, scenic routes and avoided the interstates whenever possible. The historical routes, although slower, were much more interesting. From the Washington Beltway, we connected with Branch Avenue (Maryland Route 5), which leads into Southern Maryland. This was the general escape route for Lincoln assassin John Wilkes Booth.

On the evening of April 14, 1865 (Good Friday), Booth entered the small corridor adjoining the state box at Ford's Theater in Washington, D.C. He closed the door behind him and wedged it shut with the leg of a music stand. Booth then moved to the entry door of the state box. Placing his eye to a peephole in the door, Booth spied Lincoln like a hunter waiting for a shot at game. Seated in the box along with the President and Mrs. Lincoln were their guests Major Henry Rathbone (a military aide to Lincoln) and his fiancée Clara Harris.

As an accomplished professional actor, Booth was familiar with the comedy *Our American Cousin*. He waited for a line in the play that was sure to produce an uproarious response from the audience. Taking his murderous cue at about 10:15 p.m., Booth stealthily entered the state box and fired a single-shot, .44-caliber Deringer to the back of the president's head. The sound of the pistol discharging its fatal ball was somewhat masked by the crowd's laughter.

Major Rathbone sprung toward Booth, who dropped the now empty pistol. Drawing a dagger, Booth fended off Rathbone's grip by inflicting a deep wound to Rathbone's left arm. With Rathbone still grasping at Booth, the assassin vaulted over the side of the balcony box. Catching a spur on one of the flags and bunting adorning the box, Booth fell awkwardly to the stage floor below. Springing to his feet, Booth brandished his bloody knife toward the audience and shouted, "*Sic semper tyrannis!*" The motto of the Commonwealth of Virginia translates from Latin: *Thus always to tyrants.*

Most in the audience were momentarily stunned; some believed that the real-life drama unfolding before them was part of the play. Booth, fleeing across the stage, disappeared into the back of the theater. Exiting Ford's by a rear door, which led into an alley, Booth mounted a waiting horse and galloped off toward the Navy Yard Bridge (current site of the Eleventh Street Bridge). Crossing the Anacostia River into Maryland, Booth was later overtaken by fellow conspirator David Herold.

Earlier, Herold had led co-conspirator Lewis Powell (alias: Payne) to the Lafayette Square home of Secretary of State William Seward. Powell had been directed by Booth to kill Seward as close as possible to 10:15 p.m., to coincide with Booth's attack on Lincoln. Herold was supposed to hold the reins for Powell's mount during the assault and—when the evil act had been completed—to lead Powell out of the city to the rendezvous with

Booth. There, Herold would guide the party through Southern Maryland in an escape to Virginia and the South.

At the time, Secretary Seward was recuperating from an April 5 accident. Falling from a runaway carriage, Seward suffered a broken arm and jaw along with a concussion. Powell gained entrance to the residence under guise of delivering medicine from Seward's doctor. Powell pushed by a servant and headed upstairs where he was stopped by Seward's son, Frederick. Told that he could not see the secretary, Powell drew a pistol and struck Frederick Seward several times.

Powell then charged into Secretary Seward's bedroom where he was grabbed by the attending nurse, George Robinson. Powell pulled a knife and struck Robinson on the forehead, knocking him down. Powell then began to stab at William Seward's head. Robinson recovered and struggled again with Powell. Seward's elder son, Augustus, awakened by the commotion, entered his father's room and joined Robinson in restraining the attacker. Powell broke free and ran back down the stairs, stabbing a State Department messenger on the way out.

In the commotion of Powell's savage attack, David Herold became scared and deserted Powell. Seward survived, though seriously injured with wounds to his face and neck. In the melee, four others had been wounded. Frederick Seward sustained the most critical wounds. His skull had been fractured in two places.

Without Herold's help, Powell became lost in the city. He hid out in a cemetery. Powell was arrested several days later when he showed up at the Washington boardinghouse of Mary Surratt, which led to her being arrested too.

In another part of the plot to throw the federal government into chaos, Booth had instructed co-conspirator George Atzerodt to assassinate Vice President Andrew Johnson. Atzerodt either got cold feet or never agreed to kill Johnson. No attempt was made to harm the vice president.

In the investigation and military tribunal that followed, Army prosecutors also believed that Booth had ordered an additional conspirator, Michael O'Laughlen, to assassinate General Ulysses S. Grant. But on the night of the Lincoln and Seward attacks, O'Laughlen spent the evening drinking in a Washington bar. In any case, General Grant was not in D.C. at the time of the attacks. The general and Mrs. Grant had departed on the evening train for Philadelphia. Wanting to visit their children in Burlington, New Jersey, the Grants had regretfully declined President Lincoln's invitation to accompany him and Mrs. Lincoln to Ford's Theater.

Booth and Herold reached the Surratt House and Tavern in Surrattsville, Maryland (now Clinton, Md.) around midnight. They picked up field glasses, carbines, ammunition, and whiskey from John Lloyd, an ex-D.C. policeman, who was leasing the tavern from Mary Surratt. Lloyd would later turn government witness and implicate Mary Surratt in the conspiracy. She was convicted and became the first woman hanged by the federal government.

Swigging down some whiskey, Booth tried to ease the pain of a broken leg. His left fibula was broken just above the ankle. The injury *probably* occurred when Booth leaped to the stage at Ford's Theater. There is some belief that Booth's horse might have fallen on him during the ride out to Surrattsville. In either case, Booth and Herold continued southeast to the home of Dr. Samuel Mudd, near Bryantown, Maryland. Dr. Mudd set Booth's leg and allowed Booth and Herold to rest in his home until that afternoon (April 15).

To this day, controversy surrounds Dr. Mudd as to whether he had knowledge of the plot beforehand or was just an innocent practitioner of medicine. He was convicted by the military tribunal. Avoiding the death penalty by one vote, Mudd was sentenced to life in prison at Fort Jefferson in the Dry Tortugas (islands about 70 miles west of Key West, Florida).

In 1867, an outbreak of yellow fever struck down the prison doctor. Mudd took over the medical duties and saved many souls during the epidemic. President Andrew Johnson pardoned Dr. Mudd in 1869. He returned to his Southern Maryland farm where he died in 1883.

From Mudd's farm, Booth and Herold crossed Zekiah Swamp and headed toward Bel Alton, Maryland. By midnight on the 15th, they reached the home of Samuel Cox, a Confederate sympathizer. Cox hid them in a nearby thicket for six days, while his foster brother, blockade runner Thomas Jones, brought supplies to the fugitives.

On April 21, Jones guided Booth and Herold to the Potomac River near Popes Creek, Maryland. That night, in a rowboat provided by Jones, Booth and Herold set out to cross the Potomac. Fearful of being discovered by Union gunboats, the two men became disoriented in the dark. Their boat encountered strong currents. Eventually, Booth and Herold ended up back at the Maryland shore. The next night, they successfully made the crossing.

Foraging through Virginia, Booth and Herold crossed the Rappahannock River by ferry at Port Conway. Searching the area several days later, a Union cavalry detachment showed pictures of Booth to residents. From this investigation, the cavalry received leads that led them to Bowling Green, Virginia. From there, they were directed to the Garrett Farm near Port Royal, arriving in the early morning hours of April 26.

From the Garrett family, the unit commander, First Lieutenant Edward Doherty and the two War Department detectives with him, Everton Conger and Luther Baker, learned that Booth and Herold were in a nearby tobacco barn. Surrounding the barn with his detachment, Doherty ordered the fugitives to give themselves up. Herold eventually surrendered, but Booth let it be known that he would not come out without a fight.

The barn was set ablaze, and through an opening between the slats of the structure, Sergeant Boston Corbett shot Booth in the neck. The assassin was pulled from the barn and taken to the porch of the Garrett farmhouse. Booth died several hours later, thus ending the largest manhunt in U.S. history—up to that time.

Booth's body was taken to Washington where it was further identified and autopsied. He was secretly buried on the grounds of Fort McNair in Washington. In 1869, the body was released to the Booth family and interred in Green Mount Cemetery in Baltimore, Maryland.

Herold was found guilty and hanged on July 7, 1865, along with Lewis Powell, George Atzerodt, and Mary Surratt. In addition to Dr. Samuel Mudd, Michael O'Laughlen and two other conspirators received prison terms. Mary's son John Surratt Jr., a Confederate agent, had also been implicated in the conspiracy. He fled overseas.

In 1867, John Surratt Jr. was brought back to the United States to stand trial. Since the U.S. Supreme Court had ruled in 1866 that military courts have no jurisdiction over civilians when nonmilitary courts are open, Surratt was tried in federal court at Washington, D.C. The trial ended in a hung jury and eventually all charges were dropped. Released from custody in 1868, Surratt lived in Maryland for the remainder of his life. He died in 1916 at the age of 72.

Major Rathbone, who valiantly attempted to apprehend Booth at Ford's Theater, would become a tragic figure himself. Rathbone left the Army in 1867 and married Clara Harris. He became the U.S. Consul to the Kingdom of Hanover. In 1883 after years of depression with fits of jealousy and temper, Rathbone murdered Clara and attempted to kill himself. He was committed to an asylum in Germany where he died in 1911.

Mary Todd Lincoln's remaining years were marked with delusion, paranoia, and depression. Distraught since the 1862 death of the Lincoln's 11-year-old son Willie, Mary's already troubled mental state was aggravated by the assassination of her husband. With the death of son Tad in 1871, she slipped into a fantasy world of hallucination. The Lincoln's sole-surviving son, Robert, sought medical treatment for his mother but her mental illness worsened. Mary Lincoln was committed to an asylum for several months in 1875. She died in 1882 and rests with her husband in the Lincoln Family Tomb at Oak Ridge Cemetery in Springfield, Illinois.

Sgt. Boston Corbett became known as "The Avenger of Lincoln." After the Civil War, he moved to New Jersey and then Kansas. In 1867, Corbett became an assistant doorkeeper at the Kansas State House. In February of that year, he chased state representatives and staff around with a pistol. Although he fired three shots, no one was injured. Corbett was arrested, judged insane, and committed to an asylum. He escaped to Mexico in 1888 and was never heard from again.

Leaving Route 5, Bob and I cut over to U.S. 301 at La Plata, Maryland. Continuing south on Route 301, we crossed the Potomac River via the Governor Nice Memorial Bridge. Looking upriver, we could see the wide expanse and currents of the Potomac and could better understand the difficulties that Booth and Herold faced.

South of Port Royal, Virginia, we turned around and headed back north on 301 to find the historical marker designating the Garrett Farm. Locating it along the northbound lanes, it read: "This is the Garrett Place where John Wilkes Booth, assassin of Lincoln, was cornered by Union soldiers, and killed, April 26, 1865. The house stood a short distance from this spot."

Parking along the shoulder, we followed a path into the spacious wooded median. There, we stood on the ground where Booth had died over a hundred years before. For a couple of moments, Bob wondered how American history might have been changed, if Booth had been prevented from assassinating President Lincoln. Bob enjoyed speculating on the "what ifs."

Back in Port Royal, we took U.S. Route 17 southeast to Yorktown, Virginia, situated on the York River. In 1781, the decisive battle of the American Revolution was fought at Yorktown. With the assistance of Rochambeau's French troops, General George Washington and his Army laid siege to the British under Lord Cornwallis. The blockade of the Chesapeake Bay by De Grasse's French fleet prevented the British navy from either resupplying or evacuating the British force at Yorktown. Bombarded by artillery and trapped without any prospect of relief, Cornwallis surrendered his army on October 19, 1781. Independence and freedom for the colonies was assured.

The following day, we traveled the Colonial Parkway to Jamestown (site of the first *successful* English settlement in North America). Next, we visited Williamsburg (18th century capital of Virginia) where we toured the restored historic district.

Starting back early Sunday morning, we arrived home in time for Bob to catch some sleep before his first night on the job. Bob and the other rookies had been assigned to the USPP Central District (D-1), which was responsible for the national monuments and urban federal parks within D.C. Bob was detailed to Squad A, currently working the midnight shift (11:00 p.m. to 7:00 a.m.).

Not wanting to be late, Bob dressed early in the evening, so he would have plenty of time to report to work. I took several snapshots of a smiling Bob in uniform. He was ecstatic to be finally going on patrol. A cold front had moved into the area and temperatures were predicted to drop to the low 40s. I packed a lunch pail with snacks and a thermos of hot chocolate. I also sent him off with a hug and a warm kiss.

Upon retiring to bed, I missed Bob and longed for the secure feeling of having him beside me. I realized that I would have to become use to sleeping *alone*—during Bob's midnight tours of duty.

D-1 worked out of Park Police Headquarters on Ohio Drive in East Potomac Park. Arriving early for the 10:45 p.m. roll call, Bob took a seat in the empty briefing room. Later, more officers started to arrive. Bob chatted with the other rookies from his class assigned to Squad A. All were anxious to start working the streets.

Several minutes before the start of roll call, the squad sergeant appeared. He intently reviewed some notes that were resting on the briefing room lectern. Then, he glanced at his watch, while he raised his head to view the assembled squad. It had grown in number with the addition of the rookies. After taking another look at his watch, the sergeant grabbed both sides of the lectern as he said: "Okay, listen up. We've got some new officers here tonight—fresh out of the academy. Welcome to the squad. I'm Sergeant E.P. Smith. My call sign is 102. I'll be checking on you throughout the night. You new men will be doubled up with veteran officers until you learn the foot beats."

Next, the sergeant called roll and gave out the beat assignments. He continued with the police lookouts and other pertinent information. Before the squad was dismissed, Sgt. Smith announced an inspection. Bob could tell by the bothered expressions of the veteran officers that inspections weren't very popular. This one had been scheduled due to the rookies' presence. The officers lined up and came to attention. Sgt. Smith checked each officer's uniform and equipment before he dismissed the squad for duty.

Bob introduced himself to the officer with whom he had been paired. Tonight, they would be working Beat 145, the White House (WH) sidewalk. Bob grabbed a mobile radio before heading out to the parking lot. In those days, Park Police radios were bulky, heavy (three pounds) Motorola HT-200 units that had metal telescoping antennas. The portables were carried in cases with attached shoulder straps. The radio was carried opposite one's gun side. Since Bob was a right-hander, he slung the strap over his right shoulder with the radio against his left hip.

Officers on foot patrol drove their personally owned vehicles (POV) to duty assignments. Each foot beat had a parking spot reserved for Park Police. The senior officer offered to drive, since there was only one official parking spot per beat. On the way to their post—during some small talk—the veteran asked Bob, "Are you married?"

"Yes. We have a three-year-old daughter. How about you?"

"Nope, but I have a girlfriend. She doesn't like this shift work. It's tough on a relationship. Things really aren't working out for us. Maybe it's for the best. A lot of the guys have marital problems. It takes at least a couple of years to get a piece of the weekend off. You work a lot of overtime. Your court dates have to be scheduled for your days off. It's rough on the ladies. Eventually, I'd like to get into the motor [motorcycle] unit. They work mostly days."

"Yeah, I made a deal with my wife. I promised that I would spend my time off doing family things, rather than activities with the guys or hobbies."

"I wish you luck. Anyhow, I'm happy to see you guys arrive. Maybe I'll be able to move up to a cruiser or out to another district," replied the veteran officer.

Rookies were the lifeblood of the force. They had an upward ripple effect on all officers within the rank of private. Rookies could replace foot beat officers, who could move to patrol car assignments. The more experienced and senior patrolmen could be selected for the specialized units: scooters, horse mounted, motorcycles, dog handlers, aviation, and detectives.

Arriving at East Executive Avenue and Pennsylvania Avenue, the senior officer and Bob checked in with the third relief officer (3:00 p.m. to 11:00 p.m.). He had no unusual incidents to pass on before going off duty.

Bob and the veteran officer started to patrol the White House sidewalk. Beat 145 covered the 1600 block on the south side of Pennsylvania Avenue, between East Executive Avenue and West Executive Avenue. Most of the demonstrations in Washington took place on the WH sidewalk and across the street in Lafayette Park. The sidewalk was a popular tourist spot to view and to photograph the White House. The beat was also important to White House security.

Although the Executive Protective Service and the Park Police have concurrent jurisdiction throughout D.C. (the same authority as Metropolitan Police), the three departments control varied *primary* jurisdictions. The areas in and around the White House highlight these interlocking main responsibilities.

The origins of the Executive Protective Service date back to 1922 when the White House Police force was formed at the request of President Warren G. Harding. Prior to that time, the White House and its grounds were protected by members of the Washington Metropolitan Police, augmented in wartime by the military.

Originally under the control of the military aide to the president, the White House Police—after a breach of security—were placed under the supervision of the U.S. Secret Service in 1930. During that summer, a well-dressed sightseer strolled into the White House and interrupted President Herbert Hoover's dinner. Mistaking the man for a Secret Service agent, the White House Police had let him pass through the front door of the Executive Mansion. He wandered into the dining room before being escorted away by the Secret Service.

The duties of the White House Police were expanded by Congress in 1970 to include the protection of foreign diplomatic missions in the D.C. area. With these added responsibilities, the White House Police were renamed the Executive Protective Service (EPS).

While the Secret Service and EPS (renamed USSS Uniformed Division in 1977) have responsibility for security of the White House and its grounds, the U.S. Park Police are tasked with protecting the adjacent federal parklands, which include the WH sidewalk, Lafayette Park, and the Ellipse. Adding to this delineation of police powers is the Metropolitan Police Department, which has primary responsibility for Pennsylvania Avenue.

These jurisdictions evolved through history, being further complicated by the multi-nature of the White House. Besides being the residence of our chief executive, the White House serves as the offices of the president and his staff and the site of many state functions. Since it's also a national treasure and one of the country's most popular tourist attractions, the White House was placed under the *custodial* care of the Department of Interior, National Park Service in 1933.

Although the Park Service maintains the property, the U.S. military supports the White House with communication, food, medical, and transportation services. The Marine Corps even provides a ceremonial guard at the front door to the West Wing.

Bob and the senior officer dutifully walked their beat. Bob listened keenly to the information and advice offered by the experienced footman. On one of the strolls by the White House Northwest Gate (A-4), the veteran took Bob over to the pedestrian entrance. They were buzzed in by the EPS officers on duty. Inside the gatehouse, Bob and the veteran chatted with the EPS officers.

"So, this is your first day on the street," one of the EPS officers remarked.

"Yeah, I'm happy to be out of the academy," Bob replied.

The EPS officer continued, "You're welcome to come in here anytime you need a break." Pointing to a monitor, the EPS officer emphasized, "We've got cameras covering the sidewalk, so you can even keep an eye on it, while you're in here."

Bob thanked the EPS officers for their hospitality. The veteran and Bob returned to the sidewalk. Later in the shift, Sergeant Smith pulled up to the curb and motioned for Bob to jump into the front seat of the cruiser. Extending his hand, Sergeant Smith greeted Bob: "Private Ritter, I'm E.P. Smith. Glad to have you in the squad."

Grasping the sergeant's hand firmly, Bob replied: "Thank you, sergeant. Glad to be here."

Sgt. Smith continued: "I've heard from the training folks that yours was a pretty good class, so I don't expect too many problems. And if you do your job well, you won't have any trouble with me."

Nodding his head, Bob said, "Sergeant, I want to be a good officer."

"I'm sure you'll do fine. Let me give you a quick rundown on what I'm looking for. It's important that you come to work unless you're absolutely too sick. In the coming weeks, after you new men get the swing of things, the older officers will be moving on. I won't have any extra men to cover for you.

"You need to be on time for roll calls. I pass on important information, and you don't want to miss any of it. It's also disruptive when officers come in late. And we need to make our reliefs on time. Get yourself an alarm clock that runs on batteries. It's no excuse that your power went off."

"Yes, sergeant, already have one."

"Good! You get a meal break. The rest of your shift, I expect to see you out on patrol. When we go to days, don't hang out with Park Service employees. Be visible and professional."

Again, Bob nodded his head in acknowledgement.

"The *Book of General Orders*, that's the Park Police bible to me. Learn it inside and out. Do what it says, and you won't have any problems. Okay?"

"Yes, sergeant."

Looking at Bob's nameplate, Sgt. Smith asked, "What's the 'R' for?"

"Robert," answered Bob. "Most people call me Bob."

"Okay, Bob. Any questions?"

"No, sergeant."

"All right, I'll check with you later."

Bob exited the cruiser and rejoined the veteran on patrol. The seasoned officer and Bob discussed beat responsibilities for not only the White House sidewalk, but other USPP foot beats as well. The Lafayette Park and Ellipse beats complimented the sidewalk beat. Besides providing for the safety of Park Service visitors, all three were important in providing an outer perimeter of security for the White House.

At these locations, the park patrolmen needed to be ever watchful that assassins or terrorists weren't reconnoitering the area or setting up for an assault. Additionally, the park officers were responsible for recognizing and handling mental subjects. This included medical referral to St. Elizabeths Hospital of subjects deemed to be a danger to themselves or others.

The sidewalk and Ellipse beat officers were also charged with preventing White House fence jumping. In the event the penetration could not be prevented, the park officer needed to immediately signal HQ by radio, so EPS could be officially notified. Even though the White House fence and grounds were protected by sensors and cameras, it was important to relay the confirmation of fence jumpers to EPS.

The White House sidewalk was probably the most important Park Police foot beat. The officer on duty had many responsibilities and was required to be alert and proactive. Besides being on the lookout for fence jumpers, mental subjects, assassins, and terrorists, the officer had to watch for protestors throwing items onto the White House lawn or attaching banners to the WH fence.

In addition, the Northwest Gate is accessed from this beat. The gate is used by invited guests and those with official appointments for admission to the White House. It's also where those *without* appointments come to see the president. Many of these uninvited "gate callers" hold an irrational belief that they can gain access to the president. Often, the park policeman on the WH sidewalk makes the Northwest Gate officers aware of these subjects, after encountering them on patrol. When they persist in seeing the president, EPS escorts them into a room inside the gatehouse. A Secret Service agent then responds to interview the subject and to take appropriate action.

As it was necessary for the WH sidewalk to be constantly manned, the senior officer and Bob coordinated their break with the Lafayette Park (Beat 146) officers. The 146 officers covered the sidewalk, while Bob and the veteran took their meal break in the Lafayette Park Lodge. This is a small structure on the H Street side of Lafayette Park. It has public restrooms on each end with a Park Service storage room in between. The room houses a desk, a Park Service telephone, and a chair. Inside the desk are the Park Police logbooks for Beats 145 and 146.

Looking around the room, Bob saw gardening tools, supplies for the rest rooms, and cleaning materials. The veteran remarked, "Not exactly the best atmosphere for dining, but it's out of the cold."

"Yeah, there's a chill in the air tonight," Bob added.

"They're predicting a cold winter," cautioned the veteran.

"I need to buy some long underwear," replied Bob.

"Get yourself a stretch headband too," suggested the veteran officer. "Wear it over your ears with your cap down tight against it. And some gloves. Not too bulky. You need to be able to get your finger inside the trigger guard of your revolver. Get black-colored stuff. The sergeants won't say anything as long as they're black."

Bob munched on his cold sandwich and potato chips. He was warmed by the hot chocolate and made a mental note to buy another thermos. It would be nice to have another to carry heated soup.

"I also double sole my shoes and use inner soles," the senior officer related between gulps of black coffee. "I find it helps to keep my feet warm and more comfortable. The inner soles act like shock absorbers."

The two officers finished their meal and returned to the WH sidewalk. Another important responsibility of a U.S. Park Police officer is providing information to visitors, regarding the federal parks in D.C. and other general tourist information. Bob had learned much of that in the academy. In the coming months, Bob would add to that knowledge by discovering some of the little-known-historical facts of Washington. History spoke to Bob, and he was a rapt listener.

Despite the fact Bob was on the outside looking in, he felt a tremendous sense of pride in being a part of White House security. Through the six-foot fence bordering the north side of the White House grounds with the sidewalk, Bob viewed one of the most recognizable symbols of the free world. There was much history surrounding Bob.

Even the White House fence had a story to tell. Though giving the appearance of black-painted wrought iron, it's actually made from hardened steel with bronze spear points atop the pickets. In order to make the White House more secure, the original iron fencing was replaced in 1936–1937 by the Army Corps of Engineers. The fence is solidly anchored in a foot-high sandstone curb.

In deference to history and tradition, the original Northwest Gate of the White House was allowed to remain—though it compromised security. In 1972, Bob touched his hand to the actual gate that every president since James Monroe had passed through. This was the thrill of discovering the secrets of history.

The next night, Bob was assigned to Lafayette Park since the new officers were being rotated around the foot beats. Originally part of the White House grounds as designed by city planner Pierre L'Enfant, President Thomas Jefferson separated it from the front lawn in the early 1800s. The resulting seven-acre tract of land was opened to the public and was designated President's Park. By 1822, Pennsylvania Avenue had been formally extended through the area.

In 1824–1825, Revolutionary War hero the Marquis de Lafayette visited the United States. He addressed a joint session of Congress—the first foreigner to do so. He also gave the first commencement address at the new Columbian College (now George Washington University). One of the biggest honors bestowed on Lafayette during his visit was the public celebration held for him in President's Park. Due to the notoriety of this event, the area became popularly known as Lafayette Square (later officially designated Lafayette Park).

In 1851, the recently formed Department of the Interior took over the care of Lafayette Park. Plans were drawn up for landscaping and ornamental enhancements. In 1853, Clark Mills was commissioned to produce a statue honoring Andrew Jackson, the hero of the Battle of New Orleans (War of 1812). This was seen as a unifying gesture to the rise of sectionalism. President Jackson, though a Southerner, had been a strong supporter of the Union.

For a time, the area was called Jackson Park due to the prominence of the Jackson statue. Situated in the middle of the park, this was the first equestrian statue sculpted by an American. It's noted for Jackson's rearing horse, which balances the entire weight of the statue on its hind legs.

Surrounding the limestone base of the statue are four cannon that were actually captured by Jackson from the Spanish at Pensacola, Florida in 1819. The Jackson statue was also cast from bronze melted down from Spanish cannons. With the ever-increasing popularity of the statue, Mills later cast identical replicas for the cities of New Orleans and Nashville.

Between 1891 and 1910, four other statues were erected, one in each corner of Lafayette Park. These statues commemorate Lafayette and three other foreign-born patriots (Rochambeau, Kosciuszko, and Von Steuben) who fought with the Continental Army during the War of Independence.

Lafayette Park was the scene of a notorious crime in 1859. Philip Barton Key (the U.S. Attorney for D.C. and son of Francis Scott Key) was shot and killed by Congressman Daniel Sickles of New York. Key had been having an affair with Sickles's young wife.

In the trial that ensued, Sickles was represented by a defense team that included attorney Edwin Stanton (became secretary of war for Pres. Lincoln). Claiming that Sickles had been "temporarily insane," his attorneys argued that it was justifiable homicide. It was the first case in U.S. history that such a defense was used. The jury acquitted Sickles. He became a Union General during the Civil War. Sickles lost his right leg and won the Medal of Honor at Gettysburg. You can still see Sickles's fractured right leg and the 12-pound cannon ball that caused the injury at the National Museum of Health and Medicine located in Silver Spring, Maryland. The rest of Sickles's body is buried at Arlington National Cemetery.

While patrolling the north side of Lafayette Park, a blue light drew Bob to a still functional piece of Washington history. Situated on H Street was an old police call box. The blue call box, with light atop, sat on a gray pedestal. The pedestal and box were made of iron.

Park Police officers were issued two brass keys. One unlocked police call boxes and traffic signal boxes; the other gained access to Park Service facilities. Bob opened the box and saw a phone receiver inside. This connected via a party line to MPD communications. Bob could still see the vestiges of old switches, no longer used.

The system of fire and police call boxes began in D.C. during the 1860s. They originally utilized telegraph signals. In the late 1910s, the boxes were switched over to telephone lines. The police call boxes were an important aid to public safety into the 1950s–1960s. Before police car radios and portable radios for foot beats, patrol officers had to stop at call boxes to check in with central command.

Police radio communications started in the 1930s. Originally, patrol cars were only equipped with receiving units. They could be dispatched to duties, but the officers still needed to report via the call boxes. The call boxes were also used by officers on their rounds. The patrolman would throw a switch in the box every 30 minutes, which signaled that his patrol was proceeding as normal with no assistance needed.

With the advent of two-way radio in the 1940s–1950s and the development of walkie-talkies in the 1950s–1960s, police call boxes had become dinosaurs from the past. In 1972, they were only used by officers who wanted to speak with their precincts without tying up the radio or to get an outside line. Police call boxes were phased out in the late 1970s.

In the coming weeks, Bob's squad rotated from midnights to 3–11 to days. Bob and his fellow rookies became experienced in all the permanent foot beats (White House sidewalk, Washington Monument, Lafayette Park, Ellipse, Lincoln Memorial, Jefferson Memorial, and the Kennedy Center). The senior officers moved on, and Bob's class settled into the foot beats.

On the 3–11 p.m. shift rotation, Bob got his first taste of directing traffic since the academy. A cruiser unit dropped him off at Rosslyn Circle for the afternoon rush hour. Rosslyn Circle is located on the Virginia side of the Francis Scott Key Bridge. In the old days, D.C. Transit trolleys ran there from Georgetown and used the circle to turn around for the trip back over the Potomac River. Near the circle were terminals where riders could connect to Virginia lines.

By 1972, the Rosslyn section of Arlington County, Va. had become an area of high-rise office buildings. Buses and cars replaced the trolleys. Rosslyn Circle was now a grassy area surrounded by roadways. Key Bridge had become a major commuter thoroughfare.

On the D.C. side, Key Bridge connects with M Street (U.S. Route 29), Canal Road, and the Whitehurst Freeway. At the Virginia end, it links to the George Washington Memorial Parkway (GWMP), Lee Highway (U.S. Route 29), and with Wilson Boulevard via North Lynn Street.

A Park Police motor officer arrived to brief Bob. The officer slowly dismounted his birch-white Harley-Davidson Electra Glide trimmed with black saddlebags and Park Police emblems. Equipped with two-way radio, emergency lights, and siren, a police motorcycle is an impressive machine. During winter months, the motors ran with sidecars attached. This provided increased stability, especially useful during icy conditions.

Ambling over toward Bob, the motorman's deliberate movements and red, chapped face portrayed a deep, piercing cold. Bob shuddered to think what it was like to ride a motorcycle around town on a frigid, windy winter day. The motor officer looked like a 200-pound block of ice.

"Your first time at the circle?" the motorman grunted.

"Yep."

The motor officer looked Bob over a couple of times, to size him up. Bob got the feeling he was a man about to be thrown to hungry wolves.

"Well, I guarantee you won't forget it," the motorman said in a dead-serious tone. Pointing north to the bridge, he continued: "Pretty soon, more traffic than you've ever seen is going to be coming over Key Bridge. Give it priority, so we can empty out D.C."

Bob, looking at the three lanes of outgoing traffic already on the bridge, commented, "Looks pretty heavy now."

"Trust me, son; you ain't seen nothin' yet. Don't let the cross traffic intimidate you. If they have to wait 5 minutes, so be it. Run the bridge."

"Okay," Bob acknowledged.

The officer stated with emphasis: "*Be careful*! Nobody likes going to police funerals. If you go up against thousands of pounds of rolling steel, you're going to lose every time. I guarantee it. Wait until you have a break in the traffic before you step into the travel lanes. Don't count on these people seeing you or stopping. If they don't yield, get out of their way! Stay clear of the buses and trucks. Sometimes they cause a draft that can suck you in. Any questions?"

"No, I don't think so."

"All right, get on the radio if you need anything."

The motorman roared off, leaving Bob alone against a rising tide of traffic. It was just about 4:00 p.m.; Bob put on his orange visibility vest and white gloves. Then he pulled a traffic whistle from his pocket. Cars, buses, and trucks whizzed by Bob in a never-ending parade—that was traveling at 45 mph.

The circle traffic from North Lynn and the GWMP was building up. The waiting drivers gave Bob irritated looks. Bob nodded back to show that he hadn't forgotten them. He searched for a break in the bridge traffic, but as far as his eyes could see, the vehicles were spaced too closely. Eventually, Bob decided to stop the lane nearest him first, which he could do from the curb. Then, he could step out into that lane to stop the middle lane. From the middle lane, he could stop the far lane. He used that method for most of the next two and a half hours. Seldom were there enough gaps in all three lanes to attempt to stop them simultaneously.

Bob must have been doing something right. The sergeants frequently selected Bob for the Rosslyn Circle coverage. I could always tell when he had the assignment, as his uniforms smelled of diesel fumes and were a couple of shades darker. Off to the cleaners for priority service.

During the first month that Bob's academy class hit the streets, two of the rookies left the force. One was dismissed for falling asleep on duty. He had apparently been caught sleeping on two different occasions. The circumstances surrounding the separation of the other officer were quite surprising.

Arriving home one evening, Bob asked me, "Remember the officer who saw the downed power line at Harpers Ferry?"

"Yes, how's he doing?"

"Not too good. He either got fired or was forced to resign."

"Wow! What happened?" I asked with astonishment.

"It went back to his academy days. To take the job, he moved to D.C. from out of state. The training sergeant told the officer to make sure he got D.C. tags and a D.C. permit [driver's license]. The law gives you 30 days to do this after you move. The other day, the sergeant saw the car parked at one of the beats. It still had out-of-state tags. Apparently, the sergeant had been suspicious of the situation for some time. He decided to investigate. The word is that the officer didn't have a title or registration for the vehicle."

"No!"

"Yeah, the officer claimed he bought the car from a friend who was withholding the paperwork until all of the payments were made on the vehicle."

"Wow," I said. "Can he come back, if he clears the matter up?"

"No, he's done. We have a one-year probationary period. They can let you go for just about anything. After an incident like this, they probably won't reinstate him."

"Wow, you never know," I said—still a bit shocked by the news. "Maybe that explains why you guys weren't put in for a commendation after Harpers Ferry."

On Friday, November 3, 1972, an incident of another sort took place that caught federal law enforcement officials by surprise. There were reports that a disturbance had broken out at the South Interior Building, which housed the Bureau of Indian Affairs. The Trail of Broken Treaties Caravan had arrived in Washington earlier that day. American Indian leaders wanted to present a list of grievances to BIA officials. Hundreds of American Indians descended on BIA Headquarters. When a scuffle broke out with federal guards, the Indians then took over the building, which is located at 1951 Constitution Avenue, NW, D.C.

Police made contingency plans in case forceful removal of the protestors would become necessary. Since the presidential election was only a few days away, the Nixon administration wished to settle the incident peaceably. The Indians occupied the building throughout the weekend while negotiating with government officials.

The South Interior Building had its own notable history. It was constructed in 1932 as the headquarters for the Public Health Service. During World War II, the building became the Combined Chiefs of Staff Building. Here the armed forces chiefs of staff of the United States and Great Britain planned strategic military operations. Even the top-secret details of the Manhattan Project, which created the first atomic bomb, were coordinated at the building. After the war, the newly created Atomic Energy Commission occupied the building until 1958, when the National Science Foundation (NSF) took over. In 1965, the NSF was succeeded in the building by the Bureau of Indian Affairs.

A settlement of the standoff was reached whereby the federal government promised to review the Indians' grievances. Additionally, in exchange for a $66,000 travel grant, the protestors agreed to vacate the BIA. The Indians were escorted out of town on Monday, November 3.

During the occupation, furniture and files were destroyed. Graffiti was painted on the walls, and some federal records were missing. To some, it appeared that the government had been extorted.

The following day saw President Richard Nixon and Vice President Spiro Agnew reelected in a landslide over Democratic candidates Senator George McGovern and R. Sargent Shriver. McGovern had run on a platform of withdrawal from Viet Nam for release of American prisoners of war. Sargent Shriver (John F. Kennedy's brother-in-law) replaced original Democratic vice presidential nominee Senator Thomas Eagleton of Missouri. It was revealed during the campaign that Eagleton had undergone electro-shock therapy in the 1960s for depression.

Weeks passed, and winter became more severe. Bob joked that if he didn't keep moving while on patrol, he'd freeze up. Although it was bitterly cold, Bob enjoyed the interaction with tourists. This was the interpretive aspect of being a Park Police foot patrolman at our national icons.

Interpretation is the act of providing information and meaningful experiences to park visitors. In dusty photo albums across the country and around the world, Bob can still be seen as he appeared in 1972–1973—frozen in time—standing alongside tourists who wanted a special remembrance of their visit.

Bob was routinely assigned to cover the Ellipse (Beat 143). Many tourists visit the Ellipse for the beautiful view of the South Portico of the White House. This 52-acre grassy plot was originally part of the White House grounds. It was separated from the South Grounds of the WH and became a federal park.

The Ellipse contains several monuments, including the Zero Milestone. This granite monument is 2 feet square by 4 feet high. Constructed in 1920 to replace a temporary marker, the Zero Milestone marks the point at which highway distances are measured to and from Washington.

The Army's first transcontinental motor convoy started here in 1919. Over 60 vehicles and more than 200 men departed the Zero Milestone on their two-month journey. The convoy included road and bridge building equipment. A young Army officer by the name of Dwight D. Eisenhower was one of those who made the 3,200-mile trip to San Francisco. The experience served as an inspiration for President Eisenhower's strong support of the Interstate Highway System, which he helped form in 1956.

For the holiday season, the Ellipse is transformed into the Christmas Pageant of Peace. In 1972, the pageant consisted of a Yule log, life-size nativity scene, performance stage, reindeer pen, and other exhibits. The Pathway to Peace led to the National Christmas Tree. Along the pathway were smaller trees—decorated for the states and territories.

The 1972 National Christmas Tree was a 75-foot Engelmann spruce, cut from Medicine Bow National Forest in Wyoming. Bob was one of the park policemen who provided site security for the tree lighting ceremony. Vice President Spiro Agnew with Secretary of the Interior Rogers Morton threw the switch that illuminated over 10,000 bulbs.

For the month of December, the Ellipse beat officer was augmented by personnel from the USPP Special Operations Force (SOF). During prime hours of visitation, SOF officers provided additional security for the Pageant of Peace. While assigned to Beat 143, Bob became friendly with Harold P. "Sonny" Nowlon and several other SOF officers. Sonny told Bob: "The word is SOF will be picking up some new officers early next year. Would you like me to mention your name to Captain Groves [SOF Commander]? He's been asking if we know any good officers who might be interested."

"Yeah, keep me in mind. SOF sounds like a great unit," replied Bob.

"Good, I think you'd like SOF better than one of the districts. I'll say something to Groves, and we'll see what happens."

On one of Bob's days off, he took our daughter, my mom, and me downtown for some sightseeing. During Bob's duty assignments, he had discovered some interesting, out-of-the-way places. On the Washington Monument grounds, he showed us Survey Lodge near Independence Avenue. It's actually made from stone, quarried for the construction of the Washington Monument, which opened to the public in 1888. Originally used by surveyors, the lodge housed boilers that ran the first elevator in the Monument. Pipes ran 800 feet underground to a steam engine located outside the Monument. In 1901, an electric elevator replaced the original steam-powered elevator. Survey Lodge was eventually converted to Park Service offices.

Next, we walked across the south Monument grounds. Stopping at a manhole cover, Bob told us: "Underneath is a 12-foot-tall scale model of the Monument. It's made of granite. Engineers used it as a reference point for surveying during construction of the Monument."

My mom looked at Bob disbelievingly and said: "Come on Bob, I wasn't born yesterday. There's a sewer or something under there."

Our three and a half-year-old daughter chimed in, "Daddy, you're kidding."

Bob bent down and lifted off the cover. To our surprise, there it was—just as Bob had said. My mom declared, "My, isn't that something?"

After touring the Monument, we walked down to 17th Street and Constitution Avenue. There, Bob showed us the Lock Keeper's House. This stone structure dates back to the 1830s. It was built to house the lock keeper of the Washington extension of the Chesapeake and Ohio (C & O) Canal. The lock keeper collected tolls and kept records of shipping traffic. Here, the Washington City Canal (fed by Tiber Creek) connected to the C & O Canal.

By the 1870s, railroads had taken the place of canals in commerce. Tiber Creek and the Washington Canal had also become an open sewer. Tunnels were built to carry sewage, storm water, and the flow from Tiber Creek to the Potomac. The creek and canal were filled, and Constitution Avenue constructed over the canal right of way.

Crossing the street to the Ellipse, Bob took us by the Bulfinch Gatehouses. They were designed in 1828 by Charles Bulfinch (architect of the U.S. Capitol). These sandstone structures saw duty on the Capitol grounds until 1874. Nearby are matching sandstone fence posts, which connected the original wrought iron fence of the Capitol.

Continuing north on 17th Street, we came across the Butt-Millett Fountain, erected in 1913. Bob related that it was a memorial to Major Archibald William Butt (military aide to presidents Theodore Roosevelt and William Howard Taft) and Francis Millett (a famous American painter). Butt and Millett lost their lives when the ocean liner RMS *Titanic* (on its maiden voyage) hit an iceberg and sank in 1912. The marble fountain was designed by Daniel Chester French, who sculpted the Lincoln statue in the Lincoln Memorial. The fountain was functionally designed with the added purpose of providing drinking water for U.S. Park Police horses.

The cold winter continued for the D.C. Metropolitan Area. There was little crime in federal parks that were routinely patrolled by footmen. The presence of uniformed officers was a major deterrent. Bob mostly handled parking violations, drunkenness, larcenies, and mental subjects. Occasionally, Bob got in on arrests for assaults, robberies, burglaries, and even an attempted rape.

During the evening and midnight shifts, Bob became familiar with the "night people" of D.C. This assorted cast of characters included vagrants and "bag ladies" (women who wander the streets carrying their possessions in shopping bags). Bob developed a special concern for one homeless woman by the name of Mary. She would walk around the park areas pushing a shopping cart filled with everything she owned, neatly tucked away in brown bags.

Bob tried to get Mary to go to a homeless shelter on frigid nights, but she refused. Mary said she really wasn't homeless. The streets were her home. She also worried that she'd be assaulted and robbed at the shelter. Mary claimed she was safer on a park bench with Bob on the beat than she would be in any shelter.

She regularly spent the nights at the Ellipse or in Lafayette Park. When Bob was assigned those beats, he made sure she stayed warm and opened up the public restrooms for her when needed (they were locked at dark). Bob gave her one of our old blankets. There was always the danger during extremely cold winter nights that the homeless could succumb to hypothermia.

One of the favorite sleeping spots for vagrants was a couple of large iron grates on the Washington Monument grounds. There, steam vented from underground pipes. This network of steam pipes ran throughout the downtown area, providing heat for federal buildings. The problem was that the steam soaked the vagrants with moisture, which could lead to subnormal body temperatures on bitter nights. Park Police tried to keep the vagrants off the grates as much as possible. Sadly, one of Bob's academy classmates found a homeless man dead on a Monument grounds steam grate that winter.

Many of the homeless Bob encountered had alcohol and drug problems. One had been a successful businessman, who dropped out of the "rat race." Some had mental and emotional problems. Most were impoverished, but others had sources of income such as Veterans' Affairs (VA), Social Security, and public assistance benefits.

Mary received money sent to her by relatives. She got mail via U.S. Postal Service general delivery, picking it up at the main downtown post office. This was the only contact she had with relatives or most anyone else other than Park Police. Bob described Mary as "no longer wanting to be a part of society."

In the news, 1972 ended with the American bombing of North Vietnam in a U.S. attempt to force resumption of the deadlocked Paris peace negotiations. Baseball star and humanitarian Roberto Clemente perished in a plane crash off the coast of Puerto Rico. Clemente was bringing relief supplies to earthquake-stricken Nicaragua.

The New Year brought some excitement to the airwaves. Elvis performed a live-television concert from Hawaii. Our beloved Washington Redskins played tough but lost to the Miami Dolphins 14-7 in Super Bowl VII. The win capped a perfect season for Miami, the only undefeated team in NFL history.

In Washington on January 20, 1973, President Nixon was inaugurated for his second term. For weeks, Bob had watched the construction of the presidential reviewing stands along Pennsylvania Avenue. Bob worked many hours and had his days off canceled as security was heightened leading to Inauguration Day. Counter-inaugural demonstrations took place.

Then, on January 23, 1973, President Nixon announced that a ceasefire agreement had been reached for Vietnam. The Paris Peace Accords were officially signed on January 27. U.S. troops would start to withdraw from Vietnam. American prisoners of war were to be released. It was agreed that the people of South Vietnam should decide their political future through democratic elections.

In February, Bob got some good news. He was being reassigned from District 1 to the USPP Special Operations Force. Bob's sergeant told Bob that he had earned the assignment and wished him luck. Even better days were on the way for Bob.

Chapter 10

SOF

During the late 1960s, visitation to our national parks increased in dramatic fashion. So did crime. The national park system reported more than a two-fold increase in criminal activity from 1966–1970. Even wilderness area national parks like Yellowstone, Yosemite, and the Grand Canyon posted significant increases. Major crimes such as larceny, assault, robbery, rape, and murder escalated. Accidents, both vehicular and non-traffic, were also on the rise.

The year 1970 saw two highly publicized incidents that spotlighted the issues of crime and safety in our national parks. In June 1970, a nine-year-old boy was killed when he fell into a boiling hot thermal pool at Yellowstone Park. The second incident happened in Yosemite over the Fourth of July holiday. A large number of unruly youths took over part of the park. The park rangers were inexperienced in crowd control. Violent confrontations ensued, resulting in physical injuries and a great deal of property damage.

The National Park Service responded to these challenges by creating a law enforcement division in Washington. This office was responsible for the safety and protection of park visitors. As the United States Park Police were experienced and skilled in the handling of urban crime, special events, and demonstrations, the Park Service looked to them for assistance.

In the comprehensive program that followed, senior Park Police officials (rank of captain) were assigned to each NPS regional office to coordinate law enforcement. More rangers and Park Police officers were hired. A large number of rangers were scheduled for extensive law enforcement training. Additionally, the USPP was directed to establish a strike force that could respond to any national park in emergency situations.

The U.S. Park Police Special Operations Force (SOF) was formed in 1971 as a unit that could provide temporary law enforcement assistance throughout the national park system. This was especially essential, as many of our national parks are enclaves of *exclusive* federal jurisdiction—where state and local police have no authority.

When territories were admitted into the union, exclusive legislative jurisdiction was retained by the Congress of the United States over federal reservations within the new state. Enclaves of exclusive jurisdiction also exist on federal land purchased or ceded from the states. Thus, many sites that were originally military installations and the like are not subject to state and local law.

Since the U.S. Park Police are federal officers, they can exercise police powers on Park Service lands across the United States. From 1971–1973, the USPP Special Operations Force distinguished itself in assignments to Grand Canyon, Yosemite, Rocky Mountain, and Big Bend National Parks, as well as several national monuments, national recreational areas, and national seashores.

When Bob reported for duty to the Special Operations Force in early 1973, the unit was manned by a captain, a lieutenant, 2 sergeants, and over 20 privates. The SOF substation was located in Northeast D.C. on the grounds of Fort Totten Park. Ft. Totten was one of the many forts constructed during the Civil War for the defense of Washington. All that remained of the fort were some earthen defensive works that included firing positions used by artillery and infantry.

The substation was situated in the former Park Police outdoor range building. When Park Police began using the Secret Service range in Beltsville, Maryland for firearms requalification, the USPP outdoor range became surplus property, available for the new SOF. With a firing range just outside the substation door, SOF personnel could routinely hone their firearms skills. It was also a great location for tactical training exercises.

When SOF was not responding to out-of-town law enforcement requests, it handled the many demonstrations and special events that frequently occurred in the federal parks of D.C. SOF was also used for the selective enforcement of traffic regulations and the targeting of criminal activity. Additionally, the unit maintained two Special Equipment and Tactics Teams (SETT). These officers were trained in situations involving hostages and barricaded gunmen.

Bob was honored to have been chosen for SOF. He was told that Captain Hugh Groves, the Commander of SOF, personally selected the officers for this elite unit. It was important that SOF personnel showed initiative and courage and that they were calm under pressure and able to handle stress. As SOF officers traveled and worked closely together, they also needed to be team players and somewhat like-minded.

During Bob's first weeks at SOF, he often partnered with Sonny Nowlon, one of the officers who had recommended Bob to Captain Groves. Sonny was born in the East Side of New York and raised on Staten Island. He still ordered coffee the New Yorker way by asking for "a container of coffee" rather than a cup.

Sonny had an adventuresome streak, which must have been hereditary. As a youth, Sonny's dad had been a "runner" for the Irish Republican Army. After coming to the states, his dad became disabled when Sonny was only 14. Sonny left school to support the family. For money, he worked on motorcycles and raced them until he was drafted into the Army.

Following basic training, Sonny received specialized instruction in combat engineering and explosives. He attended jump school at Ft. Benning, Georgia and was attached to Special Forces. A veteran of several tours of duty in Viet Nam, Sonny was selected for Officers Candidate School—eventually achieving the rank of first lieutenant. He served in several other military operations and also trained troops for the 101st Airborne Division at Ft. Campbell, Kentucky.

After his military service, Sonny worked several years for an intelligence agency in short term, high-risk operations. Sonny then joined the USPP. He had been in SOF since its formation and was a well-respected officer. As Bob related: "Sonny served overseas in covert operations. He knows his stuff. He's been taking me around and showing me the ropes."

"Where have you been working?" I asked.

"All over the metropolitan area," Bob answered. "That's the neat thing about SOF. We get to work in all the Park Police districts. Sonny's been taking me to the lesser-known federal parks in D.C.—like Franklin, Farragut, McPherson, Lincoln, Meridian Hill, and DuPont Circle. We've also been out to the Agricultural Research Center and the Baltimore-Washington, Suitland, George Washington, and Rock Creek parkways. It's been good familiarization, and Sonny is especially street savvy."

Bob held up some uniform items. "Today, we stopped by the Park Police Property Section at Brentwood. He got them to issue me some extra shirts and another pair of pants. As Sonny said, 'We travel out to the boonies. It can be a long drive to a dry cleaner.'"

I could tell that Bob was enjoying his work. SOF was agreeing with both of us. Although Bob still had weekdays off, the normal working hours for SOF were 10:00 a.m. to 6:00 p.m. Occasionally, they worked 6:00 p.m. to 2:00 a.m. or 4:00 p.m. to midnight. Though I wasn't looking forward to Bob's work-related travel, it was nice that he was off steady shift work and no longer had to pull a midnight shift.

However, it wasn't long until Bob was sent out on his first SOF trip. It was late February 1973. Sonny and Bob were on cruiser patrol (Car 715). While heading down North Capitol Street to the National Mall area, they stopped a vehicle for speeding. After name checking the driver, it was discovered that he had multiple outstanding warrants for moving (non-parking) traffic violations.

Sonny was up by the violator's vehicle, issuing a speeding ticket, while Bob stood by the front passenger door of the cruiser with radio microphone in hand. Bob was backing up Sonny and waiting for confirmation of the warrants. Once they were verified, the subject would be arrested and his vehicle impounded. It would be nice to get a scofflaw off the streets.

Suddenly, Bob heard the radio dispatcher call Car 702 (one of the SOF sergeants). "702," replied the sergeant.

"702, 10-25 [report to] your substation immediately," directed the dispatcher.

"10-4," the sergeant acknowledged.

Next, the dispatcher called other SOF units in turn, giving the same order—to report to the SOF substation immediately.

After receiving the message for Car 715, Bob responded over the air, "We're 10-6 [busy] waiting for confirmation of subject's warrants."

The dispatcher replied, "715, 10-22 [disregard] your traffic stop and 10-25 your substation immediately."

"10-4," Bob reluctantly acknowledged.

He called Sonny back to the cruiser and told him the news. Sonny was beside himself. "Give me the mike!" he bellowed.

"715," Sonny called into the microphone with some displeasure in his voice.

"Car 715," responded the dispatcher.

"Request MPD responds to my location to take custody of the subject."

After a brief pause, the dispatcher replied, "Car 715—*per the watch commander*—advise subject of his warrants and the need to clear them—then 10-25 your substation immediately."

"10-4," Sonny groaned into the mike.

Sonny and Bob looked up and down North Capitol Street for an MPD cruiser—without success. Where were they when you needed them. With no other recourse, Sonny informed the subject of his outstanding traffic warrants and that he needed to go to one of the MPD district stations to take care of the matter. The subject claimed no knowledge of the warrants. He promised to stop by MPD.

After clearing the traffic stop, Sonny grumbled: "He's not going to stop by MPD. I might as well told him to drive down to Central Cell Block and check in. This was his lucky day. The crap must have hit the fan somewhere."

"Yeah," Bob agreed, "must be an emergency."

Arriving back at SOF, the officers anxiously poured into the roll call area of the substation. The small building featured only two rooms. The large main room contained areas for roll call and report writing. This room was not divided by partitions; it also housed workspace for the detail clerk and supervisory personnel. Everything used by SOF: desks, chairs, file cabinets, message boxes, blackboards, and a storage vault were spread about the main room. The other room in the building was a small area used by Park Police armorers.

The substation buzzed with speculation regarding the upcoming assignment. In one corner, Captain Groves sat at his desk, writing notes on a pad of paper. Bob thought the captain looked a bit apprehensive.

After the last officers checked in at the substation, Captain Groves moved over to the briefing lectern, where Sergeant Carl Holmberg was standing.

Sergeant Holmberg rapped his hand on the side of the lectern a couple of times to get the officers attention. Then, he announced loudly, "Quiet down for Captain Groves."

The captain put his right leg up on a chair that he had pulled alongside the lectern. Leaning toward the officers, he said: "Men, you've been ordered to South Dakota. The secretary of the interior is sending SOF to Mount Rushmore. There's been a disturbance at an Indian reservation. The Park Service is worried the trouble might spread."

Captain Groves glanced down at his watch. Then, he lifted his head back toward the officers. "You're flying out tonight by military transport from Andrews Air Force Base. You don't have much time to prepare, so thanks for your cooperation." Handing some notes to Sergeant Holmberg, the captain finished with, "Sergeants Holmberg and Hill will brief you on what to pack and other particulars."

After the sergeants' briefing, the officers hurried out to their POVs for the drive home. Arriving at our apartment, Bob rushed through the front door and headed for our bedroom—slowing only enough to give me a passing kiss on the cheek.

"How come you're home early? What's up?" I asked as Bob disappeared into the bedroom. He had been scheduled to work till midnight.

"We're going to Mount Rushmore."

"We are!" I said with tongue-in-cheek sincerity while joining Bob in the bedroom.

"You're funny. SOF is going. We're leaving in an hour and a half from Andrews."

Fortunately, one of the first tips Sonny gave Bob was to keep a suitcase packed for short notice trips. Bob pulled the bag from a closet and tossed it on the bed. Already packed were two pairs of uniform pants, some uniform shirts, casual clothes, socks, and underwear. Bob grabbed his shaving kit from the bathroom and a uniform jacket from the closet. He threw some long johns, an insulated vest, and some heavy wool socks into the suitcase too.

"How long will you be gone?" I asked.

"Nobody knows for sure. The sergeants thought at least a week or two."

"A week or two," I moaned.

"Yeah, there's some trouble on an Indian reservation near Mount Rushmore. There's concern it might carry over to the park. We don't know a lot. We'll find out more when we get out there. I'll call when I can."

"Bobbie, I'm going to miss you."

"I'll miss you too, honey." Bob closed the suitcase and placed it on the floor by the bed. "I love you more than anything in the world," Bob said as he pulled me close to him. We embraced and shared a sensuous kiss. For a moment, we stayed wrapped in each other's arms. I could feel the warmth of Bob's love.

It was decided that I would go with Bob to Andrews. Wanting to see Bob off on his first SOF trip, I got a neighbor to watch our daughter. It also made better logistics. Although the military would be flying SOF out due to the emergency situation, they would be flying back via a commercial airline, probably to Washington National Airport. This way, Bob's car wouldn't be stranded at AAFB.

Bob carried his suitcase out to the car, while I held onto his free arm. Opening the trunk, Bob placed the suitcase inside and then grabbed his Park Police issued duffel bag. Unzipping it, he checked the gear inside: riot helmet, riot baton, gas mask, raincoat, and other items. "What are all those plastic strips for?" I asked.

"They're flexi-cuffs. We use those during mass arrests. The strap goes around the wrists and interlocks through the notched end."

"How do you get them off?"

"You cut them. They're one-time use."

We headed for the Beltway and the 20-minute drive to Andrews Air Force Base. Bob was told to use the main gate, which is off Allentown Road. The security policeman at the gate checked us in and directed Bob to the passenger terminal.

At the terminal, I went inside with Bob. He was one of the first officers there, since most SOF personnel lived in Virginia. Later, we spent some time with Sonny Nowlon, the officer who was mentoring Bob. It was nice of Sonny to say he would look after Bob for me. Soon, Sergeants Holmberg and Hill announced that the plane was ready for loading. Bob and I shared a goodbye kiss, and I waved to him as he departed the terminal for the tarmac.

On the drive home that evening, I reflected on this new stage of Bob's career. I was happy Bob was off on an exciting adventure yet saddened that he and I would be apart. It was Bob's first government travel since the training trip to Harper's Ferry, West Virginia. I remembered the tragic circumstances of that trip and how Bob was endangered. Now, he was off on his first law enforcement trip. I worried about Bob and what he might face. There would be many more trips to come during Bob's law enforcement career. Each one would bring new challenges for us.

Chapter 11

The Shrine of Democracy

The officers hurried across the tarmac to a waiting Douglas VC-118 airliner. The VC-118 was a military version of the propeller-driven Douglas DC-6. Powered by four 2,500 horsepower Pratt and Whitney engines, the aircraft featured "United States of America" markings and a distinguishing paint scheme. The plane was one of the oldest in the 89th Airlift Wing of the U.S. Air Force.

The primary mission of the 89th Airlift Wing is to provide special air mission (SAM) support for the president, vice president, and senior military and civilian leaders. The Park Police officers were being airlifted by the Air Force due to the special request of the secretary of the interior.

Sonny and Bob took seats in the rear of the aircraft and buckled up. Shortly thereafter, the veteran airliner was readied for departure. Each engine started in turn, resulting in a thunderous roar and a cloud of smoke. Taxiing to the runway, the flight was immediately cleared for takeoff. The engines revved mightily as the vintage bird lumbered down the runway. Finally, she rose into the evening sky and winged her way toward the West.

After being airborne for about 30 minutes, Lieutenant Turner, the deputy commander of SOF, rose from his seat in the front of the passenger cabin to address the officers. "Men, we're heading for Ellsworth Air Force Base at Rapid City, South Dakota. When we arrive, Park Police Captain Denny Sorah will meet us. He's the law enforcement coordinator for the Park Service Regional Office at Omaha, Nebraska. He'll have updated information for us. Please bear with me until then.

"In a little while, we'll be served some sandwiches. Afterwards, I suggest you try to get some rest. It's going to be a long night."

Sonny turned toward Bob and said: "That's what I like about Groves and Turner. They don't keep information from us. When they find out something, they let us know."

A few minutes later, Sergeant Holmberg moved down the aisle, stopping at the row occupied by Bob and Sonny. "Private Ritter, Lieutenant Turner would like to see you."

"He does," is all Bob could say to the surprising request.

Seated nearby, Private Jerry Delane cast a mischievous glance in Bob's direction and loudly chimed in with, "Uh-oh, Ritter's in trouble."

Sergeant Holmberg shook his head as he told Bob: "There's nothing wrong. The lieutenant just wants to speak with you."

"Okay, sarge, I'll be right up."

Sonny yelled over to Delane in a humorous tone, "Hey, Jerry, point those big ears of yours somewhere else."

"Okay, Snuffer, anything you say."

Delane had nicknamed Sonny "The Snuffer." It alluded to Sonny's checkered military career, which included special warfare operations. Delane, along with SOF Officer Tom Kaylor, was always good for a wisecrack or two, when an opportunity presented itself. Bob took it as good-natured fun. Delane and Kaylor weren't really malicious. They mostly poked fun with you, not at you.

Moving to the front of the aircraft where the lieutenant was seated, Bob reported in, "Lieutenant Turner, Sergeant Holmberg said you wanted to see me."

"Yes, Bob, please sit down," Lieutenant Turner replied with a smile, while he motioned to the empty seat next to him. "What do you think of SOF so far?"

"Great, I really enjoy being here."

"How have you found the transition?"

"Couldn't have been smoother. Everyone has been very helpful. It's a great group of guys."

"Good," replied the lieutenant. "We're more of a family than most units—since we work so closely together."

"Yes, sir, there's a camaraderie here that didn't exist in D-1. Working as a unit and in two-man patrols definitely builds teamwork and friendships."

"That's right," replied the lieutenant. "We pride ourselves in having some of the highest morale on the force."

"I'm proud to be here."

"Bob, tell me about yourself. I know what's in your personnel file. Tell me about your off-duty life."

For the next five minutes, Bob chatted with the lieutenant and related much personal information. Then, Turner asked Bob if he had any questions.

"Yes, sir. I was wondering about our authority in these out-of-town emergencies."

"Good question. Our authority is delegated from the secretary of the interior. We don't have explicit statutory authorization for law enforcement outside of the environs of the District of Columbia. That's something the Park Service is going to have to look at, sooner or later. Sometimes—like tonight—I wonder what a bunch of policemen from D.C. are doing heading out to the Wild West," Lieutenant Turner said with a grin breaking over his face. Then, the lieutenant extended his hand to Bob, "Glad to have you on board."

Bob made his way back to his seat. "What did Turner want?" Sonny asked curiously.

"He asked about me. I was impressed that he was genuinely interested in my private life and me as a person. He welcomed me again to SOF. He's a regular guy."

"Yeah," Sonny agreed, "he and Groves are the best."

About this time, Private Tom Kaylor was passing by on his way back from the restroom. Like a shark on the prowl, he suddenly eyed Bob and closed in for the attack. Sliding into an empty seat nearby, Kaylor loudly yelled out, "Hey, Ritter, who was that chick with you at Andrews?"

"My wife," Bob answered.

"I'm not buying that. She was a knockout—way too pretty for you. What did you do, Ritter, hire a model to be with you at the airport to show off?"

"She's my wife, Tom."

"What could a beautiful woman like that see in you?"

"That's what I keep asking myself," Bob replied with a smile. "I guess I'm just *lucky in love.*"

Officer Kaylor rose, shaking his head and grumbling to himself all the way back to his seat.

Sonny turned to Bob. "I want to warn you. Since you're the new man and this is your first trip, some of the guys will probably try some tricks on you. They won't clue me in—so be careful."

"Thanks, Sonny, I'll keep that in mind."

After a sandwich and some chips, Bob closed his eyes and relaxed back—deep into the seat. Massaged by the rhythmic vibrations from the massive piston engines of the plane, Bob quickly fell asleep. Some hours later, Bob awoke to Sonny's voice and a couple of light taps on the shoulder. "Bob, we're getting ready to land. We're on final."

After a smooth landing, the aircraft passed a row of Boeing B-52 Stratofortresses. Bob strained his neck to view these mighty bombers of the Strategic Air Command (SAC). As if he knew what Bob was thinking, Sonny commented: "They're loaded with nuclear weapons, ready to scramble. Ellsworth also has Minuteman II missile silos. You better believe security is tight around here."

The below freezing temperatures and wind chills bit into the park policemen as they disembarked the aircraft. The officers gathered on the ground to retrieve their bags, which were being unloaded directly from the cargo hold to the tarmac. Park Police Captain and Regional Liaison Officer Denny Sorah had rental cars ready for the men. While bags and gear were loaded into the vehicles, Sorah briefed Turner on the latest orders for SOF.

When the loading was completed, Lieutenant Turner announced: "Men, follow Captain Sorah and me. We're driving to Wounded Knee, the site of the takeover. I'm going to check in with the FBI."

Like a game of musical chairs, park policemen vied for the seats in the nearest cars, happy to get out of the cold. Within a blink of an eye, the only space left for Bob and Sonny was in the lead vehicle, operated by Captain Sorah with Lieutenant Turner riding in the right front seat. Bob and Sonny climbed in the back, joined by Jerry Delane.

"Hi, Denny, how's it going?" Delane said to Captain Sorah.

"Okay, Jerry, not counting the present situation."

Delane then turned toward Bob, "Captain Sorah and I know each other from D.C."

The caravan departed Ellsworth AFB and headed south out of Rapid City. Captain Sorah had a country music station playing on the car radio. It served as background while Sorah and Turner chatted. About 10 minutes into the drive, Delane spoke up again, "Denny, can you change the radio station?"

Sorah took a glance black in Delane's direction. "Jerry, there aren't many stations out here. All of the music ones are country. It'll grow on you."

With a pained expression, Delane shot back: "Denny, you've been out here too long. We need to get you back to D.C."

The caravan rolled on toward the Pine Ridge Indian Reservation, near the South Dakota-Nebraska border. On February 27, 1973, about 200 members of the American Indian Movement (AIM) occupied the village of Wounded Knee, located on the Pine Ridge Reservation. They originally planned to protest at the Oglala Sioux Tribal Headquarters building at Pine Ridge, South Dakota. Fearing an incident, the building had been manned earlier by a contingent of FBI agents, U.S. marshals, and BIA Police. AIM had been critical of the administration of the Oglala Sioux tribal chairman.

Finding tribal headquarters well fortified, the AIM group drove about 25 miles to the small village of Wounded Knee. There in 1890, the U.S. Cavalry massacred almost 150 Indians, including some women and children. At Wounded Knee, AIM took over the village trading post, museum, gas station, and church. They vowed to hold the village until the federal government addressed a list of grievances that included alleged BIA and tribal corruption, conditions on the reservations, and treaty rights.

Arriving at Wounded Knee, Captain Sorah and Lieutenant Turner checked in with officials of the FBI at their command post. After the meeting with the FBI, Sorah and Turner relayed information to Sergeants Holmberg and Hill. The sergeants passed to the privates that the situation at Wounded Knee had deteriorated. Gunfire had broken out between federal officers and some of the AIM occupiers.

The SOF caravan drove next to Keystone, South Dakota, near Mt. Rushmore. There, SOF had motel rooms waiting. Later in the morning, SOF would meet at Mt. Rushmore for a briefing followed by the posting of duty assignments.

As the caravan approached the Rushmore View Motel, the officers got their first look at the memorial. The gigantic, carved faces of presidents George Washington, Thomas Jefferson, Theodore Roosevelt, and Abraham Lincoln, loomed majestically in the early morning sky. "That's why we're here," Sonny said.

Inside the motel office, the sergeants told the officers to pair up in twos to register. Sonny asked Bob, "Do you snore?"

"I don't think so. I haven't had any complaints from Jan."

"Good, let's bunk together."

Bob and Sonny registered, grabbed a key, and then headed off for some much-needed rest. Later that morning, a loud ringing abruptly awoke Bob and Sonny from a sound sleep. "Geez, it can't be time already," Sonny cried out.

Bob jumped out of bed to answer the phone. After thanking the desk clerk for the wakeup call, Bob returned the receiver to the cradle and turned toward Sonny. "Afraid so, partner, time to rise and shine."

"Bob, you don't mind if I hit the shower first, do you?"

"No, be my guest."

"Thanks, that way I'll have time to get a container of coffee after I get dressed."

The officers formed up in the parking lot for the short trip to Mount Rushmore National Memorial. At the closed entrance to the park, the caravan was passed through a barricade by a ranger who directed SOF to the park visitor center. In the cafeteria at the visitor center, SOF was able to brunch before the meeting. Already enjoying the food supplied by the park concessionaire was a small group of rangers. Most had been ordered to Mt. Rushmore from other national parks in the NPS Midwest Region. These rangers were staying in accommodations on the park grounds.

The meeting was opened by the superintendant of the memorial, who thanked the rangers and Park Police for their quick response to the emergency situation. He announced that for the immediate future, Mount Rushmore would remain closed due to the Wounded Knee takeover. Thus, the outer boundaries of the visitors' area became a security perimeter.

Next, the chief ranger of the park related past incidents at Mount Rushmore. There had been Indian occupations of the mountain in 1970 and 1971. In 1970, Mount Rushmore had been occupied for several months by over 20 Indians, who camped at the top of the faces. They yelled activist slogans down to tourists and displayed a large flag that read "Sioux Indian Power."

Continuing with the briefing, the ranger detailed an incident that occurred within the past month. An AIM contingent traveled to nearby Custer, South Dakota. At the Custer Courthouse, AIM protested the killing of an Indian by a white man. A violent confrontation ensued. Several buildings caught fire and burned. Both Indians and police were injured.

Next, some troubling, recent intelligence was divulged. There was information that a group of radicals was plotting to seize the top of Mount Rushmore in support of the Wounded Knee takeover. This time, they intended to plant dynamite charges along granite veins and other key points in the carved faces. The threat of blowing up the faces of Mount Rushmore could serve as formidable leverage for extortionist demands. The force of rangers and Park Police were here to protect the memorial.

This was certainly a threat the Park Service was taking very seriously. Mount Rushmore is one of our most treasured national icons. The land it's situated on is also very significant to the Sioux (Lakota) nation. The Black Hills of South Dakota are sacred to the Sioux. They have long tried to regain the land from the federal government, which took it without just compensation. Indian militants have no love for the carvings on Mount Rushmore, which they consider defacements to sacred land.

The idea of gigantic sculptures adorning the Black Hills dates back to 1923. In that year, the State Historian of South Dakota, Doane Robinson, proposed the carving of western heroes into a granite formation known as The Needles. He suggested figures such as Buffalo Bill Cody, John Fremont, Lewis and Clark, Red Cloud, and Jim Bridger. Robinson gained the backing of South Dakota U.S. Senator Peter Norbeck and other influential parties. It was felt the sculpture would be a major attraction that would bring tourists to the state.

With support in hand, Robinson invited noted sculptor Gutzon Borglum to visit the Black Hills to discuss the project. Arriving in 1924, Borglum surveyed the area and rejected The Needles for the site of a colossal sculpture. Instead, Borglum recommended Mount Rushmore for the location of the memorial. The granite of Mount Rushmore was of a smoother grain, and the sun shone on the almost 6,000-foot-high peak for most of the day. Borglum also convinced Robinson that the carving should be a national memorial—paying homage to the spirit of America. Borglum substituted national heroes for Western ones by suggesting figures of U.S. presidents.

In 1925, the U.S. Congress and the South Dakota legislature authorized construction of the project. Mount Rushmore was first dedicated in October of that year. In the beginning, the project relied solely on private contributions. Borglum spent most of his time trying to raise money for the construction of the memorial. Unfortunately, very little was raised, and by 1927 the project was on the verge of financial collapse.

Then in the summer of 1927, the situation improved markedly when President Calvin Coolidge visited the Black Hills. Legend has it that while Coolidge was staying in a lodge at Custer State Park, Borglum hired an airplane for a fly-by. From the airplane, Borglum dropped a wreath inviting the president to a rededication of Mount Rushmore. President Coolidge accepted the invitation and became interested in the project after seeing the site. With presidential support, the U.S. Congress passed an appropriations act in 1929 that would match private contributions. Finally in 1934, the federal government took over full funding of the project to ensure its completion.

Actual work began on the memorial in 1927. Borglum chose presidents representing important milestones in U.S. history from colonial times to the 20th century. He designed a presidential grouping that included Washington, Jefferson, Theodore Roosevelt, and Lincoln. From these sculptures, he modeled working copies made of plaster, which measured five feet from bottom of chin to top of head.

To measure his plaster models, Borglum first affixed an upright shaft to the top center of each head. Attached at the base of the shaft were a protractor plate and a ruled, horizontal bar. The bar pivoted along the central axis of the protractor. A plumb bob hung from the horizontal bar. The plumb line could be slid back in forth on the bar and also raised and lowered. As a result, any reference point on the head could be measured for degree of angle, horizontal distance from the center point, and vertical distance to the top of the head.

Measurements were transferred to the mountain via a 30-foot, movable boom. Each inch on the model equaled a foot on the mountain. Thus, the faces of Mount Rushmore were carved to a scale of men 465 feet tall. The heads average 60 feet in height (as tall as a six-story building) with noses 20 feet long, mouths 18 feet wide, and eyes 11 feet across.

Mount Rushmore became a colossal, artistic medium where granite was removed by engineering technology to produce sculpture. Workers were suspended over the face of the mountain in small swing seats called bosun chairs. The seats dangled from cables attached to hand operated winches. Dynamite was used to blast within several inches of a reference point. Then, holes were pneumatically drilled about three inches apart, which honeycombed the face. The remaining rock was hand chiseled to the proper depth. The final surface was air hammered to a smooth, white finish in a process known as "bumping."

George Washington was the first to be carved into the mountain. Because of his importance as the father of our country, Washington's position in the memorial was prominent. Thomas Jefferson was included due to his authorship of the Declaration of Independence and the purchase of the Louisiana Territory, which doubled the size of the nation. Abraham Lincoln was selected for his preservation of the Union and the Emancipation Proclamation, which abolished slavery in the United States. Theodore Roosevelt gained his place on the mountain due to his international expansionism, his protection of the common man against corporate monopolies, and his conservation efforts, which included expansion of the National Park System.

The Washington head was dedicated in 1930. At that time, the phrase "Shrine of Democracy" was coined. It has been used ever since to describe the memorial. In keeping with this sentiment, Borglum also planned an entablature and a Hall of Records for Mount Rushmore. The memorial was to be a commemoration of the first 150 years of American history, not just a tribute to the lives of four presidents.

The entablature was patterned after the shape of the territory added to the U.S. by the Louisiana Purchase. A brief history of the United States from 1776–1906 would be inscribed within the outline using three-foot-high letters. This design was abandoned due to space concerns.

Originally, work on the Jefferson head began on the right side of Washington. In 1933, the partially completed Jefferson face had to be blasted away due to problems with the granite. The Jefferson sculpture was restarted at a position to the left of Washington. This necessitated the movement of Lincoln to the area of the mountain cap that had been reserved for the entablature.

Borglum started work on the Hall of Records in 1938. A great hall, measuring 80 by 100 feet with a 20 by 14-foot entrance, was to be blasted into a rear area of the mountain. The room would house bronze and glass cabinets displaying important national documents. The hall would also feature busts of famous Americans and a list of American contributions to the world. Above the massive entrance, a bronze eagle with a wingspan of 38 feet would rest.

By 1939, the chamber had been cut to a depth of 70 feet when construction was halted on the Hall of Records. Congress only authorized funds to complete the faces. On October 31, 1941, work on the memorial was finished—just days before America's entrance into World War II. Through a period of 14 years, about 450,000 tons of granite were removed to make the memorial. The debris remains at the base of the mountain, where it fell many years ago.

At the conclusion of the briefing, the chief ranger and Lieutenant Turner decided to combine the force of rangers and park policemen into two equal squads. One squad would work 6:00 a.m. to 6:00 p.m., the other 6:00 p.m. to 6:00 a.m. "Let's volunteer for the graveyard shift," Sonny suggested to Bob. "If somebody is planning to seize control of the mountain, they'll probably try it at night."

"Makes sense to me," Bob agreed.

Plans were drawn up for the posting of personnel. With the addition of the park policemen, patrol beats could be extended along South Dakota (SD) Route 244 and other areas within the almost 1,200 acres of the park. Since SD Route 244 went through federal property, park service officers had concurrent jurisdiction with state authorities. It was also decided to post officers on top of the carvings themselves, to serve as lookouts and as a last line of defense. Though being posted at the top of Mount Rushmore sounded intriguing, Sonny reasoned that the Route 244 beats would have more action. Accordingly, Sonny and Bob asked for one of those assignments.

Bob, Sonny, and the remaining personnel assigned to the second shift were told to report back at 5:45 p.m. The exception was the two officers who would be posted to the mountaintop. They were asked to return earlier, so they could climb the mountain and relieve the first shift personnel during daylight.

The day shift immediately began their duty assignments. Sonny and Bob wanted to see the summit of Mount Rushmore. They received permission to accompany the first shift officers on their climb. A Park Ranger familiar with the memorial led the four park policemen up the mountain trail through rocks, shrubs, and trees.

Along the way, Bob and Sonny remembered the climatic ending of Alfred Hitchcock's 1959 thriller, *North by Northwest*. Stars Cary Grant and Eva Marie Saint are chased by two Communist spies across the summit of Mt. Rushmore and down the faces. With the Shrine of Democracy as backdrop, Grant struggles with one of the spies and pushes him over the edge. Carrying a statue with hidden microfilm, Eva Marie Saint slips and falls. She dangles precariously from a ledge, as the second spy recovers the statue. Cary scrambles down and grabs Eva Marie one handed. The second spy tramps on Grant's other hand to loosen his grip to the mountain. At the last second, a shot is fired by a lawman from a neighboring peak, and the spy plunges to his death.

"That scene was totally shot in Hollywood," informed the park ranger. "Hitchcock did film here in 1958. Scenes were shot in the cafeteria, in the parking lot, and various shots were taken from the visitor center terraces. Hitchcock wasn't permitted to film on the heads. The Park Service prohibited that after word was leaked that a violent chase scene was planned. The film company was allowed to shoot still pictures of the memorial faces. Hitchcock was crafty. He used the stills to produce a studio mock-up where the scenes with actors were shot."

Making their way through rocks and boulders on a trail strewn with slippery Ponderosa Pine needles, the five men caught site of a mountain goat deftly traversing a ridge. "Mountain goats aren't indigenous to South Dakota," the ranger told the park policemen. "Back in the 1920s, a bunch of them escaped from a pen at Custer State Park. Over the years, they have reproduced and thrived in the Black Hills."

The Park Police were being led over the same route that Borglum's workers used to access the mountain peak. Remains of old air compressor pipes could still be seen along the trail. They also saw an old, broken drill bit. After climbing some steep metal steps (built to make the workers ascent/descent safer), the party came to a large crevice behind the heads. Here, Bob and Sonny saw the unfinished Hall of Records. It was rough-cut and tapered back to a depth of about 70 feet. Originally, Borglum planned to erect granite steps from the valley below, so tourists could visit the Hall of Records.

After scaling another steep stairway, the men arrived at the top of George Washington's head. From a vantage point 500 feet above the visitor center and almost 6,000 feet above sea level, Bob and Sonny enjoyed the magnificent view from the summit. They considered themselves very lucky to have this rare opportunity.

The ranger familiarized the first shift officers on park landmarks and their points of direction from the top of the monument. Special emphasis was given to perimeter areas where intruders might gain surreptitious entry. In the backcountry of the Black Hills, infiltration would be extremely difficult to detect and prevent. Nighttime would bring additional challenges. Thinking aloud, Sonny uttered, "Hope we have a lot of clear, moonlit nights."

Unfortunately, Park Police had no night vision (thermal imaging) equipment. In those days, the military Starlight Scope was the only device available. It was extremely expensive and designed with first generation technology. The Starlight was bulky and heavy—weighing in at 7.5 pounds. Also, the image tube could be burned out in high light conditions—like those commonly generated by the bright nighttime lights of Washington, D.C. Thus, requests for Starlights were an easy target for Park Service budget cutters.

SOF did have binoculars and some Colt AR-15 rifles that had optical scopes. In addition, SOF used Remington 700 BDL rifles chambered for the .243 Winchester cartridge for targets out to 250 yards. Beyond 250 yards, SOF utilized Sako Forrester rifles in .308 caliber. Both rifles featured bolt actions and Redfield scopes.

The ranger turned to Bob and Sonny, "Ready to head back?"

"Yeah," Sonny answered.

During the return down the trail, the ranger asked, "Do you men have anything warmer than what you're wearing?"

"No, these are our winter uniforms," Bob answered.

The midnight detail is going to freeze up here," warned the ranger. "Twelve-hour shifts are a long time, and the weather can be severe."

Sonny replied: "We'll say something to the sergeant. Maybe something can be done."

Back at the motel, Sonny and Bob found Sergeant Earl Hill, who was the night shift supervisor. First, Sonny and Bob related to Sergeant Hill the thrill of standing on top of the Shrine of Democracy. Then in Sonny's own colorful way, he added: "Earl, one of the park rangers warned that the night guys posted to the top are going to freeze their gonads off. Maybe there's an Army-Navy store in Rapid City. I volunteer to pick up some stuff, if I get reimbursed."

"I guess you would," Sergeant Hill replied. "But we better see how tonight goes first. If we have problems, we can go to Ellsworth and try and borrow some equipment from the Air Force."

"And Earl, we need a Starlight Scope. We don't have any night eyes," Sonny added.

"Yeah, I'll keep working on it. This trip definitely shows the need for one."

Bob and Sonny took a quick nap before returning to the memorial with the rest of the second shift at about 5:00 p.m. The night shift was arriving early, so they could grab some dinner. The park concessionaire was graciously keeping the cafeteria open until 6:00 p.m., even though the park was closed to tourists. Jerry Delane and a park ranger joined Bob and Sonny at their table. The ranger asked the park officers, "Did you men bring any fusees with you?"

"No," answered Bob. "The Air Force probably wouldn't have let them on board."

"That's right," replied the ranger. "Maybe we can get some from the highway patrol to get us through the night. We only have a couple boxes left at the park. We're going to need plenty at the main gate."

Waiting until the ranger left the table for a refill of coffee, Delane asked Bob, "What the hell are fusees?"

"They're flares, Jerry. Some non-law enforcement types—like railroaders—call them fusees."

"Tex, you're smarter than you look," said Delane. Since Bob's youth, some have nicknamed him "Tex"—after western film star Tex Ritter.

Later, the two officers who had been assigned to the top of Mount Rushmore for the day shift entered the cafeteria. One of the officers showed the soles of his shoes to Sonny and Bob. After only one trip up and down the mountain and about eight hours of patrol, the officer had worn holes through both of his leather soles. The issued uniform shoes weren't made for rough terrain.

The day officers also expressed concern for their relief, who would be spending the night on the mountain. There were the dangers of poor visibility, cold, and wind chill. The only shelter of any kind was Borglum's unfinished Hall of Records. For refreshments, the night relief was only able to bring up a couple of sandwiches and a thermos of coffee.

"Yeah," Sonny agreed, "we said something to Earl about it. At least they have some flashlights."

The second shift briefing was conducted by Sergeant Hill, who updated the situation at Wounded Knee. Sporadic gunfire continued between government forces and AIM militants. There were no signs that the incident would be resolved anytime soon. It was reported that AIM was building bunkers, trenches, and other defensive positions. Among the AIM contingent were several Vietnam veterans, who were establishing security to hold the village.

The 6:00 p.m. to 6:00 a.m. shift began. Bob and Sonny patrolled SD 244 and the park perimeter areas along the route. All posts and beats were radio checked every half hour. Sergeant Hill checked on his men throughout the night. The officers at the top were cold but in good spirits. The 12-hour shift passed without any major incidents.

Later that morning, Sergeant Hill drove to Ellsworth AFB to visit its supply section. The Air Force gave him parkas and jump boots for the officers assigned to the mountaintop. The gear was greatly appreciated. Eventually, Park Police issued jump boots to all SOF personnel. The boots were worn on out-of-town assignments.

As it looked like SOF would be needed at Mount Rushmore for an indefinite amount of time, Lieutenant Turner returned to his duties in Washington. The sergeants were left in charge. The next several weeks passed without any disturbances. Intelligence reports showed that Indian militants had become aware of the increased security at Mount Rushmore. The presence of SOF and the added rangers had been a strong deterrent to any unlawful actions. Also, Indian militants were primarily concerned with getting food and other supplies passed Wounded Knee roadblocks. The resupply of the Wounded Knee occupiers was a continual problem for AIM.

As things were quiet at Mount Rushmore, SOF was released from its temporary duty and returned to D.C. While I was unpacking Bob's suitcase, I found a pair of women's panties. When I asked about them, Bob smiled and said: "One of the guys put those in there as a joke. Sonny warned me something would happen since this was my first trip. And I have my suspects!"

Between late March to September 1973, SOF was called back to Mount Rushmore on three more occasions. This was due to adverse intelligence, which cropped up from time to time. In these instances, a smaller group of SOF officers was deployed. Scheduled demonstrations and other duties in Washington required keeping most SOF officers in D.C.

Bob and Sonny were selected for all of the additional Mount Rushmore deployments. In one instance, it was learned that an Indian group planned to conduct a ceremonial "Sun Dance" at the memorial. It was feared that once the group gained access to the park, they would attempt to take over the mountain. With the coming tourist season, keeping the park closed indefinitely was not an option. Park Police were needed to keep visitors and the memorial safe. As Bob said: "Most members of AIM and other Indian organizations are peaceful citizens, who are trying to improve conditions through organizing and lawful protest. That's one of the things that make our country great. Unfortunately, radical elements can often gain control of these organizations. Some want violent confrontations in order to gain headlines."

During one of the trips, Sonny and Bob along with several other park policemen were responsible for the capture of a dangerous felon. It started on a clear, moonlit night; Bob and Sonny were on patrol and had parked in an overlook adjoining SD Route 244. Suddenly, a recreational vehicle (RV) sped past Sonny and Bob's location.

"Sonny, that guy was spooked when he saw us. I think I saw a rifle barrel propped up next to his seat!" Bob exclaimed.

"Everybody carries long guns out here. There isn't a pickup *without* a loaded gun rack in the whole state. But he didn't look right to me either," Sonny agreed.

"Sonny, that rifle was located within the driver's reach," Bob added.

Sonny pulled the patrol car out of the overlook and started to follow the RV. "Bob, can you get the tag numbers?" Sonny asked.

Bob had excellent distance vision. He peered at the back of the RV like a nighthawk. "Yeah, I got it." Bob checked his briefing notes from earlier that evening. "Sonny, that's the RV that's wanted by the FBI!"

"Bob, this guy's looking back at us. I can see him in his side view mirror. Keep an eye on your side of the RV and the back window. I've got the driver."

Bob called in the tags to the park's radio dispatcher, who excitedly confirmed the felony hit. "Per the FBI, that vehicle is stolen and believed to be operated by an escaped convict. Subject was serving a life sentence for the murder of a law enforcement officer. Fugitive told associates he was not going back to prison and would not be taken alive. It's reported that he has a cache of guns to include a .308-caliber assault rifle, a 12-gauge shotgun, and several handguns and knives. Subject is deemed to be armed and *extremely* dangerous."

"Get the shotgun ready," Sonny yelled. Bob grabbed the 12-gauge pump. He worked the action, loading a double-ought-buck round into the gun's chamber.

"She's locked and loaded with trigger safety on," Bob called out.

Just then, Sergeant Hill called on the radio. "Car One, do not attempt to stop vehicle. We'll set up a felony stop on 244, at the entrance to the park. I'm at the main gate now."

"10-4," Bob acknowledged. Bob and Sonny were trailing behind the RV in a southeasterly direction. They were on the west side of the park. SD Route 244 curves south around the park like a giant horseshoe.

"Car Two, 10-25 [meet] for the 10-53 [road block] at 244 and the park entry road," radioed Sergeant Hill.

"10-4, ETA in two." Car Two had been covering the section of Route 244 on the east side of the park. Fortunately, the officers were nearby.

"Car One, how much time do we have?" Sergeant Hill asked.

"If he keeps this speed, ETA about five," Bob replied.

"10-4" replied Sergeant Hill.

Several minutes later Sergeant Hill radioed: "Car One, we're ready. When he stops for the roadblock, pull your car broadside and set up a covering position. I'll handle the arrest from this side. I have an AR-15 so watch my line of fire."

"10-4," Bob replied.

A couple of minutes later, the RV approached the roadblock. A Park Ranger vehicle and an unmarked sedan were positioned nose to nose at about a 45-degree angle across the roadway. Using the vehicles for cover, officers stood with guns drawn. The fugitive hit the brakes on the RV, and it screeched to a stop. At the same time, Sonny pulled his vehicle sideways across Route 244. Sonny and Bob both exited the car from the driver's side. With the shotgun, Sonny took a position over the hood of the vehicle. Moving to the trunk, Bob drew his Smith & Wesson Model 10 "bull barrel" revolver—loaded with 110-grain Super Vel .38 Special ammo. The new Smith had replaced Bob's originally issued Colt Police Positive.

With an AR-15 in one hand and the PA microphone from the cruiser in the other, Sergeant Hill announced in a commanding tone: "You're under arrest. Turn off the vehicle. Remove the key and place both hands out the side window. I don't want to see anything in your hands but a set of keys. Do it now!"

For a moment, the subject looked at the roadblock in front of him; then he glanced in the side view mirror where he saw Sonny and Bob blocking any retreat. "Do it now!" Sergeant Hill repeated.

The subject turned off the ignition and placed both hands out the side window. He was ordered to throw the keys to the side of the road and then to open the door of the RV using the outside handle. Next, he was directed to exit the vehicle with his hands up. Subject was told to lie face down on the pavement with arms and legs spread. He was then ordered to crawl toward the waiting officers.

Subject was handcuffed behind his back and thoroughly searched. He was given his Miranda Warning (right to remain silent and to have an attorney present during questioning). Then, the RV was searched. Weapons and ammunition were seized and cataloged. Other evidence in the vehicle was inventoried and preserved for later collection as might be needed.

After contacting the FBI office in Rapid City, the park policemen were advised to bring the fugitive to Rapid City and the Pennington County Jail. It was a federally approved detention facility. The subject would be held there until he could be presented to a state magistrate, later that morning.

Sonny and Bob transported the escaped prisoner to Rapid City. There were no "caged units" at the park, so the subject was placed in the back of a Park Ranger sedan. Sonny drove while Bob sat in the back seat to the right of the subject. This kept Bob's gun side away from the fugitive. Bob also placed a flexi-cuff around the subject's ankles to restrain his legs during the 45-minute drive. Sergeant Hill rode in the right front seat. Another officer followed behind in the stolen vehicle.

Having been captured enraged the subject. During the transport to Rapid City, the fugitive complained bitterly about going back to prison. He spoke with anger and looked at his captors with hate. The subject showed no remorse.

The park policemen wished the subject would have opened fire. He had been convicted of killing a law enforcement officer in cold blood. If necessary, the officers would have obliged the subject in his vow not to be taken alive. Sergeant Hill asked the escapee why he decided to surrender. Subject screamed: "I'm not stupid. You had a machine gun. Otherwise, I'd of shot it out with you bastards!" Subject had seen Sergeant Hill's AR-15 (semi-automatic weapon) and mistaken it for the fully automatic M-16 military version, which is similar in appearance.

At the county jail, the Park Police were met by the FBI resident agent. He filed a federal detainer on the subject until he could be presented to state authorities for extradition. Extradition is a process where the demanding state (where he is wanted) sends an affidavit to the asylum state (where he was captured). In this case, the affidavit would certify that the subject fled the demanding state to escape confinement, and a copy of the original judgment of conviction would be attached. The subject is then arraigned (brought before a judge to answer the charge) in the asylum state. Unless there's a case of misidentification or some defect in the extradition documents, fugitives are returned to the demanding state. In most cases, fugitives waive extradition and are surrendered to officers of the demanding state without legal challenge.

The FBI agent was familiar with the U.S. Park Police. The agent had previously been stationed in Washington, D.C. He congratulated the officers on the capture and promised to send a commendation to their chief. Also, an official from the South Dakota Highway Patrol stopped by the jail to offer his thanks. The apprehension of a dangerous criminal brings much pleasure and pride to the law enforcement community as well as making the streets safer for both citizens and law enforcement officers.

Bob and Sonny enjoyed the night shift. Besides the excitement, working a 12-hour overnight shift allowed them to see the tourist attractions of the South Dakota Black Hills by day. The name Black Hills translates from the Lakota (Sioux) words "Paha Sapa" (hills that are black). From a distance, the mountain range appears black due to the Ponderosa Pine that blankets the area.

The Black Hills have a rich mining history. In 1874, the U.S. Army Seventh Cavalry (commanded by Lieutenant Colonel George Armstrong Custer) explored the area and found gold at French Creek in the southern hills. When news of the discovery spread, white prospectors illegally entered the region; this land had been ceded to the Sioux by the Fort Laramie Treaty of 1868. At first, the Army forcibly expelled the trespassers. Soon, the stream of prospectors was too large for the Army to contain.

Whites demanded that the government open the area to settlement. The U.S. government attempted to gain back the land through negotiations with the Indians. These attempts were unsuccessful and war broke out. Eventually, the Indians surrendered and were forced back to their reservations. New territory was opened up to white settlement. By the 1880s, thriving towns had sprung up near the gold mining camps.

Bob and Sonny visited the famous South Dakota Gold Rush town of Deadwood. In 1876, the legendary lawman Wild Bill Hickok was murdered in a Deadwood saloon while playing poker. Hickok had joined the game late and had to sit in a chair with his back to the bar. For self-defense reasons, Hickok favored seats that would give him a clear view of the room. Unfortunately for Hickok, that chair had already been taken.

Jack McCall—a poor loser who had lost money to Hickok the day before— was drinking heavily at the bar. Without warning, McCall approached Hickok from behind and shot him in the back of the head—killing him instantly. Legend has it that Wild Bill's poker hand was black aces and eights, which became known as "The Dead Man's Hand."

Another highlight of Bob and Sonny's Black Hills travel was a visit to the Crazy Horse Memorial near Custer, South Dakota. In 1947, Lakota Chief Henry Standing Bear invited sculptor Korczak Ziolkowski to design a mountain memorial to the Lakota warrior Crazy Horse. Chief Standing Bear wanted to show that the "red man has heroes too." Ziolkowski sculpted a clay model depicting a mounted Crazy Horse pointing over his horse's mane toward the east—from where the white man came. The artwork portrays a defiant Crazy Horse saying, "My lands are where my dead lie buried."

Visiting the memorial in 1973, Bob and Sonny were greeted by a gentleman in his 60s with a graying, full beard. Attired in jeans and a short-brimmed western-styled hat, he introduced himself as "Korczak" (pronounced core-chock). Bob and Sonny also met Korczak's wife and one of their older sons. Korczak told of his promise to the Indians to carve the memorial. He envisioned a work that would be the largest man-made monument in the world. Korczak intended it to be a source of pride to Native Americans—as a symbol of their culture.

The memorial was a work in progress. The observation area was some miles away from the mountain. Through binoculars, Bob and Sonny viewed a huge ledge, which had been blasted into the mountainside. From this area, the horse would be carved. Crazy Horse's face showed no detail—only some rough crags. As Korczak's son said, "We still have a long way to go." Bob and Sonny got the feeling this was going to be a life-long project. Bob believed the expansive memorial had become Korczak's personal reparation to American Indians.

On the drive back to Mount Rushmore, Bob and Sonny discussed their aspirations. Although inspired by Korczak and his family's dedication to a towering vision, Bob and Sonny's goals were more immediate. Bob was laying the groundwork to become a Secret Service agent, and Sonny wanted to make Park Police detective. The two friends shook hands as they agreed to help each other fulfill their childhood dreams—which now appeared within reach.

Chapter 12

Car 718

Back in Washington, Bob and Sonny volunteered for SOF assignments that would further career goals. These included protective support and "soft-clothes" details. In the latter, SOF officers dressed in casual clothes and patrolled areas where criminal activity had been occurring. The idea was to blend into the background in order to catch unsuspecting criminals in the act.

Areas causing the most concern were Rock Creek Park, the Mall (since renamed National Mall), and Franklin Park. Rock Creek Park was established in 1890. It covers over 1,700 acres and is approximately four miles long by one mile wide. Beginning just above the National Zoological Park in Northwest D.C., Rock Creek Park continues north to the Maryland border. To the south, it connects to the Rock Creek and Potomac Parkway—leading to the Potomac River and the Mall area.

Rock Creek Park offered something for everyone—including criminals. There were about 15 miles of hiking trails and 14 miles of graveled bridle trails for horseback riding. The park also provided bike and jogging paths, a golf course, stables, tennis courts, athletic fields, and 70 picnic groves. In addition, the park featured a nature center (with planetarium), a Civil War installation (Fort DeRussy), a restored 1820 gristmill (mill for grinding grain), and the Carter Barron Amphitheater. On its outdoor stage, the biggest acts of the day performed during the summer season.

Fort DeRussy was one of the forts that defended Washington in July 1864. Confederate General Jubal Early's troops attacked the city from the north along the 7th Street Pike (now Georgia Avenue). Fort Stevens, supported by artillery fire from Fort DeRussy, stood in the way of Early's advance. For several days, Early's forces probed for weaknesses along the Union lines. Meanwhile, Fort Stevens was reinforced—causing Early to retreat to Virginia. Throughout the siege, President Abraham Lincoln rode out to Fort Stevens to check on the situation. On one occasion, Lincoln was almost hit by Confederate rifle fire when he peered over the parapet of the fort. Thus, Lincoln became the only president to come under *enemy* fire while in office.

The remote trails of Rock Creek Park offered cover for assaults and robberies. Park buildings provided opportunities for burglars. Special events drew crowds of people who were targeted by pickpockets and purse-snatchers. Picnic areas were the scene of domestic disturbances. Car break-ins occurred in the parking areas.

Theft from autos was also a recurring problem within the Mall. The concept of a grand mall dates back to Pierre Charles L'Enfant's original 1791 plans for the city. The Mall was envisioned as a broad avenue that would extend from the Capitol grounds to a point south of the White House—where an equestrian statue of Washington was planned. In the 1800s, the Washington Monument took the place of the proposed Washington statue.

In 1902, the McMillan Commission submitted to the Senate a broad-reaching plan for the future development of the district's federal area along L'Enfant's original ideas. One of the commission's recommendations was that the Mall be a broad, green area divided by tree-lined roadways and bordered by public buildings. Asphalt-paved roadways lined with elms were added to the Mall in the 1930s.

During Bob's tenure with Park Police, the Mall was still divided by four asphalt drives, which provided parking for tourists. The two inner roadbeds have since been covered with gravel to provide a path for walkers and joggers. Along the Mall, the National Gallery of Art and museums of the Smithsonian Institution drew tens of thousands of visitors daily. In the 1970s, thousands of cars parked along the four drives that ran through the Mall. During tourist season, most of the cars parking in the Mall were from outside the Washington Metropolitan Area.

On occasion, valuable belongings (cameras, purses, suitcases, etc.) could be seen through the windows of these vehicles. Criminals might also spy tourists placing valuables in car trunks. This served as temptation for thieves, who would punch out locks or break windows in smash-and-grab thefts.

Even if caught red-handed, perpetrators were sometimes not convicted. If a subject was caught carrying stolen property, he could say he found the items on the street. Without an eyewitness to the break-in, this type of incident would not be prosecuted due to a lack of sufficient evidence. And if tourists owned the stolen items, they could not be brought into evidence unless the owner was willing to return to D.C. to identify the items in court. Thus, street-smart thieves targeted vehicles with out-of-state tags. Even when perpetrators were convicted, they were not given jail time in nonviolent crimes. Jails and prisons were overcrowded and reserved for violent offenders.

In Franklin Park, assaults and robberies along with the solicitation of prostitution were the principal crimes committed. Dating back to the 1850s, the park is located several blocks northeast of the White House. It lies in the downtown business district between 13th and 14th Streets NW and I and K Streets NW. There are no "J" streets in Washington. Urban legend says the letter "J" was skipped because Pierre L'Enfant bore a grudge against John Jay, who negotiated an unpopular treaty with England. In actuality, the letters "I" and "J" were written very similar in L'Enfant's time and "J" was excluded to avoid confusion.

During the Civil War, General Joe Hooker's troops camped in Franklin Park and other open areas of downtown Washington. Frequented by soldiers of the Army of the Potomac, Washington's vice district became known as "Hooker's Division." Prostitutes who serviced Hooker's men were called "hookers," a term that came into its own as a popular slang expression. The hookers of the 1970s used the west side of the park to pick up their "Johns." In those days, the neighborhood surrounding Franklin Park featured sexually oriented businesses and cheap hotels. The almost five acres of Franklin Park were overgrown with trees and shrubs. This foliage provided excellent cover for criminal activity. Criminals could hide in the dense vegetation and spring out to rob passersby.

Park Police did not have enough manpower to make Franklin Park a permanent beat. SOF was called upon to selectively patrol the area in both uniform and soft clothes. Though some significant arrests were made, sporadic criminal activity continued. Eventually, the Park Service took Park Police recommendations to clear much of the thick shrubbery from the park. This opened up the park, denying criminals hiding places and concealed escape routes.

Throughout 1973 and into 1974, Bob continued to volunteer for protective support assignments. It was commonly known that Bob wanted to ultimately transfer to the Secret Service. Bob enjoyed protective assignments and gained experience in the protection of the president and other high-level officials. Park Service sites such as the Kennedy Center and Ford's Theater were regularly visited by the president, vice president, and Cabinet level VIPs.

SOF also manned Car 718, which provided outer perimeter security for the president when he stayed at Camp David—located in Catoctin Mountain Park near Thurmont, Maryland. The presidential retreat has its origins with America's December 1941 entry into World War II. Previously, President Franklin D. Roosevelt used the presidential yacht U.S.S. *Potomac* for weekend escapes. The Navy and the Secret Service felt Roosevelt's cruises aboard the *Potomac* were too much of a security risk in wartime. German U-boats operated in the Atlantic Ocean just off the East Coast of the U.S.

White House officials consulted with the National Park Service to locate a retreat for President Roosevelt that was within a two-hour drive of Washington. The site also needed to be at a high enough elevation to provide relief from summer heat and humidity. Hi-Catoctin—a remote camp in the mountains of Western Maryland—was selected for the new presidential retreat.

The log cabin camp was originally built in the mid-1930s as a federal recreation area. For the presidential lodge, Roosevelt picked a cabin with a large stone fireplace and a beautiful view of the valley below. The cabin was enlarged and remodeled with modern conveniences. Other cabins were converted into a communications building, servants' quarters, and the Secret Service command post. A gatehouse was built and roads were improved. The camp already contained a dining hall and swimming pool.

Purportedly, Roosevelt named the retreat Shangri-La after the mountain paradise in James Hilton's 1933 novel *Lost Horizon*. Roosevelt also used "Shangri-La" as a code word for secret locations. The existence of Roosevelt's Shangri-La was kept secret until after the death of FDR in 1945. In 1953, President Dwight Eisenhower changed the name to Camp David in honor of his then five-year-old grandson, David Eisenhower.

Another Catoctin Mountain site near Shangri-La also had a secret past. Camp Greentop was utilized by the War Department in World War II as a training area for Office of Strategic Services (OSS) operatives. The camp trained agents in espionage, hand-to-hand combat, marksmanship, explosives, and other areas of unconventional warfare. William Fairbairn, a designer of the famous Fairbairn-Sykes Fighting Knife, was an instructor.

Bob and Sonny were routinely assigned to Car 718. Some SOF officers didn't care for the duty. They disliked the hour and a half drive to and from Camp David. Plus, protection can be boring if you don't have the right attitude. Additionally, mountain roads could be dangerous. In the winter, roads iced up and were slippery. Throughout the year, white-tailed deer crossed the roads with little warning. There had been several accidents involving Park Service vehicles. Despite the challenges, Bob and Sonny believed it was an honor to help protect the president. They cheerfully accepted the duty and always took their responsibilities seriously.

When the president traveled to Camp David, Car 718 responded from D.C. to Catoctin Mountain Park. Although within the borders of a national park, Camp David was officially a Navy support facility. Closed to the public, Camp David is protected by a double row of maximum-security fencing and Marine patrols with guard dogs. The Secret Service presidential detail provides the inner ring of protection for the president and first family.

Upon arrival, the officers in Car 718 were provided a Secret Service radio and began to patrol the park. Special emphasis was given to the access road that led to Camp David's main gate. In spite of the sign that warned park visitors not to enter, many tourists disregarded the warning and drove up to the main gate. During times of peak park visitation, Bob and Sonny would position Car 718 on the access road to the camp. From there, they could stop and check unauthorized vehicles.

One late night, a car turned off the main road and started up the camp drive where Bob and Sonny were parked. The Secret Service agent on duty at the main gate quickly radioed Bob and Sonny that no one was expected at that hour. Our boys in blue hurriedly jumped out of their cruiser and flagged down the car. Looking inside the vehicle, they recognized the familiar faces of David Eisenhower and Julie Nixon Eisenhower. Sonny greeted them apologetically: "Good evening, folks. Sorry for the trouble. The Secret Service said no one was expected at this hour."

A sheepish look came over David Eisenhower's face as he said: "Men, it's my fault. We decided on the trip at the last minute. It was to be a surprise for the President and Mrs. Nixon. In the rush, I forgot to call ahead to notify the White House."

Bob smiled as he said: "Well, you certainly surprised us. Enjoy your weekend."

Back inside their cruiser, Sonny told Bob: "There goes the camp's namesake. It must be neat to have something named for you—while you're still alive."

"Yeah," Bob agreed. "But Camp Sonny has a nicer ring to it."

Sonny laughed and replied, "Certainly snappier than Camp Harold [Sonny's given name]."

President Nixon spent many days at Camp David during his first presidential term. It was said he liked to work on speeches and important policy initiatives in front of the fireplace in Aspen Lodge (the presidential cabin). The Nixons used the retreat for relaxation and family gatherings. President Nixon also held staff and Cabinet meetings and hosted foreign dignitaries at Camp David.

The president and first lady continued to use Camp David extensively during Nixon's second term. It served as a haven from the growing political firestorm facing the president in Washington. By the summer of 1973, the Watergate break-in (June 17, 1972) and related matters had become a national scandal for the Nixon administration. Seven men had already been convicted in the burglary. Several had ties to the Committee to Re-Elect the President (CREEP) as well as the White House. One of them, James McCord, charged in a letter to U.S. District Court Judge John Sirica that top government officials had participated in a coverup. Presidential aides H.R. Haldeman and John Ehrlichman resigned due to allegations of wrongdoings. President Nixon fired White House Counsel John Dean, who became a star witness for the Senate Watergate Committee. Additionally, Special Prosecutor Archibald Cox was investigating the matter for the Department of Justice.

Things got worse when White House official Alexander Butterfield testified to the existence of a secret taping system that recorded conversations not only in the Oval Office, but also in Nixon's working office—located in the Old Executive Office Building. Special Prosecutor Cox and the Senate committee both subpoenaed the tapes. Nixon refused to turn them over on the grounds of "executive privilege"—the doctrine that the president's conversations and correspondence with his staff are confidential.

After lengthy negotiations, Nixon agreed to permit U.S. Senator John C. Stennis (Mississippi) to review the tapes and prepare a written summary. Although the Senate committee agreed to the deal, Special Prosecutor Cox rejected the offer. The White House then directed Cox to make no further attempts to gain the tapes. Cox refused and publicly stated he would continue his efforts. This set the stage for the "Saturday Night Massacre."

On Saturday, October 20, 1973, President Nixon ordered Attorney General Elliott Richardson to abolish the office of the special prosecutor. Richardson refused the order and resigned. Deputy Attorney General William Ruckelshaus also resigned rather than carry out Nixon's order. Solicitor General Robert Bork became the acting attorney general. He issued the order closing down the special prosecutor's office. Nixon directed the Justice Department to take over the responsibility of the investigation and prosecution of Watergate matters.

The presidential firing of Special Prosecutor Cox brought strong protest from Congress, the press, and the public. Some wanted Nixon impeached. Along 1600 Pennsylvania Avenue, motorists honked horns in support of impeachment. New anti-Nixon demonstrations took place on the White House sidewalk.

Continuing objection to Cox's removal forced the appointment of a new special prosecutor, Leon Jaworski. He would take over the investigation and prosecution of all Watergate matters for the Department of Justice. Under pressure from Jaworski and Judge Sirica, Nixon released some of the subpoenaed tapes. One was found to have a gap of 18½ minutes. Our nation continued to move closer to a constitutional showdown ...

Besides the revelations of Watergate, a federal investigation into Maryland corruption spelled additional trouble for the Nixon administration. In the spring of 1973, allegations surfaced against Vice President Spiro Agnew. It was alleged that while governor of Maryland, Agnew had taken illegal payments from businesses seeking state contracts. Agnew claimed innocence and vowed to fight any charges. Agnew defiantly stated he would not resign the vice presidency if indicted.

Eventually, Agnew negotiated a plea bargain with the Department of Justice. On October 10, 1973, Agnew resigned the vice presidency and pleaded nolo contendere (no contest) to one count of tax evasion. Agnew was sentenced to probation (three years) and a $10,000 fine. Under provisions of the 25th Amendment to the Constitution ratified in 1967, President Nixon nominated Congressman Gerald R. Ford of Michigan to become vice president. Ford was confirmed by the House and the Senate and became the 40th vice president of the United States on December 6, 1973.

When the president was not at Camp David, Car 718 patrolled the Park Police Central District. This area covered the federal park areas in downtown D.C. to include the Mall and memorials. Car 718 was also called upon to handle various special assignments, which occurred from time to time.

On one occasion, Bob and Sonny were on routine patrol when the call came in: "Car 718, report *immediately* to the NPS warehouse in Alexandria for a transport. A Park Service official will have a wreath for you to transport to 141 [Lincoln Memorial]. The item is needed ASAP for a VIP visit that will take place within the hour."

"10-4," Sonny acknowledged. "En route from westbound Independence at 17th." Turning to Bob, Sonny grumbled, "Geez, you'd think they'd have made better preparations."

"Yeah," Bob agreed.

After a fast drive across the 14th Street Bridge and south on the George Washington Memorial Parkway into Alexandria, Virginia, Bob pulled the cruiser up to the NPS warehouse. A Park Service employee was waiting for them, but there was no wreath in sight.

"Where's the wreath?" Sonny asked, concerned that time was being wasted.

"It's too big for me to carry. It's in the back. I'll take you to it."

Inside the warehouse, Sonny and Bob were led past assorted boxes, crates, and cabinets. Stopping in a back corner, their guide removed a tarp from a large, freestanding object. Revealed before Bob and Sonny's eyes was a metal wreath about five feet tall by three feet wide. It gave the appearance of intertwined laurel leaves, supported by legs that were part of the one-piece design.

"Bob, you get that side," Sonny directed. "Let's get this out to the car." Sonny and Bob started to pick up the wreath. "What's this thing made of?" Sonny asked.

"Solid gold," answered the park service employee.

"Yeah, sure," scoffed Sonny. "What's it really made of—brass-plated lead? It's heavier than it looks."

"Solid gold," the park service employee answered again. "It was a gift to the U.S. from Ethiopia some years ago. The State Department called. Emperor Hailie Selassie is in town for an official state visit and wants to see it."

"Yeah, our motormen are part of his motorcade escort," Bob added.

Bob and Sonny carried the wreath out to the cruiser where their problems really began. No matter how they turned the wreath, it wouldn't fit through the doorway into the back seat area.

"Let's try the trunk," suggested Sonny. Bob popped the trunk lid on the Chevrolet Bel Air sedan. Despite the cavernous area of the trunk, our boys couldn't get the wreath to fit. The trunk contained a first aid kit, spare tire, boxes of flares, tire chains, jack, tear gas canisters, Bob and Sonny's riot bags, and a Winchester Model '94 lever-action rifle. The old .30-30 was used at Catoctin Mountain Park when the president was at Camp David.

"Bob, maybe it'll fit if we unload the trunk. What we can't get in the back seat, we'll leave here until later."

"Sonny, I don't think we'll be able to get it to fit then. The trunk hinges are going to block it. It's too long and too wide, and the legs have a big footprint. And we might damage it."

"We can tie the trunk lid down with rope," Sonny replied.

"I don't know, Sonny. If it falls out, we're going to be walking permanent midnights. If the motorcade beats us there, I don't think the emperor will want to see us pull up with it hanging out the trunk—like some cheap lawn ornament from Hechingers [a now defunct home store chain]. Why don't we call for the wagon?"

"That's a good idea." Sonny grabbed the mike and called, "718."

"718," replied the dispatcher."

"This wreath is too big for the cruiser. Request 714 responds to my location for the transport."

"718, we're getting word the motorcade could be moving shortly. They're at the State Department. Is there any way you can secure the item on board and transport it *now*?"

"*Negative*, this thing is big enough to jump through, and it's solid gold!" Sonny emphatically replied. Sonny's response brought a series of audible "clicks" on the radio—as other Park Police units pressed their microphone buttons on and off to dramatize the strange situation.

"Roger, 718. Wagon 714, respond ASAP to NPS warehouse Alexandria to assist 718."

"10-4, from 23rd and Constitution," 714 replied.

The SOF prisoner transport wagon arrived, and the wreath was loaded through the double rear doors of the unit. Bob sat in the back with the wreath, so it wouldn't fly around on the trip to the Lincoln Memorial. It was decided to expedite (with emergency lights and siren), as the motorcade was staged at the Department of State—less than a minute drive to the Lincoln Memorial.

At the memorial, Bob and Sonny hurriedly carried the gold wreath up the 57 steps to the chamber. They were met by an official from the Office of the Chief of Protocol, U.S. Department of State. The protocol officer was happy to see the wreath. "Thanks so much," she said. "You saved the day!" Pointing to a spot in front of the Daniel Chester French statue of Lincoln, she directed Sonny and Bob to place the wreath there.

"We're happy we could help," Sonny replied.

"Sorry for the last minute curve. At the State Department luncheon today, his imperial majesty asked to see the Lincoln Memorial. Lincoln is his favorite historic figure. During a past visit, he presented this wreath in honor of Lincoln. Apparently, his imperial majesty believes the wreath is kept here on permanent display. Our gift office had to scramble to sort it all out."

"No problem," Bob responded.

A few minutes later, the motorcade arrived at the Lincoln Memorial. It was a sunny, warm day in early May 1973, and Emperor Hailie Selassie stood in awe at the base of the colossal statue of his hero. Lincoln appeared to gaze down on Selassie, returning the reverence. Selassie's cherubic face shined as his eyes viewed the golden wreath. It would be Selassie's last visit. The following year, Selassie was deposed by the Ethiopian military. He was placed under house arrest and reportedly died in 1975 under mysterious circumstances.

On another occasion, Car 718 was dispatched to Dulles International Airport for escort duty. Bob and Sonny reported to an official from the National Gallery of Art. The gallery curator was frantic with worry. Surrounding him were cases of French impressionist masterpieces that had been loaned to the National Gallery from the Hermitage Museum in the Soviet Union. The curator called out to Sonny and Bob: "Thank God you're here. The armored car I contracted for has broken down. I need you men to guard the paintings until a replacement can get here. Then, you can escort us to the gallery. They said it would be at least four hours until another armored car is available."

"How much are these worth?" Sonny asked.

The curator looked around to make sure no one else was listening before he whispered, "About 35 million dollars."

"Thirty-five million dollars!" Sonny exclaimed loudly.

"Please, not so loud," cautioned the official.

"Four hours—thirty-five million dollars, how about we just load them into our car and transport them for you now?" Sonny suggested.

"That sounds better than standing here with them," replied the nervous curator. He jumped into the back seat where Bob and Sonny loaded his lap with priceless paintings. Next, Bob and Sonny filled the interior area and trunk. Paintings were stacked from floor to headliner and into the rear deck. The cruiser pulled out of Dulles and headed for Washington with one very relieved curator and 35 million dollars in cargo—just another day for Car 718.

Chapter 13

Signal 13

In many police departments, the radio code "Signal 13" means an officer needs *immediate* assistance. When a Signal 13 breaks over the air, officers get a sudden, gut-wrenching sensation because one of their own is in trouble. All too often, Signal 13s are used to report that an officer is down. The years 1973 and 1974 were an especially dangerous period for American law enforcement personnel. During those two years, 547 officers were tragically killed in the line of duty. Of the 547 line-of-duty deaths, 266 were attributable to felonious assault. The vast majority of those fatalities were due to officers being shot by armed felons.

Although trying not to show my concern, I became increasingly worried about Bob's safety. The blue uniform he wore was a target not only for violent criminals, but also for radicals, revolutionaries, and deranged individuals. The news routinely featured reports of police officers being injured and killed—some murdered in coldblooded ambushes. One of the worst incidents occurred on Sunday, January 7, 1973, when a black militant went on a shooting rampage in New Orleans, Louisiana. I watched in horror as the violence played out on national television.

I can still see the terrifying images of a high-rise Howard Johnson's Hotel. A rooftop equipment room of masonry construction provided excellent cover for a deadly sniper. For hours, he held police at bay, while he reigned down death from the barrel of a .44 Magnum caliber semiautomatic carbine. Prior to the standoff, the shooter ran through the hotel setting fires and firing at white employees and guests. He set off firecrackers for diversions to give the appearance of multiple gunmen.

Utilizing an armored CH-46 military helicopter, sharpshooters finally downed the sniper after an 11-hour siege. Fearing that the shooter had an accomplice, police waited until Monday afternoon to storm the sniper's rooftop lair. After the smoke had cleared, the dead shooter was identified as Mark James Robert Essex, a 23-year-old vocational trainee.

It was later reported that Essex had received a general discharge from the U.S. Navy on the grounds of "unsuitability." Family and friends related that Essex had encountered racism in the Navy that caused him to become embittered. After his discharge, he spent some time in New York City where he came under the influence of black-nationalist doctrine.

Further investigation linked Essex to the murders of two other New Orleans police officers that occurred on New Year's Eve 1972. Bullets removed from the dead officers matched Essex's carbine. His deadly toll after both incidents was nine dead, which included five police officers. Scores of others were injured.

To Bob, Essex was a product and symbol of the worst of American society. Confronted by a system where he was not treated equally and fairly, Essex turned to black extremism. He embraced its most violent message—armed rebellion. Enraged with hatred, he gave up on America and life. In a suicidal moment, Essex chose to take revenge on the world he would soon leave. Mark Essex wanted to make his mark on history.

I asked Bob, "Do you think he was trying to start a revolution?"

"It probably was more about hatred, revenge, and notoriety. He might have hoped his actions would serve as inspiration for others to copy."

One group inspired by the doctrine of black revolution and left-wing radicalism was the Symbionese Liberation Army (SLA), formed in the San Francisco Bay area in 1973. The group's leader was a black convict named Donald DeFreeze. As an inmate, DeFreeze had come in contact with white activists during prison-sanctioned activities. The most extreme of these activists viewed *all* minority inmates as "political prisoners."

When DeFreeze escaped from prison in the spring of 1973, he fled to Berkeley, California to hide out with his new friends in the radical underground. During this time, DeFreeze recruited white-middle-class extremists who were willing to use violence to overthrow the government. Taking the name "Field Marshal Cinque" (after the slave who led a revolt on the ship *Amistad* in 1839), DeFreeze authored a manifesto for the SLA calling for "revolutionary war against the fascist capitalistic class and all their agents of murder, oppression, and exploitation."

On November 6, 1973, Marcus Foster, the superintendant of schools for Oakland, CA, was shot and killed with bullets laced with cyanide. The following day, the SLA issued a communiqué taking full responsibility for the assassination. They stated the killing was for Foster's support of an identification card program for public school students. Foster was a popular, well-thought-of black educator and his coldblooded murder backfired on the SLA, alienating it from the public and other radical-left groups.

Two SLA members were tried and convicted of the Foster murder (one of the convictions was later overturned). The SLA rebounded by kidnapping 19-year-old publishing heiress Patricia Hearst. Patty was the granddaughter of newspaper tycoon William Randolph Hearst. For many months, the group remained in the headlines as the Patty Hearst kidnapping became one of the biggest media stories of the era. As a good faith gesture for Patty's release, the SLA demanded that Hearst's parents hand out millions of dollars worth of food to the needy. After distributing two million dollars worth of food, the Hearst family decided no more food would be made available until Patty was released.

What happened next stunned the Hearsts. In a series of SLA audio communiqués by Patty, she increasingly denigrated her family, while she became more supportive of the goals of the SLA. On April 3, 1973, another SLA audio communiqué marked Patty's conversion from prisoner of war to freedom fighter. Patty announced she had been given the option of being released or "joining the forces of the Symbionese Liberation Army and fighting for my freedom and the freedom of all oppressed people." Patty then declared, "I have decided to stay and fight." Hearst added that she had been given the name Tania (after a female comrade of Cuban revolutionary Che Guevara). Included with the tape was a photo of Hearst. Dressed in fatigues and a beret, she was pictured holding an assault rifle.

The Hearst family suggested that Patty had been "brainwashed" or coerced into making the statements. Some speculated that Hearst had been a member of the SLA from the beginning and that she had staged her own kidnapping. Bob, who had studied Marxist indoctrination in college political science courses, felt that Hearst could very well have been "programmed" by the SLA into a new identity reborn with the group's view of the world. Bob explained that revolutionaries have been adept in taking impressionable minds and molding them into true believers. With the absolute control that the SLA exhibited over Hearst, the group might have broken down Patty's resistance with drugs and/or oppressive behavior— which happened to some American POW's during the Korean War. Isolation, sleep deprivation, starvation, brutalization, and the threat of death might have made Hearst susceptible to a bombardment of SLA propaganda. This multi-step regimen could have made Patty feel shamefully guilty and worthless.

Next, Hearst's captors would encourage Patty to confess her sins and then offer a *lifeline* to release the burden. As Tania, she could choose good over evil and dedicate herself to the belief system of the SLA. Bob pointed to Patty's tapes, which seemed to lend some credence to his analysis. Hearst sternly denounced the sins of her relatives and accused her father and the FBI of wanting her dead. She seemed to have undergone a complete belief reversal.

Then on April 15, 1973, Patty Hearst was caught by surveillance cameras as the SLA robbed a San Francisco bank. Hearst was seen carrying an M-1 carbine and shouting orders to bank customers. After reviewing the film and eyewitness interviews, U.S. Attorney General William Saxbe called the SLA "a bunch of common criminals," and it was his belief that Patricia Hearst was "not a reluctant participant" in the robbery. Hearst was now wanted by the FBI as a suspect in criminal activity.

With the police and FBI manhunt intensifying in the Bay area, the SLA moved their operations south to Los Angeles and acquired a safe house. On

May 16, 1974, SLA members Bill and Emily Harris entered Mel's Sporting Goods in nearby Inglewood, California to obtain some supplies. Store personnel observed Bill Harris shoplifting a pair of socks. A scuffle broke out when the Harrises attempted to leave the scene. Patricia Hearst, who was keeping watch from across the street in a van, fired on the shop with an assault rifle to aid the getaway. To cover their trail, the trio stole several vehicles that were switched out during the escape. Eventually, the Harrises and Hearst hid out in a motel near Disneyland in Anaheim, California.

Police recovered the abandoned van, which contained a parking ticket that led authorities to the address of the SLA safe house. The next morning, police and FBI agents raided the location. The hideout was empty. With the failure of the Harrises and Hearst to return and news reports of the Inglewood incident, the remaining members of the SLA had abandoned the safe house.

Overnight, the SLA commandeered a house on East 54th Street in the Compton neighborhood of South-Central LA. On May 17, 1973, the mother of a resident of the home tipped police that heavily armed individuals had moved in. With this information, Los Angeles Police Department (LAPD) Special Weapons and Tactics (SWAT) teams and FBI agents surrounded the house, while television cameras covered the action *live*.

Police ordered the occupants to "come out with your hands up." When the SLA did not reply to calls for surrender, police fired tear gas into the home. The SLA responded with automatic-weapon fire, touching off a two-hour gun battle. More tear gas was fired into the house, which erupted in flames. When the shootout was over, Donald DeFreeze and five other SLA members were dead.

Although the incident greatly reduced the ranks of the SLA, it was not dead. The Harrises and Hearst were still at large. In a SLA communiqué, Tania eulogized her dead comrades and vowed, "I know what I have to do." To Bob, the SLA was a "political cult." It was based on the *irrational* belief that military actions by the SLA would ignite a nation-wide revolution. Then, a utopia could be formed—patterned after SLA ideals. Bob predicted the remaining members of the SLA might seek revenge for the death of their comrades. They would also most likely look for new recruits and plan future operations that would keep them in the news and before the public's eye.

Bob had his own brush with an individual who wanted revenge and publicity. It was in late 1973. Two stories dominated national headlines at the time. One was the Arab oil embargo brought on by U.S. support of Israel during the October 1973 Yom Kippur War. The cutoff of oil imports caused a shortage of gasoline. An odd-even rationing system was instituted. Vehicles with odd-numbered license plates could gas up on odd-numbered days; vehicles displaying even-numbered tags were limited to even-numbered days. Americans waited in long lines at gas stations, hoping that supplies would not run out before their turn at the pumps.

The second was the Watergate affair. After President Nixon fired Watergate Special Prosecutor Archibald Cox, there were calls for the president's impeachment. Anti-Nixon demonstrations and protests sprung up in Washington, D.C. One demonstrator demanding Nixon's impeachment was a short, stocky, middle-aged man named Samuel J. Byck. He was an unemployed salesman from Philadelphia, Pennsylvania. Byck had been turned down for a Small Business Administration loan. After the rejection, Byck became an outspoken critic of President Nixon, whom he accused of oppressing the poor.

Byck had been to Washington before with his one-man demonstration. On that occasion, Park Police had warned Byck that he needed a permit to demonstrate on the White House sidewalk. When Byck refused to get one, Park Police arrested him.

Now once again, Byck was back on the White House sidewalk and carrying a protest sign. Several carloads of SOF officers pulled up along Pennsylvania Avenue in front of the White House in order to monitor the day's demonstrations. SOF Officer Tom Kaylor recognized Byck and asked the sergeant if Byck had a permit.

"No, I don't see him on the list. Check him out. If he doesn't have a permit and refuses to stop, arrest him."

Officer Kaylor approached Byck with Bob standing by as backup. When Kaylor asked Byck if he had a permit, Byck became agitated and said he didn't need one. He refused to leave. Officer Kaylor grabbed Byck's left arm and placed him under arrest. Byck resisted Officer Kaylor's grasp, and Bob moved in to control Byck's right arm. Kaylor and Bob whisked Byck to the SOF patrol wagon where he was transported to Central Cell Block.

Unknown to Park Police, Byck had come to the attention of the U.S. Secret Service in 1972 for allegedly remarking that someone should kill President Nixon. Byck was interviewed by agents from the Philadelphia Field Office of the Secret Service. He became the subject of periodic Secret Service investigations. Unfortunately, Byck's mental state deteriorated.

On the morning of February 22, 1974 (Washington's Birthday), Samuel Byck drove to Baltimore/Washington International Airport (BWI) in Anne Arundel County, Maryland. Armed with a stolen .22-caliber handgun and a homemade gasoline bomb, Byck shot and killed an airport policeman who was screening passengers at a security checkpoint. Byck then stormed his way aboard a nearby Delta Airlines DC-9 jetliner.

Entering the cockpit through its unlocked door, Byck found the pilot and copilot readying the aircraft for a flight to Atlanta. Byck ordered the pilot to take off immediately. The pilot cautioned that he couldn't take off with the door of the plane still opened. Byck fired a warning shot into the cockpit. Two flight attendants ran off the plane, closing the main door behind them.

Byck again ordered the pilot to get the plane off the ground. The pilot answered that the wheels were still chocked and that the plane had not been cleared for departure. Upset, Byck fired another shot. Then, he grabbed a female passenger from the cabin and forced her into the cockpit to help fly the plane. Angered that the aircraft was not moving, Byck shot the pilot and copilot and returned the passenger to her seat. Byck grabbed another female passenger and dragged her into the cockpit. Again, Byck fired at the pilot and copilot.

Through the porthole of the door to the aircraft, a responding county police officer saw Byck moving between the cabin and the cockpit. The officer fired several times at the hijacker with his .38-caliber issued service revolver but couldn't penetrate the door's plexiglass window. Then, the officer fired the .357 Magnum revolver he had removed from the fallen airport policeman. Byck was hit twice. With the copilot fatally shot and the pilot severely wounded, Byck retreated into the cockpit where he committed suicide.

At the time, Byck's motives were not known. The incident looked like just another aircraft hijacking attempt. Subsequently, an audio tape was found in Byck's car. Byck had also mailed a tape recording to newspaper columnist Jack Anderson and others. On the tapes, Byck tells of "Operation Pandora's Box." Byck chillingly details his plan to hijack an airliner and to force the crew to fly it over downtown Washington, D.C. There, Byck would shoot the pilots and drive the control stick of the aircraft down toward the White House, causing the airliner to crash into the Executive Mansion. Byck's failed hijacking was in actuality an assassination attempt on President Richard Nixon.

Bob suspected that an incident that occurred only five days before might have influenced Byck. "It's the copycat phenomenon," Bob informed. "In some impressionable minds, certain incidents can inspire similar behavior. People who are unhappy with their lives, blame others for their problems, and are suicidal are especially susceptible. They see the notoriety gained by perpetrating an infamous act. The copycat sees a way to become famous and to gain some revenge. At the stage their mind is in, it seems to be the only way they can get even and get some self-satisfaction. I've got to believe that the White House helicopter intrusion affected Byck."

In the early morning hours of Sunday, February 17, 1974, Private First Class (PFC) Robert K. Preston stole an Army UH-1B "Huey" helicopter from Fort Meade, Maryland—about 25 miles east of Washington, D.C. The 20-year-old Preston had washed out of the Army's flight school and was sent to Ft. Meade to become a helicopter mechanic.

Preston flew the stolen helicopter to the restricted airspace of the White House complex. There, he flew over the White House and hovered above the South Grounds. Unaware of the origins and intentions of the helicopter, EPS officers took no action.

The Huey left the area but returned later with a Maryland State Police (MSP) helicopter in pursuit. MSP had been notified that a rogue helicopter was flying erratically in the vicinity of BWI Airport. The MSP helicopter intercepted the rogue helicopter, following it down the Baltimore-Washington Parkway toward D.C. Once again, the Huey violated restricted airspace and approached the south side of the White House near the West Wing. This time, EPS officers opened up with pistols and shotguns. The rogue helicopter landed on the White House lawn and Preston was arrested.

Preston was eventually turned over to Army authorities. He was sentenced to a year at hard labor and fined $2,400. Although the President and Mrs. Nixon were not in Washington during the incident, matters of White House security had been raised. The incident received extensive media coverage. The pilot of the MSP helicopter indicated that Preston could have flown the stolen chopper into the White House at top speed (over 100 miles per hour). The MSP trooper believed that those on the ground would have been unable to prevent it. Did the Preston incident spawn Byck's plan for an aerial assault of the White House?

Of the hundreds of police officers killed every year, dozens die in traffic accidents. Bob had a close call when his cruiser was struck from behind while stopped along the George Washington Memorial Parkway near Arlington, Virginia. An inattentive motorist rear-ended Bob at about 45 miles per hour. It was one of those things a police spouse fears most. Bob's cruiser was on the northbound side of the parkway. The impact of the accident propelled the cruiser into the air where it turned around a complete 180 degrees before landing some feet from where it had been.

Miraculously, Bob only received whiplash, back injuries, and a few bruises. The doctor at the Police and Fire Clinic put Bob on sick leave, as he had sharp pain from his neck to lower back. After a couple of days, Bob asked to be returned to duty. Bob still had pain, but he also had an exemplary work ethic. Bob's explanation: "SOF is already down a couple of officers. I need to get back and pull my weight."

The Park Police Accident Review Board judged that the accident could not have been prevented by Bob. Thus, Bob's duty record remained unblemished, and he was not faulted in any way. The Park Police official who conducted the accident investigation remarked that Bob was very fortunate. The investigator stated it was a wonder the gas tank hadn't exploded from the impact. Also, if the cruiser had been propelled in the other direction, the car would have gone over a steep, high cliff that bordered that section of the parkway. Rocks and the Potomac River lay far below. It was certain that Bob would not have survived. It was another sobering reminder of how quickly Bob could be put in harm's way. I thanked God that Bob was not seriously injured and prayed that Bob would remain safe.

These worries were something the spouse of a law enforcement officer has to live with. You might only be a knock on the door away from tragedy and grief. You never knew what the next day or night might bring. I always made sure I sent Bob off with a kiss and an embrace. It was my way of wishing him good luck, while holding him close—just in case.

An officer who went through police school with Bob was also involved in an on-duty accident—or at least his cruiser was. Responding to the vicinity of the Jefferson Memorial for a report of a suspicious person, the officer was interviewing the subject when a couple of tourists approached. While the officer was responding to the tourists' questions, the suspicious subject jumped into the officer's cruiser. The subject then sped off along the broad concrete apron that runs between the Tidal Basin and the memorial with the officer in foot pursuit. Swerving to miss a child who was in the walkway, the subject piloted the vehicle into the Tidal Basin where it made a splash worthy of any movie scene.

Bob and Sonny were working downtown in Car 718 when the 10-33 (emergency) call came in. "What did he say?" Sonny asked in disbelief.

"A cruiser went in the water near the Jefferson," Bob replied.

"I was afraid that's what he said. Let's go!" Bob and Sonny were one of the first units to arrive on the scene. They were both amazed to see a United States Park Police cruiser partially submerged, going down by the bow. "There's something you don't see every day," Sonny declared.

"That's for sure," Bob agreed.

Bob and Sonny helped secure the prisoner. Both the arresting officer and the subject were soaking wet. Sitting down in the grass, the officer started to shake his head, while he tried to wring some of the water from his trousers. Still a bit out of breath and excited, he turned toward Bob and said: "Rit, that crazy bastard stole my cruiser and drove it into the Tidal Basin! I don't believe it! Then, I had to jump in and rescue the son of a bitch. The only way I could get him out was by smashing the rear window."

The three officers watched, as the cruiser disappeared below the waterline. A gurgle could be heard as the trunk slipped under. Some of the remaining trapped air escaped and bubbled to the surface.

"Don't let that broken window worry you," Sonny told the still agitated officer.

Bob warned his former classmate: "Get it together. Soon, they'll be sitting you down and asking a lot of questions."

Bob walked over and retrieved the officer's shoes and gun belt, which he had taken off before his plunge into the water. When Bob returned, the officer nervously asked, "Rit, do you think I'm in trouble?"

Before Bob could answer, Sonny interjected with a bit of sarcasm: "No, Chief Wells doesn't mind if one of his cruisers ends up in 10 feet of water. Don't worry; he's got plenty of 'em."

A police officer never knows what the next moment might bring. This appealed to Bob's sense of adventure—but not in a thrill-seeking way. I think Bob liked the new and different challenges he faced every day. He was a man of action and took pride in handling situations and doing the best he could do. He also enjoyed helping people. These were the rewards that most satisfied Bob.

Bob and I were similar in our desire to help people and to pursue rewarding careers. I had accepted a teaching position (kindergarten) with the Prince George's County School System. Like Bob, I believed I was making a difference and helping to create a better society. We and many others of our generation had been inspired by the "New Frontier" of President John F. Kennedy. In his 1961 Inaugural address, JFK urged, "And so, my fellow Americans: Ask not what your country can do for you; ask what you can do for your country."

Like Bob, my profession was not something I got into by accident or convenience. I truly felt I was answering my country's call. Prince George's County was struggling with court-ordered desegregation. Amidst the turmoil of mandatory busing and integration, I chose Prince George's over other school systems with lesser challenges. Bob and I were committed to work for a better America.

Bob was also guided by his childhood ambitions. Having reached his two-year anniversary with Park Police, Bob focused on applying for an agent position with the U.S. Secret Service. Telephoning the Secret Service Personnel Division in Washington, Bob learned he would need to submit an application and security forms. He would have to come into the Secret Service personnel office to be fingerprinted. Bob would also need to pass a physical and the Treasury Enforcement Agent (TEA) Exam. Additionally, it was a requirement that all agent candidates be interviewed by a Secret Service special agent in charge (SAIC). Spouses of married candidates were also required to be interviewed. The Secret Service wanted to be sure spouses fully understood the demands of the position and supported their partner's career choice.

I encouraged Bob in his goal of becoming a Secret Service agent. First, I knew that he wanted to make it his life's work. Second, I felt a career as an agent would be safer than that of a uniformed police officer. As it turned out, Bob was told that the Secret Service had no immediate openings in its Washington Field Office. That fact—along with several events still to come—would cause Bob to take a detour on the road to his professional hopes and dreams.

Chapter 14

SY

Some of the protective assignments Bob received at SOF were escort duty for Department of State motorcades. By working these movements, Bob became friendly with Gene Lombardi, an agent with the Office of Security (SY), U.S. Department of State. Lombardi hailed from Buffalo, New York and was previously an officer with the Executive Protective Service. He invited Bob to the Main State building, located at 21st Street and Virginia Avenue, NW, D.C.

Meeting at the 21st and C Streets entrance, Lombardi escorted Bob to the eighth floor. After treating for lunch, Lombardi gave Bob a personal tour of the State Department diplomatic reception rooms. There, Bob saw antique American furniture, objects of art, and the desk on which the Treaty of Paris was signed in 1783. Bob rubbed his hand along the desktop where Benjamin Franklin, John Adams, and John Jay signed the treaty that officially recognized American independence from Great Britain.

Next, Lombardi led Bob to Bill D'Urso's office. D'Urso was head of the SY detail that protected Nancy Kissinger, the wife of Dr. Henry A. Kissinger, who served concurrently as secretary of state and national security advisor to the president. Normally, SY would have been protecting the secretary of state. Due to prior unusual circumstances, Dr. Kissinger was already being protected by the U.S. Secret Service. Kissinger had received Secret Service protection since late 1970.

At the time, FBI Director J. Edgar Hoover informed President Nixon of an alleged plot to kidnap Kissinger—who was then only national security advisor. According to Hoover, the plotters intended to hold Kissinger until the U.S. released political prisoners and ceased bombing operations in Southeast Asia. Additionally, the same group was alleged to have been planning to blow up underground steam pipes that provide heat to federal buildings in Washington. This was reportedly an attempt to disrupt the operations of the federal government.

After the short, informal visit with D'Urso, Lombardi took Bob to the office of Bill Decourcy, Chief of the SY Protective Services Division (PSD). Lombardi introduced Bob to Decourcy and added: "Bob's the Park Police officer I've been telling you about. He's been a big help to us and received some commendations from the chief of protocol."

Decourcy rose from his desk and extended a beefy hand: "Glad to meet you, Bob. Thanks for your assistance and good work. We certainly appreciate it." After the handshake, Decourcy relaxed back into his chair and clasped his hands behind his head. "Gene tells me you have a college degree and enjoy protective duties. We have a new counterterrorism initiative at State," Decourcy advised. "Congress has authorized the hiring of additional agents to enhance departmental security at home and abroad. Although most of the positions will be for American embassies and legations overseas, some will be stateside. We'll need more agents to protect the next secretary of state and others. While the Secret Service protects heads of state and government, SY is responsible for the protection of lesser dignitaries as directed by the secretary. Our duties will increase in future years. We could use a good man like you."

Surprised, Bob took a short while to mull over what he had just heard. "Bill, I'm flattered that you would be interested in me. But I actually want a career with the Secret Service. I'm going to be applying there soon."

Lombardi quickly interceded: "Bob, the Secret Service is a great organization. But you'll advance quicker in SY. With your police experience, you'll be able to move right into protection. There's going to be some golden opportunities here."

"That's right," Decourcy affirmed. "I'll need agents with protective skills."

After the visit with Decourcy, Lombardi led Bob to the State Department personnel office where he got Bob a copy of the hiring announcement along with an application packet. "Look Bob," Lombardi said in a reflective tone, "These are *reserve* positions for no longer than five years or the need of the department, whichever is less. After three years, you could convert to a permanent position in the Foreign Service. Maybe by that time, the department will have civil service positions for protection agents. No one's going to say anything if you use SY as a stepping stone. Stay as little or as long as you like. We have several guys now who are actively seeking positions with the FBI and CIA."

"Gene, I should probably wait until the Secret Service opens up."

"Bob, the Secret Service hiring process takes months. You could be hired here within 30 days. We do our own background checks, so we could have yours expedited. That would be a big help in your application with the Service. You'd already have a full-field background investigation completed and a top-secret clearance. You'd also have protective time under your belt. We work hand-in-hand with the Service's detail. It would be great experience, and I know you'd enjoy it."

That evening, Bob told me the news, while he pulled forms out of a large manila envelope. Spreading them out on our kitchen table, Bob asked, "What do you think, honey?"

"I don't know, Bobbie. Maybe it would be better for you to stay at Park Police and concentrate on applying to the Secret Service."

Bob didn't immediately respond to my comment. He sat there looking at the forms, while he thought over what I had just said. "Honey, obtaining a top-secret clearance would be a plus. And I'd gain some new experience. I could do it until the Secret Service opens up."

New experiences were always very important to Bob. Since I also worried about Bob's safety as a police officer, I decided to drop my reservations. "Go ahead and apply if you want to," I said.

So, Bob filled out the forms and dropped them off at the State Department personnel office along with an official "raised seal" copy of his birth certificate. A couple of days later, he went in for a "security interview." Soon after that, we heard from some friends and neighbors that they were contacted regarding Bob's background investigation. Several weeks after that, Bob received a letter that he was being appointed to a security officer position and was given a date to report. It all happened *very* quickly.

"What should I do, honey?" Bob asked.

"I guess you should show up on the date and time specified. Otherwise, they might come looking for you," I joked.

"Seriously, Jan, should I accept the offer?"

"Sure, why not? You know you want to."

"Honey, I just think this will better prepare me for the Secret Service. I don't see how it could hurt me."

Bob accepted the State Department position and notified Park Police that he would be leaving. Looking back on his several years of duty, Bob unfortunately remembered not only the good but also the bad. Residual pain would prompt thoughts of some of the latter—his car accident and an injury during a civil disturbance when rocks were hurled at him. He also had vivid memories of fatalities: car accidents, the incident at Harper's Ferry, and a suicide. His mind would never erase some of the tragedy it had seen. Bob could only hope that time would dull some of the more graphic images.

Like a bad dream, one particular mental image flashed back to Bob from his early days at SOF. Sonny and Bob had spotted something in the grass near Rock Creek Parkway. Towering majestically 125 feet above was the Calvert Street Bridge (renamed Duke Ellington Memorial Bridge). The neo-classical-designed structure was erected in 1935. It's constructed of three concrete arches, which support a 60-foot-wide roadway with 12-foot-wide sidewalks. The bridge is 825 feet long and features pedestrian overlooks.

There had been a report of a young woman sitting on the wall of the bridge. Now, Sonny and Bob confirmed their worst fears. At their feet was a lifeless, bruised, crumpled body of broken bones and internal bleeding. In a fit of depression and desperation, this soul had jumped to eternity.

As there were no vital signs and death was obvious, Bob went to the cruiser to pull a raincoat out of his duffle bag. Returning to the scene, he carefully spread the raincoat over the deceased. Shortly thereafter, paramedics arrived and confirmed that the subject exhibited no signs of life. Waiting for an MPD homicide detective to respond to take charge of the scene and investigation, Bob and Sonny wondered what triggered this horrific self-destruction. The medical examiner describes it as multiple blunt-force injuries.

Sonny was also curious as to why the Calvert Street Bridge was such a "suicide magnet." There are hundreds of bridges and countless buildings in D.C., yet the Calvert Street Bridge accounted for about half of those who jumped to their death. A similar bridge—the nearby William Howard Taft Bridge—accounted for about another quarter of the deadly total. Bob suggested that the majesty of the bridges might appeal to those with suicidal tendencies who want to go out in monumental style. Bob also theorized that "copycat behavior" might play a part. Once someone jumped off the bridges and it was publicized, others in the same frame of mind might be induced to similar behavior. Over time, these two bridges gained a continuing notoriety.

Bob and Sonny speculated as to their chances of talking the subject out of jumping—if they had arrived earlier. Could they have saved this person's life? If so, emergency hospitalization and follow-up treatment might have been successful in turning the tide. She might have been able to return to a happier life. Bob always wondered as to the "what ifs."

Sadly, they didn't get the opportunity to intervene in her affairs. They knew she must have left some family and friends behind. It would be devastating news. They didn't envy the MPD detective who would be making the notifications.

One thing Bob didn't look forward to in June of 1974 was leaving his friends at Park Police. Sonny had been promoted to detective some months before, so he had already left SOF. Bob was happy for Sonny, but the reassignment had been difficult for Bob, who dearly missed the good-natured Irishman. Occasionally, Bob was able to see Sonny in the course of official duties and during off-duty hours. Now, Bob would be saying goodbye to Sonny and others on a more lasting basis. It would be difficult to stay in personal touch with his Park Police friends—with the long hours and varied schedules they kept. Bob's spirits were lifted somewhat by the prospect of forming new friendships at State.

With mixed emotions, Bob reported to the Washington Field Office of the U.S. Department of State located at 1800 North Kent Street in Rosslyn, Virginia. In the reception area, Bob chatted with several other newly appointed security officers, who were also reporting for duty. One of them, Tim Robinson, was from Richmond, Virginia. Tim was married and had been a schoolteacher. Both men took an immediate liking to each other.

After orientation by an employment branch officer, the new agents had their pictures taken for credentials and diplomatic passports. Then, they were introduced to Joe Morton, Special Agent in Charge (SAC). Morton welcomed them and presented each a leather flip case with gold-tone badge.

Next, the men met Assistant Special Agent in Charge (ASAC) John Bacom. He introduced the new agents around the office and found them desk space. Bacom assigned a senior agent to train each new man in personnel security investigation. Agent Don Miller was paired with Bob. Miller had been an investigator with the Civil Service Commission (CSC) before coming to State. "Bob, have you done background investigations before?" Miller asked.

"No, I did code investigations when I was a housing inspector. I also have some experience in accident and preliminary criminal investigation when I was a park policeman."

"Well, you won't have any trouble doing backgrounds. Let me give you a quick overview. From the end of World War II into the early 1950s, a system of background checks and investigations was established for federal workers and those seeking U.S. government employment. Executive Order 10450 specifically requires federal employees to be reliable, trustworthy, of good conduct and character, and of complete and unswerving loyalty to the United States. The hiring and retention of federal employees is to be in the best interests of national security.

"The scope of the investigation to determine this depends on the position. Any position where the occupant could bring about a *materially adverse effect* on national security is deemed a *sensitive* position. Sensitive positions require a full-field background and periodic updates. Within sensitive positions, there are different levels of access to classified information ranging from confidential to top secret. The depth of the investigation conducted corresponds to the level of access a position permits. The higher the level, the more we have to do.

"We don't really have to worry about what is required or not." Handing an investigation request sheet to Bob, Miller explained: "See, it's clearly designated what we have to check. For this one, there's two neighborhoods, three personal references, three employments, an education check, and so on.

"Here's the manual. It specifies the information we're looking for in each of the investigative areas and what questions should be asked. We're trying to find out if the individual is honest, trustworthy, reliable, of good character, financially responsible, and a loyal American. If we find derogatory information, we report it as accurately and completely as possible. We don't make judgments. That's left to others. We just report what we find—the positive and any negative. The adjudicators will determine if the subject is suitable for federal service and whether they can be entrusted with national security information.

"Any questions so far?"

"No, Don, it looks pretty straight forward."

"Good, this afternoon, I have a security interview scheduled with a Foreign Service officer applicant. I want you to sit in on it. We conduct a security interview of all who apply for a sensitive position at State. Some agencies don't. We feel it's an important part of the process. The security interview provides us an opportunity to go over the SF-86 [Security Questionnaire] with the applicant for accuracy and completeness. We can also obtain any releases we might need. The interview also offers the subject a chance to provide an explanation for any listed adverse history and to voluntarily disclose any other derogatory information."

Bob studied the personnel security manual closely. Later that afternoon, he picked up his new credentials and sat in on the security interview that Agent Miller conducted. The next morning, Miller handed Bob a stack of security investigation requests. "Look through these and start scheduling your security interviews. After the interviews are completed, you can begin your field investigations. If you have *any* questions, don't hesitate to see me. The only dumb question is the one that doesn't get asked."

During the next six weeks, Bob worked diligently on background investigations. He earned a reputation for providing high-quality investigations quickly and efficiently. By nature, Bob was a self-starter and well organized. It also helped that Bob knew the Washington Metropolitan Area.

On the protection side of the job, Bob scored a perfect 300 on the SY firearms qualification. Because of his proficiency with firearms and prior police training and experience, Bob quickly received several short-term temporary duty assignments (TDY) with Mrs. Kissinger's detail. During the movements, Bob drove the State Department limousine utilized by Mrs. Kissinger, while a senior agent rode the right front seat. Another agent would go in advance to Mrs. Kissinger's destination and be responsible for the specifics of the visit as well as securing the arrival area. Once Mrs. Kissinger arrived and was situated, the advance agent would "leapfrog" to the next stop as needed.

Bob fit right into protection and Mrs. Kissinger's detail. Gene Lombardi soon told Bob: "Jim Barnes will be going on vacation. Since you know D.C. and have been doing a good job, we're going to ask WFO to let you fill in as advance agent. This will be a good way to get you over here."

Bob looked forward to the opportunity as he was called into SAC Morton's office. "Bob, PSD requested you for an extended TDY. I told them they couldn't have you. You're doing a good job with your cases, and I want that to continue. I'm going to rotate agents over there a couple of days at a time, so everyone can stay current on their work. And I just assigned you some priority backgrounds."

"Mr. Morton, I enjoy personnel security investigations, but I really came to State for its protective mission. My cases are current, and I promise to keep them that way. I'll do whatever it takes to both carry a good caseload and work protection too."

Morton grimaced, shook his head a couple of times, and leaned forward toward Bob. "Let me give you some advice. The way to advance in SY is through investigations. That's over 95% of what we do. Mastery of the various investigations we conduct will determine when and where you'll be assigned overseas. Investigatory skills will heavily influence your career in the Foreign Service. That's where you should concentrate your effort."

Bob came home that night and told me the news. He had no desire to serve at a foreign post. Bob had hoped to work protection until he could be hired by the Secret Service. Now, SAC Morton had decided to limit Bob's protection time. "What are you going to do?" I asked.

"Continue to turn in my cases ahead of due dates, so I'll be available for protective assignments." Opportunity knocked several days later. It was late afternoon; Tim Robinson and Bob were dictating cases for typing. Suddenly, Joe Morton popped into their work area.

"I'm glad you're still here," Morton said with a sigh of relief. "All the other agents have gone for the day. Archbishop Makarios of Cyprus will be coming to New York tomorrow. SY will be protecting him. You men go home and pack. Fly up to New York this evening and check into the Plaza Hotel. The New York Field Office [NYFO] will have a room reserved for you and further information."

"Thanks, Mr. Morton," Bob said in appreciation.

Like a father preaching to his son, Morton warned: "Go ahead and have your fun. But remember, *investigations* pay the bills around here."

Earlier that week on Monday, July 15, 1974, Archbishop Makarios had been deposed from his position as President of Cyprus via an army coup d'état. It was initially reported that Makarios had been killed, but he escaped to Malta and then flew to London. Now, Makarios was coming to New York to address the United Nations Security Council.

Bob and Tim took the Eastern Air Shuttle to LaGuardia Airport where they taxied to the Plaza—one of the most celebrated hotels in the world. Located along Fifth Avenue at Central Park South, the Plaza was distinguished by its elegant French chateau-style architecture. An iconic Manhattan landmark since 1907, the hotel featured world-class luxury and service.

At check-in, there was a message for Bob and Tim to report to NYFO Agent Jerry O'Brien at the SY Command Post (CP), which was located next to the suite reserved for Archbishop Makarios. Bob and Tim proceeded to the CP where they met O'Brien and Agent Carl Dresher, who was also from the NYFO. O'Brien informed the three agents they would be needed in the morning to assist with the archbishop's arrival. "Bossy will be here tomorrow at 8:00 a.m. sharp," O'Brien announced. "After the bomb sweep,

I'll need one of you to secure the suite until the archbishop's arrival. Any takers?"

"Yeah, I'll do it," volunteered Robinson. "By the way, Jerry, who's Bossy?"

"Bossy is the nickname for the NYPD Bureau of Special Services [BOSS]. It's the unit that coordinates support for dignitary protection and other special assignments.

"Bob, Carl, meet me in the CP tomorrow at 8:00 a.m. Bob, you'll go with me to JFK [John F. Kennedy International Airport] to assist with the airport arrival. Carl, you man the CP. After the archbishop settles in at the hotel, you guys will be released to get some rest. Starting tomorrow evening, you're scheduled to work the night shift [8:00 p.m. to 8:00 a.m.] with several other agents, who will arrive later."

After the orientation, Bob, Tim, and Carl went to the hotel's restaurant for a bite to eat. Dresher immediately ordered a "Jack Daniels on the rocks." After several drinks, Dresher started to bad-mouth SY in general and several high-level managers in particular. The more Dresher drank, the worse things got. Feeling uncomfortable, Bob finally said: "Carl, take it easy. Remember, you're on duty tomorrow morning."

The following day, Archbishop Makarios arrived in New York and was escorted by motorcade to the Plaza Hotel without incident. Makarios spent the day preparing his UN speech and receiving diplomats and members of the press. The NYFO agents provided protection during this time.

That evening, Bob, Tim, Carl, and another agent reported for the night shift. O'Brien advised the men: "Kenny Harrison from the Chicago Field Office will be joining you later. Kenny will be the assistant detail leader and night shift supervisor. The archbishop's aide says they're in for the night. In case of an unscheduled movement or an emergency, we've got two cars in front of the hotel. The keys are taped to the inside cover of the CP logbook. Carl knows the city, so he'll drive the principal's car. By the radio transmitter, there's a list of important phone numbers. For armament, the suite post has an Uzi [submachine gun] with two extra clips in the attaché case by the door."

After O'Brien finished with the briefing, he and the day shift agents left the hotel. The night shift agents began to rotate through the protective posts. There was no unusual activity until around 1:00 a.m. Tim Robinson was on the security post across from the elevator bank. Bob was in the CP with another agent, while Dresher covered the suite door. Tim radioed that he thought he heard some noise from the stairwell at the end of the hallway. Bob responded from the CP to investigate. Quietly opening the stairwell door, Bob heard the sound of footsteps coming down the stairs from the upper floors of the 19-story hotel. Bob clung to the wall adjacent to the doorway, taking a good defensive position. A short time later, a subject wearing a suit and tie appeared on the stairway landing between floors. A wide smile broke over the individual's face when he saw Bob. "I'm

Kenny Harrison. I thought I'd take the stairs to check on you men. You passed with flying colors."

On Friday, July 19, 1974, the midnight shift was held over to supplement Archbishop Makarios's visit to the United Nations. Carl worked the CP; Tim covered the hotel's lobby, while Bob was selected by Kenny Harrison to ride in the follow-up (FU) car (the security vehicle immediately behind the principal's limousine). The eyes of the world were on Makarios, as he pleaded his case to the Security Council and charged that the coup was organized by the Greek junta (a group of ruling generals). The next day, Turkey entered northern Cyprus and the threat of war between Greece and Turkey became a real possibility.

That weekend, SY received an extended itinerary for the archbishop, which included a visit to Washington, D.C. to meet with Secretary of State Kissinger. Travel to other U.S. cities was also listed. As a result, Joe Morton called the CP to speak with Bob, who was out on post. Carl Dresher relieved Bob, so he could take the call.

Bob picked up the phone and identified himself. The voice on the other end of the line said: "Bob, Joe Morton here. Was that Carl Dresher who answered the phone?"

"Yes, he's working the night shift."

"Is he carrying a gun?" Morton asked nervously.

"Yes."

"He's not supposed to be working protective assignments!"

"Why not?" Bob asked with some trepidation.

"Don't worry; I'll take care of it. The reason I called is to let you know that Scott Walker will be replacing you when you get back to D.C. I need your priority backgrounds as soon as possible."

"Okay, boss, you'll have them soon."

Kenny Harrison was unhappy but powerless to prevent Bob having to leave the detail. On the evening before the trip to Washington, Harrison took Bob into Archbishop Makarios's suite. There, Makarios sat in one of the stately armchairs that adorned his Plaza suite. Although the archbishop's tall black hat and golden staff lay on a nearby table, his posture was as if he was seated at a church altar. Makarios gracefully motioned Bob to come forward. Reaching out for Bob, the archbishop clasped both of his hands around Bob's right hand. In heavily accented English, Makarios solemnly pronounced: "The people of Cyprus thank you for your service during this tragic crisis. With providential guidance, the independence and sovereignty of Cyprus will be returned." An aide then handed Makarios a small box. The archbishop presented it to Bob. Inside was a gold-tone fountain pen with "Archbishop Makarios" deeply engraved on the barrel.

Back in Washington, Bob returned to background investigations and to TDY with the Mrs. Kissinger Protective Detail. On Capitol Hill, the House

Judiciary Committee continued to hold hearings into whether articles of impeachment should be brought against President Nixon. Earlier in the year, the House of Representatives began looking into the matter to determine if the president had been involved in the Watergate coverup and other "high crimes and misdemeanors" perpetrated through the abuse of governmental power.

The Justice Department investigation by Watergate Special Prosecutor Leon Jaworski also moved forward during 1974. In April, Jaworski subpoenaed an additional 64 White House tapes to be used in the upcoming criminal trials of seven White House aides. Instead of surrendering the tapes, President Nixon released edited transcripts. With this action, Nixon claimed that all relevant material in his possession had been turned over to investigators and that the transcripts showed no wrongdoing. Prosecutors, however, maintained that the transcripts were heavily edited and that one important tape was inexplicably missing. Federal Judge John Sirica ordered the president to immediately turn over all of the subpoenaed tapes.

The president again refused, and White House lawyers filed an appeal before the District of Columbia Court of Appeals. Seeing this as a delaying tactic, Jaworski decided to try to bypass the federal court of appeals. Utilizing a special rule in cases that were of "imperative public importance," Jaworski petitioned the U.S. Supreme Court to hear the appeal. In a rare move, the Supreme Court agreed to take the case. On July 25, 1974, the Supreme Court in the case of United States versus Richard M. Nixon upheld by a unanimous decision of eight to zero (with Justice William Rehnquist abstaining—he was a Nixon appointee) the court order requiring the president to surrender all subpoenaed tapes.

With the Supreme Court ruling against him, Nixon was forced to release transcripts of several damaging tapes. One became known as "the smoking gun." It showed that contrary to Nixon's previous assertions, he was involved in the Watergate coverup within days of the burglary. In an especially incriminating passage, Nixon told White House Chief of Staff H.R. Haldeman to have the Central Intelligence Agency tell the FBI to "put the hold" on the investigation due to matters of national security.

Soon after these details were made public, Republican congressional leaders strongly advised Nixon that he should immediately resign the presidency. If not, it was certain that he would be impeached by the full House of Representatives and eventually convicted by the U.S. Senate. On the evening of August 8, 1974, Nixon appeared on national television to announce that he would submit his resignation the following day. The nation was in uncharted waters.

On the morning of Friday, August 9, 1974, Bob drove Mrs. Kissinger to the White House to say her farewell to the president. In the East Room, President Nixon said goodbye to his staff and supporters. Afterwards on the south lawn of the White House, the President and Mrs. Nixon boarded a helicopter for the short flight to Andrews Air Force Base. From there, the Nixons would fly to their home in San Clemente, California.

At 11:35 a.m., President Nixon's resignation letter was delivered to Secretary of State Henry Kissinger (as required by federal law). Thus, Nixon became the first and *only* president in U.S. history to resign the office. At noon, Gerald Ford was sworn in as the 38th president of the United States. Ford, who had become vice president only seven months before due to the Agnew resignation, would now serve the remaining two and a half years of the presidential term.

That night, I commented to Bob how scary things had been. We were both relieved that President Nixon had decided not to stay on and fight impeachment. There had been earlier indications that Nixon would not resign. Washington had also been ripe with fears that the president might become suicidal. Even concerns regarding President Nixon's control of the military and its nuclear arsenal surfaced. To Bob, Nixon's resignation was proof that the American system eventually works—unlike some other countries where coups, dictatorships, and oppression were the norm.

On September 8, 1974, President Ford granted Richard Nixon a "full, free, and absolute pardon." Ford felt the country needed to move on from Watergate. Fearful that a criminal trial of Nixon would prolong the agony for years to come, Ford issued a pardon to bring immediate closure to the affair. President Ford also believed compassionately that Nixon had suffered enough by relinquishing the presidency.

To fill the vice presidential vacancy, Ford nominated former New York Governor Nelson A. Rockefeller. After lengthy congressional hearings, Rockefeller was confirmed by both houses of Congress. He was sworn in as the 41st vice president of the United States on December 19, 1974. For the first and *only* time in U.S. history, neither the president nor the vice president had been *elected* to the office.

Back at WFO and in the field, Bob continued to hone his interview and investigative techniques. In one case, a Foreign Service officer applicant admitted to Bob that she was no longer interested in State. Her family had urged her to keep the decision to herself, so the investigation would continue. It was hoped an appointment would eventually be extended, which would be an honor to add to her résumé. With this admission, her investigation was closed and money and effort were saved.

Bob was also surprised by the disclosure of another Foreign Service candidate. Bob had informed her: "I'll be contacting your current and past places of work, neighbors, friends, bosses, co-workers, schools, and law enforcement agencies. Believe me, I'll find out all that's *legally* relevant to your suitability for a government position and whether you can be entrusted with national security information. If there's anything that you want to add to your security application or offer an explanation about, this is your chance."

The attractive applicant was in her late 20s and an executive assistant to a well-known member of Washington's elite. The applicant directed her eyes away from Bob toward the floor. "I've been doing something naughty," she said. "I've been having a secret affair with my boss. He's married. I've recently broken it off. Serving overseas in the Foreign Service will give me a chance to move on with my life. I hope this doesn't disqualify me."

Bob took his personnel security investigations very seriously. He believed that both the government and the applicant deserved a thorough and accurate report. Bob wanted to be sure that the adjudicators had everything they needed to make informed determinations. He also wanted to work as much protection as possible—for the experience. Thus, he often worked backgrounds on his own time to stay ahead of the workload and to ensure top-quality reports. Frankly, I didn't believe Bob should be donating his time to the government, but I understood Bob's inherent need to do the best he *could do*—no matter what. At least his hard work did not go unnoticed.

Chapter 15

Trips and Transition

SAC Morton rewarded Bob by assigning him some choice out-of-town trips. In late August 1974, Bob and his friend Tim Robinson were among those SY personnel selected for the Kissingers' visit to the U.S. Virgin Islands (V.I.). While traveling to St. Thomas, V.I., the combined advance team of Secret Service and SY agents had a scare when their military aircraft was diverted to Puerto Rico (P.R.). Hurricane Carmen had been forming in the Atlantic and caught the flight as the storm moved toward the west. The propeller-driven plane was strongly buffeted and forced to land at Roosevelt Roads Naval Station (about 50 miles east of San Juan, P.R.). Eventually, Carmen would make its way to the U.S. where it caused $150 million in property damages to central Louisiana.

Departing the plane, the agents were drenched with torrential rain— driven by hurricane-force winds. The electric power had been knocked out to the base; only essential operations had generator backup. Bob and Tim spent the night in the dark at the Visiting Officers Quarters (VOQ). The next day, the advance team flew to Charlotte Amalie on St. Thomas where team personnel transferred to a ferry for the 35-minute boat ride to Caneel Bay Plantation Resort.

Located on neighboring St. John, V.I., the resort featured the crystal-clear water of the Caribbean along with pristine, sandy-white beaches dotted with coconut palms. There, the Kissingers would vacation for an extended Labor Day holiday in the sun.

Staying at the picturesque "Cottage Number Seven" as the guests of financier and conservationist Laurance Rockefeller, the Kissingers enjoyed reading, swimming, and snorkeling. The resort had a retreat-like atmosphere. There were no telephones, televisions, or air conditioning in the cottages. Ventilation was provided by ceiling fans and louvered windows. In order for Secretary Kissinger to stay in contact with Washington, a message center with telephone and teletype had been installed in number seven by the White House Communications Agency (WHCA).

During a visit to St. Thomas, Bob managed to call me from a pay phone. He emphasized how much he missed me. I wished that I were with him too, so we could have enjoyed this romantic paradise together. As I was pregnant and we were expecting our second child in late October, our separation was even more difficult.

Bob also related an incident that had occurred the previous day. Mrs. Kissinger had been snorkeling in the secluded Turtle Bay section of the resort. Bob and another agent were keeping a watchful eye from a small boat nearby. Bob saw what looked like a dozen or so long slender objects—suspended motionless underwater. Sliding over the side of the boat to investigate, Bob suddenly found himself within a school of resting barracuda. Several were a couple of feet long. Bob carefully backed away from the powerful jaws and razor-sharp teeth of the pike-like fish and retreated into the safety of the boat. He suggested that Mrs. Kissinger take a break on the beach until the barracuda left the area. Bob didn't believe in taking any chances. Concerned, I asked Bob how close he had come to the fish. "Close enough to count their teeth" was his answer.

The fall and winter of 1974 were a blur to Bob and me. SY protective assignments multiplied. Some of this was due to the opening of the 29th Session of the United Nations General Assembly (UNGA) in New York, and some was due to increasing travel by Mrs. Kissinger—both foreign and domestic.

As the foreign studies director for former New York Governor Nelson Rockefeller's Commission on Critical Choices for America, Mrs. Kissinger frequently commuted to New York. The offices of the commission were located in Midtown Manhattan. Bob would often be selected to ride on the flight deck with the pilot and co-pilot during the commercial flights to and from New York. An armed federal agent in the cockpit could serve as a last line of defense against any skyjacking attempt.

Overseas, Mrs. Kissinger accompanied her husband on some of his many diplomatic missions. Of the foreign trips Bob worked, several were most memorable. The Kissingers' October 1974 visit to the former Soviet Union (now Commonwealth of Independent States) had many unusual moments. At the time, the Soviet Union and the United States were still very much engaged in the Cold War. Soviet security forces harassed the USSS and SY advance teams on a number of occasions.

The intrigue began for Bob when he first arrived in Moscow and attempted to pass through immigration and customs. The Soviet official carefully inspected Bob's U.S. Diplomatic Passport. Then, the officer checked Bob's passport with a list of Americans arriving to advance Secretary Kissinger's forthcoming visit. A moment later, the immigration officer looked up at Bob and barked, "Your name is not on the list." Handing Bob's passport back, the official firmly stated, "You are not permitted to enter the Soviet Union."

Bob protested, "I have a diplomatic passport with valid visa issued by your embassy in Washington."

The officer called to a supervisor, who was standing nearby. "Is there a problem?" asked the supervisor in accented English.

"He is not on the official list for the Kissinger delegation," replied the immigrations officer.

The supervisor looked sternly at Bob: "Come with me. There will have to be an inquiry."

An SY agent in line behind Bob promised to send assistance after that agent cleared immigration and customs. The party was being met by the State Department assistant regional security officer (RSO). He would be sent to help Bob.

The supervisor escorted Bob to the immigration office. There, the official—with Bob's passport in one hand and a master list in the other—made his own check. Waving the list in front of Bob, the officer taunted: "This is very serious. You are not on the official list agreed between your country and the Ministry of Foreign Affairs."

Bob responded, "I have a diplomatic passport with a visa stamped by the Soviet Embassy in Washington authorizing my visit."

The official waved the list again as he reiterated: "You are not on the list. You do not have permission to enter the Soviet Union."

"Let me see the list," Bob said in an assertive tone. The officer reluctantly handed the document to Bob. On the letterhead of the Soviet foreign ministry was a multiple-page list. A column of names in English characters—arranged in alphabetical order—ran down the left side of the pages. Typed in Russian to the right of each name were what looked like governmental affiliations. Bob could not find his name in the R's. Turning back to the first page, he began to peruse the list. A name caught Bob's eye in the J's. "Look here," Bob stated emphatically as he pointed to the name. "There's a Robert *Jitter* listed. And that probably says state security. It's a typing error. It's supposed to be me, Robert Ritter."

The official snatched the list back from Bob and took a quick look. Then to Bob's astonishment, the official remarked, "No, that's Robert *Jitter*."

"We don't have a Robert Jitter. There is no *Robert Jitter*! Someone made a mistake."

The officer sat down at his desk and began to dial the telephone. "I will have to consult the Ministry of Foreign Affairs." For about 10 minutes, the immigration supervisor navigated his way through a series of telephone conversations. As the official spoke in Russian, Bob had no idea how things were going.

In the meantime, the assistant RSO arrived at the office. After the two Americans introduced themselves, Bob recapped the situation. The assistant RSO immediately turned to the immigration official and stated in a resolute voice: "I am from the U.S. Embassy. Why is this American diplomat being detained?"

The supervisor answered: "He is not on the official entry list. I am now awaiting a call from the Ministry of Foreign Affairs to determine his fate."

The assistant RSO spoke with increasing firmness: "I am familiar with the list submitted to the Soviet Embassy in Washington. Mr. Ritter was on that list and was issued an entry visa for this trip. Mr. Ritter needs to be cleared immediately. He is an *official* guest of your country."

The immigration supervisor replied in a conciliatory tone: "Please sit down. The ministry will be calling back soon."

"Mr. Ritter has proper credentials. This is becoming more than an inconvenience. You need to clear him now or a protest *may* be lodged."

Just then, the phone on the official's desk rang, interrupting the stalemate between East and West. Listening attentively to the party on the other end of the phone, the immigration supervisor only uttered a few words in Russian from time to time. Apparently, the other party was doing most of the talking. Completing the call, the officer put down the receiver, turned to the two Americans, and advised: "Okay, no problem. The ministry requires another paper [official document] to be issued to Mr. Jitter. Then, he will be cleared for entry."

Moving to an old manual typewriter that was set up in a corner of the office, the supervisor rolled a sheet of government stationery into the carriage. Striking the keys in two-finger fashion, the official took about five minutes to complete the paper. He then removed the document, signed it, and stamped it with an official seal. He folded the sheet and placed it inside Bob's passport. After handing the passport to Bob, the immigration supervisor cautioned both Americans: "Mr. *Jitter* must keep this paper with his passport until he departs the Soviet Union. The paper will be surrendered upon exit." With a sly grin, the immigration officer peered at Bob and proclaimed: "You may now proceed to customs. Welcome to the U.S.S.R."

On the way to the customs area, the assistant RSO looked over the document Bob was being required to carry. "What does it say?" Bob asked.

"Something about your passport being in error and that your true name is Robert Jitter."

"You're kidding!"

"No, the Russians aren't going to admit they made a mistake. And they might have done it on purpose to irritate us," remarked the assistant RSO.

Whether it was Soviet bureaucratic bungling or KGB (U.S.S.R. state security) gamesmanship, Bob had been officially renamed. For hotel and travel accommodations, on guest lists, at meetings, and the like, Bob was both listed and addressed by the Soviets as Robert *Jitter*—for the entire visit.

In those days, official visitors to the U.S.S.R. were tightly controlled. Accommodations were handled by the Ministry of Foreign Affairs, and the Seventh Directorate of the KGB closely monitored the movements of official guests. The Kissinger advance team was assigned rooms at the Sovietskaya, the official hotel of the Soviet Union. Located in the northern section of Moscow, the hotel was about a 10-minute drive to the Kremlin (seat of government). The Sovietskaya was erected in 1952 during the regime of Josef Stalin. Designed in a grand empire style, the hotel featured elegant-crystal chandeliers—suspended from high ceilings that were supported by ornate-marble columns.

After checking into the Sovietskaya, the SY agents went to their rooms to unpack. It was then they discovered that a number of personal belongings were missing. Wool socks, casual jeans, athletic shoes, and logo T-shirts had been removed from their luggage. Embassy personnel suspected that the items had been stolen at the Moscow airport—by either airline employees or the KGB. A thriving Soviet black market existed on such Western goods.

For the missing socks, an emergency call was made to Bill Decourcy's office in D.C. Bill arranged for the purchase of replacements and shipped them to the U.S. Embassy in Moscow via diplomatic pouch and courier. Until the articles arrived, several SY agents were seen walking around in shoes without socks during the cold Russian winter.

One of the SY agents had a problem of another sort. The agent liked to put down a drink or two and had packed a bottle of his favorite Scotch whiskey for the trip. He had wrapped the bottle inside a wool overcoat for protection. All of a sudden, Bob heard a good amount of swearing—coming from the room across the hall.

Bob quickly responded to find the agent standing over one of his suitcases and cursing loudly in disgust. The agent's overcoat was littered with shattered glass. Bob smelled the strong aroma of Scotch. The Scottish wool fabric of the imported overcoat had soaked up the Scotch whiskey like a thirsty sponge. The coat now featured an unwanted characteristic of another famous Scottish export.

Unfortunately, dry cleaning the expensive overcoat was not viable in the Soviet Union. The agent was warned it could take several weeks or more for the article to be cleaned and then it might come back filled with holes. For the visit, the agent could only smother himself with cologne in an attempt to mask the smell of the aged Scotch that permeated his outer garment and other clothes.

For Mrs. Kissinger's visit to the Soviet Union, the SY agents coordinated their efforts with Ralph Basham, the USSS lead advance agent. Whenever Mrs. Kissinger was with her husband, she fell under the Secret Service "protective umbrella." During those times, SY agents would interface with the USSS detail. The senior SY agent would work close proximity to Mrs. Kissinger, while the remaining SY agents would add an additional layer of protection outside the USSS protective perimeter.

A native of Owensboro, Kentucky, Basham was a friendly and extremely capable agent. He always took the time and effort to fully include and inform SY in all aspects of an advance. In fact, the entire USSS secretary of state detail was well run and functioned with a high degree of competence. Bob told me on several occasions how lucky he was to be able to work with the Secret Service agents and to learn firsthand the intricacies of executive protection. For Bob, it was a pleasurable and enjoyable experience—despite the long hours and out-of-town travel. For me, it became a growing burden, as I had to assume a larger portion of the family duties—necessitated by Bob's increasing absence.

The morning after the SY advance team arrived at the Sovietskaya, Bob ran into Agent Basham in the lobby of the hotel. Basham flashed a smile at Bob and greeted him with a loud, "Good morning, Agent *Jitter*."

"So, you heard," Bob replied.

"Yes, and I also heard you think your room is bugged."

"Most definitely," Bob confirmed. "Last night, another agent came to my door, and we were talking quietly. Next, we hear this crackle come from the TV set in my room. Like someone was turning up a scratchy volume control. The odd thing about it: The set was turned off, and I had unplugged it when I moved in."

"That seals it for me," Basham declared. "I'm going to ask the foreign ministry to switch us to the Hotel Rossiya. It's a modern tourist hotel and not as gloomy as this place. My guys have been experiencing problems too. One found some money in his room; another received calls from a woman inviting him to the bar for a drink. After he hung up on her several times, a man called and told the same guy he looked 'cute' and asked if they could get together. They think they can play with us. This crap has got to stop."

For the upcoming trip, the Soviet government offered Mrs. Kissinger an itinerary that included visits to Soviet cultural attractions. These movements were scheduled to coincide with the strategic arms limitation talks (SALT) that would be held in Moscow between Secretary Kissinger and high-ranking Soviet officials. Since Mrs. Kissinger would be visiting these sites without her husband, SY would be solely responsible for coordination of the U.S. advance preparations with Soviet authorities. One of the visits planned by the Soviets for Mrs. Kissinger was a trip to the city of Leningrad.

The city was founded in 1703 by Czar Peter the Great, who originally named it Saint Petersburg—after his patron saint. At the start of World War I, St. Petersburg was renamed Petrograd. With the death of Vladimir Lenin in 1924, Petrograd was changed to Leningrad in honor of the leader of the 1917 Russian Revolution and the first head of state of the Soviet Union. With the dissolution of the Soviet Union in 1991, the city changed its name back to St. Petersburg.

Situated at the mouth of the Neva River, Leningrad was built upon numerous islands that adjoin the Baltic Sea. Located about 400 miles north of Moscow, Leningrad was the Russian capital for most of the imperial period. The major cultural attractions are the State Hermitage Museum, the many palaces of the czars (former emperors of Russia), and other historical sites. The Winter Palace (former official residence of the Russian czars) and other buildings house the State Hermitage Museum. This impressive collection contains over three million artifacts.

SY Agent Greg Bujac, with Bob assisting, was selected to conduct the Leningrad advance. Greg was from Bowie, Maryland and had worked in the State Department communications section before coming to the Office of Security. Like Bob, Greg performed his duties in a no-nonsense manner.

As domestic flights within the Soviet Union were not up to international standards—cabins were not pressurized, and maintenance concerns were an issue—Greg and Bob were booked on the historic *Red Arrow*, the overnight train to Leningrad. The train departed Moscow's Leningrad Station each night at 11:55 p.m., arriving in Leningrad at 7:55 a.m. the following morning.

Greg and Bob arrived at Lenigradsky Vokzal (Leningrad Station). The classically designed structure was built in the mid-1800s. It featured pilasters (supporting columns that project out from exterior walls), arch-styled windows, and a clock tower. The two agents moved to the platform area where a conductor checked tickets and directed the duo to one of the dark-red sleeper cars of the *Krasnya Strela* (*Red Arrow*).

Boarding the train, Bob and Greg immediately smelled the odor of burning charcoal emanating from the large copper samovar (urn to heat water) located at the end of the car. After making some cups of tea, the men located their compartment and sat down on the berths, which had already been made-up for sleeping. The two enjoyed the hot beverage, while they discussed some of the *unclassified* aspects of the Leningrad advance. Soon, the train pulled out of the station. The sleeper car rolled and pitched as the train was brought up to speed. The clack of the wheels resonated into the compartment, while the train whizzed by the snowy Russian countryside.

"What do you say, Bob? Let's hit the sack. We've got a long day ahead of us."

"I'm for that," Bob agreed.

Both travelers stripped down to their underwear. Greg turned off the lights. Our boys crawled into the berths and pulled up their covers. About five minutes later, there was a knock on the compartment door. "I'll get it," Greg bellowed. Sliding out of bed, Greg retrieved his glasses, which lay nearby. He cracked the door open and was surprised by a beautiful, young blonde, who tried to force her way into the compartment. "Hold it, sister," Greg commanded as he braced the door. "This compartment is occupied."

Pushing a ticket through the door opening, the blonde responded in English: "I have a ticket. Please let me in."

"No, we have the tickets for all the berths. You need to see the conductor. Good night," Greg told the blonde as he pushed the door closed and relocked it. Greg turned toward Bob and stated emphatically: "We're both married. She's not spending the night in here!"

About five minutes later, there was another knock at the door. This time, Greg didn't move from his berth but shouted out, with some annoyance, "Who's there?"

A voice answered: "Ingrid Andersen. The conductor said the train is full. Please let me in."

"No, we bought tickets for all four of the berths, so we'd have some privacy," Greg replied. "The conductor checked our tickets earlier. Look, we need to get some sleep."

Several minutes later, the door to the compartment flew open. The conductor had used his passkey to unlock the door. The attractive blonde rushed into the compartment, carrying an overnight bag in one hand and a ticket in the other. Greg and Bob jumped out of the berths and put their trousers on.

"Wait a minute," Greg asserted. "This isn't right." Greg grabbed his and Bob's tickets and snatched the ticket from the blonde's hand. Greg moved to the corridor of the train to resolve the matter with the conductor.

In the meantime, the statuesque blonde advanced toward Bob. In a soft, sensuous voice she pleaded: "Please let me stay with you. I'm alone and frightened." She then retrieved a passport from her coat pocket and showed it to Bob. "It's okay," the blonde added. "I'm not Russian; I'm Swedish. I'm traveling back to Stockholm." Bob understood the assertion since U.S. personnel were not permitted to fraternize with Soviet nationals.

"I'm sorry," Bob replied. "You can't stay here."

"Let me stay with you—*please*." Shaking his head, Bob escorted the blonde outside to the corridor where Greg was making his case.

The conductor understood some English but seemed reluctant to become involved. Pointing to the ticket in question, Greg reiterated to the conductor: "This lady's ticket is for another compartment. Will you please help her?" The conductor finally took the blonde's ticket, examined it, and grumbled something in Russian. He then motioned to the blonde. With a look of dejection, the attractive blond stranger followed the conductor down the corridor of the train. Bob and Greg returned to their berths where they slept uninterrupted for the remainder of the night.

The next morning, they were met at the train station by the security officer from the U.S. Consulate General, which opened in Leningrad in 1973. Consulates foster trade and handle the interests of visiting Americans. They are located in popular tourist cities and cities of commerce. While there might be several U.S. consulates in a foreign country, there will be only one U.S. Embassy. The embassy will be located in the foreign nation's capital. The embassy provides a full-range of administrative services and is led by an ambassador, who serves as the official U.S. representative to the foreign government.

At the Leningrad Consulate, Bob and Greg were ushered into a "safe room" where they would brief the consul general on Mrs. Kissinger's upcoming visit. Safe rooms in U.S. embassies and consulates are really rooms within a room. They are designed to protect conversations from eavesdropping. The interior walls, floor, and ceiling of the outer room are removed to eliminate hiding places for listening devices. The inner room is constructed entirely of plexiglass. This allows one to easily see that no "bugs" have been inserted into either of the rooms. The plastic enclosure also acts as a sound attenuator. Sound masking and other techniques are also used to protect against audio surveillance.

Security advances were completed and the Kissingers arrived in Moscow. While Secretary Kissinger hammered away at SALT and the proposed Vladivostok Summit between President Ford and Secretary General Brezhnev, Mrs. Kissinger took VIP tours hosted by the Soviet government. She visited the cathedrals and palaces of the Kremlin (old citadel of the city), the Bolshoi Ballet, Red Square and Lenin's Tomb, the czar's bell and cannon, and other famous sites.

In Leningrad, Mrs. Kissinger visited the State Hermitage Museum and the palaces of the czars. Mrs. Kissinger was told at the Hermitage; if she spent one minute at each exhibit it would take 11 years to complete the tour. Fortunately for Bob and the other SY agents, Mrs. Kissinger opted for an abbreviated visit. She only asked to see some of the magnificent paintings along with Fabergé eggs and the imperial crown jewels.

When I heard all that Bob was able to see, I was a bit envious and really wished that I could have been there with him. I knew Bob was enjoying the sightseeing aspect of his work. In college, he had selected courses in the humanities and art for electives. It was certainly a golden opportunity to see things that the rest of us can only dream about.

With the Kissingers departure from the Soviet Union, the U.S. Embassy held a "wheels up" party at the restaurant/bar atop the Rossiya Hotel in Moscow. Greg Bujac and Bob stopped by to give thanks to all who had assisted with the visit. The embassy also invited the Soviet officials who had hosted the trip. One of the Soviets attending was a Russian KGB colonel, whom Bob and Greg had met during the visit.

The SY agents had been told by their Soviet counterparts that the colonel neither understood nor spoke any English. Throughout the trip, Bob and Greg had to use an interpreter to converse with the colonel. Now, he was bellied up to the bar and enjoying straight double shots of Stolichnaya vodka. When he saw Bob and Greg, the colonel cheerily called out: "Hello, my American friends. Please come and enjoy some good Russian vodka with me."

Bob responded with a grin, "Colonel, I don't know who your English teacher is, but they sure have done a good job with you in only a couple of days."

Greg added: "Yeah, colonel, I guess we don't need to find an interpreter. Thanks for the help you gave us."

The colonel's face filled with mirth as he let out a hearty laugh. "You two are funny guys. And Mr. *Jitter* is a good sport. I like Americans. It was my pleasure to help you." Then, the KGB colonel pointed to the upper-level mezzanine of the room. "Why didn't you like my sweetie?" he asked. Leaning over the railing was the beautiful blond stranger, who had tried to spend the night with Bob and Greg onboard the *Red Arrow*. She smiled and waved to our boys.

"Don't blame her, colonel," Bob replied. "We're both happily married and love our wives."

"And we're not that lucky—for it not to have been a setup," added Greg.

From Moscow, the Kissingers traveled to India. Bob leapfrogged to Tehran, Iran. In 1974, Iran was ruled by Shah Mohammed Reza Pahlavi (Shah of Iran). SAVAK, the Iranian secret police, controlled internal security. Former CIA Director Richard Helms was the U.S. ambassador to Iran. U.S. arms sales to Iran totaled in the billions of dollars. A large American advisory group trained the Iranian military in the use and maintenance of the weapons.

For a short while, all thoughts of the coming Kissinger visit were forgotten when Bob arrived at the U.S. Embassy and was handed a cablegram sent by Bill Decourcy:

"PLEASE INFORM SA ROBERT RITTER, SY, THAT HE IS THE FATHER OF A SON BORN 10:43 P.M. WEDNESDAY, 10/30/74. MOTHER AND SON ARE EXCELLENT. SON WEIGHED 9.6 POUNDS."

Bob had hoped to get home before our second child was born. Of course, it didn't work out that way. Bob celebrated the good news with Tim Robinson, Ralph Basham and the other agents on the Iranian advance. Then, it was back to business and thoughts of terrorism.

In spite of the iron hand of SAVAK, there was a guerilla movement operating in Iran that wanted to overthrow the shah and drive out the U.S. presence. Traveling in Iran was not without risk—if you were an American official. Former U.S. Ambassador Douglas MacArthur II and his wife escaped a kidnapping attempt in 1971. Four armed men stopped the ambassador's car and attempted to break out the windows with an ax. The ambassador's driver managed to pull away from the attackers. In 1972, a U.S. Air Force brigadier general was seriously wounded when he drove over a bomb, and in 1973 a U.S. Army lieutenant colonel was assassinated while traveling to work.

Trying not to become a target of opportunity, Bob sought authorization to rent a foreign car for his and Tim's travel to Isfahan, Shiraz, and Persepolis for the SY advance. When that request was turned down as being too costly, Bob asked for a nondescript car from the embassy motor pool.

The following morning, an embassy car with driver arrived at Bob and Tim's hotel. The vehicle was a late model four-door Chevrolet sedan, black in color. The driver wore black pants, a white shirt with black tie, and a black cap. Not only was the vehicle displaying diplomatic license plates, an American flag was flying from the right front fender! Tim Robinson asked the embassy driver, an English-speaking Iranian national, "Don't you have something a little less official looking?"

"No, all embassy cars the same," answered the driver.

"Well, please take the flag down," Tim directed. "We're trying not to draw attention to ourselves."

The driver moved close to Tim and stated in a low voice, "I understand— you CIA."

"No, no, no!" Tim burst out. "We're just helping with the Kissingers' visit."

While the embassy driver removed the American flag, Bob jumped behind the wheel. Tim slid in the right front seat and rode "shotgun." Bob called out to the driver: "Get in the back; I'm driving. You're going to see what it's like to be chauffeured around." As a driver for Mrs. Kissinger, Bob had received specialized training in breaking blockades and other scenarios regarding attacks on motor vehicles by terrorists. If something was going to happen, Bob didn't want to trust his and Tim's life to a motor pool driver.

Bob and Tim drove south from Tehran through the arid Iranian desert— with the embassy driver serving as guide and translator. Over 200 miles later, they pulled into the Iranian city of Isfahan. The city had its origins thousands of years ago and had been the capital of Persia during the 16th century. Isfahan featured many marvelous sites of Islamic architecture, culture, and history. Its palaces, mosques, gardens, fountains, and bridges reflected the ancient Persian expression: "Esfahan nesf-e Jahan" (Isfahan is half the world).

The U.S. Embassy had reserved a room for Bob and Tim at an Isfahan hotel. The hotel had quite an unusual feature. Like something out of *Arabian Nights*, the entry doors to the guest rooms were arch shaped with an open area both above and below the door. The distance between the floor and the bottom of the door was several feet. This allowed anyone so inclined to gain entry into the room by simply crawling under the door. Our boys were a bit uncomfortable upon retiring for the evening.

The night passed without incident, and the next morning Bob was on his way to Shiraz and Persepolis to conduct the advance along with USSS

Agent Ralph Basham. Persepolis was the center of the Persian Empire from about 518 B.C. to 330 B.C. when the city was plundered and burned by Alexander the Great. Eventually, Persepolis was abandoned. Its ruins were first studied in the 1930s when archaeologists from the University of Chicago began excavations. Among the remains were massive stone columns and buildings. The buildings, terraces, gates, and walls featured bas-reliefs and colossuses.

At the conclusion of the Persepolis visit, Bob was able to catch a ride back to Tehran with Ralph Basham via an Imperial Iranian Air Force helicopter. This would save many hours of driving through desolate and possibly dangerous territory.

A Secret Service agent, who had been assisting in the southern Iranian advance, also wanted to take the chopper rather than ride in an embassy car the almost 450 miles to Tehran. On his way to Persepolis from Shiraz, the agent radioed Basham to hold the aircraft. Ralph smiled at Bob and playfully said, "Watch this." Basham transmitted back: "The chopper captain wants to leave immediately. What's your ETA?"

"Ralph, I should be there in about 15. Please tell him to wait!"

"Standby, I'll talk with the captain." A minute later Ralph transmitted again: "You better tell your driver to pick it up, son. I could only get the captain to wait another five minutes. He says there's a dust storm brewing over the desert, and we'll have to leave in five—with or without you."

"Ralph, we're hitting top end now! Stall 'em!"

Holding back his laughter, Basham answered: "I'll try, partner. But I don't control the Iranian air force."

Just then, Bob and Ralph saw a cloud of dust appear on the road—far off in the distance. "That must be him," Bob said to Ralph.

The five minutes expired and like clockwork, Basham raised the radio to mouth level. To simulate a message from an airborne helicopter, he continuously squeezed the transmitter key on and off while talking. Basham radioed that he couldn't hold the chopper any longer and that he and Bob were en route to Tehran.

"Ralph, you're breaking up. Don't leave me! Don't leave me!" boomed from out of Basham's radio.

The agent finally arrived and found the helicopter still on the ground with Ralph, Bob, and the Iranian flight crew beaming with laughter. "Damn it, Ralph! You almost gave me a heart attack!" yelled the agent—still frantic with worry.

After the Iranian trip, Bob was able to come home for a while. It was good to have him back. Rejoicing in the recent arrival of our son, Robert Jr., we felt truly blessed to have both a boy and a girl. Providing for another child would bring new challenges and sacrifices. To meet the obligations of parenthood, our maturity continued to grow. We were now a family of four.

Back at the office in addition to backgrounds and being a regular temp with the Mrs. K. detail, Bob was now being assigned passport and visa fraud investigations. Being selected to conduct criminal investigations was advancement for Bob. He dove back into his investigations, but soon Bob was needed for yet another out-of-town, protective assignment. He headed to New York with Tim Robinson to provide protection for Imelda Marcos.

For the 1974 United Nations General Assembly, the secretary of state designated a number of attendees as "official guests" to the U.S. These high-profile dignitaries did not qualify for statutory USSS protection. One was Imelda Marcos, the wife of Philippine President Ferdinand Marcos. As first lady of the Philippines, Mrs. Marcos had survived an assassination attempt carried out by Carlito Dimailig, a 27-year-old geodetic engineer. The incident took place on December 7, 1972, and was caught "live" on Filipino television.

Mrs. Marcos was presenting beautification awards during a ceremony in Manila. As one group of recipients was leaving the presentation area, Dimailig came up on stage and approached Mrs. Marcos. Filipinos watched in horror as the would-be assassin pulled a 12-inch bolo knife from his sleeve and began to slash at Mrs. Marcos. She turned and put her arms up to block the blows—then collapsed to the stage. Agents of the Presidential Security Force rushed to her aid, fatally shooting Dimailig. Mrs. Marcos was evacuated by helicopter. At the hospital, she received 75 stitches to her right arm.

In November of 1974, Mrs. Marcos was officially traveling to New York for the UNGA and to open the new Philippine Center, which was located at 556 Fifth Avenue in Manhattan. This visit presented some memorable moments for the agents of SY.

For the Marcos arrival at JFK airport, Tim Robinson was the "baggage agent." His duties included securing Mrs. Marcos's luggage and transporting it to the Carlyle Hotel where the Marcos party would be staying. Located on the Upper East Side of Manhattan, the art deco designed Carlyle dates back to 1930. It's New York's posh hotel for the world's elite.

Assigned to the follow-up car, Bob stood on the tarmac with Tim as the Philippine Air Force (PAF) plane pulled to its parking point and the engines were shut down. Stairs were pulled to the aircraft, and its door opened. A pair of PAF airmen scrambled off and proceeded to open compartments in the underbelly of the plane in order to offload Mrs. Marcos's luggage. Tim walked over to inform them that a station wagon was standing by for the luggage transport. One of the airmen looked over at the station wagon and asked, "Is that the only vehicle you have for baggage?"

"Yes," Tim replied in a worried tone.

The airman chuckled as he told Tim, "The first lady has 75 pieces of luggage that need to go to the Carlyle."

"What!" Tim cried out in disbelief.

"You're lucky," stated the airman. "She's traveling with 150 pieces. Half of them are empty for any purchases she might make. We'll keep them on board until she needs them." Tim had to go back to the terminal and rent a box truck for the transport.

The second surprise to the SY detail came with Mrs. Marcos's schedule. Bob, Tim, and several other SY agents were assigned to the night shift; most protective personnel were scheduled for the day shift, which included two NYPD "Bossy" detectives. The "skeleton" night shift arrived at 8:00 p.m. to find the day crew sitting around bored and restless. "What did you guys do today?" Bob asked.

"Nothing," answered the detail leader. "We sat here all day. She must be recovering from her travel. There's nothing on her schedule. Looks like you men will have a quiet night."

About 30 minutes after the day shift left, an aide to Mrs. Marcos appeared from within the suite with a list of expected guests. Included were such notable names as pianist Van Cliburn and artist Andy Warhol. The guests arrived, and at about 10:45 p.m. the aide returned to announce, "Mrs. Marcos and her guests will be going out for the evening."

Bob was on the front door post and thought the aide was joking. Realizing the aide was serious, Bob advised: "We'll want to have an agent advance the locations. Can you please tell us where we'll be going?"

"Copacabana, Delmonico's, '21' Club, and possibly other nightspots."

The SY detail quickly made arrangements for the unscheduled movements. Later that night and into the next day, Mrs. Marcos and her guests visited several New York clubs—ending up at the '21' Club. There, Mrs. Marcos, who had a lovely voice, sang until the wee hours of the morning—accompanied by Van Cliburn on piano. Mrs. Marcos arrived back at the Carlyle at 6:30 a.m.

The day shift checked in at 7:45 a.m., and the detail leader joked, "How much sleep did you guys get last night?"

The night shift supervisor answered: "None! We just got back. We were out all night."

The detail leader laughed and said, "Yeah, right."

The next day was almost an exact repeat. Mrs. Marcos slept and stayed in her suite during the day. Guests arrived between 9:00 p.m. and 10:00 p.m. Then Mrs. Marcos and her guests would spend all night on the town. The night supervisor finally convinced the detail leader that it wasn't a joke, and shift personnel were adjusted to Mrs. Marcos's New York lifestyle.

There was some excitement during the visit. On Monday afternoon, November 18, 1974, the phone in Bob and Tim's hotel room rang. It was the detail leader instructing them to report to the CP immediately. There,

Bob, Tim, and the rest of the detail were briefed on an incident that had just occurred in Washington, D.C.

Napoleon Lechoco, a Philippine émigré to the U.S., had taken over the Philippine chancery (office building) at 1617 Massachusetts Avenue, NW. Lechoco was a leader of the Filipino community in the D.C. Metropolitan Area. As a ploy, he had made an appointment with the Philippine ambassador, Eduardo Romualdez. Once Lechoco gained access to the ambassador's office, he pulled a handgun from a briefcase. In the commotion, an economic attaché was shot and presumed dead. Lechoco then handcuffed Ambassador Romualdez—holding him hostage at gunpoint.

In New York, the night shift agents were being called in early to provide additional security for Mrs. Marcos in case there was a wider plot. And since the Philippine ambassador had been seized and the chancery evacuated, the U.S. Department of State had been asked by the FBI to establish contact with the Philippine government. Because Bob had been a police officer in D.C. and was familiar with the area, he was asked to serve as liaison between SY and Mrs. Marcos's security aide.

Authorities in D.C. talked with Lechoco via telephone for the purpose of negotiating the subject's surrender and the safe release of the ambassador. In New York, Bob briefed the security aide and Mrs. Marcos on the situation. Mrs. Marcos immediately expressed her deep concern for Ambassador Romualdez, who was also Mrs. Marcos's uncle.

As the evening progressed, it was learned that Lechoco and his wife had immigrated to the U.S. in 1972—without their children. In October 1974, six of the seven Lechoco children were permitted to leave the Philippines to rejoin their parents, who resided in Oxon Hill, Maryland. Mr. Lechoco was under the impression that his oldest child, a 17-year-old son, was being detained in the Philippines. Thus, Lechoco demanded that his son be allowed to leave the Philippines, so he could travel to the U.S.

Although the press reported that President Marcos had played the major role for the Philippine government during the crisis, Bob knew firsthand that Mrs. Marcos had actually made the decisions from New York. Mrs. Marcos had dispatched Philippine diplomats from New York to Washington to standby on the scene. She also directed her youngest brother, Benjamin Romualdez, to travel from Manila to Washington to assist in the negotiations—in case the incident became drawn out.

Later that night, however, Mrs. Marcos promised the following: If Lechoco would give himself up and release the ambassador unharmed, Lechoco's son would be granted an immediate exit visa and put on the next flight to the United States.

In the early morning hours of Tuesday, November 19, Lechoco threw his gun out a second-floor window of the four-story brick building nestled along Washington's Embassy Row. Lechoco and Ambassador Romualdez appeared moments later. In a fortunate surprise, they were followed by Mario Lagdemeo—the economic attaché who was thought to have been killed. He had only received a flesh wound and had feigned death during the ordeal. Mrs. Marcos was overjoyed with the good news.

Lechoco was taken into custody by the FBI and sent to St. Elizabeths Hospital for a psychiatric evaluation. Found competent to stand trial, Lechoco was convicted in 1975 of kidnapping and sentenced to 10 years in prison. Subsequently, Lechoco won an appeal for a new trial. In 1977, he was acquitted by a jury that found him "not guilty by reason of insanity." Released unconditionally, Lechoco became a free man.

Mrs. Marcos and her security aide were grateful for the help given by Bob during the incident. To show thanks, the security aide invited Bob into one of the outer rooms of the Marcos suite. Mrs. Marcos adored fresh-cut flowers. The room was literally filled with floral arrangements sent by Mrs. Marcos's many personal and official friends. The aide invited Bob to select an arrangement to give to me. Bob declined the gracious offer by saying: "Thanks very much. But I'm from out of town. So I really couldn't get them home to her."

"Then pick out one of the vases for your wife," the aide suggested.

Bob looked around the room and saw a metal vase in the corner. "Okay, thanks. I'll take that metal one. I'd be afraid the ceramic and crystal ones might break in my suitcase."

The aide went to the vase, removed the flowers, and emptied the water into another container. "Here you go, Mr. Bob—with our thanks."

Bob took the vase to his hotel room and placed it in one of his suitcases—not thinking much more about it. The next morning after being relieved from duty, Bob got some breakfast and then went to bed. Several hours later, he's awakened from a sound sleep by some furious pounding on his room door. Bob opened the door and found the Philippine security aide with a very worried look on his face.

"Mr. Bob, I'm sorry, but I need the vase back! I found out it was an official state gift to the first lady from the Saudi Arabian ambassador to the U.N. It's handcrafted from *solid silver* by artisans to the royal family! The ambassador mentioned it in a phone call to the first lady. The ambassador is coming for lunch. We need the vase for the table setting."

"Sure, I understand. Let me get it."

"Mr. Bob, I'm sorry about this. With all the flower arrangements arriving daily for the first lady, the significance of this one was not caught by our staff. Of course, you're welcome to pick another vase for your wife." When Bob returned home after his detail assignment, he told the story, as he presented me a heavy, cut-crystal vase. I had a good laugh.

It was now December 1974. Bob was waiting to hear from the Secret Service regarding his agent application. Bob had submitted the necessary paperwork, been fingerprinted, passed a physical, and scored in the 90th percentile in the Treasury Enforcement Agent Exam. In addition, we both had been interviewed at USSS Headquarters.

In somewhat of a surprise, Bob received a call from the U.S. Customs Service. Customs offered Bob an agent position in their Baltimore Field Office—starting as a GS-7. They projected that Bob would work in Baltimore for several years and then be transferred to Customs Headquarters in D.C. It sounded like Bob was being guaranteed at least five years in the Baltimore-Washington area and being penciled in for the "fast track." Bob thanked them for the offer. Saying he would keep Customs in mind, Bob related that he hoped to be hired by the Secret Service.

After the call, I remarked to Bob: "You didn't apply to Customs. How could they offer you a position?"

"They said I was one of the highest-rated applicants on the Civil Service Commission register for the TEA position. They had gotten a copy of my SF-171 [federal job application] and also knew that I had a current top-secret clearance."

In another surprise several days later, Bob was contacted by the Bureau of Alcohol, Tobacco, and Firearms (ATF) and was offered an agent position. ATF told Bob he would be sent to the next Treasury Agent class and assigned to a field office *after* graduation—probably Philadelphia. The ATF recruitment officer emphasized that ATF would be picking up our moving expenses.

Bob expressed to me with some frustration: "This is just great. I'm hearing from everyone except the Secret Service—the only agency I really applied to and want."

Finally, Bob got the call he was waiting for: "Mr. Ritter, I'm with Secret Service Personnel Division in Washington. I have some good news for you. We're offering you an entry level GS-5 special agent position with our Pittsburgh Field Office. How does that sound?"

A bit shocked, Bob replied, "Pittsburgh—I had applied for the Washington Field Office."

"I know but that's where we have an opening. It's also a *very* good office to start in. The SAIC there is Jim D'Amelio. He's one of our best, and you couldn't have a better boss to learn from."

"Ma'am, please don't get me wrong. I truly appreciate being offered a position with the Secret Service. It's what I really have wanted for a long time. The problem is my wife is a schoolteacher and has a contract with Prince George's County Schools. She started her second year in September. She knows this school system and is making good money that we need to support our family. It's going to be hard for me to ask her to quit her job, pack up and move to Pittsburgh, and then try to find a teaching position in the middle of the school year. Also, I had hoped with my experience to start out at a GS-7. In fact, Customs has offered me a GS-7 position in their Baltimore Field Office."

"Mr. Ritter, we can only start you at the GS-5 grade. It would only be for six months. When the six months are over, you'll automatically be promoted to GS-7. Since you already work in the federal government, you'll start at a step level that will be at least what you're making now."

"I understand, but I feel I'm qualified to start at the GS-7 level. If I start at a 7, I'd be a 9 in a year rather than having to wait a year and a half. Eventually, I'd reach the journeyman grade six months earlier."

"Mr. Ritter, I'm sorry, but the offer is for a GS-5 in the Pittsburgh office. I also need to tell you that the offer does *not* include relocation expenses. The move would be at your expense."

"Well, that presents another problem," Bob said. "We bought a town house only a year ago. With the closing costs we paid, we're going to lose a bundle if we have to sell it and then purchase something in Pittsburgh—all at our expense. My wife might be out of work for a while. This could be a financial hardship for us."

"Well, we would really like to have you. We only take the best. I hope you can accept the offer."

"Ma'am, may I wait until the Washington Field Office opens up?"

"Mr. Ritter, to be honest with you, we don't operate that way. We don't know when WFO might open up and what the future needs would be. Right now, WFO needs experienced agents, which we are rotating off protective details. For a new agent, we have an opening in Pittsburgh and the position is yours—if you want it."

"Okay," Bob said, "thanks! I'm honored to have been offered a position. I've thought about this since I was a kid. I'll talk to my wife tonight and call you tomorrow morning."

Bob and I discussed the offer. Bob was right; I wasn't happy at the prospect of quitting my job and uprooting our family to Pittsburgh in the dead of winter—and moving at our expense. I was upset at the news and didn't hide my feelings. We were just starting to make ends meet. Things had been coming together for us. We had our own home. I was happy with my teaching position. We had family and friends nearby. We had an excellent day care provider for Robbie.

Besides, my professional teaching certificate was for Maryland. Becoming certified in Pennsylvania and then landing a teaching position at this point in the school year would be very difficult—if not impossible. The school systems would already have their staff requirements filled and have qualified teachers on waiting lists.

There was also the problem of selling our townhouse. I handled our family finances and feared a move now would bring financial insecurity. Much of the settlement costs for the town house had been rolled back into the mortgage. And with the cost of selling the town house (sales commissions and other fees), I didn't see where we'd have any money to put down and close on another property. It would be back to renting.

At the same time, I knew how much Bob wanted a career with the Secret Service. He had actively spent the past four years preparing for the opportunity. And it had been a goal since childhood. Now, it was finally within his grasp. My heart urged me to support Bob and to forget the balance sheet. "Bobbie, go ahead and accept the offer," I declared. "It might be tough in the beginning, but we'll work it out."

Bob smiled at me and replied, "Honey, I love you, but sometimes dreams don't come true." Gazing at our newborn son, who was nestled in my arms, Bob continued: "It would be too selfish of me to ask you to make these sacrifices. I'd be making a step forward, but *we* would be taking a step backward. I should do what's best for our family."

"Bobbie, our parents told us we shouldn't get married. We got married, and we had a child. They said we wouldn't finish school. We worked hard and got our degrees. We both made individual sacrifices, but we met the challenges together, and our love has made us strong. I want you to go with the Secret Service. This will just be another one of those challenges. I don't know of two more responsible people—especially for our age. We'll do it, and we'll come out on top—like we always do."

"Jan, it doesn't work for us financially. If I'd known I couldn't have gotten a position in D.C., we could have stayed in the apartment. If we sell the townhouse now, we wouldn't clear enough to pay off the mortgage. Plus, we still have a couple of years of payments on the car. And, you'll be out of work; we won't be able to qualify for a new mortgage. We'll erase all the gains we've made the past six years. This move would put us back in the hole. Life is trying to tell us something."

"Bobbie, what about Tecumseh's Curse? I believe in you. You have a gift for this type of work. We should be celebrating. You're going to be a Secret Service agent!"

"Jan, I appreciate your support, but I'm going to accept the agent position with Customs in Baltimore. We won't have to move. After I get settled in the job, I'll look into taking law courses at night at the UM School of Law in Baltimore."

The next morning, Bob called the Secret Service and reluctantly declined the offer. I could tell that he wasn't happy. He tried to mask his disappointment with the prospect of working toward a law degree. Bob even considered asking his parents for financial help, so he could resign from the federal government and enroll in law school as a full-time student.

A couple of days passed; Bob was working the evening shift in D.C. on the Mrs. K. detail. I had arrived home from school and was changing into some comfortable clothes when the phone rang. It was the lady from Secret Service personnel. She asked for Bob. "I'm sorry; he's working late tonight. May I help you?"

"Is this Mrs. Ritter?"

"Yes."

"I've got some great news. We just received authority to hire several agents for the Washington Field Office. We're saving one of the slots for your husband. The starting date would be early January."

"You're kidding!"

"No, it just came through. Talk about luck."

"Bob's going to be *so* happy. This will be a great Christmas present for him!" I said with joy. I immediately contacted Bob through the Secret Service Kissinger Command Post and told him the wonderful news. Bob could hardly believe it. He was going to become a Secret Service agent after all. Through the phone, I could hear the other agents in the CP—both SY and USSS—congratulating Bob on his achievement.

Like a godsend, this unexpected turn of events reaffirmed my belief that a higher power was pointing Bob toward a special destiny. We went over to my mom's house on Christmas morning. She was proud that soon she would have both a son and a son-in-law in the Secret Service. We all commented about how lucky things had turned out.

Then, some disturbing news interrupted the holiday merriment. Marshall Fields, a 25-year-old taxi cab driver from Silver Spring, Maryland, had crashed a car through the Northwest Gate of the White House. Fields then drove the vehicle up the horseshoe drive to a point near the colonnaded North Portico.

Since President Ford and his family were away on a skiing vacation to Vail, Colorado, the Secret Service used compassion in responding to the threat. Eventually, Fields exited his vehicle. He wore dark glasses and an Arab kaffiyeh atop his head. Fields claimed to have dynamite inside two satchels that were strapped over his shoulders. Fields held his arms up to show the wires that ran from his gloved hands to the bags.

Using the name Abdur Rahmin, Fields told EPS officials he was the Messiah. Fields rambled for several hours about Islam and finally demanded that a local radio station (Howard University) broadcast a message that Fields wanted to meet with the Pakistani ambassador. After hearing the message on his car radio, Fields dropped his satchels, waved a white flag, and surrendered.

A search found that the suspected dynamite was actually safety flares and that Fields had no weapons or detonating devices on him. Some official documents of the Agency for International Development (AID) were found in the bags. Fields's deceased father had been an official with AID, and the family had lived in Arab countries.

Fields was committed to St. Elizabeths Hospital where he was found competent to stand trial. Charged with unlawful entry and destruction of government property, Fields was subsequently convicted and sentenced to 18 months in prison.

After the Fields incident, the Secret Service reviewed their security measures, especially as to the crash worthiness of the White House gates. Dating back to 1818, the wrought-iron Northwest Gate was no match for a speeding automobile. In 1976, all of the White House complex gates were upgraded. They were replaced with new gates made from heavy-gauge steel. A 12-inch-wide steel beam rose from the ground to reinforce the back of the gate when closed.

The year 1974 ended with some high drama for the Secret Service. With Bob onboard, what would 1975 bring?

Chapter 16

USSS

Before the Civil War, paper money in the U.S. was designed and issued by thousands of private banks, which were chartered by state governments. Thus, a note issued in New York would not be good in Pennsylvania. This multi-fragmented system of currency also presented much opportunity for fraud and counterfeiting. Since there were about 7,000 varieties of genuine notes and about 4,000 varieties of counterfeit notes, it was nearly impossible to distinguish the good from the bad.

When hostilities broke out between the Union and Confederacy in 1861, the federal government realized it needed a strong national currency to pay for the war effort. The Union issued "Treasury Demand Notes" and "United States Notes," which could be redeemed for gold or silver. Because the United States Notes were printed with green ink, they were popularly called "greenbacks."

Since the notes were new, people were unfamiliar with them. Counterfeiters turned their attention to U.S. currency and much was passed into circulation. By the end of the Civil War, it was estimated that at least a third of the currency in circulation was counterfeit. Government officials were concerned the public would lose confidence in the money, and it would become worthless.

On April 14, 1865, Secretary of the Treasury Hugh McCulloch discussed the matter with President Abraham Lincoln during a White House Cabinet meeting. McCulloch recommended the creation of a permanent force of detectives who would fight counterfeiting. Lincoln liked the idea and gave McCulloch approval to set up the operation within the Treasury Department. It was one of the last major decisions the president made. That evening at Ford's Theater, President Lincoln was shot by John Wilkes Booth and died the following day.

During the next several months, McCulloch put the plan in operation. On July 5, 1865, William P. Wood was sworn in as the first chief of the United States Secret Service. Although originally formed within the Treasury Department to suppress counterfeiting, the U.S. Secret Service soon became the first general-investigative arm of the federal government.

As the Justice Department did not have its own investigators, Secret Service operatives (as they were then called) were regularly loaned to Justice and other executive branch departments for various federal law enforcement inquiries. These included matters such as: land fraud, illegal lotteries, oil lease corruption, contract fraud, bank fraud, and the terror perpetrated by the Ku Klux Klan. During the Spanish-American War and World War I, operatives of the Secret Service were also tasked to conduct counter-espionage and intelligence operations.

Presidential protective duties began *informally* in 1894 when the Secret Service learned of threats against President Grover Cleveland and of an alleged kidnapping plot directed against his children. In order to keep President Cleveland and his family safe, the Secret Service stationed operatives at the White House and at Cleveland's summer home (Gray Gables on Cape Cod, Massachusetts).

During the Spanish-American War, the Secret Service provided protection for President William McKinley. This *part-time, unofficial* protection continued after the war. In fact, several Secret Service operatives were with McKinley when he was assassinated during a visit to Buffalo, New York in 1901.

Following the McKinley assassination (the third presidential assassination in U.S. history), Congress gave tacit approval to the Secret Service to provide *full-time* protection for the president. Starting in 1902, Secret Service operatives were assigned to President Theodore Roosevelt, although legislation directly funding presidential protection was not passed until 1906.

In 1907, Secret Service operative Joseph A. Walker was killed in the line of duty. His murder spotlighted the work conducted by the Service for agencies outside of Treasury. Walker was investigating Western land fraud when he was shot and killed near Durango, Colorado. The Secret Service uncovered massive fraud in the implementation of the federal homestead program. Companies were fraudulently filing for personal homesteads, which were then illegally harvested of timber, mined for coal, or used for cattle grazing. Secret Service investigations returned millions of acres to the government and a large number of individuals were convicted. Even several U.S. senators and a congressman were charged with criminal activity.

Objecting to the fact that members of Congress had been investigated by the executive branch, Congress passed legislation prohibiting the loan of Secret Service operatives to agencies outside the Treasury Department. In a countermove, President Roosevelt transferred nine Secret Service operatives to the Department of Justice. These nine agents became the core of a new U.S. investigative arm. This office eventually became the Federal Bureau of Investigation (FBI).

Through the years, Secret Service investigative responsibilities increased. By way of congressional appropriations and departmental and executive orders, the Service picked up investigative responsibility for the forgery of U.S. government checks, bonds, and other federal obligations. In 1917, a federal law was passed (18 U.S.C. Section 871) making it a felony to threaten the life of or threaten to do bodily harm to the president. Investigative jurisdiction for this statute was given to the USSS.

However, the greatest and most important increases to the Secret Service mission during the first 75 years of the 20ᵗʰ Century were due to added protective duties. In 1913, Congress authorized protection for the president-elect. Congress extended protection to the president's immediate family in 1917. The Service took over supervision of the White House Police in 1930 and the Treasury Guard Force in 1937.

President-elect Franklin D. Roosevelt was the first "official" protectee of the Secret Service to come under an assassin's gun. The attempt took place on February 15, 1933, in Miami, Florida. Roosevelt had just finished a 10-day vacation and deep-sea-fishing cruise on board Vincent Astor's yacht, the *Nourmahal*. The president-elect was scheduled to address an outdoor reception given in his honor at Bayfront Park and then depart Miami via train for New York.

That evening, Roosevelt's motorcade pulled up to the stage of the park amphitheater. Thousands of people had turned out to catch a glimpse of the incoming president. Due to the paralysis of Roosevelt's legs—caused by polio contracted at the age of 39—the president-elect did not mount the stage but addressed the crowd by microphone from the rear of an open touring car. After a brief speech, Roosevelt shook hands and chatted with Chicago Mayor Anton Cermak. Shortly thereafter, five gunshots rang out.

Roosevelt was unharmed, but Mayor Cermak and four others were wounded. Secret Service agents and police quickly apprehended the shooter, who was later identified as Giuseppe (Joe) Zangara—a 33-year-old unemployed bricklayer. Zangara emigrated from Italy in 1923 and became a U.S. citizen in 1929.

Since childhood, Zangara complained of stomachaches (thought to be psychosomatic). Zangara believed the pains were a direct result of the work his father forced him to do as a child. As a result, Zangara developed a hatred for authority, political leaders, and the rich and powerful. During his service in the Italian army, Zangara considered killing King Victor Emmanuel III of Italy but never got the opportunity.

Zangara blamed the Great Depression, which began in 1929, on American capitalism. He transferred his hatred of capitalists to the president—as symbolic leader of the country. By February 1933, Zangara had decided to travel to Washington, D.C. to kill President Herbert Hoover. This act would be retribution for all the perceived ills caused by the president. Also by killing the president, Zangara believed his stomach problems would end.

On February 13, 1933, Zangara bought a .32-caliber revolver at a Miami pawnshop. The next day, he read in the newspaper that President-elect Roosevelt would visit Miami the following evening. Zangara decided not to take the bus to Washington where his stomach pains might be aggravated by the cold weather. Zangara would stay in Miami and kill Roosevelt instead.

By the time Zangara arrived at the park, the amphitheater was already jammed with people. He could only force his way to a distance of about 30 feet from Roosevelt's car. The ceremony was winding down and Zangara had to make his move. Zangara, who was only five feet two inches tall, jumped on top of a chair to take aim at the president-elect. Zangara fired. Several bystanders grabbed for Zangara's arm and the chair wobbled. Roosevelt was spared.

Zangara came close to changing history. One can only imagine what might have happened if Roosevelt had been struck down by an assassin's bullets in 1933. Would there have been a "New Deal." Would the outcome of World War II been changed.

Zangara's only remorse was that he hadn't succeeded in killing Roosevelt. Five days after the attempt, Zangara appeared before a judge and pled guilty to four counts of assault with intent to commit murder. Zangara was sentenced to 80 years in prison at hard labor. Mayor Cermak was critically wounded in the attempt and did not recover. He died on March 6, 1933. Zangara was then charged with first-degree murder, and again he pled guilty. Zangara was sentenced to die in the electric chair. Defiant and unrepentant to the end, Zangara was executed on March 20, 1933. His remains were buried in an unmarked grave on the grounds of the Florida State Penitentiary at Raiford.

There would not be another armed assault on a Secret Service protectee for 17 years. On the afternoon of November 1, 1950, the eyes of the nation focused on President Harry S. Truman and the Secret Service. Two Puerto Rican nationalists, Griselio Torresola and Oscar Collazo, attempted to assassinate Truman. The duo hoped the president's assassination would draw American attention to Puerto Rico and the nationalists' quest for independence.

During this period, the President and Mrs. Truman were residing at the Blair House—located across Pennsylvania Avenue from the White House, which was undergoing major renovation (1949–1952). On the morning of the day of the attempt, Torresola and Collazo walked by the Blair House in order to familiarize themselves with security posts and to devise a plan to enter the building. The Blair House outer protective perimeter consisted of two security booths—located along the sidewalk at the east and west approaches to the property. These stations were manned by White House Police officers. Another uniformed officer stood post at the steps leading to the front door of the Blair House. Torresola and Collazo devised a simple plan: Storm the front door; find the president, and shoot him dead.

At about 2:20 p.m., they put their plan into action. Torresola approached from the west, while Collazo advanced from the east—passing the east security booth where Agent Floyd Boring (senior agent) was checking with

Private Joseph Davidson. When Collazo reached the canopied-covered Blair House steps, he drew a German-made Walther P.38 semiautomatic pistol from his waistband. Collazo pointed the gun at Private Donald Birdzell, who was facing away from Collazo. Suddenly, Officer Birdzell heard a metallic "click," which was the unmistakable sound of a gun dry firing. Birdzell turned and saw Collazo—who was inexperienced with semiautomatic pistols—frantically hitting the slide of the P.38 in an attempt to get it to discharge.

Apparently, the weapon must have been cocked and "off safe," while Collazo wrongly believed the safety was "on." When Collazo flipped the combination safety/de-cocking lever, he actually activated the safety. This would have automatically dropped the hammer of the gun without firing. To get the gun to fire now, Collazo had to flip the safety/de-cocking lever back to off. Then, he could either pull the trigger in double action, or manually cock the hammer and fire with single action. That is unless a round was not in the chamber. In that case, Collazo would have had to pull the slide of the gun back to chamber a round and cock the hammer. Then, the gun could be fired in single action. After the first shot, all successive rounds in the magazine would fire in single action—with the recoil of the action automatically chambering a round and cocking the hammer.

Without warning, the P.38 discharged with a *bang*! A 9mm bullet tore into Officer Birdzell's right knee. In order to keep pedestrians out of harm's way and to distance himself from Collazo, Birdzell limped out to the middle of Pennsylvania Avenue while returning fire. Collazo fired another round at Birdzell and missed.

By now, Agent Boring and Officer Davidson were shooting at Collazo from the east security booth area. Boring and Davidson were briefly joined by Agent Vincent Mroz, who had heard the shots and ran out the east basement door. Mroz fired one shot and then ran back inside. Through a basement corridor, Mroz sprinted to the other side of the building in order to flank the shooter from the west.

Collazo emptied his gun at Boring and Davidson—missing on all shots. Using the wrought-iron fence and shrubbery as cover, Collazo crouched on the Blair House steps to reload the P.38 with a spare magazine.

A few seconds after the shootout erupted at the Blair House steps, Torresola approached the west security booth, which was manned by Officer Leslie Coffelt. Torresola pulled a German-made Luger P.08 and fired at Coffelt. Three 9mm bullets found their mark, hitting Coffelt in the left side and abdomen. Officer Joseph Downs was entering the west basement door of the building when he turned toward the shots and reached to draw his gun. Torresola quickly pumped three shots into Downs, who tumbled inside the basement hallway. In spite of his wounds, Officer Downs was able to secure the door behind him.

Next, Torresola turned his attention to Officer Birdzell, who was firing at Collazo from the middle of Pennsylvania Avenue. Torresola took aim and fired the Luger. Amazingly, the bullet struck Birdzell in the left knee. Now with disabling wounds to both knees, Birdzell fell flat to the pavement and passed out. The Luger was empty; Torresola kneeled to reload with a fresh magazine. At that moment, the mortally wounded Coffelt—displaying *unparalleled* valor—managed to lean out of his booth and fire one shot. The bullet hit Torresola in the head, killing him instantly.

The sounds of gunfire awakened President Truman, who was taking a nap in a second floor bedroom. Secret Service *legend* says Truman went to a window to see what was going on. Also inside Blair House was Secret Service Agent Stewart Stout. He grabbed a .45-caliber Thompson submachine gun and stood guard in the first floor hallway—covering the front door, elevator, and stairway.

Back at the Blair House steps, Collazo was reloading the P.38. He had been shot through his hat, with the bullet causing a flesh wound to the head. Now, Collazo felt a bullet rip into his chest. Collazo collapsed at the foot of the Blair House steps. The shootout was over. The final tally: White House Police Officer Leslie Coffelt was dead as was his killer, Griselio Torresola. White House Police Officers Donald Birdzell and Joseph Downs were wounded. Both would recover and return to duty.

The wounds to would-be presidential assassin Oscar Collazo were not serious. He was charged as an accessory in the murder of Officer Coffelt and with assault with intent to kill President Truman and Officers Birdzell and Downs. Collazo was found guilty and sentenced to death. President Truman commuted the sentence to life in prison. Pardoned by President Carter in 1979, Oscar Collazo returned to Puerto Rico where he died of natural causes in 1994, at the age of 80.

In the media reports regarding the Blair House shooting, it was publicized that the Secret Service did not have statutory authority for its investigative and protective responsibilities. The Secret Service had been receiving its authority annually with congressional passage of the Treasury Appropriations Act. Congress remedied this in 1951 by passing Public Law 82-79, codified as 18 U.S.C. Section 3056 (Powers, authorities, and duties of United States Secret Service). The Service received permanent authority for its protective and investigative mission, and the statutory right to carry firearms, make arrests, and other law enforcement activities. The authority to protect the vice president—at his request—was also added to Secret Service duties.

In 1962, the law was changed so that the vice president and vice president-elect received automatic protection. Congress also authorized the protection of former presidents at their request—for a reasonable amount of time—after they left office. In 1965, this was amended so that former presidents and their spouses received protection during the president's lifetime. Unless declined, protection of widowed spouses of a former president and their minor children would continue for four years after the president's death.

The Secret Service was not given the responsibility of protecting major presidential and vice presidential candidates and nominees until after the assassination of Robert F. Kennedy in 1968, although a 1912 incident foreshadowed the danger. In that year, presidential candidate Theodore Roosevelt survived an assassination attempt by John Schrank (an ex-bartender from New York City).

Roosevelt had been elected vice president in 1900 and succeeded to the presidency with the 1901 assassination of William McKinley. In 1904, Roosevelt won his own four-year term as president. Choosing not to run in 1908, Roosevelt supported fellow Republican William Howard Taft, who defeated Democrat William Jennings Bryan. Subsequently, Roosevelt and Taft had a falling out—especially over the weakening of Roosevelt's conservation and antitrust policies.

Upset at Taft, Roosevelt tried for the Republican nomination in 1912. Roosevelt did well in the primaries, but the vast majority of convention delegates were chosen by party leaders who were loyal to President Taft. The party officials deciding contested delegates were also Taft supporters. Thus, Taft easily won the Republican nomination. Feeling that the nominating process had been undemocratic, Roosevelt and his supporters split from the Republicans and formed the Progressive Party (commonly called the Bull Moose Party). The new party chose Roosevelt as their standard-bearer.

The attempt took place during a campaign stop in Milwaukee, Wisconsin. On the evening of October 14, 1912, Roosevelt exited the Hotel Gilpatrick (present site of Hyatt Regency Hotel) and was about to depart via automobile for Milwaukee Auditorium (present site of Milwaukee Theater) where a speech was scheduled. While Roosevelt was standing in the vehicle and waving to his supporters, a shot rang out from close range. Immediately, the gunman was seized by Roosevelt aides and the police. Roosevelt was hit in the chest with a .38-caliber bullet, yet he refused to go to a hospital.

When Roosevelt arrived at the auditorium, doctors conducted a cursory examination and recommended that Roosevelt cancel his speech and seek emergency treatment. Disregarding medical advice, Roosevelt placed a handkerchief over the wound and proceeded to the stage. During the introduction for Roosevelt, the crowd of about 10,000 was told that the former president had been shot but would attempt to make his speech. When someone from the crowd yelled "fake," Roosevelt removed his vest to reveal a bloodstained shirt. Roosevelt then smiled at the crowd as he said, "It takes more than one bullet to kill a bull moose." Roosevelt then made an hour and twenty-minute speech.

When he was later treated at hospitals in Milwaukee and Chicago, x-rays showed that the bullet had penetrated the chest cavity but had not damaged the lungs or caused serious injury to the ribs. Miraculously, the bullet had spent much of its energy going through a heavy overcoat, a folded 50-page speech, and the steel case that carried Roosevelt's eyeglasses. With no vital organs in danger, surgeons decided it would be safer to leave the bullet in place. Roosevelt carried it within him the rest of his life.

Before finding the opportunity to strike in Milwaukee, John Schrank had followed Roosevelt on the campaign trail through seven states. Schrank wanted to kill Roosevelt to avenge the assassination of William McKinley. In several dreams, the ghost of McKinley told Schrank that Roosevelt was responsible for McKinley's murder. Besides being McKinley's avenger, Schrank wanted to stop Roosevelt's bid for an unprecedented third term as president. It was Schrank's belief that a third term would be the first step in establishing a dictatorship. Schrank also feared that if Roosevelt were not elected, he would claim that a fraud had been committed and plunge the nation into another civil war.

In a pre-trial competency examination, it was the opinion of five doctors that Schrank was insane. He was committed to the Northern Hospital for the Insane near Oshkosh, Wisconsin. Later, Schrank was transferred to the Central State Hospital in Waupun, Wisconsin where he died in 1943 at the age of 67.

To recover from the wound, Roosevelt was forced to leave the campaign trail for several weeks during the height of the presidential contest. Although soundly defeated by Democrat Woodrow Wilson, Roosevelt prevented Taft from winning reelection. Taft—who finished third to Wilson and Roosevelt—suffered one of the worst defeats in U.S. history for a sitting president. The election of 1912 was also the only time that a third party candidate succeeded in polling more votes than the candidate of either the Democratic or the Republican parties.

Fifty-six years later, Congress reacted to the tragic death of presidential candidate Robert F. Kennedy by authorizing Secret Service protection for presidential and vice presidential candidates. Also in 1968, Congress amended the law that provided USSS protection for the spouses and children of former presidents. Spouses of former presidents would now receive protection until their death or remarriage. Children of former presidents would receive protection until 16 years of age, unless protection was declined.

In 1970, the White House Police force was renamed the Executive Protective Service (EPS). With the new name came the added responsibility of protecting foreign diplomatic missions in the Washington, D.C. area. And in 1971, Congress authorized the Secret Service to protect visiting heads of state or government.

From a small force of operatives formed in 1865 to combat counterfeiting, the Secret Service evolved into one of the most prestigious and revered law enforcement agencies in the world. Entering its 110th year in 1975, the Service had earned its enviable and well-deserved reputation with a heritage of sacrifice and success. Its dual full-time mission of criminal investigation and protective functions was unique in American law enforcement.

Bob couldn't have hoped for a better way to start the New Year; he was finally fulfilling a lifelong ambition and becoming a special agent of the United States Secret Service.

Chapter 17

First Day

On Monday, January 6, 1975, Bob reported to the Personnel Division of the U.S. Secret Service, Room 912, 1800 G Street, NW, Washington, D.C. There, Bob met the other newly appointed Washington Field Office (WFO) agent. His name was Tom Conaty. A graduate of the University of South Carolina, Tom was married and had been an artillery officer in the U.S. Marine Corps (Vietnam 1971–1972). After leaving the military, he became a stockbroker with a large national firm. Tall and lean in stature, Tom wore a steady smile that reflected an easygoing personality.

Bob and Tom were taken to the Secret Service Visual Information Branch (VIB) where pictures were taken for their commission books and White House passes. Returning to the personnel office, they received a "new employee" briefing. Next, both men filled out the paperwork needed for withholding, insurance, retirement, emergency notifications and the like.

After lunch, they reported to Director H. Stuart Knight's office, which was on the eighth floor at 1800 G Street. In 1973, Knight was appointed the 15th Director of the United States Secret Service by President Richard M. Nixon. Born in Ontario, Canada, Director Knight was raised in Detroit, Michigan. He volunteered for the U.S. Army in World War II and was awarded two Purple Hearts, a Bronze Star, and a Silver Star for gallant action in the Pacific Theater. After the war, Knight was naturalized a U.S. citizen. He graduated from Michigan State University and joined the Secret Service in 1950. Starting in the Detroit Field Office, Knight subsequently worked his way through the vice presidential and presidential protective divisions. Before becoming director, Knight had served in various high-level field and headquarters positions.

Escorted into the director's inner office by an administrative aide, Bob and Tom observed dimly lit display cases containing Secret Service memorabilia. The office was noticeably dark. Heavy drapes were drawn across the windows and the overhead lights were off. The only direct light in the work area of the office came from a single lamp on top the director's desk.

"This is cool," Tom commented.

"Yes," Bob added, "the lighting and display case items give a sensation of journeying back in time."

"The director only uses the desk lamp," remarked the aide. "He says it helps him focus better. Feel free to look at the exhibits and then make yourself comfortable. The director should be back shortly. I'll be outside if you need anything. Welcome to the Secret Service." Bob and Tom examined the displays. They were thrilled to see vintage badges, commission books, and other historical items of the Secret Service.

Afterwards, they took a seat at the conference table adjacent to the director's desk and engaged in small talk. About ten minutes later, Bob and Tom sprung to their feet when the director entered the office through the backlit doorway. "Hello, men, I'm Stu Knight." He shook hands with Bob and Tom and invited them to return to their seats.

"The swearing in of new agents is one of my most pleasant duties," the director related. "The tradition dates back to 1865. In the early years of the Service, the oath was administered by the chief in his office on the fourth floor of the Treasury Building. As the Service grew and offices spread across the country, the agents in charge administered the oath outside of Washington. Except for a few years in the 1870s when headquarters was temporarily moved to New York and in 1971 when the first women agents were sworn in by the assistant secretary for law enforcement, the tradition of being personally sworn in by the head of the Secret Service has continued for agents starting their careers in Washington."

Director Knight then asked the new appointees about themselves and their families. When the chat was over, the director requested Bob and Tom to stand and to raise their right hand. "Please repeat after me," he said.

As required by Article VI of the U.S. Constitution and subsequent federal law, Bob recited the oath of office:

"I, Robert Ritter, do solemnly swear that I will support and defend the Constitution of the United States against all enemies, foreign and domestic; that I will bear true faith and allegiance to the same; that I take this obligation freely, without any mental reservation or purpose of evasion; and that I will well and faithfully discharge the duties of the office of Special Agent United States Secret Service. So help me God."

With a broad smile, Director Knight shook hands with the agents, as he congratulated them. Next, the director presented Bob and Tom their Secret Service credentials—a black leather case that displayed the badge and held the agent's commission book. Bob looked at the gold badge with pride. It was designed in the shape of a shield with an eagle atop. The Secret Service five-pointed star rose from the center of the shield. Inside the star were the words: "The Department of the Treasury." The star points represented courage, duty, honesty, justice, and loyalty. Inset within the shield were gold letters in a blue-enameled background that read: "United States Secret Service."

The commission book certified as follows:

UNITED STATES SECRET SERVICE
TREASURY DEPARTMENT
ROBERT RITTER
Special Agent

is commissioned by the United States Secret Service, Treasury Department, to protect the President of the United States and others as authorized by statute; to detect and arrest any person violating federal laws relating to coins, obligations, and securities of the United States and foreign governments, and in performance of these duties, to arrest any person committing any offense against the United States. This person has Top Secret Clearance and is commended to those with whom official business is conducted as worthy of trust and confidence.

Washington, D.C.

The background of the commission featured blue-inked impressions of the Treasury Building and the Secret Service star. Affixed to the commission book was Bob's picture. The commission was signed by both the director and Bob.

After the headquarters swearing in ceremony, Bob and Tom's next stop was the Washington Field Office (WFO), which was located several blocks away at 1900 Pennsylvania Avenue, NW. The abbreviation "WFO" was pronounced either with its letters spelled out (W-F-O) or as one word, "wŏŏfō."

The building housing the field office was a modern concrete and glass structure built in 1972. It was owned by George Washington University and commonly called the Pepco Building—after its largest tenant, the Potomac Electric Power Company (Pepco). The field office occupied the sixth floor (Suite 600) of the nine-story building. The location of the Washington Field Office and USSS Headquarters within several blocks of the White House was by design. In the event of an emergency, agents could quickly respond to the White House complex.

Bob and Tom reported to their WFO supervisor, Lubert "Bert" de Freese. He was an assistant to the special agent in charge (ATSAIC or AT) and supervisor of the Special Investigations (SI) Squad. A Navy veteran of World War II, de Freese served in the Pacific. After graduating from Colorado State University, he joined the National Park Service in 1950. In 1956, de Freese transferred to the Secret Service and worked in the Chicago

Field Office. De Freese spent most of his Secret Service career in Washington with the White House Detail, including the protection of President Dwight D. Eisenhower's grandchildren. Bert was the middle-aged father figure for WFO. It was appropriate that he supervised and guided beginning agents.

While inviting Bob and Tom to take a seat, de Freese reached for one of the briar pipes that rested in a rack on his desk. He placed some tobacco in the bowl of the pipe and tamped down the mixture. Lighting the pipe produced an aromatic smoke that drifted through the air with a sweet, full scent.

"I feel like I know you men already," de Freese related between puffs of tobacco smoke. Talking slowly and softly, he continued: "In the SI Squad, we mainly conduct background investigations for new and current employees. I reviewed the backgrounds done on you men, and the Service is fortunate to have you onboard."

"Thank you," both Tom and Bob replied.

De Freese turned to Bob, "You're Art Rehkemper's brother-in-law."

"Please don't hold that against me," Bob quipped.

De Freese smiled as he said, "You know we think highly of Art here."

De Freese then handed each agent a thick loose-leaf binder. "This is your Secret Service Manual [SSM]. It was instituted in the early 1950s by Chief Baughman. It covers every investigation and procedure. I want you to start your reading with the section on the Special Investigations and Security Division [SI&SD] and personnel security investigations. As soon as you men learn the material and qualify with your weapons, you'll be assigned cases.

"During your first year, I'll be assigning you further readings and guiding your on-the-job training [OJT]. In the old days, OJT was the only training agents received. Now, it supplements the Treasury and Secret Service schools."

Just then, the intercom on de Freese's desk rang out, "Bert, are the new agents here?"

"Yes, Frank, they're with me now."

"Send them down to my office. Charlie wants to see them before he leaves for a meeting at headquarters."

"I'm sending them now." De Freese directed the new agents to Assistant Special Agent in Charge (ASAIC) Frank Cavanaugh's office.

In the Secret Service, the abbreviation SAIC was usually pronounced S-A-I-C by articulating each letter. That was different from FBI offices where special agent in charge was abbreviated SAC and pronounced as a single word. Another difference between the Secret Service and FBI was the term "unknown subject." USSS agents never abbreviated the term in reports or in speech. The FBI used the acronym "UNSUB." The Bureau also used acronyms for the names of major case files; the Service used letters and numbers. For example: The FBI file name for the 1971 Northwest Airlines hijacking (D.B. Cooper) was "NORJACK." That was formed from the words Northwest hijacking.

Secret Service agents pronounced the ASAIC abbreviation as either "A-SAC" or "A-S-A-I-C." ATSAIC was usually pronounced "AT-SAC" as one word, but commonly the abbreviation was shortened to AT and enunciated "A-T."

Bob and Tom entered the ASAIC's office. Cavanaugh looked over each man several times before gruffly uttering: "I'll be taking you to see Mr. Gittens. Just a few things before we go. While you're in the SI Squad, ATSAIC de Freese will oversee your work and training. Your chain of command *stops* at ATSAIC de Freese. Don't go over his head. If you make him happy, you make me happy. And you're going to want to make me happy.

"And one more thing, this is a *field office*. Your work is on the street. I only want to see you in the office when you're locking up bad guys and writing reports. Understand?"

"Yes, sir," both men responded in unison.

At SAIC Gittens's office, Cavanaugh tapped on the open door and announced, "Mr. Gittens, I'm here with the new agents."

"Good, bring them on in," Gittens replied in a Bostonian accent as thick as New England fog. The SAIC's office was on the northeast side of the building with windows overlooking 19th Street and Pennsylvania Avenue. Immediately in front of Gittens's executive-style desk was a conference table with chairs. On the wall to the right were multiple dry-erase boards lined up in a neat row. They listed: squads, personnel, duty status, and assignments. The other walls of the office displayed awards and pictures. United States and USSS flags stood in their bases like silent sentries. A wooden bookcase and credenza rounded out the furniture.

A native of Cambridge, Massachusetts, Charles L. Gittens was the first black special agent hired by the U.S. Secret Service (1956). He was a graduate of North Carolina Central University where he majored in English and Spanish. Prior to joining the USSS, Gittens had been a musician (trombonist) in the U.S. Army and a high school teacher. Gittens worked in the New York and San Juan (P.R.) field offices before becoming the WFO-ASAIC in 1969. He was promoted to SAIC-WFO in 1971.

Gittens rose from his desk and flashed a toothy smile. He was trim and stylish in his tailored sharkskin suit, silk tie, and wellington boots. After introductions and handshakes, Gittens welcomed the new agents to the Secret Service and the Washington Field Office. Looking at Tom Conaty, Gittens remarked, "You interviewed with me last year."

"Yes, sir," Tom affirmed.

Gittens—with a blank look on his face—looked directly at Bob and asked, "Did I interview you?"

"No, sir," Bob replied. "I interviewed at headquarters."

"Good," Gittens sighed with relief. "I only remember the exceptional applicants. The ones I don't remember usually *aren't* hired," Gittens said as he cracked another wide grin. Gittens spent several minutes chatting with Bob and Tom, and then ASAIC Cavanaugh quickly ushered our boys back out to the hallway.

Returning to the SI Squad and ATSAIC de Freese, Bob and Tom were assigned desks and safes where they could secure their manual, equipment, and investigative work. Next, de Freese instructed the new agents in the Treasury Department Firearms Policy:

"A firearm may be discharged only as a last resort when in the considered opinion of the officer there is danger of loss of life or serious bodily injury to himself or another person."

Guidelines for the use of warning shots and other firing situations were discussed. Each agent signed the policy and guidelines and was given a copy.

Then, de Freese sent the agents to Special Officer (SO) Dave Green for the issuance of Secret Service equipment. Special officers were generally retired military or retired police officers, who performed support duty with the USSS as a second career.

Special Officer Green handled the equipment and technical operations for the Washington Field Office. Bob and Tom were issued Smith & Wesson Model 19, .357 Magnum revolvers with two and one-half-inch barrels. Green also issued each agent handcuffs with keys and carrying case, a Motorola HT-220 radio with microphone and standard ear piece, an ammo pouch, 12 rounds of ammunition, a holster for the Model 19, and a "linen tester." This device was a pocketsize magnifier used to examine suspected counterfeit notes.

Placing the holster, handcuffs case, and ammo pouch back on the special officer's desk, Bob stated, "I prefer to use my own leather—made by DeSantis."

Green smiled and replied: "I have to issue them to you. Keep them in your desk drawer until you retire."

Next, Green gave the agents the address of a local hearing aid shop. There, Bob and Tom would be fitted for custom-molded earpieces. Green then issued the agents their USSS identification pins. Each serial-numbered set contained four lapel pins of the same design but with different accent colors. In case a pin was lost during a protective assignment, agents could immediately switch to a different-colored pin for security purposes.

Lastly, Green assigned an official government vehicle and issued a government driver's license to each agent. Due to the long hours USSS special agents worked and their being subject to after-hours recall, agents were authorized with home to work driving privileges.

The next stop for Bob and Tom was the United States Treasury Department Building at 1500 Pennsylvania Avenue, NW, D.C. The first Treasury Building was burned by the British in 1814. The replacement building suffered a similar fate. It was burned down by arsonists in 1833. In 1836, Congress authorized the construction of a "fireproof" building for the Treasury Department. Designed in the Greek revival style of architecture, the new building featured a granite exterior with massive classical columns. The east and center wings were completed by 1842. In the 1850s and 1860s, the building was expanded with the construction of the south, west, and north wings. The Treasury Building is the third oldest federal building in D.C.—only the White House (1792) and the Capitol (1793) are older. The Treasury Building appears on the reverse of the $10 bill.

Entering the Treasury Building (commonly called Main Treasury) via the 15th Street entrance, our boys made their way to the Treasury Firearms Range, which was in the basement on the north side of the building. There, Treasury law enforcement agents, officers of the Executive Protective Service, and officers of the Treasury Security Force (renamed Treasury Police Force in 1983 and merged into the USSS Uniformed Division in 1986) went for firearms qualification.

Secret Service agents in the Washington area were required to qualify monthly on the Standard Qualification Course (SQC). Bob had not shot the SQC since police school. All of his shooting since then—both qualifying and recreational—had been of the practical variety. Bob was a firm believer that law enforcement personnel should practice as realistically as possible. In Bob's opinion: Using a target shooter's stance, a one-handed hold, and a single action mode to fire wadcutters (target rounds) at bull's-eye targets did not correlate to law enforcement combat situations.

On a quarterly basis, however, the Service did require agents to shoot the Practical Pistol Course along with combat courses for the Remington Model 870 shotgun and Uzi submachine gun. These qualifications were conducted at the USSS Beltsville Training Center (renamed James J. Rowley Training Center in 1983).

Bob and Tom had no problems qualifying with the model 19s. Tom had pistol and rifle training when he was in the military and had routinely qualified with a sidearm. Initially, Bob shot the SQC using the techniques of a competitive marksman. After achieving an "expert" score, Bob switched to a two-handed grip and fired the course in double action to practice combat shooting techniques.

Following the qualification session, Bob and Tom examined the massive burglarproof vault doors that lined the north hallway of the Treasury basement. Earlier in our nation's history, the vaults stored gold, silver, currency, coins, bonds, and securities. At the beginning of World War II, a number of the vaults were converted to a temporary bomb shelter for President Franklin D. Roosevelt and his staff. This was a precautionary measure until a permanent shelter could be constructed under the then new East Wing of the White House. A tunnel was built between the ground floor of the White House and the Treasury Building for quick access to the makeshift shelter. Securely locked steel doors protect both ends of the tunnel from unauthorized entry.

Later that evening, I heard a short siren blast from in front of our townhouse. I went to the window and saw a red light flashing from the dash of a four-door sedan. Bob was home, so I hurried out to meet him. "Hi, honey, I'm just checking out the equipment in my 'G-ride.' See, I've got a fireball that plugs into the cigarette lighter receptacle, a siren, and a two-way radio. What do you think?"

"It sure beats having to use our car," I happily replied. At the State Department, Bob had to use our Buick V-8 not only for security investigations but also for *criminal investigations*. The federal mileage rate hardly paid for the gas and maintenance yet alone compensated for the wear and tear.

"How did your first day go?" I asked excitedly.

"Great! I'll tell you all about it at dinner tonight." Bob then took out his new credentials and proudly showed me his badge and commission book. I was happy for Bob. He had worked hard and earned this moment.

Chapter 18

WFO

Bob arrived at the Washington Field Office bright and early the following morning. Opening his SSM, Bob read the section regarding the Special Investigations and Security Division. Later that morning, the intercom buzzed in Bob's office. It was Bert de Freese. "Bob, will you please come to my office."

"Yes, sir," Bob respectfully replied.

As he stepped into the ATSAIC's office, Bob heard a radio playing softly in the background. "Sounds like Brahms to me," Bob remarked.

"Do you like classical music?" de Freese asked.

"Yes, I also like jazz and rhythm and blues."

"I don't listen to classical all the time," de Freese said. "Mostly, I listen to Harden and Weaver [D.C. radio personalities] in the morning. Once in a while, I like to hear some good country music—not the twangy hillbilly stuff, but traditional country and western."

Motioning to Bob, de Freese continued: "Please sit down. I wanted to let you know I'll be assigning you some cases today. By next week, you'll be carrying a full caseload."

"Great!" Bob said as he slid into a chair. "I'm ready to earn my keep."

"The office is down from its authorized strength. We're short-handed in the squad," de Freese informed. "Headquarters sends a lot of *specials* over here. They want to bring someone onboard immediately or update a security clearance for a promotion, transfer, or special intelligence access. Applicant investigations have a 60-day due date, but they always want them completed as soon as possible [ASAP] too."

"It was the same over at State," Bob commented. "They even coined a term over there, 'Soonest.' They use to stamp it above the ASAP on the investigation request. It meant that particular ASAP case had priority over all your other ASAPs.

"Once, I had a couple of *Soonests* and three or four regular ASAPs, and at the same time I was sent out on a protective assignment. So, the SAC calls me and asks, 'What more needs to be done on that priority case of yours? Headquarters is asking.' I answered *which one*? I wasn't trying to be wise, but headquarters was making almost *everything* some type of priority."

De Freese laughed and said: "Your supervisors at State gave you some pretty high recommendations. With your experience, you'll be able to step right into these without missing a beat. Have you read the SI&SD pages in the manual?"

"Yes, I finished them this morning."

"Good, I'm sure it's very similar to what you did at State. In the Service, we use the Standard Form [SF]-1588 memorandum report [M/R] to write up investigations. I have a couple of samples to give you that show how we do the synopsis and investigative details section for backgrounds," de Freese said as he handed the sheets to Bob. "If you have any questions, see me or Ted Wilkes."

"Yes, sir," Bob acknowledged. "As soon as I get the cases, I'll hit the street."

WFO agents were grouped into five squads: Protective Intelligence (PI), Criminal, Protection, Forgery, and Special Investigations (SI). The Protective Intelligence Squad provided PI teams for protective movements and investigated threats against USSS protectees. The Criminal Squad mainly handled investigations of the counterfeiting of U.S. obligations. The Protection Squad conducted protective surveys and coordinated protective operations for the field office. As the name implies, the Forgery Squad investigated the forgery of government checks and bonds. The SI Squad conducted security investigations and other special investigations: employee vehicle accidents, tort claims, and losses in Treasury shipments.

The Washington Field Office was configured so that each squad had its own area. Squad ATSAICs were GS-14s on the federal pay scale and had single offices. The workstations for squad clerks were situated outside the ATSAICs' offices. File cabinets and safes for case control documents and active cases, etc., were also located in these open areas. Offices for squad agents ranged in size from small (two desks) to large (three to five desks).

Office meetings were held in a centrally located, large multi-purpose room officially called the "conference room." It contained tables with chairs, a lectern, agent mailboxes, file cabinets, and a library.

Interview rooms and the prisoner processing area were in the Criminal Squad area. There, subjects were interrogated, and prisoners fingerprinted and photographed.

The WFO duty agent office was on the Pennsylvania Avenue side of the building. The small room contained security monitors, alarm readouts, telephones, and the console for radio communications.

Near the office for the SOs, a secure room stored surveillance equipment, weapons, ammunition, battering rams, and judicial evidence.

One of the most important rooms in every Secret Service field office was the teletype room. Here the TWX (teletypewriter exchange service) machine printed out investigative referrals, requests for protective manpower, transfers, promotions, and the day-to-day business of the Secret Service. Initial PI investigative reports, protective surveys, preliminary counterfeit notifications, and other time-sensitive traffic were often sent to headquarters by TWX.

In the SI section, Bob and Tom shared an office with four desks. Two of the desks were vacant. Returning from the visit with de Freese, Bob found Tom Conaty intently reviewing yesterday's closing stock quotes in the morning paper. "Can't get it out of your blood, huh?" Bob remarked.

"No, old habits are hard to break. I enjoyed being a broker. Might still be doing it if it hadn't of been for the bear market."

Tom folded the newspaper and set it aside. "What did Bert want?"

"He's assigning me some backgrounds today because I did them at State."

"Bob, what should I know about background investigation that's *not* in the manual?" Tom asked.

Bob opened his briefcase and pulled out an atlas of the D.C. Metropolitan Area. "Get yourself one of these. You can pick them up at any People's Drug Store. It'll save you a lot of time in finding places and in lining up your stops. Streets are alphabetically indexed and cross-referenced to a point on a map page.

"For the field interviews, make a checklist until you memorize what's needed. That way you won't forget to ask any required questions. Write down responses as the interviewee answers. Don't trust your memory. You don't want to be repeating stops. And stay in control of the interview. Keep them focused on what's relevant.

"The rest is in the manual. Read it a couple of times, and you'll be doing these in your sleep."

About an hour later, the SI Squad clerk dropped off several cases at Bob's desk. "After this," she told Bob, "your newly assigned cases will be placed in your mailbox in the conference room. When your reports are ready for typing, put them in the in-box on my desk." Bob looked over the cases and started to plan his fieldwork.

Hours for WFO personnel were 9:00 a.m.–5:30 p.m. with Saturdays and Sundays off. Agents received premium pay for working at least 469 hours of administratively uncontrollable overtime (AUO) per year. That averaged out to about 10-extra hours a week. Premium pay was figured at 25 % of the rate of a GS-10, step 1. It was added to the agents' biweekly salaries. USSS agents called premium pay "PL," which was the abbreviation for public law, the type of legislation that authorized the compensation.

Bob arrived home late the next two nights. He was spending the evening interviewing references and conducting neighborhood checks for his assigned security investigations. Bob was making good progress.

By Thursday afternoon, Bob was already writing up one of the cases when he was called to Bert de Freese's office. Seated in the office with de Freese was senior Agent (GS-13) Tom Dailey. Tom coordinated protective assignments for WFO personnel. "Bob, there's a presidential movement to the Washington Hilton this evening," de Freese informed. "The office is short on available agents. Tom wants to use you as a post stander, and I agree. Normally, we don't like new agents working protection until they've at least graduated T-school or have some OJT under their belts. I'm not concerned in your case since you were a police officer and SY agent. Just don't shoot anyone who's wearing a lapel pin," de Freese joked.

Passing a slip of paper to Bob, Dailey stated: "Here's your assignment notification with reporting instructions. I'll tell the advance agent to make sure you're well briefed."

That afternoon, Bob reported to the International Ballroom of the Washington Hilton Hotel (1919 Connecticut Avenue, NW, D.C.). The hotel was built in 1965 and designed in the shape of a double arch (as viewed from the air). It had become one of the most popular convention hotels in the city. The ballroom seated over 1,000 guests for banquets and featured tall, majestic ceilings. Designed with no supporting pillars, the ballroom presented unobstructed views.

The site advance agent started the security briefing by introducing Bob to the other WFO agents. Then, the agent proceeded with the protective details for the event—American Football Coaches' Association Coach of the Year Banquet. The president was scheduled to arrive at 9:30 p.m. Security would be put in effect at 6:00 p.m. to allow time for the bomb sweep, which needed to be finished before the doors could be opened to guests. The advance agent ended the briefing with: "This is a big event for the president. He was a varsity football player at the University of Michigan and a coach at Yale University. Be on your toes tonight. I've been told some headquarters heavies might drop by for this one."

Bob was posted outdoors at the T Street side of the hotel. The advance agent briefed Bob as to the duties of the post. This area contained VIP and public entrances. President Ford would be arriving by motorcade at the VIP entrance. This entrance opened into a private area, which housed an elevator and a spiral stairway. One floor down, a corridor led to the stage entrance of the ballroom. Smaller meeting rooms were also accessed here. One room was designated a holding room for the president, while another was the Secret Service command post.

The T Street public entrance led into the terrace level of the hotel. From this level, guests could access the other floors of the hotel via stairways and elevators. Both public and VIP entrances were accessed by a single driveway and sidewalk that were just off T Street.

T Street had been posted earlier with "Emergency No Parking" signs. Now, T Street was being closed between Connecticut and Florida Avenues. A rope line had been set along the sidewalk to block entry into the presidential arrival area and to funnel guests into the T Street public entrance.

Later that evening, an older agent stopped by Bob's post. Bob thought the individual was probably from headquarters. The agent extended his hand and introduced himself. "I'm Bill Foster from Protective Forces."

"Glad to meet you, sir. I'm Bob Ritter."

"Bob, I've been told you just transferred from SY."

"Yes, sir, I was sworn in on Monday."

Foster broke a nervous laugh as he said: "This might be some kind of modern-day record—working presidential protection after only a couple of days on the job. What protective experience do you have?"

"I worked foreign dignitaries and Mrs. Kissinger's detail at State. Before that, I was a Park Police officer. I worked protective movements and at Camp David. I also walked the White House sidewalk, Ellipse, and Lafayette Park beats."

"Good," Foster said—looking a bit relieved. "Then you're familiar with the *basic* principle of Secret Service protection."

"It's a system of concentric security perimeters that provide 360-degree protection," Bob answered.

"That's right," Foster affirmed, looking even more relieved. "Keeping that in mind, what are the duties of your post?"

"I'm controlling access to the arrival area and observing everyone coming in and out of the hotel—looking for anyone suspicious. I'm also watching the windows in the building across the street. When we get near the time the presidential motorcade will depart the White House, the site advance agent will close this side of the sidewalk at Florida Avenue. An agent will secure the T Street public doors from the inside, so no one can come out who's not cleared. I'll be out here with MPD making sure this side of the street is clear of anyone who isn't authorized. The public area will then become a credentialed press area for the president's arrival. After the president is inside, we'll reopen this side of the sidewalk and the T Street public entrance. We'll close them back down again for the president's departure."

"Very good, nice meeting you, Bob, and good luck in your career," Foster said.

Bob continued to be called upon for post standing duties. The Washington Field Office was short of agents—especially in the journeyman grade (GS-12). The Service was having problems filling vacant senior agent positions at the WFO. After doing a tour on a protective detail or headquarters assignment, most agents wished to transfer to one of the 64 USSS districts *outside* of Washington. The Washington Field Office with its heavy protective burden was not a prime choice for agents who wanted to get back to criminal investigation and a less hectic pace. Only agents who wanted to remain in the D.C. area asked for reassignments to WFO.

A peculiarity of the Washington Field Office was that it had more female special agents than all other Secret Service offices combined. The first-five women to be appointed Secret Service agents started at the WFO in December 1971. All five had been with the Executive Protective Service, which opened its ranks to female officers in 1970. The practice of starting most female SAs at WFO continued through the 1970s. SAIC Gittens was a firm believer in equal opportunity. The women agents were treated no differently than the men.

In the coming weeks and months, Bob and Tom welcomed other rookie agents to the WFO. Agents Barbara Riggs and Charles Fowler joined Bob and Tom in the SI Squad. Charlie had been an MPD officer prior to joining the Service. He sported a mustache that was made more prominent by a prematurely receding hairline. Looking more like a CPA than a federal agent, Charlie spoke slowly and chose his words wisely. His addition added another black agent to the WFO roster.

Bob was supportive of the hiring and advancement of minorities and women. He figured that varied backgrounds, views, skills, and ideas were essential, so the culture of the Secret Service could adapt to modern day challenges. At Park Police and the Department of State, Bob had witnessed firsthand the benefits of cultural diversity. In his opinion, both organizations were more effective because of it. Working alongside women and diverse ethnicities, Bob treated them fairly and objectively. Bob was rewarded by gaining new perspectives and insights. He wanted to work with people who have "good hearts" and who "perform their duties competently." That was more important to Bob than race, religion, gender, sexual orientation, and the like.

Barbara Riggs was the 10th woman special agent to be hired in the then 110-year history (1865–1975) of the U.S. Secret Service. A graduate of Cornell University, Barbara had majored in International Studies and Spanish. She was bright, intelligent, and vivacious. Bob knew Barbara had what it takes to break glass ceilings and to become a top agent.

When Barbara found out Bob was a former SY agent, she confided to him: "I was thinking about entering the Foreign Service. My parents hosted foreign exchange students. I traveled and lived in Latin America. I also considered going to law school."

Bob responded: "Barb, you're a lot like me. You need adventure. Being a Foreign Service officer or an attorney wouldn't be exciting enough for you. This will be a perfect fit."

"I don't know, Bob. But, I'm going to give it a try."

Coming home one night during his first few weeks on the job, Bob appeared to be on edge. "Is everything okay?" I asked.

"I met Art [my brother] downtown after work. He wanted to welcome me to the Service."

"And," I said.

"I'm kind of down."

"Why?" I asked in surprise.

"He told me I needed a 'rabbi.' "

"A rabbi," I said in a confused tone.

"Apparently, that's what they call a *hook* in the Secret Service—someone high up who can help your career advance. I met Art at this bar where HQ agents go after work until traffic clears up. Art suggested I stop by from time to time and build some relationships."

"What did you tell him?"

"I'm a field office agent. I have protection assignments and investigations in the evenings. I'm not going to have the time. And the spare time I get, I promised to spend with you and the kids. And even though I'm drinking straight Coca-Cola, I don't think ASAIC Cavanaugh is going to want to hear that one of his new agents hangs around a bar before he hits the road in a G-ride or reports for a protection assignment. I told Art if hard work and forward thinking isn't going to get me ahead then I'm going to be a terminal 12."

"What did he say to that?"

"Art said my plan *might* work, but it's going to take a 'whole hell of a lot more time and effort.' "

"Bobbie, do you think he was putting you on?"

"No, he had the best of intentions. I told him thanks for the advice, but it's not my way. It's just disheartening to me if that's the way the Secret Service operates."

And it wasn't Bob's way. To Bob, the journey and day-to-day achievement were more important and much more satisfying. Bob wanted to earn his rewards. Any other way wouldn't be right.

Soon it was March 1975. Bob, Tom, Barbara, and Charlie reported to the Consolidated Federal Law Enforcement Training Center (CFLETC) for one of the last Treasury agent schools held at 1310 L Street. The CFLETC would move that summer to Glenn County (Glynco), Georgia and be renamed the Federal Law Enforcement Training Center (FLETC). A delay in constructing permanent CFLETC facilities in the D.C. area caused the center to be relocated (in a cost-cutting measure) to a surplus military base, the former Glynco Naval Air Station near Brunswick, Georgia.

Criminal Investigator School Number 734 consisted of 50 agents from the following Treasury agencies: Secret Service; Customs Service; Alcohol, Tobacco and Firearms; and the Internal Revenue Service. The 12-week course covered the following topics: interviewing, surveillance, undercover operations, search and seizure, arrest techniques, federal criminal law, defensive tactics, marksmanship, and dignitary protection.

ATSAIC de Freese offered Bob a deal. Bob could keep the government car during training as long as he would do some backgrounds in the evenings and on weekends. At the same time, Bob would be able to qualify for his PL. And, he wouldn't have to use our car for home to school. Bob accepted the offer.

The 12 weeks rolled by. Bob attended school, worked backgrounds in his spare time, and studied. A comical moment occurred during one of Bob's homework assignments. Bob had been issued a Pentax 35mm camera to photograph some pretend crime and accident scenes. Our seven-year-old daughter volunteered to model. Carrie posed motionless on our living-room floor, while I spread some ketchup on her forehead. Bob and I were busily staging the scene when we were surprised by a neighbor, who had come to our open front door and peered through the glass-paneled storm door. Seeing Carrie lying on the floor with eyes closed and what looked like a head injury, our neighbor threw open the door and excitedly cried out, *"What happened?"*

Our daughter sprang up like a jack-in-the-box and answered: "Don't worry. I'm okay. I'm just helping my daddy become a *secret agent*."

Graduation day arrived. I was especially proud of Bob when he received the class award for highest scholastic average. Barb Riggs told me that Bob even beat a law school grad and former assistant U.S. attorney in the law exam. Bob was also the *first* person to have graduated from both the CFLETC Police School and the Criminal Investigator School.

School ended on a Thursday, so out-of-town agents could use Friday as a travel day. For Bob, Tom, Barb, and Charlie, it was back to business as usual at the WFO. On Friday, May 2, 1975, they carpooled with other WFO-SAs to Winchester, Virginia. The President and Mrs. Ford would attend the 48th Shenandoah Apple Blossom Festival. The Ford's daughter, Susan, was chosen to be queen of the festival.

After the coronation ceremony, the President and Mrs. Ford rode in the Firemen's Parade. Comedian Bob Hope was the grand marshal. It was the first time since the JFK assassination in Dallas (November 22, 1963) that a president and first lady rode together in an open-car motorcade. The Secret Service provided parade security and counter-sniper coverage. Assigned as agent liaison to an EPS counter sniper team, Bob spent that sunny and warm afternoon on a rooftop watching the crowd and buildings along the parade route through a pair of binoculars.

In a turnabout that could only happen to a Secret Service agent, Bob spent the next day underwater in a submarine. Bob was one of the WFO agents who were sent via helicopter to Norfolk, Virginia for President Ford's participation in the commissioning ceremony of the nuclear aircraft carrier USS *Nimitz* (CVA-68). The keel laying for the *Nimitz* was in June 1968, and she was launched in May 1972. Three years later with sea trials behind her, the *Nimitz* was ready to take her place in the fleet.

For the occasion, the *Nimitz* was docked at Pier 12, Norfolk Naval Station with the other vessels in her nuclear-powered task force: the guided-missile cruisers USS *California* (CGN-36) and USS *South Carolina* (CGN-37) and the fast-attack submarine USS *Ray* (SSN-653).

The *Ray* was commissioned in April 1967. She was 292 feet long and had a speed in excess of 20 knots. Designed with a teardrop hull and sailplane contour for maximum underwater speed and maneuverability, the *Ray* featured four torpedo tubes that could fire Mk 48 torpedoes and anti-submarine rockets (SUBROC). In those days, the SUBROCs carried 5-kiloton *nuclear* warheads. The *Ray* was also equipped with the latest in sonar and electronic countermeasures for her hunter-killer mission.

Since the cruisers and submarine had formidable weapons systems and were "ready to go to war," the Secret Service placed an agent aboard each for liaison purposes. As portable radios were useless within the hull of a submarine, the agent would have to communicate via the secure control center of the *Ray*. Bob was chosen because he had been granted sensitive compartmented information (SCI) access while at SY and had knowledge of CRYPTO operations.

Reporting to the end of Pier 12 where the USS *Ray* was tied up, Bob presented his credentials to security personnel. Bob was cleared and crossed over a gangway to the deck of the *Ray*. There, he stepped into a hatchway and climbed down a ladder into the operations compartment of the sub. He was met and welcomed aboard by the executive officer (XO) of the *Ray*. After verifying Bob's credentials, the XO gave Bob a tour of the sub, which included a peek at a locked-down weapons console. Afterwards, Bob settled in at the officers' wardroom (dining area) until the presidential movement was over.

Later that evening back in D.C., Bob and some of the other WFO Norfolk post standers reported to the Washington Hilton for yet another protective assignment. President and Mrs. Ford attended the 61st Annual White House Press Correspondents' Association Dinner. Other USSS protectees attending were Vice President Nelson Rockefeller, Secretary of State Henry Kissinger, and Treasury Secretary William Simon. Bob didn't arrive home until after midnight. This was the type of day that foreshadowed the coming 1976 presidential campaign for agents of WFO.

In international news, the year 1975 finally brought an end to U.S. involvement in Vietnam. Although U.S. combat troops had departed Vietnam in March 1973 as stipulated by the Paris Peace Accords, the U.S. continued to support the South Vietnamese government with military and economic aid. The peace treaty also provided for the return of U.S. prisoners of war, a ceasefire, and for the eventual reunification of Vietnam.

However, hostilities resumed, and in April 1975 North Vietnamese forces pushed into South Vietnam capturing city after city on their way to Saigon. President Ford instituted "Operation Frequent Wind," which became the biggest helicopter evacuation in history. About 7,500 American and South Vietnamese personnel were airlifted to safety. On April 30, 1975, Saigon fell to North Vietnamese forces.

The fall of South Vietnam and the communist Khmer Rouge military takeover of Cambodia was a hot topic of discussion around WFO. Then on May 12, 1975, the Khmer Rouge seized a U.S. merchant marine container ship, the SS *Mayaguez*, which had been operating in international waters well off the coast of Cambodia. The Khmer Rouge suspected the *Mayaguez* was carrying military cargo. Before the *Mayaguez* was boarded and seized, her captain was able to send a distress signal. Forced to sail to the island of Koh Tang, the vessel anchored offshore. The crew of the *Mayaguez* was then removed to the island.

Fearing another incident like the USS *Pueblo*, whose crew was put on trial and imprisoned by North Korea in 1968, President Ford ordered a military response to Cambodia's "act of piracy." On May 15, a U.S. Navy destroyer pulled alongside the *Mayaguez*, and a boarding party of U.S. Marines secured the abandoned ship.

With naval and Air Force support, Marines invaded the island of Koh Tang in an attempt to locate and rescue the hostages. The Marines encountered heavy resistance, and three U.S. helicopters were shot down. Unknown to U.S. authorities, the 39-member crew of the *Mayaguez* had already been removed from Koh Tang to the Cambodian mainland and then to another island where they were released prior to the start of hostilities. A fishing boat then carried the *Mayaguez* crew to a U.S. Navy warship.

With the seamen freed, the U.S. command recalled the force of Marines from Koh Tang. During the battle and subsequent withdrawal from the island, 15 U.S. military personnel were killed, and 50 were wounded. Three Marines were listed as missing in action (MIA). It was believed that the MIAs were eventually captured and executed by the Khmer Rouge.

Bob stood posts for protective movements and continued to work SI cases through the hot Washington summer. On Friday afternoon, September 5, 1975, Bob was at the Washington Field Office closing out his casework in preparation for the USSS Special Agent Training Course (SATC) that he was scheduled to begin on the following Monday. With the abruptness and intensity of an afternoon thunderstorm, alarming news passed through the office. Someone had attempted to shoot President Ford in Sacramento, California.

The president's morning began with a motorcade to the Sacramento Community Convention Center for a breakfast speech to business and civic leaders. President Ford then returned to his suite at the Senator Hotel to freshen up for engagements at the California State Capitol where he would cap the visit with an address to a joint session of the legislature. Opting to walk to the nearby capitol building through an adjoining park, the president, accompanied by staff and Secret Service, departed the hotel at 10:02 a.m.

Along the way, Ford shook hands with onlookers who gathered for a chance to see the president. Also in the crowd was 26-year-old Lynnette "Squeaky" Fromme. As Ford neared Fromme, she pulled a .45-caliber Colt semiautomatic pistol from a holster strapped to her thigh. The gun was hidden by a long red robe and floral-print dress. Fromme pointed the gun at Ford, but it did not fire. Immediately, USSS Agent Larry Buendorf wrestled Fromme to the ground where she was disarmed and handcuffed. Agents of the presidential detail whisked Ford through the park area into the safety of the capitol building.

Although not implicated in the horrific Tate-LaBianca murders of 1969, Squeaky Fromme had been a follower of Charles Manson since 1967. She sat outside the Los Angeles Courthouse during the murder trial (6/70– 1/71) of Manson and other family members. To draw attention to her protest, she shaved her head and carved an "X" in her forehead.

After Manson's conviction and imprisonment, Fromme and some other Manson family members formed the International People's Court of Retribution. They warned corporate executives to stop polluting or die.

Subsequently, Fromme moved to Sacramento to be near Manson, who was incarcerated at Folsom State Prison. Bob believed Fromme used the opportunity of Ford's Sacramento visit to make headlines. Shooting the president would give Fromme worldwide notoriety to draw attention to Manson's imprisonment and her extremist views on environmental pollution.

Fromme was the first woman to attempt to assassinate a U.S. president. She was also the first person to be convicted and sentenced under the provisions of 18 USC Section 1751. The law was passed in 1965 because of the JFK assassination and the aftermath in Dallas. Before that time, it was not a federal violation to kill, kidnap, or assault a U.S. president or vice president. The law also provided penalties for anyone convicted of conspiring or attempting to kill, kidnap, or assault a president or vice president.

Fromme was convicted of attempting to kill the president; she received the maximum sentence: life imprisonment. On December 23, 1987, Fromme escaped from the Federal Prison Camp in Alderson, West Virginia. She was recaptured two days later within several miles of the prison. Fromme reportedly escaped in order to see Charles Manson, who was rumored to be ill. In July 2008, Fromme was paroled, but another 15 months were added on for the prison escape conviction. With time credited for good behavior, Fromme was released in August 2009.

Tom Conaty and Bob reported to the U.S. Secret Service Training Division (1717 H Street, NW, D.C.) for Special Agent Training Course Number 58. The Fromme assassination attempt of the preceding Friday was the hot topic. USSS training instructors revealed that the pistol Fromme used contained a loaded magazine, but there was no round in the firing chamber. In order for a semiautomatic pistol like the Colt Model 1911 to be made ready for firing, the slide must be pulled to the rear, which cocks the exposed hammer. When the slide is released, it springs forward to pick up a round from the magazine and deposits it in the chamber. If the safety is off, the gun can now be fired with a pull of the trigger. Once the weapon is fired, the blowback from the round's discharge will automatically ready the pistol for the next shot.

It was believed Fromme either manually cocked the hammer or pulled back and released the slide before inserting the magazine. In either case, the gun could not fire, and Ford and the Secret Service were *extremely* fortunate. Firing .45-caliber rounds at the president from such close range would surely have been fatal.

Agent Buendorf received the U.S. Secret Service Valor Award for his courageous action. Without hesitation, Buendorf charged Fromme when the weapon was drawn. He then tried to insert his thumb between the cocked hammer and frame of the gun, so the hammer could not strike the firing pin. At the same time, Buendorf drove Fromme to the ground and disarmed her.

Buendorf's heroic response served as inspiration for Bob, Tom, and the other 34 agents in the SATC as they dove into the course material. The SATC was a seven-week school of specialized USSS training. Topics included: USSS history and legal authority, USSS forms and reports, interviewing and interrogation, forgery investigation, handwriting analysis, U.S. coins and currency, counterfeiting, special investigations, protection, protective intelligence, 10-minute medicine, technical security, and assassination. As Bob said: "This is the essence of what a Secret Service agent is. It's important that it's learned inside out."

On the evening of September 18, 1975, Bob and I were recapping our day over dinner when a news flash broke. Kidnapped heiress Patricia Hearst and three members of the Symbionese Liberation Army had been arrested in San Francisco, California. The FBI followed the trail of several SLA associates that eventually led to two San Francisco apartments. Bill and Emily Harris were arrested at one of the hideouts when they returned from jogging. Hearst and Wendy Yoshimura were taken into custody at the other. Hearst's capture ended one of the largest and most famous manhunts in history. When asked during booking what her occupation was, Hearst responded, "Urban guerilla."

In 1976, Hearst went on trial for federal bank robbery and weapons violations. Her defense attorney, F. Lee Bailey, argued that Patty had been brainwashed and coerced. Three psychiatric experts testified for the defense that Hearst was not responsible for her actions at the time of the bank robbery. Expert witnesses for the government testified that Hearst voluntarily participated in the crime.

Hearst was subsequently found guilty and sentenced to seven years in prison. On February 1, 1979, after serving almost two years in federal prison, Patricia Hearst's sentence was commuted to time served by President Jimmy Carter. In 2001, President Bill Clinton, on the last day of his presidency, granted Hearst a full pardon.

After hearing the news of the SLA arrests, Bob mentioned that President Ford was embarking on another California trip, and coincidentally one of the stops was San Francisco. It would be the first trip back to California since the September 5th assassination attempt. Thinking of the president's safety, I remarked to Bob, "It's a good thing they were captured before Ford's visit."

"Yes, but it's one of those things that might prompt others to act," Bob replied cautiously. "And, you have the recent Fromme attempt. The copycat phenomenon can come into play with someone who identifies with Fromme or Hearst and wants to make a statement and become famous at the same time." We finished eating our dinner, and I thought no more about it.

Four days later on Monday, September 22, 1975, President Ford was winding up his West Coast trip with a visit to San Francisco. Earlier in the day at the Hyatt Regency Hotel, the president addressed the 58th Annual Convention of the AFL-CIO Building and Construction Trades Department. Although only a block away, the president took no chances and decided to motor—rather than walk—to his next stop. The motorcade took less than a minute to reach the St. Francis Hotel. There, President Ford attended receptions and gave remarks to the World Affairs Council of Northern California. After the address, Ford gave a videotaped interview to KPIX-TV.

At 3:28 p.m., the president wrapped up the interview and proceeded to the motorcade area. While exiting the St. Francis for the presidential limousine, a single shot rang out from across the street. Ford was pushed into the armored limo by Secret Service Agents Ron Pontius and Jack Merchant, and the motorcade sped off for San Francisco International Airport. With Ford safely aboard, *Air Force One* departed for Andrews Air Force Base, Maryland. At Andrews, the president transferred to *Marine One* for the short helicopter flight to the White House South Grounds.

Back in San Francisco, 45-year-old Sara Jane "Sally" Moore was in federal custody. Moore was a divorcee and mother of a nine-year-old son. She had been a bookkeeper for the People In Need (PIN) 1974 food giveaway, which had been funded by the Hearst family in hope the SLA would release Patty Hearst. Two million dollars worth of food was distributed. Moore had given information regarding fraud in the PIN program to San Francisco Police. She had also been a sometime FBI informant into the radical movement.

Of late, Moore had purchased a Charter Arms .44 Special revolver from Mark Fernwood, reportedly a member of the right-wing John Birch

Society. Moore had passed details of the transaction to police and the Bureau of Alcohol, Tobacco and Firearms for possible gun violations.

On Saturday, September 20, 1975, Moore called Inspector Jack O'Shea, a San Francisco Police Department (SFPD) detective she had known since her PIN days. According to O'Shea, Moore complained about "the system" and said she was "going to Stanford to test it." Moore also told O'Shea that she was going to ask him something that would make him "recoil in horror." Moore then asked O'Shea if he could have her arrested. Surprised, O'Shea said he could if Moore was carrying the gun she had recently purchased.

The "Stanford" reference worried O'Shea, as President Ford was scheduled to visit Stanford University (Palo Alto, California) the next day for the dedication of a new law school building. O'Shea notified the FBI and the Secret Service of the information.

On Sunday, September 21, O'Shea sent two San Francisco police officers to Moore's apartment—just in case. Moore wasn't at home. She was taking an undercover ATF agent to Mark Fernwood's residence in Danville, California. The agent wanted to check out Fernwood's operation. After looking over Fernwood's gun collection, Moore and the ATF undercover agent departed.

When Moore arrived home at about 2:30 p.m., the SFPD stakeout officers asked if she was carrying a weapon. She acknowledged that she had one in her purse. The officers seized the unloaded .44 Special revolver and some rounds of ammunition from her handbag. Several boxes of .44-caliber ammunition were also confiscated from Moore's car. Moore was placed under arrest and booked for possession of a concealed weapon, which was only a misdemeanor offense.

SFPD called the Secret Service to see if they wanted Moore detained until the USSS could interview her. Secret Service advised that wasn't necessary, as they would contact her later that evening. Moore was released and returned to her apartment. Since it was late in the day, Moore had missed the opportunity to drive out to Stanford for the presidential visit.

That night, Moore was picked up at her residence and taken for questioning to the USSS San Francisco Field Office (SFFO) by agents Gary Yauger (USSS Intelligence Division, Washington, D.C.) and Martin Haskell (USSS-SFFO). During the interview, Moore telephoned Inspector O'Shea and expressed concern for her situation. O'Shea advised her to tell the agents what she had told him, and she'd be all right. Later, Agent Yauger also talked with O'Shea regarding Moore.

Agent Yauger's initial evaluation was that Sara Jane Moore was "not of protective interest." She was free to go and no arrangements were made to keep her under surveillance. A protective intelligence background investigation was initiated to look at Moore further.

The next morning (Monday, September 22, 1975), Moore drove back to Danville, California. She used a ruse to purchase another handgun. Moore told Fernwood she wanted a handgun for a woman friend. The friend would be leaving shortly for a backwoods outing and needed a gun for self-defense. When Fernwood said he wanted to meet the woman, Moore answered that her friend didn't have the time. Moore assured Fernwood that the woman knew how to handle a firearm. Fernwood sold Moore a nickel-finish Smith & Wesson .38-caliber pistol and some wadcutter target loads.

Then, Moore drove back to San Francisco. She parked her 1970 Toyota in a garage near the St. Francis Hotel. Along with hundreds of others, Moore waited behind police barricades for the presidential departure. She kept her hands in the pockets of the blue raincoat she was wearing.

At approximately 3:30 p.m., President Ford appeared at the Post Street exit of the St. Francis. A cheer arose from the crowd. Ford smiled and waved. Moore drew the revolver from her purse, took aim with a two-handed hold, and fired one shot at Ford from about 40 feet away. Police and Secret Service agents rushed toward Moore and subdued her. Ford escaped injury and was evacuated from the scene.

Oliver Sipple, a former Marine who served in Vietnam, may have deflected Moore's aim and prevented her from firing follow-up shots. Sipple was in the crowd and lunged at Moore when he saw the gun. In any event, Moore's shot missed the president. The bullet hit a concrete wall, expending most of its energy before it ricocheted off. Striking a bystander, the bullet failed to penetrate and caused no serious injury.

Moore told investigators she would have gotten Ford if her .44-caliber revolver had not been confiscated. Moore, who claimed to have received firearms training during a stint with the Women's Army Corps (WAC) in the early 1950s, was accurate with the .44 during recent target practice. The assassination attempt was the first time Moore was able to shoot the newly acquired .38-caliber revolver. Unfamiliar with the shooting characteristics of the gun, Moore's shot missed its mark.

Sara Jane Moore was the first person to fire a bullet at a president since the JFK assassination of 1963. Since Moore had been interviewed by Secret Service agents the night before the attempt, Congress scheduled a review of USSS procedures and actions. There were specific concerns regarding the information given to the Secret Service by the SFPD, the subsequent USSS interview of Moore, and Agent Yauger's decision not to place Moore under surveillance. A hearing into the matter was held by the Senate Subcommittee on Treasury, Postal Service and General Appropriations with Senator Joseph Montoya (Democrat-New Mexico) presiding.

San Francisco Police Inspector Jack O'Shea testified that he informed both the FBI and Secret Service that Moore "might be another Squeaky Fromme." O'Shea added that he had six enlargements made of Moore's driver's license photo for the Secret Service, but they failed to pick them up. O'Shea stated that any belief by the Secret Service that he was not concerned about Moore must have been a misunderstanding.

USSS Agent Gary Yauger would testify that he asked O'Shea: "Do we need anything else? Do we have a problem?"

O'Shea's memory of the conversation was that Agent Yauger asked instead, "Is there anything else?" Both men agreed that O'Shea answered, "No." Yauger believed that O'Shea was saying Moore was not a problem, and O'Shea believed that he was only replying that he had no additional information.

Agent Yauger emphasized to the subcommittee that Sara Jane Moore showed no signs of mental instability. Additionally, Moore displayed no animosity toward the president. With the facts he had at the time of the interview, Yauger believed his evaluation of Moore was correct; he'd make the same decision again.

U.S. Secret Service Assistant Director (AD) James Burke testified that Moore exhibited nothing to warrant her being followed. AD Burke revealed that an internal review of the Moore case had affirmed that the agents' judgment and actions were proper. It was the official position of the U.S. Secret Service that Sara Jane Moore was not a danger to President Ford at the time of the interview. In spite of Secret Service testimony to the contrary, Chairman Montoya wrapped up the two-day hearing by concluding, "What did happen proved to be erroneous human judgment."

Sara Jane Moore was indicted for attempting to murder the president of the United States (18 USC Section 1751). Found competent to stand trial, Moore entered a guilty plea to the attempted assassination charge and was sentenced to life imprisonment. On February 5, 1979, Moore escaped from the Federal Prison Camp at Alderson, West Virginia. She was recaptured several hours later. Convicted of the prison escape, Moore was sentenced to an additional three years to run consecutively. On December 31, 2007, Sara Jane Moore was released from federal prison.

Back at the Special Agent Training Course, Bob and Tom enjoyed the informative field trips, which highlighted the school's schedule. Visits to Crane & Company of Dalton, Massachusetts, the Bureau of Engraving and Printing (BEP) in Washington, D.C., and the U.S. Mint in Philadelphia, Pennsylvania were part of the counterfeiting block of instruction.

Crane & Co. began providing paper for the production of U.S. currency in 1879. They became the sole supplier of currency paper for the Department of Treasury. The trade name for the special paper is "Marathon." It's composed of 75% cotton and 25% linen. Embedded within the paper and visible to the naked eye are red and blue rayon fibers, which act as a security feature.

Bob showed me how you can pick these fibers out with a pair of tweezers. "That's a good field test to help determine if a note is genuine," Bob explained. "Most counterfeiters print red and blue lines to resemble the fibers or leave them out altogether. With the counterfeit printed red and blue lines, you can scratch them off with your nail or rub them off with an eraser."

Bob did warn that some counterfeiters have bleached genuine $1.00 bills to remove the ink from the paper. Next, they print higher denomination (20, 50, and 100) counterfeit bills on the genuine paper. These counterfeit notes can be especially deceptive since they have the feel of genuine notes and feature the red and blue security fibers. Accordingly, it's a federal felony violation to possess blank currency paper or any paper identical in composition.

An interesting fact I learned from Bob is that the average life of a dollar bill is about 18 months. Likewise, notes can be folded approximately 4,000 times before tearing. Federal Reserve System member banks remove worn notes from circulation and return them for destruction and replacement to the regional Federal Reserve Bank.

Bob also divulged some of the physical characteristics of U.S. currency. Uncirculated notes weigh about one gram and stack 233 to the inch. There are roughly 490 notes to the pound, so a million dollars in singles would weigh approximately 2,000 pounds.

Since July 1929, the dimensions of U.S. currency have been approximately 2.61 inches by 6.14 inches. Before that time, notes were larger at about 3.12 inches by 7.42 inches. Bob said we have the Philippines to thank for the smaller size notes. When the Philippines were still a possession of the United States, the BEP manufactured the peso for use in the islands. So as not to confuse the two currencies, the Philippine notes were designed to be one-third the size of U.S. currency. The smaller size notes were more easily handled and became popular with Americans who lived in the Philippines.

It was suggested that U.S. currency be reduced to the smaller, more convenient size. The Treasury Department studied the matter and agreed. The smaller notes were also cheaper to print. The faces and backs could be printed in power presses at 12 notes per sheet. The backs of the large notes could only be printed at eight notes per sheet. Then, the original sheet of large notes had to be split in order to fit hand presses to print the faces at only four notes to the sheet. The small notes also lasted longer because they didn't have to be folded as much to fit into wallets and purses. Additionally, the small size currency stacked and stored better in bank vaults and took up less space in cash registers.

After relating the above, Bob said: "Okay, here's one for you. If you get this right, we'll go out for dinner tonight. Who was the first woman to be pictured on U.S. paper money?"

"I know this one," I confidently replied. "It's a trick question. There's never been a woman's portrait on U.S. currency. And I'm picking the restaurant."

"We'll still go out to dinner," Bob announced. "But the correct answer is Martha Washington. She first appeared on notes printed in 1886."

"Gosh, they should have chosen Dolley Madison. At least she saved the White House silver!" I grumbled.

Bob continued to enjoy the SATC and the information he learned. At the same time, the adventure continued for President Ford and his Secret Service White House Detail. During an October 14, 1975, visit to Hartford, Connecticut, the presidential limousine was struck broadside by another vehicle. It happened a little before 10:00 p.m., while the president was en route to Bradley International Airport after attending a Republican fundraiser at the Hartford Civic Center.

Fearful of another assassination attempt, Secret Service agents charged out of the follow-up vehicle with guns drawn. Agents covered the occupants of the striking vehicle, while the situation was assessed. A short time later, the presidential limo continued on its way to the airport. The limo had to travel at reduced speeds because the right front fender had been rammed into the adjacent tire.

Subsequent investigation ascertained that the incident was accidental and resulted from a police mistake. Motorcycle officers were responsible for closing off side streets, so the presidential motorcade could travel unimpeded. Somehow, they missed one intersection.

The presidential limousine entered the unsecured intersection on a red light. On the cross street, 19-year-old James Salamites was driving some friends in his mother's 1968 Buick LeSabre. Salamites had the green light and right of way. He continued into the intersection and collided with the presidential limo. The president and accompanying guests were thrown to the floor by the impact and sudden stop. Only one injury resulted from the mishap. One of the president's guests broke a bone in his hand when it slammed into the partition that separated the front and rear seat areas.

Bob had been a Secret Service agent for less than a year and already there had been two assassination attempts and an automobile accident involving the president. It was believed to be the first time ever that the Secret Service had a motor accident with the president aboard. And, only the second instance that a president was involved in a vehicular accident.

In 1902, William Craig was the first Secret Service operative killed in the line of duty. At the time, Craig and President Theodore Roosevelt were traveling in a horse-drawn carriage near Pittsfield, Massachusetts. A speeding trolley collided with the carriage. The force of the impact ejected Craig and the president from the open-air vehicle. Operative Craig died at the scene. President Roosevelt received only minor cuts and bruises.

Concerned at the recent events, I mentioned to Bob, "You might have to rethink Tecumseh's Curse."

"Jan, I know things have been wild lately. Yet, these three incidents only confirm the past 135 years of history. Since 1840, every president elected or reelected in a year ending in zero has died in office—four by assassination. Presidential assassination attempts and other incidents outside of these parameters have been unsuccessful. If history is *allowed* to repeat itself, the president elected in 1980 will die in office, and there's about a 60% chance the cause of death will be by assassination."

Chapter 19

Death in Dallas

The protective block was the last course material covered in Secret Service school. Hands-on training at Beltsville, Md. in driving armored limousines and working the follow-up was an exciting part of the instruction. A visit to the USSS Transportation Section (1310 L Street, NW, D.C.) was also scheduled. Another interesting subject for the agents was a review of presidential assassinations and attempts, especially the John Fitzgerald Kennedy (JFK) assassination. Of special interest to Bob was the section on protective intelligence.

The agents were surprised to learn of a little-known plot against JFK that occurred in 1960—three years before his assassination in Dallas. Richard Pavlick, a 73-year-old retired postal worker from Belmont, New Hampshire, had a known dislike for Catholics and the Kennedy family in particular. This resentment intensified when Pavlick became convinced that JFK's father, Joseph (Joe) Kennedy, had stolen the 1960 presidential election. Concluding that JFK's narrow victory over Richard Nixon was due to the power and wealth of the Kennedy family, Pavlick became incensed and decided to take matters in his own hand. Pavlick would prevent JFK from being inaugurated.

After giving away his small home and property to a local youth organization, Pavlick drove south to find the president-elect. Pavlick purchased dynamite, blasting caps, cans of gasoline, and detonating wire to use in a suicide bombing. He checked Kennedy family homes in Hyannis Port, Massachusetts and the Georgetown section of Washington, D.C.— looking for an opportunity to strike. Finding none that suited him, Pavlick followed the president-elect to Palm Beach, Florida. From the street, Pavlick carefully watched the Mediterranean-style mansion owned by Joe and Rose Kennedy at 1095 North Ocean Boulevard.

Pavlick planned the attempt for Sunday morning, December 11, 1960. Wiring his car with dynamite, Pavlick intended to ram JFK's limousine and detonate the explosives as the president-elect left his parents' home for church. Seeing Jacqueline (Jackie) Kennedy with children Caroline and John-John outside with the president-elect, Pavlick had a change of heart. He would wait for another opportunity.

Fortunately, Pavlick did not get a second chance. Pavlick had sent postcards back to his hometown hinting of a future calamity and that he would be heard from "in a big way." The postmaster recognized that the cards were mailed from cities the president-elect had been visiting. The Secret Service was notified.

A nationwide lookout was posted for Pavlick and his 1950 Buick. On December 15, 1960, Pavlick was arrested in Palm Beach, Florida. A search of Pavlick's vehicle and motel room discovered 10 sticks of dynamite and other bomb paraphernalia. Pavlick was charged with making threats against the president-elect (violation of 18 USC Section 871) and federal explosives violations.

Found incompetent, Pavlick was committed to a federal mental hospital in Springfield, Missouri until such time he could be tried. After JFK's death in 1963, federal charges against Pavlick were dropped, and he was transferred to the New Hampshire State Hospital at Concord. Pavlick was subsequently released in 1966 and died in 1975 at the age of 88.

Bob again considered the "what ifs" of history. If Pavlick had been successful in 1960, how might our past have changed? Lyndon Johnson would have become president three years earlier. U.S. involvement in Vietnam, the Bay of Pigs Invasion, and the Cuban Missile Crisis were only a few of the tough Cold War problems Johnson would have decided. Adding the domestic issues of the time, one can see how our history might have been drastically altered.

SAIC Winston "Win" Lawson of the USSS Liaison Division was a guest speaker on the JFK assassination for Bob's SATC. Lawson was a graduate of Buffalo University and had served in the Army as a counterintelligence agent. He was appointed to the Secret Service in 1959 and was initially assigned to the Syracuse Field Office.

Transferred to the White House Detail (WHD) in 1961, Lawson was the lead advance agent for JFK's ill-fated Dallas trip. Lawson added an emotionally moving dimension to the course material. Having a president assassinated during one's watch is the worst that could happen to a Secret Service agent. Lawson and the others working the motorcade that day are the *only* agents to have lost a president to assassination since the Secret Service began formal, full-time protection in 1902.

In November 1963, JFK and his advisors were laying strategy for the 1964 presidential campaign. Wins in Texas and Florida were crucial for reelection. Texas was problematic, as conservative and liberal leaders within the state Democratic Party were feuding. In 1960, Kennedy-Johnson barely took the state. In fact, they were outvoted in Dallas, which was a conservative stronghold. It was decided that the President and Mrs. Kennedy would visit Texas in a whirlwind two-day swing, which would encompass five cities. It was hoped the trip would unify Texas Democrats.

This would be Mrs. Kennedy's first extended travel with the president since the death in August of their infant son, Patrick. Born prematurely, Patrick had difficulty breathing and died when he was just two days old.

JFK looked forward to having Jackie accompany him. Loved by the American people as a figure of grace and elegance, Mrs. Kennedy was sure to capture the enthusiastic attention of both the public and the press.

On November 21, 1963, the president and first lady arrived at Kelly Air Force Base in San Antonio, Texas. They were welcomed by Texas Governor John Connally, Vice President Lyndon Johnson, and U.S. Senator Ralph Yarborough. All three would accompany the president throughout the Texas visit. Motoring to Brooks Air Force Base, JFK dedicated the USAF Aerospace Medical Center.

Next, the President and Mrs. Kennedy flew to Houston. After a motorcade through streets lined with onlookers, the Kennedys arrived at the Rice Hotel where they addressed the League of United Latin American Citizens (LULAC). Mrs. Kennedy electrified the crowd by delivering her speech in Spanish. That evening in the Sam Houston Coliseum, the president gave remarks at a testimonial dinner for Congressman Albert Thomas. The presidential party then flew to Fort Worth where they spent the night at the Hotel Texas.

The following morning, Friday, November 22, 1963, JFK spoke briefly to a crowd of several thousand well-wishers, who had gathered in a parking lot near the Hotel Texas. Returning inside the hotel, JFK addressed a breakfast gathering of the Fort Worth Chamber of Commerce. Afterwards, the president and first lady with Governor and Mrs. Connally motored to Carswell AFB. The President and Mrs. Kennedy departed via *Air Force One* (Boeing 707-tail number 26000) for the short flight to Dallas.

To prevent a double tragedy and for continuity of government (COG) reasons, the president and vice president do not travel in the same automobile, helicopter, airplane, etc. Accordingly, the Vice President and Mrs. Johnson flew from Fort Worth to Dallas aboard *Air Force Two* (Boeing 707-tail number 86970). The vice presidential aircraft arrived at Love Field at 11:30 a.m.; the touchdown of *Air Force One* was a short time later.

After the president and first lady were officially welcomed to Dallas, they moved to a nearby fence line to shake hands with some of the spectators who had turned out for the occasion. As she glided along the crowd, Jackie looked stunning in a pink wool suit trimmed in a collar of navy blue. A signature pillbox hat accented the ensemble.

At 11:55 a.m., the presidential motorcade departed Love Field en route to the Trade Mart where JFK was scheduled to give a luncheon speech to business and civic leaders. The motorcade route chosen by Agent Lawson was suggested by SAIC Forrest Sorrels of the Dallas Field Office. Sorrels was a living legend. He started with the Secret Service in 1923 and became the special agent in charge of the Dallas Field Office in 1935. Sorrels had been providing presidential protection in Dallas since FDR's 1936 visit.

The White House staff had allotted 45 minutes for the initial motorcade to the Trade Mart. It was planned to be a *slow*-moving procession along a route that afforded the public the best opportunity to see the President and Mrs. Kennedy. For downtown Dallas, Main Street was utilized, as it featured heavily populated buildings and was a wide thoroughfare.

After the procession through downtown Dallas, the motorcade would need to take the Stemmons Freeway, which was the most direct route to the Trade Mart. Unfortunately, the ramp to the Stemmons Freeway could not be accessed from Main Street. A concrete median prevented this. Thus, the motorcade would have to take a right onto northbound Houston Street and then a left onto westbound Elm Street, which connected to the Stemmons Freeway. This maneuver would bring the motorcade in view of additional buildings and people. One of these buildings was the Texas School Book Depository (TSBD), a seven-story brick structure with windows overlooking Elm Street.

The presidential limousine used for the Dallas stop was Secret Service (SS) 100-X, a 1961 Lincoln Continental convertible. The vehicle was modified by custom coachbuilder Hess and Eisenhart of Cincinnati, Ohio. Thirty-three inches were added to the frame to give the car a 154-inch wheelbase. The vehicle weighed in at almost 8,000 pounds with a body length over 21 feet. The interior was custom upholstered, appointed with presidential seals, and configured with foldaway jump seats. The rear trunk was fitted with handrails and the rear bumper with steps, so Secret Service agents could ride at the back of the limo as needed.

A custom "bubbletop" consisting of six-interconnecting pieces of plexiglass had been designed to cover the car's occupants from inclement weather. The clear plastic allowed the president to be seen during processions and parades in spite of the weather. Contrary to the popular belief of the day, the bubbletop had no significant ballistic properties. The plexiglass was only a quarter-inch thick and was not bulletproof. When not in use, the bubbletop stacked neatly in the trunk.

SAIC Lawson related to the agents of SATC Number 58 that since the bubbletop was *not* considered a protective-security feature, the decision to use it or not was based solely on the weather and the wishes of presidential staff. On the morning of November 22, 1963, Lawson had been advised by WHD-ASAIC Roy Kellerman that presidential aide Kenneth O'Donnell had requested the bubbletop to be off if the weather was clear and not raining. Although it had been raining earlier in the day, the sky cleared in time for President Kennedy's Dallas arrival. It was sunny with temperatures in the 70s. The bubbletop stayed in the trunk.

In hindsight, it was suggested by some agents that the bubbletop might have prevented the assassination. They believed that Oswald might have thought the bubbletop was bulletproof and not fired. Some speculated the plastic might have distorted Oswald's aim or deflected the fatal bullet's trajectory.

Motorcycles and a pilot car led off the Dallas motorcade. Staying about a quarter mile ahead of the lead car, these units served as a forward guard. The motorcycle officers and pilot car alerted police along the route of the motorcade's progress and assured that cross street traffic was stopped and that the roadway was clear. Additionally, they watched for any signs of trouble and were able to communicate with the lead car if an alternate route needed to be taken.

The lead car functioned as a mobile command center and guided the presidential limousine as to the route to follow. Lawson rode in the lead car since he was the WHD advance agent. The lead car was driven by Dallas Police Chief Jesse Curry. The vehicle also carried SAIC Sorrels and Dallas County Sheriff Bill Decker.

Following the lead car was SS 100-X with the president in the right rear. Mrs. Kennedy sat to the president's left. Governor and Mrs. Connally occupied the right and left jump seats respectively. The presidential limo was driven by SA William Greer with WHD-ASAIC Roy Kellerman in the right front.

The USSS follow-up car (call sign: Halfback) was a 1956 Cadillac convertible (SS 679-X). It was driven by SA Sam Kinney with WHD-ATSAIC Emory Roberts in the right-front position. Agents George Hickey and Glen Bennett sat in the right and left-hand sides of the rear seat respectively. Presidential aides David Powers and Kenneth O'Donnell occupied the jump seats. Agents John "Jack" Ready and Paul Landis occupied the right running board with Ready at the front position. SA Clint Hill (First Lady Detail) was positioned on the front of the left running board with SA William McIntyre at the rear.

Four motorcycles operated by members of the Dallas Police Department were near 100-X and 679-X—two on each side of the motorcade. Their mission was to keep the streets open and to discourage spectators from dashing out to the president's vehicle. As the engines were extremely loud, the motorcycles stayed in a position to the rear of the presidential vehicle until needed at the front or sides.

The vice presidential vehicle (1964 Lincoln Continental convertible on loan from Ford Motor Company) was next in line. The vice president rode in the right-hand side of the rear seat with Mrs. Johnson in the middle. Senator Ralph Yarborough sat to the left of Mrs. Johnson. The vehicle was driven by Texas Highway Patrolman Hurchel Jacks. Vice Presidential Detail (VPD) SAIC Rufus Youngblood rode in the right front.

The vice presidential follow-up (four-door sedan) was driven by Joe Henry Rich of the Texas Highway Patrol. Agent Jerry Kivett, VPD advance, rode the right-front position. VPD-ATSAIC Thomas "Lem" Johns rode in the right rear, while SA Warren "Woody" Taylor sat on the left side of the rear seat. Vice presidential staffer Clifton Carter occupied the middle of the front seat.

Behind the vice presidential follow-up were vehicles carrying dignitaries, press, White House Communications Agency personnel, and White House staffers. A police car was at the end of the motorcade. It kept the motorcade intact and prevented unauthorized vehicles from joining the procession.

Throughout the downtown area of Dallas, the president and first lady were warmly received. Thousands of well-wishers crowded the sidewalks and some surged out into Main Street for a closer look at the President and Mrs. Kennedy. Thousands more watched from windows.

Eventually, the presidential limo approached the end of the downtown area and turned right onto Houston Street, traveling one block north to Elm Street. SS 100-X was moving at an estimated speed of 12–15 miles per hour. Slowing to make the sharp-left turn onto Elm, the presidential vehicle continued down the street—passing the School Book Depository on the right. Halfback followed closely behind.

In the lead car, SA Lawson had just given the 5-minutes-out radio signal to alert Secret Service personnel at the Trade Mart of the impending arrival. It was about 12:30 p.m. The agents in the motorcade observed that the crowd had thinned out along this part of the route. There was no need for any of the follow-up agents or motorcycles to advance toward the presidential vehicle, since there was no danger of people pushing out into the street. Soon, the president's motorcade would be picking up speed and entering the Stemmons Freeway. The risky parade segment of the motorcade would be over ...

Suddenly, a loud report sounded. Agents turned to the right and rear—in the direction of the sound. To most, it sounded like a firecracker, the backfire of a motorcycle, or a tire blowout. The president made some unnatural movements. Two more discharges sounded. Several agents observed a hit to the right side of the president's head. The motorcade was under fire!

In the presidential follow-up, SA Clint Hill sprinted off the running board toward 100-X. SA George Hickey rose with an AR-15 semiautomatic rifle and scanned the building and crowd to the right. ATSAIC Roberts radioed to the lead car: "Halfback to Lawson, the president has been hit. Escort us to the nearest hospital, fast but at a safe speed."

In the presidential car, ASAIC Kellerman leaned toward SA Greer and ordered: "Let's get out of here. We are hit." Greer put his foot into the accelerator and 100-X took off. Next, Kellerman radioed the lead car: "Lawson, this is Kellerman. We are hit; get us to the hospital immediately."

Agent Hill lost his footing but managed to climb onto the back of 100-X as it was sharply accelerating. Mrs. Kennedy had risen up and was leaning over the trunk. Hill stretched across the trunk and pushed Mrs. Kennedy back into the rear seat. SA Hill then used his body to shield both Mrs.

Kennedy and the president. It was obvious that the head wound to the president would be fatal. Hill shook his head and gave an anguished "thumbs down" to the agents in the follow-up. SA Hill along with ASAIC Kellerman also observed that Governor Connally had been injured.

Seated in the vice presidential vehicle, SAIC Youngblood didn't know if the first report was a "firecracker, bomb, bullet, or other explosion." Instinctively, Youngblood shouted, "Get down!" and reached back for Vice President Johnson, pushing him down into the rear seat. Then, Youngblood vaulted into the back of the vehicle and used his body to cover the vice president.

The presidential car arrived at Parkland Memorial Hospital at approximately 12:35 p.m. The president and Governor Connally were placed on stretchers and wheeled into the emergency room. Doctors attending the president observed wounds to the head and neck. The first priority was to establish an airway. A tracheotomy was performed to improve respiration. Blood and fluids were administered. Chest tubes were inserted for drainage of blood and air. Cardiac massage was given.

After about 15 minutes of treatment, it became apparent that the president was not going to be resuscitated. The president exhibited dilated and unresponsive pupils. There was no pulse or heart beat. An electrocardiogram machine connected to the president registered a flat line. A priest was called to administer last rites, and President John F. Kennedy was pronounced dead at 1:00 p.m. local time.

Nearby in an adjacent trauma room, Governor Connally was being treated for a sucking chest wound. A bullet had entered Connally's back and exited his chest, causing the right lung to collapse. To re-expand the lung, rubber tubes were inserted between several ribs. The lung and lacerated muscle was sutured back together. Later that day, Connally was also operated on for wounds to his right wrist and left thigh. After several weeks at Parkland, Connally was transferred to a hospital in Austin where he stayed for five days. Subsequently, Governor Connally was released and following several months of rehabilitation made a full recovery.

The Dallas Police Department, the Federal Bureau of Investigation, and the U.S. Secret Service began investigations into the assassination. About 45 minutes after the assassination, Dallas Police Officer J.D. Tippit was shot and killed while on patrol in the Oak Cliff section of Dallas. Thirty-five minutes later, a suspect in the Tippit murder, Lee Harvey Oswald, was apprehended in a movie theater where he had taken refuge. Oswald pulled a .38-caliber revolver on officers and forcibly resisted arrest.

Investigation soon developed Oswald as a suspect in the JFK assassination. Oswald was an employee of the Texas School Book Depository and had left the building shortly after the assassination. He had been seen on the sixth floor of the TSBD where an Italian-made 6.5-millimeter Mannlicher-Carcano carbine (with telescopic sight), spent cartridge cases, and a bag made of wrapping paper and tape had been found. Earlier, Oswald had carried a similar-looking bag into the TSBD. He claimed it had contained "curtain rods." No curtain rods were found at the TSBD.

On the evening of November 22, 1963, Oswald was formally charged with the murder of Officer Tippit. Eyewitness testimony had identified Oswald as the shooter of Tippit and as the subject who was seen leaving the scene of the crime with gun in hand. A jacket belonging to Oswald was also found along the getaway trail.

The following morning (November 23), an additional charge was levied against Oswald for the murder of JFK. The FBI had traced the carbine found on the sixth floor of the TSBD to Oswald. Though purchased using the alias A. Hidell, the carbine was shipped to a Dallas post office box rented by Oswald. At the time of arrest, a Selective Service card and a Marine Corps certificate of service were found in Oswald's wallet in the name of Alek James Hidell. The counterfeit Selective Service card featured a photograph of Oswald. In addition, a handwriting examination of the documents used to purchase the carbine had identified Oswald as the true writer.

During the interrogation at police headquarters, Oswald denied any involvement in the Tippit and Kennedy murders. When asked questions he could not readily explain, Oswald routinely answered falsely or refused to discuss the matter. Since the sessions with Oswald were unproductive, Dallas police decided to transport Oswald to the county jail, which was customary procedure after a subject had been charged with a felony. It was publicly announced that Oswald would be transferred to the county jail on Sunday morning, November 24.

Handcuffed to Dallas Police Detective A.J. Leavelle, Oswald was led into the basement garage area of the Police and Courts Building at 11:21 a.m. It was planned that Oswald would be loaded in a nearby car and taken to the county lockup. Press coverage was permitted for this part of the transfer and approximately 50 news people with cameras and microphones crowded the area. More than 70 police officers provided security.

In front of a live national television audience, Jack Ruby, a Dallas nightclub owner, emerged from the crowd and pointed a snub-nosed, .38-caliber pistol toward Oswald's abdomen. The nation watched in disbelief as Ruby fired one shot. Oswald grimaced and fell to the floor mortally wounded. Oswald was transported to Parkland Memorial Hospital where he was pronounced dead at 1:07 p.m., a little over two days after the death of President Kennedy.

With the murder of Oswald, it became impossible to resolve the charges brought against him in a court of law. Facts became intertwined with rumor. Doubt and speculation took over the consciousness of a nation looking for answers. Conspiracy theories were advanced. In this climate of shock, grief, uncertainty, and suspicion, President Johnson, with the advice of congressional leaders, decided an all-encompassing national investigation was needed.

On November 29, 1963, the President's Commission on the Assassination of President Kennedy was created by executive order. Commonly known as the Warren Commission (after its Chairman, Chief Justice Earl Warren), the body was empowered to subpoena witnesses and evidence and to compel testimony, if necessary, by granting immunity to witnesses. The commission was also authorized to inquire of and utilize any federal agency as needed.

After an extensive fact-finding investigation where the Secret Service alone conducted 1,550 interviews and submitted 800 reports totaling 4,600 pages, the commission presented its final report to President Johnson on September 24, 1964. The report totaled 888 pages. In addition, 26 volumes of testimony and exhibits were released. The commission's main conclusions were as follows:

1. The shots that killed President Kennedy and injured Governor Connally were fired from the Texas School Book Depository.
2. Lee Harvey Oswald fired the shots that killed President Kennedy and injured Governor Connally.
3. Lee Harvey Oswald killed Dallas Police Patrolman J.D. Tippit.
4. No evidence was found that either Lee Harvey Oswald or Jack Ruby was part of a conspiracy to assassinate President Kennedy.

These conclusions were based on the evidence as previously mentioned along with other incriminating testimony and items gathered during the course of the commission's investigation. Some of the most important additional evidence included:

1. The bullet found on Governor Connally's stretcher and the bullet fragments (large enough to be identified) found in the presidential limousine were fired from the 6.5-millimeter carbine that was found on the sixth-floor of the TSBD.
2. The three shell cases found on the sixth-floor of TSBD were fired from the 6.5-millimeter carbine.
3. Oswald's palmprint was found on the barrel of the 6.5-millimeter carbine.
4. Two photographs were recovered that show Oswald posing with a carbine and holding up newspapers of the Communist Party, U.S.A. and the Socialist Workers Party. Oswald is also seen in the pictures carrying a revolver in a belt holster. Oswald's wife, Marina, testified that she took the pictures.

5. Oswald's fingerprint and palmprint were found on the paper bag believed to have been used by Oswald to carry the carbine to work.

6. Oswald's fingerprint and palmprint were found on cartons that appeared to have been moved to arrange a sniper's nest on the sixth floor of the TSBD.

7. A witness to the presidential assassination saw a man who resembled Oswald fire a rifle from the sixth floor of the TSBD.

8. Cartridge cases found near the scene of the Tippit murder were fired from the .38-caliber Smith & Wesson revolver that was taken from Oswald at the time of his arrest.

9. Oswald's Smith & Wesson revolver was purchased using the alias A.J. Hidell. Handwriting examination determined that Oswald forged the purchase order. The revolver was sent to the same Dallas post office box where the carbine was delivered.

10. Marina Oswald testified that her husband had previously attempted to assassinate Major General Edwin Walker of Dallas. On the evening of April 10, 1963, a rifle bullet was fired into Walker's home, just missing the general. Walker was a staunch anti-communist, who resigned from the U.S. Army while being investigated for distributing right-wing propaganda to his troops. Photographs of the rear of Walker's home (where the shot was fired) and a note to Marina advising what to do in case Oswald was killed or captured in the Walker attempt were found among the Oswalds' possessions.

Through the years, Bob had read the Warren Commission report several times from cover to cover. With the recent look at the JFK assassination in Secret Service school, I asked Bob what his thoughts were on the subject. "Well, the Secret Service officially accepted the conclusions and recommendations of the Warren Commission," Bob advised. "In fact, the implementation of a number of commission recommendations brought about a modernization of the Service. That's probably the Warren Commission's most significant legacy."

"What about Oswald?" I asked. "It's been about 11 years since the Warren Commission's report. Do you think there was a conspiracy?"

"The way I look at something like this is to go back in history—start at the beginning and see where the facts take you. Starting with preconceived notions and working backward might cause you to jump to conclusions."

"Okay, Bobbie, start at the beginning. But I need to warn you. Dinner will be ready soon."

"All right," Bob laughed. "I'll try to keep it short. Lee Harvey Oswald was born in New Orleans. He was the product of a broken home. His dad died before Oswald was born. Oswald's mother was forced to work and could give little time to her son. At the age of three, Oswald was sent to an orphanage for a year. Oswald's two older brothers spent these years in orphans' homes.

"When Oswald was five years old, he moved to Dallas with his mother, who remarried. Oswald's brothers were sent to boarding school. About three years later, Mrs. Oswald's stormy marriage ended in divorce. Oswald lost a father figure. Oswald's brothers were in turn forced to leave school and to help provide for the family. Both eventually joined the armed forces.

"During his formative years, Lee Harvey Oswald had no permanent roots. His mother moved frequently. Oswald attended a multitude of schools. He spent these years mostly alone. Oswald woke up to an empty house and came home to one after school. He had to take care of himself and fell into a solitary routine, which usually didn't include activities with other children. He was starved for attention and affection. It wasn't a normal childhood. To compensate, he turned inward.

"Things took a turn for the worse when Oswald and his mother moved to New York City to live with Oswald's married half brother. The relationship was strained. Oswald allegedly pulled a knife on his brother's wife during an argument and also struck his mother. Oswald and his mother were asked to leave; they moved to an apartment in the Bronx.

"Oswald was teased in junior high and became a disciplinary problem. He stopped going to school. His mother couldn't control him. He was charged with truancy, temporarily placed in a youth facility, and referred for psychiatric observation and evaluation. Oswald was found to be withdrawn, evasive, and emotionally disturbed. It was recommended that Oswald receive psychiatric follow-up. Before any treatment was undertaken, Oswald's mother moved to New Orleans where Oswald was enrolled in school.

"In New Orleans, classmates poked fun at Oswald. He was involved in fights. He made no close friends and was generally a loner. He started to spend his time reading. During this period, Oswald became interested in communism and read books on the subject. Oswald was a mediocre student but completed the eighth and ninth grades.

"The following year, 1955, Oswald left school to work. Soon afterwards, he began to espouse the communist line. He blamed his problems and those of the working class on capitalists. Oswald believed a revolution was coming where the workers of the world would 'throw off their chains.' He spoke admiringly of Soviet Premier Khrushchev and the Soviet Union. Oswald suggested to a co-worker that they join the Communist Party, U.S.A.

"Oswald reportedly also mentioned that he would like to kill President Eisenhower because he was exploiting the working class. That bears repeating: Oswald said, apparently in all seriousness, that he would like to kill President Eisenhower because he was exploiting the working class. This was in late 1955 or early 1956, about eight years before the JFK assassination."

"Geez," I blurted out.

"In 1956, Oswald followed in his older brother's [Robert] footsteps and joined the Marines. Although this might seem illogical for someone who was turning away from his country, the Marine Corps served as a *lifeline*. Oswald didn't want to live with his mother, and he was tiring of the workplace. The Marine Corps was an escape.

"In the Marines, Oswald's basic training included rifle and pistol marksmanship. He was eventually trained as a radar operator. He continued to have personality problems and stayed to himself. Oswald routinely read communist literature and taught himself some elementary Russian. He studied foreign affairs. He used this knowledge to attract attention to himself and to stroke his ego. It fueled his inner feelings of superiority, and he wanted to be different.

"Oswald's Marine Corps service was problematic. He was court-martialed in 1958 for accidentally shooting himself with an unauthorized firearm. Later that year, he was again court-martialed for an argument with a superior. Oswald was reduced in rank and spent some time in the brig.

"Instead of changing his behavior to resolve relationship difficulties, Oswald blamed others for his problems. He believed people picked on him unfairly because of his political views. Oswald became a committed Marxist and espoused the doctrine that the U.S. system of capitalism made workers slaves and used the military for international aggression. To Oswald, it all started with capitalism. He blamed the U.S. economic system for forcing his mother to work and for their troubled relationship.

"Oswald spoke admiringly of Russia and Castro Cuba. He lost interest in the Marine Corps. In 1959, Oswald applied for and received an early release—purportedly to care for his mother, who had been injured at work. Oswald was honorably discharged to the Marine Corps Reserve. After several days with his mother, Oswald put into play his next escape.

"Using the ruse that he would be attending school in Switzerland, Oswald traveled overseas where he received a tourist visa to visit Russia. Once in Moscow, Oswald declared that he wanted to defect and become a citizen of the Soviet Union. When Oswald was told that he would have to leave Russia, he cut a wrist in an apparent suicide attempt. Oswald was hospitalized and after his recovery, affirmed to Soviet authorities that he still wanted to become a Soviet citizen.

"Growing impatient with Soviet bureaucracy, Oswald appeared at the American Embassy where he surrendered his passport and attempted to renounce his U.S. citizenship. Oswald added that he had offered to tell the Soviets what he knew about U.S. military radar. Embassy officials tried to dissuade Oswald from taking any hasty action. Oswald was told he could come back in a couple of days and personally renounce his citizenship then.

"Oswald probably played out this scene at the American Embassy to impress Soviet authorities. Oswald wanted to prove his sincerity to the Soviet government and to sway them in permitting him to remain in Russia. He also began writing a 'historic diary', which contained both real and exaggerated events and self-serving statements. To me, this is evidence that Oswald had *delusions of grandeur.*

"Oswald was eventually allowed to remain in Russia and sent to Minsk where he worked in a factory, which made radios and televisions. By now, he had broken off relations with his family. Oswald fell in love with a Russian woman, who worked at the factory. She spurned his marriage proposals. To mend his hurt ego, Oswald courted another woman, Marina, whom he met at a worker's dance. Soon, Marina and Oswald were married, and she became pregnant.

"By early 1961, Oswald had become increasingly disillusioned with Soviet life. He's tired of factory work and the limited recreational opportunities available. Missing the freedom he had grown accustomed to in the U.S., Oswald didn't like the compulsory activities of the 'Kollective.' Oswald was also disgusted with the better life afforded Communist Party officials, whom he blamed for corrupting and subverting the socialistic revolution. Disappointed with communism, Oswald began negotiations with the American Embassy for a return to the U.S.

"In reality, Lee Harvey Oswald was a square peg in a world of round holes. He wasn't going to fit in or be happy anywhere. He didn't want to work, and he didn't like authority. But, he wished to be seen as a great intellect and as someone ahead of his time. Oswald had a superiority complex, and he wanted a place in history. He also wanted to be provided with a comfortable living.

"Disappointed with life in the USSR, Oswald looked for his next escape. In June 1962, Oswald and Marina with their new baby girl arrived in the U.S. They first stayed in Fort Worth, Texas with Oswald's brother Robert. Then, Oswald's mother moved to Fort Worth and invited Lee and his family to stay with her. Soon tiring of living with his mother, Oswald moved his family to their own apartment. In fact, he ordered Marina to keep his mother out of the new residence.

"Oswald was interviewed several times by the FBI, which was standard procedure for returning defectors. Oswald complained to the FBI about the "undesirable" discharge he had received from the Marine Corps Reserves— after his 1959 defection had been reported by the national press. Oswald was also upset at the interest shown to him by the FBI. He was overly defensive—probably somewhat paranoid.

"It didn't take long for Oswald to remember why he had left the United States. Oswald disliked having to work menial jobs to make a living, and he couldn't stand his mother. Lying to Marina that he had been fired, Oswald quit one job after several months work.

"Lee and Marina had marital problems. He was jealous of attempts by the Russian-speaking community to help Marina and the baby. Oswald's superego was hurt. Marina was seen with a black eye. With the rent overdue and money for food and other household goods lacking, Oswald relocated to Dallas to try to find a job. Marina stayed in Forth Worth—moving in with friends.

"In Dallas, Oswald found a job as a graphic arts trainee. During this period, he most likely prepared the phony 'Hidell' documents. Alek was a name he used in Russia, and "Hidell" was probably a play on *Fidel* Castro, who was a hero to Oswald.

"In November 1962, Marina reunited with her husband in Dallas. Soon afterwards, their marital difficulties resumed. Marina testified that Oswald became nervous and irritable, and the least thing provoked him. They continued to fight. Marina moved out for a short period, but returned when Oswald again promised to change his ways.

"Oswald corresponded with the Soviet Embassy, Communist Party, U.S.A., and the Socialist Workers Party. He subscribed to communist newspapers. He continued to read literature by Marx and Engels.

"Using the 'Hidell' alias, Oswald ordered the .38-caliber pistol and 6.5-millimeter carbine by mail. He received them in March 1963. Soon after, Marina photographed him holding a carbine and carrying a .38 revolver in a belt holster. In the picture, Oswald displayed copies of the Communist Party and Socialist Workers Party newspapers.

"Then on April 10, 1963, Oswald attempted to assassinate General Edwin Walker of Dallas. Oswald later rationalized this action to Marina by saying that Walker was a fascist and that many lives could have been saved if someone had killed Hitler before World War II. Marina admonished her husband for the act.

"After being fired from the graphic arts firm for poor performance and an inability to get along with fellow workers, Oswald was persuaded by Marina to relocate to New Orleans to look for work. She actually wanted to get him out of Dallas because of the Walker incident.

"In May 1963, Oswald was hired as a machinery oiler for a New Orleans company. He rented an apartment and sent for Marina. By July, Oswald was fired from this job too. He applied for unemployment compensation. Oswald renewed his passport, and he and his wife mailed visa requests to the Russian Embassy. Marina later testified that Oswald really wanted to go to Cuba and was using the pretense to return to Russia as a way to get to Cuba. Oswald was an admirer of Castro Cuba and probably figured that Marxist principles and revolutionary fervor were still alive and well there. Oswald was planning his *next escape* from the realities of life.

"In New Orleans during the summer of 1963, Oswald actively and publicly began his pro-Castro activities. He had "Hands off Cuba" circulars printed and formed a one-man "Fair Play for Cuba" chapter. Oswald handed out his leaflets on the city streets. Oswald also tried to infiltrate an anti-Castro organization. After he's found out, a scuffle ensued and Oswald and three Cuban exiles were arrested. Oswald gained more public exposure by debating a local anti-Castro leader on New Orleans radio. However, Oswald was exposed as a Communist defector on the show, and his comments lose credence.

"It's my belief Oswald engaged in these activities to prove his devotion to the cause. He wanted to be able to impress Cuban authorities and in turn receive favorable treatment from them. He didn't want a repeat of what happened in Moscow. For the same reason, it's also possible Oswald's attempted infiltration of the anti-Castro community was reconnaissance in search of a worthy assassination target. Marina testified that during May of 1963: She observed her husband dry firing the carbine at night on the porch of their New Orleans apartment. Oswald had missed General Walker the month before. I think Oswald believed the murder of Walker or of an anti-Castro leader would be the ultimate act to gain the admiration of Cuban officials. The eventual assassination of JFK might have been the final chapter in that plan."

"Wow!" I exclaimed.

"By late summer, Oswald had an *overpowering and uncontrollable* desire to go to Cuba. He was *desperately* looking for his next escape. Marina testified to the Warren Commission that Oswald even contemplated hijacking an airplane to take him to Cuba. Oswald tried to have Marina, who was pregnant with their second child, assist him in the skyjacking. That showed how *desperate and dangerous* he had become.

"Marina decided to return to Dallas with a friend, Ruth Paine. In late September 1963, Oswald traveled to Mexico City for the purpose of gaining entry into Cuba. Mexican authorities required a Cuban visa before an American would be permitted to board a plane for Cuba. Oswald appeared at the Cuban Embassy and told them he wanted to return to Russia through Cuba. He applied for a transit visa. He was told he must first have a Russian visa. He became distraught when he found out it would take four months to obtain a Soviet visa. He argued with a Cuban consular officer, but to no avail. Follow-up visits to the Russian and Cuban embassies were unproductive.

"Oswald returned to the U.S. dejected. His trip to Mexico was a failure. He got a room in Dallas and lived by himself. Marina preferred to stay with Ruth Paine in Irving, Texas—waiting for the new baby to be born.

"A neighbor of Mrs. Paine mentioned that the Texas School Book Depository had a job opening. The neighbor's brother, Buell Frazier, worked there. Oswald got the job and began work at the TSBD on October 15, 1963. Oswald rode out to Irving with Frazier for weekend visits with Marina.

"During early November, the FBI visited the Paine residence on two occasions to interview Oswald. He wasn't there but became angry when he heard the FBI had been out to see him. Oswald ordered Marina to get the tag numbers of the FBI vehicle.

"On November 15, 1963, a Dallas newspaper mentioned that the president would be visiting the Trade Mart. The next day, it was reported that the presidential motorcade would parade through the downtown area. Subsequent news reports detailed the presidential visit and motorcade route.

"For the weekend of November 16–17, Marina asked Oswald not to come out to Irving. Since Oswald had visited the previous three-day holiday weekend [Veterans Day], Marina didn't want to impose on Mrs. Paine's hospitality.

"On Sunday the 17th, a call was made to Oswald's rooming house by Mrs. Paine and Marina. They were told no one lived there by the name Lee Harvey Oswald. When Oswald phoned Marina the next day, she asked about this. Oswald became upset and admitted to using an alias. He told Marina not to call him there again.

"On Thursday, November 21, Oswald caught a ride after work with Buell Frazier and showed up unexpectedly at the Paine residence in Irving. He told Frazier that he needed to pick up some "curtain rods." Marina thought Oswald was there to make up for the latest argument. Oswald asked Marina to move back to Dallas with him. She refused and had little to do with Oswald that evening.

"The next morning, Friday, November 22, 1963, Oswald rode to work with Frazier. Oswald carried a package with him. After the assassination, a police search of the Paine garage discovered that Oswald's carbine was missing. It was found on the sixth floor of the Texas School Book Depository. No curtain rods were ever found. An empty package made of brown wrapping paper and tape was found near the carbine."

"So, what do you think?" I asked.

"I believe President Kennedy's visit to Dallas with his motorcade passing by the Texas School Book Depository was the chance of a lifetime for Oswald. A chance he couldn't pass up. He had been a committed Marxist since his teens. He considered himself a visionary and believed in Marxist revolutionary doctrine. Oswald hated capitalism, and he saw the American president as the leader of an unjust society. Destiny had given Oswald an opportunity to prove his greatness, to further history, and to gain entry to Cuba. Marxism was the most important influence on Oswald's life, and he boldly acted on its principles.

"Fidel Castro was one of Oswald's Marxist heroes. President Kennedy had long supported the overthrow of Castro and the establishment of a democratic government in Cuba. JFK was president during the U.S. backed Bay of Pigs Invasion in April 1961. Kennedy also confronted Soviet Premier

Khrushchev during the Cuban Missile Crisis in October 1962. The president had enacted a naval quarantine around Cuba. Khrushchev backed down and removed Soviet nuclear missiles from Cuba.

"In December 1962, President Kennedy and Jackie addressed the surviving Bay of Pigs freedom fighters at the Orange Bowl in Miami. Kennedy proudly received the brigade's battle flag and told the crowd of 40,000, 'I can assure you that this flag will be returned to this brigade in a free Havana.' The president's speech featured U.S. support for Castro's ouster and for a free Cuba.

"With the time Oswald spent in Russia, his steady diet of radical newspapers, and his contact with the anti-Castro community in New Orleans, I believe Oswald thought President Kennedy was contemplating another U.S. backed invasion of Cuba. During visits to Tampa and Miami, Florida on November 18, 1963, the president continued to make public declarations calling for Castro's downfall. Oswald had to have viewed President Kennedy as an *enemy* of Castro Cuba.

"Oswald had probably targeted General Walker for similar reasons. Walker was strongly critical of Castro Cuba and the Soviet Union. Walker was a staunch anti-communist. Oswald had the motive. With Walker living in Dallas, Oswald had been presented the opportunity. After Oswald received the carbine, he had the means. Oswald took advantage of the opportunity and attempted to assassinate General Walker—but failed. On November 22, 1963, Oswald was presented with another opportunity—the opportunity of a lifetime for a devout Marxist.

"Depressed from his failed mission to Mexico City, his unsatisfying and stormy relationship with Marina, and his aversion to work for a living, Oswald saw the assassination of President Kennedy as not only a way to make history, but also a way to escape from a troubled life. By assassinating President Kennedy, Oswald would prove to Cuban authorities that he was a true revolutionary. Oswald might have fantasized he would receive a hero's welcome in Cuba and be handsomely rewarded for the remainder of his days. It was also a means of taking revenge on an America Oswald detested."

"Okay, then why didn't he proudly admit to the assassination? Why did he deny everything?" I asked a bit confused.

"Because, he hoped he could beat the charges. And Oswald was secretive and a liar. In reality, Oswald had a ninth grade education and didn't even have a driver's license. He wasn't as smart as he thought. He was severely emotionally disturbed and had plenty of anger and hatred. Oswald acted on impulses and had a distorted view of the world and his place in it. I believe the *final* decision to assassinate JFK was not made until the night before when he visited Marina in Irving. Had she agreed to move back to Dallas with him the next day, who knows how history might have been changed.

Instead, Oswald left his wedding ring on the dresser and took the carbine to work.

"The JFK assassination, in my estimation, was an impulsive crime of opportunity. That's why Oswald had so little time to think it out and to prepare. For example after the assassination, Oswald had to take the time to stop by his Dallas rooming house to pick up his .38-caliber revolver. If he had been set on the assassination for any great time, Oswald would have already made arrangements to have the pistol with him.

"Plus, Oswald was captured within an hour and a half of the assassination. He didn't get very far and apparently didn't have any help. His escape was a failure, and he might have had inner suicidal thoughts of going out in a blaze of glory. This would have been the ultimate escape from an unhappy life. Remember, Oswald was trying to pull a gun when officers were arresting him.

"I do believe, however, that Oswald was probably trying to make his way to Cuba after the assassination. He *might* have decided to carry out his earlier plan of skyjacking an airliner. That would be why he had to get the revolver from his rooming house. And why he didn't bother to pick up his passport when he was there. Oswald wouldn't need a passport to board a domestic flight and then skyjack it to Cuba or to storm his way on an airliner at gunpoint. Once in Havana, Oswald would ask for political asylum. Having executed JFK, Oswald believed he would be welcomed in Cuba with open arms.

"But along the escape route, he's stopped by Officer Tippet. Oswald's next action showed clearly that he wasn't an innocent 'patsy' and that he didn't want to be caught. The evidence shows that Oswald mercilessly pumped four bullets into Tippet—killing him instantly. Oswald's getaway to Cuba was sidetracked. He's forced to hide out in a movie theater. After he's arrested, what else could Oswald do? His only hope was to fight the charges and to win an acquittal in court."

"So, you don't believe there was a conspiracy?" I asked.

"I'm a federal agent. I deal in facts and evidence. The facts and evidence pointed directly to Oswald. There was overwhelming probable cause that Oswald assassinated President Kennedy and murdered Officer Tippet. As a criminal investigator, I don't see evidence that would return an indictment of conspiracy on anyone. That doesn't mean that others weren't involved.

"In Secret Service school, they told us that President Johnson *privately* believed Cuba was behind the JFK assassination. This was based on Oswald's activities in Mexico City before the assassination. LBJ was apparently afraid the American public would demand that Cuba be invaded if there were strong suspicions that Castro was involved. This could possibly have set off World War III with the Soviets defending Cuba. Therefore, LBJ supposedly directed the FBI and CIA not to pursue some leads that might have led to Cuban intelligence. Of course, this would have also protected sensitive U.S. intelligence sources. It would also have provided some cover as to what the CIA and FBI did and did not know about Oswald's Mexican trip—before the assassination."

"So, what do you think about Cuban involvement?"

"Jan, the problem with the JFK assassination is one could develop very plausible scenarios that would implicate Soviet or Cuban intelligence, anti-Castro Cubans, rogue elements of the CIA, organized crime, or even certain private and public individuals.

"That being said, the most likely contact point for conspiratorial activity would have been when Oswald was in Mexico City in late September 1963. Oswald was somewhat paranoid and the kind of person who would be very suspicious of cold contacts from anyone. So, if he was going to be influenced by someone, it would most likely have been in the periods when Oswald was making outward contacts himself. During his Mexico City visit, Oswald made multiple contacts with the Cuban and Soviet embassies. From my SY experience, those visits would have come to the attention of intelligence operatives of both foreign governments.

"The problem is that President Kennedy's visit to Dallas hadn't been firmed up yet. Oswald's later hiring at the Texas School Book Depository seemed to be by chance. No one could have plotted this in September 1963. After Mexico City, Oswald went to Dallas and lived in several rooming houses. It would have been unlikely that foreign agents could have found him when the president's visit was finalized. In any case, I firmly believe Oswald was the triggerman. Yes, he could have been worked. There could have been a conspiracy. Yet, I don't see *probable cause* that would put the cuffs on anyone other than Oswald."

"How about the CIA?" I asked.

"The CIA had to be aware of Oswald. He was a defector to the Soviet Union. They must have known about his return to the U.S.—as did the FBI. Oswald publicly supported Castro Cuba in New Orleans and encountered anti-Castro Cuban exiles. Oswald traveled to Mexico City and contacted foreign embassies. That would have caused him to come to the further attention of the CIA. So, there were opportunities for rogue agents and anti-Castro Cubans to have known about Oswald too.

"After the Bay of Pigs fiasco, President Kennedy shook up the CIA. Some anti-Castro Cubans blamed Kennedy for not sending in U.S. air cover and troops when the invasion was failing. During the Cuban Missile Crisis, JFK pledged to Khrushchev that the U.S. would not invade Cuba. The most militant Cuban exile leaders saw that as surrender to Castro. U.S. support was withdrawn from some anti-Castro activities. There was mistrust of Kennedy in the anti-Castro community.

"A plan could have been devised by a CIA type or Cuban exile to manipulate Oswald into assassinating Kennedy. They would have represented themselves as Cuban intelligence and offered Oswald safe passage to Cuba for assassinating President Kennedy. This would have gotten rid of Kennedy and at the same time made the assassination look like an operation of Cuban intelligence. When that became public, America would have demanded a reckoning with Cuba."

"Okay, if that was the plan, wouldn't you want Oswald to talk and lay the blame with Cuba? You wouldn't want a Jack Ruby to silence Oswald."

"Yes, unless you were afraid if Oswald started talking, he might relate information that upon close investigation would uncover the real conspirators and their true loyalties. There's no hard evidence Jack Ruby was anything more than a modern day vigilante, who wanted fame. Yet, there's one thing that continues to trouble me about Ruby."

"What's that?" I asked excitedly.

"Ruby used a little-known point shooting technique to kill Oswald. The method was taught to commandos in World War II. Agents of the OSS, the forerunner of the CIA, were schooled in it."

"What!" I blurted out.

"Yeah, I noticed it some years ago when I watched footage of the Oswald killing. The photographs taken at the time of the shooting confirmed it. Ruby knew what he was doing, or he had some very good coaching. As he sprung out of the crowd toward Oswald, Ruby extended his right arm. In his hand was a snub-nosed Colt revolver. Unlike how most everyone else grips a handgun, Ruby had his index finger, which is the normal trigger finger, pointing along the frame of the gun in line with the barrel. He used his middle finger on the trigger. Since he wasn't using the sights, Ruby didn't need to bring the gun to eye level. This allowed him to keep the gun low and to move in quickly with stealth. This is a very effective means of accurately engaging a moving target at close quarters. Pointing his right index finger where he wanted to shoot, Ruby dispatched Oswald with one shot."

"Jeez!"

"Yeah," Bob remarked, "the shooting of Oswald looked more like a professional hit. I don't know where Ruby picked up the technique. He spent almost three years in the Army Air Corps, but his specialty was aircraft maintenance. Ruby didn't learn it in mechanics school!"

"Bobbie, did the Warren Commission report make mention of this?"

"Not in regard to Ruby's point shooting technique."

"How could they have missed something like that?" I asked—a bit bewildered.

"That's a *very* good question. Jan, do you smell something burning?"

"Oops, it's dinner time."

Chapter 20

PI

With Treasury and Secret Service schools completed by the fall of 1975, Bob received some good news from ATSAIC de Freese. Bob was being reassigned to the WFO Protective Intelligence Squad. Packing his belongings, Bob moved to an empty desk in one of the offices of the PI area.

After settling in, Bob reported to Special Agent Carl Williams. Carl had a reputation as a smart and savvy street agent. He was temporarily filling in at the ATSAIC position. This gave Williams an opportunity to gain some administrative experience.

"Hi, Carl," Bob said as he took a seat in Williams's office. Bob was already acquainted with Williams and several other PI Squad agents. In the past, Bob had served as back up for the agents, while they were conducting a risky field interview or making an arrest. Bob had also assisted agents in the Criminal and Forgery Squads. Being a former Park Police officer, Bob and others with police experience were occasionally used to accompany agents who were making arrests or responding to potentially dangerous situations.

"Hey, Bob, welcome. I'm glad Frank [ASAIC Cavanaugh] decided to send you to PI. We've got our hands full. As you know, one of our agents is on indefinite medical leave. Another will be transferring soon. We've got loads of work to spread around and too few bodies."

"I'm excited to be here."

"Good, we'll start you out with some gate caller cases. These subjects were interviewed by ID at the Northwest Gate, and you'll be following up. Some were deemed *dangerous to themselves or others* and referred to St. E's. Others were sent on their way following the interview. After the collateral investigations and record checks are in, you'll make a final evaluation as to whether the subjects are of protective interest."

"Sounds good," Bob enthusiastically replied.

"We'll also start using you in PI teams. After you get some time in the squad, I'll add you to the PI duty agent rotation. By then, you'll be handling anything that comes up. In the meantime, I want you to ride along with senior agents when they go out on casework. Hook up with Steve Reynolds, he has some interesting cases."

"10-4," Bob affirmed.

Around the WFO, Steve Reynolds was known as "The Professor." He had studied psychology and was part cop and part clinician. Reynolds had a wealth of PI experience under his belt, and a primary influence in his evaluations was an analytical look at the subject's mental state. Steve spent much time discussing mental illness with Bob as it related to the protective function of the Secret Service. Bob also accompanied Reynolds in field interviews, and Steve took Bob by St. Elizabeths Hospital to meet some of the doctors who handled the "White House cases." Acting as a mentor, Steve imparted knowledge to Bob gained by years of practical experience.

Another agent who helped Bob was Richard "Dick" Corrigan. He had been with the Secret Service for about five years. Corrigan was a college graduate and former military officer. With a tour on a protective detail in between, WFO was Corrigan's second field office. Bob and Dick routinely backed up each other. A collegial relationship developed between the two that soon led to a strong bond of friendship.

The Washington Field Office had the most active Protective Intelligence Squad in the country. The everyday demands of protection within the WFO district bore heavily on the squad. In addition to a large and important investigative caseload, agents were needed for PI teams. A PI team (two agents) was assigned to all movements of the president and vice president. For the movements of other protectees, PI teams were used as circumstances warranted. In the Washington area, USSS protectees included the president, first lady, vice president, secretary of the treasury, and family members of the president and vice president. In the mid-1970s, the USSS was also charged with protecting Dr. Henry A. Kissinger.

One of the PI team members also served as the protective intelligence coordinator for the protectee visit. This entailed liaison with the site advance agents, the running of name checks, a review of current intelligence, the submittal of intelligence situation reports, and the presentation of intelligence information at the security briefing. During the movement, the PI team would respond to all incidents of a protective nature.

Dick and Bob were often partnered as a protective intelligence team. Each day and night Secret Service protectees were visiting somewhere in Washington. The most frequent stops were speaking engagements at one of the many convention hotels. PI coverage was also extended to the numerous airport departures and arrivals of protectees. These occurred mainly at Andrews Air Force Base in Maryland though some took place at Washington National Airport (now Reagan National Airport).

Being the nation's capital, Washington received an infinite number of foreign dignitary visits. When the dignitaries were chiefs of state or heads of government, they qualified for Secret Service protection. On state visits to Washington, foreign heads of state or government were extended the courtesy of staying at the Blair House, the President's Guest House (1651 Pennsylvania Avenue, NW, D.C.).

Dating back to 1824, the Blair House was originally built by Dr. Joseph Lovell, the first surgeon general of the United States. It was designed in the Federal style. In 1836, the house was sold to newspaper publisher Francis Preston Blair, who was a member of President Andrew Jackson's "Kitchen Cabinet."

In 1859, Blair built an adjacent townhouse at 1653 Pennsylvania Avenue for his daughter Elizabeth and her husband, Samuel P. Lee, a naval officer and third cousin to Robert E. Lee. It was at the Blair House in 1861 that General Robert E. Lee was sounded out by Francis Preston Blair as to taking command of the Union Army. General Lee would subsequently resign his U.S. commission and fight for his home state of Virginia and the Confederacy.

In 1941, the federal government purchased the Lee House. The Blair House was acquired by the U.S. in 1942 for the Department of State, which turned it into an official guesthouse for visiting heads of state. In 1948, both townhouses were combined and simply referred to as the Blair House. From 1949–1952, President Truman and his family resided at Blair House because the White House was being renovated. It was at the Blair House in 1950 that the unsuccessful assassination attempt by two Puerto Rican nationalists took place.

In 1969–1970, the U.S. bought two more townhouses next to the Blair House on Jackson Place, NW. All four townhouses were eventually interconnected and formed the Blair House complex. Managed by the Office of Chief of Protocol, U.S Department of State, the Blair House has décor, amenities, and service fit for a sultan or queen—including conference and meeting rooms, kitchen and dining facilities, library, hair salon, and exercise room.

Bob and Dick became fixtures at the Blair House, being regularly assigned to provide WFO protective intelligence support for foreign dignitary visits. One got to be the coordinator, while the other filled out the team. As a PI team, Bob and Dick not only had to cover the dignitary's movements around Washington, but also the scheduled events held at the Blair House or other residence utilized by the protectee. On private visits to Washington, dignitaries stayed at hotels or at their respective countries' embassies.

The USSS Dignitary Protective Division (DPD) coordinated the security for visiting heads of state and government with the Department of State, which had the primary responsibility for the visits. The DPD had supervisory personnel who served as detail leaders for the visits. Special officers were also on staff. Their duties included the issuance of trip identification, the handling of baggage, and the operation of the Secret Service armored limousines used in foreign dignitary visits.

Once a foreign leader accepted USSS protection—it could be declined—field offices whose districts would be visited would conduct the physical advance and provide protective intelligence coverage. To complete the detail, the DPD requested agents for temporary duty from field offices nationwide.

Bob and Dick worked protective intelligence for one foreign dignitary's extended stay at the Blair House that became memorable. Dan DeAngelo of DPD was the detail leader. On the first day of the visit, DeAngelo told our boys he wanted PI coverage from eight in the morning to twelve midnight, daily. Corrigan explained that it was the standard practice of WFO—barring adverse intelligence—to provide only one PI team for visits and movements, even presidential movements. DeAngelo clasped his hands together as he firmly said, "I only want one PI team—at any one time."

"Dan," Corrigan replied, "there's no one to relieve us. You're asking for 16-hours-per-day coverage. We have casework too. Normally, the PI team reports to the residence at 9:00 a.m., our regular starting time, unless there's an earlier movement. During blocks of downtime in the protectee's schedule, we try to keep on top of our casework. After the protectee is in for the evening, we're usually released. If something comes up after hours, we can respond from home."

After thinking over what had been said, DeAngelo instructed Corrigan: "Go over to the field office during the next break and tell Frank Cavanaugh I said to schedule you for 12-hour days. Tell him the itinerary justifies it and that the detail is getting SOT [scheduled overtime]. I'll let the advance agents go when we're in for the night but want you men to stay late. Besides standing by for PI, you can cover any unscheduled late night movements. Getting you some extra money will help with the long hours."

Later that day, Dick and Bob walked the couple of blocks to WFO. ASAIC Cavanaugh's secretary got our boys in to see the second in command. Cavanaugh took a pause from some paperwork and glanced up toward the two agents standing before him. "What's up?" Cavanaugh asked. Corrigan repeated what DeAngelo had said. Bob saw the ire grow in Cavanaugh's face as he replied: "I've *never* seen a foreign dignitary with a firm itinerary. I'm not signing off on SOT for foreign dignitary visits."

Corrigan dipped his head a bit, while he softly said: "Sir, Detail Leader DeAngelo wants us from eight in the morning to midnight for the entire visit. Our work schedule is firm."

"Is that so," Cavanaugh replied angrily. "Then let him pay you out of his budget! Look, if you guys don't want to do this job, I'll get two in here who will."

"No, sir, we're happy with the assignment," Corrigan quickly declared.

Cavanaugh bristled as he growled back: "You misunderstood me. If you don't like working for the Secret Service, you two can leave your guns and badges on my desk on your way out!"

"Sorry to have bothered you, sir," Bob stated with conviction. Grabbing Corrigan by the arms, Bob whisked him out the door.

Safely outside in the hallway, Corrigan gasped, "That didn't go very well, did it?"

"No, we should have asked DeAngelo to call Cavanaugh. What were we thinking?" Bob uttered.

"I thought we were just following DeAngelo's orders. I should have known better," Corrigan said, shaking his head.

Back at the Blair House, Corrigan told DeAngelo that ASAIC Cavanaugh would not be scheduling overtime for the PI team. DeAngelo frowned and replied: "I'm sorry you won't be getting SOT like us. I still would like to have you men stay late every night. When you're not here, I don't feel we're as safe nor have as many options." With that, Dick and Bob agreed to arrive early each day and stay until they were released by DeAngelo. During this assignment, I didn't see much of Bob. He arrived home after midnight and was out the door a little after I got up in the morning. Unfortunately, there would be many more days and nights like this to come.

Out of necessity, Bob was soon placed into the duty agent mix. After hours, the WFO phone line was transferred to the Treasury Department switchboard. When an emergency call came in, the Treasury operator forwarded it to the WFO duty agent. That agent in turn notified the appropriate squad duty agent. The WFO duty agent and the squad duty agents were rotated on a weekly basis. There were only five agents in the PI Squad at the time. With agents out on TDY assignments and the like, Bob was frequently scheduled to be the agent on call for the PI Squad.

There were no pagers. The WFO duty agent and squad duty agents were required to stay home at nights and on weekends. For most squads, it wasn't more than an occasional imposition. For the agents in PI, it was a relentless burden. Routinely, someone in the Washington area was coming to the protective attention of the Secret Service. It seemed that the nighttime brought out the PI subjects like stars in the sky. Our phone rang on many a late night and early morning. No matter how many times it happened, I never got use to it. Startled, I would awake nervous and uneasy. The ringing warned that Bob would soon be taken from my side and the safety of our home.

Jotting down the information, Bob planned his action accordingly. Then, Bob hurriedly got dressed, attaching his gun, handcuffs, radio, ammo case, and badge to his pants belt. For his badge, Bob had a special holder, which clipped to the belt. Wearing the badge to the left of the holster, Bob could flip back his suit coat to expose the badge when he identified himself to suspects. This kept the right hand near the holster in case Bob had to draw his weapon. Watching Bob put on the Secret Service star in the middle of the night always reminded me of the danger inherent in law enforcement.

Sometimes I got back to sleep, and sometimes I lay restless—worrying about Bob as he disappeared into the darkness.

Many times, I didn't see Bob until the next evening. In spite of having to work all night on the new case, he was still expected to work his regular-day hours and assignments. All protective intelligence cases were important. Threat cases received the highest priority. Like homicide investigations, threats against Secret Service protectees were investigated immediately, and the cases were worked until a preliminary resolution could be attained.

Bob worked 36 hours straight on one *direct threat* case. These were cases where the subject clearly threatened (spoken or written) the president or other protectee. *Indirect* or *conditional threats* were dependent on stipulations and marked with uncertainty. Examples of indirect threats are as follows: (1) If the president doesn't change his ways, he will be struck down, (2) I might shoot the president if he gets us in another war, and (3) If the president were here, I'd punch him in the nose.

Conditional threat cases were not prosecuted by the U.S. Attorney's Office unless agents could show that the subject *intended* to inflict bodily harm. An element of the crime (18 U.S.C. Section 871) was that threats had to be made "knowingly and willfully." In 1969, the U.S. Supreme Court decided in Watts v. United States (394 U.S. 705) that appellant's statement, "If they ever make me carry a rifle, the first man I want to get in my sights is L.B.J.," was not a true threat. The Supreme Court remanded the case back to the U.S. Court of Appeals with a judgment for acquittal.

The Supreme Court reasoned that the subject made the statement in the context of an anti-war rally and that it was "political hyperbole." The court also noted the conditionality of the statement: The subject would first have to be drafted into the Army. It was ruled that political hyperbole, words spoken in jest, and idle talk were constitutionally protected speech.

Mental illness, lack of intent, the inability to carry out the threat, and intoxication were other prime factors used by assistant U.S. attorneys in deciding the prosecutorial merit of threat cases. Bob spent many a night tracking down subjects who had engaged in "bar talk" of a threatening nature toward the president or other protectee. Most of the time, the subjects claimed they had been intoxicated and didn't mean what they had said. One was a soldier of fortune wannabe, who had tried to impress the ladies.

Bob took all of these cases seriously. He remembered that Samuel Byck had been reported to the Secret Service for sounding off in a bar. It was alleged that Byck had said words to the effect that someone should kill President Nixon. Byck ended up trying to assassinate Nixon in a bizarre aircraft-hijacking attempt where he planned to crash the plane into the White House. Even though Byck's "Operation Pandora's Box" never got off the ground, Byck killed two innocent people before committing suicide during the failed attempt.

Since the president resided at the White House, all roads led to Washington for protective intelligence subjects who were having mental episodes. Those who didn't have cars most often traveled to D.C. via bus or train. These modes of transportation were cheaper than air travel. PI subjects were commonly out of work and low on funds. In some of these cases, the Secret Service was tipped off to the subject's travel to Washington. Dick and Bob were regularly called to meet these subjects upon their arrival in D.C.

A major portal to the city was the Greyhound Bus Terminal at 1110 New York Avenue, NW. Built in 1940 of limestone over reinforced concrete, the structure was a striking example of art deco architecture. The nearby Trailways Terminal (1200 I Street, NW) was the other major bus gateway to Washington. Between the two facilities, hundreds of buses arrived daily.

Traveling by rail, PI subjects disembarked at Washington's magnificent Union Station. Designed in a Beau Arts classical style, the station opened in 1907. Constructed of marble and granite, the building featured a grand facade with columns and arches, 96-foot-high vaulted ceilings, colossal statues, and other allegorical adornment.

During the golden age of railroading, Union Station was one of the busiest terminals in the nation and saw its share of presidential arrivals and departures. In fact, the station was designed with a presidential suite, which offered safe access and security. This innovation was the result of President James A. Garfield's 1881 assassination. Garfield was shot while walking through the waiting room of Washington's old Baltimore and Potomac Railroad Station. Although the suite at Union Station hadn't been used by a president since Eisenhower's time, it stood as a reminder to Bob of the potential danger a president faced when traversing a public area.

The 18 tracks and platforms of Union Station handled hundreds of trains and many thousands of passengers a day. The station's grand concourse was big enough to hold the Washington Monument if laid on its side. In those days, passengers were not required to give names or show identification when purchasing tickets. It was a difficult and time-consuming task to intercept persons of interest unless detailed travel information was available.

Often, PI subjects made their way to the White House or to a site that the president might be visiting. PI subjects also telephoned the White House and mailed letters to the president. Even though these appearances and communications might not be overtly threatening, they could still earn a Secret Service interview if bizarre behavior, irrational ideas, or an insistence to gain personal access to the president was exhibited.

If they appeared to agents to be mentally ill and a danger to themselves or others, subjects were referred to St. Elizabeths Hospital to be observed by a psychiatrist. At St. E's, the subjects could voluntarily sign themselves in for treatment, be committed involuntarily by a doctor, or be released from custody.

A good number of the subjects PI agents came in contact with were what the Secret Service loosely termed as *cranks*. These subjects, due to some mental disorder or other psychological problem, had an abnormal direction of interest toward Secret Service protectees. Most of these individuals were not dangerous. They were nuisances, who consumed a disproportionate share of the Service's valuable PI resources. Nuisance cranks are not to be confused with ordinary citizens, who have legitimate reasons for contacting high government officials and who present their comments in an appropriate manner.

A majority of the cranks had severe disorders, which markedly affected thought and behavior. Being out of touch with reality characterized these types of psychotic disorders. Most of the subjects suffered from *paranoid schizophrenia*. Symptoms included *delusions* and *hallucinations*.

Delusions are beliefs that have no basis in reality. In delusions of grandeur, paranoid schizophrenics think they are gods, kings, prophets, or some other important figure. They often believe they're on a mission to save the world. Subjects experiencing delusions of persecution feel others are plotting against them. Even relatives and friends might be thought of as enemies.

Hallucinations are reactions to circumstances that do not exist and are not real. Paranoid schizophrenics might claim to hear voices, to see things that are not there, or to imagine sensations that are not physically possible.

Bob soon became a valuable asset to the PI Squad. He had a knack for protective intelligence matters. When making contact with subjects exhibiting abnormal or disturbed behavior, Bob first assessed whether the subject presented an *immediate* danger. Bob listened to the subject for verbal clues and closely watched his or her hands and demeanor. Looking for bulges and other signs of concealed weapons, Bob would frisk the subject if conditions warranted.

Next, Bob attempted to establish rapport. Intently listening to the statements made by subjects, Bob showed concern for their plight. Many PI subjects felt frustrated, and they were seeking relief from problems that overwhelmed them. Although these problems might be imaginary and the subjects' concerns unfounded, they were all too real to individuals with psychotic disorders. Outwardly disagreeing with demented individuals or trivializing their concerns could provoke anger and violent behavior. As Bob said, "It does little good to try and reason with an irrational mind."

Utilizing strategies during the interview that did *not* incorporate obvious pretext, Bob got the subjects to provide the needed identifying and personal history information. It was important that agents did not lie to mental subjects, even if it succeeded in getting the subjects to comply with a resented course of action. Once subjects realized they had been deceived, they could feel threatened and become uncooperative and even violent.

Some PI subjects continued to come to the attention of the Secret Service on repeat occasions. It would be that more difficult to handle the subject the next time if he or she felt betrayed. It was essential that PI subjects held positive thoughts toward the president and the Secret Service. Otherwise, subjects might turn their fear and suspicion to the president or USSS agents and resort to offensive actions.

Bob was particularly successful in diverting subjects from their attempts to talk with the president and to submit to the prescribed course of action. Even though the subjects did not accomplish their mission to have an audience with the president, Bob made them feel that they had achieved the essential part of their goal. For example, Bob assured subjects who were not a danger that the information would be presented to higher authorities and that all appropriate action would be taken. Thus, subjects could return home knowing they had done everything that was necessary and possible.

Bob would then notify the subject's family for assistance in making travel arrangements. Bob and Dick put many a PI subject on a bus back to their hometown. With these subjects, the main goal was to get them out of Washington, so they wouldn't be tempted to return to the White House.

With subjects that were being referred to St. Elizabeths, Bob advised that the first step in the process of getting this information to higher authorities was that the information had to be verified and evaluated. The subject would have to be seen by a person who specialized in these matters.

Of the mentally ill subjects who had a direction of interest to the president, Bob found that their discourse fell into two broad categories. In the first, subjects believed they had the solution for some pressing world problem, or they wanted to warn of some impending catastrophe or apocalyptic event. These ranged from irrational ways to solve issues such as world hunger to dire warnings of a sneak attack by the Soviets or by aliens from outer space, etc.

In the second category, subjects complained of imaginary ailments and accused others of causing them harm. Often, subjects complained that their homes were bugged and that they were being spied on. In severe cases, government agencies were blamed for bombarding the subjects with radar waves and the like for mind control. Subjects wanted the president to order the responsible parties to stop these intrusions. It was not uncommon for subjects to place aluminum foil inside their hats or clothes to ward off the imaginary rays.

The most potentially dangerous paranoid schizophrenics were those who heard voices ordering the elimination of something or someone for the good of society. Command hallucinations coupled with persecutory delusions could be a lethal mix.

Next to paranoid schizophrenia, the most common psychosis medically diagnosed for PI subjects was manic depression. Commonly called bipolar disorder today, subjects generally came to the attention of the Secret Service during the manic phase of the illness. These episodes were characterized by overactive behavior—both physical and mental. Racing thoughts, poor judgment, rapid speech, impulsiveness, over-estimation of true abilities, arrogance, exaggerated sense of well-being, restlessness, and insomnia were some of the symptoms.

The delusions of bipolar subjects in manic episodes normally focus on grandeur. In this exalted state, subjects could quickly become irritated, angry, and violent when their activities were blocked by authority figures. Frenzied thoughts and behavior could produce elevated strength and stubborn resistance.

On one occasion, it took Bob and two police officers five minutes to subdue a manic-depressive subject and to get him safely into the transport wagon. This was an especially dangerous operation. The subject had to be taken into custody at his residence. A law enforcement officer never knows where the subject might have a weapon hidden. Plus, there's always the danger that the subject might be able to wrestle a handgun away from an agent or officer. Until one can get handcuffs on a subject who is resisting arrest—especially a charged-up mental subject—lives can be in jeopardy.

While all PI investigations can be dangerous, a few had some comic moments. In one instance, Dick Corrigan was assigned a case that involved a check made payable to the president for a moderately large sum of money. A private citizen had mailed the check to the president on several occasions. Each time, the White House returned the check to the sender. When it showed up once again in the White House mailroom, the problem was turned over to the Secret Service.

First, Dick called the bank that the check was drawn on. Surprisingly, it was found that the subject had enough money in her account to cover the amount. Deciding to return the check in person, Dick asked Bob to accompany him. While Dick didn't think the individual was dangerous, it was always a good idea to have a witness along when contacting a female who might have mental problems.

During the drive uptown, Dick expressed: "I'm going to suggest she send the money to her favorite charity. Hopefully, this lady is just a bit eccentric and not a full-blown mental case."

"Yeah, if she has delusions of grandeur toward the president, we could have a problem on our hands. Right now, it seems her favorite cause is POTUS [president of the United States—pronounced pō-tus]," Bob reasoned.

Parking the government car near the apartment building where the subject resided, Dick and Bob took the stairs to the fourth floor. Police and federal agents never rode the elevators in residential buildings in certain neighborhoods. A couple of guys getting out of a plain four-door Ford sedan and dressed in suits and ties were a tip-off to wanted persons and juvenile troublemakers that "The Man" had arrived. If the power was turned off to the elevator during operation, law enforcement personnel could be trapped inside for hours, since the emergency phones inside the cab might also be inoperable.

Arriving at the subject's apartment, Dick rapped a couple of times on the door. From within, a woman's voice called out, "Who's there?"

"Mr. Corrigan, ma'am."

"What do you want?"

"I've been sent by the White House. I'd like to talk with you." Suddenly, the sound of footsteps could be heard inside the apartment. Reaching the door, the subject cracked it open to the length of the safety chain. She peered perplexingly at the two men. Holding his commission book to the opening, Dick announced: "I'm Mr. Corrigan and this is Mr. Ritter. May we come in?"

Without saying a word, the subject unlatched the chain and motioned the visitors inside. She was in her mid-30s with a stocky build. "Ma'am, the White House sent us to personally thank you for your generosity," Dick declared. "It was a wonderful gesture." Pulling the check from his pocket, Dick continued, "Unfortunately, the president isn't allowed to accept gifts such as this." Corrigan extended the check to the subject.

The subject's face changed from confusion to anger. "I want to give my money to the president. You take the check back," she commanded.

"Ma'am, your thoughtfulness toward the president is enough." Dick countered. "He'd like you to donate it to your favorite charity."

The subject snarled, "No, you tell the president to keep it."

Dick tilted his head back and forth toward the door, giving Bob a sign to start moving that way. Backpedaling to the door, Dick said in a soothing voice: "All right, ma'am, I don't want to argue with you. The White House can't accept this; we have to leave it with you. Please accept our regrets." With that, Corrigan dropped the check inside the apartment as he followed Bob out the door.

Bob and Dick ran down the hallway to the fire door. They hurried down the stairs. At about the third floor landing, Dick and Bob heard the sound of quick footsteps hitting the steel treads above them. "Step on it Bob; she's moving!" Corrigan shouted.

At the street, Bob and Dick ran for the government car, with the lady in hot pursuit, waving the check out in front of her. Just that moment, a Metropolitan Police cruiser came around the corner. Seeing the show before them, the MPD officers pulled to the curb. One of the officers called out with a chuckle, "Secret Service or FBI?"

Corrigan, somewhat embarrassed, pulled out his commission book and answered, "Secret Service."

At the same time, the subject threw the check at Bob, who was trying to get into the passenger side of the government vehicle. Then without fanfare or warning, she removed the skirt she was wearing and threw it on the sidewalk, revealing a full girdle. "What do I have to do?" she screamed. "Send my clothes to the president too!" Then she started to unbutton her blouse.

"No, no," Bob cried out. Knowing he and Dick were fighting a losing battle and only making things worse, Bob picked up the check and tried to calm the subject: "We'll take the check back. Please keep your clothes on."

Seeing the check in Bob's hand, the subject did an about-face and headed back to the apartment building, not bothering to pick up her skirt or to refasten her blouse.

"Do you need assistance?" the officer inquired, still smiling.

"No, I think we're okay now. I was afraid for a moment we might have to commit her," Corrigan answered.

Back at the office, Dick closed out the case by sending the check back to the White House with a suggestion that it be shredded.

Another humorous moment occurred when Bob and a female agent were sent on a Saturday afternoon to stake out the Sky Terrace of the Hotel Washington (515 15th St., NW, D.C.—since renamed the "W"). The hotel's rooftop bar and grill overlooks the Treasury Building and the White House. A waitress reported that while serving two male subjects lunch, she overheard them trying to determine the distances from the bar to targets within the White House complex. It was recounted that the subjects had made the comments in the context of the range a sniper would zero in on. The waitress described the two subjects as in their mid to late 20s with medium length brown hair. The waitress also noted that one of the subjects said he would be back later that day.

Attired in casual clothes, Bob and the female agent took up a position at one of the tables and looked like any other young couple enjoying each other's company on a Saturday afternoon. They sipped iced tea from highball glasses, while they waited for the subject to return. As the afternoon progressed, the bar filled up with hotel guests, tourists, and others seeking refreshment and a birds-eye view of the city.

A person who brought some concern to the female agent suddenly entered the bar. "Oh, no! There's an agent I know from headquarters who just entered the bar," she informed. "We went through SS school together. I might have to go over and tell him we're working, so he doesn't blow our cover."

Just then, the HQ agent caught site of Bob's partner. Coming to the table, the agent loudly greeted her, "Hey, Sally, how's things over at the field office?"

The female agent responded softly, "Mark, this is Bob Ritter from WFO; we're here working an investigation."

"Sally, we're friends. You're here having a couple of drinks on a Saturday afternoon. I know the Secret Service hierarchy frowns on agents seeing each other. You don't have to worry about me; I won't tell anyone."

"Mark, we're not on a date. There's only iced tea in these glasses. Bob's happily married. We're working a PI investigation. A couple of guys were in here earlier talking about ranges to the White House for sniper shots."

"Now I believe you," the agent said as he sheepishly dipped his head. "That was Joel Smith and I. We met for lunch." Bob and Sally looked over to see the waitress frantically confirming that the HQ agent was indeed the subject in question. All three agents had a good laugh over the double case of misunderstanding.

The months rolled by for Bob. The year 1975 ended with a major incident of international terrorism. On December 21, Ilich Ramirez Sanchez, the Venezuelan terrorist known as Carlos, led a raid on the headquarters of the Organization of the Petroleum Exporting Countries (OPEC), located in Vienna, Austria. Wielding machine guns, Carlos and five other terrorists stormed the second-floor meeting room where OPEC was in session. In the assault, two security officers and a Libyan official were killed. One of the terrorists was seriously wounded in the exchange of gunfire.

The terrorists took 11 oil ministers and scores of others hostage. Issuing a pro-Palestinian communiqué calling for the solidarity of all Arab nations against Israel, the terrorists demanded that they be flown out of Austria with the 11 ministers and their delegations. Otherwise, all of the hostages would be killed and the building blown up.

The siege ended 20 hours later when Austrian authorities permitted the terrorists to fly to Algeria with their hostages—after all of the OPEC employees were released. In Algiers, members of the non-Arab delegations were freed. Next, the plane was refueled and flew to Tripoli, Libya where the Libyan delegation and some others were released. Airborne again, the terrorists were denied landing in Tunisia. They eventually returned to Tripoli where the remaining hostages were set free after arrangements were made for a sizeable ransom.

At home, the United States looked forward to its 200th birthday. The bicentennial year would bring additional challenges to the beleaguered Washington Field Office Protective Intelligence Squad.

Chapter 21

The Bicentennial

Dick Corrigan and Bob started out the bicentennial year by receiving some recognition for the successful handling of several high profile cases. One was an important threat case in which Bob received a conviction. In another, Dick and Bob's previous evaluation of a subject proved to be highly accurate.

That case began in 1975 when the subject sent a rambling letter to the secretary of the treasury with language that could be construed as a veiled threat. The subject had been accused by the Securities and Exchange Commission (SEC) of defrauding $200,000 from investors. Subject's attorney agreed to present his client for an interview by the Secret Service as long as the subject was not asked about the pending SEC case.

Even though the attorney was present and had advised the subject to answer the questions, the individual was uncooperative and verbally combative. After naming some politicians and others he didn't like and ranting about what was wrong with America, the subject stormed out of the attorney's office. Dick stayed to talk with the attorney, while Bob followed the subject outside. Bob observed that the individual was walking with a limp. "How did you hurt your leg?" Bob asked.

"In a parachute jump," answered the subject.

"Were you in the military?"

"I went to a civilian jump school," the subject replied angrily.

"Look, we don't want to add to your troubles. We're just trying to resolve the matter of this one letter," Bob remarked.

"I don't want to talk about it," the subject stated emphatically as he reached his car door.

Using a different tack, Bob quickly asked, "Who do you like?"

The individual immediately answered, "Gary Cooper, now there's a *real* American hero." With that, the subject jumped behind the wheel, started his car, and drove out of the parking lot. Bob wrote down the tag number of the vehicle.

Later, Dick and Bob interviewed the subject's wife and found her to be elusive too. She was prone to break down in tears. Bob had the feeling that she was hiding something. Bob also noticed men's adventure magazines on the coffee table at the couple's residence.

In the days that followed, Corrigan was informed by the subject's attorney that his client did not want to be further interviewed by the Secret Service. The attorney also remarked that the subject was upset that his wife had been questioned by Dick and Bob.

Next, the individual sent another letter to the secretary of the treasury. This time, the subject threatened some form of retaliation if either he or his wife were contacted again by agents of the Treasury Department. With this turn of events, Dick and Bob gathered to discuss the case. Dick's preliminary evaluation had been that the subject did not present a danger to Secret Service protectees. "What do you think, Bob?" Dick asked.

"I think this guy is of protective interest. He's a hot head, who doesn't like his country. He's been accused of some serious criminal activity. He's writing letters with conditional threats. His emotional state is deteriorating. The world is closing in on him. In his desperation, he might resort to some sort of senseless act that would incorporate violence."

"Bob, I have the feeling he's just a lot of talk. Do you think he presents a danger to the secretary?"

"He certainly has a direction of interest toward the secretary."

"Do you think he's for real?" Dick asked.

"Yes, I think he's capable of reckless, dangerous behavior."

"Okay, there's no need to take chances. We'll go with your instincts. I'll write him up as being of protective interest for the time being."

Several weeks later, Dick received some alarming news from the U.S. Attorney's Office. The subject had just been arrested by the FBI for extortion. He was charged with attempting to extort a large sum of money from an interstate bus company. It was alleged that the subject had threatened to blow up some of the buses of the company unless a payment was made. It was believed that the subject had sent a package containing explosives to the bus line. The parcel exploded in a Washington, D.C. post office before it could be delivered. Fortunately, no one was hurt.

The news was an affirmation of Dick and Bob's evaluation. Hearing Dick relating the recent events brought to Bob's mind one of the most famous cases in the annals of crime. It was as if all the pieces of a jigsaw puzzle were suddenly coming together. "Sit down Dick and let me run something by you," Bob burst out excitedly. "This might sound a bit farfetched, but I've been troubled about our guy for some time. There's something about him I haven't been able to put my finger on—until now."

As he took a seat, Dick interjected: "I'm a believer. Lay it on me, my brother."

"Dick, remember the FBI circular regarding D.B. Cooper?"

"Yeah, the Feebies [FBI] sent some information about the skyjacking to law enforcement agencies in hope Cooper could be identified."

"I looked over the circular pretty thoroughly," Bob stated. "I think you should write up our man and submit him to the FBI; they might want to take a look at him in the Cooper case."

"Tell me why you think so," Dick mused—intrigued by what he had just heard.

"About four years ago on Thanksgiving eve 1971, a white male purchased a ticket for a Northwest Orient Airlines flight from Portland to Seattle," Bob began. "D.B. Cooper is a misnomer that the press got hold of early in the investigation, and it stuck with the public. According to the FBI, the hijacker actually used the name *Dan Cooper* when purchasing his ticket."

"Bob, you're kidding me. Why didn't the Bureau correct the mistake?"

"Maybe they wanted an easy way to weed out hoaxers," Bob speculated. "In any case, our guy's name is *Dan*. It's worth mentioning that his given name is Dan, not Daniel.

"And when I followed him from the attorney's office," Bob continued, "I noticed he walked with a limp. He told me he injured his leg in a parachute jump. Since he had told us plenty of things and people he didn't like, I tried the other side of the coin. I asked him whom he did like. Without hesitation, he answered, 'Gary Cooper.' I didn't think much about it at the time."

"The movie star Gary Cooper," Dick intimated.

"I can only assume so because our guy referred to Cooper as a 'real American hero.' Gary Cooper was an action film hero. With our subject's recent caper, his answers could take on new meaning. If you take our guy's first name and Gary Cooper's last name, you might have an alter ego, *Dan Cooper*. I saw men's adventure magazines at our subject's residence, like *Argosy* and *True*. This guy might be living out his fantasies.

"His physical description is similar to the hijacker in the Northwest Airlines case. Our guy is about 175 pounds, around six feet tall, and with dark hair. The problem is the age. Our man was 30 in 1971, while the hijacker was described as mid-40s. But our subject looks older than he is with his receding hairline. In a business suit and dark glasses, he probably would look even older. Plus, Cooper might have disguised himself to look older. And from my experience, eyewitness testimony—especially descriptions—can be extremely inaccurate."

"Yeah, I can vouch for that," Dick echoed.

"Taking this further, the $200,000 Cooper extorted from Northwest Airlines is the *same* amount our subject is accused of swindling," Bob added. "And our guy just got arrested for trying to extort money from an interstate transportation company with threats to blow up their vehicles. That's a similar MO [modus operandi]."

"Bob—on that point—why would our man risk doing something like that now?"

"He was probably trying to score some quick cash to flee the country. He's becoming more desperate, and he's looking for a way out."

"You're probably right."

"One more thing, Dick—the Northwest flight that was hijacked by Cooper on the Portland to Seattle leg—where do you think it originated from?"

"Where?"

"Washington, D.C.," Bob answered with a smile. "Maybe Cooper was from the D.C. area and had flown the flight before."

"Bob, the circumstantial evidence you presented is more than enough to justify alerting the FBI. I'll write it up and send it to Liaison for forwarding to the Bureau."

At the end of January 1976, further validation of our boys' evaluation surfaced. The subject attempted suicide before his court date by taking an overdose of sleeping pills. Bob came home that night and told me how he and Corrigan were being praised for their accurate assessment of the subject. He had certainly proven to be dangerous.

"Bobbie, do you think this guy could really be D.B. Cooper?" I asked.

"Yes, if Cooper is still alive. But, I have to honestly say I think the odds of Cooper surviving the jump are 50-50 or less."

"Why?"

"Because it *appears* that he jumped out of the plane at night without knowing precisely where he was. Because it was cold and raining and the terrain was treacherous. According to the FBI, Cooper jumped into high winds and freezing temperatures wearing only a business suit, trench coat, and street shoes. Even if he got his chute open, clouds covered the ground. He had little control over his drop zone. He could have landed in trees, rocks, or water."

"So you think he didn't know what he was doing," I inferred.

"Well, he knew the aft stairs on a 727 could be lowered in flight. He knew enough to tell the captain to stay below 10,000 feet, so the cabin would be unpressurized. Cooper directed the captain to fly with his landing gear down and the flaps at 15 degrees. That would enable Cooper to ensure that the aircraft was being flown at a safe speed for deployment of the aft stairs and for jumping.

"And, Cooper chose a $200,000 ransom payable in $20 notes. That was a sum that was manageable to tie around his waist and to jump with."

"Bobbie, how much does $200,000 in twenties weigh?"

"There are about 490 notes to the pound. So, 10,000 twenty-dollar notes would weigh approximately twenty and a half pounds," Bob figured.

"If he didn't survive, wouldn't they have found some trace of Cooper by now?" I asked.

"Not if he landed in water or his chute didn't open. He could have hit the ground in a remote area and animals could have taken care of the rest," Bob theorized.

"Yikes!" I said.

"Yeah, and it would have been a fitting end for Cooper," Bob reasoned. "He's no hero in my book. He's a criminal, who endangered a lot of people for greed or some other selfish motive."

"Why does the public think of him as a folk hero?" I asked.

"I believe it's because they partly identify with him. They see him as a Robin Hood type. People love to root for the underdog. They think Cooper was probably a regular Joe, who after striking out with the system decided to strike back. They'd love to have the same daring.

"And because many people *don't* think it's wrong to steal from corporations or the government. That's why we have so much white-collar crime and income tax evasion. People all too easily rationalize larcenous behavior.

"Unfortunately, the press and the public also romanticize and idolize the notorious and the infamous. D.B. Cooper has become a folk hero—our generation's John Dillinger. Because there's been no trace of Cooper since he jumped, many think he got away with it. This all adds to the mystique. And after Cooper, there were a lot of copycats. So many that airlines were directed by the FAA [Federal Aviation Administration] to institute passenger security screenings."

"But you don't think Cooper made it," I said.

"I think it's more likely he died in the attempt. I see several main possibilities regarding Cooper—with lots of variations. One, he was caught up in some type of serious situation that required some quick money. Maybe he owed some big gambling debts to the mob. Maybe Cooper defrauded some folks out of $200,000. When he thought he might be found out, he needed another 200K to cover the amount in question. If the hijacking succeeded, it was a way out. If not, then his death during the attempt was another way to escape his troubles. The risk involved was secondary. The pressure of the situation forced him to take chances. He was desperate. Cooper might have been out of practice or known just enough about parachuting to get himself killed. *Desperate* people are *dangerous* people.

"Or, Cooper might have been an experienced though daredevil sky diver, paratrooper, or smokejumper, who had the qualifications to make such a risky jump. In this case, Cooper might have done it for the thrill, and the money was his prize."

"Smokejumper!" I cried out. That possibility had not occurred to me.

"Yeah, those guys are as tough as paratroopers," Bob continued. "Jumping out of airplanes into danger is a daring way to make a civilian living. Smokejumpers routinely parachute into dense forests where they land in trees. They're trained for that. They carry equipment sacks around their waists, so a bank bag full of money shouldn't have been a problem. And since most forest fires are started by lightning, smokejumpers have plenty of experience parachuting during bad weather. If Cooper was a smokejumper, he might have even worked the forests along the flight path. The forests of Oregon and Washington are prime smokejumper territory."

Bob was always thinking. The breadth and depth of his knowledge never ceased to amaze me. "Wow! Bobbie, how else could Cooper have gotten away with it?" I asked.

"Besides being really, really lucky."

"Yes."

"He would have needed to be familiar with his jump area. Being a pilot would have been a plus. Cooper might have deduced the flight path flown by the speed, altitude, and destination requirements he gave the Northwest crew. By dead reckoning, he could have figured out *approximately* where to jump.

"Cooper might have had thermal clothing underneath his business suit. He might have had an altimeter, compass, and other helpful items with him. The supposed explosives were probably safety flares. Cooper could have ignited them and thrown them from the aft stairs just before he jumped—to check wind conditions. Maybe Cooper had an accomplice on the ground in a clearing—watching for the flares with binoculars and then turning on a homing beacon. Maybe there was a break in the cloud cover. Maybe Cooper survived the jump. But that's a lot of maybes.

"Even an experienced skydiver would have had problems with the way the incident unfolded. First, the plane landed about 30 minutes late in Seattle. Cooper had ordered the pilot to circle until the money and parachutes were ready on the ground.

"After the passengers were traded for the ransom money and chutes, Cooper ordered the plane refueled. When everything was said and done, the plane spent over two hours on the ground and didn't depart Seattle until about 7:45 p.m. I think Cooper made a severe miscalculation on how long he would be on the ground.

"He might have chosen an afternoon short-hop flight, so authorities wouldn't have a lot of time to dispatch chase aircraft. And that it would be just about dark when he jumped. That way, spotting his parachute and any subsequent ground search would be difficult. As it was, the flight crew believed Cooper jumped sometime after 8:00 p.m. That was probably later and darker than Cooper planned. But there was no turning back, so he jumped into the wind, rain, and darkness—more likely to his death.

"The fact that none of the bills have turned up in circulation points to Cooper not surviving," Bob reasoned. "Although it's possible he lost them during the jump."

"Bobbie, couldn't he be holding the ransom money until the banks get tired of checking?"

"Anything's possible. But the heat is *never* going to die down on those 10,000 serial numbers. The notes originated from the San Francisco

Federal Reserve Bank. Its serial numbers begin with the prefix 'L.' Even if Cooper laundered the money overseas, eventually the notes would wear out and be returned to the Federal Reserve or the Treasury for destruction. Believe me, any $20 Federal Reserve Note with a serial number that begins with an 'L' and with the series date of the ransom money will be checked before being destroyed."

Several weeks passed; Dick and Bob's subject had one more trick up his sleeve. He escaped from the custody of U.S. marshals while being transported between the federal courthouse and jail. Although Bob received a tip that the subject was hiding out in Greenwich Village, New York, the FBI believed the subject had fled to Canada. In any case, the FBI and Marshals Service had primary jurisdiction over the subject. Bob, Dick, and the rest of the agents in the PI squad had plenty of other subjects, visits, movements, and events to worry about.

The major event of 1976 for the Washington Field Office was the American Revolution Bicentennial celebration. The new ASAIC, Radford "Rad" Jones, was personally supervising WFO bicentennial preparations. Jones played varsity baseball at Michigan State University while earning a degree in criminal justice. He started with the Secret Service in 1963 at the Buffalo Field Office. Later, Jones worked at the Kennedy compound in Hyannis Port, Massachusetts and was one of the first agents assigned to the Intelligence Division. Jones came to WFO from the Louisville Field Office where he had been the ASAIC.

Bob was surprised when he was called on the intercom and asked to come to the ASAIC's office. Jones greeted Bob with a smile and invited him to sit down. "Bob," Jones began, "I want to compliment you on your handling of the Singleton case. I've also been hearing some good comments from DPD on the PI advances you've been doing over there."

"Thank you, sir."

Jones looked Bob squarely in the eye and continued: "I'm putting together WFO's bicentennial team. Washington will have major events that the president and vice president will participate in. We're also expecting visits from some prominent foreign dignitaries. I can't overstate how important the overall protective intelligence arrangements for the bicentennial will be. I need someone who'll get the job done. I'm selecting you to be the WFO-PI coordinator for the bicentennial."

"Wow, I appreciate the faith you have in me. This is totally unexpected. I know we're short-handed in PI, but I figured one of the senior agents would get the assignment."

"Bob, I chose you because I know you'll do an excellent job for us. From what I've seen and heard: You're a bright, hardworking agent, who doesn't put off until tomorrow what can be done today. That's more important to me than GS grade.

"I also know you're a former park policeman and have good contacts there. With your local police experience, you'll be able to establish good working relationships with MPD, the FBI, and other agencies. With the Church Committee stirring up things on Capitol Hill, establishing contacts with intelligence sources and getting *meaningful* information will be a challenge. I feel you'll be up to the task."

"Thank you, sir. I won't let you down."

"I know you won't," Jones stated emphatically. "Bob, I'll want you to keep me personally advised of your progress. Also, we'll need to send preliminary situation reports to headquarters every 30 days—sooner if intelligence dictates."

"Yes, sir, no problem."

"OK, Bob, do you need anything from me?" Jones asked.

"Yes, I'd like to start attending the COG [Council of Governments] monthly law enforcement planning meetings."

"You got it."

That afternoon, a teletype was sent to headquarters naming Bob the USSS Washington area coordinator for bicentennial intelligence. A national coordinator was chosen in the Intelligence Division, and area coordinators were selected for Philadelphia and New York (other cities where major bicentennial events would be attended by USSS protectees).

Bob lost no time in making personal visits to area law enforcement agencies to establish liaison. He visited his old Park Police unit, SOF. It was a homecoming for Bob. SOF supervisors promised to work closely with Bob and to share whatever intelligence was developed.

Next, Bob dropped by the Metropolitan Police Department Special Operations Division (SOD). Bob knew several high-ranking officers at SOD. Although not optimistic as to how much they could contribute, the SOD contacts pledged full cooperation. Nonetheless, the MPD was walking a fine line regarding intelligence operations.

The MPD Intelligence Division had been all but dismantled due to privacy and civil liberty concerns. During the civil rights and Vietnam War demonstration years, MPD had collected intelligence of a political and partisan nature—including surveillance of activists. Since that time, MPD had sharply curtailed their intelligence gathering due to internal directives and D.C. Council civilian oversight. The primary guideline was that intelligence operations should not be conducted unless laws have been violated, or there is strong belief that they will be.

It was more of the same at the Washington Field Office of the FBI. Domestic intelligence investigations had become a dirty word at the FBI, and it was pronounced "COINTELPRO" (Counterintelligence Program). The first public knowledge of the secret program surfaced in 1971 when an FBI resident agency office in Media, Pennsylvania was burglarized. Documents exposed that the FBI had engaged in domestic spying against radical and civil rights groups. This led to allegations of improper wiretaps and break-ins.

A Freedom of Information Act (FOIA) lawsuit produced more disclosures in 1973, which caused both the FBI and the Justice Department to look into COINTELPRO. A subsequent joint investigation under Assistant Attorney General Henry Petersen resulted in the November 1974 public release of a summary of COINTELPRO. The Petersen committee reported that over 2,000 COINTELPRO operations were conducted from 1956–1971 (when COINTELPRO was terminated by J. Edgar Hoover). The vast majority of these operations were found to be proper and legal. About one percent of the activities were deemed "abhorrent in a free society."

FBI operations characterized as "troubling" centered on activities to disrupt dissident groups and their members. These included sowing dissension within the groups and the collection and dissemination of derogatory information on certain leaders. These new disturbing revelations caused the Senate to conduct its own investigation via a select committee.

Commonly called the Church Committee after its chairman, Senator Frank Church of Idaho, this body began its inquiry in 1975. The committee conducted a broad investigation, encompassing both foreign and domestic intelligence operations. The CIA, FBI, and National Security Agency (NSA) were scrutinized. In early 1976, the final report of the Church Committee was being prepared for public release.

Uneasy as to what the findings and recommendations of the Church Committee would be, supervisors at the FBI-WFO gave Bob general assurances of cooperation but little specifics. The FBI was in an unenviable situation. Although COINTELPRO had been officially terminated in 1971, there were accusations that similar activities had continued—especially since Hoover's death in 1973. Some believed these operations had been kept from subsequent FBI directors as well as Justice Department officials.

Into this sea of uncertainty, Bob dove headfirst in his quest to do everything that was legal and ethical to ensure that the Washington, D.C. bicentennial celebration would be safe for Secret Service protectees. For the months leading up to the bicentennial, Bob worked many hours "staying ahead of the intelligence curve" as he called it. He even established intelligence contacts with police in New York, Chicago, Miami, South Dakota, and Puerto Rico.

Some of the best international intelligence came from a sister Treasury agency, the U.S. Customs Service. Bob was a frequent visitor to Customs Headquarters at 1301 Constitution Avenue, NW. There, Customs agents in the Office of Enforcement Support provided useful data to Bob. Concerned with attempts to smuggle weapons and explosives into the U.S., Customs had compiled information on domestic and international terrorist organizations.

Bob believed the biggest threat to the American bicentennial would be from domestic terrorist groups who used bombings as a means of violent protest. Customs and the FBI agreed with the assessment as did Bob's friends at the Department of State's Bureau of Intelligence and Research (INR). The best hope for any advance warning and prevention of such bombings would be through investigations conducted by the FBI and local authorities.

In March 1976, Attorney General Edward Levi proactively issued guidelines for domestic security investigations. The Levi guidelines set standards for the internal security investigations conducted by the FBI and took effect on April 6, 1976. A *full* domestic intelligence investigation could now only be conducted when there were "specific and articulable facts giving reason to believe that an individual or group is or may be engaged in activities that involve the use of force or violence."

With its public release in April 1976, the final report of the Church Committee documented the COINTELPRO abuses of the FBI. The committee concluded that such tactics should be banned. The report also listed 96 recommendations regarding the gathering of intelligence by federal agencies. Church Committee recommendations for the FBI often exceeded the Levi guidelines and were generally more specific and restrictive. The Church Committee proposed that its recommendations be enacted by law.

Because of the Levi guidelines and fear that Congress might pass overly restrictive legislation, FBI officials conducted fewer internal security investigations and less information was being passed to the Secret Service. Due to the fallout over improper COINTELPRO operations, the FBI seemed to retreat from some of the legitimate crime prevention aspects of intelligence investigations.

One recommendation of the Church Committee had a particularly chilling effect on the Bureau. It stated: "The Committee has found serious abuses in past FBI investigations of groups. In the conduct of these investigations, the FBI often failed to distinguish between members who were engaged in criminal activity and those who were exercising their constitutional rights of association. The Committee's recommendations would only permit investigation of a group in two situations: first, where the FBI receives information that the avowed purpose of the group is soon to engage in terrorist activity or hostile foreign intelligence activity; or second, where the FBI has information that unidentified members of a group are soon to engage in terrorist activity or hostile foreign intelligence activity."

Without reservation, Bob championed the protection of the civil and constitutional rights of U.S. citizens. However, it was a legitimate function of law enforcement to detect criminal activity and to prevent ongoing criminal acts. Bob worried that the FBI was overreacting to the Levi guidelines and the proposals of the Church Committee. It seemed the FBI was moving toward a threshold where full-scale intelligence investigations would only be conducted when there was evidence that a *violent* crime *had already* been committed.

In addition, the Church Committee criticized the FBI on its use of "covert human sources" (informants). The Committee recommended that informants should only be used when absolutely necessary and only upon approval of the Attorney General or his designate based on a *probable cause* standard. And those informants should only be used for 90 days, although a 60-day extension may be granted for "compelling circumstances." Finally, it was noted that informants should not engage in any activities that violate law.

This was a major disqualifier for FBI informants who had infiltrated terrorist groups. It was impractical for sources to retain their cover if they refused to participate in *any* act that might be a violation of law. And a *probable cause* determination of criminal activity *before* an informant could be used would be devastating on crime prevention. Thus, information from the FBI specifically forewarning of violent activity by groups or members of groups was diminished by quantity and quality, as the Bureau sharply reduced its domestic intelligence exposure. The FBI did not want to do anything that would prompt Congress to pass legislation requiring a *court order* before an informant could be inserted into a group.

Among the groups law enforcement was concerned with regarding the safety of bicentennial events was the Fuerzas Armadas de Liberación Nacional (FALN). The group's Spanish name translates to Armed Forces of National Liberation. This clandestine, paramilitary group first surfaced in October 1974 when they left a communiqué in a New York City telephone booth claiming credit for seven bombings. Five of the bombs exploded outside Manhattan banks, and two detonated in an alley between the city hall and police headquarters of Newark, New Jersey. No one was injured in the blasts.

The FALN sought Puerto Rican independence from the U.S. Like other terrorist groups, the FALN used revolutionary rhetoric to rationalize the use of violence. Besides immediate independence for Puerto Rico, the group also demanded the release of five imprisoned Puerto Rican nationalists. Four of the nationalists had fired shots inside the U.S. House of Representatives in 1954. Five Congressmen were wounded in the assault. In addition, the FALN wanted the release of Oscar Collazo, who had attempted to assassinate President Truman in 1950.

In December 1974, the FALN made headlines again. A New York City police officer was blinded in the right eye and suffered disabling injuries when a booby trap exploded at the entrance to a vacant building. The officer had been lured to the location by a pretext call. The FALN took credit for the act—stating it was revenge for the death of a youth while in a

Puerto Rican jail. Puerto Rican authorities claimed the youth's death had been a suicide.

In January 1975, the FALN escalated the violence with an explosion at the historic Fraunces Tavern complex in lower Manhattan. A bomb was planted inside the doorway of the redbrick Federal-style annex to Fraunces Tavern. The tavern had its origins in 1719 and served as a meeting place for Revolutionary War patriots. After resigning his commission in the Continental Army in 1783, General George Washington bade farewell to his officers at the tavern.

Estimated to have been the explosive force of 10 sticks of dynamite, the bomb killed four people, while scores were injured. In a communiqué, the FALN said the bomb was in retaliation for a recent "CIA ordered bomb" that killed and injured several Puerto Rican independence supporters in Puerto Rico. The message warned, "You have unleashed a storm from which you comfortable Yankies [sic] cannot escape."

The Fraunces Tavern bombing was followed by other FALN bombings in New York, Chicago, and Washington. On October 27, 1975, bombs exploded outside the U.S. Department of State and the Bureau of Indian Affairs buildings in D.C. No one was injured.

The D.C. devices were believed to have been two or three sticks of dynamite connected to a timing device and taped to a propane cylinder. The bombs were then placed in carry-on bags or briefcases. The use of propane cylinders in the devices was a signature of the FALN. Bomb experts believed the FALN added propane in an attempt to start fires with the explosion. The steel cylinders also served as a source of shrapnel.

Bombings had become the favorite tool of domestic terrorist groups. Bombings received front-page newspaper and prime time radio and television coverage. This guaranteed the group's message was brought before the public. Nothing defined terror better and created more fear and panic within the citizenry than the horrific toll a random bombing could ignite.

That point was tragically brought home to the city of New York on December 29, 1975. At 6:33 p.m., a bomb exploded inside a terminal at LaGuardia Airport. Jammed with holiday travelers, a first-floor baggage claim area suddenly became the scene of mass death and destruction. Eleven persons died and seventy-five were injured. Estimated to have been equal to 25 half-pound sticks of dynamite, the explosive force punched a hole approximately 12 feet in diameter through the 6-8 inch reinforced-concrete ceiling above the blast area. The bomb was planted in a coin-operated public locker and was detonated by a timing device.

It was one of the most deadly explosions in New York history, second only to the 1920 Wall Street bombing, which took the lives of 40 people and injured over 100. There were no credible claims of responsibility for the LaGuardia bombing. The NYPD and FBI conducted a massive investigation but were unable to bring anyone to justice. To this day, no one has ever been charged or prosecuted for the crime.

As the bicentennial approached, several militant groups threatened the celebration. There were warnings to "blow out the candles on the nation's birthday cake," and to "turn the bicentennial upside down." While there were no specifics or any hard intelligence, Bob knew what the language suggested. The bicentennial presented an opportunity for terrorist groups to achieve worldwide notoriety for their cause through the use of violence.

Amidst this backdrop of threats and uncertainty, law enforcement officials prepared for the biggest weekend in U.S. history. Since there would be little advance warning of trouble, authorities took security measures to negate any possible violence—especially as to bombings. One of the initiatives was a strong suggestion to transportation companies to close down public lockers at passenger terminals. Amtrak was one of the major carriers who shut down their coin-operated baggage lockers in the Northeast corridor during the bicentennial weekend. This denied terrorists the chance of planting bombs in them.

Fortunately for the Secret Service, it was supported by Explosive Ordnance Disposal (EOD) technicians from the U.S. military. All areas where USSS protectees would visit were thoroughly searched for explosive devices. The Secret Service established security perimeters that ensured areas cleared by EOD remained safe for the protective movement. This was standard operating procedure (SOP). Three hundred and sixty-degree coverage was the basic principle of Secret Service protection. The goal of "three-sixty coverage" was to provide the protectee with a safe zone—free from any hazard or threat.

Less than a month before Independence Day 1976, the security procedures of the Secret Service were tested by an assassination scare. It was the evening of June 7; President Ford had just concluded an address to about 600 students at Bowling Green State University in Bowling Green, Ohio. The president was heading for the exit of Anderson Arena when he paused to shake hands with some students. A student pointed a camera at the president. Suddenly, there was a loud report. President Ford's face went pale, and his knees buckled. The president's detail immediately grabbed Ford and shielded him. Other agents rushed to the student. President Ford was quickly evacuated from the area. It was all an innocent accident. The camera's flashbulb had exploded with a sound like a gunshot.

Although the Secret Service was criticized as *overreacting*, Bob told me agents did exactly what they were trained to do. He explained: "One of the most important points learned from the JFK assassination was that agents should react spontaneously when an explosive sound is heard. If the object posing the threat is within *hands reach*, you move to neutralize it. If not, you *cover* your protectee and *evacuate*. You don't have time to determine whether it's a shot, firecracker, flashbulb explosion, or whatever. If it's an assassination attempt, the shooter already had one free shot. The more your reaction is delayed; the more advantage an assassin would have."

The bicentennial finally arrived. For D.C., the major observances would be held on Saturday, July 3, through Sunday, July 4, although President Ford did have an important appearance before the Independence Day weekend. On July 1, Ford dedicated the new $40 million National Air and Space Museum of the Smithsonian Institution, which opened on the Mall. It was America's gift to herself. The ceremony featured a space age twist. The ribbon to the museum was cut by a mechanical arm identical to the one on board the *Viking 1* space probe. The command to activate the arm was relayed from the actual *Viking 1*, which was on its way to Mars.

The Saturday schedule began with the American Bicentennial Grand Parade. Vice President Nelson Rockefeller led off the action. When Rockefeller reached the end of the parade route, he was escorted to the VIP reviewing stand located in the 1600 block of Constitution Avenue, NW. From the best seat in D.C., Rockefeller watched the remaining two and a half-hour spectacle that featured about 200 units and 10,000 marchers. Approximately 500,000 spectators lined the parade route.

That night, President Ford attended an "Honor America" celebration at the Kennedy Center. The program was entitled "Let Freedom Ring Again" and featured the Mormon Tabernacle Choir. Comedian Bob Hope introduced the president. Hope got a laugh from the audience when he referred to recent congressional sex scandals. "They may not be the best congressmen, but they sure are the most affectionate," Hope chided.

President Ford accompanied by his daughter, Susan Ford, spent Sunday, July 4, at bicentennial events in Pennsylvania and New York. They flew by helicopter to Valley Forge, Pennsylvania where they attended a program sponsored by the Pennsylvania Bicentennial Commission. At Valley Forge State Park, the president and Susan toured the encampment area for the Bicentennial Wagon Train Pilgrimage.

Next, they traveled to Philadelphia, Pennsylvania where they participated in a program at Independence Hall (where the Declaration of Independence was signed) and attended a luncheon at the Bellevue-Stratford Hotel.

Later that afternoon, the president and his party flew by helicopter to the flight deck of the aircraft carrier USS *Forrestal* (CV-59), which was anchored in New York Harbor. The president and Susan were met by First Lady Betty Ford. In the ceremony that followed, the president rang the Bicentennial Bell (a gift from Great Britain) 13 times and addressed the VIPs (from the Diplomatic Corps) who had assembled to view "Operation Sail 1976."

Transferring via helicopter to the USS *Nashville* (LPD-13), the Fords were briefed on the ships participating in Operation Sail. Then, from an honor position on the flight deck, the presidential party watched the parade of international tall ships.

Back in Washington, Bob gave the final intelligence briefing to the agents who were working the July 4 celebration. About 75 agents had been brought in from out of town to work the bicentennial weekend, which culminated with the Sunday night fireworks spectacular.

The largest crowd ever to have assembled in Washington packed the Mall and the Washington Monument grounds for our nation's Independence Day bicentennial. Officials estimated the crowd to have been over a million strong. A spacious fenced-in safety zone had been constructed from the eastern part of the Reflecting Pool to the southwest side of the Washington Monument grounds. A stage and VIP stand were situated within the safety zone on the Monument side of 17th Street.

The "Pageant of Freedom" kicked off at 6:00 p.m. with a performance by the Grambling University Marching Band. They were followed by country singer Johnny Cash and his band. Next on the program was a patriotic concert by the U.S. Army Band and Chorus, followed by the Mormon Tabernacle Choir. Vice President Rockefeller delivered the featured address at about 8:45 p.m. The Army Band concluded the musical program with a rousing rendition of John Philip Sousa's "The Stars and Stripes Forever," which led into the fireworks.

At the time, the D.C. fireworks spectacular was billed as the largest and loudest pyrotechnical show ever to have been set off in the United States. About 33½ tons of explosives were launched from eight barges anchored in the Tidal Basin and from platforms by the Reflecting Pool and on the grounds of the Washington Monument. The president and first lady returned to Washington in time to view the 45-minute display from the Truman Balcony of the White House. Several hundred yards away on a blanket, the kids and I marveled at the fireworks too. The White House South Grounds were opened to White House pass holders and their families. Bob met us at the gate and got us cleared for entry. The evening concluded with a replica of the Liberty Bell tolling 200 times.

When it was all over, the score was 3-0 in favor of the law enforcement teams of Washington, Philadelphia, and New York. The terrorists did take one in Boston, Massachusetts. In the early morning hours of July 2, 1976, several bombs exploded in the Boston area. One blast destroyed an Eastern Airlines four-engine turboprop Electra airliner that was parked at Logan Airport. No one was hurt in the blasts.

On the international scene, Israel struck a dramatic blow against state-sponsored terrorism. An Air France flight from Tel Aviv to Paris had been hijacked on June 27, 1976, after a stopover in Athens, Greece. The hijackers were supporters of the Popular Front for the Liberation of Palestine.

After refueling in Benghazi, Libya, the plane continued to Uganda, a nation controlled by strong-arm dictator Idi Amin. Landing at Entebbe on

June 28, the hijackers were reinforced by Arab terrorists who were waiting on the ground. It appeared that the hijackers had the full backing of the pro-Palestinian Amin.

The hostages were transferred to the old terminal building at Entebbe. The hijackers demanded the release of 40 criminals being held in Israel and an additional 13 that were imprisoned in France, West Germany, Switzerland, and Kenya. Otherwise, the hostages would be killed and the aircraft destroyed. A deadline of 11:00 a.m. July 1 was set by the terrorists.

Through Idi Amin, the French ambassador began negotiations with the hijackers. On June 30, Israel advised the French that it would consider the release of prisoners. With Israel joining the diplomatic negotiations, the terrorists extended the deadline to July 4 and freed about 50 children, who were then flown to France. The next day, about 100 non-Jewish hostages were also freed and flown to safety. More than 100 hostages remained in custody. This group consisted of the Jewish passengers along with the crew of the French airbus, who valiantly refused to leave until the last of the hostages were released.

While the Israeli Cabinet was considering the exchange of prisoners for hostages, the Israeli Defense Forces (IDF) was developing military options. After dry runs in the Israeli desert, a rescue plan was formalized and put into effect on July 3. Final governmental approval for the operation came as the commandos flew south in their Hercules C-130 aircraft. Israeli officials were convinced that the use of force had become necessary. The terrorists were refusing to negotiate as to the location of the proposed exchange. The hijackers had insisted the exchange be conducted in Uganda rather than a neutral nation. That brought Israeli skepticism as to whether the terrorists would keep their word.

After an eight-hour flight covering over 2,000 miles, the C-130s of the IDF utilized unconventional landing methods to affect a surprise attack during the overnight hours of July 3-4. A motorcade consisting of a black Mercedes limo and escorting Land Rovers rolled off the ramp of the lead C-130—while it was still moving. Masquerading as a motorcade of President Idi Amin, the Israelis took Ugandan sentries by surprise.

The old terminal building was quickly stormed and the hostages extracted. Other IDF units secured the remainder of the airport, and over 10 MIG fighter planes of the Ugandan air force were destroyed on the ground during the ensuing action. Within an hour, the first C-130 was back in the air with the hostages safely onboard. An IDF covering party was the last unit to depart Entebbe. It had remained on the ground long enough to ensure that the rescue party would not be pursued.

When the 90-minute operation was over, about 20 Ugandan soldiers and 7 terrorists lay dead. The only IDF fatality was the leader of the initial strike team, Lt. Colonel Jonathan Netanyahu (brother of future Israeli Prime Minister Benjamin Netanyahu). Sadly, three hostages were killed in the crossfire. Another hostage was not at the airport when the rescue mission took place. That hostage had been taken to a local hospital after becoming ill. Following the raid, the hostage disappeared and was presumed to have been killed on orders of a distraught Idi Amin.

The 1976 raid on Entebbe is remembered as one of the most famous and one of the most successful counter-terrorist operations of all time. The Israeli achievement prompted the U.S. to establish its own counter-terrorist unit, the U.S. Army 1st Special Forces Operational Detachment-Delta—commonly known as Delta Force.

With the end of the bicentennial weekend, I could tell that Bob was truly relieved. Yet, there was no break in the work. On July 7, 1976, Queen Elizabeth II of Great Britain and her husband, Prince Philip, the Duke of Edinburgh, arrived in Washington for a state visit in honor of the American Revolution Bicentennial. It was the Queen's first visit to the U.S. since 1959. The royal couple's bicentennial visit to the U.S. received a wildly enthusiastic response from the American press and public. Americans were awe-struck with the monarch and turned out in great numbers. Everyone wanted to see the Queen.

Protection for the Queen was provided by the Secret Service. Concerns were compounded at some of the sites due to the simultaneous presence of the president, first lady, vice president, and other protectees. British security was represented by a gentleman who was titled the "Queen's Police Officer." He was an inspector from the Special Branch of London's Metropolitan Police. Popularly known as "Scotland Yard," the Metropolitan Police force dates back to 1829 and was originally formed to provide police services for Greater London. Throughout its rich history, additional duties and responsibilities of national scope were added to the mission of the Metropolitan Police. These include the protection of royalty, certain public officials, and heads of government who visit the UK.

During advance arrangements for the Queen's visit, British officials emphasized that U.S. security was to be low-key and unobtrusive. For example, the British wanted the Queen to ride in a Rolls Royce instead of a USSS armored limo. They also advised that the Queen would venture where she wanted when out on movements. The British did not want the Queen's access to crowds restricted.

The situation had become tense; British authorities were reluctant to accede to USSS policy. There was even a possibility the British might decline Secret Service protection. Bob found that many British officials had a casual attitude toward security. They didn't seem to think the Queen was in any danger while in the U.S.—even though their Washington embassy had been a past target of terror. In 1973, a letter bomb exploded at the British Chancery (3100 Massachusetts Avenue, NW). The device was rigged to detonate upon opening. The blast severed the left hand of a secretary who worked in the office of a senior military attaché.

With the support of the incoming U.S. Chief of Protocol, Shirley Temple Black, the Secret Service held firm. The British eventually deferred to American protective methods. Queen Elizabeth would ride in a Secret Service armored limousine. Crowds would also be divided and controlled as to access level, and barriers would be utilized. The Secret Service did agree to use minimally intrusive controls such as rope lines. At the Embassy of Great Britain, red-plastic chain links were strung between stanchions.

The British were only getting back some of what they handed out on their own shores. When USSS protectees visited the United Kingdom during these years, the Brits were unwavering regarding one very important protective issue—the carrying of firearms within the UK. In those days, the Secret Service was limited to the use of only *one* handgun. That single weapon had to be shared among all the agents of the detail. It was usually carried by the supervisory agent in close proximity to the protectee or rotated through the suite doorpost when the protectee was in their temporary residence.

Highlights of the Queen's D.C. visit included a White House arrival ceremony featuring a 21-gun salute and a State Dinner held in the White House Rose Garden. Normally, official dinners are held in the State Dining Room of the White House. Since the State Dining Room could only seat 150 guests, First Lady Betty Ford moved the dinner outside to the Rose Garden. A large white tent with clear vinyl sides was erected in the Rose Garden to accommodate an expanded guest list of 250. The tent featured air-conditioned comfort and a wooden floor covered with red carpet.

After dining on Lobster en Bellevue and Roast Saddle of Veal, guests were entertained in the White House East Room by comedian Bob Hope and recording artists The Captain and Tennille. Hope, who was born in England, got a smile from the Queen when he joked, "My folks were English; they were too poor to be British." After the show, there was late night dancing in the State Dining Room.

The guest lists for the White House State Dinner and the reciprocal dinner and reception at the British Embassy read like a cultural who's who. Besides the elite of the Ford administration, national politicos, and diplomats; famous personalities from entertainment, sports, business, high society; and the media added sparkle to the events. Celebrity invitees included: Helen Hayes, Greer Garson, Cary Grant, Bob Hope, Muhammad Ali, Telly Savalas, Ella Fitzgerald, David Brinkley, Bill Blass, Dorothy Hamill, Julie Harris, Willie Mays, Barbara Walters, and many more.

The Queen also visited the Lincoln Memorial, Smithsonian Institution Castle, National Gallery of Art, Washington National Cathedral, Capitol Rotunda, and the District Building. Bob got tickets for me and the kids to see the Queen at another one of her stops, Arlington National Cemetery.

Petite and looking younger than her 50 years, the Queen presented a regal picture in a lavender silk dress and hat accented by white gloves and shoes. Assisted by Prince Philip, who was attired in a naval uniform of white, her majesty placed a wreath of red and white carnations at the Tomb of the Unknowns. Afterwards, members of the ceremonial unit of the U.S. Army, "The Old Guard" (3rd Infantry), ended the commemoration with drum rolls and the playing of taps. It was a solemn and touching occasion and sadly reminded me of my father's military funeral.

Around this time, another occasion aroused some mixed emotions in me. Bob and I had moved from the District Heights townhouse to a spacious four-bedroom, split-foyer home in the Kettering Subdivision of Largo, Maryland. The community was multicultural and looked to be a great place to make new friends and to raise a family. There were good schools, parks, a swimming pool, youth athletic teams, and other activities.

We hosted a housewarming party and many of Bob's Secret Service friends were able to attend. Everyone was having fun and the party was moving into the late evening. Bob finally had to remind his colleagues that he was leaving on a ten-day trip early the next morning. Bob did it with a wink of the eye and a nod in my direction. The meaning was clear, and it was a sweet gesture on Bob's part. As we made love later that night, I was truly thankful for the loving relationship we shared. At the same time, I dreaded that Bob was going away. The two diverse feelings were symbolic of our marriage. The needs of the Secret Service were determining my private life—and my emotional well-being—more and more.

Chapter 22

Long Days and Lonely Nights

B ob considered the Washington Field Office to be the busiest Secret Service district in the country—and with good reason. Protective responsibilities were a bottomless drain on WFO manpower. That burden spread to out of district assignments. The WFO was unique in that it *routinely* supplied post standers for presidential and vice presidential visits throughout the nation. This was due to the fact that the limousines and follow-ups needed for out-of-town trips were flown via the Air Force from Andrews Air Force Base, Maryland.

For these airlifts, C-141A transport planes were utilized. The Lockheed C-141A Starlifter was a four-engine jet aircraft, which could cruise at over 500 miles per hour. The plane featured clamshell rear doors and a loading ramp. A good portion of the 145-foot length of the aircraft was devoted to cargo area. The C-141s could carry about 50,000 pounds of payload nearly 4,000 miles without refueling. An armored limousine (12,000 pounds) and a follow-up (5,000 pounds) were no problem for the C-141. Even with two vehicles chained down in the cargo compartment, there was room to install rows of aft-facing seats for passengers. That's how the "car plane," as USSS agents called it, was configured for Air Force special air missions (SAMs) in support of the Secret Service. For the USSS, it was a convenient and cost-effective method of sending post standers where needed.

Being a WFO junior agent, Bob missed very few car plane trips. Even when Bob was the PI Squad duty agent, he was still sent out on weekends. During the week, Bob would be called out at night for PI matters. Then on approach of the weekend, Bob would fly out of town via the car plane to be a post stander in cities across the country. A senior PI agent would then fill in for the weekend duty. I never thought this was fair. Yes, there were PI calls on the weekend, yet the weekend duty agent did get some time at home. It seemed to me that Bob was drawing the short end of every assignment.

Along with out-of-town post standing and TDY assignments, in town PI advances, PI team coverage, and PI caseload, Bob was routinely assigned to USSS protectee arrivals and departures at Andrews Air Force Base. Because we lived close to Andrews, Bob was scheduled for most of the late-hour AAFB arrivals/departures—either as a post stander or as a member of a PI team.

Tom Dailey, the agent who made the assignments, asked Bob if he didn't mind taking more than his share since most of the WFO agents resided in Virginia. In fact, one WFO agent lived in the Front Royal, Virginia area—about 65 miles from Washington. When the agent was hired, he asked SAIC Gittens if it was all right to live that far from the office. Gittens gave the green light by answering, "I don't care if you live in Atlanta as long as you get to work on time."

Of course, Bob readily agreed to take on the extra work. He was willing to help his fellow agents. Never mind that protectee arrivals/departures were all hours of the day and night and that Bob consistently maxed out his premium pay (PL) hours.

PL was a great bargain for the Secret Service. It was figured at the pay rate of a GS-10, step 1, times 40 hours a month for administratively uncontrollable overtime (AUO). Bob consistently worked 60 or more PL hours a month. Each month, he gave at least 20 hours (half a workweek) to the Secret Service. These were hours taken out of his private time and away from his family.

Because it had somehow designated special agent positions as "exempt from the Fair Labor Standards Act" (FLSA), the Secret Service decided its own criteria for non-PL overtime. To be paid at time and a half, hours above the normal workday and workweek had to be scheduled overtime (SOT). And to be eligible as SOT (pronounced: S-O-T), the Secret Service decided the hours had to be *recurring*. Therefore, the same hours had to be scheduled for at least several days in a row to be payable as SOT. While agents on protective details received SOT, WFO agents were rarely scheduled for overtime pay.

PL was supposed to be for hours that could not be administratively scheduled in advance. During a normal workday, an agent might have to initiate surveillance, track down a subject, make an arrest, and other investigative duties that would necessitate working over one's regularly scheduled hours. If Bob was running down a PI subject who had threatened the president, he couldn't call it quits because it was 5:30 p.m. That was understandable.

Yet, Bob was given many protective assignments—*well in advance*—that required him working after hours and on days off. Although he was scheduled for the assignments, he was not scheduled for the overtime. WFO supervisors used the excuse that the hours were "not recurring." As a result, these assignments were counted as PL hours.

For every PL hour worked in excess of 469 per year, Bob received no pay. That amounted to hundreds of unpaid hours per year. The weekend car plane trips were a perfect example of agents being scheduled for travel and work without being scheduled for the overtime. I had suspicions that the SOT policy of the Secret Service had been crafted to avoid paying just compensation. SOT had more loopholes than a used car warranty. Yet, Bob never complained. He was loyal to the Secret Service. When I mentioned that the overtime policies of the Park Police and State Department seemed fairer, Bob grinned widely as he replied, "I'll see what I can do about that—*if I ever become director.*"

Although the bicentennial celebration was the event of the year for the Washington Field Office, the major operation for the Secret Service during 1976 was the presidential campaign. The Secret Service was required to protect major presidential candidates. This responsibility stretched Secret Service manpower and resources to the breaking point since a record number of candidates had thrown their hats into the ring. The USSS enlisted special agents from ATF and other Treasury agencies to supplement the candidate details.

During the campaign, Bob was temporarily assigned to various USSS presidential primary state operations centers. Bob spent time in Florida, Illinois, North Carolina, New York, Arizona, Indiana, and Ohio. He conducted PI advances for presidential candidates.

In the Republican primaries and caucuses, incumbent President Gerald Ford faced strong competition from former Governor Ronald Reagan of California. On the Democratic side, a large number of politicians vied for the presidential nomination including: former Governor Jimmy Carter of Georgia, Senator Henry "Scoop" Jackson of Washington, Alabama Governor George C. Wallace, Senator Birch Bayh of Indiana, Senator Frank Church of Idaho, former Senator Fred Harris of Oklahoma, Congressman Morris "Mo" Udall of Arizona, former Director of the Peace Corps Sargent Shriver, Senator Lloyd Bentsen of Texas, and former California Governor Jerry Brown.

Bob took these assignments very seriously. He remembered Robert Kennedy's assassination during the 1968 presidential campaign and the assassination attempt by Arthur H. Bremer against George Wallace in the 1972 presidential campaign. The latter incident left Wallace paralyzed from the waist down, yet he was back with his fourth try at the nomination.

There had already been one assassination scare in the '76 presidential campaign. On November 20, 1975, Ronald Reagan was working the crowd at a campaign event in Miami, Florida. Suddenly, a 20-year-old college dropout pulled a toy gun and pointed it directly at Reagan from only a few feet away. Secret Service agents wrestled the subject to the ground and arrested him. The replica resembled a snub-nosed .38-caliber revolver. Had the subject been a real assassin bent on taking Reagan's life, he would have had a clear shot. To Bob, it was more proof that improvements were needed in Secret Service protective operations.

Always a student of history, Bob explored the past for answers to the future. In 1972, Bob watched the Wallace shooting as it replayed again and again on television. With an eye toward prevention, Bob told me the answer was "in the crowd." Since that time, Bob had become a Secret

Service agent. The knowledge and experience gained led to a better understanding of the problem. This insight helped Bob to refine his ideas and strategies.

The two assassination attempts against President Ford in 1975 added to Bob's database. Bob believed the historical evidence showed that the procedures used by the Secret Service in working a principal—which hadn't changed significantly since the 1940s—could not prevent a determined assassin from firing shots at deadly range.

In fact, most agents of the Secret Service believed it was impossible to prevent the death or serious injury of a principal by an assassin who was willing to give his or her life in the attempt. That was part of the culture of the Secret Service.

Bob's own research yielded some interesting statistics. During the period 1835–1976, there were 13 assassination attempts with a direction of interest toward the office of the presidency. Of those 13 attempts, nine were made on sitting presidents, and three took place against presidential candidates. The other incident targeted a president-elect.

Handguns were used in 11 of the 13 attempts. Eight of the handgun attempts were made at close range. Two other pistol attacks occurred at ranges of approximately 30 and 40 feet. The other handgun assault took place on the sidewalk in front of Blair House. A rifle was utilized in one of the assassination attempts. In another, a commercial airliner was the intended weapon.

Five of the 13 attempts were successful. Four presidents (Lincoln, Garfield, McKinley, and JFK) and one presidential candidate (RFK) were assassinated. Two of the 13 attempts were partially successful in that targeted principals were wounded (Theodore Roosevelt and George Wallace). Handguns were used in six of the seven attempts that were either successful or partially successful. In the 13 attempts that Bob examined, six others also lost their lives—including two law enforcement officers, two bystanders, and two perpetrators. A Puerto Rican terrorist was fatally shot by a mortally wounded White House policeman during the 1950 Truman assassination attempt. And in 1974, Samuel Byck committed suicide during his failed attempt.

Thus, in only two of the above 13 incidents did assailants lose their lives. And those deaths occurred during *unsuccessful* attempts. It was clear that suicide missions were not necessary. In fact, two presidential assassins were able to escape the scene of the crime (Booth and Oswald).

Although Secret Service protection was in effect during eight of the 13 attempts, in only two instances did Secret Service agents and/or police fire weapons. That was during the 1950 assault on Blair House and the initial stage of the 1974 attempt by Samuel Byck.

After an analysis of these past events, Bob disclosed an alarming prediction for the future. "It's *more likely* the next presidential assassination attempt will be by a lone gunman using a handgun at close range," he told me. "It will probably happen in or near a public area, and the subject will be waiting to strike. And the scary part: The Service doesn't have a reliable method to prevent it from happening.

"In the United States," Bob continued, "government leaders frequently choose to come in close contact with unscreened individuals in the course of public activities—especially during political campaigning. The freedoms enjoyed by American citizens and the nature of the U.S. political system make it impossible to provide absolute protection. Assassins always seem to have the advantage of surprise. An assassin might be in any crowd waiting to strike."

That was a deadly problem for the Secret Service, and Bob was working on ways to help neutralize the threat. In particular, Bob noted that movements to two Washington hotels regularly presented opportunities for would-be assassins to come within inches of the president. Due to the physical layout of these sites, President Ford usually opted to access the ballrooms via the lobbies rather than the secure back routes preferred by the Secret Service. The president did this in order to shake hands with the public and to provide the White House press corps with photograph opportunities (photo ops). The two hotels were the Statler Hilton (renamed Capital Hilton) at 1001 16th Street, NW, and the Mayflower (now Renaissance Mayflower) at 1127 Connecticut Avenue, NW.

Bob had worked both hotels as a PI team coordinator on many occasions. The Statler opened in 1943 and was of neoclassical design. Its presidential ballroom was designed with wartime concerns in mind. A six-foot wall of steel-reinforced concrete protected the head table area. A large service elevator was installed to lift President Roosevelt's limo to and from the second floor where the ballroom was located.

Fondly known as the "Grand Dame of Washington," the Mayflower opened in 1925 and quickly became a favorite of presidents. Both Franklin D. Roosevelt and Harry S. Truman had resided at the elegant hotel. The Mayflower had also been one of FBI Director J. Edgar Hoover's favorite spots for lunch.

As PI coordinator for presidential visits to sites such as the Statler Hilton and Mayflower, Bob checked the names of everyone who would be working or attending the function as well as other civilians who might come in close proximity to the president. A criminal or mental record might cause a subject to be excluded. Obviously, a known PI subject would be a "Do Not Admit." Bob also had to submit an intelligence situation report, which was prepared after a check with MPD and ID of the latest intelligence information. These facts along with any lookouts would be passed to the post standers during the intelligence briefing.

As part of the protective advance, the ballroom, holding room, and preferred entry/exit ways would be swept by EOD for explosive devices and the areas secured by agents. An identification system with clip-on lapel pins would be utilized for host committee members and hotel staff personnel. Host committee officials—backed by agent personnel—would check tickets to insure that no gatecrashers were admitted to the function. It was extremely important that only authorized guests were permitted access to secure areas.

The Secret Service had been thoroughly embarrassed by a professional gatecrasher during the 1961 Inaugural of President John F. Kennedy. Stanley Berman of Brooklyn, New York gained access to the presidential box for the inaugural ball held at the D.C. Armory. Berman was seen on national television sitting next to the president's father, Joe Kennedy. Berman succeeded in getting JFK's autograph before being reported to the Secret Service by Kennedy family members. Sitting in the seat reserved for Robert Kennedy, Berman was only a few feet away from *both* President Kennedy and Vice President Johnson. It was a significant lapse in security. One can only wonder what would have happened if Berman had been an assassin bent on wiping out the new administration.

Further protective arrangements for D.C. presidential movements included: the checking of purses and briefcases before guests could enter the function room. In addition, a "package room" was established on site, so deliveries could be examined by EOD before being allowed into the secure area. Even the food and beverages offered to the president were checked and randomly selected by the USSS. Thus, a 360-degree protective zone was established with concentric rings of security. The police manned the outer area with Secret Service agents securing the middle perimeter, which were mainly checkpoint posts. The agents of the presidential detail provided the inner security, which was the last line of defense.

With all of these arrangements, the ballrooms of the Statler Hilton and Mayflower were reasonably safe for presidential visits. The major problem was in the hotel lobbies, as they were neither swept for bombs nor secured by agent personnel. It was impractical for the Secret Service to secure such large public areas. Accordingly, these areas were *not* intended to be used in presidential movements.

Nevertheless, President Ford routinely chose to work his way through the crowded, unsecured lobbies. Like most politicians, Ford enjoyed meeting the public and shaking hands. It happened so often that folks began to expect it. On one occasion, over 100 people waited in the lobby of the Statler Hilton to greet President Ford.

Bob felt it was always a potentially dangerous situation and an illogical one at that. Bob would run name checks on guests, committee members, entertainers, and hotel staff. On occasion, subjects with criminal, mental, and/or Secret Service records would be excluded from working or attending the respective function. Yet in the lobby, 100–125 people who had *not* been cleared were allowed to come in close proximity to the president. The site advance agents told Bob this was okay because the president's decision to pass through the lobby was not made in advance. It was "impromptu."

Bob wasn't buying it. "Impromptus" were *stops* that were neither scheduled nor announced. They usually occurred during out-of-town campaign trips and were decided on the spur of the moment. The president might be in a motorcade and decide to drop by a coffee shop or similar spot for a couple of minutes. This was a good way to present the president as a regular person, who was interested in average Americans. They were always good photo ops for the evening news.

True impromptus were random and unpredictable. They were considered safe as the chance of a presidential assassin being there at the same time was virtually impossible. But movements that were officially on the president's schedule and announced in the morning newspaper were another matter. Bob worried that a potential assassin would find out the president's schedule. If there were a movement to either the Statler Hilton or Mayflower, a gunman among the crowd in the lobby would have a dead-on shot at the president.

And to Bob, it wasn't an implausible scenario. PI subjects frequently came to Washington to see the president. On a good number of occasions, they showed up at sites where the president was attending a function. Since PI subjects didn't have tickets for the private events, they gravitated to the public areas. Bob felt a would-be assassin could do the same. Bob reasoned that a subject who had decided that the president must die would not wait for POTUS to visit his or her city or town. He or she could board a plane and be in Washington in a matter of hours.

History supported Bob's rationale. Washington, D.C. has seen two presidential assassinations (Lincoln and Garfield). Unsuccessful attempts against presidents Jackson and Truman have also occurred in the nation's capital. In addition, an attempt against the life of President Nixon was planned to culminate at the White House.

Bob also considered that Giuseppe Zangara, who shot at FDR in 1933, originally intended to travel to Washington to assassinate President Herbert Hoover. At the time, Zangara was living in Miami, Florida. When he read in the newspaper that President-elect Roosevelt was coming to Miami, Zangara canceled the D.C. trip and switched his gun sights to FDR.

To counteract the threat the lobbies of the Statler Hilton and Mayflower posed, Bob suggested to the squad ATSAIC that two PI teams be assigned to these sites for presidential visits. Two teams could cover more area. And if one of the teams became tied up with an interview, there would still be a team available to work the public areas where the president was vulnerable.

Bob's research reflected that would-be assassins often arrive in advance of the actual attempt. PI teams working the lobbies would have a good chance of recognizing a nervous individual or one with a bulge or some other visual cue. Historically, many assassins have been paranoid. Just giving a paranoid individual "the eye" might induce some telltale behavior. Gaining articulable suspicion, agents could pat down the subject for weapons. Agents in the lobbies could also be on the lookout for unattended packages and other suspicious items.

Bob strongly believed that *prevention* should be the single most important objective of protection. In Bob's mind, prevention could not be overemphasized. Because assassination attempts were all too successful, would-be assassins needed to be stopped beforehand. Bob called it "preventive intelligence."

In regard to protective movements, PI agents would eyeball everyone in the public areas and guests as they lined up to enter the function rooms. Suspicious persons would be checked. During movements through public areas, PI agents would establish a mobile protective zone outside the perimeter of the presidential detail agents. The PI agents would work the crowd, looking for anything and anyone suspicious. Inside the crowd, PI agents could better detect and counteract untoward actions.

Believing his methods to be sound, well-reasoned, and supported by history, Bob was disappointed when his suggestions were dismissed outright. Bob's ATSAIC simply said, "We're already overextended."

To that, Bob suggested that the teams be made-up of an MPD detective and a PI agent. That way, no additional agent personnel would be needed. The AT replied, "I don't see the need for this." The AT also did not want to institute any new guidelines for PI teams. The ATSAIC mirrored the PI mission as taught in Secret Service school. PI teams *respond* to protective intelligence subjects and incidents. The proactive role Bob proposed was not part of the agency's culture.

In all frankness, Bob believed the manpower shortages of the Washington Field Office, and the operational demands of the MPD had precluded a fair consideration of his ideas. A proposal that called for the deployment of additional bodies was probably seen as heretical.

Still, Bob used his PI techniques in D.C. when able. Some agents liked Bob's ideas. Some didn't think it made much difference. Bob thought the latter to be somewhat "fatalistic." In truth, Secret Service agents nationwide (including many supervisors) were generally critical of protective intelligence. They viewed much of the PI investigative workload as a waste of precious time. The overwhelming majority of PI subjects would never be more than recurring nuisances. Yet, the Service spent thousands of man-hours each month handling these individuals.

It seemed that the most dangerous subjects did *not* come to the attention of the Secret Service. And in the two assassination attempts by subjects who were of prior Secret Service record (Samuel Byck, Sara Jane Moore), the USSS did not deter these individuals from carrying out their attacks.

Some agents even believed that Sara Jane Moore's USSS interview actually prompted her attempt.

Continuing to hone his PI strategies in the presidential primaries, Bob was regularly assigned PI advances for Ronald Reagan, Jimmy Carter, and Governor Wallace. Bob reasoned that a minimum of two PI teams were needed for most campaign appearances, due to the number of unscreened individuals who came in close proximity to the protectee. Bob would liaison with state and local authorities and work out his manpower requests so that he always received at least three plainclothes officers. One of the officers would work with Bob, while the other two would comprise the second team. Both teams would work the crowd, especially at large outdoor events. In multiple events, the second team would leapfrog ahead to the next stop.

Bob telephoned me from the road when he got a chance. He mentioned that his PI methods were being enthusiastically received by police. I was proud of Bob. In 1972, he had theorized some strategies for enhanced executive protection. Now, he was actually putting them into effect. It was proof positive what can be accomplished when one sets goals and works hard to achieve them. Bob believed that assassinations could be prevented. Presidents and those seeking the office did not have to die in a blaze of gunfire. Bob was making a difference.

Although Bob missed the children and me, he enjoyed his presidential primary advance work. He was gaining experience in different parts of the country, and it was exciting. There were always some humorous moments too.

During one Southern advance, Bob arrived in town and was told by police that an explosive device had been found in the city's auditorium—several days before. The device had been deactivated without injury. The police believed the bomb had been placed due to a labor dispute. They were convinced it had no direction of interest to the impending presidential candidate's visit.

Still, Bob didn't want to take any chances. He immediately notified the lead advance agent and the Intelligence Division. Next, Bob anxiously awaited the arrival of the EOD team assigned to the visit, to inform them of the news. Bob had worked with this particular team on prior advances. The team leader was an Army sergeant first class, who was a couple of months from retirement. He was a short timer, who was looking forward to life after the military. The other team member was a young corporal, who carried the bags and did all the heavy lifting.

Bob was waiting for the team as they pulled up to the entrance of the hotel where the advance party was staying. It was a warm, sunny day and the front windows of the team's rental car were down. The corporal was driving, while the sergeant sat relaxed in the passenger's seat, blowing smoke from a dollar cigar and looking more like a chauffeured millionaire.

These were good assignments for enlisted personnel. EOD teams in support of the Secret Service wore civilian clothes, flew commercially, drove rental cars, and stayed in major hotels.

Leaning out the window, the sergeant greeted Bob with a broad smile and a handshake. Bob got right to business. "Men, we need to check out an explosive device that was found at the civic center. It's ..."

Before Bob could finish, the sergeant began to wail like a wounded boar: "Oh—sh-t! Only 57 days to retirement. I should have stayed in the office. No, I had to hit the friggin' road! Serves me right. Oh, sh-t!" The sergeant then turned to the corporal and barked, "Son, when we get there, you grab the equipment and do exactly like I tell you."

"Sarge, settle down!" Bob stated with authority. "The device was found a couple of days ago. It was made safe by the sheriff's department. It's at the bomb squad's office. I want us to look at it for technical details. Then we can go to the civic center to see exactly where it was found. Afterwards, I need to get a teletype out to headquarters."

"Oh, okay—understood," the sergeant said, gaining some composure. The junior member of the team just shook his head.

During the Illinois primary, Bob worked Ronald Reagan's visit to the northern part of the state. The advance team did an early morning check in at a hotel in Waukegan, Illinois (on the shore of Lake Michigan) and then headed out to conduct the advance. It was off-season and the hotel was just about deserted. When they returned that evening, a television crew was set up out front. The lobby was bristling with activity, and people were waiting to be seated in the restaurant of the hotel. "What's going on?" Bob asked a pair of ladies, who were sitting in the lobby.

"The Secret Service is staying here for Ronnie Reagan's visit," one of the gals answered excitedly. "It's been all over the radio and TV. We thought we'd come on over and check it out. Who are you with?"

"Just a traveling salesman," Bob answered. Apparently, not much happened in Waukegan during those days.

An especially moving moment occurred between Bob and me during the North Carolina primary. Bob called late one night from Asheville, North Carolina. He had just finished working Ronald and Nancy Reagan's visit to the Biltmore House. George W. Vanderbilt, an heir to railroad magnate Cornelius Vanderbilt, built the home in the 1890s. Designed after French Renaissance chateaus, the four-story brick mansion features a 780-foot facade and 250 rooms. It stands on a 125,000-acre estate in the western mountains of North Carolina.

Recounting the candlelight tour, Bob said the Reagans looked like "a couple on their honeymoon." Their eyes "sparkled with romance." Bob could see the deep love the Reagans had for each other. Bob said it reminded him of our love. I told Bob I loved him and asked him to be safe.

"The toughest thing I face every day is being away from you and the kids," Bob declared. Bob touched my heart. I missed him very much.

Bob kept busy in the primaries and was occasionally called out at night. In one instance, he drove over a hundred miles to a highway patrol station for an important investigation. A person had given a statement to police regarding a plot by two unknown subjects to assassinate President Gerald Ford. The individual had been found along the side of the interstate by a highway patrolman. Claiming to have escaped with his life, the subject exhibited evidence of having been beaten. A national lookout was issued.

Bob arrived and began an intensive interview with the complainant. Concerned with certain parts of the story, Bob continued the questioning for several hours. Finally, the interviewee admitted he had made-up the part about the assassination plot. In reality, the complainant was hitchhiking when he was picked up by two males. The two unknown subjects were sharply critical of President Ford but made no threats. A fight broke out between the hitchhiker and one of the subjects. The car was stopped, and the hitchhiker was thrown from the vehicle. Angry with the subjects, the complainant decided to "really get back at them."

On another occasion, Bob called me from the road with worry in his voice. He had just seen the movie *Taxi Driver*. The Martin Scorsese directed film was released in February 1976. It starred Robert De Niro as Travis Bickle, a mentally troubled Vietnam War veteran. Actress Cybill Shepherd's screen role was that of Betsy, a campaign worker for a fictional presidential candidate. Jodie Foster portrayed Iris, a young prostitute. The story unfolded in Manhattan.

Bob suspected that certain story elements were influenced by Arthur H. Bremer's journal, *An Assassin's Diary*. Entries in the diary cover the approximately six weeks leading up to Bremer's 1972 assassination attempt on George Wallace. Bremer had originally stalked President Richard Nixon. Unable to find a surefire opportunity to assassinate the president, Bremer switched to an alternate target, Governor Wallace. Bremer had also considered shooting Secret Service agents en masse.

Looking for clues to detect would-be assassins, Bob had studied Bremer's life and diary in detail. Bob saw similarities between the character Bickle and the real-life Bremer, and it wasn't just that both last names started with a "B" and contained six letters. Travis Bickle hails from the Midwest. He's a loner with serious emotional issues. Bickle does not have satisfying relationships with females and cannot achieve sexual fulfillment. He endures severe headaches. After rejection, Bickle feels he has to do something "big." He buys weapons, stalks a presidential candidate, and engages in a dangerous game of cat and mouse with the Secret Service. Both stories end in violence.

Concerned with the copycat phenomenon, Bob was afraid some vulnerable misfit would identify with the Travis Bickle character. "This country has plenty of alienated ne'er-do-wells who are anti-social and anti-authority," Bob warned. "Troubled, impressionable minds might try to emulate what they see in *Taxi Driver*. The film presents a violent prescription for those who would want to shock society into noticing them. Through cold-blooded murder, the lead character gains fame and *even* receives some exoneration," Bob said in a tone of disgust. "They turned a suicidal sociopath into a hero."

"Bobbie, it's just a movie," I replied.

"To you and me and most everyone else, it's just a movie. To a few, it might be the fantasy to kill and to die for," cautioned Bob.

In August 1976, Bob became the case agent for Gerald Bryan Gainous Jr., whose recurring actions had possibly served as inspiration for copycat behavior. Gainous had just been arrested for jumping the White House fence an unprecedented fourth time. USSS Headquarters was in an uproar. Something had to be done. Bob was called to the ATSAIC's office.

It was the policy of the Secret Service *not* to publicize protective incidents such as these. The notoriety these events received could spawn similar behavior. Normally, the USSS Office of Public Affairs would not release a statement unless a press inquiry was made. And when statements were released, they were usually brief and to the point. The Service did not want to spawn further irrational activity, either by the same subject or by others.

During Gainous's first White House intrusion (November 1975), he was able to make his way to a cluster of bushes near the South Portico—about the same time Susan Ford was arriving back at the White House. While Susan was unloading camera equipment from her car, the subject approached from out of the shadows. He was confronted by Secret Service agents and arrested for unlawful entry. Gainous said he was seeking a presidential pardon for his father.

The first intrusion received no press coverage. In December 1975, Gainous scaled the White House fence again. This time, he was captured immediately. During inquiries regarding the second incident, the media also learned details of the first penetration. A furor was set off by the press. White House and congressional officials wanted to know how the subject had managed to get so close to the president's daughter. Media coverage was heavy; Gainous was even interviewed on television.

About six weeks later (January 17, 1976), Joseph Cruz, a native of San Juan, Puerto Rico, climbed over the White House fence onto the South Grounds where he was arrested. And in April 1976, New York City resident James Hackett was arrested after he scaled the north fence of the White House. Then in June 1976, Gerald Gainous—who had been released on nine months probation for his earlier two incidents—once again jumped the White House fence. He was promptly arrested.

This had been the most fence jumping activity anyone at the Secret Service could remember. Had the copycat phenomenon come into play?

Tragically, there was more to come. On July 25, 1976, a local cab driver, Chester Plummer, climbed over the White House fence at its northeast corner. Brandishing a three-foot length of iron pipe, Plummer ran toward the Executive Mansion. He was intercepted by an EPS officer, who repeatedly warned Plummer to stop and to drop the weapon. Plummer continued to advance toward the officer and attempted to strike him with the pipe. In self-defense, the EPS officer fired one shot at Plummer, who died en route to the hospital. Bob wondered if Plummer had been motivated by the flurry of White House intrusions and the resulting press coverage.

Bob reviewed the Gainous file with the PI Squad ATSAIC. "Headquarters is giving us heat on this one," the AT groaned. "Yesterday, Gainous was sentenced to two years probation on the condition that he leaves town and stays out of trouble. Today, he goes right back to the White House and jumps the fence for a fourth time. He cut his leg going over, and it took six stitches to sew it up. And he's turned violent. Gainous punched an EPS sergeant during the arrest. Gainous is going to get himself killed. We have to stop it *now*. Rad thought you'd be the guy to get it done."

After a short period of contemplation, Bob suggested: "Boss, the judge isn't going to be happy to hear about this latest escapade. I'll go down to the U.S. Attorney's Office and speak with the Deputy USA of the Criminal Division. Instead of handling this like completely new offenses, I think the Service should ask for Gainous's probation to be revoked. We'll ask the judge to send Gainous to Lorton [prison] to do the time. That should get Gainous off the streets, so he can't hurt himself or serve as a poster boy for fence jumpers international."

The strategy worked. Gainous was eventually sentenced to two years at Lorton Reformatory. Several weeks after Gainous's fourth penetration of the White House grounds, Helen Puchalski, a 29-year-old mental patient from Norwood, Massachusetts, climbed over the WH fence at the northwest pedestrian gate. Puchalski was on a weekend pass from a Massachusetts mental hospital. She was arrested without incident. It was the eighth time in 10 months that the White House fence had been scaled.

By mid-August 1976, both the Republican and Democratic parties had chosen their candidates for the presidential faceoff. Jimmy Carter locked up his party's nomination by winning a vast majority of the Democratic primaries and caucuses. At the Democratic National Convention held in New York City (July 12–15), almost 75% of the delegates voted for Carter—giving him an easy first ballot win. Carter selected Minnesota Senator Walter Mondale to be his vice presidential running mate.

The Republican National Convention was held in Kansas City, Missouri from August 16–19. President Ford had slugged it out in the primaries with Governor Reagan. Ford entered the convention with a majority of the delegates in his column, but his nomination was not assured. Reagan was a close second. Both candidates vied for the votes of uncommitted delegates. In a first round ballot, Ford narrowly edged Reagan for the Republican presidential nomination. Since Vice President Rockefeller did not wish to run, Ford chose Kansas Senator Robert Dole to be his running mate. Carter-Mondale and Ford-Dole would face each other in the fall presidential race.

The work kept coming for Bob. He was out of town more than he was in. And when he was in, he was home very little during waking hours. I looked forward to the end of the presidential campaign and to the beginning of a new year. It had to be better than 1976—so I hoped.

Chapter 23

Descent into Darkness

In early September 1976, Tom Dailey asked Bob if he would like an overseas TDY assignment with the USSS protective detail for Secretary of State Henry Kissinger. Dailey knew that Bob had served on Nancy Kissinger's State Department detail. Bob didn't particularly want the travel but thought it would be fun to work again with some of his old friends.

Secretary Kissinger was in London working on a British-American peace initiative for Southern Africa. Kissinger would soon embark on a diplomatic mission to Europe and Africa to consult with foreign leaders on the worsening racial strife in South-West Africa (Namibia) and Rhodesia (Zimbabwe). There was serious concern that full-scale war with Cold War overtones would erupt in the region. Due to the need for heightened security and the number of agents out on advances, the Kissinger Detail supplemented its working shifts with agents from the field.

Bob was to fly to London where he would join in transit the protective shift led by Agent Ken Clark. Bob was booked with Clark's shift for a commercial flight to Zurich, Switzerland—Secretary Kissinger's next stop. Bob was told to pack his gun and HT-220 radio in his carry-on bag and not in his suitcase, which was vulnerable to being lost or stolen. At Heathrow Airport, Bob would give his weapon and radio to an agent whose shift would be flying to Zurich via USAF car plane. The agent would secure Bob's revolver and radio in the detail's command post locker (equipment trunk), which was being transported by car plane.

Bob's flight was over an hour late getting into Heathrow. By the time he was able to meet Clark, the connecting flight was being called for boarding. The car plane agent had already left the airport. That plane was departing from a USAF base some distance away.

With a handgun in his carry-on bag, Bob quickly found himself at the airport's security checkpoint for departing flights. In the United Kingdom, gun laws are taken very seriously. Ken Clark told Bob to get out his diplomatic passport and USSS credentials. Ken picked out a security line that a matronly-looking official was manning. She looked a bit indifferent and bored. "Maybe she'll go easy on us," Clark expressed with some hope.

Clark went through the line first. After his carry-on was inspected and cleared, Clark showed his badge and diplomatic passport to the officer and announced: "Ma'am, I'm the supervisor of the man behind me. We're agents of the United States Secret Service and are on a diplomatic mission. Agent Ritter just arrived from the States and is transiting to Europe and then Africa. He has a handgun in his bag—an official duty weapon."

That perked up the security official. "He has what in his bag?" she asked in a lively cockney accent.

"His official duty weapon—a Smith and Wesson revolver," Clark answered calmly.

The security officer looked sternly at Bob. "Place your bag on the table and present your identification." After carefully checking Bob's credentials, she then searched the carry-on bag and removed Bob's holstered handgun *and* HT-220 radio. "I'll have to take these," she said decisively.

"This man needs his gun and radio for our protective mission," Clark protested.

The checkpoint officer doggedly replied, "We always take them."

"You always take them," Clark stated in disbelief. "Ma'am, that's expensive United States property. Our director isn't going to be happy when he hears this. This man is a U.S. Secret Service agent," Clark affirmed. "He's useless to me without his gun and radio."

"Thanks, boss, for that display of confidence," Bob murmured.

The security officer let out a short chuckle as she explained: "I'm putting them in a manila envelope. The envelope will be sealed and then given to the aircraft captain. Your man will be able to collect it after you reach your destination. I can't let *anyone* board with firearms or two-way radios. That's a rule we strictly adhere to."

"You had me worried for a minute," Clark expressed with much relief.

As it turned out, Bob got his gear back sooner than expected. Once the plane was airborne and out of British airspace, the captain of the Swissair flight invited Bob to the flight deck where he handed him his gun and radio. "I'd feel safer with you having your side arm back in the passenger compartment. If anyone tries to hijack this flight, they'll be in for a big surprise," the captain declared with a wide smile.

Bob's shift worked midnights in Zurich. They stayed in the same hotel as Secretary Kissinger—the Dolder Grand. Situated on a mountainside overlooking Lake Zurich, the castle-like hotel first opened in 1899. At this picturesque retreat, Secretary Kissinger negotiated for several days with Prime Minister John Vorster of South Africa.

Then, Kissinger flew back to London to advise Prime Minister James Callaghan of the results. Bob's shift flew to Secretary Kissinger's next stop, Paris, France. Kissinger hoped to gain support for the peace initiative from French President Giscard d'Estaing.

After Paris, Kissinger was off to the Federal Republic of Germany (Hamburg) to discuss the Vorster talks with Chancellor Helmut Schmidt. This was supposed to be Secretary Kissinger's last European stop before continuing to Africa with his "shuttle diplomacy."

Bob's shift was directed to fly ahead via USAF car plane to Lusaka, Zambia—one of Kissinger's first African stops. The cargo area of the C-141 Starlifter was loaded with an armored limousine and a station wagon follow-up. The vehicles were secured to the deck with sturdy steel chains. To assure a reliable supply of fuel, drums of high-octane gasoline were strapped along the sides of the cargo area along with other security gear and personal luggage.

The C-141 headed south from Europe toward the African continent. It was estimated to be about a nine-hour flight. Diplomatic clearances had been requested from nations the C-141 would flyover. One African country did not respond in time. The C-141 had to be vectored around that nation's territory. This added extra time to the flight, but more importantly the aircraft consumed a greater amount of fuel.

There was not much to do on car plane flights. Since the C-141 was not engineered for passengers, accommodations were Spartan. The only portholes were in a pair of paratroop doors. The noise generated by the Starlifter's four jet engines was deafening, even with the issued earplugs. The lighting was harsh. It was difficult to fall asleep. Meals consisted of bland TV dinners.

Aboard the car plane, Kissinger detail agents wiled away the time playing poker. With a blanket thrown over its spacious hood, the limo became a card table. A deck of cards and a set of poker chips were as indispensable on car plane flights as guns and ammo. With agents' wallets filled with travel advance money, the games went on nonstop.

It was early morning when the C-141 approached Lusaka International Airport—about 35 minutes till sunrise. To the shock of the aircraft's crew, the airport was dark. The runway lights were off and there were no navigational aids operating. The flight crew rechecked their directory of international airports and confirmed that the listing for Lusaka International showed it was operational 24 hours a day.

Attempts to raise the airport's control tower via radio were unsuccessful. Finally, a voice responded—presumably in the Zambian language of Nyanja. The pilot asked for someone to come to the mike who could speak English. Several minutes later, an English-speaking voice broke over the radio, "This is Lusaka, go ahead." The pilot informed the ground party of the flight specifics and that the military attaché at the U.S. Embassy had passed all to the Zambian government and appropriate permissions had been granted. The pilot emphasized in no uncertain terms that the approach and runway lights needed to come on immediately, as the C-141 was low on fuel. The reply from the airport was unnerving: "Airport operations won't commence until later this morning. There are no scheduled flights for hours."

"Lusaka, get your lights operational. We have proper diplomatic clearance and need to land now!" boomed the C-141 pilot.

"There's no one here but the cleaning crew. I'm speaking with you from the radio set in the maintenance office," replied the voice on the radio.

"Roger, Lusaka. Get whatever airport lights on you can. Then line up all the vehicles available along the sides of the runway, so their headlights can shine on the tarmac. Be as quick as you can because this bird is coming down in two-zero minutes—one way or another."

"WILCO [will comply]," came the reply from the ground.

The loadmaster of the C-141 scrambled around the compartment, double-checking that the cargo was secured and that all of the agents were belted tightly in their seats. Agents were briefed on bracing techniques and other rough-landing procedures.

Along with several other agents, who were in the first row of seats, Bob sat directly in front of the black Cadillac armored limo. The cargo compartment of the C-141 was 10 feet wide. The limo filled Bob's peripheral vision like a 12,000-pound monster. "This must be the last thing someone sees when they're run over by a Cadillac," Bob joked to those around him. Bob's head was about hood high with his legs only inches from the bumper of the black behemoth—close enough to reach out and touch the license plate.

The loadmaster informed the agents that the aircraft would circle as long as possible to allow ground personnel time to illuminate the field and for the approaching sunrise. With the flight engineer closely monitoring the gauges, the minutes ticked away, while the pounds of fuel in the tanks dropped to the minimum required for safety. The aircraft commander announced that he was bringing the plane in.

The sun was just rising along the eastern horizon. The aircraft quickly descended, and without warning the landing gear forcibly collided with the runway. The shock wave of touchdown energy penetrated through Bob's back like a jackhammer. Suddenly coming to life, the massive Cadillac sprung from the cargo deck. The steel chain links tightened and strained to their limits. For a couple of rapid heartbeats, Bob feared the chains might break, savagely unleashing 12,000 pounds of steel. Just as rapidly as the Cadillac had risen, it thundered back down to the deck with a roar and shuddered considerably. "This is the roughest landing I've ever seen," yelled the agent next to Bob. "I thought we crashed!"

The muscle spasms that immediately flared in Bob's back proved the point. Bob felt the heightened pain. Bob's lower back pain had never completely gone away since his Park Police cruiser accident. And his back was further aggravated during a State Department counterterrorist driving school. The practical exercises consisted of actual vehicle ramming and the like.

During the unloading of the C-141, it was discovered that several suitcases had been damaged during the rough landing. The suitcases had been secured with tie-down straps; the force of the landing caused the straps to slice through the hard shell sides—more evidence of the brute energy that came into play.

The vehicles were offloaded along with the other USSS equipment and personal luggage, and the shift checked into the Intercontinental Hotel Lusaka. Agents were posted to four-hour shifts to guard the limo and follow-up, which were being kept in the hotel's parking lot. When not safeguarding the vehicles, the agents were free to catch up on sleep or to do some sightseeing.

The next day, Ken Clark held a shift meeting in his hotel room. He had just arrived back from the American Embassy with the latest news. "Do you want the bad news or the *really* bad news first?" Clark asked his agents.

One of the agents piped up, "Don't we have any good news?"

The furrows in Clark's forehead rippled with tension. "No," Clark answered tersely. After a brief pause, Clark began: "The bad news is there's intelligence that rebel forces might try to steal the armored limo and follow-up. I'm going to double-up our security coverage. From now on, two agents will be assigned to each four-hour shift. I want you to take all of the shoulder weapons out of the follow-up and store them with you in the armored limo. If anything should happen, get the word out over the radio and drive the limo to the American Embassy. The rest of us will meet you there."

"Ken, there's a truck load of Zambian troops in the parking lot and sentries around the hotel. The embassy in Lusaka doesn't seem to be that secure. It's right off the street with only one local guard out front and a Marine inside. Wouldn't we be safer at the hotel if something goes down?" one of the agents asked.

"That brings me to the *really* bad news," Clark replied. "When black African leaders became aware of the secretary's meeting with the South African prime minister in Zurich, they decided to hold their own summit in Tanzania. Guerilla leaders were included in the meetings as well as the presidents of Mozambique and Angola. They're backed by the Soviet Union and Cuba. It's feared the conference might have taken a hard line. It's believed the revolutionaries and their supporters want to tie the problem of South African apartheid [official policy of segregation] with the other issues. That would be a deal breaker with the South Africans and kill any chance for peace. Dr. K. decided the time isn't right to begin mediation in Africa. He's returning to Washington to consult with President Ford and to see what plays out. The trip to Lusaka has been postponed for at least a week."

Groans and moans broke out from the assembled agents. Some expletives were uttered. "Listen up," Clark ordered. "There's more. The car plane left early this morning. A tire and possibly the nose gear were damaged during the landing. It's flying to a base in Europe to be checked and repaired. It will return, but for the time being we're stranded. Since Dr. Kissinger postponed his trip, the Zambians pulled the plug on the troops at the hotel. We're on our own and in a region that might break out in war at any moment."

More expletives were spoken. One of the agents blurted out what most were thinking, "Man, are we sh-t out of luck."

With Dr. Kissinger returning to Washington, a State Department envoy was dispatched to Dar es Salaam, Tanzania to consult with President Julius Nyerere on the British-American initiative and to report on the specifics of the African summit. President Nyerere embraced radical black nationalists and was influential with them. It was hoped Nyerere could be persuaded to welcome a resumption of Kissinger's diplomatic mission.

In Lusaka, Bob and the other agents guarded the cars 24 x 7. To keep the batteries charged and to run routes, the vehicles were driven around Lusaka in a two-car motorcade on several occasions. Zambians watched in wonder as the big, black Caddy and black Mercury station wagon—both sporting Washington, D.C. tags—cruised around the streets of the city. A fun part of one of the outings was when the motorcade stopped at a local playground. The children flocked to the cars for a peek inside and to get some bubblegum and candy bars from the agents.

The word from Tanzania was that President Nyerere was not optimistic about the chances for peace. The Africans wanted black-majority rule now *and* an end to apartheid. Otherwise, there were threats "to fight to the last man." President Nyerere did agree, however, that Kissinger should continue on his mission.

On September 14, 1976, Dr. Kissinger and his party arrived in Dar es Salaam. The next day, Kissinger consulted with President Nyerere, who was suspicious of U.S. intentions. Nyerere parroted the Soviet Union's position that Kissinger's trip might really be a last-ditch attempt at keeping white governments in power. Nyerere challenged the U.S. to provide military aid to the black "freedom fighters" if the "racist regimes" will not transfer power peaceably.

Secretary Kissinger's next stop was Lusaka where he conferred with Zambian President Kenneth Kaunda. Bob stood in the halls of the Zambian State House, which resembles a small-scale White House, while Kissinger sought acceptance for the British-American plan. Kaunda, a moderate on black-white issues, advised the U.S. secretary of state that time was running out. Kaunda warned that Southern Africa was only days—not weeks—away from an escalation to full-scale warfare.

After several days of negotiation, Kaunda gave his blessing to Secretary Kissinger to travel to Pretoria, South Africa. Kaunda felt this was the last chance for peace, and that overruled his aversion of giving any recognition to the white-minority regime in Pretoria. Thus, Secretary of State Kissinger became the highest American official to visit the Republic of South Africa. The nation was the target of U.N. sanctions and international isolation due to its human rights violations. Besides institutionalizing apartheid within its own borders, South Africa administered racist policies in South-West Africa, which it controlled in violation of a U.N. resolution. The South African government also supported, both economically and militarily, the white-minority regime in Rhodesia.

The peace plan presented by Secretary Kissinger for Rhodesia called for a two-year transitional period to majority rule. An interim biracial government would be established, leading to black rule and insuring that white financial interests were protected. A fund would be established by the U.K. and U.S. to compensate for the property of whites leaving the country and for property that might be expropriated from whites who wished to remain.

It was felt that Vorster would pressure Rhodesian Prime Minister Ian Smith to accept the plan. South Africa wished to ease the tensions within its own country. In return for Rhodesian acceptance of the plan, the "front-line" black presidents of Southern Africa would pressure guerillas to end their attacks in Rhodesia and South-West Africa. There would also be an effort within the U.N. to ease sanctions on Rhodesia.

For South-West Africa, the British-American plan proposed a transition to full independence and black-majority rule with the protection of the rights of the white population. A conference would be held in Geneva to work out the details. The South West African People's Organization (SWAPO) would be included in the negotiations as a primary partner. South Africa had previously refused representation to SWAPO.

In Pretoria, Kissinger negotiated with Vorster, listened to the concerns of South African black leaders, and ultimately met with the Rhodesian prime minister. In the meantime, Bob's shift flew via car plane to Kinshasa, Zaire to prepare for the secretary's upcoming visit with Zairian President Mobutu Sese Seko. Kinshasa (formerly Leopoldville, Belgian Congo) sits within the Zaire River basin and receives over 50 inches of rain a year. Hit with a one-two punch of high temperature and oppressive humidity, Bob sweltered in the stifling mist of a tropical rain forest.

Secretary Kissinger arrived in Kinshasa with high hopes. He had received indications from both Vorster and Smith that they favored the proposed peace plan over warfare. Adding the positive reactions of presidents Nyerere and Kaunda, the prospect of moving toward nonviolent resolutions of Southern African racial problems looked much better. President Mobutu received the good news with relief. Pleased with Kissinger's progress, Mobutu—in an unexpected move—invited the secretary for a dinner cruise on the Zaire River (also known as the Congo River).

One of the longest rivers in the world, the Zaire runs almost 3,000 miles and has depths over 500 feet. The river was the setting for Joseph Conrad's 1902 novel *Heart of Darkness*. In 1976, river steamers still plied the Zaire between Kinshasa and Kisangani (formerly Stanleyville). When word reached the Secret Service command post that Kissinger had accepted Mobutu's impromptu invitation, Ken Clark announced to his agents with much concern: "Great, now we've got to do a last minute advance of a steamboat. Does *anyone* know *anything* about steamboats?"

Clark was surprised when Bob volunteered the following: "Ken, I don't know about steamboats as such, but I did have instruction on boilers when I was a housing inspector. Many of the apartment buildings have some pretty big ones."

Clark looked at Bob with some amazement: "You're with me. We'll grab the EOD man and get Nkulu [Zairian official who was the USSS advance contact] to run us over there. The secretary and Mobutu will depart in an hour or so."

A short time later, the men pulled up to a small pathway that led from the road to the bank of the Zaire River. The path was about three feet wide and cut a swath through the dense vegetation, which covered the riverside. As the advance party stepped down the trail, Clark caught sight of some men moving around in the underbrush. "Nkulu," Clark said, "who are those men? We have to get them out of there—for security reasons."

Nkulu looked at Clark without expression and responded in a matter-of-fact way, "They are catching killer snakes, so Mr. Kissinger does not get bitten and die." Just then, one of the bushmen lifted up a pole with a three-foot serpentine shape clinging to it. He deftly dropped his catch into a large burlap bag and continued to pole through the brush. Three sets of American eyes quickly scanned the trail, as Ken, Bob, and Rich, the EOD man, suddenly realized that street shoes and a business suit don't offer much protection against the razor-sharp fangs of venomous snakes.

"Nkulu, those men may stay there!" Clark affirmed loudly. "What types of poisonous snakes are found here?"

"Mambas and vipers," answered Nkulu. "If you are bitten, you have no more than one-half hour to reach hospital for antivenin."

The party quickly moved to the riverbank where a gangplank had been dropped from the steamer, an aging stern-wheeler. A relic from a by-gone era of European colonialism, the ship now reflected the stark reality of third-world economics. Her white paint was grimy from years of equatorial service and lack of upkeep. Smoke belched from rusted smokestacks as the lady was being readied for yet one more run.

"Bob, do a safety inspection of the engine room," directed Clark. "Rich, start your EOD sweep. Nkulu and I will head for the wheelhouse where we'll coordinate with the captain. I don't see any lifeboats or life vests. I've got a lot of questions."

Bob went below deck to the engine room. What he found was a scene that could have come out of *The African Queen*—the 1951 action-adventure film, which starred Humphrey Bogart and Katharine Hepburn. The story was based on the 1935 novel by C.S. Forester and set along a dangerous stretch of the Congo in war torn 1914. The engine room Bob entered more resembled that earlier period than present day. Everything in it looked original. The boiler was an old, hand-riveted one. Steam escaped from loose-fitting rivets and from pipes connected to the boiler. The water in the boiler was heated by wood.

The ship's engineer was an elderly gentleman. He stood by watching pressure gauges as a young assistant threw wood into the firebox to get up steam. Bob nodded to the engineer and moved alongside of him. The gauges were old and worn. Most troubling, the main safety gauge was not operating properly. Its needle fluctuated wildly between low and high-pressure readings. It would be impossible to obtain an accurate reading to warn of dangerous redline pressure buildup.

As the boiler moaned and groaned, Bob checked it for cracks and signs of stress. He inspected the leaking pipe joints, literally bandaged with cloth bindings. There were no certificates of inspection or maintenance records to be found. No safety equipment could be seen. To sum it up, the engine room was an inspector's *worst* nightmare.

Bob moved to the wheelhouse where Ken—with Nkulu interpreting—was not finding the captain very receptive to USSS inquiries. Needing a breather, Ken motioned Bob to the outside deck. "How did it go?" Clark asked.

"Ken, this boat's a relic. It's probably been decades since anyone opened up the boiler and inspected it. I didn't see any signs of maintenance. The main pressure gauge is shot. We've got leaks from rivets and pipes. There's rust everywhere."

"That bad, huh?"

"Yep."

"Okay, Bob, help out Rich with the EOD sweep. I'll stay here with Nkulu and see what I can learn from the captain. It looks like this tug doesn't have radar, a two-way radio, emergency equipment, or anything else."

Bob found Rich on the main deck, watching three Zairians in a rowboat. Well, only two of them were actually in the boat. The other was in the water. He was being held underwater by the ankles while the third man paddled the craft along the side of the steamboat. "Rich, what are those guys doing?" Bob asked a bit bewildered.

Portraying a *now I've seen everything* look, Rich answered, "I *think* they're checking the hull for explosives."

Bob assisted Rich in finishing the EOD sweep and the two men met up with Clark and Nkulu in the ship's dining room. "I'm worried about the hull inspection," Rich stated to Nkulu. "We need divers to check under the boat."

"Crocodiles may be nearby," Nkulu replied. "Better to stay in dinghy."

"Nkulu, besides poisonous snakes and crocodiles, what other dangers are there?" Clark asked.

"Upriver, there are cannibals. But we won't be going that far."

"Good, let's stay well clear of the cannibals," Clark emphasized. "Will we have escort craft from the military with us on the cruise?"

"We should have a patrol boat join us," Nkulu answered.

"Nkulu, will you please check in the galley to see what is being prepared for Dr. Kissinger. Later, I'll need to select the actual meal and beverage that will be offered," Clark advised.

After Nkulu left the table, Clark asked Rich about the EOD sweep. "A local looked under the hull. I can't guarantee that it's clean. I did the best I could in my sweep. Without a dog, divers, and more time, something could still be planted."

"Guys, I'm recommending the secretary passes on this stop," Clark announced. "We've got too many potential dangers here. We'd need days to make this safe." Clark then radioed the detail leader and advised him of the particulars. In spite of Clark's warning, Secretary Kissinger decided to continue on the outing. The cruise was mercifully cut short, however, when Kissinger was called back to the U.S. Embassy for some important cable traffic regarding other global issues. Although the problems of Southern Africa were paramount at the time, Secretary Kissinger had to be concerned with other hot spots and diplomatic problems around the world.

After Zaire, Dr. Kissinger traveled to Nairobi, Kenya where he consulted with President Jomo Kenyatta. Then it was back to London to review the past several weeks of mediation with British Foreign Secretary Anthony Crosland.

In London, Bob received a scare. As he was dressing one morning, he bent down to tie his shoelaces. Suddenly his back froze in pain, and he couldn't straighten himself. Bob's back had gone out as muscles contracted in excruciating spasms. After a day of medication and rest, Bob was able to continue to Washington.

Back in D.C., Bob returned to the field office. It was good to have Bob home, but the joy didn't last. As the presidential campaign was in its final weeks, Bob was sent on the road and worked the *next 33 days straight.* Working no less than 12-hour days, Bob crisscrossed the country wherever he was needed. He pulled many 16-hour days.

Both presidential candidates experienced poll-changing moments down the stretch. Jimmy Carter lost some support when he gave an ill-advised interview to *Playboy* magazine. The devoutly religious Carter admitted that he had lusted in his heart for other women and had committed adultery in his mind on occasion. Carter livened up the interview with the use of several colloquialisms, which some deemed inappropriate and not presidential.

President Ford floundered during the second presidential debate. The series of presidential debates were the first televised since 1960. Millions watched as our nation's chief executive and commander in chief stated with conviction, "There is no Soviet domination of Eastern Europe, and there never will be under a Ford administration." That statement and Ford's follow-up comments led many to believe that Ford was soft on the communist threat and unknowledgeable in foreign affairs.

The race tightened and became too close to call. Finally on November 2, 1976, Democrat Jimmy Carter defeated incumbent President Gerald Ford. Carter was the first president to be elected from the Deep South since Zachary Taylor (Louisiana) in 1848. The election was not decided until the early morning hours of November 3. Carter-Mondale edged Ford-Dole by only two percentage points in a popular vote of over 81 million. Although Carter-Mondale took only 23 states and the District of Columbia to Ford-Dole's 27 states, the Carter-Mondale team won more of the populous states and was elected by a 57-vote margin in the Electoral College.

I was happy to see the campaign year come to an end. Bob's total hours for 1976 amounted to almost a year and a half of what normal people worked. I hoped and prayed that 1977 would be easier on Bob and me. I couldn't see how it could be any worse. Our nation's 200th anniversary coupled with a presidential campaign was a back breaker for the Secret Service and especially the Washington Field Office, which had too much work for too few agents. Bob had spent so little time with the kids and me; it became a perpetual hardship. Although 1976 was one of the worst years of my life, I continued to support Bob. Yet, I was being worn down, little by little.

Chapter 24

Deacon

It was a weekday morning in January 1977, a little before 9:00. Working at his desk, Bob was dictating some PI reports for typing. Bob's office was adjacent to the private door used by agents to enter and exit the field office. Suddenly, someone appeared in the hallway. The individual held a pad of paper and a pencil. Without speaking a word, he stood in the hallway for about 10 minutes, making a check mark for every agent who entered the field office after 9:00 a.m.

Later that morning, a general meeting was held to meet the new ASAIC of the Washington Field Office, Curt Gallagher. Bob recognized Gallagher as the person who had been checking the arrival of agents earlier in the day. After introducing Gallagher, SAIC Gittens made a hasty departure from the room. Bob knew something was up. Gittens usually stayed for the entire meeting.

Gallagher wasted no time tearing into the agents. With a permanent frown chiseled on his face, Gallagher scolded all as if they were a bunch of lazy clock-watchers. "From now on, everyone's going to work or else," Gallagher warned. "I was sent here by headquarters to straighten out this office." Gallagher then summarily dismissed the agents and stormed out of the room.

When Bob recounted the meeting to me later that evening, I could hardly believe my ears. The agents of the Washington Field Office were sworn law enforcement personnel. Their commission books confirmed top-secret clearance and informed that the bearer was "worthy of trust and confidence." These agents were entrusted with federal criminal investigations and presidential protection. They had just finished a very challenging year. WFO personnel worked demanding hours—some of which were uncompensated. Bob had the blood squeezed out of him in '76. The year was especially hard on our family. Personal sacrifices and hardships were many. How could anyone say such things and be so out of touch with the *real* situation.

Bob tried to play it down by saying that he was trying not to take the comments personally. He thought the new ASAIC had gotten carried away in an attempt to assert himself as an authoritarian and disciplinarian. Yet, I could tell that Bob was disheartened and disappointed. "I believe this is Gallagher's first ASAIC position. He's also never worked at WFO and doesn't know the office," Bob said. "Hopefully, he'll see what we do and get to know us and soften some." Bob was fearful, however, that Gallagher's managerial style was one of intimidation and confrontation. ASAICs were in charge of personnel and day-to-day operations. Bob wondered how such a person could be placed in the number two position at WFO—one of the most important—if not most important—field offices in the country. It certainly couldn't help morale.

The protective work kept coming for WFO. The field office was making security arrangements for the presidential inauguration of James Earl Carter Jr. Presidential inaugurations date back to 1789 when George Washington was sworn in as the first president of the United States under the Constitution. The ceremony took place at Federal Hall in New York City, which was then the seat of the national government.

Thomas Jefferson was the first president to be inaugurated (1801) at the nation's new capital, Washington, D.C. Accompanied by a military unit, congressmen, and friends, Jefferson walked from his boarding house to the Senate chamber of the U.S. Capitol where he was sworn in by Supreme Court Chief Justice John Marshall.

For the 1809 inauguration, President James Madison was the first to have an "official" inaugural ball held in his honor. First Lady Dolley Madison hosted the gala at a hotel on Capitol Hill. Four-hundred guests paid $4.00 each to dance, dine, and celebrate. Music was provided by the United States Marine Band, fondly known as "The President's Own."

William Henry Harrison's 1841 inaugural parade from the Capitol to the White House featured public marchers and floats. Up to that time, only military units had been an official part of inaugural parades.

President Ulysses S. Grant began the tradition of reviewing the processions. After leading the parade up Pennsylvania Avenue, Grant watched the 1869 and 1873 inaugural parades from a stand that was constructed in Lafayette Square. President James A. Garfield was the first to review an inaugural parade from a presidential stand erected in front of the White House. He set that precedent in 1881. The first president to review an inaugural parade (1897) from a glass-enclosed reviewing stand was William McKinley.

President James K. Polk's 1845 inaugural address was the first to be sent by telegraph; Samuel F. Morse did the honors. James Buchanan's 1857 inauguration was the first to be photographed. The first to be covered by motion picture was William McKinley's 1897 inauguration. Calvin Coolidge's 1925 inaugural ceremony (oath of office and address) was the first to be broadcast *live* over radio. The first moving pictures with sound (newsreel) were taken at Herbert Hoover's 1929 inauguration. Harry S. Truman's 1949 inaugural was the first to be broadcast via the new medium of television.

Warren G. Harding was the first president to ride in the parade by automobile. During the 1921 inauguration, he was transported in a sleek Packard Twin Six.

For the 1977 inaugural advance, Bob assisted with the surveys of the buildings along the parade route. In the weeks leading up to the inauguration, scores of buildings had to be thoroughly checked. Building managers and security officials were contacted. Occupants who would be in the buildings during the parade were name checked. Building supervisors were advised that windows were to remain closed during the inaugural parade. Rooftop access was to be secured.

Preparations for the 1977 inaugural parade marked one of the earliest uses of Executive Protective Service counter sniper (CS) teams in Washington *outside* of the White House. The EPS Counter Sniper Unit had been formed in the early 1970s. Besides providing protective support for the White House, CS teams were utilized in out-of-town movements of the president when needed. It was important that the Secret Service had dedicated CS capabilities for the 1977 inaugural parade. President-elect Carter informed the Secret Service that he intended to *walk* the parade route. Accordingly, the USSS advance team planned to place EPS-CS teams on the rooftops of several buildings to protect the president during the inaugural parade.

MPD Special Operations Division Commander Robert Klotz was informed of this at an initial meeting held to coordinate inaugural security. After hearing this, Captain Klotz became visibly upset. "No one's getting on top a roof with a rifle in this city unless they're a member of the Metropolitan Police Department," Klotz declared. Secret Service supervisors presented their reasoning for the move, but Klotz remained adamant in his objection. Klotz viewed the Secret Service proposal as an infringement of MPD's jurisdiction. The meeting ended in deadlock.

Captain Klotz was a 22-year veteran of the force. Bob had established rapport with Klotz and earned his trust during intelligence coordination for the bicentennial. After the meeting, a USSS supervisor who was aware of the relationship asked Bob to follow up with Klotz in an attempt to persuade him to drop his opposition.

Bob stopped by SOD Headquarters the following morning. He appealed to the captain that counter-sniper support was something the Service desperately needed in D.C. With all the presidential movements within the city, the USSS was playing "Russian roulette" without it. Another Dallas could happen at any time. Bob also reasoned that MPD did not have enough Emergency Response Teams (ERT) to provide for both the needs of the city and the never-ending schedule of presidential movements. Bob concluded his comments by advising Klotz that USSS-CS teams are specially trained to support protective movements. An agent is assigned with each team for communications and coordination with USSS-PI teams. The goal is to detect and prevent a sniper from firing a shot.

Another meeting was held where Klotz and Deputy Chief Robert Rabe were given a full presentation regarding the capabilities of the CS teams and their rigorous training and qualification standards. In the end, Klotz did the right thing and did not press his objections. Klotz and Rabe were also reluctant realists; the Metropolitan Police Department didn't have the resources to take on presidential counter-sniper duties. EPS-CS teams were used for the inaugural parade and plans were made for their future use in presidential movements throughout D.C. for arrivals and departures.

Additional inaugural parade protective arrangements included the use of Secret Service Technical Security Division (TSD) personnel along with EOD teams to check the sewers under the street. Manhole covers were welded shut. Anything that could contain a bomb was removed from along the parade route. Inaugural reviewing stands were constructed. Street and traffic lights were removed by D.C. public works, so parade floats and balloons would have unobstructed clearance.

Assigned to PI duties for the inauguration, Bob worked the *New Spirit Inaugural Concert* held at the Kennedy Center Opera House on inauguration eve. It was the first inaugural gala ever televised. The show was taped and broadcast later that evening by CBS. President-elect and Mrs. Carter and Vice President-elect and Mrs. Mondale were entertained by a galaxy of stars including: Bette Davis, Redd Fox, Paul Newman, Loretta Lynn, John Wayne (taped appearance), Shirley MacLaine, Warren Beatty, the Alvin Ailey dancers, Beverly Sills, Muhammad Ali, Jean Stapleton, the National Symphony Orchestra, Chevy Chase, and Dan Aykroyd—who did his trademark Jimmy Carter impersonation.

The First Lady of Soul Aretha Franklin led off the evening's final number, Irving Berlin's "God Bless America." She was joined on stage by the entire cast, and the audience was invited to sing along. It was a rousing and patriotic prelude to Inauguration Day.

At 12:00 noon on Thursday, January 20, 1977, James Earl Carter Jr. was sworn in as the 39th president of the United States by Chief Justice Warren Burger. It was a sunny day with temperatures below freezing. For the oath of office, Carter placed his left hand on a family Bible held by his wife, Rosalynn (pronounced: rose-uh-lynn).

To start his 1,228-word inaugural address, Carter thanked former President Ford "for all he has done to heal our land." President Carter told the 150,000 spectators gathered on the east lawn of the Capitol: "This inauguration ceremony marks a new beginning, a new dedication within our government, and a new spirit among us. A president may sense and proclaim that new spirit, but only a people can provide it." Drawing upon religious and American ideals, Carter urged, "Let us create together a new national spirit of unity and trust." The president shared his vision of a rebirth of the founding principles of our nation and his dedication to apply these values to domestic and international policy. The president called on us to have a "fresh faith" in the American dream.

Later that afternoon, the President and Mrs. Carter departed the Capitol via motorcade for the inaugural parade staging area. Against Secret Service advice, the president and first lady walked the entire length of the parade, approximately a mile and a half. With their nine-year-old daughter Amy, the Carters wowed the crowd of 250,000 spectators with a humble march to the White House, smiling and waving all the way. Carter was the first president in history to walk the *entire* parade route.

This brought some uneasy moments for the Secret Service. Bob was one of the agents who walked along the sides of Pennsylvania Avenue, preceding the presidential party. Bob had memorized the photographs of all quarterly investigation (QI) subjects within the WFO district. QIs were persons the Secret Service currently evaluated as being dangerous to protectees. These cases were reviewed and updated *quarterly*—sooner if circumstances warranted. Although most QIs were institutionalized, Bob kept his eyes open. If someone escaped from St. E's, he or she might be in downtown Washington before notification could be made. There was always the potential danger of *out-of-pocket* QIs. That's how Secret Service agents described QIs whose whereabouts became unknown.

Once inside the solar-heated White House reviewing stand, the Carters and Mondales watched the one hour and forty-five minute procession of floats and marching bands from behind panels of bullet-resistant glass. The first use of "bulletproof" glass in a presidential reviewing stand was for the 1965 inauguration of Lyndon Johnson.

That evening, the Carters and Mondales stopped by the many inaugural balls held in their honor. The balls were called "parties" in keeping with President Carter's theme of a *people's inaugural*. Black tie was optional. Of course, peanuts were in good supply. The first lady wore a gold-embroidered sleeveless coat over a blue chiffon dress trimmed in gold. Designed by Mary Matise, the gown was six years old and had originally been worn by Mrs. Carter to the ball celebrating her husband's inauguration as governor of Georgia. Dominic Rompollo designed a new ice-blue wool cape to update the ensemble and to offer protection from the cold Washington winter.

For the night of the inaugural parties, Bob was partnered with Dick Corrigan for general PI response. This team would handle any PI incidents that might occur within the WFO district. Bob persuaded his ATSAIC to let the team cover the evening's presidential arrivals when they weren't busy handling calls. Bob's team complemented the PI team assigned to each inaugural party site. After the presidential party settled in, Bob and Dick leapfrogged to the next site.

In a touch of Jeffersonian democracy, the president and first lady held receptions at the White House on the Friday and Saturday following Inauguration Day. About 7,500 people were personally greeted by the Carters and their family in the cross hall of the White House underneath the presidential seal. Punch and cookies were served in the East Room, which was festively decorated with a variety of floral arrangements. Guests ranged from members of Congress and celebrities to the general public and Carter's "Peanut Brigade" of volunteers. Bob spent the weekend on the White House grounds watching the long line of guests for anyone suspicious.

The new president brought a new outlook to Washington and new challenges for the Secret Service. Carter's common-man approach to the presidency was imbued with symbolism. For example, the president did away with the playing of "Hail to the Chief" before his entrance at official functions. He believed this tradition reflected an imperial presidency.

Directing his Cabinet to cut the "frills," Carter specifically tasked his department heads to reduce the number of chauffeured limousines and to economize on travel and other expenses. The president wanted his team to reject the customary extravagances of office. He suggested that his Cabinet fly commercially when possible and in coach-class accommodations. To that effect, Carter ordered a reduction in the number of Air Force planes reserved for government VIPs. Cabinet members were urged to cut back on the privileges of rank and to stay close to the people they served.

Leading by example, President Carter reduced the White House motor pool and terminated the custom by which senior White House aides were driven to and from work in government limos. The president also vetoed the Secret Service procedure of sending armored limousines abroad for Vice President Mondale's late January 1977 trip to Western Europe and Japan. Carter believed the vice president could use vehicles supplied by the host nations without endangering security.

Along similar lines, Carter told the Secret Service that he did not want presidential limos flown around the country for him. The president said he would use whatever was available in the local Secret Service offices. Since most USSS offices had no vehicles suitable for presidential protection, presidential limos and follow-up cars had to be transported via truck for visits outside of Washington.

Additionally, President Carter disliked the black presidential limos. He thought them too ostentatious. Carter wanted to use the presidential fleet's "off-the-record" vehicle whenever possible. Previously, this vehicle had only been used for private (off-the-record) movements of the president. Appearing less formal with a tan body and brown vinyl top, this modified Lincoln Continental did feature a full complement of security enhancements.

USSS Director H. Stuart Knight was tasked by President Carter to conduct a full review of presidential protection. In keeping with his goal to reduce the White House staff by one third, Carter requested Knight to eliminate any procedures and personnel that would not compromise security. In particular, the president questioned the need for agents to move around with him within the White House. Carter did not think it was necessary.

As a result, the Secret Service presidential detail reduced its visibility to the president. When Carter walked between the Executive Mansion and the West Wing, he was only followed from a distance by a single agent. In addition, agents no longer went above the state floor (first floor). Access to the residence floors were controlled from the ground and first floors. Other steps were taken within the White House to afford the Carters more privacy while still providing a secure inner zone of protection.

As to protective measures outside the White House, the president wanted fewer agents around him and asked that they give him more room during movements. President Carter was informed protective procedures for presidential trips could not be drastically altered without an adverse effect on security. The Service would modify what they could, but the president would have to be closely worked by the White House Detail in public crowds and other potentially dangerous situations.

Like a submarine on a torpedo run, Carter's cut-the-frills campaign set sights on another target, the presidential yacht *Sequoia*. Built in the mid-1920s, the 104-foot craft featured a wooden hull and mahogany trim. She was designed by famed naval architect John Trumpy and first saw use as a private yacht. Purchased by the federal government in 1931, the *Sequoia* initially served as an inspection craft for the Department of Commerce, which was then charged with shipboard safety.

An avid angler, President Herbert Hoover took a liking to the vessel and used her for excursions on the Potomac River. Commissioned by the Navy in 1933 to serve as the presidential yacht, the *Sequoia* became a favorite of President Franklin D. Roosevelt. FDR used her for weekend cruises on the Chesapeake Bay.

In 1936, the larger and safer U.S.S. *Potomac* (165 feet in length) replaced the *Sequoia*. The *Potomac* was built of steel and less a fire hazard. The *Sequoia* was retained in federal service for use by the secretary of the Navy and other governmental leaders.

After President Roosevelt's death in 1945, the *Potomac* was herself replaced by the oceangoing 244-foot U.S.S. *Williamsburg*, which served President Harry S. Truman. The *Williamsburg* was decommissioned in 1953 during Dwight D. Eisenhower's presidency. Eisenhower preferred the smaller and more economical *Lenoir*. Ike renamed the 92-foot craft the *Barbara Anne* in honor of one of his granddaughters.

Originally built in 1931 as a private yacht for Montgomery Ward Chairman Sewell Avery, the *Lenoir* was pressed into service as a Coast Guard cutter during World War II. In 1945, the craft was assigned to the U.S. Navy and became an escort vessel for the presidential yacht *Williamsburg*. As the *Barbara Anne*, the yacht was mainly used by Eisenhower after his 1955 heart attack—during vacations to Newport, Rhode Island.

When John F. Kennedy became president in 1961, the *Barbara Anne* was renamed the *Honey Fitz*, in honor of John Fitzgerald, JFK's maternal grandfather. Fitzgerald obtained the nickname "Honey Fitz" while serving as mayor of Boston, Massachusetts and as a U.S. Congressman. The *Honey Fitz* was used by President Kennedy and his family on numerous occasions, including Potomac River cruising and vacations to Hyannis Port and Palm Beach. An accomplished yachtsman, JFK loved the sea and prized his time on board the *Honey Fitz*. The Kennedys also sailed aboard the yacht *Sequoia*.

After JFK's tragic death, Lyndon Johnson assumed the office of president. At first, Johnson announced he would not use the yachts but changed his mind after cruises on the *Sequoia* and *Honey Fitz*. The *Sequoia* became LBJ's favorite, and he used it extensively.

With Richard M. Nixon's 1972 election to the White House, the *Honey Fitz* was sold in an economy move. The *Sequoia* became the sole remaining presidential yacht. Through the years, the *Sequoia* had proudly served presidents Hoover, Roosevelt, Kennedy, Johnson, Nixon, and Ford. At times, Cabinet meetings were held onboard and foreign dignitaries entertained. The classic craft offered a relaxing and comfortable escape from the pressures of Washington.

Many believed this tradition would continue with President Carter, a U.S. Naval Academy graduate and former naval officer. The *Sequoia* was readied. Wood was polished and brass was shined. Everything was made shipshape—down to the smallest detail. The proud crew looked forward to serving the new president.

In anticipation of Carter's use of the *Sequoia*, Secret Service personnel in the Washington Field Office updated procedures for "Watch Guard." This was the call sign for the WFO vehicle that shadowed the *Sequoia* on land. When deployed, Watch Guard was manned by a pair of agents. Bob was one of the agents who had been selected for Watch Guard duty.

In case of an emergency necessitating the evacuation of the president, Watch Guard would move to a prearranged pickup point. Once on shore, the president could be transported as needed. During normal operation, the agents assigned to Watch Guard would keep a sharp eye out for any suspicious activity and respond appropriately.

Bob was chosen due to his Park Police experience and knowledge of the installations and shoreline along the Washington Channel and Potomac and Anacostia Rivers. Watch Guard was a challenging assignment, as the vehicle was often operated off road and in hilly terrain.

As it turned out, the new president did not use the *Sequoia*. To Carter, the yacht was just another extravagance. The crew of the *Sequoia* was shocked when they learned that Carter wanted the craft put up for public auction. Some historians and conservationists objected, citing that the *Sequoia* was a national treasure. Regardless, the *Sequoia* was marked as government surplus. She was sold to a private party on March 25, 1977. One of the grand ladies of the sea, the *Sequoia* still sails today.

The sale of the *Sequoia* meant one less thing the Washington Field Office had to worry about on the protective side. Yet, there were new drains on WFO manpower for the protective coverage of President Carter, whose radio call sign was "Deacon." Radio call signs are actually suggested by the White House Communications Agency with the Secret Service making the final selection. Deacon was a fitting choice for President Carter, who was a born-again Christian and real-life deacon.

During his presidential term, Carter often taught adult Sunday school and regularly worshiped at the First Baptist Church of Washington (1328 16th Street, NW, D.C.). The church was founded in 1802; President Harry S. Truman attended religious services there from 1945–1950.

Given the duty of establishing protective intelligence liaison with the church, Bob met with its pastors and office staff. He provided PI guidance and security advice. In the succeeding months, the First Baptist Church was deluged with tourists and other out-of-town visitors who wanted to attend church services with the president. Besides the personal visits, the church also received numerous phone calls and letters regarding the president. Some of these contacts were from individuals who exhibited emotional and/or mental problems or wanted access to the president. That's when Bob had to step in.

The Washington Field Office supplied post standers and PI teams for President Carter's visits to the stately church, a tall stone structure designed in the neo-Gothic style with beautiful stained-glass windows. Counting the preliminary preparations and actual length of the visits, Bob usually worked at least a half day each time he was assigned the PI advance. If he had to interview a subject and take follow-up action, Bob could be gone for most of the day.

During Sunday services, the church was routinely filled to capacity with members of the congregation and visitors. The church became a Sunday morning stop for tourist buses. On occasion, several hundred people gathered outside the church just to catch a glimpse of the president. The 16th Street arrival/departure point became a potentially dangerous area. Bob recommended that a secure off-street area near a private entrance to the church be used in future presidential movements. The Presidential

Protective Division (PPD) and WFO advance agents agreed; the change was made.

In 1977 alone, President Carter attended service at the First Baptist Church of Washington over 25 times. Eventually, the basement of the church was turned into an area where tourists could watch the services on video monitors.

WFO also supported PPD agents who were assigned to first family members such as Amy Carter (code name: Dynamo). The president and first lady enrolled Amy at Stevens Elementary School (1050 21st Street, NW). The school was built in 1868. Named after abolitionist and U.S. Congressman Thaddeus Stevens, the school was the first to offer a public education to the black community of D.C.

With Amy's daily attendance at Stevens Elementary, WFO was called upon to provide a "trail car" during the school year. This vehicle was manned by WFO agents. It followed Amy's limousine, which was operated by agents from the family detail.

Bob described Amy as: "Just like any other fourth grader. She carries a Snoopy book bag and loves pets." Amy Carter was the first child of a president to attend public school in the District of Columbia since 1908. In that year, President Theodore Roosevelt's son Quentin received his sixth grade education in a D.C. public elementary school. The following year, Quentin Roosevelt transferred to a private school in Alexandria, Virginia.

March 1977 was quite an unusual month for the Secret Service—especially for the agents in Washington. On Saturday, March 5, the president conducted a two-hour radio call-in show in conjunction with the CBS radio network. Moderated by CBS newsman Walter Cronkite, the show was named "Ask President Carter." Americans were given the opportunity to call the White House on a special toll-free number for a chance to speak with President Carter. If selected, the caller would be able to ask the president a question *live* on the radio. After the president's reply, callers would be permitted a follow-up question if needed.

Although not censored as to subject matter, the calls were screened for location and authenticity to insure geographic balance and genuineness of purpose. Callers had to identify themselves to operators by name, telephone number, and hometown; this information was verified through local directory assistance. Prospective callers were also name checked by the USSS Intelligence Division.

Bob was one of the WFO-PI agents who assisted USSS-ID personnel during the program. Agents were standing by in case callers became obscene, abusive, or threatening. The radio show was broadcast on a seven-second delay. This allowed time for callers to be cut off before inappropriate language was sent out over the airwaves. In that event, the calls would be transferred to the Secret Service for follow-up.

Additional agents were also needed to handle the extra volume of *trouble calls* that were expected via the regular White House lines. Out of the several hundred thousand people who tried to get through on the toll-free line, only 42 were able to speak with the president on the radio. The whole concept of a president giving the public *direct* telephone access to him was new to the Secret Service. It hadn't been done before. It was felt the president's radio show could spark an increase in the number of trouble calls that are routinely placed to the White House—calls whose content prompt them to be referred to the Secret Service.

In the course of a normal day, the White House switchboard receives tens of thousands of calls. Many of these calls are for the president. The only calls actually put through to the president—after the callers are verified—are those from family and friends, government and private sector leaders, and other important persons whom the president wishes to speak with. The vast majority of people calling the White House are average citizens who want to express an opinion or sentiment to the president. These calls are directed to the White House Comment and Greeting Office. This office is predominantly staffed by volunteers, mainly retired federal workers. They respectfully write down the caller's comments, which are then compiled for the president.

All too often, White House operators receive calls from individuals who *insist* on speaking with the president. They have an irrational belief that their calls are important enough to command the personal attention of the president. Often, these callers make incoherent and troublesome statements or even voice threats against the president. These calls are transferred by White House operators to the Secret Service Protective Intelligence Division.

Bob came home that evening and expressed concerns that he and some other agents had in regard to the president's radio show. Bob understood that the president wanted to get close to the people. The exchange allowed the president to hear what was on the mind of the average American. Moreover, it gave the citizenry a chance to hear the positions of the president. Bob felt it was a nice gesture. But, he was concerned that the publicity surrounding the radio event would cause irrational minds to be even more determined to gain access to the president by phone, letter, and in person. As Bob said to me, "Every action has consequences; some of them can be bad."

Bob believed one of those negative consequences actually occurred only two days later. On March 7, Corey Moore, an ex-Marine and unemployed auto worker, stormed into a suburban Cleveland (Warrensville Heights, Ohio) police station and took a female clerk and a police captain hostage at gunpoint. Moore wanted publicity for his wacky agenda, which included the demand that "all white people should get off the planet." After 11 hours, Moore traded the female hostage for a television set, so he could watch the media coverage of the incident. He then demanded a telephone call from President Carter. Moore wanted to *personally* present his list of grievances to the president. Bringing the president into the incident would also gain Moore maximum media exposure.

Police passed Moore's demand to the USSS, who informed the White House. Although the Secret Service advised that it would be a dangerous precedent to set, the White House announced on the evening of March 8 that President Carter would be glad to phone Mr. Moore *after* the last hostage was released. This was confirmed by the president during his nationally televised press conference on the following morning (March 9). With a public assurance that the president would call, Moore released his hostage and surrendered peaceably. President Carter kept his promise and telephoned Moore that afternoon. Moore was subsequently found guilty of kidnapping, robbery, and extortion. He was sentenced to 5-25 years in prison.

Wednesday, March 9, 1977, is better remembered for the acts of terrorism that took our nation's capital by surprise. At about 11:00 a.m. that morning, seven men stormed into the B'nai B'rith (Jewish service organization) building at 1640 Rhode Island Avenue, NW, D.C. Wielding guns and machetes and searching floor by floor, the intruders rounded up over a hundred people and forced them into an eighth-floor conference room. There, the captors bound their hostages and forced them to lie face down on the floor. The windows of the conference room were painted over to cut off the view from the outside.

About an hour later, three armed men entered the Islamic Center at 2551 Massachusetts Avenue, NW, in the heart of Embassy Row. Twelve hostages were seized. The abductors tied up their captives and held them at gunpoint. Hostages had now been taken at two D.C. locations.

While this was going on, Bob and a handful of other agents were on their way to the headquarters building of the Central Intelligence Agency, located in Langley, Virginia (a short drive from D.C.). The agents were assigned to provide protective support for President Carter's visit to the CIA.

Upon his arrival at 1:26 p.m., President Carter was escorted to a seventh floor conference room where he met with intelligence officials. Later, the president made his way to the agency's auditorium and participated in the swearing-in ceremony of Admiral Stansfield Turner as the new Director of the CIA. The oath of office was administered by Byron R. White, Associate Justice of the U.S. Supreme Court. The president then addressed the approximately 450 persons in attendance.

With the president's 2:49 p.m. departure from CIA Headquarters, Bob and the other agents were released to return to Washington. During the drive back, Bob was called on the radio and ordered to respond to the District Building (renamed John A. Wilson Building in 1994) located at

1350 Pennsylvania Avenue, NW, D.C. Apparently, a shooting had just occurred at that location. Bob was dispatched to the scene to monitor the situation. The building was *only* a couple of blocks from the White House.

Bob checked in at the police command post, which had been hastily set up in a room on the fourth floor of the District Building. One floor above, two men were holding 13 persons captive within the offices of the D.C. City Council. One of the men was armed with a shotgun; the other brandished a machete.

During the initial takeover, two shotgun blasts were fired at security officers. One of the officers was wounded, while a bystander, WHUR-FM news reporter Maurice Williams, was killed. D.C. Councilman Marion Barry was wounded by a ricochet. The pellet struck about an inch above his heart but most of its energy had already been expended.

Shots broke out again a few moments later when city police arrived on the scene. During this exchange, the gunman shot a hostage, who was lying face down on the floor. It was a warning to police that innocent lives were in danger. Hearing the terrified cries of hostages, police held their fire and a standoff ensued.

With the seizure at the District Building, well over a hundred hostages were being held at *three* separate D.C. locations. Fear and panic was spreading throughout the city. Security was tightened in government buildings. Fearing additional takeovers, officials closed the Municipal Building (300 Indiana Avenue, NW) as well as the Washington Monument and Lincoln and Jefferson Memorials.

Bob learned that all three of the incidents were connected. The hostage takers were members of the Hanafi Moslems, a small religious sect, whose members were mostly black Americans. The organization had its headquarters in a house at 7700 16th Street, NW, D.C. The home was purchased for the group by then Milwaukee Bucks basketball star Kareem Abdul-Jabbar, who was a member of the sect. The founder and leader of the order, Hamaas Abdul Khaalis, was one of the seven men who were now holding hostages at the B'nai B'rith building.

Khaalis had been a former member and official in the Nation of Islam (NOI). He left that organization in 1958 over religious differences. Khaalis moved to Washington and formed his own order in the mid-1960s. In 1972, Hamaas Abdul Khaalis sent an open letter critical of NOI leader Elijah Muhammad to a number of Black Muslim mosques.

In January 1973, seven members of the Hanafi were brutally murdered in their 16th Street home. All were relatives of Khaalis. Five of the victims were children; one was a nine-day-old baby. Three of the children were drowned in a bathtub—another in a basement sink. The remaining child and two adults were shot and killed. Two other women were shot in the head but survived. One had permanent brain damage. It was the largest mass murder and one of the most brutal crimes in Washington history.

Eight men from the Philadelphia area with ties to the Black Muslim community were eventually charged with the murders. Prosecutors argued that the killings were retribution for the inflammatory letters authored by Khaalis. One of the men died of natural causes awaiting trial. Five of the remaining seven were tried together as codefendants. The sixth man was scheduled to be tried separately, as he was expected to be a government witness in the trial of the five. After the sixth man changed his mind and refused to testify, the judge acquitted one of the codefendants for lack of evidence before the case went to the jury. The remaining four were convicted. The eighth man—who had been on the run—was subsequently captured, tried, and convicted. The defendant who refused to testify was murdered in prison in 1974 to insure his silence. Thus by March 1977, five men had been convicted of the murders. Four were serving lengthy prison sentences, while the fifth had his conviction overturned. He was awaiting a new trial.

Hamaas Abdul Khaalis believed the murders of his family had been executions ordered by certain Black Muslim leaders. He was critical of police and government officials for not pursuing these allegations. He also blamed the trial judge (who was of Jewish faith) for acquitting one of the defendants and for ordering a new trial for another. In addition, Khaalis was upset that those convicted of the murders had not been executed. And with the tragedy that had befallen the Hanafi, Khaalis felt that elected city officials had not shown the proper deference that he and his sect deserved.

Now, Khaalis and his followers had taken matters in their own hands. Khaalis wanted to extract his own justice under the principles of Islamic law. Early on during negotiations with D.C. Police Chief Maurice Cullinane and Deputy Chief Robert Rabe, Hamaas Abdul Khaalis demanded that the murderers of his children and of Malcolm X be handed over to the Hanafis. It soon became clear why some of Khaalis's men carried machetes. Khaalis was engaged in a jihad (holy war) and wanted blood for blood. If the killers were not delivered to him, Khaalis threatened to behead hostages.

Supported by specialists from the Department of Justice, State Department, and the Behavioral Science Unit (BSU) of the FBI, Cullinane and Rabe attempted to establish trust and rapport with Khaalis. The MPD officials wanted to set in motion a negotiation process that would preclude the setting of ultimatums and deadlines and eventually lead to a peaceful resolution of the crisis.

Cullinane and Rabe were also aided by the ambassadors of Egypt, Pakistan, and Iran. Egyptian Ambassador Asraf Ghorbal was the first to volunteer. Egyptian nationals were among those being held at the Islamic Center. Ghorbal enlisted the aid of Pakistani Ambassador Sahabzada Yaqub-Khan and Iranian Ambassador Ardeshir Zahedi. Yaqub-Kahn and Zahedi were on the board of governors of the Islamic Center.

On Wednesday evening, the three ambassadors were brought to the MPD Command Center in the Municipal Building where they made a series of telephone calls to Khaalis. Yaqub-Kahn, a retired Pakistan army general with a Ph.D. from Harvard, did most of the talking for the ambassadors. He appealed to Khaalis's Islamic faith and read passages from the Quran that expressed peace, compassion, and mercy.

Reporters from all over the world also called B'nai B'rith. Wanting to get his message out to the public, the Hanafi leader told the media what had happened to his family and that those responsible had not been brought to justice. He warned that things could get much worse. Washington, D.C. newsman Max Robinson (WTOP-TV) talked with Khaalis several times. During one live newscast, Khaalis sternly voiced some of his demands.

Bob called home to say he wouldn't be able to leave the District Building until midnight—when his relief was expected. It looked like the takeovers would not end anytime soon. He emphasized that "patience" is the key strategy employed by police negotiators in such incidents. "Hostage takers are given time to cool off, so the situation can be defused," Bob advised. "Negotiators talk around demands that can't be met in order to keep the conversation moving in a positive direction and to buy more time to wear down the hostage takers."

To show good faith, authorities agreed to several of Khaalis's demands. They succeeded in halting the showing of the film *Mohammad, Messenger of God*. The film was pulled from New York theaters. Khaalis thought the film to be sacrilegious. And the $750 Khaalis paid in attorney fees for a contempt of court hearing during the 1973 murder trials was refunded to him by the city. To establish mutual trust, police agreed not to storm the buildings if Khaalis would not harm any more hostages.

The MPD official in charge at the District Building was Captain Robert Klotz, the Commander of the Special Operations Division. Klotz took Bob up to the fifth floor to view the scene. Dried blood could still be seen on the hallway floor. MPD officers armed with rifles and shotguns and wearing ballistic helmets and vests crouched behind conference tables that had been turned on their sides for makeshift barricades. The glass surrounding the double doors that led into the reception area of the council offices had been shot out. The doors themselves showed damage from gunfire as well as some of the inner walls. A female hostage could be seen sitting in a chair immediately inside the doorway of the office where the hostages were being held. Her arms were bound; she was being used to shield the movements of the two abductors.

On the return to the police command post, Bob reminded Klotz that British Prime Minister James Callaghan would be arriving at the White House South Grounds at 10:30 a.m. the following morning (March 10). It was the beginning of an official state visit. Bob was scheduled to work the arrival ceremony, which would include a 19-gun salute. The Presidential

Salute Battery of the 3rd U.S. Infantry (The Old Guard) renders the honors for White House ceremonies. They utilize World War II vintage artillery, which fire a 75-millimeter blank shell containing a pound and a half of powder. The guns make quite a roar.

The hostages were being held in the northwest corner of the District Building, just off 14th Street and Pennsylvania Avenue. There was nothing but open park area diagonally between that corner of the building and the White House South Grounds where the salute would be fired. Captain Klotz immediately picked up on Bob's concern and asked that the salute be canceled. The sound of the guns firing might spook the hostage takers into harming their captives.

Bob called the USSS Washington Field Office, the Presidential Protective Division White House Command Post (W-16), and the Department of State Office of the Chief of Protocol and relayed MPD's request. Bob received assurances from all that the salute would not occur.

The following morning, Bob reported to the South Grounds to serve as a PI team member for the arrival ceremony. He saw the Army cannon teams arrive at the Southwest Gate (B-3). The officer in charge said they decided to report to the White House "just in case." As the situation at the District Building had not been resolved, the salute battery returned to Fort Myer. It was the first time anyone could remember that the traditional salute honors had not been rendered.

After the arrival ceremony, Bob relieved the midnight agent at the police command post in the District Building. It was learned that earlier that morning, Khaalis had asked to meet with the three ambassadors. The ambassadors had worked through the night and had gone home to rest. During the time police were making contact with the ambassadors to discuss the proposal, Khaalis changed his mind, and the tone of the negotiations took a bad turn.

Through the news media, Khaalis learned that a national Black Muslim leader had recently arrived in Washington to offer his assistance in the crisis. Khaalis viewed this individual as an enemy and one of those responsible for the murders of his family. Khaalis was infuriated and the situation quickly escalated. He now wanted this Black Muslim brought before him too. Khaalis accused the police of not taking him seriously. He warned that unless the murderers of his family are turned over to him, "Heads will roll, and blood will run ankle deep."

Cullinane and Rabe advised Khaalis that authorities had no part in the Black Muslim leader coming to Washington. They assured Khaalis that the individual's actions had caught them by surprise too. The ambassadors reestablished their dialogue with Khaalis. They attempted to calm Khaalis and asked him to be merciful.

Later that afternoon, Ambassador Ghorbal invited Khaalis to meet with the ambassadors and police officials at a "table of peace." Khaalis consented to the meeting and preparations were made. A conference table was set up on the first floor of the B'nai B'rith building. Although Khaalis originally wanted to be armed and accompanied by several followers, he eventually agreed to come alone. It was also decided that none of the parties would bring weapons to the meeting.

When told of the meeting by Attorney General Griffin Bell, President Carter expressed deep concern for the safety of the ambassadors. Carter had called MPD Chief Cullinane early on during the incident to offer the full assistance and cooperation of federal authorities. The president also gave his assurance to Chief Cullinane that federal officials would not take over the incident. Final decisions would be left in the hands of local authorities. In keeping with that pledge, Carter did not block the ambassadors from attending the face-to-face meeting though he held grave reservations.

At about 8:10 p.m. on Thursday evening, March 10, the trio of ambassadors along with Cullinane, Rabe, and Captain Joseph O'Brien, Commander of the MPD Homicide Division, sat down with Hamaas Abdul Khaalis. O'Brien participated in the meeting because he had maintained contact with Khaalis since the 1973 murders, and some trust had been established between the two. Khaalis's son-in-law, Abdul Azziz, who was not a participant in the takeovers, was also allowed to sit in on the talks. The day before at the order's 16th Street headquarters, Azziz had issued press statements on behalf of Khaalis. It was believed that Aziz would bring another trusted face to the table.

During the talks, Chief Cullinane pronounced that it was beyond his control to present the murderers of Khaalis's family. At the same time, Ambassadors Ghorbal, Zahedi, and Yaqub-Kahn continued to appeal to Khaalis's orthodox Moslem beliefs. Citing Islamic principles of peace and goodwill, the Moslem diplomats reinforced on Khaalis the need to treat the hostages with compassion and mercy. The ambassadors also acknowledged Khaalis's great loss. They grieved with the Hanafi leader over the senseless murder of his family. To ease the tension of the standoff, the ambassadors reiterated that Khaalis had made his point. He had been successful in getting the story of the tragedy out to the world and in attaining most of his demands.

Khaalis finally came to the realization that the individuals he sought would not be brought to him—*no matter what*. For the release of the hostages, Khaalis next asked for immunity from prosecution for himself and his men. Cullinane replied that the Justice Department would *never* agree to that. Emphasizing that they were negotiating in good faith, police officials said they would *not* make promises they could not keep.

After three hours of discussion, police negotiators found an opening to end the crisis. A weary Khaalis expressed a desire to go home. Chief Cullinane and Deputy Chief Rabe seized the opportunity. They offered

Khaalis a deal. If he and his men surrendered, Khaalis would be permitted to await trial at home. During arraignment, the government would ask that Khaalis be released on his personal recognizance (no cash).

In the early morning hours of Friday, March 11, Khaalis and his band of men laid down their weapons and surrendered at all three locations. The hostages were free after almost 40 hours of captivity. Some were taken to hospitals for medical treatment, while others were reunited with family and friends. Church bells tolled that morning as news of the hostage release spread throughout the city.

The hostage takers were transported to police headquarters and processed. Later that morning, they were arraigned in D.C. Superior Court. Most were held over for trial in lieu of hefty surety (cash) bonds. In accordance with the agreement to end the crisis, Hamaas Abdul Khaalis was freed without bond. He returned to his 16th Street residence. The terms of release stipulated that Khaalis must surrender his passport and not leave the District of Columbia. Khaalis also had to turn over any firearms that might be on the 16th Street property and to refrain from breaking any laws.

The release deal brought criticism from the public, some congressional leaders, and even a law enforcement official from a neighboring jurisdiction. They believed that deals made under duress should not be kept. Promise anything to end the crisis but don't bow later to extortion.

The critics pointed out an incident that occurred earlier in the year in Indianapolis, Indiana. Forty-four-year-old Anthony Kiritsis walked into a mortgage banking office and took a senior executive hostage. Kiritsis accused the firm of trying to steal land from him through foreclosure. A shotgun was wired to the hostage's neck and rigged to go off if Kiritsis was felled. The kidnapper forced police to transport him and his hostage to Kiritsis's apartment, which was booby-trapped with a gasoline bomb. A 63-hour standoff ensued.

To secure the safe release of the hostage, authorities bowed to Kiritsis's demand for absolute immunity from prosecution. Yet after he freed his captive, Kiritsis was immediately arrested by police. Charged with kidnapping, armed robbery and other crimes, Kiritsis was held on $850,000 bond. The prosecutor announced that government authorities never intended to honor the terms of the deal. Critics felt the same thing should have been done with Hamaas Abdul Khaalis.

Bob, however, felt Cullinane and Rabe had done the right thing. The deal ended the crisis without further harm to any of the hostages. Bob said police found a small arsenal of weapons and over 10,000 rounds of ammunition when they searched the B'nai B'rith building. The Hanafis had to rent a truck to transport it all. An execution room had also been readied at the B'nai B'rith site. Seven heavily armed men could have caused much murder and mayhem. Plus, there were two other hostage locations to contend with. Since one person had been killed at the District Building, police worried that Khaalis had been forced beyond the point of no return and would have nothing to lose if he carried out his threats.

Considering the circumstances, Bob thought the pretrial release for Khaalis was a small price to pay for a peaceful end to the standoff. Bob knew that the FBI had a court-ordered wiretap on Khaalis's phone and that MPD Emergency Response Teams had surveillance on Khaalis's residence. There was no danger that Khaalis would be able to flee prosecution or put into play some new terrorist plot.

Bob compared it to the way he dealt with protective intelligence subjects. It was important to establish trust and to keep one's word. "Most of these people are already pretty paranoid," Bob said. "If you lie to them, the next time they come in contact with me or another agent could spell serious trouble. The police are in the same boat in hostage situations. Once it gets out that police and government prosecutors don't keep their word, it'll make future hostage situations that more difficult to negotiate. Subjects will not believe anything the police say and violence could rule the day."

It took Hamaas Abdul Khaalis a little less than three weeks to violate the terms of his pretrial release. Khaalis threatened to kill people during several alarming telephone conversations that were overheard on the FBI wiretap. As threats to do bodily harm are a violation in the District of Columbia, Khaalis was arrested on March 31, 1977, and held without bond.

Two months later, the trial of the 12 Hanafis began in D.C. Superior Court amidst some of the tightest security ever seen. Facing overwhelming evidence, defense attorneys virtually conceded the armed kidnapping charges their clients personally participated in but pursued a vigorous defense against conspiracy charges of murder and kidnapping. The law states that each member of a criminal conspiracy can be held liable for the crimes committed by other members in the furtherance of the conspiracy. Athough only one defendant pulled the trigger on the shotgun blast that killed reporter Maurice Williams, the other 11 codefendants were charged with the murder as well. Each codefendant was also charged with additional counts of kidnapping that were incurred from the two sites where they were not present.

On July 23, 1977, a jury of ten women and two men found all 12 Hanafis guilty of multiple counts of armed kidnapping. Only Khaalis, as leader of the conspiracy, and the two individuals at the District Building were found guilty of second-degree murder. The three were also found guilty of assault with intent to kill. The *minimum* sentence handed out to the 12 Hanafis ranged from 24 to 78 years in federal prison. Hamaas Abdul Khaalis was sentenced to 41–123 years. He died in 2003 at the Federal Correctional Complex at Butner, North Carolina. Abdul Muzikir, the triggerman at the District Building, received the longest sentence—78 years to life.

March 1977 presented the USSS with yet one more surprise. On March 24, First Lady Rosalynn Carter, accompanied by her personal secretary, slipped away from the White House for a secret shopping trip to New York City. Neither the Secret Service nor the first lady's press secretary was notified of the visit. Mrs. Carter shopped the fashion houses along Seventh Avenue. She purchased dresses, gowns, suits, and coats for her spring and summer wardrobe.

Agents of the First Lady Detail only became aware of the situation when the New York Field Office (NYFO) called W-16 to check on the whereabouts of Mrs. Carter. The NYFO had received a report that the first lady had been spotted in the city. The White House Communications Agency maintains a system of computer monitors that list the locations of the president, vice president, and other Secret Service protectees. The W-16 agent advised that the locator screen showed the first lady at the White House. At the same time, members of the White House press corps were calling the first lady's office to find out what was going on. The New York press was reporting that Mrs. Carter was in Manhattan.

With confusion mounting, the NYFO dispatched agents to check on the reports. They caught up with the first lady along Seventh Avenue. That evening, they escorted Mrs. Carter to LaGuardia Airport where agents accompanied her back to Washington. While the flight was being readied for takeoff, a stewardess moved a package that was protruding into the aisle. The owner of the parcel told the flight attendant, "Be careful with that; there's a bomb in it!" With that remark, the flight was delayed while the subject was escorted off the plane by police. The package contained a ceramic vase. The individual said he made the remark in jest and was unaware that Mrs. Carter was aboard the aircraft.

Paired with Dick Corrigan, Bob worked the WFO-PI team that covered the first lady's arrival back at Washington National Airport. When he got home that night, Bob related how unbelievable the whole day had been. To think that the first lady could leave the White House unnoticed and that an aide would arrange a trip to New York without protection seemed almost impossible—especially only several weeks after the Hanafi takeovers. As unlikely as it may have been, that's exactly what happened. Bob was relieved that the first lady was back safely at the White House. The portion of the trip made without protection had exposed Mrs. Carter to potential danger by making her a target of opportunity.

Chapter 25

Darkness Falls

For quite some time, Bob had been thinking about ways to better assess the dangerousness of protective intelligence subjects. There were no established procedures for reliably predicting violent behavior. During his time in the WFO-PI Squad, Bob developed a strategy that he believed made for more accurate evaluations. He was currently in the process of writing up his method for submission to the USSS Employee Suggestion Program that was administered by the Office of Public Affairs.

Gary Yauger, the USSS-ID agent who interviewed Sara Jane Moore the evening before her attempted assassination of President Ford, transferred to the Washington Field Office. Bob had become acquainted with Yauger during temporary assignments to the Intelligence Division. A seven-year veteran of the Secret Service and a GS-13, Yauger was a bright and conscientious agent. At WFO, Yauger was assigned as a Forgery Squad group leader.

Bob invited Yauger to lunch. "I'd like to run some PI stuff by you," Bob added. The two met in an Italian restaurant near the field office. After placing their orders, the men updated each other on their personal lives. Yauger was a friend of my brother Art and knew that Bob was Art's brother-in-law. After some more small talk, Bob thanked Gary for meeting with him.

"No problem. I've been brown bagging. It's good to get out of the office."

"Gary, I have a checklist that I use when I'm evaluating whether a subject warrants protective interest," Bob began. "You and Marty Haskell are the only two people in history to have interviewed and evaluated a subject just prior to an assassination attempt. I'd like your opinion on what I've come up with. With your unique experience, I can't think of anyone better qualified."

"Shoot."

From a suit coat pocket, Bob pulled out a Xerox-copy of a hand-typed form and slid it across the table toward Yauger. The document was titled: "Protective Interest Evaluation Review (PIER)." Yauger glanced at the paper and a smile broke over his face.

"The form lists key actions taken by presidential assassins prior to their assaults—gathered from the historical record," Bob advised. "These would be the significant events that furthered the progression of the assassination or attempt. Next to each event, there's a check box to mark if that particular action matches the subject you're evaluating. Each entry has a corresponding point value, which is weighted as to the significance of the behavior. When you've completed the review, you total up the score. The higher the score—the more your subject's actions are similar to past assassins. I see a high score as an indication and prima facie evidence that the subject warrants protective interest."

Yauger spent a moment perusing the form. "Bob, you know the Service doesn't have much faith in psychological profiling. Squeaky Fromme and Sally Moore showed the inadequacy of the assassin's profile a government research group came up with in the late 60s. Assassins could only be males according to that study."

"Exactly the reason I took a *behavioral* approach. I based my form on factual, real-world events. Many are common to most assassins. Some are absolutely necessary for an assassination."

"Headquarters believes personal interviews followed up by background investigations are the best tools to use for evaluating PI subjects," Yauger stated. "I don't think they'll go for a form that takes the final evaluation away from the professional judgment of agents. An experienced agent's gut feeling is more accurate than any profile."

"This is only another tool to *help* in the evaluation process, though there are some acts—like 'Acquiring Weapons'—that are red flags by themselves," Bob informed. "The purpose of the checklist is to make sure any telltale signs pointing to my subject being the real deal are detected and considered. It's like the checklist a commercial pilot uses before takeoff.

"Gary, you and Marty are two of the best we have," Bob continued. "You evaluated Moore as not being dangerous. Based on our training and methods, the decision was correct and every other PI agent in the Service would probably have made the same decision. That's the problem. Less than a day after your evaluation, Moore went out and tried to kill the president. Comparing Moore's behavior with those of known assassins is a method to bring some concrete reasoning to agent intuition."

"With what I knew about Moore then, I don't see anything on your form that would have changed my mind," Yauger asserted. "At the time I interviewed her, she didn't present a danger. I'd make the same decision today and not lose any sleep over it. Most of the people we deal with are kooks. They don't know themselves what they're going to do next. My interview and the attention we gave her may have prompted the attack."

"Yeah, our evaluations are more art than science," Bob readily agreed. "Yet, I think Moore was ready to do the deed before you talked with her. Moore's arrest on Sunday might have prevented her from making the attempt that afternoon when Ford visited Stanford. I don't believe your interview caused her to take a shot at Ford. The copycat effect of Squeaky Fromme's attempt and the capture of Patty Hearst and the other SLA members were probably contributing influences on Moore—along with Ford's opportune return to California.

"Moore's life had become desperate," Bob suggested. "She originally gave information to police in order to combat the corruption she witnessed in the PIN program. During the time she provided information to the FBI, she fully converted to the ideals of the far left. Since she had betrayed her radical friends, Moore felt guilty and confessed her sins. She hoped for forgiveness. Instead, Moore was exiled from the new world she desperately wanted to stay a part of. She had a lot of internal conflict. In my opinion, this was heightened by a grandiose personality. She believed her actions were more important than they actually were. She pictured herself as an actor on a world stage.

"I think the Fromme attempt showed Moore a way out—a chance for personal redemption. Moore thought she could absolve her sins by doing Fromme one better. At the same time, she'd strike a blow for the revolutionary left and gain worldwide fame. Desperate people are *dangerous* people."

"You have the entry 'Acquiring Weapons' heavily weighted," Yauger pointed out. "You mentioned this would be a red flag by itself. Bob, a lot of people have firearms."

"It would have to be a recent purchase. Simply having access to firearms would only be a yellow flag," Bob explained. "Recent target practice or dry firing would be another concern. Of course, the form needs to be taken in the context of the subjects who come to our attention.

"In Sara Jane Moore's case, the form would have indicated she was of protective interest based on what was known at the time of your interview. She had contacted a law enforcement officer about testing the system and going out to Stanford. This showed her intent to appear at a site the president would be visiting and to take *some* type of abnormal action.

"But the red flag warning was 'Acquiring Weapons.' Moore purchased a .44 Special revolver right around the Fromme attempt. Moore bought the weapon and *practiced* with it because she suddenly had a need for one. People buy things they intend on using. The acquisition of firearms, explosives, and the like by a *PI subject* shows me that he or she is preparing to commit a violent act. Based on that, I would have asked the police to keep an eye on her until after the end of the visit."

"Yeah but Bob, Moore said she purchased it for protection. She had been an informant and was fearful for her life. She carried it in her purse. She also told police and ATF about the purchase."

"Gary, she wasn't going to tell you the truth about her intentions. That's the advantage of this form. It's not swayed by deception. Moore's actions spoke louder than her words. It had been a year or so since she first disclosed that she was giving information to the FBI. And some months since she gave *public news interviews* about her activities. Yet, she only purchased the .44 several weeks before her attempt on Ford. And when she was arrested with the gun in her possession the day before the attempt, it wasn't loaded. An *unloaded* gun doesn't give any protection. She couldn't have been too worried about her safety."

"That's a good point—a really good point," Yauger conceded.

In spite of Gary Yauger's comments regarding the checklist," Bob placed the suggestion in the PI Squad ATSAIC's inbox for review and forwarding to the Office of Public Affairs. The following morning, Bob was called into the AT's office. He wasn't even asked to sit down.

Handing the submission packet back to Bob, the AT stated in a curt, businesslike tone: "I'm not sending this on. Believe me; I'm doing you a favor. ID has staff people who work on these things, and they use computers and consultants. You don't want to come off that you know more than headquarters. A junior agent doesn't want that reputation. The suggestion program is mainly for the use of clerks in regard to administrative matters.

"If you want to make changes in PI procedures, put your time in at WFO and try and get a transfer to ID. Then if you still think this is of value, you can present your suggestions directly to those who make the decisions."

Bob was clearly discouraged when he arrived home that evening. He figured it wouldn't be easy getting his ideas accepted, but he didn't know it would prove to be an impossible task. Bob had submitted two suggestions during his tenure at WFO and neither received much consideration—if any. Bob had struck out on both.

Walter "Walt" Bothe was another senior special agent who transferred to the Washington Field Office during this time. Bothe started with the Secret Service in 1966. A deep, gruff voice more resembling a grizzled beat cop belied the fact that Bothe had earned a master's degree in criminal justice from Michigan State University. His checkered career took him to field offices (New York and Los Angeles) on both coasts. Bothe made a name for himself in criminal investigation as well as protection, working organized crime strike forces and on the protective detail for Henry Kissinger.

Bothe put his heart and soul into Dr. Kissinger's protection, accompanying him throughout the world for a good number of years. In October 1974, Bothe was wounded when an Uzi submachine gun accidentally discharged, while Kissinger's plane was taking off from Cairo, Egypt. The attaché case carrying the Uzi fell to the floor from an overhead storage rack, firing off a round. The bullet struck Bothe in the arm and grazed his head. Initially, Bothe thought the plane was under attack. He showed his mettle when he called out to fellow agents, "Don't worry about me; cover the secretary!"

As a State Department agent assigned to Nancy Kissinger, Bob had worked with Bothe and the two respected each other. At WFO, Bothe was assigned to the Criminal Squad. He had been there a couple of days when he stopped by Bob's office. "I've got some bad guys I need to run down and get off the streets. Bob, I know you have your own workload but would really appreciate the help. Joe [PI Squad AT] said it would be okay. And it won't be a one-way street. We can work on your cases too."

"Sure, give me a minute to put on my vest [ballistic]," Bob answered.

"I'll meet you at the elevators in 10," Bothe said.

Agent Bothe was on the hunt for an individual who was wanted for the passing of counterfeit currency. It was hoped the subject would ultimately lead Bothe to the source of the "funny money."

On the way to check some of the subject's haunts, Bothe thanked Bob for the assistance and then revealed, "You know I wanted to get you over to the secretary's detail—if Ford would have won, and Dr. Kissinger would have stayed on."

"Thank God Ford lost!" Bob joked. "The TDY assignments were tough enough on my wife. A permanent assignment would have finished us."

When Bothe was done laughing, he turned to Bob and said: "Seriously, you're an agent I trust. When I go out to put the cuffs on someone, I don't want just anyone covering my back. I have a lot of respect for you. You served with one of the best police forces in the country. I've seen you in action; I know you can handle yourself."

Over the next several months, the two continued to help with each other's casework as circumstances and time permitted. As a result, Walt became a willing mentor to Bob. Several events showed the personal relationship that had quickly developed. Bothe grabbed Bob one morning and took him to SO Dave Green's office. "Dave, what's the story on that two-door gold Pontiac I saw in the garage at 1800 G?" Bothe asked.

"We just got that in a transfer from another field office."

"I thought so!" Bothe said enthusiastically. "I seized that car in a counterfeiting case when I was in New York. It was new at the time. It's a nice car; I drove it for a year. Dave, can we get the car assigned to Bob? He's been helping me in some criminal cases, including stakeouts. The Pontiac would be better than the four-door Ford he drives. With the Ford, he might as well put a banner on the door that reads: 'Federal Agent on Duty.' "

"No problem," Green replied with a laugh. "The Pontiac's unassigned. Bob, go ahead and make the switch. The keys are in it."

"Great," Bothe said. "Bob, I'll come down and help you. Then, I could use some help in Southeast."

At the garage, Bothe opened the trunk of the Pontiac and showed Bob a secret compartment. "That's where they hid the counterfeit plates," Bothe informed. After the transfer of Bob's belongings, Bothe jumped behind the wheel. "Let me drive for old-time sake. This car brings back memories."

His face beaming, Bothe recounted some "war stories" involving the vehicle. With a sparkle in his eye, Bothe fondly reminisced about his old days in the New York Field Office; Bob didn't miss a word.

"Did your old car have a *people's radio?*" Bothe asked Bob, referring to the AM-FM radio installed in the Pontiac.

"No, Walt, my car only had a Secret Service radio."

"Well, you got one now," Bothe said with a smile. "In this car, the Service radio is hidden in the glove box."

Later that afternoon, the two men stopped for dinner. Bob had to work an evening PI team; Walt would work late running out some leads. During dinner, Bothe divulged the following: "Well, I've decided to do it. It's final. I'm going to leave the Service."

"We've all been hearing the rumors," Bob said. "I hate to see you go, but let me be one of the first to wish you luck."

"Thanks, I appreciate that," Bothe replied. "It was a tough decision, but the right thing to do. Dr. Kissinger is out of government, and his Secret Service detail will be ending. He needs me. I'll be heading up his private protection. It's a good deal too. I'll get an executive salary and benefits. They've got it worked, so the Marshals Service will be deputizing me. I have a couple of guys lined up to help out. It's the opportunity of a lifetime."

The weeks went by. Bob assisted Bothe in the arrest, transport, and interview of criminal subjects. Bob even got credit for an arrest in a case where multiple subjects were apprehended. Finally, it was Walt Bothe's last day as a Secret Service agent, and Bob treated him to lunch. "Thanks for everything you taught me and for letting me share your final months in the Service," Bob expressed. "I'll never forget it."

"Partner, I enjoyed working with you." Bothe reached across the table toward Bob. The two men shook hands in a warm manner that served as a testament to the camaraderie that had developed.

"The honor was mine, Walt."

Bob stayed very busy during 1977. His work never seemed to let up. Thanks to President Carter, the car plane trips stopped for a while since limos and follow-ups were being transported by truck. Thus, I got to see Bob on more of the weekends although he frequently served as the PI duty agent. We couldn't go anywhere since Bob was on call. He was often gone on a moment's notice, most of the time not returning for hours.

Saturday, April 23, was one of those days. Shep Kelly, a State Department SY agent and friend of ours, stopped by the house to see us. Kelly was leaving SY and moving out of the area to take a position with the State of Illinois. Shep wanted to personally say goodbye.

We invited Shep to stay for lunch. I had just put some sandwiches on the dining room table when the telephone rang. "I hope it's not work," I cried out. Bob answered the phone and immediately reached for the pad of paper and pencil lying nearby. "Darn it, another Saturday ruined," I moaned.

A couple of minutes later, Bob returned the receiver to the cradle and turned to Shep and me. "I'm sorry," Bob said. "A bomb exploded this morning at Washington National. It was near the VIP gate. A man was killed. I have to go."

"Bob, do you mind if I follow you over? I'll get the info for SY. You know we use that area too," Shep said.

"Of course not, let me grab a suit and say goodbye to the kids."

"In the meantime, I'll call my Ops desk," Shep announced.

A short time later, Bob appeared with a hang-up bag over his shoulder. Not wanting to take the time to change, Bob was responding in casual clothes. But he always made sure he had a dress shirt, tie, and business suit with him—in case he would later have to work a protective assignment. "I'll call when I can," Bob promised. Then he kissed me goodbye.

Shep gave me a parting hug. "I want you guys to visit me in Springfield."

"Be safe," I called as Bob and Shep charged out the door with sandwiches in hand. Bob was off on another adventure.

Located on the Virginia side of the Potomac River, Washington National Airport first opened in June 1941. It stands on land once owned by George Washington's adopted stepson, John Parke Custis. The Main Terminal was designed with columns and other architectural accents influenced by Mount Vernon, Washington's beloved home.

Through the years, National grew into a major regional airport with over 10 million passengers using its facilities annually. The Main Terminal was expanded in 1950. In 1958, the new North Terminal opened followed by the Commuter Terminal in 1970.

From 1941–1987, National Airport was operated by the Civil Aeronautics Board (CAB) and its successor, the Federal Aviation Authority (FAA). In 1987, the control of National Airport, along with Dulles International Airport, was transferred by Congress to a newly created Metropolitan Washington Airports Authority. In 1998, the airport's name was officially changed to Ronald Reagan Washington National Airport.

Bob and Shep parked near the airport's VIP gate in spaces reserved for law enforcement vehicles. USSS motorcades used this entrance to pass directly to and from the tarmac. This allowed protectees to board and disembark aircraft without having to pass through waiting rooms and other public areas that were potentially dangerous.

Entering the nearby south extension of the Main Terminal, the two men made their way to a public corridor near the Eastern Air Shuttle waiting room. An FAA policeman directed them to a door that opened into a hallway within the restricted area of the building. There, they were met by the lead investigator, who was from the Alexandria Field Office (AX) of the FBI. The agent reviewed Bob and Shep's credentials and entered the identifying data in the Bureau's crime scene book. "You're just in time," the FBI man said. "You'll be able to see the room before it's hosed down. It's right around the corner. We're finishing our evidence collection and will be releasing the area to airport personnel."

Bob and Shep were then led into the scene of the explosion—a men's locker room used by the airport's custodial staff. There was a trail of dried blood on the floor, which led to an adjoining room. Powder burns could be seen on some of the lockers. There were marks on the ceiling and walls where shrapnel had been embedded. Some ceiling tiles were missing. They had been collected by the FBI as evidence.

"The bomb exploded at about 11:00 a.m. this morning," the lead FBI agent advised. "From the fragments, we believe the device was a pipe bomb—black powder packed into a three-inch-diameter pipe about eight inches long. The bomb was hidden in a gray-steel Craftsman toolbox, which had been placed in a shipping carton. The bomb was rigged to detonate when the toolbox was opened.

"The decedent was an airport janitor. He was either sitting in a chair with the toolbox in his lap or standing next to a table with the toolbox on top. When he lifted the lid to look inside, the bomb exploded. The decedent staggered through an adjoining kitchen to a supply room where he was found on the floor.

"From our preliminary investigation, we don't believe the decedent was the maker or the target of the bomb. He was 51 years old and had worked at the airport since 1970. He was a widower and lived by himself in Southeast, D.C. He was friendly and considered a good worker. He had no known enemies.

"Tracing his morning activities, we believe the decedent found the shipping carton somewhere within the Eastern Air Shuttle area or the FAA restricted area. Police have checked the remainder of the airport for explosive devises with negative results. No one has claimed responsibility for the bombing.

"The locker room is used by about 50 employees," continued the FBI agent. "Though the door to the FAA restricted area is not secured, there is a cipher lock on the locker room door. Our best guess is the device was intended for an individual or group of individuals. A pipe bomb set as an entrapment device [booby trap] is personal. A terrorist bomb directed against the airport would more likely have been constructed of dynamite or plastic explosives and detonated with a timing device.

"We're checking out FAA personnel and Eastern employees who work in the vicinity to see if one of them might have been the intended target. The only thing we've come up with so far is an incident that happened last night. An individual arrived late and missed the final shuttle flight of the evening to New York. Apparently, he became quite upset, and police were summoned. Eastern Air Shuttle doesn't require reservations. They guarantee that everyone who shows up for one of their hourly flights will get a seat—even if they have to add an additional plane and crew. But that doesn't apply to passengers who show up late."

The Bureau agent handed Bob a slip of paper with the subject's name and other identifying information. "The guy lives in D.C. Bill Thomas from our Washington Field Office is checking him out."

"I've worked with Bill on some cases," Bob said. "I'll give him a call."

When the briefing was concluded, Bob and Shep headed to the FAA Police office where they borrowed a couple of desks and phones. Shep informed SY of his findings, while Bob reported the information to the USSS Intelligence Division. Bob asked ID to run a record check on the subject who was involved in the Friday night incident. Bob almost fell out of his chair when he heard the results. An ID computer screen synopsis of the subject's criminal record revealed he had been convicted in 1970 of attempted first-degree murder and aggravated arson.

"Pull the subject's hard file," Bob said. "I'll be there in 15 minutes." Bob said goodbye to Shep and drove across the 14th Street Bridge to USSS Headquarters. After showing his credentials to the special officer on duty, Bob was buzzed into an inner hallway. Bob activated a four-digit cipher lock and entered the duty desk area of the USSS Intelligence Division.

Bob anxiously reviewed the subject's file. It contained police reports and newspaper clippings. Bob could hardly believe what he was reading. As a juvenile in 1970, the subject had apparently come under the influence of black revolutionary ideology. Police became suspicious of the individual after he was found injured near the scene of a bombing. Authorities suspected the subject had planted the device and that it detonated prematurely.

In the same Midwestern city 10 days before, a bomb had exploded in the women's restroom of a downtown department store. The device contained a two-pound stick of dynamite detonated by a timer. A woman was seriously injured in that blast, sustaining permanent injuries to her lungs. While police were checking the scene, they found another device hidden in a nearby locker, which fortunately had failed to detonate. This bomb contained 10 two-pound sticks of dynamite. Its purpose was to injure and kill the police and firemen who had responded to the first explosion.

On the day of the bombing, witnesses spotted a suspicious male—dressed as a woman—carrying a package into the department store. This individual's description was similar to the subject. Additionally, a friend of the subject informed police that the individual had bragged about planting the bombs. With this information, police applied for and received a search warrant for the subject's residence. Manuals on bomb making and urban warfare were found.

In the ensuing trial, the subject was convicted of attempted first-degree murder and aggravated arson. The subject was sentenced to 20 years. He served about three years in a state reformatory. After his release, subject moved to Washington, D.C. to pursue journalistic ambitions. The Secret Service had a file on the subject because he had been on the guest list for several White House functions.

Bob telephoned the Washington Field Office of the FBI and told the government operator that he was a Secret Service agent and needed to speak with Agent Bill Thomas as soon as possible. "Is this for real?" the duty operator asked incredulously. Bob gave the operator assurances that this wasn't a crank call.

A short time later, Thomas called Bob at the Intelligence Division. "Bob, Bill Thomas here. What's up, buddy?"

"Bill, I'm covering the National Airport bombing investigation for the Service. Headquarters is especially concerned since the gate we use for motorcades is at the south end of the Main Terminal. It's not known where the device was originally left or for whom it was intended. I just came from the scene and was told you're looking into a guy who was involved in an incident there last night."

"That's right. I'm at the field office getting my facts lined up before I take a run out to see him. The individual has felony priors in the Midwest. I'm getting an agent out there to see if he can pull local records on a Saturday. We might have to wait until Monday."

"Bill, I've got some good news for you. I have a copy of the subject's police file in front of me along with some newspaper accounts. He was convicted of a department store bombing. A device with a two-pound stick of dynamite activated by a timer went off in a women's restroom. A woman was seriously injured. An entrapment device was found hidden in a storage locker in the restroom—10 two-pound sticks of dynamite. Fortunately, it had a faulty timing mechanism and didn't explode."

"Holy crap!" Thomas cried out. "Bob, can I come over and take a look at the file?"

"Sure, come to the eighth floor of 1800 G and ask for me."

Thomas arrived at USSS Headquarters, and Bob escorted him to ID. "Ten two-pound sticks of dynamite," Thomas repeated several times. "That would have caused a lot of death and destruction." Thomas reviewed the subject's file and made detailed notes. "Ten two-pound sticks of dynamite," Thomas said once more while shaking his head. "This kid had a lot of anger."

"Yeah, he bought into the revolution in a big way," Bob expressed in agreement.

"Bob, let's go see if he's at home," Thomas said. Bill was a regular guy, and a rapport had developed between the two. Bill welcomed Bob's company. Besides providing backup, Bob offered an investigative perspective that was outside the Bureau. It also saved Thomas time. On the first case the two went out on, Bill told Bob: "This saves a lot of phone calls. You can see for yourself exactly what I'm doing on the case."

The agents arrived at the apartment building where the subject resided. It was typical of the thousands of brick, multi-unit structures that sprung up in Washington on every vacant lot during the 1940s and 50s. Thomas rapped loudly on the subject's door four or five times and called out, "Hello, anyone home?" There was no answer from within. "Boy, I'd love to get inside and take a look around," Thomas remarked.

"Drop me back at headquarters first," Bob declared.

Thomas chuckled and said: "I was just wishing out loud. We don't do that anymore—really."

On the way back to 1800 G, Bob suggested: "Maybe this guy took a shuttle flight to New York this morning. That would have placed him at the airport. Even if he has no connection to the blast, he might have seen something."

"Yeah, I was thinking about that too. I'll get Alexandria to check with the airline."

Agent Thomas and Bob weren't able to find the subject at home until the following week. Cracking the door about a foot, the subject peered out at the two men. Bill held up his credentials and announced: "Agent Thomas from the FBI. We'd like to talk with you."

The subject immediately looked surprised and uneasy. "No, I don't speak with the FBI," he replied with some anger in his voice.

"Look, we need your help in a matter," Thomas explained.

"No, I'm not talking with you." The subject then shut the door on the two agents.

"That wasn't very friendly—was it?" Thomas remarked to Bob.

"No, he didn't act like someone whom the system has truly *reformed*," Bob replied.

"I think this guy still has a big chip on his shoulder," Thomas expressed.

The next day, Bill Thomas telephoned Bob with yet another twist. "Bob, I got a call from New York. You're going to love this. The subject's brother was arrested at LaGuardia Airport on December 28, 1975!"

A light bulb went off in Bob's head. "That was right around the LaGuardia bombing!" Bob cried out.

"You're good. It was the day *before* the blast," Thomas informed. "Some coincidence, huh."

With the subject's refusal to talk, many unanswered questions remained. Nevertheless, there was no hard evidence to link the subject to the National Airport bombing, and he was never elevated to suspect status. As with the LaGuardia explosion of 1975, the Washington National Airport bombing of 1977 remains unsolved to this day.

Bob received a pleasant surprise during the spring of 1977. His ATSAIC approved a training request for Bob to attend a two-week USSS Firearms Instructor Training Course (FITC No. 53) at Beltsville, Maryland. Bob was told it was a reward for the good work he had been doing. Yet, Bob had to be on call during evening and weekend hours. He also had to agree to take no leave during the summer months. Of course, that was the only time I had off from my school-teaching position. Still, it was nice to have Bob home at regular hours for a couple of weeks. The time that Bob spent in training reminded me of what married life could have been like if Bob had chosen a normal career.

Bob was in heaven. He and the other 11 agents and officers in the class shot pistols, shotguns, submachine guns, and some special weapons. In the classroom and on the range, topics included marksmanship fundamentals, ballistics, analysis of shooting errors, and techniques of combat shooting. Bob graduated with the highest shooting average, and he was awarded the marksmanship trophy for the course.

Back in the real world, a large number of foreign dignitaries descended on Washington during 1977 to meet with the new U.S. president. Mexico, Canada, Israel, Great Britain, Japan, Jordan, Saudi Arabia, Australia, Venezuela, West Germany, Italy, and France were some of the countries whose heads of state/chiefs of government made official visits to consult with President Carter. In addition, a number of heads of state or government made nonworking visits to Washington. A Latin American dictator was one of those who made a private trip to our nation's capital in 1977. The foreign leader asked for Secret Service protection for the visit; Bob was given the PI coordinator assignment.

Frank Brown, the supervisor selected to head the dignitary's Secret Service detail, called Bob to inquire about an individual. The subject's name had been given to Brown by a member of the foreign advance team, a colonel in that country's security forces. According to the colonel, the subject resided in the U.S. and posed a "grave threat" to the safety of the visiting dignitary. Brown asked Bob to check on the subject.

Bob headed for the Foreign Intelligence Branch (FIB) of USSS-ID where he name checked the individual. Finding the subject to be of record, Bob pulled the file, which was classified "SECRET" and marked "NOFORN" (Not Releasable to Foreign Nationals). A review of the file revealed a good amount of sensitive information regarding the subject—including some past intelligence activities. However, Bob saw nothing that would indicate the subject posed anything more than a *political* threat to the visiting leader.

Bob telephoned Brown and reported the following: "Frank, the subject's file is classified, so I can't brief you over the phone. I can tell you that the subject was not evaluated a danger to our protectee in past visits. Why are they so concerned about this guy now?"

"I was only told that he posed a 'grave threat.' "

"OK, I'll want to talk with the colonel to get some specifics. Then I'll pass what we have to the FBI. We'll get them on board too. The subject's last known address is out of the Washington district. I'll request a collateral investigation for an interview, and we'll update the file. Frank, give me a time when I can come up to DPD and brief you on this guy and the rest of the intelligence I have for the visit."

"Are you at ID now?" Brown asked.

"Yes."

"I'll pick you up in front of 1800 G in about 30 minutes. Bring the file with you; I want to see it."

Bob reviewed the file several more times, making sure not to miss anything. When he was done, Bob signed out the case file and then proceeded to the sidewalk in front of 1800 G. A short time later, a Secret Service vehicle carrying four individuals pulled to the curb. A USSS special officer drove the vehicle. Detail leader Brown was on the passenger side of the front seat. Bob was surprised to see two Hispanic males in the rear of the vehicle. Bob jumped in the back, and the car pulled away.

"Bob, this is Colonel Garcia and Captain Mendez. They're handling the security for his Excellency. They were able to join us. You had some questions you wanted to ask them," Brown said.

"Yes, what specific information do you have that this subject presents a danger to his Excellency?" Bob asked.

"The subject is a mortal enemy of our nation," Colonel Garcia declared. "We have received information that the subject would like to see his Excellency deposed by any means necessary. He is dangerous and presents a grave threat to his Excellency."

"Colonel, do you have any particulars as to a plot, other conspirators, and the like? How reliable is the information?"

"Our sources are good. We know that the subject is somewhere in the United States. He would be acting alone. If he gets a chance, he would kill his Excellency."

"Colonel, we'll check this man out and take all appropriate action to ensure his Excellency's safety," Bob assured.

The colonel then looked Bob in the eye and said in the tone of a command, "We need to know where this man is living and see any other information you have on him."

"Colonel, there are national security and privacy regulations I have to follow. I promise we'll look into this very closely, and I'll *personally* advise you of the outcome," Bob affirmed.

Suddenly, Brown reached over his seat into the rear of the vehicle and snatched the subject's file out of Bob's hands. The file jacket had a red-letter "SECRET" cover sheet stapled to the front of the file folder. This denoted that the file contained documents up to the secret level. Inside the folder, pages containing classified information were marked at the top and bottom with the appropriate security classification. These pages also had the intelligence control marking "NOFORN."

Brown looked at the file for several minutes. Then in a move that shocked Bob, Brown handed the file folder to Colonel Garcia. "Frank, there's classified intelligence information in there," Bob warned.

"It's all right, Bob. Colonel Garcia has a need to know," Brown replied.

"Frank, the file's checked out to me. There's information that's *not* for foreign dissemination."

Bob started to reach for the file to retrieve it. Brown grabbed Bob's arm and angrily said: "The colonel can look at the file. I'll take the responsibility. That's an order!"

For the next five minutes, Bob sat in disbelief as the colonel spoke in Spanish to his aide, who made entries in a pocket notebook. Finally, the vehicle arrived back at the hotel where the officers were staying. When the colonel was finished perusing the file, he returned it to Brown. The officers then said their goodbyes and exited the vehicle.

Brown handed the classified intelligence file back to Bob. "Ritter, don't *ever* challenge my authority again," Brown admonished. "When we travel overseas, we depend on the cooperation of the host country. We rely on their security services. We would want them to do the same thing I did."

"Frank, I had a duty to protect the classified information in this file. With the "NOFORN" marking, it's not to be disseminated to foreign nationals, even those *with* the proper U.S. clearance and a need to know. Only the originating intelligence agency has the authority to make those determinations," Bob said in his defense.

Brown frowned at Bob and waved a hand as if to summarily dismiss Bob's concerns. No more words were spoken on the way to WFO where Bob was dropped off.

At his desk, Bob typed a "Memorandum for the Record." Bob recounted the incident and recommended that the agencies that had compiled and classified the information be notified of the unauthorized disclosure. Bob reasoned that they would want to assess the harm done, if any. Bob was just finishing the memo when the intercom rang. "Agent Ritter," called the voice from the speaker.

"Yes," Bob answered.

"This is ASAIC Gallagher. Come down to my office—now!" Bob took off like a rocket to the northeast corner of WFO and the ASAIC's office, passing other agents as if they weren't even there. It was the fastest he had ever moved through the hallways. Reaching his destination, Bob tapped lightly on the open door. "Come in and close the door behind you," Gallagher barked. Closing the door softly, Bob maneuvered to a position in front of Gallagher's desk.

Gallagher gave Bob a cold and angry stare. "I just got off the phone with Frank Brown," Gallagher began. "He said you were insubordinate with him. He wants you off the advance team. What do you have to say for yourself?"

"Sir, I wasn't *insubordinate*. I was only trying to prevent the release of national security information."

"That's what this is about?" Gallagher uttered.

"Yes, Brown asked me to check out an individual's file from ID. A security officer from the visiting country claimed the subject was a threat. Brown wanted to review it. The file was classified "SECRET" and had a "NOFORN" handling control. Over my protest, Brown handed the file to two foreign security officers. Now they know where the subject lives, who his associates are, and that he's passed information to U.S. intelligence agencies, and the like. This guy is a political enemy of the regime in power; he could end up in an alley with a bullet in his head.

"Plus, sensitive intelligence methods and sources might have been compromised. I had a responsibility to protect the classified information. I'm finishing a memorandum now to apprise ID of the unauthorized disclosure."

Gallagher bristled: "You'll do nothing of the kind! Put that memo in a burn bag and don't mention this to *anyone*. Take the file back to ID like nothing happened. You'll stay on the assignment. I'll handle things with Brown."

"Sir, there was a disclosure of national security information. I have a duty to report it."

"Ritter, what are you going to do when I transfer you to New York." Gallagher stated authoritatively.

Bob understood the meaning of the rhetorical question. Although Gallagher had never been assigned to the New York Field Office, he was always telling agents how much tougher it was than WFO. Gallagher liked to threaten agents who didn't toe the line with a transfer to New York.

"I can't believe this is happening," Bob remarked with exasperation.

"I'll say this one more time. Listen *carefully*. Take the file back to ID and forget this ever happened. Keep your mouth shut or else," Gallagher warned. "Remember, a supervisor may not always be right, but he's *always* the supervisor."

"Yes, sir," Bob acknowledged.

That evening at home, Bob was still in shock and disbelief as to the day's events. "He threatened you with a transfer to New York," I remarked.

"Yes, threats are one of his management tools."

"Bobbie, don't let it get you down," I expressed in sympathy. "It wasn't your fault. You didn't do anything wrong."

"But I did," Bob said. "I should have stood my ground and taken back the file in spite of what Brown said."

"Bobbie, you were just following orders. Please don't worry about it."

"Yeah, but I know better. Jan, there's a saying in the Secret Service: 'He thinks this is for real.' It's said as a putdown of those agents who some think take things too seriously. The truth is; it is for real. Secret police from banana republics play for keeps."

Bob worked the dignitary's visit and acted as if nothing had happened. Although Frank Brown was not pleased with Bob's presence, Brown made no mention of the file controversy. The special officer who had been present during the file incident drove the USSS armored limo during the visit. He was retired military. The SO took Bob aside during a private moment. "You did the right thing the other day," the SO told Bob. "Frank shouldn't have let them see the file. He likes to curry favor with people."

The subject who had caused all the concern could not be located by the Secret Service for an interview. As a precautionary measure, Bob had photos of the subject reproduced and distributed to detail agents. The subject was made a *lookout*. In spite of the earlier dire warnings, the foreign dignitary's visit concluded without any problems. There were no protective incidents.

The summer of '77 is remembered in New York for an apocalyptic-like event that took place in the city amid a sweltering heat wave. On the evening of July 13, 1977, a series of lightning strikes and power company missteps plunged the five boroughs of New York into total darkness. The power blackout would last up to 25 hours in some areas. Airports, subways, and tunnels were closed. Looting and arson became widespread. Over 2,000 stores were ravaged. Especially hard hit were the Bronx, Queens, and Brooklyn. Even Manhattan was the scene of looting. Over 1,000 fires burned—resulting in the deaths of three civilians. The cost of the shutdown totaled in the hundreds of millions of dollars counting lost revenue, property damage, theft, and overtime to firefighters and police. More than 3,000 arrests were made.

The blackout came at a bad time. The city was already panic-stricken. New Yorkers were in deadly fear of a serial killer. The press first dubbed the murderer "The .44-Caliber Killer" referring to the .44-caliber pistol used in the attacks. In May 1977, the killer became known as the "Son of Sam" after he sent *New York Daily News* columnist Jimmy Breslin a macabre letter that was signed "Son of Sam."

The terror wave began in July 1976 when 18-year-old Donna Lauria was shot and killed outside her home in the Bronx. She had been driven home by a girlfriend, 19-year-old Judy Valenti. The two were chatting in the car when a white male approached the vehicle and opened fire without warning. Valenti was wounded in the thigh during the assault.

Over the next 11 months, the killer calling himself Son of Sam struck six more times. Four would die in the attacks, while five were wounded, some seriously. Son of Sam targeted young females, most often teenagers with long brown hair. In mortal terror, tens of thousands of young women had their hair cut short and dyed blond or resorted to wigs.

In the early morning hours of July 31, 1977, Son of Sam struck for an eighth time. The horror continued. Parked along a Brooklyn lover's lane, a young couple embraced and kissed. Suddenly, a white male walked up to the car and fired several shots before disappearing into the darkness. Twenty-year-old Robert Violante was shot twice in the face; his date, 20-year-old Stacy Moscowitz, received a fatal head wound. Moscowitz died 38 hours later—becoming Son of Sam's sixth murder victim. Robert Violante survived but lost an eye.

The NYPD caught a break in the Moscowitz-Violante crime. Detective James Justus was checking out parking tickets that were issued in the area on the night of the murder, hoping to gain a lead. One of the ticketed car owners was identified as David Berkowitz of Yonkers, New York. Justus called Yonkers Police for help in contacting Berkowitz. As luck would have it, Dispatcher Wheat Carr took the call. She was the daughter of *Sam* Carr. The Carr family was suspicious of Berkowitz, who happened to live in their neighborhood. They believed Berkowitz had sent them threatening letters and had shot their dog.

Miss Carr put Justus in touch with a Yonkers police officer who had more information concerning Berkowitz's alleged bizarre behavior. Officer Thomas Chamberlain told Justus that Berkowitz was a suspect in another dog shooting, other threatening letters, and in several arson cases. The two policemen compared notes. The letters believed to be written by Berkowitz were similar to those written by Son of Sam. It was thought that the *Sam* in "Son of Sam" might be Berkowitz's delusional reference to Sam Carr.

The next day, August 10, police converged outside of Berkowitz's Yonkers apartment building. A visual check of Berkowitz's car revealed what appeared to be a submachine gun in plain view (it was later determined to be a semiautomatic rifle). The officers then searched the vehicle and seized the weapon along with ammunition, an incriminating letter threatening further murders, and maps of the crime areas.

For the arrest, police decided it would be safer to wait until Berkowitz, a 24-year-old postal clerk, departed his residence. At about 10:00 p.m. that evening, Berkowitz emerged carrying a paper bag. He was taken into custody without incident. The paper bag contained a Charter Arms .44-caliber Bulldog revolver. Subsequent ballistics testing indicated that Berkowitz's revolver was the one used in the Son of Sam crimes.

Under police questioning, Berkowitz admitted to the Son of Sam murders. Other evidence against Berkowitz included finger and palm prints found on the Son of Sam letters and at crime scenes. Furthermore, there were witness identifications.

David Berkowitz was found competent to stand trial. He pled guilty to six counts of murder along with multiple counts of attempted murder and assault. Berkowitz received the maximum sentence of 25 years to life for each of the murders and shorter sentences for the lesser charges. He is incarcerated at the Sullivan Correctional Facility in Fallsburg, New York.

Six days after Berkowitz's arrest for the .44-caliber killings, the world of entertainment suffered a tragic loss. On the afternoon of August 16, 1977, Elvis Presley, "The King of Rock 'n' Roll," was found unconscious on the bathroom floor of his Graceland Mansion located in Memphis, Tennessee. Presley was transported to Baptist Memorial Hospital. Attempts to resuscitate him failed. He was pronounced dead at 3:30 p.m. Elvis Presley was only 42 years old; the world mourned his loss.

Shelby County Medical Examiner Dr. Jerry Francisco ruled Elvis's death was of "natural causes" and that no foul play was evident. At the request of the Presley family, Francisco performed an autopsy on Elvis's body. Preliminary findings listed the cause of death as "cardiac arrhythmia," an irregular heartbeat that resulted in a heart attack. Later, Presley's cause of death was specifically attributed to "hypertensive heart disease with coronary heart disease as a contributing factor."

President Jimmy Carter released the following statement regarding Presley: "Elvis Presley's death deprives our country of a part of itself. He was unique and irreplaceable. More than 20 years ago, he burst upon the scene with an impact that was unprecedented and will probably never be equaled. His music and his personality, fusing the styles of white country and black rhythm and blues, permanently changed the face of American popular culture. His following was immense, and he was a symbol to people the world over of the vitality, rebelliousness, and good humor of his country."

Late August 1977 found the Washington Field Office along with the Dignitary Protective Division busy with the security advance arrangements for the upcoming signing of the Torrijos-Carter treaties. The treaties between Panama and the U.S. were a culmination of 13 years of diplomatic negotiations regarding long-standing issues involving the Panama Canal.

The first attempt at building a canal to link the Atlantic and Pacific Oceans occurred from 1880–1893. A French company excavated land on the Isthmus of Panama, which was then a province of Columbia. The project was abandoned due to engineering difficulties and widespread disease (malaria and yellow fever), which killed thousands of workers.

With eyes on having its own canal, the United States backed a revolution in which Panama won its independence in November 1903. In the 1903 Hay-Bunau Treaty with the new nation of Panama, the U.S. received the right to build a canal across the Isthmus of Panama and to control a 10-mile-wide Canal Zone in *perpetuity.*

After purchasing the excavations and equipment of the old French company, the U.S. started construction on a canal that eventually featured a system of dams and locks, whereas the French had tried to build a sea level waterway. After years of grueling work and an investment of hundreds of millions of dollars, the canal was completed and officially opened in August 1914. It is often called "The Eighth Wonder of the World."

Through the decades, Panama grew to resent the U.S. presence. Panama wanted more say in the administration of its own territory. Panama also believed that it wasn't getting its fair share of canal revenues. Relations between the two nations worsened in the 1960s, heightened by the anti-American sentiment that spread through Latin America.

In January 1964, riots broke out along the border of the Canal Zone. The hostilities were sparked by Panamanian demonstrators who attempted to fly their nation's flag within the Canal Zone. During the action, the Panamanian flag was torn. Agitators seized upon the incident to ignite several days of rioting. Four U.S. soldiers and over 20 Panamanians were killed. Hundreds were wounded.

The government of Panama charged the U.S. with aggression. Panama severed diplomatic relations with the United States and appealed to the Organization of American States (OAS). In April 1964, the U.S. and Panama agreed to an OAS resolution whereby the two nations would settle their differences by negotiation. Diplomatic relations were restored, but progress toward a settlement of the issues was elusive. Ultimately, both sides agreed that a new treaty was in order.

The Johnson, Nixon, and Ford administrations took part in treaty negotiations with Panama with little success. Disagreements on a number of key points prevented a resolution of the matter. The major stumbling blocks involved matters of Panamanian sovereignty and the right of the U.S. to defend the canal.

President Carter made the negotiation of new accords a top priority. Beginning in February 1977, American and Panamanian officials met in Washington and talks proceeded in earnest. By mid August, major compromises had been reached, and it was announced that both sides had come to terms regarding two newly proposed treaties.

Under the terms of the first, the "Panama Canal Treaty," the 1903 treaty and other prior agreements would be nullified. The Canal Zone would cease to exist; Panama's territorial sovereignty was recognized. The U.S. was granted rights to operate and manage the canal under a new commission comprised of five American directors and four Panamanian directors. An American would serve as the canal's administrator through December 31, 1990. After that time, a Panamanian would be the administrator.

Panamanians would be trained to assume canal duties and the American workforce would be reduced. The treaty set forth procedures for the gradual handing over of the canal to Panama by December 31, 1999, the date of the treaty's expiration. Panama was guaranteed at least $10 million a year in revenues during the transition to complete Panamanian control.

The U.S. Army retained the primary responsibility for the defense of the canal during the life of the treaty with the Panamanian military contributing to joint planning, training, and tactical operations as needed. By the treaty's end date, all American military personnel were to be removed from Panama, and all U.S. military bases turned over to the Panamanian Defense Forces.

A 30-month transition period was established whereby American nationals would come under the legal jurisdiction of Panamanian authorities. Panama would assume the responsibility for police, fire, courts, prisons, postal, and other civilian services within the old Canal Zone.

The second agreement: "Treaty Concerning the Permanent Neutrality and Operation of the Panama Canal," declared, "The canal, as an international transit waterway, shall be permanently neutral. ..." Vessels of all nations whether in war or peace would be treated on terms of equality. Due to the special relationship between the U.S. and Panama, vessels of both nations were entitled to travel the canal "expeditiously." In addition, the U.S. was given the right along with Panama to maintain the canal's neutrality.

Like the "Panama Canal Treaty," the neutrality treaty would take effect six months after both nations exchanged ratification documents. The neutrality treaty, however, was open-ended. Therefore, the U.S.—although all of its military forces would have to vacate Panama by December 31, 1999—would still have the right to insure the neutrality of the Panama Canal into the future.

The signing of the treaties by President Carter and Panamanian chief of government General Omar Torrijos was scheduled for September 7. The ceremony would take place at the Headquarters of the Organization of American States (17th Street at Constitution Avenue, NW). Also known as the Pan American Union (building), the structure opened in 1910. President William Howard Taft spoke at the dedication ceremony.

While predominantly Spanish colonial in design, the building reflects the architectural and cultural influences of the Americas. A facade of marble with three arched entry gates made of bronze highlights the exterior of this monumental building, one of the most beautiful in Washington. Inside the spacious courtyard, a sliding, glass roof insures that tropical vegetation flourishes year-round. A centerpiece pink-marble fountain and red-tile floor adorn the indoor garden. The first floor of the building also houses the Simón Bolivar Room where the Permanent Council of the OAS meets. Here, representatives from member nations discuss matters of regional importance.

Marble stairways lead to the second floor and the historical Hall of Flags and Heroes. National flags of all OAS member states are proudly displayed along with the busts of legendary heroes such as George Washington, Simón Bolivar, and José de San Martin. From the hallway, one gains entry to the magnificent Hall of the Americas through five pairs of stately glass-paneled doors. The room features a 45-foot-high vaulted ceiling supported by massive columns. Tiffany-designed crystal chandeliers add to its majesty.

Within the Hall of the Americas, General Torrijos and President Carter would formally sign the treaties in an internationally televised event. Witnessing the ceremony would be the heads of state or government of 26 other Western Hemisphere nations along with their delegations. First Lady Rosalynn Carter, former President Gerald Ford, and the widow of LBJ, Lady Bird Johnson, would also attend.

The security arrangements for 27 simultaneous state visits along with those of the president and other protectees were staggering. Not since President Kennedy's state funeral in 1963 had Washington seen so many foreign leaders at one time. While the State Department was responsible for protocol and the security of lesser dignitaries, the USSS had to provide protective details for 27 foreign heads of government/state.

Bob was tasked with the intelligence coordination for all 27 visits as well as the events pertaining to the treaty signing. Bob was also assigned to cover all movements of General Torrijos during his visit to Washington. In preparation, Bob spent an entire day at the Intelligence Division reviewing the files pertinent to all 27 protectees. He spent hours checking with the FBI, State Department, CIA, and police in New York and Miami—and hours more attending advance meetings and in other preparations. For the days leading up to the visits until their conclusion, Bob was like a ghost. I saw signs that he had been home, but I never caught sight of more than an apparition in the darkness of late night or early morning shadows.

Bob was concerned about the demonstrations that were being planned to coincide with treaty events. There was always the chance agitators could provoke violence. Some groups prepared to protest the signing of the treaties—charging that America should not give away the canal. Others planned to protest human rights violations within Latin America.

More worrisome was the potential for bombings. The presence of so large a number of Latin-American leaders coupled with the worldwide attention the Panama Canal treaties were receiving set the stage for such activity. Within the past several years, a number of anti-Castro Cuban exile groups had joined under umbrella organizations. They were in a continuing revolutionary struggle with Castro and anyone who supported diplomatic relations with the Marxist regime. A number of bombings and other violent incidents had taken place.

In fact, one bomb had gone off inside the OAS building in November 1974. At the time, the OAS was meeting in Quito, Ecuador to discuss the organization's economic embargo against Cuba. The device exploded in a phone booth located on the second floor of the building, outside the Hall of the Americas. The blast caused over $100,000 in damages to the building including a hole blown through the roof. Luckily, no one was hurt.

In May 1975, the Permanent Council of the OAS was meeting in Washington. Mexico and several other countries were proposing a resolution that would lift the OAS sanctions imposed on Cuba in 1964. During the session, bombs exploded outside the business office of the Soviet airline Aeroflot (16th and K Streets, NW) and at the Mexican Chancery (2829 16th Street, NW). Both devices were small and damage was minimal.

Another incident occurred in D.C. about two months later in July 1975. The Costa Rican ambassador was leaving the embassy offices (2112 S Street, NW) for the day. As he walked toward the street, a bomb exploded about three feet away. It was a small charge that resulted in nothing more than noise and smoke. The purpose of the device was more likely to intimidate and to warn; the ambassador was not harmed.

The ministers of foreign affairs for OAS member nations were meeting in Costa Rica. Although OAS sanctions were not lifted against Cuba, a resolution was passed that allowed members "to normalize or conduct their relations with the Republic of Cuba at the level and in the manner that each State deems advisable, in accordance with each one's national policy and interests."

A thorough review of the past and present led Bob to believe that at least one bomb and possibly several would be detonated in Washington during the week of the treaty activities. This assessment was based on the history of certain anti-Castro Cuban exile organizations. Bob did not think they would pass up the opportunity that was being presented them. Thus, Bob's intelligence situation report warned of demonstrations, bomb threats, and bombings with the prediction it was "more likely than not that one or more bombs would be detonated in D.C. during treaty week."

Bob explained that on U.S. territory, the usual modus operandi of these groups was to explode a bomb late at night or in the early morning hours. Sites were targeted for the purpose of sending a powerful protest message and warning, while times of detonation were chosen to reduce the risk to innocent bystanders.

Bob noted that the embassies of OAS nations that have diplomatic relations with Cuba were of primary risk. Another potential target was the Cuban Interests Section, which had recently opened in the former Cuban Embassy building at 2630 16th Street, NW. In May 1977, the U.S. under the Carter administration had agreed to exchange "interests sections" with Cuba. While not a restoration of diplomatic relations, the interests sections would conduct consular matters. Diplomatic relations with Cuba were severed in 1961.

Of course, the OAS building, embassies of OAS members, and the Cuban Interests Section would be well protected during the treaty signing. And the Embassy of the Soviet Union, the nation that provided the most support to Cuba, was always well protected by the Executive Protective Service and under the surveillance of the FBI. Thus, Bob reasoned that terrorists were more likely to select safer targets—as happened in May 1975 when a bomb exploded outside the Aeroflot business office.

After Bob's situation report was received at USSS Headquarters, an intelligence research specialist (IRS) from the Foreign Intelligence Branch called Bob. "What *hard* information do you have that bombs are going to be exploded in D.C. during treaty week?" she asked. "We didn't get anything about that from the FBI." Bob explained his rationale—as stated in the report—was based primarily on past activity. "So your assessment is purely *speculative*," she said.

"I'd describe it as a credible prediction based on well-reasoned analysis," Bob replied.

General Omar Torrijos arrived at Andrews Air Force Base on the evening of Monday, September 5. He was welcomed by Secretary of State, Cyrus R. Vance. General Torrijos and his family were transported by USSS motorcade to the Jackson Place residence of the Blair House complex where they would be the guests of President Carter. Later that evening, Bob gave a personal intelligence briefing to Torrijos's chief security aide, Lieutenant Colonel Manuel Noriega.

Twenty-six other heads of government/state and their delegations arrived in Washington on that Monday and Tuesday. Numerous motorcades crisscrossed the Embassy Row and downtown areas. Sirens wailed and emergency lights flashed in motorized movements choreographed by protocol and security. Washingtonians and tourists alike gazed at flag-bedecked limos—hoping to catch a glimpse of the international elite.

The official events of Panamanian treaty week began Tuesday evening at the Pan American Union building with a formal reception hosted by OAS Secretary-General Alejandro Orfila and his wife, Helga. About 1,500 guests attended. First Lady Rosalynn Carter represented the White House. President Carter spent the day in the Oval Office meeting bilaterally with a number of Latin American leaders.

During the early morning hours of Wednesday, September 7, Bob and I were awakened by a phone call from the WFO duty agent. Two bombs had exploded in D.C. One high-explosive device detonated at about 2:40 a.m. in a driveway behind the offices of the Soviet airline Aeroflot. No one was injured, but the shock wave of the blast sucked out dozens of windows in nearby buildings, including the Capital Hilton Hotel and the Washington Post Building.

The other device exploded at about 3:00 a.m. on the northeast side of the Ellipse, near the Executive Office Building (EOB) and the White House. Although the blast was heard in the darkness, it took police some time to find the actual site of the bombing and to make sure no other bombs had been planted. It was eventually discovered that the bomb had exploded in a large concrete flowerpot that borders the Ellipse near E Street. The device caused property damage only; however, the blast would have been fatal to anyone standing within 20 feet of the explosion.

Anti-Castro Cuban exile groups took credit for the bombings. The first call came into the Washington Bureau of United Press International (UPI) at about 2:55 a.m. The caller claimed to be a member of the Pedro Luis Boitel Commandos (named after a student who died in a Havana prison in 1972). The caller stated they had just bombed Aeroflot and warned of bombs set near the White House. The subject condemned the Soviet Union for its support of Cuba.

The second call came into UPI's Miami Bureau at about 6:00 a.m. (when the office opened for the day). The caller claimed the Washington bombing was the work of the Cuban commando El Condor. The subject stated the bombing was in retaliation for giving away the Panama Canal to communists.

At daybreak, Bob responded to both crime scenes to observe the damage first hand and to gather the particulars. While he was at the site of the Ellipse blast, John Simpson, USSS Deputy Assistant Director (DAD) Office of Protective Operations (PO), arrived on the scene. Bob was on a first-name basis with the DAD. Simpson had previously served as the SAIC of the Dignitary Protective Division. Bob had provided intelligence support for many of the foreign dignitary details headed by Simpson. DAD Simpson was a native of the Dorchester section of Boston, Massachusetts; his first USSS assignment was to the Boston Field Office. With a syrupy New England accent, Simpson bestowed the title of "Brother" to those who had served under him.

"Brother Ritter," Simpson called out, "why here?"

"With the present level of security, this is about as close as you can get to both the OAS building and the White House without being detected," Bob answered. "To the perpetrators, this is a commando operation. An action here targets *both* the OAS and the U.S. The Cuban-exile groups aren't happy about our exchange of interests sections with Cuba and our plans to turn over the canal to Panama. They're also not happy with any of the nations that have relations with Castro Cuba, especially those within Latin America."

Bob noticed that Simpson looked worried. "John, cheer up. This is what we expected," Bob continued. "Fortunately, no one was injured by either blast. They've made their statement and gotten their headlines. We probably won't hear any more from them this week."

Simpson looked a bit surprised. "John, did you get a copy of my situation report on 'treaty week'?" Bob asked.

"Yes, I read it," Simpson replied. "But I didn't believe it!"

Later that day at the Kennedy Center, a noon luncheon was hosted by the Council of the Americas for visiting heads of government/state. It served as a prelude to the pre-signing reception that would be held at OAS

Headquarters that evening. About 20 demonstrators marched outside the Kennedy Center representing groups opposed to Latin American political oppression.

As the afternoon unfolded, groups targeting Latin American right-wing dictators also demonstrated across from the OAS on the Ellipse, on the White House sidewalk, and in Lafayette Park. At times, smaller groups of protestors marched to and from the Capitol.

About 1,500 protestors massed on the Ellipse. Park Police and MPD officers kept the crowd safely in check. EPS officers manned posts in front of the OAS building. Seventeenth Street was closed to all but official traffic.

At the White House sidewalk, about 500 people protested in conjunction with several hundred in Lafayette Park. Isabel Letelier—the widow of Chilean exile Orlando Letelier—spoke at the Lafayette Park rally, which was organized by the Coalition Against Repression in the Americas. Orlando Letelier was assassinated on the streets of Washington, D.C. on September 21, 1976. A former ambassador to the U.S., Letelier later held key Cabinet positions in the Chilean government of socialist Salvador Allende.

After the Chilean military coup of 1973, which deposed Allende and brought General Augusto Pinochet to power, Letelier was imprisoned. He was released in 1974 and exiled from Chile. Given political asylum in the U.S., Letelier became a fellow at the Institute for Policy Studies—an international relations think tank headquartered in D.C. Letelier accused the Pinochet military junta of human rights violations and lobbied foreign nations and companies to withhold investment capital from Chile.

Orlando Letelier was killed on his way to work as he drove his car around Sheridan Circle along Washington's Embassy Row. A bomb attached to the undercarriage of Letelier's Chevrolet Chevelle was detonated by remote control. The device exploded with enough force to lift the vehicle off the pavement and into a parked car. A colleague of Letelier, 25-year-old Ronni Moffitt, was also killed in the blast. The FBI suspected that an agent of the Chilean secret police (DINA) had carried out the assassination with the help of several Cuban exiles.

Other rallies that day focused on the canal treaty. Conservative groups protesting the turnover of the canal held a rally on the east side of the U.S. Capitol. Speakers included U.S. Congressmen Robert Dornan (Republican-California) and Larry McDonald (Democrat-Georgia). Using strong language, they called for the repudiation of the treaties.

Throughout the day, bomb threats were called in against a score of downtown buildings including several hotels and the Washington Monument. Due to the alleged threat, the Monument closed down at 5:00 p.m. and did not reopen for the reminder of the day. Police searches at all sites turned up no explosive devices.

Finally at 7:30 p.m., Wednesday, September 7, President Carter and General Torrijos met in the Hall of the Americas and signed the Spanish and English texts of the two canal treaties in front of the leaders of the Western Hemisphere.

Afterwards, a White House dinner was hosted by the President and Mrs. Carter for the 27 heads of state or government. The remaining dignitaries attended a dinner given at the Department of State by Secretary Vance. After dining on Maine Lobster en Bellevue or Roast Saddle of Veal, White House guests were entertained by opera star Martina Arroyo, violinist Isaac Stern, and pianist Andre Previn.

The following day, Mrs. Carter hosted a luncheon cruise for the wives of Latin American dignitaries aboard the Wilson Lines 103-foot-long catamaran *America*. Also invited were wives of key U.S. senators whose support would be needed for the ratification of the Panama Canal treaties.

The ship was decked out in red and pink geraniums accented by laurel leaves of green. Entertainment was provided by the Marine Corps Dixieland Band and the Sea Chanters of the U.S. Navy. Maryland Crab Supreme and Roast Rack of Lamb were the entrees.

Bob and his buddy Dick Corrigan worked PI as the first lady and her guests arrived at Pier 4 (6th and Water Streets, SW, D.C.). As the *America* departed for its cruise down the Potomac, Bob and Dick leapfrogged to the vessel's destination, Mount Vernon. After being welcomed by the music and marching routines of a fife and drum corps, the first lady and her party were given an exclusive tour of Washington's estate. When the afternoon was over, the first lady returned to the White House by USSS motorcade, while guests traveled back to Washington via private auto.

Treaty week was coming to an end. Dignitaries departed the U.S. for their home countries. General Omar Torrijos met with the Senate Foreign Relations committee before returning to Panama; supporters of the treaties faced strong opposition. The agents of the Washington Field Office returned to their standard hectic pace.

Bob was catching up on his paperwork when he received a phone call from senior Agent Tom Barry (GS-13), who had been reassigned from WFO to the Office of Public Affairs. Tom and Bob had shared a two-man office in the PI Squad. Barry was impressed with Bob's knowledge of American history and especially his expertise regarding the recorded past of the Secret Service. Bob had read every book written about the Service multiple times.

Tom invited Bob to stop by Public Affairs. Agent Barry showed Bob file cabinets crammed with documents and memorabilia. Bob pulled out one file folder that bore the notation: "Buffalo 1901." Inside, Bob discovered a handwritten letter authored by Secret Service Operative George Foster. The correspondence had been penned on hotel stationery and was addressed to Secret Service Chief John E. Wilkie. Operative Foster was with President

William McKinley in Buffalo, New York on September 6, 1901, when the president was assassinated by anarchist Leon Czolgosz. The report detailed the assassination and its aftermath. Bob's fingers tingled as he held the pages in his hands. He felt the pain that Foster must have felt as he recounted the tragedy to Chief Wilkie. Bob was touching history, and it moved him greatly.

"Some stuff, huh?" Barry said. "We've got tons of it around here."

"Yeah, this is unbelievable—priceless, one-of-a-kind original source documents, the history of the Service, right here in these file cabinets. I could look through these for hours," Bob expressed with zeal.

"Funny you should mention that," Barry said. "I know how history excites you and how neat and organized you are. Jack (Assistant to the Director (ATD) for Public Affairs Jack Warner) wants someone to go through everything we have here at Public Affairs. It needs to be reviewed, categorized, organized, and protected. Some of it should probably be sent to the National Archives for safekeeping. The rest would need to be properly stored and readily available for use in answering the inquiries we get and for review by authors and journalists. Right now, it's tough to find anything, and the documents and other items are not properly conserved."

"Yes, the documents should be in protective sleeves," Bob concurred.

"None of us here want to do it," Barry related. "There's been some talk about creating a new position. But we'd have to hire through personnel and all that red tape. We've been thinking about bringing in someone already on board for the project. I immediately thought of you. The assignment would be for no more than a year; then you'd be rotated back to the field or a protective assignment. This *wouldn't* be a promotional opportunity to a 13," Barry emphasized.

"Tom, I understand. I'd love to do this. Some of the irreplaceable items should be transferred to the National Archives. VIB [Visual Information Branch] could make copies to keep here for reference. I'd devise an agent-friendly filing system that would speed the retrieval of information. I have some other ideas too."

"I knew I had the right man," Barry sighed in relief. "I sure don't want to do it." Tom Barry introduced Bob around the office including a brief visit with ATD Warner. Everyone seemed enthused, as they now had a willing answer to a long-standing Public Affairs problem.

Bob arrived home that night with a smile on his face and enthusiasm in his voice. He told me about the opportunity, and I was ecstatic. I anticipated that Bob would be able to keep more regular hours in the new assignment. Bob projected how he would also like to send out questionnaires to selected former agents and even tape record some of those who remained in the Washington area. Bob wanted to gain valuable insight and firsthand accounts from those who had gone before. He was always thinking of ways to improve things.

The next afternoon, Bob was called down to ASAIC Gallagher's office. Gallagher had a deep frown on his face. This can't be good, thought Bob. "Ritter, ATD Warner from Public Affairs called. He wanted you reassigned there. I told him no. You don't merit a position like that. You haven't put in the time to earn it; you don't deserve the transfer."

"Sir, I have the educational background and love of history to do the job that needs to be done. This is a special assignment to catalog, organize, and preserve their holdings. It's not a Public Affairs general agent position. It's for a limited time, and there's no promotional opportunity."

"No, too many other agents are more deserving; my decision is final."

"Yes, sir," Bob said as his heart filled with despair. Bob did an about-face and headed back to his office. Bob felt like a kid on a merry-go-round who had the brass ring in hand. Then inexplicably, the ring slipped away. And there was nothing he could do about it. Unfortunately, the worst was yet to come.

About 10 minutes later, Bob received a call from Tom Barry. "Bob, I just heard that Gallagher doesn't want to release you from WFO."

"Gallagher already gave me the bad news, Tom."

"I'm going to call Gallagher and try to reason with him. He has the wrong idea about this. Don't give up yet," Barry said. "I'll be in touch." This breathed new life into Bob's hopes. Barry had known Gallagher for some years. Tom had as good as chance of anyone in turning things around.

A short time later Bob anxiously picked up the receiver to take Tom's call back. "I think I might have made things worse," Barry began. "Gallagher is dead set on keeping you at WFO. While we were talking, I mentioned that you had been over here, and I think he got the wrong idea. He became pretty angry. I tried to reason with him."

"Tom, don't worry about it. I appreciate you trying to get me to Public Affairs," Bob said in gratitude.

"Bob, I'm sorry. We sure could have used you." Bob could feel the frustration in Tom's voice. It was matched by the deep disappointment Bob felt.

Moments later, Bob was again called down to the ASAIC's office. This time Gallagher was visibly upset. "Ritter, what are you doing hanging out at Public Affairs?" Gallagher asked in an accusatory tone.

"Sir, I don't hang out at Public Affairs. Tom Barry and I use to share an office in the PI Squad. Tom knew that my minor in college was American history. He also knows that an interest of mine is the history of the Secret Service.

"Tom invited me to visit him at PA. Several days ago, I dropped by on my *lunch break*. He told me they need someone to categorize, organize, and preserve their material. Nobody at PA wants to do it. Tom thought of me as someone who would be able and willing to do the job. He recommended me to ATD Warner."

"I'm not convinced that you haven't been hanging out at headquarters to ingratiate yourself," Gallagher stated. "From now on, Public Affairs is off-limits to you. In fact, I don't want you anywhere at headquarters unless you have official business. If I hear you're over there socializing, I'll fire you!" Gallagher angrily warned.

That evening at home, Bob was about as low as I've ever seen him. He was absolutely in despair. Bob was angry that the Secret Service would place someone like Gallagher in such a critical position. Gallagher jumped to conclusions and seemed to believe the worst about people. Bob joined the growing list of those whom Gallagher marked for special attention.

Chapter 26

Off Track

Fall 1977 found Bob preparing for the state visit of Shah Mohammad Reza Pahlavi (The Shah of Iran) to Washington. Bob's responsibility was to monitor the demonstrations that were being planned to coincide with the shah's visit. The shah and his wife, Farah Pahlavi (The Shahbanou of Iran), would visit Washington in mid-November.

Groups both in support of and in opposition to the shah had received demonstration permits. Pro-shah groups included those backed by U.S.-Iranian businessmen, the Armenian and Assyrian ethnic communities, and Iranian military personnel who were training in the United States.

About a thousand Iranians were receiving military instruction in the States under a U.S.-Iranian aid agreement. A large number of the trainees would be coming to Washington to welcome the shah, who had not visited the U.S. since May of 1975.

The Armenian and Assyrian cultural groups were actively supporting the shah's visit due to a recent policy change within Iran that liberalized the use of the Assyrian language. Additionally, the shah permitted the Armenian and Assyrian minorities to practice Christianity in Iran, a predominantly Moslem nation.

Bob closely watched the intelligence that was being developed by the FBI regarding the scheduled demonstrations. It was the first time that pro-shah demonstrations had been organized. In previous visits of the shah, only anti-forces (mainly Iranian students) had rallied. There was always the concern that violence could break out, especially if opposing groups come in contact with each other.

Bob was the USSS-WFO representative to the intelligence planning meetings held for the shah's visit by the region's Council of Governments. Bill Thomas was one of the FBI agents attending the sessions. The Metropolitan Police Department was represented by officials from the Special Operations Division. An intelligence analyst attended for the State Department. The Department of the Interior was represented by a ranger from the National Park Service, which had issued the demonstration permits for the shah's visit. This ranger represented the National Park Service's National Capital Parks as well as the U.S. Park Police.

As the shah's visit approached, the FBI received hard intelligence that members of an anti-shah group were intending to disrupt the activities. An informant revealed that a large number of militants planned to attack supporters of the shah. The assault would occur on the Ellipse and coincide with the official White House arrival ceremony welcoming the shah. In the action, anti-shah protestors would use the sticks attached to their signs as improvised clubs. According to the source, the militants were also told to carry beverages in glass bottles that could later be used as missiles.

Although it was the first time this confidential informant (CI) had been used by the FBI, the information was deemed credible. The FBI corroborated that the CI had in fact attended the meeting where it was alleged that the strategy had been discussed. It was also verified that the group had purchased supplies of lumber.

In COG meetings regarding the upcoming demonstrations, the FBI warned that a violent confrontation could occur. Although the information was not sufficient enough to justify canceling the permit of the protesting group, it was made clear that law enforcement needed to use enough resources to deter the assault and any other violent behavior that might erupt during the shah's visit. On several occasions, Bill Thomas and Bob personally expressed this to the ranger representing the National Park Service. He assured both men that the information had been passed to the U.S. Park Police.

Bob sent situation reports to U.S. Secret Service Headquarters. The intelligence regarding the anticipated violence was disseminated to all Secret Service protective details and to the Executive Protective Service (renamed USSS Uniformed Division effective 11-15-77). Appropriate precautions for the upcoming demonstrations were taken by all concerned.

On Monday, November 14, 1977, the shah and shahbanou (empress) arrived in the U.S. and toured Williamsburg, Virginia where they remained overnight. The following morning, the royal party flew by Marine helicopter to Washington for the 10:30 am White House arrival ceremony.

Prior to the shah's South Grounds arrival, Bob picked up Agent Bill Thomas at the Bureau's Washington Field Office. The two agents would monitor the day's demonstrations together. First, they would check in with the law enforcement agencies working the visit.

The agents dropped by the MPD Special Operations Division staging area. In a location near the White House, 75 officers from the Civil Disturbance Unit (CDU) were standing by to assist the USPP and USSS as needed. MPD-SOD Captain Joseph Mazur stated his force was ready to roll.

At the Blair House, where the shah would be staying overnight, the agents established liaison with the onsite U.S. Secret Service Uniformed Division officials. Bob congratulated the UD personnel on their new name. They were now a full-fledged division of the USSS.

The Secret Service had invoked the 500-foot rule (District of Columbia Code 22-1115) around the "President's Guest House." This regulation prohibited certain acts within 500 feet of an embassy or other building utilized by a foreign government. No sign could be displayed that would bring the foreign government in "disrepute." Additionally, groups who might cause a security threat were not allowed to "congregate." For security reasons, the sidewalk was closed in front of Blair House, and UD officers were prepared to close down Pennsylvania Avenue when needed.

Next, Bob and Bill headed for the Ellipse to be on the ground with the U.S. Park Police force that separated the pro- and anti-shah demonstrators. The group supporting the shah was permitted to sit in bleachers on the northern part of the Ellipse. From there, they would be able to view the White House arrival ceremony. Anti-shah protestors were limited to the eastern side of the Ellipse. A snow fence stood between the two opposing groups.

En route, Bob noticed that his old unit, the USPP Special Operations Force, was parked along the northern side of Pennsylvania Avenue adjacent to Lafayette Park. He observed that the officers were in "soft hats" and appeared to be at a low level of readiness. Bob knew immediately that something was wrong.

Bob made a U-turn on Pennsylvania Avenue and pulled his car behind the last Park Police cruiser. With Bill Thomas in tow, Bob sought out Sergeant Earl Hill, who was supervising the SOF contingent. "Earl," Bob called out, "Why isn't SOF down at the Ellipse?"

"We're keeping it low-key since no trouble is expected. We've been stationed here to keep an eye on Lafayette Park and the White House sidewalk."

"No trouble is expected!" Bob cried out in disbelief. "The FBI has an informant who stated the antis are going to attack the pros at the beginning of the arrival ceremony. We've talked about it at the COG meetings and the ranger from the Park Service said the intelligence was passed to Park Police. We thought you guys would be spearheading a strong show of force to keep things peaceful!"

"That's right," Bill Thomas added.

"That's the first I've heard of it," Hill responded. "I was told this morning there was no unfavorable intelligence."

"Earl, somebody dropped the ball. The antis are going to use their signs as clubs, and they've been told to carry glass bottles to use as missiles," Bob informed.

"Okay, I'll raise the watch commander [WC] on the radio and get us redeployed," Hill stated.

"Hurry, Earl, the arrival ceremony will be starting soon," Bob warned.

Bill Thomas and Bob overheard the exchange of radio traffic between Sergeant Hill and the Park Police watch commander, who was reluctant to relocate the SOF detail. The WC wanted to keep the SOF in reserve at their present location. He firmly stated that no adverse information had been relayed to him and that there were no problems at the Ellipse. Sergeant

Hill countered that he had agents with him from *both* the Secret Service and the FBI warning of an impending violent confrontation.

With that news, the watch commander finally ordered the SOF to the Ellipse. Sergeant Hill directed his officers to don riot helmets and to have riot batons and gas masks ready. The officers scrambled to get the riot gear from their equipment bags, which were stored in the trunks of the cruisers.

Just then, the 21-gun salute welcoming the shah began to fire. Soon afterwards, a frantic call blared over the Park Police radio. A large number of anti-shah protestors had suddenly charged the supporters of the shah. The snow fence had been breached, and the anti-forces were attacking the pro-shah group with sticks.

A small force of Park Police footmen and horse-mounted officers were bravely trying to keep about 4,500 anti-shah demonstrators from several thousand shah supporters. Pro-shah individuals were being clubbed to the ground by hundreds of stick-wielding militants. In the melee, the antis also assaulted police with sticks and thrown bottles. The situation was extremely tense. The police feared for the safety of the pro-shah group, which included women and children.

With lights flashing and sirens screaming, the SOF motorcade along with Bob and Bill arrived at the Ellipse. The scene was one of pandemonium. The small contingent of Park Police had been overrun and overwhelmed. An all-out riot was taking place. It reminded Bob of the anti-war years.

Sergeant Hill quickly marshaled his forces and the SOF unit charged into the fracas supplying much needed reinforcements. After several minutes of hand-to-hand action, the Park Police reestablished a picket line. Tear gas was used to help disperse the combatants. The Park Police force of horse-mounted and foot officers steadily drove the anti-shah militants back to the eastern side of the Ellipse. Other Park Police reinforcements arrived to assist.

The incident was an embarrassment for the Carter administration. The president and the shah witnessed the brawl from the South Grounds. Tear gas drifted onto the White House ceremony causing some attendees to wipe their eyes. When the smoke cleared, 96 demonstrators and 28 police officers had been injured. Ten civilians were treated at George Washington Memorial Hospital with the most severe injury being a fractured skull. Eleven protestors were arrested.

Stunned by the violence, President Carter ordered the Justice Department to coordinate the planning for the remaining demonstrations scheduled for the shah's visit. Deputy Attorney General Peter Flaherty met with law enforcement officials to assess the situation. The MPD complained that they were not called by Park Police to lend assistance at the Ellipse. They also questioned the low profile of the Park Police. MPD officials reasoned that a very strong show of force should have been displayed to keep the groups well separated and to deter any violence.

Officials of both the FBI and State Department informed Flaherty that the Park Police had been warned about the possibility of a significant action during pre-planning meetings. Park Police Chief Jerry Wells denied that his force had received any information regarding the possibility of a clash. Park Police stated that without intelligence to indicate otherwise, the low-key stance they took was correct so as not to provoke hostile elements.

For the remainder of the day, helmeted police with riot batons stood shoulder to shoulder, while they watched anti-shah forces on the Ellipse and in Lafayette Park. Wearing their trademark cardboard masks to hide their identities, the Iranian students angrily chanted, "The shah is a U.S. puppet; down with the shah!" as they marched in serpentine columns.

The permit for anti-shah groups to demonstrate on the White House sidewalk was canceled for the following day (Wednesday, November 16). Park Police cited that the protestors presented "a clear and present danger to public safety." The protestors were mainly confined to Lafayette Park and the Ellipse with marches to Embassy Row and Capitol Hill. Supporters of the shah were permitted to congregate at Pennsylvania Avenue and 17th Street where they could see the Blair House arrivals and departures of the shah.

With police keeping the opposing groups well separated, the second day's demonstrations and marches were more orderly and peaceful. Sticks and poles not affixed to signs or placards were considered weapons and seized by police. Protestors were met by a strong show of force everywhere they went. One incident did erupt in Lafayette Park. Protestors threw sticks and stones at Park Police who were responding to an individual's cry for help. In the ensuing action, several protestors were injured and some arrests were made.

The shah's two-day Washington visit ended when he departed Andrews Air Force Base on the evening of November 16. The militants opposed to the shah had gotten their headlines. The violence that played out for news cameras and reporters was carried around the world. Protestors wanted to portray the shah as a hated despot, and they hoped to incite unrest in Iran. Like bone-dry travelers seeking a desert oasis, militants thirsted for an Iranian revolution.

About a week after the shah's visit, Sergeant Earl Hill called Bob to thank him for the warning regarding the anticipated Ellipse violence. Hill stated that Bob's quick action had prevented many more injuries. Due to Bob's alertness, the SOF was able to turn the tide at a critical time. Hill confided that the situation had become extremely dangerous. Some Park Police were close to drawing their duty revolvers. The arrival of the SOF in riot gear and with tear gas saved the day.

Sergeant Hill further related that he had submitted a commendation recommendation praising Bob's action, but it had been reluctantly declined. Apparently, the Park Police feared a lawsuit from those injured.

Even rank and file officers were openly critical of the Park Police hierarchy. They charged that not enough officers had been initially deployed to the Ellipse. In addition, police stationed at the Ellipse were told to leave their riot gear in their vehicles—thus exposing the officers to unnecessary injury.

In a lawsuit against Park Police management, all records pertaining to the Ellipse incident would be subpoenaed by the plaintiffs. Park Police had steadfastly said that *no* warnings of any violence had been received by them. A commendation to Bob would present Park Police with a major problem. Even though Bob's warning had only been given about ten minutes before the outbreak of the violence, a commendation would confirm that the USPP had indeed received prior notification. This fact would contradict their previous assertions and raise further questions.

Consequently, it was found out that the ranger attending the COG meetings did not *personally* pass the intelligence to the USPP. The information never left the Park Service. The ranger assumed erroneously that Park Police had been advised. With this dangerous mix-up, the Park Service decided to have a Park Police official attend future COG sessions.

Though the shah's visit was history, Bob continued to work long hours. There *never* seemed to be a lull in activity for the Protective Intelligence Squad. One investigation during this time is remembered for its peculiarity and uniqueness. It began one Saturday afternoon when the USSS Intelligence Division duty desk supervisor called Bob at home. An incident had just occurred at Andrews Air Force Base. Although Bob was not the PI Squad duty agent that weekend, he was being called because we lived close to Andrews.

The pilot of a private aircraft with two other persons on board had declared an emergency and had landed at AAFB. Once on the ground, the pilot stated he was a CIA operative with highly sensitive national security information. The intelligence needed to be *immediately* delivered to the White House Situation Room.

Inside the terminal building, the subject ordered up an Air Force staff car for the drive to the White House. By now, the deputy base commander had been called to the scene. The colonel talked briefly with the subject and believed him to be genuine. While a car was being readied, the colonel called the White House to advise them of the emergency. Eventually, USSS-ID received the call. They asked the colonel to keep the subject at Andrews until an agent could respond. The colonel agreed but warned that the subject claimed to have time-sensitive compartmented information. The subject was quoted as saying, "Many lives are in jeopardy."

Bob grabbed his gear and ran out of the house to the government car. After expediting to Andrews with lights and siren, Bob arrived at the passenger terminal where he checked in with the deputy base commander and his chief of security police, an Air Force captain. "Where's the subject?" Bob asked.

"All three subjects are inside this office," replied the captain as he pointed to a nearby door.

"Let's put them in separate rooms. I'd like to talk to each of them individually. Have they been patted down for weapons?" Bob asked.

"No, sir," answered the captain. "I didn't see any bulges. I do have driver permits for all three."

"Has the aircraft been checked for explosives?"

"Negative," said the captain—looking a bit uneasy.

"Under the circumstances, can we get a dog to sniff out the aircraft?" Bob requested.

"Certainly," replied the captain, who then called his control center via a portable radio and relayed the request.

Next, the three subjects were separated into different rooms. Two of the men were in their 40s while the remaining man was 19 years old. Bob ran the subjects through ID and NCIC (National Crime Information Computer) with no record found. The plane's tail number was checked through NCIC. There were no wants.

"I'll start with the teenager first," Bob advised.

"May I sit in on the interview?" asked the colonel.

"Of course," Bob replied.

Bob entered the room followed by the colonel. Bob pulled a chair over to the desk where subject number three was sitting. After identifying himself, Bob informed the subject, "I want to advise you that under federal law you're an adult, so there's no misunderstanding." Bob then followed up with the Miranda warning. Afterwards, subject number three signed a waiver, stating he wanted to talk with Bob and without an attorney present.

"Do you have any weapons, explosives, or contraband on you or in the plane?" Bob began.

"No, sir!" replied the subject—shaking his head a couple of times for emphasis.

"Okay, give me the short version as to how you got to be here today."

"I was at the Mercer County Airport this morning. That's near Trenton, New Jersey. I'm taking lessons to get my private pilot's license. My instructor, Mr. Davis, came to me and offered me a chance to get some extra flying time. A man was renting a plane for a trip to Washington. Mr. Davis would be going along. He asked if I wanted to go too and fly the plane back."

"Who flew the plane down here?" asked Bob.

"The guy who rented the plane," answered the subject. "I don't know his name. He didn't talk much."

"What happened when you got into the Washington area?"

"We flew around for a while. Mr. Davis didn't know what was going on. He asked the man what airport we would be landing at. The guy mumbled something about the White House. Then he gets on the radio and declares an emergency. Mr. Davis asked what was going on. The man said he had to get to the White House. Then, he lands us at an Air Force base."

Next, Bob interviewed Mr. Davis, subject number two. He gave the same story with a bit more detail. Davis was the operator of a flying service. Subject number one showed up this morning wanting to rent an aircraft. The subject had a current pilot's license and a valid credit card. Davis rented him a plane.

Davis got worried when he observed the individual over revving the engine and making other errors on the taxiway. The subject appeared to be out of practice and was not cleared for takeoff.

After subject number one said he needed to get to Washington in a hurry, Davis offered to accompany him in order to ensure the safe and proper operation of the aircraft—and its return. Davis invited a student pilot along, so he could get some flight time too.

Once in the Washington air corridor, subject said he needed to get to the White House. After flying around for a while, subject number one finally saw the runways at Andrews AFB. Davis was speechless when the subject radioed the tower at AAFB and declared an emergency.

Bob and the colonel then moved to door number one. The subject claiming to be a CIA operative had a New Jersey driver's license in the name of Arturo Gonzales. Bob showed his credentials and White House pass to the subject. After advising Gonzales of his Miranda rights and receiving a signed waiver, Bob started the questioning. "Tell me why you have to get to the White House."

"I can't divulge that to you," the subject stated in a Spanish accent. "This is highly sensitive information. I've been involved in a CIA operation and barely escaped with my life. This is urgent national security information that needs to be personally relayed to the duty officer at the White House Situation Room—*immediately*. The longer you keep me here with these games, the more likely many people are going to die!"

"Then you better tell me what it is," Bob stated authoritatively. "I have top-secret clearance with unqualified SI access. The colonel is fully cleared too. You made an emergency landing at a restricted military installation. You're representing yourself as a government agent, who has official business at the White House. Until you satisfy us, you aren't going anywhere."

"Okay," said the subject, "you win. But what I say stays in this room. This morning, I escaped from Russian agents. They were holding me captive—somewhere in New Jersey. The Soviet Union has developed a top-secret device that they plan to activate tomorrow at 2:00 p.m. sharp. This machine will send the Moon into a collision course with the Earth. They have it set, so the Moon will strike only the United States and wipe us out. I must get this information to the White House Situation Room! It means life or death for all of us!"

Bob rose from his chair and opened the door to the corridor where the AF security police captain was standing. "You can cancel the staff car. Order up Mr. Wheels [police transport] for our man instead," Bob advised. "He'll be visiting St. E's first."

Bob then obtained the subject's background, and filled out the referral papers for the hospital. Since Andrews was a federal installation within the "environs of the District of Columbia," Bob could refer the subject to St. Elizabeths. Bob finished the interview by taking some mug shots with a Kodak Instamatic camera. All PI agents carried them in the field.

The two other men received a stern warning from the colonel and Bob—especially to be more cautious about whom they ride with in an airplane. They were released and allowed to return in the aircraft to New Jersey.

Bob called ID and notified them of the outcome. Then he packed up his paperwork and rose to say goodbye to the deputy base commander. The colonel extended a hand in gratitude: "Thanks, I can't believe I almost sent that guy to the White House in an official vehicle. You saved my career. If there is anything I can *ever* do for you—short of treason—let me know."

Back at the field office, tension continued to mount due to ASAIC Gallagher's management style. His mistrusting personality and confrontational attitude permeated through the Washington Field Office. It seemed like the worst was being brought out of some agents. A few played up to supervisors by informing on the alleged missteps of their fellow agents. And some supervisors—especially those who cared most about their own careers—unfairly blamed agents in their respective squads rather than stand up to Gallagher.

Bob was the victim of this on one occasion. A GS-14 supervisor had been reassigned as the PI Squad ATSAIC. The individual had never worked PI before. He had no idea as to the number of calls the squad received after regular hours or to the procedures followed for notifications.

Bob was the PI duty agent during the AT's first week in the squad. A subject from Manassas, Virginia made several late-night telephone calls to the White House. No threats were made, but the caller rambled incoherently, and his diatribe was laced with disturbing imagery. Bob made the long drive out to the subject's residence and conducted the interview. Bob's initial evaluation was that the subject did not present a danger to USSS protectees. The Intelligence Division was advised, and Bob returned home.

That morning per normal procedure, the case was referred to the WFO for the follow-up investigation regarding the subject and a final evaluation. ASAIC Gallagher had seen his copy of the referral and decided to put the new AT on the spot. During the ASAIC's morning meeting, Gallagher grilled the AT as to the overnight case. Of course, the AT had no knowledge of it; the teletype was still sitting in his inbox—unread. The AT used the excuse he had not been advised by the squad's duty agent.

Thoroughly embarrassed, the new ATSAIC decided to take his anger out on Bob. "You should have called me at home," the AT complained bitterly.

"We get these all the time—at least two after-hours cases every week," Bob apprised. "We notify ID as to the initial action. They send a teletype over here with the details and the requested follow-up investigation. We haven't been notifying the AT on routine call outs. ID has the same policy; they don't call us after Northwest Gate interviews—even if the subject is committed."

"I don't care. From now on when you're called out, you phone me at home after the notification to ID," the AT ordered.

"You got it," Bob said.

It didn't take long to put the new procedure in effect. Two nights later, Bob was out intercepting a PI subject at the Greyhound Bus Terminal in D.C. After the subject was found, interviewed, and referred to St. E's, Bob notified the Intelligence Division.

Next, he dropped a dime and a nickel in the pay phone and dialed the AT's residence. A female answered the phone; she sounded startled. "Ma'am, this is Agent Ritter from the Washington Field Office. I'm sorry to have disturbed you, but I need to make a notification to your husband."

Bob heard some muffled words spoken between the ATSAIC and his wife. It sounded like neither of them was very happy. The AT got on the phone and angrily barked, "Do you know what time it is?"

"Sir, I'm sorry to disturb you, but I intercepted a PI subject at the Greyhound Bus station. He was referred to St. E's. You wanted me to notify you."

"It's 2:30 in the morning!" the AT yelled. Then, there was dead silence. The AT had hung up on Bob.

Later that day, Bob was called into the ATSAIC's office. "Don't call me at home again," the AT commanded. "You woke up my wife; she couldn't get back to sleep."

"I'm sorry," Bob apologized. "You said you wanted to be notified after I called ID."

"From now on, either be at the office or phone me here at 9:00 for the notification. During the weekends, notify me during daytime hours."

"Yes, sir," Bob answered.

When Bob recounted the story to me, I couldn't help but think of all the times I had been aroused from a sound sleep due to late-night call outs. And all the times I'd laid restless in bed—worrying about Bob.

ASAIC Gallagher intimidated the agents under him. He acted as if a good number of them were trying to beat the Service out of a paycheck. Bob was one whom Gallagher watched with a mistrusting eye. Since Bob's performance was solid, Gallagher resorted to petty concerns to keep Bob in check. One of these non-issues pertained to Bob's membership in the Association of Former Agents of the U.S. Secret Service (AFAUSSS).

The AFAUSSS was founded in 1971 in order to bring together former and *current* Secret Service employees for comradeship and for help in times of need. Bob became a member, so he could learn more about those who had served before him. Bob wanted to know everything he could about the rich legacy of the Secret Service. The association published a newsletter, which featured the memorable cases and protective activities of former agents. Bob also thought it would be good to support the organization's benevolent outreach.

What have I done now thought Bob when he was summoned to ASAIC Gallagher's office. Bob couldn't have been more surprised when he heard Gallagher say: "Floyd Boring [emphasis on *Boring*] was in here the other day trying to drum up support for the retired agents' association. He mentioned you were a member."

"Yes, sir, I've only been able to attend a couple of meetings. It was on my own time," Bob preemptively declared.

"It's probably a good idea if you don't spend a lot of time with those guys. The Service has changed since their day. We don't operate like that anymore. I don't want them leading you astray. I can't order you not to belong, but it would be better if you didn't," Gallagher stated. Bob was dumbfounded.

Later when I heard the story, I couldn't understand why Gallagher would say that. Bob suggested that Gallagher was probably being defensive. Many of the association's members still had powerful Secret Service connections and were well thought of. Gallagher didn't want his agents complaining to retired personnel who could pass it to headquarters.

During the winter of 1977–1978, a new grassroots protest organization sprung up on the national scene. The American Agricultural Movement (AGR) was formed by family farmers demanding better prices for their produce. AGR spokesmen warned that American farmers were heading for bankruptcy. A national farmers' strike was called. Some farmers refused to plant crops until prices were raised to a level of profitability.

Traveling to our nation's capital in "tractorcades" to lobby Congress and the Carter Administration was another part of their strategy. From their campground on the Mall, farmers sought public support for congressional action to ensure profitability. During the farmers several months of sporadic protests, goats were let loose on Capitol Hill, and a sit-in was staged at the Department of Agriculture Building to gain headlines. Secretary of Agriculture Robert Berglund was evacuated during the initial rush of the building. By April 1978, most of the farmers had left D.C., and the Mall settled down in time for the beginning of the tourist season.

As cherry blossoms bloomed along the Tidal Basin, Bob worked with WFO senior SA Dan Mitchell in updating protective surveys. Mitchell was a GS-13 in the Protection Squad and had been the lead advance agent for many of the foreign dignitary visits to Washington during the past several years. In a good number of these, Bob had served as the PI coordinator. A collegial relationship developed. The two respected each other's abilities and work ethic.

Bob was chosen by Mitchell to be the PI member for his protective survey team. The team conducted a lengthy survey of the President's Guest House. Next, Mitchell's team was tasked to conduct surveys of the major hotels visited by the president. The Washington Hilton was one of the first to be updated, since it was a popular convention hotel and frequently hosted functions attended by the president.

Al Fury, a retired Metropolitan Police officer, was the hotel's director of security. For some time, Fury had complained about the Secret Service's policy of closing down the Washington Hilton's T Street entrance for the president's arrivals and departures. The old survey called for a 10-minute window of closure before arrivals/departures. With departure delays from the White House, the entrance was sometimes closed for an inordinate amount of time. Fury reiterated that this was a major inconvenience to hotel guests.

Bob suggested to Dan Mitchell that the initial closure could wait until the actual departure of the presidential motorcade from the White House. As to the departure at the end of the function, Bob likened it to Elvis. The entrance could be left open until five minutes to the president's scheduled departure. After that, folks would have to wait until the president left the building. This new procedure would minimize the inconvenience as much as possible while still protecting the president.

Bob also suggested that two PI teams be included in the site's manpower requirements. Bob felt that the policy of having only a single PI team at presidential sites was inadequate. Two teams could provide better coverage, especially as to public areas. If one team became tied down with an interview, there would still be another team available.

Bob was disappointed when he stopped by Dan Mitchell's office to review a draft of the Washington Hilton protective survey. There had been no increase in PI coverage. The number of teams remained at one. "I was told to try to reduce the number of agents, not add to it," Mitchell explained.

Disappointment turned to disbelief when Mitchell revealed that he was discontinuing the closure of the hotel's T Street entrance for arrivals and departures. This reduced the number of agent post standers, but the area would no longer be secure. The credentialed press area for arrivals and departures would now be open to the public—and potential *assassins*.

"Dan, you can't do this," Bob implored. "We're losing three-sixty protection."

"They have to be able to get people in and out of their hotel. It's been a real hardship. It's all about cooperation and trade-offs. We have to work around it," Mitchell stated.

"Dan, anyone will be able to set up within 15 feet of the president—with firearms or explosives. POTUS goes up there all the time. We're going against the basics of protection."

"Bob, stop worrying. We'll put a police officer on the rope line. It'll be okay."

Bob couldn't believe what he had just heard. Dan Mitchell was an experienced and able agent. He had served in the Presidential Protective Division. Bob held Dan in the highest regard. Yet now, Mitchell seemed to have abandoned protective principles for the convenience of the Washington Hilton.

Bob went to see his immediate supervisor, the ATSAIC of the PI Squad. Unfortunately, Bob had lost some respect for the current AT. He seemed to care most about getting a promotion to a GS-15. One of the AT's tactics was to take credit for the investigative successes of his agents, even when it wasn't warranted. So it was with some trepidation that Bob entered the AT's office.

"Sir," Bob began, "I'm concerned about the protective survey I'm working on with Dan Mitchell. It's for the Washington Hilton. Mitchell's decided to bow to the hotel's request to open up the T Street entrance. Currently, it's closed down during presidential arrivals and departures. What used to be a credentialed press area would now become an unsecured public area within 15 feet of POTUS."

"What does that have to do with protective *intelligence?*" the AT questioned.

"It sets up a dangerous area—one that PI teams will have to be continually concerned with."

"Why would PI teams have to be concerned with it?"

"If it becomes a public area with no agent posts, someone's going to have to cover the crowd."

"Ritter, I don't see that this concerns PI. You made your suggestions. The responsibility and final decision is Mitchell's and his ATSAIC's. They know what they're doing."

"Sir, to make that area public violates the basic principles of protection."

"This isn't a PI matter. We have enough to worry about. *That's all,*" said the AT as he returned to the paperwork on his desk. Bob wasn't surprised by the AT's response. He wasn't going to concern himself with a matter that might create some professional controversy. He wouldn't put himself at risk.

Bob considered his next move. One of the principal tenets of Secret Service culture is "Thou shalt not go over the head of one's supervisor." With the AT's refusal to look into the matter, Bob weighed his available options. It would be improper to go to the Physical Protection Squad AT or to ASAIC Gallagher.

Bob decided to talk with several senior agents who were friendly with Mitchell. One was a newly promoted GS-13. The agent did not want to get involved. The other agent was no more receptive. He suspected that Bob might be unconsciously "trouble shooting" the survey in order to look good. Since Gallagher had become ASAIC, suspicion and mistrust had taken over the office.

Desperate, Bob stopped by to see Bert de Freese, who had been Bob's first AT and his WFO training officer. De Freese was now the WFO Operations Branch supervisor. Bob related his concerns to de Freese and sought his advice. De Freese and Mitchell had known each other for quite some time. De Freese volunteered to have an *informal* talk with Mitchell.

Several days later, Bob was called to Mitchell's office. "You won. You got your way," Mitchell said.

Bob immediately felt an immense sense of relief. "That's great, Dan," Bob said. "You had me worried. Opening up the T Street entrance would have been a huge mistake."

Mitchell looked at Bob with some indignation. "You're getting two PI teams. The primary responsibility for one of the teams will be to give special attention to the T Street entrance area and to cover the crowd during arrivals and departures."

"You mean you're still going to open it up?" Bob said very worriedly.

"I told you we have to work around that. Our previous procedure is *unacceptable* to the hotel's management. This isn't Russia."

"Then we should go through the garage or something."

"I've looked at that. Considering the alternatives, this is the most secure and practical way to reach the stage."

"Then at least keep a post in the area to keep the public moving. No one except credentialed press would be permitted to view the arrivals and departures. The area could only be used by the public for *direct* ingress and egress to the hotel."

"That wouldn't work. Besides, the survey's already been submitted and approved," Mitchell informed. "The additional PI team is a better solution. I thought you'd be happy. This can be a precedent to get two-team coverage for the other hotels."

"Dan, this isn't right. I'm going to have to go over and talk with someone at PPD."

"I've already discussed this with PPD-Ops. They're okay with it."

"They must not have looked at this closely," Bob said. As Bob walked back to his desk, he couldn't believe what had happened. How could experienced, able agents not see the inherent danger the survey presented. To Bob, it was like playing Russian roulette with the president's life.

Later that morning, the PI-ATSAIC charged into Bob's office like a wounded elk. The AT was thoroughly upset. "Ritter, what don't you understand about me being your boss! You disobeyed me and went over my head!" yelled the AT. "Now we're tying up two teams at the Hilton!"

"Sir, I didn't go over your head. I was worried, and I went to Bert de Freese for some advice. He talked with Mitchell."

"You just couldn't leave it alone!" screamed the AT. Then, he turned on his heels and stormed back to his office. Bob was shaken. He had never seen a supervisor so angry. Several agents had come to the hallway to see what the commotion was. Bob knew he was finished in the PI Squad.

Bob later found out that the Protection Squad AT had referenced the Washington Hilton survey during the ASAIC's morning meeting. One of the points mentioned was that a second PI team would be needed. The PI-AT assumed Bob—in defiance of a direct order—had talked with the ATSAIC of the Protection Squad regarding the Hilton survey. Bob's AT smoldered until the meeting was over. Then he erupted on Bob with full fury.

That afternoon, Bob was summoned to the ASAIC's office. "I'm sending you to the Forgery Squad," Gallagher declared. "I want you to know it's not because of your performance. I'd send you back to PI tomorrow if need be. Right now, this is the best move for you.

"I do want to counsel you on one thing. I've seen this myself. When a superior makes a decision, the time for discussion is over. It's time to follow orders. You're going to have problems if you don't learn that."

Chapter 27

Forgery Squad

As upset as Bob was with the circumstances that had overtaken him, he was more worried about the changes to the Washington Hilton protective survey. Bob had completed several temporary duty assignments with the Presidential Protective Division. He was acquainted with a number of PPD agents. "I'm thinking about talking with one of the supervisors I know on PPD," Bob said.

"No, Bobbie, please don't do that," I begged. "You did all you could. They're not going to want to get involved. You'll only get yourself in more trouble."

"Yeah, you're probably right," Bob said reluctantly

"Bobbie, please promise me you won't do anything more about this."

"Okay, honey—I promise."

To be honest, I thought Bob was probably overreacting as to the potential danger the change might cause. Bob was an absolute perfectionist and believed in taking no chances. If Bob had his way, the president would *never* walk by an unscreened public area.

I knew Dan Mitchell. I had met him at office functions, and he had helped us during our house move. Dan was an outstanding person. Bob looked up to Dan as one of the top WFO agents and more importantly as a friend. It just didn't seem possible to me that Dan and his WFO superiors would do anything that would put the president in harm's way.

I had been approached before about Bob's tenacity. One of Bob's co-workers, Agent Barbara Riggs, had come to me at a WFO Wives' Club meeting. Barb was concerned that Bob was taking the job too seriously. "Work is a means of supporting my avocation," Barb said. "It allows me to provide for my horses. I'd rather be out riding than here. Jan, you know I think the world of Bob, but I'm afraid he's going to burn himself out. He worries too much about work and especially things he can't change."

I knew that Bob wouldn't burn out. He was on a calling and thrived on the challenges he faced. My candle, however, was burning down. Bob's time in the PI Squad had taken a toll on me. The past two and a half years had been an endless action-film serial of late night call outs, long hours, no days off, and out-of-town travel.

The silver lining to the recent incident was Bob's transfer to the Forgery Squad. I hoped Bob would be able to keep hours that were more regular.

There were about 40 agents in the WFO Forgery Squad, which was the largest and busiest in the Secret Service. In fact, the squad was larger than most USSS field offices.

Within the Washington area, millions of U.S. Treasury checks (T-checks) were issued each year to federal workers, military personnel, federal retirees, and Social Security recipients. Treasury also issued the payroll and public assistance (welfare) checks for the District of Columbia, since these were federal obligations.

This made for a huge pool of U.S. government checks available to be stolen from the mail, especially in the impoverished sections of Southeast and Northeast Washington. Add to this, the number of U.S. Savings Bonds stolen from the mail or in burglaries. A large squad was needed to investigate the endless stream of forgery cases referred to WFO from Treasury.

While the Postal Inspection Service investigates mail theft, the Secret Service has primary investigative jurisdiction for the forgery (signing to deceive) and uttering (fraudulent cashing) of U.S. government checks. Due to the fact most forged T-checks are stolen from the mail, postal inspectors and USSS agents often conduct investigations hand in hand. Local police also have a stake in these crimes, since state and D.C. theft and fraud statutes can come into play.

Because of its size, the WFO Forgery Squad was divided into five groups. No other squad was organized that way. Bob's group leader, Jim Smith, was a GS-12. Smith was being given a chance to gain some administrative experience to bolster his promotional opportunities. Group leaders assigned and reviewed cases. The other four group leaders were all GS-13s. It was the policy of the Secret Service that all agents below GS-14 were nonsupervisory. Therefore, the *official* supervisor of forgery agents was squad ATSAIC Don Murphy, a GS-14.

Group Leader (GL) Smith seemed wary of Bob. Rumors circulated around the office that Bob had gotten in trouble with the PI Squad ATSAIC. In the retelling, misunderstandings became embellished. Who knows what was being whispered behind Bob's back.

Bob didn't receive much of a welcome from Smith. Bob was curtly told to pick out an empty desk in the forgery bullpen and to be ready to start receiving cases. Since Bob was one of the few agents to reside in Maryland, he was assigned to cover a large section of Prince George's County (P.G. Co.) and the bordering sections of D.C. That was fine with Bob. He wanted a territory he could call his own.

Immediately, Bob paid a visit to the Prince George's County Police Check and Fraud Squad to establish liaison. He received an unexpected and very cold reception. The sergeant of the squad flatly stated that no one wanted to work with the Secret Service anymore. "Why?" Bob asked.

"The agent you're replacing couldn't be trusted," related the sergeant. "He had agreed not to make any arrests in a joint case until the investigation was played out. Your agent comes back from an out-of-town assignment and needs some stats. He pops a couple of arrests in the case. This tipped off several other suspects that we had an interest in for local offenses. They've fled the area; our case was ruined. We wasted a lot of time and effort."

"I apologize for that," Bob said. "I don't operate that way. I'm a former police officer and respect the sovereignty of local law enforcement. I understand your concerns and wouldn't do anything that we didn't have a consensus on."

The sergeant and Bob talked for another five minutes—with Bob trying to allay the sergeant's fears. Softening a bit, the sergeant introduced Bob to Detective Rich "Rabbit" Donnelly, the investigator who handled check fraud. Bob eventually won over the sergeant and Donnelly. Bob promised to cooperate fully and pledged to make no arrests in shared cases without Donnelly's concurrence.

With the fire out, Bob returned to the field office and stopped by to talk with GL Smith. "I wish you would have warned me about P.G. County Check and Fraud, so I would have been prepared," Bob said. "When I went out there, I was told they didn't work with the Secret Service anymore."

Smith acted like Bob was hallucinating. "They couldn't have said that," Smith maintained. "I straightened that problem out myself."

"I don't make this stuff up," Bob said. "They were ready to show me the door. Call Sergeant Bender if you don't believe me."

Smith backpedaled, "Maybe they were just playing with you."

"No," Bob stated. "They were angry."

Smith continued to dismiss Bob's concerns and contended that nothing wrong had been done anyway. "We needed to make the arrests," Smith declared. "We can't sit on federal felonies forever."

Bob then realized that GL Smith had probably pressed for the arrests and was trying to play down the ill will it had generated. "Anyway, I smoothed things over," Bob said. "I'll keep us on good terms."

On the way back to the bullpen, Bob silently vowed to treat his local law enforcement partners as equals. Bob would keep the cases he worked jointly "close to the vest." He would tell the group leader as little as possible regarding those investigations. Keeping the GL in the dark would prevent him from pressuring for premature arrests.

Bob's next visit was to Largo, Maryland where Postal Inspector William "Bill" Solomon had his office. Bill's investigative territory included Prince George's County and Southern Maryland. Bill was happy to see some new Secret Service blood. The two hit it off right away. Bill offered to notify Bob whenever there were any mail thefts. Bob volunteered to give Bill an investigative hand. Solomon mentioned that he often worked with Detective Donnelly. Bob suggested that the trio meet for lunch.

The following Friday afternoon, Bob, Bill, and Rich gathered at the Shady Oak Inn in District Heights, Maryland. Each of the three talked about their professional lives. Bill Solomon was a couple of years from retirement. He longed for one more big case. Rich Donnelly was a corporal, who hoped to make sergeant. All shared a burning desire to clear the streets of criminals.

The theft and criminal negotiation of someone's payroll, public assistance, or Social Security check wreaked financial havoc on that individual and their family. It could be a month or more until a replacement check could be sent. A claim form had to be filled out, sent in, and reviewed before a new check could be cut. The Secret Service was often required to submit a "settlement report" before Treasury issued a substitute check. This report verified that the rightful payee had neither received the check nor cashed it. For folks living from check to check, any delay in payment was a severe personal hardship.

Bob suggested that the three men work together as a team. Bob reasoned that the criminals they were after touched all of their investigative jurisdictions. Bob pledged to work tirelessly with Bill and Rich to run out any and all leads. Bill and Rich liked what they heard. In the past, too many Secret Service agents had been part-time investigators, letting their casework slide when hit with protective assignments. Bob promised to do "whatever it takes."

The major problem with forgery investigations is that they're "cold cases" from the start. By the time the Secret Service receives the case, it's been weeks and in some instances months since the crime. The trail is stone cold. Most of the people who handled the transactions don't remember them. If they didn't note a physical description or some identifiers on the check, there was usually no information regarding the presenter.

To help combat this, the WFO Forgery Squad set up a continuing "sting operation." The owner of a local photography shop was a paid WFO informant. When suspicious individuals came into the shop wanting photo identification cards made, the informant would surreptitiously notify the WFO as to the names and addresses to be placed on the IDs.

Agents in the field would then check out the addresses. Sometimes the individuals answering the door would verify that they were expecting a Treasury check. The true payee would confirm that no one should be requesting an identification card with the recipient's name and address.

In these or similar circumstances, a surveillance team of agents would be assembled. The agents would follow the subjects when they left the photography shop. Often, the subjects ended up at a liquor store where they would forge and utter stolen T-checks with the help of the false IDs. After witnessing the violations, the surveillance team would make the arrests. The subjects arrested believed it had been their bad luck to pick a location that was under the surveillance of the Secret Service. They never linked the operation back to the photography shop.

Bob was only in the squad for a couple of weeks when a bullpen mate returned to the office one afternoon with a very worried look on his face. "What's wrong?" Bob asked.

"I had a rough morning in court," answered the agent.

"What happened?" Bob asked with concern.

"I was testifying in one of the photography shop arrests," the agent related. "It was a preliminary hearing. The defense attorney objected to our use of an unidentified informant to help establish probable cause in the case. The defense argued that they should be able to subpoena the informant for the trial. The judge agreed and ordered me to name the informant. The AUSA was new and inexperienced. She left me hanging."

Oh, no," Bob said, "you didn't."

"Yes, I gave up our informant. I didn't see what else I could do."

"You could have taken the Fifth until the AUSA woke up and objected to the motion or dropped the charges. You should tell ATSAIC Murphy about this."

The agent left the bullpen and returned a short time later. "I talked with Jim Smith. He said it was no big deal and not to worry about it."

"No big deal!" Bob said. "The informant's safety could be in jeopardy. Smith's a GS-12 just like you and me. You should talk with Murphy. That's what he gets the big bucks for."

Eventually, the agent advised AT Murphy of the matter. The AT said he would notify the informant as to the disclosure. Murphy would also ask the U.S. Attorney's Office to drop the charges in the case, so the informant would not have to testify in open court.

Later, Bob was warned by Group Leader Smith not to mention the incident to anyone. Smith said AT Murphy did not want the matter spread around the office.

Over the next six months, Bob worked with Rich Donnelly and Bill Solomon in Maryland. Within D.C., Bob partnered with Postal Inspector John Sternberg. Bob and John were college fraternity brothers and old friends. During one investigation in the field, Sternberg nostalgically remarked, "Bob, when you and I were throwing down beers together at The Varsity Grill, did you ever think we'd be running down bad guys together in Southeast D.C.?"

Bob closed his share of cases and made some arrests, but the vast majority of cases he was assigned contained no significant investigative leads. These cases had to be closed unsolved. Bob saw a pattern developing. Good identification appeared to have been used when uttering the forged checks. Most of the checks were cashed at "mom and pop" liquor stores and convenience marts that did not have transaction cameras. The description of subjects presenting the checks, when available, varied greatly. A large number of checks had been forged and uttered in this manner. Bob believed this pointed to an organized check-cashing ring. Bill Solomon and Rich Donnelly thought Bob might be onto something.

During the summer of 1978, a string of U.S. Postal Service (USPS) vehicles were broken into at various locations in Northeast and Southeast, D.C. and P.G. Co. Md. The modus operandi was the same; the side windows of USPS Jeeps were forced open and mail bags stolen. The dates of break-ins coincided with the delivery dates for U.S. government checks. Bill Solomon and Bob decided to employ an old and basic investigative tool: the neighborhood canvass.

Bob and Bill canvassed the areas in Maryland where the vehicle break-ins had occurred. The two agents hoped to gather some leads while the trail was still hot. Pounding shoe leather and knocking on doors is a laborious, time-consuming technique, especially on sultry summer days. A week's worth of work and a pound of sweat went by with no information developed.

Then, Bob took a run out to a Prince George's County neighborhood where a number of T-checks had turned up missing in the past. The section had rural-type mailboxes affixed to posts. Bob circulated the area, asking if anyone had seen anything suspicious. Some hours later, Bob caught the break he needed. One resident had seen a young man in his 20s driving through the area following a mail truck on its delivery route. The subject was opening the mailboxes and inserting flyers. The eyewitness thought the action to be suspicious because the subject seemed to pause at each of the boxes longer than necessary. "Like he was going through the mail?" Bob asked.

"Exactly," answered the witness.

Bob got a description of the subject and his vehicle. Luckily, the witness still had one of the flyers. It was an advertisement for a Prince George's County nightclub. Investigation at the club yielded the subject's identity. The subject was name checked with no record found. An operator's permit check revealed the subject's residence. Bob contacted Bill Solomon and Rich Donnelly with the information. It was decided that the three would attempt to interview the subject that evening.

The individual resided in a garden-type apartment complex in Hillcrest Heights, Maryland. The subject would not invite the officers in; he preferred to talk at the door. After being advised of his Miranda rights, subject stated he delivered flyers for local businesses. He denied any involvement in mail theft. When told he was spotted following a postal truck and lingering at mailboxes, the subject claimed that he always tried to time his service with the mail delivery. This allowed him to insert the flyers within the postal bundle, so the advertisements would be taken into the recipient's home with the day's mail.

Bill Solomon started to close out the interview, "Okay, we'll be back in touch if we need anything else."

Bob wasn't buying it. "No one works that hard for a couple of cents a flyer," Bob asserted. "You're going through people's mail looking for T-checks. Look, I'll give you one chance to come clean with me, and I'll do what I can to help you. If we go the full 10 rounds, I'm going to work even harder to put you away for as long as possible."

"Whoa, Bob!" Solomon interjected. "It's been a long day." Solomon then gave one of his business cards to the subject and concluded the interview.

The three investigators gathered in the parking lot by their cars. "You think he's dirty, Bob?" Solomon asked.

"Yes, he's not taking all that time just to insert flyers."

Solomon turned to detective Donnelly, "What do you think, Rabbit?"

"I think it was a line of crap too," Donnelly replied.

"Okay," Solomon uttered, "I guess I'm getting old—and soft. I almost believed the kid."

"Here's what we'll do," Solomon advised. "Rabbit, I'll meet you at your office at 8:00 in the morning. We'll run out here and pick this kid up. We'll take him to the Postal Inspection office in D.C.

"Bob, you drop by at 11:00. That'll give Rabbit and me some time to work on him first. We'll be the 'good cops.' If we can't break him, he won't have any problem seeing you as the 'bad cop,'" Solomon expressed with a chuckle.

The following morning, Solomon and Donnelly began the interrogation of the subject. "Agent Ritter's pissed at you," Solomon warned. "I wouldn't want that man on my ass. He's with the Secret Service. He doesn't have the time for your crap. Not only does he investigate federal crimes; he also has to protect the president.

"Agent Ritter's coming over here later. The only chance you have of staying out of jail is to cooperate with Detective Donnelly and me. Tell us everything you know, and if you're truthful we'll see what we can do. Otherwise, we're going to hand you over to Agent Ritter.

"He plans to arrest you for violation of 18 U.S.C. 1725, placing *unstamped* matter in a mailbox," Solomon continued. "He's got an ironclad case. Every mailbox you put a flyer in is an additional count.

"He'll put you in cuffs and take you to his office where you'll have to give handwriting samples until your fingers fall off. After you've been interrogated, printed, and photographed, it'll be too late for you to see a judge today. You'll spend the night in Central Cell Block. The drunks and weirdos will love to get a piece of you."

Solomon and Donnelly had never seen a suspect fold so quickly. "Okay, I'll tell you what you want to know. Just don't let Agent Ritter take me!" The subject then proceeded to give details about a large check-cashing ring that had been operating in the region for the past year and a half. Solomon and Donnelly couldn't take down the information fast enough.

For a chance to plea to lesser crimes and a probation recommendation, the subject was willing to become an informant and to provide incriminating evidence on a continuing basis. The subject claimed that some members of the ring were also into burglaries, robberies, drug dealing, stolen cars, credit card fraud, fencing, counterfeiting, financial schemes, white-collar crime, and prostitution.

Away from the subject, Donnelly suggested to Postal Inspector Solomon that MPD Detective Robert Pleger be brought into the case. Donnelly vouched for Pleger's ability and integrity. Having Pleger onboard would gain a valuable ally within the Metropolitan Police Department, whose cooperation would be needed.

Bill Solomon called Bob to tell him the good news. "Our man's spilling his guts over here. You got us a good break, Bob. You were right about the check ring. This is going to be a huge case!"

The next day, Inspector Solomon drove a Postal Inspection Service surveillance truck around Prince George's County Maryland and Southeast D.C. In the back, Bob along with detectives Donnelly and Pleger debriefed the informant. The subject directed the law enforcement officers to locations where mail had been stolen and to businesses where checks had been uttered. The informant also led our men to recreational playgrounds and other hangouts where subjects involved in the ring frequented. The informant revealed that the public basketball courts of D.C. had become open-air markets for drugs and meeting places for criminals.

From the truck's one-way windows, Bob took pictures of suspects, while Rich and Robert noted identifying information. The informant described a criminal ring of about a dozen primary members. Over 50 others were used as needed in the criminal negotiation of the checks. Most of the participants were drug addicts.

One piece of information stuck in Bob's mind. The informant mentioned that a ring member known only as "Clay" had worked at an area bank. The informant did not know the name or location of the bank.

Bob had a hunch. That evening, he worked late at the office going through the check forgery photostats for the past year. He struck pay dirt. Bob discovered that over 50 District of Columbia pay roll checks had been fraudulently negotiated at a particular Northern Virginia branch of a major bank. Closer examination revealed that six of the checks had been cashed at the branch on the same day! Also noted was the fact that the branch was not near any of the mailing addresses on the checks. In fact, the addresses on the checks varied greatly in geographical location and did not coincide with the mail routes where USPS vehicles were broken into. These facts suggested two things to Bob: (1) There was a "dirty" teller at the bank branch; (2) The checks were stolen *before* they were mailed—probably out of a D.C. Government payroll office or mailroom.

The following morning, Bob met with the bank's head of security at their headquarters location in downtown D.C. The security chief, a retired FBI agent, checked the bank's transaction records regarding the checks in question. As Bob had suspected, one teller had handled all of the transactions. The teller was identified as Clayton Davis. The subject had worked for the bank for six months and then suddenly quit. "He probably didn't want to press his luck," Bob theorized.

"Yes, and you've given me pause for thought," voiced the security chief. "We're going to have to figure out a way to catch this type of thing in the future."

"So are we," Bob said.

During the next several months, Bob carefully reviewed the statements given by the informant. There were many pages of leads to run out. Bob checked the WFO photostat file for checks that were cashed at locations favored by the ring. He hoped to associate the cases through handwriting analysis to known forgers. Bob worked with the Forgery Squad agent who was a questioned document expert. WFO indices were searched for the individuals named by the informant as ring members.

Second endorser interviews were conducted at the businesses that had cashed the forged checks. When a suspect was developed, Bob showed a "photo spread" to the person who had handled the transaction. Bob would *spread* out pictures of 10 different individuals. One of the photos was of the suspect. The witness would be asked if he or she recognized any of the photos.

Persistence and hard work paid off. Several male and female forgers were positively identified and additional suspects were developed. A good number of forged and uttered checks were consolidated into Bob's parent case. Bob requested the original checks from the Check Claims Division (CCD) of the Department of Treasury. The checks would be sent to the U.S. Postal Crime Laboratory for handwriting and latent finger and palm print analysis.

The U.S. Attorney for the District of Columbia designated the ring an "organized crime group" operating within the Washington Metropolitan Area. Two AUSAs were assigned to coordinate the investigation and prosecution of ring members. The AUSAs directed the continuing undercover operations of the informant. The investigative team was compiling a wide array of evidence for presentation to the grand jury of substantive violations by a number of group members.

Bob was in the middle of all of this when he came home one evening in December. While Bob and I shared a late dinner, I asked him his thoughts on the Jonestown, Guyana tragedy, which had been in the headlines for several weeks. On November 18, 1978, Congressman Leo J. Ryan (D-

California) was assassinated in Port Kaituma, Guyana. Four persons traveling with Ryan were also murdered (including three members of the media); ten others were wounded.

At the time of the assault, Ryan and his party were attempting to depart Port Kaituma via two chartered aircraft. Representative Ryan had made a fact-finding trip to Jonestown, Guyana, an agricultural cooperative established by the charismatic Reverend Jim Jones and his Peoples Temple (no apostrophe). Complaints from relatives of some of Jones's followers prompted the inquiry. It was charged that members were being kept at Jonestown against their will and that living conditions had become intolerable. Ryan's party was comprised of staff, news media, concerned relatives, and an official from the U.S. Embassy.

The Ryan delegation arrived at Jonestown on November 17. They were given a tour of the facility and talked with Peoples Temple members. By the afternoon of November 18, about 15 persons let it be known that they wished to leave Jonestown. Congressman Ryan was going to stay one more night, while the remainder of the party would fly back to Guyana's capital city, Georgetown.

Through the State Department, Ryan arranged for the defectors to depart Jonestown with the official party. One Jonestown family was split about leaving. While the husband and wife argued, a Peoples Temple member suddenly assaulted the congressman with a knife. The attacker was subdued without any injury to Ryan.

With tensions running high, the State Department official traveling with Ryan ordered the congressman to proceed immediately with the official party and defectors to the airstrip at Port Kaituma. After one of the aircraft was boarded, a "supposed" defector opened fire on the passengers with a handgun. Two persons were wounded before the gun jammed. At the same time, a contingent of Peoples Temple security men suddenly appeared at the other aircraft and began the murderous assault on Congressman Ryan and his group. After the attackers left the scene, survivors hid in the jungle until their later rescue by the Guyanese army.

Back at Jonestown, Jim Jones was putting into action his "White Night" plan for the mass suicide/murder of the Peoples Temple flock. Under the constant urging of Jones, the inhabitants of Jonestown filed by a large vat where they were given cups containing a grape-flavored drink laced with cyanide. The poison was first administered to the children. Some of the adults voluntarily committed suicide. Others were coerced to drink by armed security guards. Some were injected with the poison. Several were shot. When the White Night ritual was completed, over 900 men, women, and children lay dead.

"It makes no sense to me why mothers would kill their children and why so many would end their lives," I told Bob.

"It was a socialistic cult founded on the principles of Marxism with apocalyptic overtones," Bob stated. "Jim Jones used control techniques—financial, psychological, physical, situational, and the like—to exert absolute power over his followers. They were reborn with Jones and believed he was a prophet. Jones substituted himself for religion. He was seen as the one and only true and legitimate leader, and his orders went unchallenged.

"The Secret Service is actually involved with the remnants of Jones's Peoples Temple. There's been an allegation some members are planning to assassinate certain American politicians. Supposedly, they're upset at what they believe was U.S. government persecution of the sect and want retribution."

"Really," I said.

"Yeah, the FBI and Service are looking into it," Bob advised. "The Bureau has also sent us a copy of an audio tape that was recorded during a portion of the suicides. I saw some of the transcript. Jones was extremely paranoid. He became resolute when told of Congressman Ryan's assassination. Jones warns his followers they'll be assaulted and tortured for the killing of the congressman. He orders the mass suicide as a way to defeat their enemies and as a vehicle for transformation to a better world. Jones uses the term 'revolutionary suicide.' Their deaths would be a final act of protest.

"Jones had his temple practice the White Nights on previous occasions," Bob continued. "For some time, Jones had prophesized that the Peoples Temple was going to be attacked by outsiders. Apparently, he had thought about moving his temple to Cuba or the Soviet Union. Jones was seeking a socialistic Utopia. But in his paranoia, he moved closer to his self-fulfilling prophecy of apocalyptic confrontation.

"With Congressman Ryan's visit, Jones became more desperate. He was afraid of governmental intervention from both the U.S. and Guyana. It disturbed him greatly that some of his followers deserted him. The assassination of the congressman sealed the fate of the Peoples Temple."

"What can we learn from this tragedy?" I asked.

"It's my understanding that authorities had been advised of the White Night suicide exercises but did not take them seriously. I certainly would have. People don't practice something that they don't intend on putting to use someday. To me, it wasn't a matter of if but a matter of when.

"Taking concerned relatives and press into Jonestown certainly aggravated Jones's paranoia and was probably seen by him as an invasion. But the fatal mistake I believe was Congressman Ryan's decision to arrange for the Jonestown defectors to depart with his official party. Jones's strictest rule was that one does not leave the Peoples Temple. The defectors were seen as traitors. Jones was worried they would reveal the true story to the world, and Jonestown would be destroyed. I believe Jones was already somewhat suicidal, and the congressman's assassination left him no way out. Honey, Jim Jones was *desperate*, and you know what I always say."

"Yes, desperate people are dangerous people!" I recited.

The New Year saw more upheaval in Iran. Mass demonstrations and nationwide strikes had plagued the country since August 1978. The Iranian students were getting their wish. On January 16, 1979, the shah and his wife left Iran for Egypt. Prime Minister Shahpour Bakhtiar was appointed by the shah to establish a civilian government to institute reforms in Iran. At the same time, the exiled Ayatollah Ruholla Khomeini was plotting a return to Iran and the establishment of an Islamic republic.

Bob was called into the office of SAIC Gerald Bechtle, who had taken over the top WFO spot in 1978. Bechtle was a graduate of Bob's and my alma mater, the University of Maryland, where he had been a star basketball player. He started with the Secret Service at the Washington Field Office in 1962. Bechtle quickly moved into protection with the Vice Presidential Detail. Subsequently, he served in the Presidential Protective Division and became the SAIC of PPD during the Ford presidency.

"Sit down, Bob," Bechtle said as he motioned to a nearby chair. "I've got a special assignment for you. I know you have a major forgery case, but I need you on an important intelligence matter."

Bechtle tossed a teletype to Bob. "As you know from your PI time, a militant wing of the Iranian students operates out of Northern Virginia. The FBI has information that they're planning a takeover of the Iranian Embassy in D.C. The Bureau's Alexandria office has the investigation.

"Curt Gallagher tells me you've established good liaison with the FBI in the past. I need you to monitor the FBI investigation as closely as possible. Headquarters is going 'ape' over this. Your job will be to see that the Bureau gives this a 'good shake' and that we get everything they develop. Don't let them 'spin you,' " cautioned Bechtle. "Both of our careers could depend on the job you do.

"You already know that the Bureau plays foreign and domestic intelligence cases close to the vest," Bechtle continued. "Recently, our agents have complained about the lack of information they've been receiving. The FBI has been disclosing very little as to the actual investigation conducted, often citing the Attorney General's guidelines, privacy restrictions, or national security regulations. A lot of cases are being closed with the FBI field agent simply saying that FBI Headquarters has decided no further investigation is warranted."

"Sir, I believe that's a reaction to the ongoing federal prosecution of former Director Gray and the two other FBI officials [Mark Felt and Edward Miller] for civil rights violations. The current FBI hierarchy doesn't have a clear and consistent view as to what is and isn't permissible in intelligence investigations. They're afraid of doing something now and being prosecuted for it in the future. So they're doing, documenting, and disclosing as little as possible. I think it's also a bit of a silent protest. They're opening up fewer intelligence cases and not investigating them as fully as in the past."

"That's a fair assessment of the situation," Bechtle stated. "For this case, I want you to establish liaison *directly* with the Alexandria SAC, Bob Kunkel. You'll be personally representing me and Director Knight."

"I'm to say I'm representing Director Knight?" Bob asked with some disbelief.

"Yes, so you're not blocked as to national security information and as a means of showing how important this is to us. For this case, you have 'need to know' and access as the director would. When they ask you if you have this and that access and have been read into this or that program, you say yes. They've been playing games like that with our agents. Headquarters has approved this, and Liaison has been advised."

"Okay, I understand," Bob replied.

"Are you familiar with Kunkel's background?" Bechtle asked.

"Yes, sir, he used to be the SAC of the Bureau's Washington Field Office. He got in trouble in the early 70s with then Director Gray. There was an incident on the Capitol grounds where an undercover FBI agent was overpowered by some anti-war demonstrators and had to be rescued by other agents. It was alleged that guns were drawn. Kunkel was accused of glossing over the incident. Apparently, he was censured and reassigned to Alexandria, a much smaller and less important office."

"Yes, and he was the Washington SAC during the initial Watergate investigation," Bechtle pointed out. "Some suggest that he didn't play ball with the White House and that was the *real* reason for the transfer."

"I'll keep that in mind," Bob said.

"I want *daily* updates," Bechtle ordered. "Give your reports directly to Sheila for typing. Any questions?"

"No, sir, I'll get right on this."

Bob headed back to his desk where he called the Alexandria Field Office of the FBI and requested an appointment with SAC Kunkel. The following morning, Bob arrived at Kunkel's office. He was greeted by the FBI agent who was the "security officer" for the Alexandria office. After checking Bob's credentials, the FBI security man announced: "We've already verified your TS clearance with SCI eligibility. The boss would like me to check on your special access authorizations."

"No problem," Bob replied.

After he satisfactorily answered all of the FBI agent's questions, Bob was ushered into SAC Kunkel's inner office. Kunkel rose from behind a massive mahogany desk and extended a hand to Bob. After exchanging handshakes, Kunkel invited Bob to sit down. "What can I do for you?" Kunkel asked as he peered at Bob from behind a pair of large-framed black glasses, which accented the FBI-SAC's silver-gray hair.

"Sir, I'm here on behalf of Secret Service Director Stu Knight and WFO-SAIC Jerry Bechtle. They send their warm regards and request your assistance in a matter that is currently being investigated by your office. It pertains to intelligence sent to Director Knight from the FBI regarding a militant group of Iranian students who are operating in your district. The information alleges that some members are planning a takeover of the Iranian Embassy.

"As you know, the Secret Service is responsible for the protection of the Iranian Embassy. The situation at the embassy is already tense. The new civilian government in Tehran stands in opposition to those who strive for a theocratic Iran and a clean break from the shah. The diplomats and military attaches at the Iranian Embassy are jockeying for survival. Throw Iranian students into the mix and the violence and bloodshed in Iran could be transformed to D.C.

"Director Knight and SAIC Bechtle have asked me to personally relay their concern regarding the intelligence your office has developed. They sincerely appreciate your cooperation in the full investigation and resolution of this matter. The director has tasked me to be his 'eyes and ears.' The director requests that I have full access to the investigation, so I may keep him and SAIC Bechtle personally advised on a continuing basis."

"I understand your concerns," Kunkel affirmed, "but we weren't planning on doing much more on this. We reported the informant's allegations and planned to keep a lookout for anything more concrete. This is the kind of information that we probably wouldn't open a full intelligence investigation on until a law was violated."

"Sir, has your source proven to be reliable in the past?" asked Bob.

"Yes," answered Kunkel.

"The name of the game for us is prevention and preparedness," Bob remarked. "If a reliable informant is reporting that criminal activity is being planned for the Iranian Embassy, the director would respectfully request that everything that is legal and ethical be done as soon as possible.

"Earlier this month, Iranian militants stormed the home of the shah's mother and sister in Beverly Hills, California," Bob stated. "Fires were started; a police car was overturned; rocks and bottles were thrown, and over 30 persons were hospitalized."

Kunkel thought for a moment. "I met Director Knight a couple of times when he headed up your Washington office. At the time, I was the SAC of our WFO. If he's that concerned about this, we'll go ahead and open up an investigation for you."

"Thank you, sir. The Secret Service is in your debt," Bob said with sincerity.

Kunkel summoned a supervisory agent from the squad that handled domestic intelligence. Kunkel authorized the agent to initiate a full intelligence investigation into the informant's allegations. The agent was directed by Kunkel to allow Bob complete access to the investigation.

The supervisor took Bob to the squad area and introduced him to the case agent who would be handling the investigation. The three men discussed the case and how the investigation would proceed.

For the next 10 days, Bob worked his forgery cases and maintained close liaison with SAC Kunkel and the lead FBI agent. Bob stopped by the Alexandria office several times a day. He was given unprecedented access to the ongoing investigation. This included actually being taken to an FBI surveillance post, while it was operational. Bob was also permitted to talk with the FBI's confidential informant over the phone, so Bob could make his own assessment of the subject. Bob made sure he thanked Kunkel frequently for the excellent cooperation.

Bob briefed SAIC Bechtle daily. Toward the end of the investigation, Bechtle seemed worried. Bob tried to assure the SAIC that everything that could legally be done was being done. Bechtle said he'd like to accompany Bob on one of his visits to SAC Kunkel—just to be safe. "Believe me, boss, you know everything the FBI knows, but it would be a nice gesture for you to personally thank Kunkel for his help." Beaming a wide smile toward Bechtle, Bob stated, "At the same time, you can confirm for yourself the *terrific* job the FBI and I have been doing."

The following morning, Bob drove to the Alexandria Field Office. He asked Kunkel's secretary if it would be all right to bring SAIC Bechtle by that afternoon. She looked at Bob and broke out laughing. "What's so funny?" Bob asked.

"That's a really odd request for us," she replied. "In the FBI, there's a *strict* pecking order among SACs that correlates to field office size. The SAC of our WFO would *never* drop by here. He'd be insulted if it was even suggested. Mr. Kunkel would be summoned over there."

"I see," Bob said.

The secretary looked at Kunkel's appointment book. "His schedule is clear this afternoon."

"I'll get Mr. Bechtle here around 1:00 p.m.," Bob advised.

Kunkel's secretary flashed Bob a skeptical look. "I'll believe it when I see him walk through the door," she said.

Bob arranged to pick up SAIC Bechtle in the garage of the Pepco Building. Bechtle opened the door to the car and announced to Bob's great surprise, "Since we've got some extra time, I'm going to conduct a vehicle inspection."

"Boss, you're kidding—right?"

"No, I want to check your car out. The inside looks pretty good."

"I just had it washed and vacuumed. Rumor has it I'm driving the SAIC to Alexandria," Bob said with a grin.

"Bob, open the trunk."

Bob exited the vehicle and opened the trunk for Bechtle's inspection. Bob noticed that Bechtle's eyes got as big as silver dollars, and he took on an even more serious demeanor. "Bob, open that briefcase for me," Bechtle ordered.

Bob immediately became suspicious. "Okay, what's up?" Bob asked.

"An Uzi is unaccounted for. That's the type of case they're carried in. A supervisor saw you with this and notified me."

"So that's what this is about! When I was a State Department agent, we kept our Uzis in Samsonite cases. To avoid confusion in an emergency, we all bought American Tourister attachés for personal use. Since it's exactly opposite in the Service, I keep the American Tourister in my car. It contains forms and other items I use in my investigative work. I brought it up to the office the other day to restock a large number of forgery forms for the 'S' case I have."

Bob then opened the gray-colored American Tourister attaché to reveal its contents. The tension in Bechtle's face eased when he saw that the case in question was a stock briefcase with no Uzi. Bechtle thumbed through the compartments of the case. "Man, you've got every form there is—and neatly organized. I don't think I've ever seen anyone so prepared. Bob, what's in that metal case?"

"It's a finger-printing kit originally made for the military for field use. I got it at Sunny's Surplus. It comes in handy now and then. When I was in PI, I must have been called out a zillion times. When it's 3:00 a.m., this attaché case turns my car into a rolling office."

"Bob, I didn't think you had the missing Uzi," Bechtle stated somewhat apologetically. "But it was my job to check it out."

"I understand," Bob said. "I'm not taking it personally."

With the inspection over, Bob and SAIC Bechtle departed for Alexandria.

"I didn't know you were an SY agent," Bechtle remarked.

"I was also a U.S. Park Police officer."

"Hmm, I thought you came to the Service straight out of college," Bechtle reflected.

"No, I had about five years of professional experience before joining the Service."

Bob had great respect for Bechtle, seeing him as a fair and capable SAIC. In June 1978, Bob had suggested at a general office meeting that gun lockers be installed in the WFO prisoner processing area. Bob felt that agents should have the *option* of locking up their weapons before processing prisoners. Jails are set up that way. This ensures that prisoners won't be able to gain access to firearms.

Several other agents had told Bob they would back him at the meeting. However, when Bob brought up the suggestion, one of the ATSAICs immediately scoffed at Bob and ridiculed the idea. The AT said words to the effect that anyone who couldn't control their own weapon shouldn't be an agent. With the AT's barrage of disparaging comments and others joining in on the attack, Bob's backers deserted him and remained silent. With no one supporting Bob, SAIC Bechtle quickly dismissed the idea.

About a week later, two Prince George's County (Md.) Police officers were tragically shot and killed by a 15-year-old juvenile, who had been arrested for petty larceny. While the juvenile was being booked, he was able to strip the arresting officer of his weapon. The subject then fired three shots. One struck the arresting officer in the chest causing a fatal injury. Hearing the shots, two other officers rushed into the booking area. The juvenile opened fire on them with the remaining three rounds of the stolen revolver. One of the responding officers was mortally wounded.

Because of this double tragedy, SAIC Bechtle called a special office meeting. Bechtle said with some emotion: "We were all too quick to dismiss Bob's suggestion. I'm guilty like everyone else. I think we owe him an apology."

Bechtle then directed Bert de Freese to order several gun lockers for the WFO processing area. Bob was moved by Bechtle's admission. There weren't too many Secret Service bosses who would stand up in front of a roomful of their subordinates and admit to an error in judgment.

Bob and SAIC Bechtle arrived at the Alexandria Field Office of the FBI and proceeded to SAC Kunkel's office. After Bob introduced Bechtle to Kunkel's secretary, she laughed and shook her head a couple of times. "It's an FBI thing," Bob told Bechtle. "I'll explain it to you later."

Meanwhile, Kunkel had seen the two Secret Service men outside his office and invited them in. Bob introduced his SAIC to Kunkel, who asked both men to take a seat. Bechtle handed Kunkel a business card and then swung a foot into the side of a nearby couch. "I just came over to kick my batteries," Bechtle said with a grin. The FBI-SAC smiled at Bechtle, who was joking that Kunkel's office had been "bugged" by the Secret Service.

"I want to thank you for the cooperation you've given us in this investigation," Bechtle began. "I really appreciate it. As Bob has told you, this is a very important matter to the Service. Bob's been keeping us informed, but I wanted to personally touch base with you to be sure we haven't missed anything," Bechtle told Kunkel.

"Your boy's been living over here," Kunkel declared. "I've been in the Bureau since 1942, and I can't remember anyone outside the FBI being granted more *operational* access to one of our sensitive intelligence investigations. We've done everything that's permissible, and he's been a shadow to my agents. It wouldn't surprise me if Bob showed up on payday looking for a check."

Bechtle laughed. The two top agents then discussed the Iranian situation. Bechtle and Kunkel concluded with some friendly "small talk" and promised to continue to collaborate in matters of joint interest.

February brought bitter cold to the Washington area. Several snowstorms hampered Bob's fieldwork. Then a blizzard hit the Washington area on February 18–19. Over 18 inches of snow fell. It was the largest 24-hour accumulation of snow in Washington since 1922. Drifts measured up to five feet in height. Schools and government offices were closed for days. Even Metrorail trains were unable to run for three days.

The following month, the worst nuclear accident in U.S. history occurred at Three Mile Island (TMI) Nuclear Power Station. Situated on a large island in the Susquehanna River about 10 miles southeast of Harrisburg, Pennsylvania, the plant operated two nuclear power generating reactors. The first TMI reactor entered service in 1974. Reactor number two became operational in late 1978.

At about 4:00 a.m. on Wednesday, March 28, 1979, pumps supplying water to the steam generating system of reactor number two inexplicably shut down. Steam was used to drive the turbines, which ran the generators that produced electricity. The water fed into the steam generating system passed over tubes that carried the extremely hot water of the reactor cooling system. The feeding water heated up and turned to steam. The reactor water was cooled in the exchange. It returned to the core of the reactor to renew the cooling of the nuclear fuel.

With the flow of cold water through the steam generating system stopped, the reactor coolant could not dissipate its heat. Temperatures in the reactor spiked. Steam bubbles formed. Water expanded and started to fill the reactor cooling system's pressurizer tank. High-pressure readings caused a relief valve to open automatically.

After the release was made and pressure returned to a safe level, the valve should have closed automatically. Although a control board light indicated the valve had closed, it was actually stuck open. This allowed reactor coolant to escape through the open valve.

Plant operators compounded the problem. They believed that the high levels in the pressurizer were caused by too much water circulating within the cooling system. They turned off the emergency water pumping system, which had started automatically. This proved to be a *major* mistake.

In reality, coolant water was being displaced in the core by steam. The continuing loss of coolant exposed the core, and fuel rods began to rupture. Nuclear fuel pellets were exposed. A meltdown had begun.

It took several hours for the plant operators to discover that the relief valve had malfunctioned. Eventually, they closed a backup valve. It took about another hour for them to realize that water might have been lost from the cooling system of the reactor. Finally, the emergency pumps were turned back on and system water levels rose.

Because of the core meltdown, radiation levels increased inside the reactor building. Alarms sounded. A "general emergency" was called. All nonessential employees were evacuated from the building. Local, state, and federal authorities were notified.

During the next several days, plant operators were still unaware as to the severity of core damage. Although the reactor had somewhat stabilized, officials were still worried as to the possibility of significant releases of radiation to the environment. Uncertainties and misinformation complicated the issue.

On Friday, March 30, officials of the Nuclear Regulatory Commission (NRC) recommended a public evacuation out to 10 miles downwind of the plant. That recommendation was rescinded when plant radiation readings improved and were better understood. A transfer of radioactive gases that morning to a processing tank had released some radiation into an auxiliary building and the atmosphere.

On advice of the NRC and health officials, Pennsylvania Governor Richard Thornburgh did recommend a voluntary evacuation for pregnant women and pre-school children living within five miles of TMI and the closing of schools in that zone. The governor also advised that people living within 10 miles of the plant should stay indoors.

A team of NRC officials arrived at Three Mile Island. They were under the direction of Harold Denton, chief of the Division of Nuclear Reactor Regulation. Denton was sent as President Carter's personal representative. The team was dispatched from NRC Headquarters in Bethesda, Maryland to coordinate the response to the accident. The NRC sought the advice of government and industry experts in bringing the incident under control.

With so much conflicting information given out to the media by different officials, it was decided that Denton would be the sole spokesperson for technical matters. Denton established personal liaison with Governor Thornburgh and kept him briefed on the situation at TMI. A communications system was also set up that directly linked the White House, TMI, the NRC, and the governor's office.

A major issue developed on Friday and Saturday. A large gas bubble had formed within the reactor. Besides the problem this posed with cooling the core, some scientists and engineers worried that the free hydrogen in the bubble might explode. It was calculated that oxygen was also being formed in the reactor as radiation broke down water molecules. Thus, it was predicted that an explosive mixture of hydrogen and oxygen could be formed. Deciding when the hydrogen might explode and a means of preventing it became Harold Denton's biggest problem. A related issue was the force such an explosion might produce. Would it be enough to breech the reactor and the four-foot-thick walls of the containment building?

Adding to the concern was President Carter's decision to visit Three Mile Island. Carter's visit was meant to alleviate the anxiety of residents regarding the true status of TMI and the risk to the surrounding area. The threat of a hydrogen explosion had been reported by the media. This produced new worry for residents. The NRC believed that it would be some days before enough oxygen could be produced to set off the hydrogen. Still, Denton had the president of the United States coming to TMI, and opinions differed significantly among some of the experts.

Bob was one of the agents contacted for possible use as a post stander for the presidential visit. The Service was asking WFO for volunteers. Bob volunteered but was told a few hours later that headquarters had decided to send only "unmarried agents."

On the afternoon of Sunday, April 1, 1979, the President and Mrs. Carter flew by helicopter from the South Grounds of the White House to Middletown, Pennsylvania. The president and the first lady then motored to Three Mile Island. On arrival, they placed yellow protective covers over their shoes and pinned dosimeters (devices to measure radiation) to their jackets. President Carter and the first lady then inspected the plant and received a briefing in the reactor's control room.

Later that afternoon, the president made a statement to several hundred reporters, who gathered at a Middletown public hall. Carter assured all that the reactor had stabilized and that radiation levels were "quite safe."

It wasn't until the following day that most experts agreed that the hydrogen in the reactor could not explode. It was their consensus that any oxygen produced would recombine with hydrogen to form water molecules. Thus, there would not be enough free oxygen in the reactor to support an explosion. The fear that the hydrogen might explode had been unwarranted.

Either way, the courage shown by the President and Mrs. Carter in visiting TMI was sincerely appreciated by the residents of the region. It turned the tide at a crucial time and prevented the escalation of anxiety and fear into panic. Bob and I were proud of the leadership shown by the Carters in calming the situation.

That April, I received a questionnaire from the Secret Service. Dr. Frank Ochberg, a psychiatrist from the National Institute of Mental Health, had been commissioned by the Service to study the effects of stress on agents and their families. Wanting to be frank and open in my answers, I carefully considered my thoughts. Some of the questions brought out the inner hostility I had been suppressing regarding Bob's career choice.

In spite of all the hours worked—the travel, the responsibility, and so on—Bob had handled the stress remarkably well. He loved his job and was a dedicated agent. The only "gripes" I had ever heard Bob make were about certain supervisors and the "culture" of the Secret Service. Most troubling to Bob was his belief that some supervisors were not receptive enough to suggestions and change.

On the other hand, I was showing the accumulative effect of years of dealing with the fallout of being married to an absentee husband. For the past four years plus, Bob had worked an extremely inordinate amount of hours. His years in the Washington Field Office and the Protective Intelligence Squad had to have been among the highest total hours worked of anyone in the Secret Service, yet alone normal jobs. If I hadn't been so deeply in love with Bob, major marital problems would certainly have developed. Realistically, I didn't know how much more I could endure.

During the spring of 1979, Bob, Bill Solomon, Rich Donnelly, and Bob Pleger presented evidence in three jurisdictions regarding their check cashing ring investigation. Arrests were made, search warrants served, and criminals brought to justice.

One search warrant executed in Suitland, Maryland resulted in the seizure of a complete Polaroid identification system consisting of a commercial ID camera, backdrop, cutter, and laminator. Along with the ID equipment, hundreds of blank D.C. operator permits were recovered. The ring had an "inside man" who stole the permit stock directly from the department of motor vehicles. With genuine blank driver licenses and professional photo equipment, the ring could make up authentic-looking IDs in the names and addresses of the true payees with the likenesses of the forgers/utterers. Such organization and sophistication had never been seen before in forgery investigations.

By August, over 25 arrests had been made with a sizable number of defendants convicted. An organized crime ring responsible for the theft of over a quarter of a million dollars had been broken by four hard-working investigators. Ringleaders were either behind bars or on the run. For his part, Bob received a USSS commendation and commendations from several outside agencies. It had been the biggest mail theft and forgery ring that anyone could remember.

With the success he had earned in the Forgery Squad, Bob asked his AT for a transfer to the Criminal Squad. Bob wanted the experience and a change of pace. Bob had worked many hours over the past year on the check ring.

Several days after making the request, Bob was called down to ASAIC Gallagher's office. Invited to sit down, Bob was cautiously optimistic that his request was being approved. Bob figured he would have been left standing if Gallagher had decided to deny the transfer. Bob was caught off guard when Gallagher said, "Bob, if anyone over at ID asks if you can investigate a case, you tell them Curt Gallagher says you can."

"Excuse me," Bob replied.

"You're being transferred to ID effective next Monday. Your orders will be coming through this afternoon."

"Great! Did they request me or was it just the luck of the draw?"

"They asked for Frank O'Donnell, but you have a year and a half more time in. You deserve the spot."

"I want to go to ID, but I don't want to stand in Frank's way," Bob remarked."

"You've been here almost five years. You're overdue for a transfer."

Bob remembered how he had felt when Gallagher denied him a transfer to Public Affairs. Bob felt sorry for O'Donnell but couldn't argue with Gallagher's reasoning. A good number of agents with less time in the Service had already been transferred out of WFO or their starting offices. Bob wanted to go to ID, so he could present his PI ideas, especially as to his "Protective Interest Evaluation Review" form.

Later that afternoon, Bob was given a copy of his orders. The transfer was official. About 30 minutes later, Bob received a call from one of the intelligence research specialists assigned to ID. She wasted no time in blasting Bob. "I just called to let you know that no one wants you over here. Frank O'Donnell is the agent who should have been transferred. You're going to have a tough time in ID."

"I didn't ask for this transfer, and I personally had nothing to do with the decision," Bob responded. "But I do deserve it. I worked PI for two and a half years and had some major cases, including some commendations from ID. I've also been at WFO for close to five years. It's unfair that anyone should resent me anything. I like Frank. He's a great agent, but I have a career too."

The IRS backed off some. "Well, I just wanted to let you know how disappointed we are."

"I know you're unhappy," Bob replied, but "I'm not to blame. Don't hold a grudge against me."

When Bob related the incident to me that evening, I was upset. I couldn't understand how someone could be so vindictive and unprofessional.

I was also hit with the news that we were going to have to buy a second car in the next couple of days. With the transfer to ID, Bob would lose his government vehicle. It couldn't have come at a worst time. The instability in Iran had caused their oil production to be drastically reduced. With a drop in oil supply and price increases by OPEC, the U.S. was experiencing another energy crisis. The price of gasoline rose, while long lines formed at the pumps.

"Does this mean you won't be called out at night?" I asked.

"Yes," Bob answered.

"Good!" I enthusiastically declared.

Chapter 28

ID

The Intelligence Division of the United States Secret Service dates back to the early 1940s. Known then as the Protective Research Section (PRS), it originally consisted of a small staff of agents and specialists. Its mission was to process and disseminate information received from USSS field offices, the FBI, state and local law enforcement agencies, and other intelligence sources. Of primary concern were individuals who made spoken or written threats against USSS protectees. Groups that believed in the use of violence to accomplish their goals also received PRS attention.

The assassination of President John F. Kennedy in 1963 brought the PRS into the modern age. Technological advancements were made, especially regarding data processing. Additional agents were added to the PRS to conduct *direct* intelligence liaison with federal agencies and to serve as members of presidential advance teams. A PRS agent would now travel to cities visited by the president in order to coordinate protective intelligence activities. This included establishing intelligence liaison with the district offices of the FBI and other local law enforcement agencies. The PRS agent would also check on any subjects the Service considered dangerous to protectees.

The PRS grew into a major division of the Office of Protective Research (PR). Renamed the Protective Intelligence Division, it was commonly referred to as ID (pronounced I-D).

On his transfer date, Bob reported to Frank Cavanaugh, Deputy Special Agent in Charge (DSAIC) of the Intelligence Division. Cavanaugh had been Bob's first ASAIC at WFO. Bob entered the DSAIC's office and stood in front of Cavanaugh's desk. Without looking up, Cavanaugh grunted a brusque, "Sit down." A few seconds later, Cavanaugh remarked: "We didn't ask for you, but we got you. So, we'll have to work you into our plans."

"Sir, I know you wanted someone else. But I'm a good agent too. Of my almost five years at WFO, two and a half years were spent in the PI Squad. Before WFO, I was a State Department agent and Park Police officer. I have the knowledge, experience, and *desire* to become a valuable addition to ID. All I ask for is a fair chance to succeed."

Cavanaugh turned his eyes toward Bob. "I remember you. You were a good agent. We've all been upset over not getting O'Donnell. The plan was to groom him for FIB. The IRSs really liked him."

"I understand," Bob said, "but this is a career organization. Making me feel unwanted isn't going to help anyone. I want to be here, and I want to do a good job."

"You make a good point," reflected Cavanaugh. "Unfortunately, I'm not going to be able to help you attain your goals. I'm being transferred to Philadelphia to become the new SAIC."

"Congratulations."

"Ron Claiborne will be taking my place. Your first assignment at ID will be the duty desk. Wilber Rainey is the Operations ASAIC. He's expecting you. He'll go over everything with you and get you started."

Bob reported to ASAIC Rainey's office. Rising from his desk, Rainey smiled and extended a hand toward Bob. "Welcome to ID," Rainey cheerily announced in a smooth Southern accent that flowed like a bubbly mountain stream. "Glad to have you on board."

"Thanks, I was getting worried that you didn't want me here either," Bob remarked. Bob then related the call from the IRS, and the conversation with DSAIC Cavanaugh.

"Don't worry about that, Bob," Rainey said. "They'll get over it."

Before graduating from Memphis State University in 1964, Wilber Rainey had a short stint as an FBI clerk in Washington, D.C. Rainey started his Secret Service career in 1965 with the Memphis Field Office. In 1969, Rainey was transferred to the Intelligence Division. Four years later, Rainey left ID for the Dallas Field Office. In 1976, Rainey became the USSS resident agent (RA) in Knoxville, Tennessee. Rainey had recently been promoted to a GS-14 and reassigned to ID as the Operations ASAIC.

"Bob, here's how we run the duty desk. When a GS-12 position opens up in ACB [Analysis and Control Branch], the agent with the most time on the desk will be rotated off," Rainey explained. "The way things are going, you won't spend more than a year on the duty desk. You'll also be conducting out-of-town advances. Have you worked the duty desk before?"

"Yes, I did a full week TDY and a bunch of fill-ins, some a couple of days at a time," Bob advised.

"Good," Rainey said. "On the wall to your right is the Operations [Ops] Branch board. It lists agents assigned to the duty desk and those out on advances. As you can see, you're starting out on the day shift. The shifts rotate every week. Your normal days off will be Wednesdays and Thursdays. This Wednesday, you're working your day off to fill-in on the 3–11 shift. Due to advances and leave, you're always subject to rescheduling. I try to contact agents when their assignments are being changed, but it's your responsibility to check the board daily—including on your days off."

"No problem, I worked shift work at Park Police. We had the same rules over there," Bob related.

Rainey then took Bob around the Intelligence Division to introduce him to the rest of the staff. The first stop was the Foreign Intelligence Branch. Due to the classified material stored there, the room contained security vaults and was only accessible from the main hallway via a single entry door, which incorporated a combination lock. FIB also had a secure telephone, which was linked to other intelligence agencies. Bob received a chilly reception; FIB had pushed for the transfer of SA O'Donnell.

Next, Bob visited the Analysis and Control Branch. This branch was organized into four geographical regions, which correlated to the time zones of the United States—starting on the East Coast with Region I and working to the West Coast and Region IV. ACB sent out the domestic PI investigative referrals and reviewed the casework submitted from the field offices. The regions also maintained watch lists of those individuals considered dangerous to USSS protectees.

The last stop was the "duty desk" where Bob met the agents working the day shift. Normally, two GS-12s and a GS-13 worked the 7–3 and 3–11 shifts. On midnights, only two agents worked (a 12 and a 13). The GS-13 senior agents served as the duty desk supervisors.

The duty desk area consisted of a raised platform situated within the large room that was the Operations Branch. The duty desk was enclosed with waist-high cabinets on three sides. The cabinets were topped with counters. Access into the duty desk area was controlled by two gates. The wall end of the duty desk area contained three identical workstations. The duty desk supervisor sat at a desk in the middle of the platform.

Bob took a seat at the empty workstation. Each station contained a desk/console, which featured an electric typewriter, telephone, computer terminal, and a radio receiver/transmitter. A television was recessed into the paneled wall. The TV could be used to monitor network news and other events. The duty desk also featured news teletype machines and a monitor that showed the locations of USSS protectees.

Later that morning, Bob ran into Ron Claiborne, who was taking over the DSAIC position from Frank Cavanaugh. Bob had worked with Claiborne during the 1976 American bicentennial. Claiborne had been the USSS national coordinator for bicentennial intelligence. At the time, Claiborne had praised Bob for the job he had done as the WFO intelligence coordinator.

"Hi, Ron," Bob said. "Congratulations on the new position." Claiborne acted like Bob was invisible. "Ron, remember me. I'm Bob Ritter."

"I know who you are," Claiborne said in an angry tone as he brushed by Bob. Apparently, the new DSAIC was upset at Bob's transfer too.

The weeks and months rolled on. Bob proved to be a very competent duty desk agent. The duty desk received calls from USSS field offices across the country. Field agents checked names through ID and related information regarding subjects who had come to their attention. The duty agents typed up the information and submitted it to the duty desk supervisor for forwarding to either ACB or FIB. Intelligence Division duty agents also called field offices outside of business hours to initiate investigations as needed.

In addition, the Uniformed Division notified ID when persons exhibiting irrational behavior showed up at the Northwest Gate of the White House. Most of these subjects attempted to have a private audience with the president. When they persisted, a duty desk agent would respond for the interview and take appropriate action. Since Bob had handled every PI case imaginable, he had no difficulty in performing his duties.

The Intelligence Division duty desk also served as the Command and Control Center for the USSS after hours and during emergencies. Receiving information, taking appropriate action, and making notifications were a big part of the job. The ID duty desk and the watch officers in the USSS Communications Division were the only Secret Service units other than permanent protective details and the Uniformed Division that functioned 24 hours a day, 365 days a year.

ID duty agents also received the "trouble calls" transferred from White House operators. A red light flashing on top of the duty desk consoles signaled that a caller to the White House had made a threat. A duty desk agent would immediately pick up the White House line and push a button to start a tape recorder rolling. The agent taking the call would try to obtain the identity and location of the caller and other information. Keeping the caller on the line gives the duty desk supervisor time to run a trace with the telephone company.

In October 1979, the Iranian situation flared up again on the international scene and was the hot topic in the Foreign Intelligence Branch. The shah of Iran's exile had taken him to Egypt, Morocco, the Bahamas, and to Mexico. On "humanitarian grounds," the deposed shah was granted permission to enter the United States for medical treatment.

On October 22, the shah arrived in New York and was admitted to New York Hospital-Cornel Medical Center. The shah underwent surgery for removal of his gallbladder and several kidney stones. At this time, it was also confirmed that the shah was suffering from advanced lymphoma (cancer of the lymph glands). Doctors prescribed a treatment program of chemotherapy and irradiation.

About a week later, the Ayatollah Khomeini, who had returned to Iran in February 1979 to lead the Muslim clerics, spoke out against the United States. Khomeini feared the shah had actually gone to the U.S. to plot a return to power. Anti-shah groups planned protests for Washington and New York.

Then on November 4, news was received at USSS-ID and around the world that the American Embassy in Tehran had been stormed by Iranian students. Over 60 U.S. citizens were seized and held captive. In exchange for the safe release of the hostages, the students demanded the shah's extradition to Iran to face trial. At first, the Carter administration believed that the civilian government in Iran would intervene and release the Americans. As time passed, it became evident that Ayatollah Khomeini supported the takeover and the students' non-negotiable demand for the return of the shah.

In fact, Khomeini did not trust Iran's moderate civilian government. He sought to control the reins of power within his Revolutionary Council. The embassy occupation and holding of American hostages rallied the Iranian people behind Khomeini. Parading blindfolded hostages and burning American flags before news cameras showed the world that Iran had struck back at "The Great Satan" America. It energized the Iranian revolution and solidified Khomeini's hold on the country.

On November 28, 1979, 38-year-old Suzanne Osgood brought a scare to the USSS. Osgood entered the Capitol Hill suite of Senator Edward M. Kennedy (D-Massachusetts), located in the Dirksen Senate Office Building. Without warning, Osgood screamed and pulled a six-inch hunting knife from her coat. Secret Service Agent Joseph Meusberger, who was posted to the reception area, seized Osgood and disarmed her. During the struggle, Meusberger received a slight cut to his left wrist.

Secret Service protection had been afforded Senator Kennedy since late September 1979 when he announced that he was considering a run for the 1980 Democratic presidential nomination. President Carter authorized the early protection due to concerns regarding Kennedy's safety. Senator Kennedy had lost two brothers to assassination. As Bob said, "Senator Kennedy presents a tempting target to someone who wants to go down in history."

It was reported that Osgood had a history of mental illness and had attempted suicide on several occasions. She had been staying in Washington for about a month. She was arrested and charged with assault on a federal officer. Osgood was ordered to St. Elizabeths Hospital for a 60-day psychiatric evaluation.

The New Year brought tragedy to the Secret Service family. On January 14, 1980, Denver Field Office Special Agent Stewart Panson "Perry" Watkins was shot by 31-year-old Joseph Hugh Ryan, a former mental patient with a direction of interest toward U.S. presidents. Ryan was of record with the Secret Service dating back to 1974 when he showed up at the White House seeking to become an undercover narcotics agent. That visit earned Ryan a committal to St. Elizabeths Hospital.

Ryan had recently moved to the Denver area from Sacramento, California. He appeared at the USSS Denver Field Office complaining that he had been threatened by former President Nixon and was being harassed by the Secret Service. Since Denver agents were not familiar with the subject, a quick call was made to the ID duty desk.

The duty desk agent gave a synopsis of the subject's record, which included recent psychiatric treatment (1979). It was also noted that during a 1979 interview by Secret Service agents, the subject was found to be carrying a loaded .357 Magnum revolver, which was confiscated.

With that information, Denver agents asked if the subject was armed. Subject replied that he was. The interviewing agents kept an eye on the subject, while the Denver Police Department was called for assistance.

In the meantime, Agent Watkins entered the reception area. Ryan suddenly jumped to his feet and pulled a .45-caliber semiautomatic pistol from under his coat. Watkins grabbed for the weapon but was shot twice with hollow-point bullets. Watkins then pulled his revolver and fired one shot into Ryan before falling to the floor. With Watkins out of the line of fire, one of the interviewing agents shot Ryan four times to end the assault. Ryan died from his wounds. Agent Perry Watkins died later that evening during surgery. It was a *very* bad day for the Secret Service.

Bob and I talked about the tragic event the following day. Suddenly, the abstract fear of Bob dealing with mental subjects hit home with lethal reality. A Secret Service agent had been shot dead by a PI subject. With the force of a tidal wave of emotion, a rush of anxiety engulfed me. Bob had dealt with PI subjects hundreds of times and continued to come in contact with them during Northwest Gate interviews and out-of-town advances.

"Was the agent married?" I asked.

"He had a wife and two teenage sons," Bob replied.

"Oh, no!" I cried out. I immediately felt a sense of the horror the agent's family must be going through. Tears fell from my eyes. I grabbed Bob and hugged him. "Bobbie, please be careful," I implored.

"Don't worry about me," Bob said. "I take every precaution to prevent this type of thing from happening. My job is to prevent anyone from having to become a hero. If it comes to that, then I've failed. And I don't intend on failing."

"Bobbie, what would you have done in this situation?"

"Actually, a *somewhat* similar situation happened to me several years back. A subject showed up at WFO wanting to speak with an agent. He said that voices told him to come to Washington *to make something big happen.* I scanned his body for bulges and didn't see any. I had another agent run his name through ID.

"The agent came back and slipped me a piece of paper with the results of the ID check hastily written on it. The subject was a former QI from another district. He had been arrested several years before within a block of the president. At the time of the arrest, he was carrying a loaded .45

automatic. I still remember the note like it was yesterday. The words '.45 automatic' were in big letters and underlined.

"I nodded to the other agent in acknowledgement of the note and slid my right hand inside my suit jacket to grip my revolver. I then asked the subject if he was carrying a weapon. He answered no. Since he had been convicted of a gun violation in the past, I asked permission to conduct a 'pat down.' He agreed, and no weapons were found.

"If he had said he was armed, I would have drawn my weapon and ordered him to grab the wall. His admission to carrying a weapon would have been all I needed to disarm him. I don't know why that didn't happen in Denver, especially since the subject was paranoid and showed hostility to the Secret Service. It's always better if agents control the situation and not the subject. People carry things that they intend on using."

Bob was back into shift work. The 3:00 p.m.–11:00 p.m. shift was the most difficult for me. Bob would be gone before either the kids or I arrived home from school; he'd come home after midnight. When I arose in the morning, he'd be sound asleep. With Bob working weekends as regular days, we spent little time together as a family.

Bob had also been rotated into the pool of agents assigned to out-of-town advances for President Carter and Vice President Mondale. Depending on the complexity of the visit and whether protectee overnights were involved, teams *usually* traveled four days in advance of vice presidential visits and five days in advance of the president.

The advance teams consisted of Secret Service agents from the respective detail, the district to be visited, the Technical Security Division (TSD), and ID. Non-USSS members of the team included a political advance agent, a member of the White House Communications Agency, and other military personnel to coordinate *Air Force One/Two* and *Marine One/Two* (helicopters) as needed.

On foreign advances, two agents were sent from ID. One agent worked the movements, while the other agent maintained an intelligence watch at the embassy's communications center. The State Department security officers and other embassy personnel assisted in foreign advances.

Bob took his advance work very seriously. Besides the normal procedure of confirming the whereabouts and updating the status of all QI subjects within a respective district, Bob studied pictures of all quarterly investigation subjects who were *unconfined* in the U.S. QIs could board a plane, train, or bus and show up anywhere in the country in a matter of hours. QIs could jump in a car and travel across country in a matter of days.

Bob used techniques he had developed during advances for the 1976 presidential campaign and for foreign dignitary and presidential visits in Washington. These included a series of checklists and forms he designed for use during advances. Bob also devised a comprehensive PI folder, which was kept in the Secret Service command post for review by detail agents. And like a NASCAR driver walking the track before race day, Bob personally familiarized himself with every area the president would pass through on foot.

Establishing intelligence liaison with federal, state, and local authorities and running out any adverse information developed were other very important duties for ID trip advance agents. Bob visited as many agencies as he could in person. He believed the personal touch resulted in better cooperation and established goodwill for the USSS. To save time, most PI advance agents used the telephone to make their notifications.

An advance in one Southern city had the potential for trouble regarding one of Bob's personal notifications. The Secret Service field office and other federal law enforcement agencies were located in a large federal building. Bob stopped by the FBI office and talked with the agent who handled intelligence. Next thing Bob knew, he was being taken to meet the FBI-SAC. After a nice conversation, Bob left the FBI office and proceeded to make the rounds of other agencies such as ATF, INS, IRS, DEA, Customs, and the Marshals Service.

When Bob arrived later that morning at the USSS district office, the field agent assigned as Bob's counterpart was anxiously waiting. "SAIC Granger wants to see us," he stated with some nervousness. "Granger said you paid a visit to the FBI."

"Yes, I made the trip notification. I talked with Agent Stanley and got a general intelligence briefing. I also met the SAC."

"Bob, our SAIC and the FBI-SAC haven't talked for years. There's bad blood between them. The Bureau SAC came up here earlier and spoke with SAIC Granger. I've never seen the FBI-SAC step foot in our office before."

"What did they talk about?" Bob asked.

"That's what we're about to find out. Let's go."

Bob followed the field office agent into the SAIC's office. It was like stepping back in time. The furniture and wall coverings were right out of the 1950s. Symbols of a bygone era, a neatly creased, stylish homburg hung from an oak and brass hat rack. SAIC Granger was an old-time Secret Service legend.

"Sit down, men," Granger said. "SAC Gifford from the FBI was up here this morning. He was very impressed that Agent Ritter had *personally* stopped by to notify them of the upcoming visit. Gifford thanked me for the courtesy and offered any help that we might need. It was nice of the old 'coot' to come in here with an olive branch." Granger looked at Bob and said in appreciation, "You caused this to happen; I owe you my thanks."

"Yes, sir," Bob responded, "my pleasure."

"I told Gifford that the main thing we need was just letting us know of any intelligence that might affect the visit," Granger advised. "He said he would personally stay on top of that for us. He also insisted on sending us his ASAC for the day of the visit. How should we use him?"

"I suggest we station him in the command post for liaison purposes," Bob replied. "If there's an attempt, bomb threat, or any other FBI matter, he'll be aware of it as it happens and can start to marshal his forces."

"Good idea," Granger declared. "Let's do that."

A new dimension was thrust into the 1980 presidential primaries. On March 15, 1980, the Chicago headquarters of the Carter-Mondale campaign as well as the Manhattan campaign offices of Republican candidate George H.W. Bush were invaded by armed intruders. The masked raiders bound the hands of campaign workers and then proceeded to vandalize the offices. Phones were ripped out; files and campaign materials were tossed about. The slogan "Statehood Means Death" was spray painted on the walls along with the initials "FALN." The intruders then fled the scene.

Suspected of involvement in over 100 bombings, the Fuerzas Armadas de Liberación Nacional had escalated their actions to armed confrontation. Bob reasoned that the attacks were in response to the recent presidential primaries in Puerto Rico. Bush favored statehood for Puerto Rico, while Carter was noncommittal on the issue. Any position other than Puerto Rico becoming a sovereign nation was detested by the FALN.

The December 1979 Soviet invasion of Afghanistan was an important foreign policy concern of the Carter administration. In the president's State of the Union address, he warned that the U.S. would boycott the 1980 Moscow Summer Olympic Games unless the Soviet Union withdrew from Afghanistan within 30 days. Congress overwhelmingly approved Carter's boycott threat.

The Soviets did not comply. In the East Room of the White House on March 21, the president announced to the U.S. Olympic Team and the nation that the U.S. would officially boycott the 1980 Moscow games. With the United States leading the boycott movement, 65 nations chose not to attend the games. Some of those countries permitted athletes to compete individually under the Olympic banner. The U.S., however, warned that Americans competing in defiance of the ban would have their passports revoked.

Meanwhile, the Iranian hostage crisis was fast becoming the defining issue of Carter's presidency. Diplomatic relations were severed with Iran. The president ordered an embargo on Iranian oil, and Iranian financial assets in American banks were frozen. The U.S. moved for the support of the United Nations and the World Court. Iran held firm in its demand that the shah must be returned to Iran. Otherwise, U.S. hostages would be put on trial. Winter turned to spring and the crisis continued without any sign of ending.

In the early morning hours of Friday, April 25, 1980, the White House released public notice of a failed U.S. military attempt to rescue the

American hostages held in Iran. At 7:00 a.m. that morning, President Carter appeared on network television to notify the nation of the operation, which had been conducted in the strictest secrecy.

During the evening hours of April 24 (Tehran time), six U.S. C-130 aircraft and eight RH-53 helicopters entered Iranian airspace in the first stage of "Operation Eagle Claw." The transport planes had taken off from a base in Egypt with a stop in Oman. The helicopters were flown from the aircraft carrier USS *Nimitz*, which was operating in the Arabian Sea.

Immediately, the rescue attempt ran into problems. A sand storm caused one of the helicopters to become separated from its formation. The crew developed vertigo and became disoriented. The helicopter returned to the *Nimitz*. A warning light on another helicopter signaled a cracked rotor blade. That helicopter was abandoned in the desert. Its crew was picked up by one of the other RH-53s. Eventually, the six remaining helicopters and six C-130s rendezvoused at a remote site code named "Desert One."

There, the helicopters were to be refueled by three of the C-130s. The helicopters would then fly Delta Force commandos to within striking distance of Tehran. The commandos would be transported by truck to safe houses located within the city. The following night, they would converge on the U.S. Embassy and the Iranian Foreign Ministry to initiate the rescue of the American hostages. The troops and hostages would move to a nearby soccer stadium where they would be evacuated by helicopter. Next, the RH-53s would fly to an Iranian air base, which was to be secured in advance by a force of U.S. Army rangers. The helicopters would be destroyed, and the hostages and U.S. troops evacuated by two C-141 aircraft.

The plan never moved past the initial stage. One of the helicopters at Desert One experienced a hydraulic malfunction and was unable to continue the mission. With only five helicopters remaining, it was recommended by the on-scene commander that the mission be aborted. The operational plan called for a minimum of six helicopters to evacuate everyone from Tehran. Any additional helicopter losses in the remainder of the operation would necessitate a large number of Americans being left behind. The Pentagon and the president agreed; the order was given to abort the mission.

During the refueling operation—which was being conducted in total darkness utilizing night vision gear—the rotor blades of one of the helicopters accidentally struck the tail section of a C-130 tanker. The helicopter then crashed into the C-130 and its cargo of fuel ignited and exploded in a fireball visible for miles around. Eight U.S. servicemen were tragically killed. Four servicemen received serious burns.

Due to the immense heat, rounds of ammunition on board the burning C-130 and RH-53 were going off indiscriminately. It was feared other aircraft might catch fire. Under these dangerous conditions and with the threat of being discovered, the entire force including the helicopter crews was loaded aboard the remaining C-130s for an evacuation from Iranian territory.

The operation was an embarrassment for the U.S. military and the Carter administration. Iranian authorities displayed the charred bodies of American servicemen to the news media. The American hostages were removed from the U.S. Embassy and divided among several locations throughout Iran to prevent another rescue attempt. The helicopters left behind became prizes for the Iranian military. Operational plans for the secret mission were found in the abandoned RH-53s. These details compromised CIA assets within Iran. The failed mission raised many questions regarding the capabilities of the U.S. military to mount counter-terrorist operations. Secretary of State Cyrus Vance resigned in protest. He had opposed the military rescue operation.

In June 1980, President Carter, accompanied by the first lady and Amy, set off on his first foreign travel since the taking of the American hostages. After an audience with Pope John Paul II at the Vatican, the president would join the heads of the major industrialized nations for an economic summit in Venice, Italy. Afterwards, the Carters would travel to Yugoslavia, Spain, and Portugal.

Bob along with ID Agent Dan Meyer conducted the PI advance for the Carters' visit to the Socialist Federal Republic of Yugoslavia (SFRY). The president accepted an invitation to visit the nation's capital (Belgrade) after receiving criticism from his own advisors and U.S. allies for not attending the funeral of Josip Broz Tito, who died on May 4. Carter sent Vice President Mondale to represent the U.S. at Tito's state funeral.

A hero of World War II and a long-time Communist, Tito led the Partisans (resistance movement) against the Nazi occupation and succeeded in liberating Yugoslavia. After the war, Tito became Yugoslavia's prime minister and moved the nation into the Eastern bloc. In 1948, Tito broke with Soviet Premier Joseph Stalin and the U.S.S.R. Tito envisioned a socialist state free of Soviet domination. In 1953, Tito became president of Yugoslavia, a position he would hold for life. A founder of the nonaligned nations, Tito maintained a foreign policy of neutrality toward both the East and West.

With the death of Tito, Yugoslavia was being ruled by a *collective* presidency. The presidency was comprised of eight members, one each from the six republics and two provinces of Yugoslavia. The president of the presidency rotated annually. Cvijetin Mijatovic, a Serbian leader from Bosnia-Herzegovina, was currently serving as Yugoslavia's head of state.

When conducting an overseas advance, American law enforcement officers have no legal authority. They may only do what the host country allows. It is extremely important that advance team members establish friendly and effective liaison with their foreign counterparts.

It was the practice of PI advance agents to give their opposite numbers appreciation gifts. The gifts were presented at the first meeting, since there was usually no time to do so at the conclusion of the visit. It was also the belief of many that giving gifts upfront resulted in better cooperation.

After learning that their contact in the Yugoslav secret police liked fine Scotch whiskey, Bob and Dan purchased several large bottles of premium Scotch at the embassy commissary. Our boys presented the gift-wrapped bottles to the officer at their initial meeting. The Yugoslav colonel tore off the wrapping paper with the eagerness of a child opening birthday presents. When the Scotch was revealed, the colonel grasped our boys in a bear hug of gratitude and appreciation. Genuine Scotch whiskey was expensive and hard to come by within Yugoslavia.

The colonel seemed genuinely touched and invited Bob and Dan to be his guests for lunch. Later that day, the interpreter provided by the Ministry of the Interior took Bob and Dan about 10 miles south of Belgrade to Mount Avala. They would meet up with the colonel at the top of the mountain, accessible by a winding road through a forest of oak, beech, and pine.

At the summit, Bob and Dan paid their respect at the Monument to the Unknown Hero, which honors the soldiers who died fighting for Yugoslavia in World War I. They enjoyed a breathtaking view of the beautiful countryside and the city of Belgrade, which lies at the confluence of the Sava and Danube Rivers. They gazed at the nearby 666-foot-tall Avala TV tower. An architectural marvel, the tower was supported by a tripod of concrete legs, which stood upon the 1,700-foot-high mountain.

Next, Bob and Dan visited a memorial commemorating a deadly plane crash, which occurred on the western slope of Mt. Avala. The statue—designed in the shape of broken aircraft wings—was emotionally moving. On October 19, 1964, a Soviet Ilyushin-18 turboprop airliner slammed into Mt. Avala amid rain and fog and exploded in a fireball of death and destruction. The plane carried Marshal Sergei S. Biryuzov, Chief of Staff of the Soviet army, 6 other high-ranking Soviet officers, and 11 others. There were no survivors.

At the time of the crash, the aircraft was making an instrument approach to Surcin Airport, located eight miles west of Belgrade. The aircraft had wandered significantly off course and was at too low of an altitude to overfly the mountain. The Soviet military delegation had flown from Moscow to attend a celebration commemorating the 20th anniversary of the liberation of Belgrade during World War II.

While Bob and Dan were walking back from the memorial, they were met by the Yugoslav colonel, who was showing the effects of having imbibed too much of his new gifts. His movements were unsteady; rosy cheeks accented a broad smile. The colonel pointed to the monument in the distance and with slow, faltering speech made some remarks in his native Serbo-Croatian.

The interpreter looked bewildered by what he had just heard. "The colonel says he was part of the force that brought about the crash. He says they placed temporary radio beacons on the mountain and turned off the navigational equipment at the airport. That caused the Russians to home in on the mountain."

"He's telling us a story," Bob said to the interpreter in disbelief.

"I've been with the colonel for many years. I've never heard this before. I believe he's being truthful," stated the translator.

"Ask him why they would have done that," Bob inquired.

After the exchange of question and answer, the translator related: "The colonel says the Partisans liberated Yugoslavia, *not* the Russian army. The Russians invited themselves to the celebration. It was worried that the true purpose of their visit was to meddle in our affairs and threaten us with invasion."

"Isn't that something," remarked Dan Meyer.

Another startling event occurred the following day. Bob and some other members of the advance team were driving to one of the stops proposed for the presidential visit. Suddenly, there was a loud *pop*, and the windshield of the vehicle imploded—showering the occupants with hundreds of pieces of glass. Several of the agents thought someone had taken a shot at them.

An inspection of the car showed no evidence of a bullet. Bob's subsequent investigation of the incident revealed that Yugoslavia did not require autos to have laminated (safety glass) windshields. They used tempered glass, which is designed to shatter into small pieces when struck. It was believed the windshield was hit by a stone thrown up from the gravel road.

Bob was nearing his one-year anniversary on the duty desk, and the 1980 presidential election was fast approaching. Since 1840, every president elected or reelected in a year ending in zero has died in office. And in a majority of those instances, the cause of death has been by assassination. The main reason Bob had become a Secret Service agent was to help end this historical trend. Now, the time was almost at hand.

"Bobbie, does anyone mention Tecumseh's Curse down at work?" I asked.

"No, and I'm not bringing it up. Otherwise, I'll be committed to St. E's!"

In reality, Bob had thought long and hard about ways of defeating what he saw to be the most likely threat to the president's safety—a lone gunman using a handgun at close range. Bob decided to submit an idea to the Employees' Suggestion Program administered by the Office of Public Affairs.

Bob had already caused the police radio frequencies to be changed on the duty desk console to ones more useful for USSS purposes. Having shown that initiative, Bob was asked by Wilber Rainey to update the duty desk manual. After completing that task, Bob thought the time was right to submit a written suggestion that magnetometers (metal detectors) be used to screen guests at presidential events. Rainey signed off on the proposal, and it was forwarded to Public Affairs.

A couple of days later, Bob was called to ASAIC Rainey's office. Rainey held up Bob's magnetometer suggestion. "Bob, you've got a whole bunch of people stirred up over this. Headquarters has asked that you remove your suggestion from consideration."

"You're kidding," Bob replied.

"No, it's an issue they don't want to broach. Headquarters is worried about civil rights complaints, political concerns, and budgetary constraints. They don't think the Carter administration would go for it. Headquarters doesn't want to take an official position on your suggestion. If they turn it down and something happens, the Service would be open to criticism and second-guessing. And apparently, they looked into using them at the White House in World War II, so your idea isn't new."

"A lot has changed since World War II!" Bob remarked. "I'll take the suggestion back, but the Service is missing the boat. The public has grown to accept metal detectors in air travel and at courthouses. Presidential protection should be no less important. We search briefcases and handbags, but someone could easily conceal a weapon on their person. The magnetometers could prevent that. We should be on the cutting edge of technology.

"Anyway, I do have some other things I'd like to submit. When I was at WFO, I developed a checklist to help me assess whether subjects are of protective interest. It's based on research I did into the behavior of assassins leading up to their attempts. You compare your case subject's actions and behavior with those of known assassins.

"The other is a permission form I created for the authorization of telephone traps. I use it on presidential trips. When bomb threats are called in, the trap can capture the telephone number of the caller. We got an arrest in the Cleveland visit using the procedure. I also have a suggestion for the way statistics are kept for PI commitments."

"Bob, go ahead and write up the telephone trap form, and I'll send it on. For the assessment form and the other suggestion, speak with Ron Porter. He's the one at ID who can help you with those types of things."

"Great, thanks for the help."

Bob stopped by ASAIC Ron Porter's office. Porter managed ID's information system and oversaw the computers. "Ron, I'd like to make an appointment to talk with you regarding some PI ideas I have," Bob requested.

"Have you run them by Wilber?" Porter asked.

"Yes, he suggested I speak with you."

"Okay, come on in and sit down. I have some free time."

"I devised a checklist to help in my evaluations as to whether PI subjects are of protective interest," Bob began. "It's based on research I did into the behavior of presidential assassins leading up to their attempts. Behaviors and actions such as: acquiring weapons, target practice, dry firing, stalking protectees, keeping diaries, feelings of desperation, suicidal thoughts, desire for notoriety, and so on. The behaviors are point weighted. Some actions, like the recent acquisition of weapons, are red flags by themselves."

"Bob, research has shown there isn't really a common set of characteristics that can predict violent behavior. There's no single profile for assassins. The things you mention would be noted on the interview form we now use. They would be considered by agents in the evaluation process. I don't think we need a special form to figure out we should make a subject a QI if he's out buying weapons, stalking protectees, and the like."

"You'd think so, but it didn't happen with Sara Jane Moore. She told a police detective that she was going to Stanford to 'test the system.' It was also known by the interviewing agents that Moore had recently purchased a .44 Special revolver. In fact, she was arrested for carrying it in her purse on the very day of President Ford's visit to Stanford. Yet, she was interviewed that night and judged not of protective interest. The attempt by Squeaky Fromme and its copycat effect could have been factored in. Plus, Moore had radical beliefs. These facts were all known by the interviewing agent.

"A big deal was made at the Senate hearing that Moore didn't exhibit any animosity toward the president," Bob continued. "The benefit of a behavioral checklist is that it's not swayed by deception and falsehood. Actions speak louder than words. The recent acquisition and carrying of a handgun by a PI subject, the historical weapon of choice for most presidential assassins, is a red flag in itself."

"The director and AD Burke don't agree with you," Porter stated. "An extensive internal review was made after the Moore attempt. It's the official position of the Secret Service that Moore was *not* dangerous at the time of the interview and that *no* surveillance was warranted."

"That's the problem with circling the wagons," Bob remarked. "If we don't admit shortcomings, we never look for a better way. We keep doing the same thing."

"Do you have something else?" Porter asked.

"Yes, when an agent refers a subject to mental health authorities, the Service should keep a record as to whether the subject is admitted or not. A percentage could be kept for each PI agent. Right now, there's no statistics as to how well agents are assessing dangerousness. It's like fielding a baseball team without keeping batting averages—or keeping arrest stats without convictions."

"Bob, we don't keep that number due to legal concerns. The Service has been sued in the past for the committals we make. Most subjects are sent for professional evaluations *against* their will. Keeping a record of how many times doctors don't agree with us isn't a good idea."

Bob was disappointed that his "Protective Intelligence Evaluation Review" form had been dealt a final deathblow. He still felt that the form facilitated a more accurate evaluation and could have prevented the Moore attempt. The culture of the Secret Service, however, seemed solidly entrenched in its ways and somewhat fatalistic.

Instead of routinely evaluating protective procedures and techniques and making improvements where needed, the Secret Service sometimes *blamed its own protectees*. Bob remembered the instructor in Secret Service school who said: "Kennedy didn't want agents on the back of the limo. They could have saved his life."

In the shooting of George Wallace and the Fromme attempt against Ford, it was said that both protectees took unnecessary risks. Wallace left the stage to work the crowd, and Ford walked through a public park. In the Moore attempt, the USSS took pride in the fact it had advised Ford not to cross the street and shake hands with the crowd. If he had, Sara Jane Moore would have had a dead-on shot at the president. It was pointed out that Ford's life was spared because he took the Service's advice.

Bob thought a major point was being missed in all these rationalizations. Procedures and techniques needed to be developed to handle these types of movements in safety. Bob believed a proactive and preventive role for PI teams would be helpful as well as the use of magnetometers for most movements. Guests could be checked for weapons before entering functions. Areas could also be roped off where the president could shake hands with the general public *after* they've been screened for weapons.

Bob couldn't understand why the Secret Service hierarchy had done little to make public areas safe. Would it take another tragedy before new procedures would be considered? Could the Secret Service survive the loss of another president?

These were some of the thoughts in Bob's mind when he was called into ASAIC Rainey's office in September 1980. Bob had been in ID for 13 months and was next in line to be rotated off the duty desk. I looked forward to Bob's transfer to ACB, whose office hours were 9:00 a.m. to 5:30 p.m. with weekends off.

"Bob, I have some bad news for you," Rainey began. "Richards [SAIC-ID] has decided to jump Ken Powell over you. He's going to take the position that's opening up in ACB. I know it's not right. You have your time in and are one of my best agents. I was overruled."

"Wilber, this can't be happening. Powell's only been here six months. I've served twice the time on the desk."

"Richards must have Powell in line for promotion. He needs to get him to a region for seasoning," Rainey explained.

"I know they didn't want me here, but I've done a good job. I don't deserve this crap."

"Bob, I sympathize with you. I did my best. Richards admitted that established policy wasn't being followed, but he said that's the way it's going to be. Between you and me, I've lost some respect for him."

I was *furious* when Bob told me the news. I was fed up with the Secret Service. It didn't care about Bob, and it sure didn't care about his family. I remember the joke SAIC Gittens told at one of the WFO Wives' Club meetings, "If the Service would have wanted its agents to have families, they would have issued them." But, it was true. The needs of the Service always came first. Spouses and family life came second. Everything outside of the job was a personal problem.

I was upset that Bob was being taken advantage of. Like the Sirens of Greek mythology, the Secret Service was an enticing and relentless seductress. I was worried our marriage was heading for the rocks. If Bob had been seeing another woman, I could have won that fight. Yet, I had no chance against the Secret Service. She was the ultimate mistress. Sometimes, I felt Bob loved the Secret Service more than he loved me.

Bob was working the duty desk night shift during the early morning hours of September 19, 1980, when news flashed over the teletype of the explosion of a Titan II missile near Damascus, Arkansas. Vice President Mondale was spending the night in Arkansas, less than 60 miles away from the blast site. Mondale had made a campaign appearance in the state.

The news reports had no information as to whether the missile was carrying a nuclear warhead. With the vice president in the area, Bob called the National Military Command Center (NMCC) at the Pentagon for details. It was learned that the missile had been undergoing routine maintenance when a wrench socket weighing eight pounds fell from a work platform. The socket fell about 70 feet. It hit the side of the silo and ricocheted into the fuel tank of the missile, puncturing its skin. Fuel leaked onto the bottom of the launch silo.

A fire started. Sprinklers were activated; eventually the silo was evacuated due to the buildup of toxic vapors. At about 3:00 a.m., a violent explosion erupted. The 750-ton launch doors blew off the silo. Flames and debris shot hundreds of feet in the air.

"Was the missile carrying a warhead?" Bob asked

"Yes," the NMCC colonel confirmed. "It has a nine-megaton yield. Each megaton is equivalent to the explosive force of a million *tons* of dynamite."

"What's its status?" Bob asked.

"We don't know. We haven't found it yet. It was ejected from the missile. We have teams looking for it."

"Is there any danger of it detonating?"

"We've never had this happen before. The condition of the warhead is unknown. It's believed the warhead's shield should be strong enough to protect the thermonuclear device. The shield is made to withstand the extreme temperatures of reentry. But, we're in unknown territory," the colonel remarked.

"What's the worst-case scenario?" Bob asked.

"That the warhead explodes, and we lose a lot of good men. State authorities are evacuating civilians out to a 10-mile perimeter. If the device detonates, we would also have a major release of radiation."

"Would the vice president be in any danger?"

"It all depends on which way the wind is blowing?" answered the colonel.

"Okay, colonel, please keep us advised of any and all updates."

Bob immediately got with duty desk supervisor Chuck Krall and the two agents began to make appropriate notifications. Bob called the USSS vice presidential command post in Arkansas and advised them of the situation. The VPPD supervisor decided to take some precautionary measures. The crew of *Air Force Two* was roused from sleep; they responded to the aircraft to prepare for takeoff—just in case. The vice president's military aide was also awakened. Somehow in the confusion of the emergency, he had not been advised by the NMCC of the explosion.

About an hour later, the NMCC colonel called to inform that the warhead had been found. It was intact and had been made safe. The crisis was over. Tragically, one airman died from injuries suffered from the blast; 21 others were injured. For his action, Bob received written commendations from Assistant Directors John Simpson (PO) and Robert Burke (PR).

In the 1980 presidential election held on November 4, Republican Ronald Reagan and his running mate George H.W. Bush defeated Carter-Mondale in a landslide. Reagan-Bush took 44 states (489 electoral votes) and finished almost 10 percentage points ahead of Carter-Mondale in the popular vote. It was one of the worst defeats in history for an incumbent president.

The ongoing hostage crisis, the failed rescue attempt, inflation, and other economic woes spelled defeat for President Carter. In the presidential debate held a week before the election, Ronald Reagan asked, "Are you better off than you were four years ago?" The electorate voted a resounding "no."

Twenty years had passed since JFK's 1960 election. Former California Governor and film star Ronald Reagan would be the next president to face Tecumseh's Curse. With the Reagan-Bush win, USSS-ID started to advance the trips of the president and vice president-elect. Bob was the ID advance agent for several of these visits.

One was to a Western city covered by a USSS resident agency. In those days, resident agencies were one or two-man offices set up within USSS districts. The resident agency was an extension of the controlling field office. Resident agents were domiciled in the far reaches of large districts as necessitated by caseload and travel time from the home field office. RAs were GS-13 senior agents.

Bob handled all of the QI reviews and a new case that sprung up during the visit. Bob was praised by the psychiatrist who was the director of the state hospital. Local law enforcement also commented favorably on Bob as well as the office secretary. The RA and Bob got along very well during the advance.

When the visit was over, the RA told Bob that the office had been approved for an assistant resident agent (GS-12) to help handle the increasing caseload. He asked if Bob was interested. Bob responded with an enthusiastic "yes." It was Bob's desire when his tour was done at ID to be transferred to a resident agency. The varied investigative work of a resident agency was more appealing to Bob than the prospect of being transferred to a field office where he would be pigeonholed to specific investigations.

Bob was ready to leave Washington. The SAIC and DSAIC of ID had never wanted Bob. He was stuck on the duty desk, and his PI ideas had been shot down in flames. Bob arrived home from the trip with a smile on his face. He told me about the "great opportunity" he was being considered for. I was lukewarm about the news.

"Jan, this is what we've been aiming for," Bob declared. "We have a chance to get out of D.C. to a less hectic life. This is one of the top RAs in the country. The area is beautiful; the cost of living is low. You'll love it."

I don't really know why I wasn't enthusiastic about the opportunity. At the time, I guess it was because the move involved the Secret Service, which had been sucking the happiness out of my life. In hindsight, what I said next would prove to be a major mistake: "If you get the job, go ahead and move out there. We'll join you this summer when school is out."

"Honey, that's not going to work. We'd need to put the house up for sale, find one in the new area, and do the move when we find a buyer. We can't wait until summer. I'd have to rent for at least six months; I don't want to be away from you and the kids that long."

"I'm sorry. I just can't do all this during a school year," I stated decisively. "We need to do this over the summer; the kids and I will join you later."

"Well, I probably won't get the transfer anyway. The RA would have to get the approval of the SAIC of the district office; then there's *headquarters*. They probably already have someone *penned* in for it."

Several days passed; Bob was working the duty desk when the call came in from the RA. "Bob, I've got great news. Everything's been approved. Give me the word and the teletype will be cut this afternoon. I'm looking forward to you joining me out here. Congratulations!"

Bob was faced with a crossroad decision. Bob enjoyed criminal investigation and he felt that getting out of the Washington grind would be the best thing for both of us. Yet, he didn't want to leave us behind—especially for six months or more. Bob thanked the RA but had to give his regrets. "Bob, you're making a big mistake passing up this transfer," the RA emphasized. This is one of the best investigative positions a 12 could have. And it will set you up for a 13."

"I know," Bob said. "I know."

On the evening of Monday, December 8, 1980, former Beatle John Lennon was shot and killed in New York City. He and his wife, Yoko Ono, were returning to their apartment from a Manhattan recording studio. Mark David Chapman, a 25-year-old security guard from Honolulu, Hawaii, fired five shots at Lennon's back. Four .38-caliber, hollow-point bullets found their mark.

In the days that followed, Bob saw the information that came into ID regarding Chapman. I told Bob that I couldn't understand why anyone would want to kill John Lennon. "A picture is unfolding of a guy who idolized Lennon at one time," Bob related. "Then Chapman becomes a born-again Christian. For Chapman, hero worship turns to betrayal when Lennon said the Beatles are more popular than Jesus Christ.

"Chapman has a history of mental problems and drug use including heroin and LSD. He's attempted suicide in the past and continued to have suicidal thoughts. Recently, Chapman has had major problems with keeping a job and in his relations with others.

"He has an obsession with Salinger's *Catcher in the Rye,* identifying with the Holden Caulfield character. There's a part in the book where Caulfield sees himself catching children before they fall off a cliff.

"I think Chapman thought it his duty to protect today's youth from Lennon, who had become a false prophet in Chapman's mind. Lennon just released a new album, which has been popularly received. At the same time, Chapman becomes instantly famous by murdering a cultural icon. In Chapman's grandiose mind, he might have thought the act would make him a hero.

"The most important thing to come out of this for me," Bob continued, "was that Chapman visited New York in October with the intent of killing John Lennon. He didn't go through with it then. Chapman returned to Honolulu and told his wife all about it. He even showed her the gun and ammunition. Like Lee Harvey Oswald's wife, she didn't notify authorities. It's important that relatives and friends pass this type of information to law enforcement. These people *don't* get better by themselves.

"The other problem is the copycat effect. Chapman has received a lot of notoriety. We're going to have a new president next month, and I hope someone isn't moved to emulate Chapman."

Mark David Chapman was deemed competent to stand trial. Rejecting his attorney's advice to plea "not guilty by reason of insanity," Chapman pled guilty to second-degree murder. He was sentenced to 20 years to life and is currently incarcerated in the Attica Correctional Facility, Attica, New York.

Bob received some good news in late December; his telephone trap authorization form was approved and adopted by the USSS. Bob received a commendation from Director Knight and a $100 cash award, minus federal withholding tax. The use of telephone traps became routine for out-of-town presidential trips.

In the Iranian hostage crisis, President Carter continued to press for the release of the 52 Americans still being held captive in Iran. After leaving the U.S. in December 1979, the shah traveled to Panama and then to Cairo, Egypt where he was granted permanent asylum by Anwar Sadat. With the shah's death from lymphoma on July 27, 1980, the demand that he be extradited to Iran became moot. With that obstacle out of the way, the U.S. was secretly negotiating with Algerian officials who acted as an intermediary for the Iranian government. Iran wanted the release of billions of dollars in frozen Iranian assets held in U.S. banks. Iran needed money to fight the war that had broken out with neighboring Iraq.

In Washington, advance arrangements for the inauguration of Ronald Reagan had begun in earnest.

Chapter 29

Rawhide

Ronald Reagan's code name was "Rawhide." It was a fitting call sign for a man who had starred in Hollywood westerns, owned his own California ranch, and loved horses. And like the buckaroo heroes of yesteryear, Reagan was riding into town to marshal in a new era. The theme for his inauguration was "A Great New Beginning."

USSS Headquarters decided that Intelligence Division agents would assist the Washington Field Office with the PI advances for a number of the 1981 inaugural events. Tim Halfman, an agent in the Liaison Branch of ID, coordinated the efforts. Because of Bob's WFO experience, he was selected to conduct the PI advance for the Presidential Inaugural Gala to be held at the Capital Centre (demolished 2002) in Landover, Maryland.

Tim Halfman then asked Bob which inaugural ball he wanted to work. Inaugural balls were being held at ten Washington locations: five Washington hotels, the Kennedy Center, three Smithsonian buildings, and at the Pension Building (now called the National Building Museum). Without hesitation, Bob chose the Washington Hilton Hotel. "There's an unsecured public area that borders the arrival and departure point," Bob explained. "It's a potentially dangerous spot. The protective survey places the burden on the PI teams to cover the area."

"You got it," Halfman said. "You'll be getting two teams from the pool of agents coming to D.C. to work the inauguration. For the gala, let me know your manpower request."

The 1981 Presidential Inaugural Gala was billed as "The Beginning of a Great New Beginning." Bob was able to get a pair of tickets for the event. On the evening of Monday, January 19, my mom and I along with over 18,000 other guests streamed into the Capital Centre for a pre-inaugural celebration with President-elect Reagan, Vice President-elect Bush, and their families.

Johnny Carson emceed the event and set the tone as he said in jest, "This is the first administration to have a premiere." Looking around at the large crowd, Carson continued the fun, "Mr. Reagan, if your movies drew crowds like this, you wouldn't have had to get into politics."

Frank Sinatra was the producer and entertainment director of the show; he also performed. Sinatra thrilled the crowd with a song dedication to Nancy Reagan. Ol' Blue Eyes adapted the title and lyric of one of his standards: "Nancy (With the Laughing Face)" to "Nancy (With the Reagan Face)."

Other stars performing included: Donny and Marie Osmond, Mel Tillis, Ben Vereen, Ethel Merman, Charlton Heston, Debby Boone, Jimmy Stewart, Charley Pride, Rich Little, and Bob Hope. Funnyman Hope wisecracked: "Ronnie Reagan's great. He's not a politician; he's an actor. He doesn't know how to lie, exaggerate, or cheat. He's always had an agent for that."

Earlier in the day, President Carter announced that a settlement had been reached between the U.S. and Iran for the release of the American hostages. Carter, Vice President Mondale, and Treasury Secretary William Miller along with their advisors spent the night in the Oval Office trying to finalize the deal. The Iranian side had a last-minute objection to some of the wording in the agreement. It was hoped the hostages could be released before Carter left office. Even with a final approval, the transfer of billions of dollars through the international banking system would take some time to accomplish.

At high noon on Tuesday, January 20, 1981, Ronald Wilson Reagan was sworn in as the 40th president of the United States by Chief Justice Warren Burger. It was the first presidential inauguration to take place on the West Front of the Capitol Building. The move permitted more spectators to view the ceremony. It also allowed the new president a spectacular view of the Washington Monument, Jefferson and Lincoln Memorials, and Arlington National Cemetery. Reagan referenced each in his inaugural address and paid tribute to their namesakes and to our fallen heroes enshrined at Arlington.

The president's 2,452-word address targeted the economic woes of America. Reagan highlighted a program that would reduce federal spending and the regulatory power of the federal government. He promised a budget that would lower the federal deficit and reduce inflation. President Reagan vowed to get the U.S. economy moving and American citizens back to work. President Reagan pledged, "Together with God's help we can and will resolve the problems which now confront us."

News reached Washington that the plane carrying the 52 American hostages had finally departed Tehran's Mehrabad Airport at about 12:33 p.m. Eastern Standard Time. It was said that the Iranians delayed the takeoff, so the hostages would not be released on Carter's watch. The Ayatollah Khomeini blamed Carter for precipitating the crisis by allowing the shah entry to the U.S. At about 2:00 p.m. (EST), the aircraft left Iranian airspace. After 444 days, the American hostage crisis was over. The news that our hostages had been freed spread throughout the land and heightened the joy of the inaugural celebration.

Later that afternoon, hundreds of thousands of happy spectators proudly waved American flags as they watched the inaugural parade along

Pennsylvania Avenue. The president and first lady waved to their admirers from an open-top armored limousine.

Due to Reagan's love of horses, the procession featured a large number of equestrian units. There were also floats and balloons, and over 30 bands high stepped to the parade's brisk 110-beat-per-minute pace. The pageant was organized to be symbolic of American history from the Revolutionary War to the 1900s.

Afterwards, television personality Willard Scott hosted a free concert on the West Front of the Capitol. The musical entertainment concluded with a U.S. military band playing Aaron Copeland's "Fanfare for the Common Man" as fireworks blazed over the dome of the Capitol.

That evening, nine white-tie presidential inaugural balls and a youth ball were held in Washington. Through the technology of closed-circuit television, the festivities were transmitted to over 80 locations across America. This enabled many thousands of additional revelers to take part in the celebration.

For the Washington Hilton inaugural advance, Bob name checked over a thousand people. Concerned about the president's safety, Bob suggested to the site advance agent that President Reagan wear his ballistic topcoat during the arrival/departure. "Do we have some adverse intelligence?" the site agent asked.

"No, and if history holds true, we probably won't have any before the next assassination attempt," Bob answered. "But, the T Street entrance to the hotel closely borders the arrival site. I'll have a PI team in the crowd, but it's a public area with a clear shot at POTUS."

The site advance agent looked at Bob with some surprise. "Okay," he said, "I'll pass it on, but I can't promise you anything."

Bob also added the warning to his intelligence situation report. The Washington Hilton was unique. Bob knew of no other site survey that brought the president so close to a public area. At other locations, POTUS would have to decide to use a non-survey route or opt to venture into public areas to shake hands.

After the security briefing for the event, Bob personally walked his PI teams around the hotel for familiarization and to assign them their duties. None of the agents had worked PI at the Washington Hilton before. One team was given the responsibility for coverage of the International Ballroom and PI response as needed. The other team was assigned to the public area adjacent to the arrival/departure site.

Bob emphasized to the latter team that POTUS and FLOTUS (first lady of the United States) were scheduled to arrive around 9:00 p.m. The Vice President and Mrs. Bush would visit later in the evening. Bob wanted this PI team to devote most of the evening to the outside arrival area. He especially wanted them in the area no later than 20 minutes before arrivals and to remain there until the departures.

Bob stood at the rope line that led to the T Street entrance of the Washington Hilton. "On the other side is the VIP entrance to the hotel where our protectees will be arriving," Bob informed. "Once inside the door, they have a secure path to the holding room and the stage area. If anything is going to happen, it will go down out here. For departures, they back up the limo and point it out toward T Street, which provides an even closer shot at POTUS—about 12–15 feet. And God forbid that he would walk over and shake hands along the rope line. Either way, an assassin would have a dead-on shot. If you see *anyone* acting suspiciously or with bulges, check them out." Bob then moved the rope line and stanchions, so they curved farther down the sidewalk. "That'll give us a couple of extra feet," Bob explained.

As ID coordinator for the site, Bob tried to handle what he could by himself. With Bob resolving ticket problems, inebriated guests, and the like with host committee staff and police, the PI teams were free to function more effectively.

The ballroom filled and dinner was served. Charlton Heston emceed the inaugural program. Glen Campbell, Tanya Tucker, and the Woody Herman Orchestra provided the evening's entertainment.

Shortly after 9:00 p.m., the President and Mrs. Reagan arrived at the Washington Hilton. Mrs. Reagan was elegant in a white satin and silk gown designed by James Galanos. The gown bared Mrs. Reagan's left shoulder and was hand embroidered with beads to form a fern-like pattern. Long white gloves, a white clutch purse, and beaded white shoes accented the gown.

The first couple spent about 25 minutes at the Hilton. The president thanked everyone for coming and informed the crowd that the 52 "prisoners of war" had just landed in Algiers on the last leg of their trip to Wiesbaden, Germany. There, they would recuperate at a U.S. Air Force facility before coming home. Mr. Reagan also proudly notified the guests that the National Christmas Tree had been lit to celebrate the release of the hostages.

The visits by the Reagans and the Bushes to the Washington Hilton were without incident. In fact, the visits to all 10 inaugural sites were completed without any major problems. It was after midnight when the Reagans visited their last ball at the Smithsonian Institution Museum of American History. The president and first lady arrived back at the White House at about 12:45 a.m.

A week after the inauguration, Washington was once again the scene of a historic celebration. The 52 freed American hostages arrived at Andrews Air Force Base about midday on January 27 aboard an Air Force Boeing 707 dubbed *Freedom I*. They were greeted by Vice President Bush, Secretary of State Alexander Haig, and Secretary of Defense Caspar Weinberger. Former hostage Richard Queen joined the group. Queen had been released earlier by the Iranians after 250 days of captivity. At the time, Queen had experienced some paralysis and other medical problems.

A caravan of buses was loaded with the freed Americans and their families for the 12-mile trip to the White House. Along the Suitland Parkway, which leads to the South Capitol Street Bridge, over 50,000 well-wishers greeted the hostages with American flags and yellow ribbons.

In Washington, hundreds of thousands lined the motorcade route and peered out of windows for a glimpse of the hostages and to cheer them on. The caravan made its way through the streets of Southwest Washington to Pennsylvania Avenue where the inaugural parade route was followed. Throughout the journey, the motorcade traveled between 5–15 miles per hour. The freed Americans and their families waved to the multitude of cheering onlookers from the open windows of the buses.

Upon their arrival at the White House, the freed hostages were greeted in the East Room by President Reagan. The presidential party then proceeded to the South Grounds where an official welcoming ceremony was held in honor of the returning Americans. Over 5,000 guests attended.

Afterwards, a reception was hosted in the East Room for the hostages, their families, and the families of the eight servicemen killed in the ill-fated hostage rescue attempt. American flags were presented to each of the hostages. Fourteen and one-half months of crisis had been officially laid to rest.

Basking in the goodwill created by the release of the hostages and the support of a majority of the American public, President Reagan moved forward in the succeeding weeks and months on his revolutionary economic package. Reagan's first executive order placed a federal hiring freeze on civilian positions. The freeze was made retroactive to November 5, 1980, the day after the presidential election. Reagan then tasked his Cabinet secretaries to reduce by at least 10 percent the operating budgets of the Carter administration. Only the Department of Defense (DOD) was exempt from the cuts. DOD received a 16 percent increase.

On February 18, 1981, the president presented his budget for the 1982 fiscal year to a joint session of Congress. In the nationally televised address, President Reagan called for over $40 billion in spending reductions. The cost-cutting measures fell heaviest on programs that aided the poor and needy such as: food stamps, Medicaid, subsidized housing, and unemployment compensation. Other budget reductions were proposed in the grants and subsidies provided to the states and private sector.

Besides spending cuts, the other two main features of Reagan's economic recovery program were regulatory reform and tax cuts to stimulate the economy. To help make up for the lost tax revenue, an increase in certain government fees was planned. Reagan projected that his plan would reduce inflation, create jobs, and eventually balance the budget. He emphasized that the time for change was now. The president warned that the national debt was approaching one trillion dollars. Reagan stated the sum was "difficult to comprehend" but tried to put it in perspective by describing it as equal to "a stack of $1,000 bills 67 miles high."

In the international arena, President Reagan accused the Soviet Union of engaging in a foreign policy of falsehood and deceit. Reagan charged that the leadership of the Soviet Union believed in the use of armed conflict to promote worldwide communism. The president warned that those who engage in international terrorism would face "swift and effective retribution," including the nations that support it.

The Reagan administration soon focused on El Salvador as a major trouble spot for East-West détente. The president accused the Soviet Union of supplying weapons to the Salvadoran guerillas in an attempt to overthrow the U.S. supported government. It was alleged that the Soviet Union was smuggling arms into El Salvador with the help of Cuba. The Reagan administration made it clear they were willing to go to the source to stop the flow of weapons.

President Reagan advised that any future negotiations with the Soviet Union in strategic weapons reduction and other important issues would be linked to all matters dividing the two nations and to the actions of the Soviet Union within that broader range.

On March 10–11, President Reagan made his first foreign trip since taking office. In a state visit to Canada, Reagan consulted in Ottawa with Canadian Prime Minister Pierre Trudeau. The first American president to visit Canada since Nixon's 1972 trip, Reagan and his top advisors discussed issues of mutual interest such as: a fisheries treaty, the conflict in El Salvador, the proposed American-Canadian natural gas pipeline, and acid rain. The president was heckled by demonstrators protesting American policy toward El Salvador and cross-border pollution from the U.S.

Bob continued to work the ID duty desk. He was working the day shift on Monday, March 30, 1981. Monday mornings were always busy as calls streamed into the Intelligence Division for the start of another workweek. The morning hours passed quickly.

The president's schedule showed an afternoon movement to the Washington Hilton Hotel. He would be speaking to the Building and Construction Trades Department of the American Federation of Labor-Congress of Industrial Organizations (AFL-CIO), which was holding their annual convention in D.C. Coincidentally, this group was one of the organizations that President Ford spoke to on the day of the assassination attempt by Sara Jane Moore.

Bob adjusted the radio at his workstation to the channels that would be utilized for the presidential visit. He selected USSS Charlie frequency in order to monitor the communications of the presidential detail. Bob also punched up the appropriate USPP and MPD radio frequencies.

Accompanied by Secretary of Labor Raymond Donovan, the president departed the South Grounds of the White House at 1:45 p.m. for the five-minute ride to the Washington Hilton. At 2:03 p.m., President Reagan began his address to the 4,000 convention delegates. The mostly Democratic audience was polite but unenthusiastic regarding the planks of Reagan's economic program.

At the conclusion of the speech, the president exited the International Ballroom for his return to the motorcade area. At about 2:27 p.m., Bill Green, PPD site advance agent, gave the signal that the president was coming out. About 10 seconds later, word came over both the USSS and police frequencies that gunfire had erupted and that there had been some injuries. On one of the police bands, Bob heard, "Shots fired; officer down!"

Bob immediately alerted duty desk supervisor Jim O'Neill, who had been busy with some paperwork. O'Neill glanced at the other duty agent, Steve Rutledge, who confirmed the report with a nod of the head. Without saying a word, O'Neill headed for SAIC Richards's office.

In the meantime, PPD-SAIC Jerry Parr radioed: "Rawhide is okay, follow-up. Rawhide is okay." From the PPD follow-up vehicle (Halfback), ATSAIC Ray Shaddick asked Parr if they were going to the hospital or back to the White House. Parr notified that Stagecoach (the presidential limo) was en route back to Crown (the White House).

A sickening feeling came over Bob. He knew the Washington Hilton and its arrival/departure point all too well. Bob feared that his worst nightmare had become terrifying reality. Someone must have fired at President Reagan as he was leaving the hotel.

Even though SAIC Parr had relayed that the president was okay, Bob was still worried. A voice in the back of Bob's mind warned that the president might have been hit. The voice reminded Bob that bullet wounds can be hard to detect, especially if made by small-caliber ammunition. A bullet can pierce clothing—leaving only a small hole that may be overlooked. If the bullets stay in the body, there are no exit wounds. It's not like the movies; blood doesn't gush from entry wounds. However, the bullets can cause life-threatening internal bleeding.

Jim O'Neill returned with SAIC Richards. Both were relieved to hear that the president was apparently okay and on his way back to the White House. Suddenly, Bob's nightmare took a frightening turn. The driver of the presidential limo (Agent Drew Unrue) notified the lead car agent (Mary Ann Gordon), "We want to go to the emergency room of George Washington." After Gordon acknowledged the message, Unrue added, "Go to George Washington fast!"

Bob hoped that the visit to the emergency room of George Washington University (GW) Hospital was just a precaution—to make sure the president hadn't been injured. Twenty seconds later, the change in destination took another ominous turn. Jerry Parr asked that a stretcher be ready on arrival. Halfback then asked the PPD command post W-16 (code name: Horsepower) if they copied that Stagecoach was now en route GW. Horsepower acknowledged that the hospital had been notified. Parr then radioed, "Let's hustle."

Had Tecumseh's Curse struck again? With the thought of the Secret Service losing another president to assassination too terrible to contemplate, Bob tried to reason other possibilities. Maybe Parr had been wounded. In the initial rush of adrenaline, Parr might not have realized he had been hit. Could it be that Jerry Parr was being dropped off at GW for treatment? In any case, Bob said a silent prayer.

SA O'Neill divided the notifications to be made by the duty desk agents. Thus, within minutes of the shooting, the Intelligence Division began to notify all headquarters offices and divisions, all protective divisions, and the Washington Field Office of the incident. Those notified were responsible for passing the information within their respective divisions/offices and to take appropriate action as needed.

Although the president's condition and details of the incident were still uncertain, ID advised that shots had been fired during the president's departure from the Washington Hilton and that the presidential limo had expedited to GW Hospital. Duty desk personnel stated that updates would be forthcoming as soon as they were available.

It took Stagecoach less than four minutes to reach GW. Minutes later, PPD agents at the hospital confirmed Bob's fears. The president had indeed been shot. At first, it was believed that the president had escaped unharmed. SAIC Parr had valiantly covered the president and pushed him into the back of the presidential limousine at the first sounds of gunfire. Parr landed on top of Reagan with the president's chest striking the transmission hump.

As Stagecoach roared away from the Hilton and down Connecticut Avenue, Parr used his hands to probe Reagan for injuries. None were found. Soon, however, the president complained of chest pain and difficult breathing. In response to Parr's queries, Reagan responded that he didn't think he had been shot nor was he having a heart attack. Reagan believed a rib might have been broken when he was thrown into the limo.

Bringing a handkerchief to his lips, the president noticed some blood and thought he had cut his mouth. SAIC Parr observed that the bright red blood on Rawhide's lips was frothy. Parr recognized this as a sign of an injured lung. By now, Stagecoach was entering the tunnel under Dupont Circle. Parr was afraid Rawhide's lung had been punctured by a broken rib. Parr ordered Stagecoach to divert to GW.

Upon reaching GW Hospital, the president attempted to walk in under his own power but soon collapsed. He was carried into Trauma Bay 5, and his clothes were quickly cut away. Reagan's blood pressure was dangerously low. An intravenous (IV) drip was hooked up to the president and fluids began to flow. Blood was ordered. While the president was being rolled on his side, medical personnel observed a small slit under Reagan's left armpit. It was a gunshot wound!

Further examination revealed that the president's left lung had collapsed. The first objective of the emergency medical team was to raise Reagan's blood pressure to prevent him from going into shock. The president received oxygen. Next, a tube was inserted into the president's chest to drain blood in order to permit the damaged lung to re-expand. Reagan continued to receive fluids and blood was administered.

In the meantime, radio transmissions were overheard that a suspect in the shooting had been transported by Secret Service agents to MPD Central Cell Block. Bob wondered why the subject hadn't been taken to the USSS Washington Field Office for release to the FBI. Due to the events that occurred in Dallas after the 1963 assassination of John F. Kennedy, it had become a federal offense to assassinate, assault, or kidnap the president or vice president or attempt to do so (18 U.S.C. 1751). Lee Harvey Oswald had been shot and killed in the basement of the Dallas Police and Courts Building on live national television. With his death, it became impossible to close the case to the satisfaction of many. Conspiracy theories abounded and persist to this day. The investigative jurisdiction for violations of 18 U.S.C. 1751 was given to the FBI. The statute also gives federal investigation and prosecution *precedence* over state and local authorities.

One of the main responsibilities of a PI team after an assault on POTUS was to take action that would maintain an "interim federal presence." Until the FBI could take over, the crime scene needed to be preserved, witnesses detained, and a federal chain of custody begun. If an assailant or assailants were apprehended, they needed to be questioned as to the possibility of other co-conspirators. It was of prime importance to ascertain if a conspiracy existed and to what extent. Were others standing by to launch another assault on the president in case the first attempt failed or to attack the vice president and others in the line of presidential succession?

It didn't take long for the news of the assassination attempt to break over radio and television. After all, the White House Press pool had covered the ill-fated departure. It did take them about 45 minutes to find out that President Reagan had been taken to GWU Hospital for treatment. The media originally reported that the president had *not* been injured and had returned safely to the White House.

President Reagan spent approximately 40 minutes in the trauma area of the GW Emergency Room. During this time, a large amount of blood drained from the tube inserted into the president's chest. X-rays confirmed the presence of a bullet, possibly within Reagan's lung. With the president continuing to bleed internally, the decision was made to operate. SAIC Parr and PPD shift agents quickly donned surgical scrubs, so they could provide protection for the president during surgery.

The Intelligence Division swelled with the arrival of the 3-11 duty desk shift and with the addition of some headquarters personnel. The latter had responded to ID when it was activated as the USSS Command and Control Center. A major problem soon arose; it became almost impossible to obtain an outside telephone line. With news of the assassination attempt being spread far and wide, telephone circuits in downtown Washington were quickly overloaded.

It was even extremely difficult to obtain a White House signal line. The White House Communications Agency signal board had been swamped by heavy usage. Bob took the initiative and spoke with a WHCA supervisor. It was emphasized that ID was trying to determine if additional shooters and conspirators might exist. The WHCA supervisor promised to give ID priority. Bob made a similar call to the White House switchboard. Priority status was obtained for ID's White House extension.

An agent was dispatched to WFO in order to establish and to keep open a line between the field office and ID. The problem continued well into the evening. Dial tones were not readily available on commercial lines. This proved to be a major obstacle in receiving and passing on updated information. Had it not been for the WHCA signal board and the White House switchboard, the Intelligence Division would never have been able to be as effective as it was during the early hours of the incident.

ID was advised by the Washington Field Office of the identity of the shooting suspect. His name was John Warnock Hinckley Jr., a 25-year-old white male with addresses in Lubbock, Texas and Evergreen, Colorado.

After a short stay in a holding cell, the suspect was moved to the MPD Homicide Branch. With USSS-SA Dennis V.N. McCarthy looking on, an MPD homicide detective advised Hinckley of his rights and asked if the subject wanted to answer questions. Hinckley replied that he thought he should talk with an attorney first. The suspect did give some identifying data.

Around 5:00 p.m., Hinckley was turned over to the FBI. The U.S. Attorney's Office authorized the FBI to charge Hinckley for violations of 18 U.S.C. 1751 and 18 U.S.C. 111 (Assault on a Federal Officer). USSS-SA Tim McCarthy (no relation to Dennis V. N. McCarthy) along with White House Press Secretary James Brady and MPD Police Officer Thomas Delahanty were also wounded during the assault on the president.

Inside Operating Room 2, the president was anesthetized. Dr. Joseph Giordano then performed a "peritoneal lavage" to detect if the president's abdominal cavity had been injured. Giordano was concerned that the bullet or a fragment might have tracked through the abdomen. In addition, there was the danger that the president had been harmed when he was forcibly thrown into the limo. An incision was made and a saline solution rinsed about. The fluid was then drained and analyzed for the presence of blood. The test was negative.

Next, Dr. Benjamin Aaron opened up the president's chest in search of the bullet and the source of the bleeding. It took several hours to locate the bullet and to remove it. A bleeding artery was sutured back together. The president was wheeled to the recovery room at approximately 6:45 p.m. During the evening, the president's condition continued to stabilize. The word from the hospital was that the president would survive. It was great news!

John Hinckley was taken to the Washington Field Office of the FBI and again given a Miranda warning. USSS-SA Stephen Colo sat in on the interview. Hinckley did not want to speak about the day's events until he could talk with his parents. He did answer questions regarding his travels, family, education, employment, medical history, and other general background information.

Hinckley divulged that he had received treatment from several mental health professionals. Most importantly, Hinckley identified a telephone number found in his wallet as one that connected to a Yale University dormitory. Hinckley said it was actress Jodie Foster's telephone number. Foster was enrolled at Yale, which is located in New Haven, Connecticut. Hinckley stated he had talked with the actress several times on the phone and that tapes of the calls were in a suitcase at his hotel room.

When Bob heard Jodie Foster's name mentioned, he excitedly turned to SAIC Richards and suggested, "This guy might be playing out the Travis Bickle role!" The blank look on Richard's face revealed that the reference was not understood. "The Travis Bickle character from *Taxi Driver*," Bob added. Richards still did not comprehend the meaning. Bob gave Richards a quick summary of the film and the significance of the roles played by Robert De Niro (Travis Bickle) and Jodie Foster (Iris). Richards then hurried off to relay the information to the supervisors who were in contact with WFO and the other USSS field offices that were monitoring FBI investigations in Denver, Lubbock, Dallas, and elsewhere.

It now seemed more certain that Hinckley was a troubled individual, who had acted alone. Later that night, a search of Hinckley's D.C. hotel room confirmed the assessment. FBI agents with USSS agents assisting executed a search warrant at Room 312 of the Park Central Hotel, 705 18th Street, NW. It was ironic that the hotel was located only a block away from Secret Service Headquarters and often housed agents who were on temporary assignments to Washington.

The search revealed a note written by Hinckley an hour before he left for the Hilton. Addressed to Jodie Foster, the letter professed Hinckley's deep love for the actress and his desire to live out his life with her. Hinckley wrote that by shooting President Reagan, he hoped to gain Foster's respect and love.

Thus, the attempt on the life of the 40th president of the United States appeared to be an irrational scheme concocted to impress a young film actress and to live out a fantasy.

Chapter 30

3-31-81

As Bob drove to work on the morning after the Reagan assassination attempt, he reflected on what more could have been done to prevent the previous day's assault. A would-be assassin had exploited a weakness in Secret Service protection. Bob put a large amount of the blame squarely on his own shoulders. He was one of the agents who participated in the 1978 update of the Washington Hilton protective survey.

To accommodate the hotel's management, a potentially dangerous change was made to the survey. This created a breach in the 360-degree protective perimeter. Bob tried to have the decision reconsidered. A modification was made; a PI team was added to cover the exposed area, yet the breach remained. Now, guilt squeezed Bob's conscience like a steel vice. He should have done more he told himself, even if it would have significantly harmed his career. President Reagan came *very* close to dying.

Seeing the movie *The Tall Target* stirred Bob's childhood fascination with presidential assassination and its prevention. The film's hero, played by actor Dick Powell, was a New York Police detective named John Kennedy. In the film, Kennedy's warning of an assassination plot against Lincoln is ridiculed by Kennedy's superior. Kennedy has to take matters in his own hands. The character was *dramatically* based on John Alexander Kennedy, the actual superintendant of the New York City Police Department during the Civil War.

In February 1861, John A. Kennedy received information alleging an assassination plot against President-elect Abraham Lincoln. The attempt was supposed to take place as Lincoln traveled through Baltimore on the way to Washington for his inauguration as the 16th president of the United States. At the same time, Allan Pinkerton, founder of the Pinkerton National Detective Agency, also developed information regarding the plot. On account of this, Lincoln secretly took the night train through Baltimore and arrived safely in Washington.

To Bob, it was ironic that the president elected 100 years after Lincoln's 1860 win was named John Kennedy, the same as the main character who had inspired Bob in *The Tall Target*. And like Lincoln, JFK was murdered by an assassin's bullet. Tecumseh's Curse haunted American history for 120 years (1840–1960). Bob joined the Secret Service and dedicated himself to breaking the curse for the president elected in 1980. By chance or fate, Bob had been on the survey team that almost cost this president his life. If Bob had shown the same resolve the Kennedy character did in *The Tall Target*, the assassination attempt on President Reagan would not have happened.

Uncanny thoughts continued to pass through Bob's brain as he walked from his Ellipse parking spot to 1800 G. My birthday was the same month and day (November 22) as the JFK assassination, and I was born in San Antonio, Texas, the first city visited by JFK in his ill-fated Texas trip. My brother and husband were Secret Service agents. Bob's initials, "RR," were the same as the president elected in 1980, Ronald Reagan. Both Bob's (Robert) and President Reagan's first and last names contained exactly six letters each. Had Bob been living in "The Twilight Zone?"

Bob took his place at the duty desk and reviewed the overnight developments. Further evidence of John Hinckley's irrational infatuation with Jodie Foster was revealed. It was also believed that Hinckley might have stalked Jimmy Carter. In fact, Hinckley had been arrested in Nashville, Tennessee on October 9, 1980, while attempting to board a commercial airliner. *Three* handguns were seized from Hinckley's suitcase. Hinckley paid a fine and was released. It was viewed as a routine arrest by local authorities and the FBI. The arrest information was not passed to the Secret Service even though President Carter was in Nashville conducting a "town meeting" on that date.

At about 8:45 a.m., Bob was called into SAIC Richards's office. DSAIC Ron Claiborne was also present. "Bob, Tim Halfman mentioned that you had been concerned about the Hilton—that it was a dangerous site," Richards queried.

"Yes, the protective survey was changed in 1978. Before that, the T Street entrance and that side of the block were closed down for arrivals and departures. What used to be a credentialed press area became a full-time public area," Bob stated. "The security director of the hotel complained that the temporary closures were too much of a hardship."

Both Richards and Claiborne were taken aback from what they had just heard; a momentary silence fell upon the room. "Bob, the director is worried," Richards said in an undertone. "There's already been press inquires asking how Hinckley was able to get so close to the president. Questions have also been raised whether the area was a press area and about the positioning of the limo."

"A concrete island separates the VIP drop-off area from T Street," Bob explained. "After the arrival, they back up the limo, so it can pull straight out to T Street. That brings the limo and the president's departure path closer to the rope line. Otherwise, the limo would have to pull forward from the VIP entrance and negotiate a sharp turn to connect with the hotel's main driveway and then out to Connecticut Avenue.

"Being that close to the rope line was never a problem when that side of the street was closed to the public," Bob continued. "It was a designated press area for arrivals and departures from the opening of the hotel in 1965 to the survey change of 1978. They still shepherd the press there for close-ups and that causes the confusion."

"Bob, we want you to interview the WFO-PI agents who worked yesterday's movement and also the squad's AT, Ed Dansereau. The director wants to know if there were any problems with the PI coverage."

"Sir, I don't know," Bob mused. "I don't have the grade to be reviewing the actions of others—especially a superior. Shouldn't Inspection be doing this?"

"Inspection is busy taking statements from everyone who worked the Hilton yesterday," Richards replied. "The director asked the ADs to conduct in-house investigations to find any problem areas. If mistakes were made, the director would rather get out in front of them before the congressional hearings. You know the drill for the Hilton; they won't be able to give you the runaround."

That evening, I anxiously bombarded Bob with questions regarding the assassination attempt and especially John Hinckley's motives.

"Hinckley identified with the Travis Bickle character from *Taxi Driver*," Bob related. "He was playing out the script with himself as lead. He bought guns and traveled around the country. He was obsessed with Jodie Foster and wanted to impress her. Hinckley thought the assassination of the president would win Foster's love. He also wanted to be somebody. He had been under psychiatric care, and the doctor advised Hinckley's parents to sever the ties to their son, so he could stand on his own. They said goodbye to him and cut off his money. John Hinckley Jr. became desperate. He was either going to live with Jodie Foster on earth or live without her in heaven."

"So, are you a hero?" I asked.

"The heroes are Tim McCarthy, James Brady, Officer Delahanty, and Jerry Parr," Bob replied.

"I meant are you getting recognition for your opposition to the changes made at the Hilton. You were the only one who saw the danger and tried to do something about it."

Bob grimaced and answered with a terse, "No."

"Why not?" I asked in a disappointed tone.

"The higher-ups don't want that information to get out," Bob replied with some emotional agitation.

"What!" I blurted out.

"There's more; I was sent to WFO this morning to assess the PI coverage at the Washington Hilton," Bob related. "Two PI teams were originally assigned to the Hilton as required by the protective survey. One of the agents called in sick. Instead of finding a replacement or taking the assignment himself, the GS-13 who schedules the squad's assignments canceled one of the teams."

With anguish in his voice, Bob continued: "The remaining team didn't pick up the slack. They can be seen in the news video coming out of the VIP entrance only *a few short seconds* before the president. When I asked why they hadn't come outside in time to check the public area, the team's senior agent claimed that the president finished his speech early. 'What could we do?' he said.

"I told him he could have asked Jerry Parr to keep the president in the holding room until the area was checked and deemed safe. Jerry is one of the most easy-going supervisors ever.

"The truth is: Presidential movements within Washington have become routine. Some agents have grown complacent. Before yesterday, the last presidential assassination attempt in D.C. was in 1950. That's long before any of today's agents started their careers and before some were born. The agents work movement after movement in D.C.—day in and day out. For some, it becomes monotonous; the job takes on an unreal quality. Sooner or later, they're going through the motions on autopilot.

"If there's no adverse intelligence, some let down even more. I go on the assumption that each and every movement is going to be the time that we're challenged. I prepare for the worst and look for ways to prevent it. I give it my all; you can't turn back the clock if something goes wrong. Yesterday should never have happened. It was taken for granted by some that the movement was going to be a *milk run*."

"That's not good," I said.

"There's still more. I wrote up my findings and gave them to the administrative assistant of ID to be typed. She came to me later in the day and said she wanted to 'warn me.'"

"Warn you of what?" I asked.

"She's been around a long time. She started in the Chicago Field Office and worked there during the JFK assassination. She told me that 'funny things' went on back then and that she has the same feeling again."

"What kind of *funny things*?"

"I don't know; she wouldn't elaborate on that. She did say that SAIC Richards told her to type only an original of my report. No copies were to be made, not even the standard agent's copy. And she was ordered to shred my original handwritten submission! She knew how strange that was. She wanted to warn me to look out for myself."

"The Secret Service is playing you for a sucker," I said in anger. "You need to do something about this!"

"I did drop in to see Richards when I was pushed off the duty desk at the end of my shift. I asked for a copy of the report for my records. He got angry and ordered me not to mention anything about the report or what was in it ever again—*even to other agents*. When I started to protest, he told me to keep quiet, or I'd ruin my career. He then ordered me out of his office."

"What are you going to do?" I asked.

"Nothing—what more can I do," answered Bob.

I filled with anger. Bob had given so much to the Secret Service. The sacrifices that he *and I* had made were superhuman. I had taken over all of the day-to-day family responsibilities. My professional and personal life had suffered. Bob had been a part-time husband and father for too long— *and for what?*

The Secret Service didn't care about anything but its image. Bob had been a lone voice warning of the danger caused by the changes to the Hilton survey. Dozens of visits had been made to the Washington Hilton since the changes of 1978. Yet, no one from PPD or WFO ever questioned them— except Bob. Now, Bob would be denied any recognition of his foresight, and his career was in jeopardy to boot. Bob had been unfairly treated when he was passed over on the duty desk, but this latest episode was the epitome of raw deals. It was also the final slap in the face I was going to take.

Maybe Bob wasn't going to do anything about our lives, but I sure was. The discontent had been growing inside of me for years. My emotions raged, and my feelings finally boiled over. I quickly fell into an abyss of despair. I deserved better I told myself. I had to do something and *do it now*.

I concluded that I wanted Bob and the Secret Service out of my life. He came home one night, and I told him in a matter-of-fact way that we were through. I wanted him to move out. He was shocked. Things had been going south for us for some time, but he never expected this. Somehow, our love had always carried us through—but *not* this time.

Bob refused to move out. He asked that we go to marriage counseling instead. I resisted the suggestion. I wanted out of the relationship—the sooner the better. I thought the love had gone out of my heart.

I called my mom and asked if she would watch the kids from time to time, so I could start going out. My mom could hardly believe her ears. I think she was more shocked than Bob. "I'm not doing that!" she stated emphatically. "I'm not going to help you throw away your marriage."

She told me that I was making the biggest mistake of my life and that I needed to rethink my actions. "Go to counseling," she advised. "You two can work out your problems." She emphasized that she couldn't have asked for a better son-in-law. She revealed the poignant conversation when Bob had asked for her consent to our marriage. Bob allayed my mom's fears and personally promised that I would graduate from college. He told her that she would always be a close part of our lives. And, Bob pledged that he would always treat me with love and respect and *never* cheat on me.

I was unhappy over my mom's refusal to baby-sit the kids but took her marital advice to heart. Bob and I did have an almost 12-year relationship.

At this point, I didn't feel the marriage could be salvaged, but Bob made me a good offer. If I still wanted to dissolve our marriage after a reasonable period of counseling, Bob agreed to move out and to give me an uncontested divorce. That seemed fair.

At our first counseling session, the councilor's eyebrows raised when I said I wanted to have my own social life. She asked that neither Bob nor I do any "extracurricular activities." It was sure to be "counterproductive." She requested that both of us give the counseling a fair chance.

When I look back at this sad period in my life, it is still *very* emotionally disturbing. I don't like to think about it and usually never do. For several weeks, I hardly spoke to Bob and resented his very presence. I knew he was also deeply hurt by my sudden desire to end our marriage, but he never gave up on me and us.

The sessions continued. I eventually realized that I wasn't myself. There had been some serious emotional changes in my makeup that affected my reasoning. I had become totally stressed out, irritable, and blamed Bob for most of our problems. It hadn't been pretty. It was like falling off the top of a mile-high cliff. I fell head over heels into extended free fall. I was out of control and grasping for a lifeline.

Over the next several months, I pieced my life back together and took control of my emotions. I knew deep in my heart that Bob was the true love of my life. We were destined to spend our lives together. Even though he had a demanding occupation, I had taken him *for better or for worse*.

It wasn't as if Bob was running around. Through the years, he had spent most of his non-working hours with me and the children. The very qualities that made Bob a superior agent also made Bob a loving, caring husband and father. He would give his life for the kids and me just like he would for his country.

Unfortunately, his devotion to the Secret Service coupled with his job assignments had placed a very heavy burden on our relationship. That was the downside of Bob's extreme loyalty. His super dedication came at a personal cost to his family life. I needed to accept it. It was part of Bob's being and that was the way it was. I stop letting things neither of us could control be personal affronts and worrisome baggage. I let go of the pressure. Once again, we became one.

During this time, Bob was *finally* transferred off the duty desk and that was a big help. He was reassigned to the Liaison Branch of ID. SA Tim Halfman was the 13 with Bob the 12. The office hours were 9:00 a.m. to 5:30 p.m. with weekends off. Bob loved the position. Duties included keeping the SAICs and other high-level supervisors of PPD and VPPD briefed on the latest protective intelligence information. The branch also maintained intelligence liaison with the Uniformed Division and all other divisions and offices of the Secret Service in the D.C. area.

In addition, Tim and Bob were responsible for the evidentiary collection of any threat letters mailed to the White House. The letters were picked up from the White House Office of Correspondence, which is located on the fourth floor of the Old Executive Office Building (since renamed Eisenhower Executive Office Building). The letters were initialed, dated, placed in document protectors, and brought back to ID for investigation.

One of Bob's first initiatives as a liaison agent was to make the interview room at the Northwest Gate safer. He coordinated efforts to have the chairs in the room bolted to the floor, so they couldn't be used as improvised weapons. Other security enhancements were made and interview procedures updated.

Another important duty of the position was maintaining close liaison with the USSS freedom of information and privacy act officer. Requests to the Secret Service for disclosures under the Freedom of Information Act were searched through the various divisions and offices. For the Intelligence Division, Tim and Bob conducted the searches. When found, the records were reviewed and delivered to the freedom of information and privacy act officer for a determination of what could be released.

In addition, Bob became the ID contact for the Secret Service continuity of government (COG) officer. Bob was "read into" the program, which included the evacuation of the president, vice president, and other senior civilian leaders to safe relocation centers outside of Washington in times of national emergencies.

Bob also participated in nuclear/radiological exercises with the Nuclear Emergency Support Teams (NEST) of the Department of Energy. Field exercises were run with terrorist, extortionist, and post attack/nuclear accident scenarios. Bob marveled at some of the equipment utilized by the teams to include briefcase-size radiological detection devices.

After one of these exercises, the head of the White House Military Office, Edward Hickey Jr., invited Bob to lunch at the Navy Mess, located on the ground floor of the West Wing. Hickey was a former Secret Service agent, former State Department agent, and former director of the California State Police where he supervised Reagan's security during his years as governor.

"I want to thank you," Hickey said.

"For what?" Bob asked.

"Your alertness and quick action during the Arkansas missile explosion showed that the military office needed a shake-up. My position was created to provide coordination and direction. I owe you my job."

"No, problem," Bob responded. "Thanks for lunch."

"My pleasure. Maybe I can do more for you someday," Hickey replied.

Bob earned his keep in the Liaison Branch. In the weeks and months following the Reagan assassination attempt, the copycat phenomenon kicked in with a vengeance. Over a dozen subjects were arrested for making threats against President Reagan. Tim and Bob spent much time familiarizing themselves with active cases and passing the intelligence to SAIC Parr of PPD.

One case stood out in particular. This individual closely emulated John Hinckley Jr. The subject traveled to New Haven, Connecticut and watched Jodie Foster perform in a Yale University play. He sent a letter to Foster with the warning, "I will finish what Hinckley started." He also left a note in a New Haven hotel room that read, "I depart now for Washington, D.C., to bring completion to Hinckley's reality." Subject was arrested in a Manhattan bus terminal while attempting to board a bus for Washington. At the time of the arrest, he was carrying a loaded revolver.

An assassination attempt on another world leader took place that spring. On Wednesday, May 13, 1981, Pope John Paul II was shot while making his weekly appearance in St. Peter's Square, Vatican City. The Pontiff was being driven around the square in his "Popemobile" when a 23-year-old Turkish national, Mehmet Ali Ağca, opened fire with a Browning Hi-Power 9 mm semiautomatic pistol. John Paul II was hit in the arm and hand and struck twice in the abdomen.

The Pontiff was rushed to the hospital where he underwent emergency surgery to repair wounds to the small and large intestines. Fortunately, vital organs had been missed and bleeding was controlled. Over the next several months, Pope John Paul II would make a full recovery. Two bystanders were also injured in the attack, one seriously.

The pope's assailant was immediately apprehended. Mehmet Ağca was the subject of a prior Interpol lookout. Incarcerated for the 1979 murder of a Turkish journalist, Ağca escaped an Istanbul prison and fled to Europe. A letter found on his person stated that he planned to kill the pope to underscore "the imperialistic crimes committed by the Soviet Union and the United States ... in El Salvador and Afghanistan."

Mehmet Ağca admitted to the shootings and was given a life sentence. In 1983, Pope John Paul II visited Ağca in prison and personally forgave him. Italian President Carlo Ciampi pardoned Ağca in 2000. Ağca was extradited to Turkey where he resumed serving the sentence for the 1979 murder. Mehmet Ali Ağca was released from custody in 2010.

With President Reagan recuperating in the White House after his discharge from George Washington University Hospital, presidential travel was minimal. Vice President Bush picked up some of the presidential trips but tried to spend more time in Washington until the president was fully recovered. Even though Bob was subject to out-of-town advances, there was a brief lull in travel. Bob still had to fill in on the duty desk when needed, but it was nice to have him off steady shift work.

The summer of 1981 saw air travel interrupted. On August 3, approximately 12,000 air traffic controllers walked off their jobs in a dispute with the federal government over wages, benefits, and working conditions. Charging that the Professional Air Traffic Controllers

Organization (PATCO) and striking members were in violation of federal law (5 U.S.C. 7311 and 18 U.S.C. 1918), President Reagan ordered the controllers back to work with the warning that those who did not return would be fired and banned from future federal employment.

About 10,000 controllers refused to return until labor negotiations were restarted on a new contract. The Reagan administration kept their promise and began terminating striking controllers. The Justice Department also filed judicial action against PATCO and its leaders. In a matter of days, the Federal Aviation Authority (FAA) turned their attention from settling a labor dispute to the hiring and training of personnel to replace striking controllers. Supervisors and military controllers also helped to fill the void. It would take years before the system fully recovered.

PATCO was decertified by the Federal Labor Relations Board. Saddled with millions of dollars in fines to the federal government and additional millions in judgments to airlines that sued for compensation for lost revenue due to flight cancellations, PATCO was forced to file for bankruptcy protection and ultimately ceased to exist.

As fall was returning to the Northeast, the United States and the world lost a good friend and a champion of peace. On October 6, 1981, President Anwar el-Sadat of Egypt was assassinated while reviewing a military parade commemorating the 1973 October War. As Egyptian air force jets flew overhead, an artillery truck suddenly stopped in front of the reviewing stand. The unit commander exited the truck and faced the presidential box. President Sadat, in military uniform, came to his feet in preparation of returning the officer's salute. Without warning, the artillery commander lobbed grenades toward the presidential box, while three soldiers rose from within the truck and began to fire at Sadat with AK-47 automatic rifles. The initial firing was followed with a running assault where the attackers fired point-blank at Sadat from the front of the reviewing stand.

President Sadat and seven others were killed in the attack. Twenty-seven were wounded. The four assassins were captured. The leader was an active duty military officer. Another was a reservist; the remaining two were civilians disguised as soldiers. All of the gunmen were Muslim fundamentalists, who believed the taking of Sadat's life was justified. All would be tried, found guilty, and executed.

The death of Sadat by extremists caused alarm and worry within the Reagan administration and among U.S. allies. Anwar Sadat shared the 1978 Nobel Prize for Peace with Prime Minister Menachem Begin of Israel. With the encouragement of President Jimmy Carter, the two Mideast leaders negotiated the Camp David Accords in September 1978. These agreements culminated in the 1979 signing of an Israeli-Egyptian peace treaty. Sadat's assassination placed the future of Egypt and the Middle East in jeopardy. With regimes in power in Syria, Iran, and Libya hostile to

Israel and the West, U.S. leaders worried that Egypt might renounce the 1979 peace treaty with Israel and move back into the Soviet camp.

Because of the failure of Egyptian security and the uncertainty of the situation, it was deemed too risky for either President Reagan or Vice President Bush to attend the fallen leader's funeral. Secretary of State Alexander M. Haig Jr. along with former presidents Richard Nixon, Gerald Ford, and Jimmy Carter were sent to Cairo to offer their condolences and to pay the respect of the American people.

During the visit, Secretary of State Haig assured Sadat's apparent successor, Egyptian Vice President Hosni Mubarak, that the U.S. would support both Egypt and its neighbor Sudan if Libya decided to subvert either's sovereignty. For his part, Mubarak pledged to continue the peace process begun by Sadat and to honor previous agreements. Haig also promised that the U.S. would speed up arms sales to Egypt and Sudan due to Libya's desire to destabilize nations friendly to the U.S. At the time, Libya was engaged in armed intervention in Chad.

The Libyan dictator, Colonel Mu'ammar al-Qadhafi, had a long history of troubled relations with the United States. He rose to power via a 1969 military coup, which deposed King Idris. Afterward, Qadhafi closed American military bases and partially nationalized the Libyan oil industry. In 1972, the U.S. removed its ambassador from Tripoli in protest of Qadhafi's support for international terrorism and subversion.

Relations with the U.S. came to a boiling point in December 1979 when the U.S. Embassy in Tripoli was ransacked and burned by a Libyan mob. Consequently, the U.S. declared Libya a "state sponsor of terrorism." U.S. diplomats were recalled to the United States.

In May 1980, four Libyan diplomats were expelled from the United States for engaging in a campaign of harassment and intimidation toward exiled opponents of Qadhafi. Claiming that they had done nothing wrong, the Libyans refused to leave and a standoff ensued. The Libyan mission was ringed with police and FBI agents. Qadhafi threatened to cut off oil supplies to the U.S. over the dispute. Eventually, an agreement was reached between both nations. The four Libyans were recalled and departed the United States. Diplomatic relations were severed with Libya.

From 1980 through 1981, a number of Libyan dissidents were killed in Europe and the Middle East. Intelligence sources suspected that Libyan "hit teams" were eliminating anti-Qadhafi exiles. Two former CIA officers were indicted on charges of supplying Libya with arms and explosives. It was also believed that several former U.S. Army Green Berets had provided special operations training in Libya.

It was within this background that the Reagan administration met Qadhafi head-on in the Mediterranean Sea. Libya claimed the entire Gulf of Sidra as territorial waters and airspace. The Gulf of Sidra extends over a hundred miles into the Mediterranean. The U.S. only recognized the three-mile limit denoted by international law. On August 19, 1981, U.S. naval forces were conducting exercises centered several hundred miles off the Libyan coast. About 60 miles offshore, two U.S. Navy F-14 Tomcat jets were patrolling the southern perimeter of the area used for the war games. Suddenly, they were attacked by two Libyan fighter jets. In the ensuing dogfight, both Libyan jets were shot down.

After the incident, both nations released official statements. The U.S. warned that "any future attack against U.S. forces operating in international waters and airspace will also be resisted with force if necessary." Libya blamed the U.S. for provoking the incident and warned that Libya would take "all measures ... to safeguard its airspace and territorial waters."

On October 9, 1981, NBC news broadcast that President Ronald Reagan would not be attending Anwar Sadat's funeral due to a report that Colonel Qadhafi had ordered Reagan's assassination. It was alleged that the order for the assassination had been issued after the August incident in which two Libyan planes were shot down by the U.S. A USSS spokesperson denied the validity of the report. It was the first time a Libyan assassination plot targeting President Reagan appeared in the news. It wouldn't be the last.

In late November through December 1981, a number of news reports circulated that Qadhafi had dispatched a "hit squad" to the U.S. Targets listed were President Reagan, Vice President Bush, the secretaries of State and Defense, and White House aides. Some reports mentioned that two "death squads" had been sent. They were described as either five or seven members each. Several news dispatches stated the teams had already entered the U.S. Others cited the teams as poised to enter via Canada or Mexico. It was said that the assassination squads were armed with rocket-propelled grenades and surface-to-air missiles. Thus, both the presidential limo and *Air Force One* were in danger according to the media.

Anonymous intelligence and administration officials were cited as describing the original source of the information as a *credible informant*. When questioned by reporters about the plot, President Reagan advised that "the threat was real" and that "we have *complete* confidence in it." Colonel Qadhafi and the Libyan government denied the charges in the strongest of terms.

It was Bob's duty as a Liaison Branch agent to stay on top of the investigations surrounding the so-called "Libyan hit teams" and to keep the SAICs of PPD, VPPD, and UD senior officials updated on the latest revelations. For his part, Bob was privy to and had knowledge of all information regarding the alleged assassination teams. Bob was on board from the very beginning.

Bob told me that he believed the entire affair was taking on a "life of its own." I have firsthand knowledge of some of this. Our phone rang at about

4:00 a.m. one morning in early 1982. It was the ID duty desk asking Bob to come in as soon as possible. Upon arrival, Bob was anxiously told by the duty desk supervisor, "A Libyan hit team is in the Washington area!"

Bob reviewed the information that had come in overnight. The previous evening, a radio hobbyist had overheard some strange transmissions while operating a newly purchased scanner at his home, located near the George Washington Memorial Parkway and Washington National Airport. The transmissions were being sent over the Citizens Band (CB) with an alteration in the frequency, so standard CB radios would not be able to hear what was being said. With "Libyan hit teams" all over the news and the conversations sounding like a Middle Eastern dialect, the hobbyist recorded the transmissions and rushed them to the Department of State in D.C. There, an interpreter translated the conversations as at least three different individuals checking positions and distances.

When the intelligence alphabet agencies (CIA, FBI, and NSA) got hold of this, it was feared that a Libyan hit team had arrived and that it was triangulating positions for a motorcade attack. Of course, questions were raised as to what other locations the assassination team might have checked and when they would strike.

WFO, W-16, the VPPD command post, the UD command post, other protective details, and headquarters officials were notified by USSS-ID. The SAICs of both PPD and VPPD or their representative were asked to come in early in order to receive a special briefing from Bob. Assassination fervor swept through the Secret Service like a desert sand storm.

Fred Mann, the agent from the Foreign Intelligence Branch, arrived. He had been called in to prepare a teletype for transmittal to area law enforcement agencies. When Mann heard the news, he acted as if he had just won the lottery. Displaying a broad smile, he beamed with joy. He had consistently evaluated the Libyan hit team threat as real and this news was the validation he had hoped for. "They're here!" he excitedly told Bob.

Bob thought another explanation might be more likely. Fred and Bob headed for the Technical Security Division where they listened to a copy of the tape. They were told that the radios had been specifically tuned to the same nonstandard frequency for privacy. "This couldn't have happened on its own," the TSD specialist remarked. "It must be a Libyan hit team."

"Yes," Mann eagerly agreed.

To Bob, the transmissions sounded like they originated from *moving* vehicles. If the subjects were triangulating firing positions, Bob reasoned that they would have been stationary. "Guys," Bob said, "I think I know what this is. There are a lot of gypsy cab drivers operating in Northern Virginia. Many are here illegally; they don't have hack licenses. I know from my experience as a former U.S. Park Police officer that they communicate with each other via Citizen Band radios. They cruise about looking for fares and keep each other informed as to their location. They try to stay clear of the police and hide their activities." Mann looked at Bob as if he had just shot down Santa's sleigh.

TSD passed Bob's information to the State Department. With this new outlook and a different interpreter, it was discovered that the subjects were reporting their locations to each other and where they had found *passengers*. It was confirmed that Bob's hypothesis was correct. A cadre of gypsy cab drivers had been mistaken for a Libyan assassination squad.

Bob walked over to the Executive Office Building and passed the information to Jerry Parr, who had a good laugh over the false alarm. At the EOB offices of the Vice Presidential Protective Division, Bob informed the supervisor on duty, Frank Brown, of the resolution of the overnight scare. Brown was no stranger to Bob. Some years before, Brown had tried to have Bob unjustly disciplined. The action resulted from Bob's reluctance to hand classified national security information to foreign nationals.

Brown looked solemnly at Bob. "We still have to be vigilant. The teams are out there—somewhere," Brown stated with conviction.

"The information has to be taken seriously—for sure. I wouldn't put anything pass Qadhafi," Bob agreed. "He's a murderous dictator. The Service and the FBI are leaving no stone unturned, but so far we haven't been able to corroborate the key details of the informant's story."

"We're hearing a different tune over here," Brown declared. "Staffers are telling us that the information has been confirmed and is reliable."

"Staff people and national security types are not criminal investigators, and I think that's where the confusion begins," Bob remarked. "They have a layman's knowledge and understanding of criminal investigations. Because polygraph examinations of the source showed no deception or were inconclusive, the non-law enforcement types immediately took that as corroboration and evaluated the information and informant as reliable. We as criminal investigators can't do that—especially with a new informant who has no track record of reliability. That's against federal procedures.

"When you also consider that the source demanded a large sum of money *upfront* and that many foreign cultures don't have a stigma about lying, the informant's story and polygraph results should be questioned even more."

"They're pretty sure this is the real deal," Brown asserted. "Maybe they have access to more of the intelligence."

"I've read every piece of information on this," Bob replied. "There's no hard evidence that this informant's story is true. We've been checking every possible angle. I and other ID agents have volunteered a lot of off-duty time reviewing tens of thousands of Customs declarations and Immigration forms. Other indices have been checked too. We haven't had one worthwhile hit on any of the names we've been given.

"Frank, you're welcome to drop by ID and review the files for yourself. I'll be happy to set it up for you."

"No, that won't be necessary," Brown replied.

Returning to ID, Bob spoke with DSAIC Ron Claiborne. "Ron, I just got back from VPPD. They've been told by staffers that the Reagan hit team information is reliable and credible. Intelligence, administration, and sources on Capitol Hill have also been reported as confirming the existence of the teams. Even President Reagan has publicly expressed confidence in the information. With the Secret Service taking the lead in the domestic part of the investigation, I'm concerned there may be some fallout on us. We haven't corroborated the informant's story."

"Don't worry about it," Claiborne snapped. "Richards and I have attended National Security Council meetings on this. They're happy with what they've been hearing. If they're reading more into it than there is, it's a win for us. The Reagan assassination attempt and Libyan death squads are the justification we need for more money and agents. The Service is submitting a budget request for an additional shift for PPD, so they can be routinely rotated through assault on the principal [AOP] exercises and other in-service training. We've also been asking for funds for counter assault teams [CAT] and magnetometer screening. And UD wants funding to make the Ellipse patrol car permanent."

As the weeks went by without any trace of the hit teams, initial reports were questioned by the press, Congress, and the public. Eventually, it was suggested by diehards that the assassination squads had been recalled due to the uncovering of the plot. No detailed information supporting the existence of the Reagan hit teams was ever released by U.S. authorities.

A double dose of tragedy struck the Washington area on Wednesday, January 13, 1982. With a major snowstorm moving into the region that afternoon, federal workers were released from work early. Schools and businesses closed. With temperatures in the 20s and snow falling, the slick roads soon filled with commuters.

Then at about 4:00 p.m., disaster struck. An Air Florida Boeing 737 (Flight 90 to Tampa, Fla.) stalled on takeoff from Washington National Airport. With ice on the wings and its engine de-icers inexplicably turned off, the twin-engine jetliner fell from the sky, crashing into the northbound span of the 14th Street Bridge. The plane came down on top of vehicles, caught fire, and plowed its way through the side barrier of the bridge into the icy waters of the Potomac River. The aircraft broke into pieces and started to sink.

Only six people were able to make it out of the fuselage. Five of the survivors were pulled from the frigid water by the heroic efforts of the flight crew of *Eagle One*, the Bell JetRanger helicopter of the U.S. Park Police. The sixth individual slipped below the icy surface and drowned. He had courageously passed the lifeline dropped from the helicopter to others. Seventy-eight souls perished in all, including four motorists.

Rescue and recovery operations forced the closing of not only the northbound span of the 14th Street Bridge but also the southbound span out of the city. With one of the major traffic arteries in and out of Washington shutdown indefinitely, the Virginia side of the Potomac as well as downtown D.C. developed massive gridlock. Most commuters didn't arrive home until late in the evening. Many gave up and spent the night in hotels.

Adding to the day's terror and to the burden of emergency workers, a second disaster occurred about 30 minutes after the first. A Metro subway train derailed between the Federal Triangle and Smithsonian stations. A malfunctioning switch shifted the train onto the wrong track. When a supervisor attempted to back the train onto the correct track, the front wheels of the lead car jumped the rails. The lead car was dragged back sideways, and the front of the passenger compartment was crushed when it collided with one of the reinforced concrete support columns of the tunnel. Three passengers were killed and over 20 were injured. Portions of the Blue and Orange lines were closed, and Metro passengers had to be rerouted by bus. This added to the nightmare the evening rush hour had become. Metro riders were stranded for hours.

Six days later, tragedy again struck American skies. On January 19, four U.S. Air Force Thunderbird pilots were killed during an exercise near Las Vegas, Nevada. The Thunderbirds were practicing a four-abreast backward loop when the horizontal stabilizers of the lead plane jammed. Diving at 400 MPH, the command pilot was unable to pull out of the loop. Maintaining their precision formation, the remaining three pilots followed their leader into the desert floor and a fiery explosion.

The major happening in Washington during the spring and early summer of 1982 was the trial of John Hinckley Jr. in U.S. District Court. Hinckley faced charges of attempted assassination of the president and 12 other counts of assault and weapons violations. The jury of seven women and five men listened to six weeks of testimony. Attorney Vincent Foster of the law firm Williams and Connolly argued that Hinckley was legally insane at the time of the crimes. Defense psychiatrists testified that Hinckley was not criminally responsible for his acts.

Assistant U.S. Attorney Roger Adelman portrayed Hinckley as an individual who desired fame and notoriety. Calling Hinckley "a hunter, a stalker," Adelman stated that Hinckley was in control of his behavior and able to choose his actions. Expert witnesses for the prosecution testified that Hinckley exhibited no serious mental problems.

Judge Barrington Parker instructed the jury that the burden of proof fell on the government to prove Hinckley was sane at the time of the offenses. To the disappointment of federal prosecutors and investigators, the jury returned a verdict of not guilty by reason of insanity for all 13 counts.

John Hinckley Jr. was remanded to St. Elizabeths Hospital until he is no longer dangerous to himself or others due to mental illness. Beginning in 1999, hospital personnel took Hinckley on day visits within the Washington area. Upon testimony that Hinckley's mental condition had improved, a federal judge ruled in 2003 that Hinckley could leave St. E's under parental supervision for some limited day visitation. In the years following, Hinckley has been permitted to make overnight visits with his parents and to stay with his mother for extended periods in Williamsburg, Virginia. All of Hinckley's movements away from St. Elizabeths have been monitored by the Secret Service.

With federal lawmakers and the public upset over Hinckley's acquittal, an insanity reform act was passed in 1984. The new law shifted the burden of proof to the defense. Now, they have to prove with clear and convincing evidence that their client was insane at the time of the crimes. The prosecution only has to show that the defendant was aware of what he or she was doing. Psychiatric testimony is limited to direct observations and severe mental disease has to be shown for insanity. The new federal standards served as a model for many state legislatures, which toughened laws relating to the insanity defense.

In April 1982, Bob graduated from a two-week "Questioned Document Course" put on by the Secret Service. Always wanting to gain more knowledge and to better himself, Bob learned the basics of handwriting analysis. By obtaining and comparing known writing with disputed writing, Bob could help determine the authorship of various questioned documents. This was extremely helpful in Secret Service investigations involving forgery and in intelligence cases dealing with threatening letters. Bob studied techniques for breaking down writing into individual characteristics that show differences and similarities in compared writings.

It didn't take long for Bob to put his new knowledge to use. He was transferred to the Analysis and Control Branch of ID. Bob took over the GS-12 agent position in Region IV, assisting his friend Chuck Krall, who was the 13. Region IV handled the Western field offices.

Bob meshed smoothly into his new assignment and became a valuable asset in the referral and review of intelligence cases. Chuck Krall handed Bob one case, asking him to write it up for submission to the Behavioral Science Unit of the FBI for their evaluation and assistance. "Put your gloves on," Krall joked. "This one's *really* cold." At the time, it was the oldest unsolved threat case in Secret Service files.

The case dated back to the mid-1960s when President Lyndon Johnson received threatening letters from an anonymous writer. The unknown subject was coined "The Traveler" by the Secret Service because the letters were mailed from different locations across America. Since some of the locations were places where LBJ had visited, it was believed the subject was stalking the president. The subject was evaluated as presenting a danger to President Johnson.

Through the years, investigation failed to determine the identity of the writer. The individual continued to mail in threats directed against the presidents who succeeded Johnson: Nixon, Ford, Carter, and Reagan. Even though it became apparent that the subject was more interested in blowing off steam than burning up gunpowder, the individual had committed numerous federal felonies and had been a long-time nemesis to the Secret Service.

It took two large file folders to hold all the paperwork that had been generated in the case. The two folders stacked about six inches high. "Chuck, let me go through these first to see if I can find some leads we can explore," Bob requested. "I'd like a shot at it before sending it off to the Bureau."

"Okay, Bob, you got it," Krall agreed.

Bob had done his own profiling when he worked PI at WFO. Although he had the highest respect for the Bureau and its BSU, Bob felt confident he could produce a psychological profile just as meaningful. Drawing upon his experience in threat assessment, Bob reviewed the many threatening letters and pages of reports before him. Bob stayed late that evening until a picture of the anonymous writer came to mind. Bob saw an aging white male who jumped around from town to town and job to job. The subject had no pension plan and was just eking out an existence. The subject would be dependent on Social Security for a lifeline in his later years. The subject had opinions about everything and Social Security would be no exception. The subject was angry at the cards he had been dealt. Threats made him feel powerful, and he gained some revenge. The subject enjoyed knowing the Secret Service was jumping through his hoops. The subject saw this as a game he was continually winning, and it added to his feeling of superiority.

It was time for pay back. Bob wrote a referral for the field office in the city where one of the threatening letters had been postmarked. Bob noted several distinguishing individual characteristics found in the unknown subject's writings. He requested that the field office show a copy of the unknown subject's latest handwritten letter to the local Social Security office as well as other governmental offices covered by the originating zip code. Bob believed it was likely that the individual had written "complaint type" letters to other authorities.

The next afternoon, Bob was coming back to his desk from a late lunch. Chuck Krall greeted Bob with a broad smile. "Bob, guess who just called and was saying good things about you?"

"Director Simpson," Bob replied facetiously.

"Danny Gibson called. They caught 'The Traveler.' "

"For real," Bob replied.

"Yeah, they arrested him this morning," Krall confirmed. "They took the letter to the Social Security office. The office manager took one look at it and said, 'That's Melvin Griggs.'

"They get Griggs's address and take a run out to his apartment. Griggs opens the door and Gibson identifies himself. Griggs says, 'How did you find me? After all these years, I didn't think I'd ever get caught!'

"Nice job, Bob. Gibson wanted me to pass his compliments to you. He said several times, 'This is the way ID should work.' "

Later that afternoon, Chuck Krall told Bob that he was wanted in SAIC Thomas's office. Thomas was in his first week as SAIC of the Intelligence Division. He had replaced former SAIC Richards, who moved into a deputy assistant director position at headquarters.

"Bob, I think Thomas wants to commend you," Chuck said. "You brought to justice a violator who we've been after for almost 20 years." Bob smiled at Chuck and hoped he was right. It was good timing that Bob would crack a decades old case with a new SAIC on board. Maybe Bob's luck was about to change. Richards certainly hadn't helped Bob's career; maybe it would be different with the new SAIC.

Bob knocked on the half-open door to SAIC Thomas's office. "Yes," answered a voice from within.

Bob peeked his head through the opening; "Sir, I'm Bob Ritter; you wanted to see me."

"Yes, come in." Bob entered the office and stood before the SAIC. Thomas stated in a monotone, "Give me your dream field office, and I'll do my best to get you there."

Thoroughly astonished, Bob replied, "Sir, I don't understand."

"Well, I thought you would from what I just heard," remarked Thomas with some surprise. "I just got an earful from SAIC Wilson of VPPD about you being burned out. We need to get you out of headquarters and back to the field."

"Sir, I don't know what you're talking about."

"I got a complaint that your work in and out of D.C. has been *less than desired*. Burnout happens to the best of us. It's nothing to be ashamed of."

"I've had superior evaluations and commendations. Any suggestion that I haven't been doing a professional job is news to me. I strongly refute the charge and ask for a chance to defend myself; there's two sides to every story," Bob asserted. "I like it in Region IV."

Thomas thought for a moment. "Since you want to stay in ID, I'll look into this further. In the meantime, decide which field office you'd like to transfer to. It can be Honolulu, San Diego, Miami, or wherever. Tomorrow, I'll let you know what I find out and my decision."

"Sir, when I leave D.C., I want to go to an RA. I don't want to go to a field office," Bob said.

"That's not going to be an option. This would need to be a quick transfer. Once you get to a field office, then you can work on an RA," Thomas advised.

"Things have been going on here that you don't know about," Bob stated. "I'm not going down without a fight."

"Let me look into this first," Thomas said. "We'll talk more tomorrow."

Bob came home that night, and he was as low as I have ever seen him, excepting the months that we were experiencing marital problems. I felt sorry for Bob and for us. I couldn't help but think about the time Bob had turned down a position in a picturesque Western resident agency due to my reluctance to move during the school year. It turned out to be a big mistake.

"What are you going to do?" I asked.

"I'm going to fight it. There's no basis to the charge. This is character assassination," Bob replied with anger in his voice.

"Which field office are you going to choose?"

Bob thought for a while then answered, "I'm hoping it doesn't come to that."

The next morning, Bob was called back to SAIC Thomas's office. Moving boxes were still stacked in the corner; the walls were bare. Thomas still hadn't found time to unpack yet.

"Bob, I really have no choice," Thomas began somewhat apologetically. "Even though I found a whole lot of nothing, SAIC Wilson thinks you're burned out. I can't have someone here that I can't assign to VP advances. Give me your top field office, and I'll make the call."

"Sir, this isn't fair. What are the specifics? I should have the right to defend myself," Bob asserted.

"They claimed you didn't take the Libyan hit teams seriously—that you had a cavalier attitude. They specifically mentioned that your performance during the VP's visit to Denver was troublesome."

"My call to Denver didn't find any evidence of that," Thomas continued. "SAIC Griffiths [Denver Field Office] said his two PI agents and the local police related that you did an excellent job. He added that no one from the VP detail made any complaints to him. In fact, they told him everything went fine. Griffiths said you're welcome back in his district anytime. I mentioned this to Wilson, but the bottom line is they've lost confidence in you."

"This is unfounded," Bob stated. "Frank Brown might be behind this. He was one of the VP supervisors for the Denver trip. He tried to have me unfairly disciplined some years ago."

"That may be, but I can't let this become a distraction for ID. You've been here three years. I made my decision. It'll be best for you to move on with your career. Bob, *you're not going to be promoted here.*"

The last comment was the coup de grace for Bob's ID career. Bob would not be recommended for promotion. Bob's superior work, sacrifices, and successes flashed by in an instant—all for naught. The only thing left was his good name, and he didn't want to lose that. "I'm going to fight this," Bob said with stern conviction.

"You don't have grounds for that," Thomas said. "This is *not* a disciplinary action. It's a routine career transfer. Nothing's going in your file.

"From what I've seen, you've done a good job here and that's what I'm telling your next SAIC. Which field office do you want to go to?"

"WFO," Bob replied.

"Okay, you got me on that one. I did tell you *any* field office. The intent was to get you away from Washington. I didn't think WFO would be in your dream list."

"I didn't think so either," Bob responded.

"I'll make the call today," Thomas promised.

Chapter 31

Back to WFO

Bob said he picked WFO, so we wouldn't have to relocate. We could wait for an opening at a resident agency without having to make an extra move. And Bob intended on fighting the smear campaign that had been leveled against him. It would be easier to seek redress while still in the Washington area.

Bob had conducted 43 out-of-town advances (mostly presidential) while assigned to ID. He had received superlative comments in a good number of these. He had performed admirably in all his assignments, including an *extra* seven months on the duty desk. With commendations, a director's award, and excellent evaluations in Bob's personnel file, the events of the last 24 hours were almost unbelievable.

Looking back on the Denver advance, Bob remembered a brief conversation with Frank Brown as the vice presidential party was boarding *Air Force Two*. While Bob and his Denver Police Department PI counterpart, a detective sergeant, were standing on the tarmac, Brown approached them and asked, "Why wasn't that PI subject removed from the motorcade area?"

"Frank," Bob answered calmly, "she wasn't a PI subject; she was a bag lady, well-known to the local PD. She was checked out. She was in the next block up from the hotel and presented no problem to the VP."

"We don't roust the homeless in this city," the detective sergeant added. "The press and the ACLU would have had a field day."

Brown looked at the detective and commented, "I didn't want you to move her." Pointing to Bob, Brown continued, "I wanted him to." Brown then turned and boarded *Air Force Two*.

Bob quickly forgot the exchange, but it now appeared that Brown must have lodged a complaint with the SAIC of VPPD. Bob knew he had made the right decision. The original radio message from Brown stated that a "staffer" had reported seeing a PI subject. Homeless persons are not PI subjects. People living on the streets of cities are a fact of American life. They may be an *embarrassment* to politicians, but they pose no physical threat. If they're not breaking the law and their behavior doesn't present a danger to themselves or others, law enforcement officers have no legal authority to move them against their will.

Homeless persons; lawful, peaceful demonstrators; non-dangerous mental subjects; and the like have civil rights just like everyone else in our society. The Secret Service has no legal justification to forcibly remove citizens who are lawfully exercising their constitutional rights. That's what makes us different from most countries in the world. Bob and every other Secret Service agent took an oath to *support and defend* the Constitution of the United States. Bob took his oath seriously.

Bob also knew that the potential danger for the vice president laid in the crowd that had assembled for his departure. Plus, nearby windows and rooftops could become sniper nests. If Bob and the police detective had been tied up running off a bag lady, they wouldn't have been able to cover the departure. That lesson should have been learned from the Reagan assassination attempt. Since no mistakes were admitted to by the Secret Service, its protective intelligence culture didn't change. PI teams continued to be looked upon as primarily a reactive asset.

It didn't take long for Bob's transfer. He finished up at ID that Friday and reported to WFO on the following Monday morning. Assigned to the Criminal Squad, Bob shared a two-man office with his long-time friend Dick Corrigan. Bob still had good police contacts in the area and made a smooth transition back to the street. It was just like the old days.

Robert (Bobby) DeProspero was the squad's AT. A graduate of West Virginia University and an Air Force veteran, DeProspero began his Secret Service career in 1965 at the Washington Field Office. Since that time, DeProspero served with the Protective Support Division, VPPD, PPD, and the Office of Inspection. This was his second tour at WFO as an ATSAIC.

DeProspero had a reputation of being an effective and fair supervisor, who elicited the best from those under him. With a poker face and reserved demeanor, DeProspero kept his subordinates guessing. He said little, but when he did—you listened. Never knowing for sure where they stood with DeProspero, most agents gave more than they might have otherwise. DeProspero's managerial style presented no problem for Bob; he always gave his best.

Bob got off to a great start. He solved some major cases and led not only the squad but also the office in monthly arrests. One case involved a Uniformed Division officer who discharged his gun while on duty. The officer claimed a subject had tried to run him over with a motor vehicle. The officer fired at the vehicle in self-defense. This occurred on a midnight shift, and some USSS supervisors suspected that the officer had accidentally fired his weapon and invented a "phantom car" assault for a cover story.

Bob interviewed the UD officer, and a reenactment was conducted at the scene of the crime, a foreign mission located in upper Northwest D.C. The officer stated he was on foot patrol when he observed a vehicle circling the neighborhood. When the officer stepped into the street to stop the suspicious vehicle for a check, the driver sped up and drove right at the officer. The officer dove out of the way while pulling his service revolver and discharging it at the vehicle.

The automobile was occupied by two subjects in their early 20s—a male driver and a female passenger. The officer believed the female cried out "Gil" during the incident. The officer described the vehicle as an older model two-door with Virginia tags.

Bob thought "Gil" was most likely the driver's nickname. Bob ran the name along with "Gilbert" through Northern Virginia police departments and through the Virginia Department of Motor Vehicles. Over a dozen possible suspects were discovered in the region. Bob systematically eliminated each one until he struck pay dirt.

Gilbert "Gil" Payne was a 22 year old, who resided in Fairfax County, Virginia. Investigation revealed the name of Payne's girlfriend. Under interrogation, the suspect's girlfriend admitted that she was the female passenger during the incident in question. She stated that Payne had been drinking and had "lost his head." Fearing that the officer had gotten the tag number, Payne left the vehicle at a friend's residence in Arlington, Virginia. The subject then left town for places unknown.

Bob recovered the subject's vehicle, which had a bullet hole in the right-rear quarter panel. With the physical evidence and the sworn statement of the girlfriend, Bob submitted a criminal complaint to a U.S. magistrate. An arrest warrant was issued. From toll records of calls placed to Payne's girlfriend, Bob ascertained a Miami telephone number. The number was listed to a pay phone outside a Miami eatery.

Bob sent a collateral investigation to the Miami Field Office (MFO). MFO agents responded to the restaurant and discovered that Payne was working there as a waiter. He was arrested and taken before a federal magistrate. The defendant waived extradition, and the U.S. Marshals Service transported him back to D.C. for trial. Payne subsequently pled guilty to assault charges. For his effort, Bob received commendations from USSS Assistant Inspector Dick Hartwick and from Gerald Bechtle, who was now the Assistant Director for Inspection.

In another high profile case, Bob investigated the theft of an agent's service revolver. The agent claimed that the weapon was stolen from the glove box of his POV, while it was parked at his residence. Again, there was suspicion of misconduct. Bob received a call from one headquarters official who advised: "Give this one a good toss. This guy could have gotten rolled in a bar or something. The story as to how his gun was stolen might be fiction.

"I want to emphasize to you how important it is that you recover the weapon and sooner than later," the official continued. "We don't need a Secret Service handgun being used in the commission of a robbery or murder."

"I'll keep working until I find it," Bob assured.

An interview of the agent whose gun was missing did not generate any leads. The agent had no idea who might have taken the weapon. Bob believed the agent was telling the truth as to the circumstances of the theft.

A check with local police revealed that the community where the agent resided had been previously free of burglaries and car break-ins. Next, Bob canvassed the agent's neighborhood. He developed the names of several young teenagers who had been suspected by one resident of committing juvenile pranks such as painting graffiti.

On a hunch, Bob decided to interview these subjects. In the presence of their parents, the juveniles admitted to stealing the revolver. They knew the vehicle was owned by a Secret Service agent, and decided to go through the car's interior. They were surprised to find a firearm in the glove box.

The juveniles took the weapon to a local gravel pit where they fired off a shot. The kick and noise generated from a Treasury Department high-velocity round fired through the short barrel revolver were too much for our young desperados. As they were returning home, the juveniles scattered the remaining five rounds through a wooded area. One of the subjects retained the pistol, hiding it in his bedroom closet.

Within two days of the reported theft, Bob had recovered the weapon and four of the rounds tossed in the woods. The fifth round was never found, even after many hours of searching by Bob and an EOD team utilizing a mine detector.

In lieu of federal prosecution, the teenagers pled guilty in state juvenile court to larceny charges. The agent whose duty weapon was recovered dropped by WFO to thank Bob. The agent was happy his name had been cleared. The agent knew supervisors had speculated he had lost the weapon under unsavory circumstances.

Although Bob enjoyed working criminal cases, he was still upset over having been unfairly forced to vacate his Region IV position in ID. Bob had also been made an unwilling part of the USSS coverup regarding the missteps leading to the Reagan assassination attempt. While the Secret Service could claim that it had saved the president's life, it was responsible for putting him at risk in the first place.

Bob consulted with an attorney, whom Bob had known since his Park Police days. The attorney wanted to file suit against the Secret Service seeking either Bob's return to the Intelligence Division or his transfer to a resident agency. Counsel would argue that SAIC Thomas's decision was derived arbitrarily and that the charges laid against Bob were unjust and fueled by a supervisor who may have been seeking retribution. Additional claim would be made that Bob's knowledge of the Reagan attempt coverup and of the hype spun regarding the "Libyan hit teams" contributed to the situation.

The attorney made it clear that he needed to introduce the latter evidence to bolster Bob's case. After all, Bob had been warned that his career would be in jeopardy if he disclosed the truth about the assassination attempt. The attorney would represent that Bob's hasty departure from ID might have been a preemptive strike against a potential whistle-blower. It was significant that the original intent of the field transfer was to get Bob out of D.C. without delay. The new SAIC of ID folded on Bob fairly quickly. What part did former SAIC Richards and DSAIC Claiborne have in the decision?

Bob considered his options. He knew information damaging to the Secret Service would be made public when the case went to trial. There was a strong probability that these revelations would lead to a Congressional hearing. The whole matter might become embroiled in partisan politics. Who knows what harm might come to the Secret Service. Bob could win the battle but lose the war. Many of his fellow agents would see Bob as a traitor.

Six months went by; Bob couldn't bring himself to filing suit. Instead, he continued to rack up arrests and convictions. Fiercely loyal to the Secret Service, Bob changed his strategy. He would stay in WFO and strive for a promotion to a GS-13. Many more resident agent positions are available for 13s than 12s.

There was one major problem with the plan; Bob couldn't shake the feeling that he was responsible for the president's near assassination and for the tragedy that struck down White House Press Secretary James Brady. Since 3-30-81, Bob's remorse at not having done more to prevent the Hilton arrival/departure point from being opened to the public became overwhelming.

If President Reagan had died, the truth would have come out. National mourning would have turned to national anger. Losing two popular presidents within 20 years would have been a deathblow to the protective mission of the USSS. In all probability, the Secret Service would have been stripped of its protective duties.

With the president's narrow escape from death and his rapid recovery, Secret Service management seized the opportunity and turned near failure into success. Treasury and USSS officials stated that no clear security mistakes were made. Although the Secret Service rationalized away wrongdoing, it quietly took steps to prevent a similar tragedy. A magnetometer screening program was instituted for the White House and for presidential visits. And at the Washington Hilton, a tent-like structure was used to enclose the presidential limousine and VIP entrance during arrivals and departures. No longer would presidential arrivals/departures be in plain sight of the public. It took the near assassination of President Reagan for the Secret Service to finally move forward.

These were needed and welcomed changes, but lost in all of the heroics of saving the president's life was the "Devastator" bullet that exploded deep inside Jim Brady's brain. Brady nearly lost his life. What was left of it was severely handicapped. Brady spent eight months in GWU Hospital. He experienced multiple major surgeries and developed infections, pneumonia, seizures, convulsions, and memory loss. Brady underwent grueling physical therapy, yet remained paralyzed on his left side. Unable to perform many everyday activities, he spent much of his time in a wheel chair. Brady's future looked bleak.

Bob knew he could have prevented the tragedy. Bob continued to fault himself for not doing more in 1978 to have the Washington Hilton survey changed. He should have aggressively challenged USSS culture. The opening of the T Street entrance area to the public during arrivals and departures was a *major* mistake, plain and simple. It almost cost two people their lives, one of them the leader of the free world. Not only did the survey change provide an easy opportunity for an assassin, it also helped to prompt the assassination attempt in Bob's estimation.

Would-be assassins like Arthur Bremer, Sara Jane Moore, and John Hinckley Jr. view lax Secret Service security as a call to action. It reinforces their delusions and compulsions and psychologically empowers them to seize the moment. It's the final piece of the puzzle that locks in their destiny and fate, the grand opportunity they've been waiting for to achieve their fantasies and their place in history.

On March 30, 1981, John Hinckley Jr. waited outside the Hilton Hotel for the departure of the president. Carrying a loaded handgun in his pocket, Hinckley could hardly believe his luck. No one from the Secret Service paid any attention to him. There were no agents inside the public area scrutinizing the crowd—as the protective survey called for.

Suddenly, President Reagan exited the hotel for the presidential limousine. The repositioning of the limo caused Reagan to come within 15 feet of Hinckley. At this close range, Reagan looked larger than life. The president waved to the crowd; Hinckley believed the gesture was meant for him alone. It was the affirmation of Hinckley's starring role. With the stage set, Hinckley's distorted mind started to roll. A voice from within cried out *action*. Hinckley pulled his weapon and fired it at the president. The president and three others were hit. President Reagan and Secretary Brady barely escaped with their lives. James Brady was permanently injured. It was all too easy—and all preventable.

If Bob had worked PI at the Hilton that day, *it never would have happened*—even with a flawed survey. Hinckley would have been found out and arrested. Or seeing the heightened security, he would have fled the area as Travis Bickle did in *Taxi Driver*. Of this, *I'm certain*.

Bob tried to get over his guilt, but he couldn't. Maybe senior executives of the Secret Service could live with the omission of the truth, but Bob couldn't. Maybe others could feel no responsibility for James Brady's tragic outcome, but Bob couldn't. No one was harder on Bob than Bob. He needed closure.

Bob came home one night and announced that he had given two weeks' notice to the Secret Service. I was at a loss for words. I never saw it coming. Bob informed me that he was transferring to the Department of Health and Human Services (HHS), Office of the Inspector General (OIG).

Former Secret Service Agent Charles "Charlie" Maddox was the Director of the Security and Protection Division at HHS. Maddox needed a qualified and experienced agent to assist in the protection of the secretary of HHS. Besides providing personal protection for the secretary, the position would entail the establishment of professional procedures, the writing of protective manuals, and the everyday coordination of the protective effort. It would be a new beginning for Bob and get his mind off the Secret Service demons that haunted him. Bob needed a *lifeline*.

I honestly didn't think it would happen. Bob loved the Secret Service almost as much as he loved his family. He was totally dedicated to the Service, and I couldn't see him leaving voluntarily. In his second tour at WFO, Bob was a well-respected agent, who was performing superlatively. He had worked hard during his Secret Service career. Both of us had sacrificed and had persevered for the Secret Service; it had become a big part of our existence.

As the days passed, Bob said little about the coming transfer. On the evening before his scheduled last day, Bob looked very apprehensive. I knew what was troubling him. "Are you really going through with it?" I asked.

"I don't know, Jan," Bob answered. "Tomorrow will tell."

"Bobbie, what about Tecumseh's Curse?"

"Tecumseh's Curse has been *broken*," Bob answered. "The Secret Service has finally come of age."

After dinner, Bob went into the living room and cued up Vince Guaraldi's "Cast Your Fate to the Wind" on our stereo's turntable. He played the tune about 10 times in a row. Each time, Bob closed his eyes and relaxed to the song's beautiful melody. He appeared to be deep in thought. The imagery of the song was not lost on me.

The following morning, I sent Bob off with a hug and a kiss and told him that whatever he decided would be fine with me. I fully believed that Bob would change his mind and stay with the Secret Service. I knew better than anyone else what the USSS meant to Bob.

I was truly surprised when Bob called me at school that afternoon and asked to be picked up at the Metro station. I knew then that Bob had done it. He had signed the papers, turned in his equipment, and dropped off the government car. As I drove Bob home, I remarked with some astonishment and disbelief, "Bobbie, I didn't think you would do it."

"I almost didn't," Bob admitted. "It was one of the toughest decisions I ever made. SAIC Buskirk called me to his office this afternoon and asked why I was leaving. I told him I was the victim of some dirty dealing during my time at ID and left it at that.

"Buskirk said he was sorry to hear that and complimented me on the 'great job' I had done at WFO. He said he didn't want to lose me and asked me to reconsider. For a couple of heartbeats, I was going to tell him that I would stay. It was a moment of truth. Then, honor and principle came to the forefront. I knew I couldn't go on working there everyday living a lie. I'm willing to confess my sin and shame at not having fought harder to change the Washington Hilton survey. But no one else is willing to admit to their mistakes. I can't live in that culture. So, I told Buskirk, regretfully, that I was still leaving.

"SAIC Buskirk did tell me that I was welcome back if I ever change my mind. 'Don't think you can't come back,' he said. 'Just pick up the phone and call me.' "

"That's good news," I said. "That can be an option for you. Maybe someday you can put this all behind you and return to the Secret Service."

"Yeah, maybe," Bob replied with some hope in his voice.

Leaving the Secret Service was not something Bob wanted to do; it was something he had to do. Bob cared more about the Secret Service than he cared about his own happiness. He sacrificed his personal career for the good of the Service. He knew that if he stayed, it would only be a matter of time until he would have to make known publically the information regarding the USSS coverup. Bob had too much integrity for his own good ... and his own peace of mind.

A NEW BEGINNING

ABOUT THE AUTHORS

Jan and Bob Ritter live on the shores of the Chesapeake Bay in Southern Maryland. Both are graduates of the University of Maryland and longtime residents of the Washington Metropolitan Area.

Jan is retired from the teaching profession where she specialized in early childhood education and Reading Recovery. When not walking the boardwalk for exercise, she enjoys shopping, antiquing, reading, and working crossword puzzles.

Bob is a retired federal criminal investigator (GS-1811) with a wealth of law enforcement and protective experience. A born collector, Bob loves history and the music of the 1940s–60s. He takes pleasure in watching the wildlife and ships that pass by the couple's bay-front condominium. Bob is a member of the Association of Former Agents U.S. Secret Service, the Federal Law Enforcement Officers Association, and the Fraternal Order of Police.

Jan and Bob relish spending time with family and friends, especially the couple's five granddaughters. With over 40 years of marriage, Jan and Bob deeply love one another and cherish each day together.

Breaking Tecumseh's Curse is the story of their early years together.